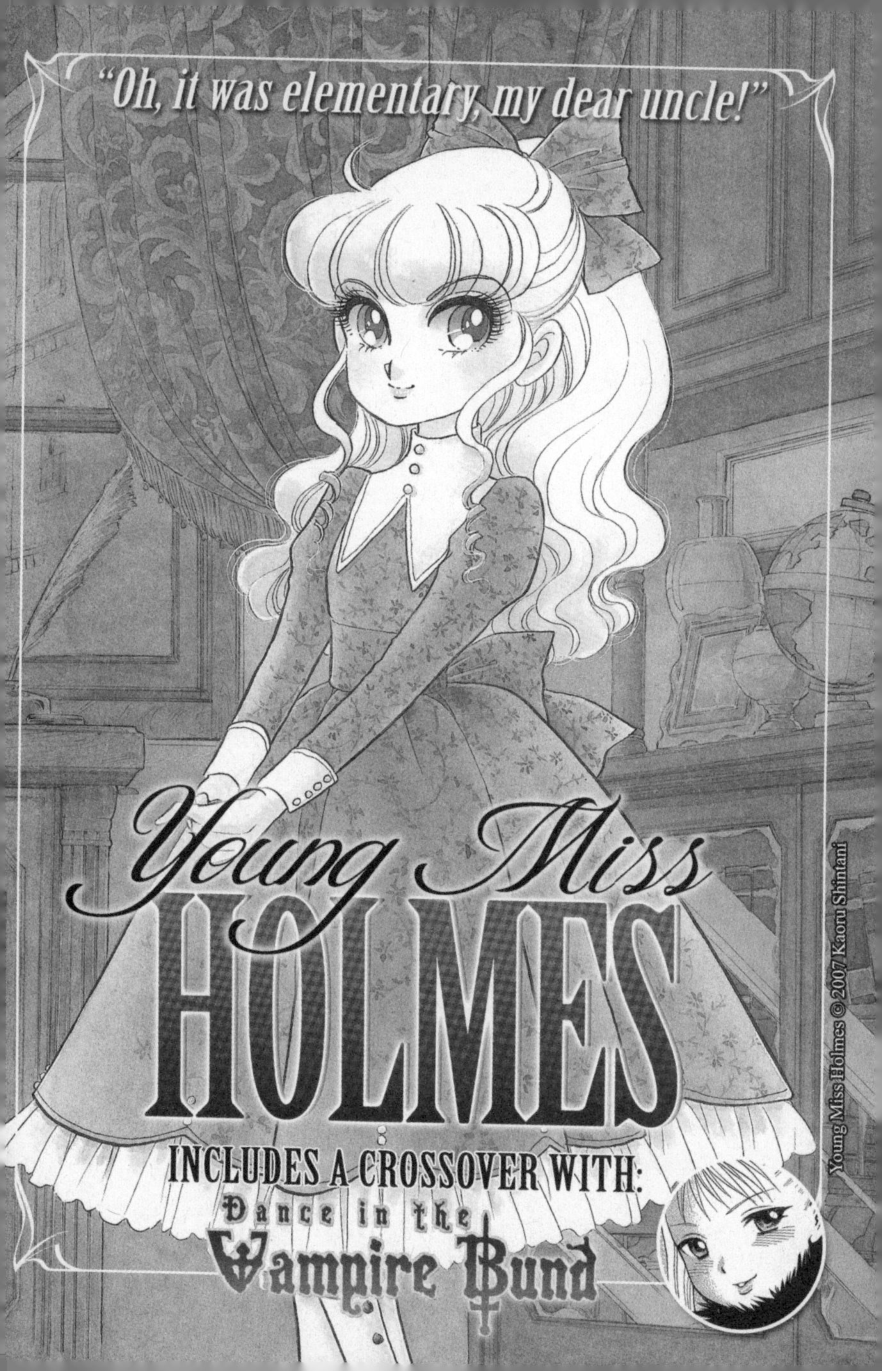
"Oh, it was elementary, my dear uncle!"
Young Miss
HOLMES
INCLUDES A CROSSOVER WITH:
Dance in the
Vampire Bund
Young Miss Holmes © 2007 Kaoru Shintani

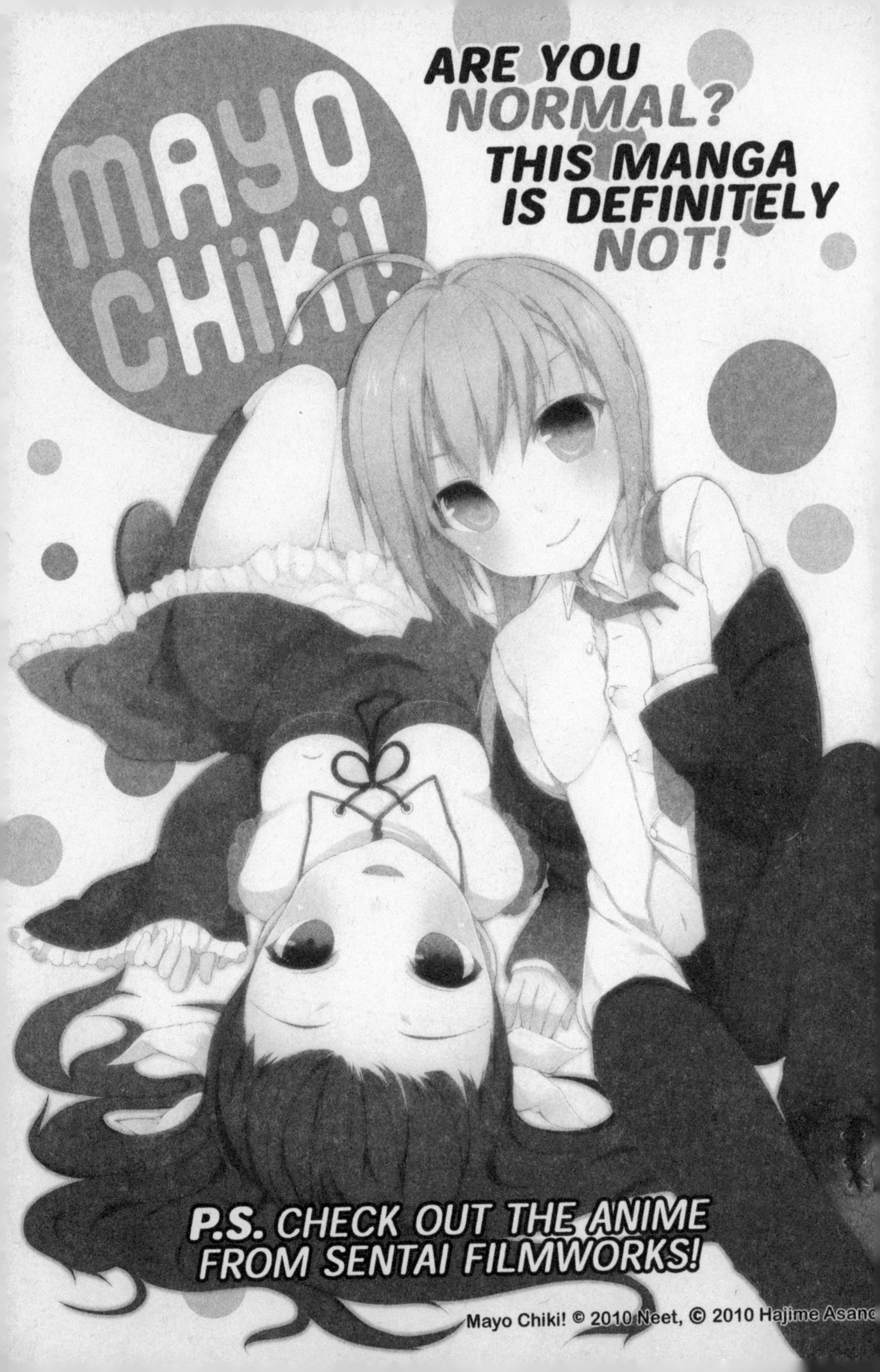
MAYO CHIKI!
ARE YOU NORMAL?
THIS MANGA IS DEFINITELY NOT!
P.S. CHECK OUT THE ANIME FROM SENTAI FILMWORKS!
Mayo Chiki! © 2010 Neet, © 2010 Hajime Asano

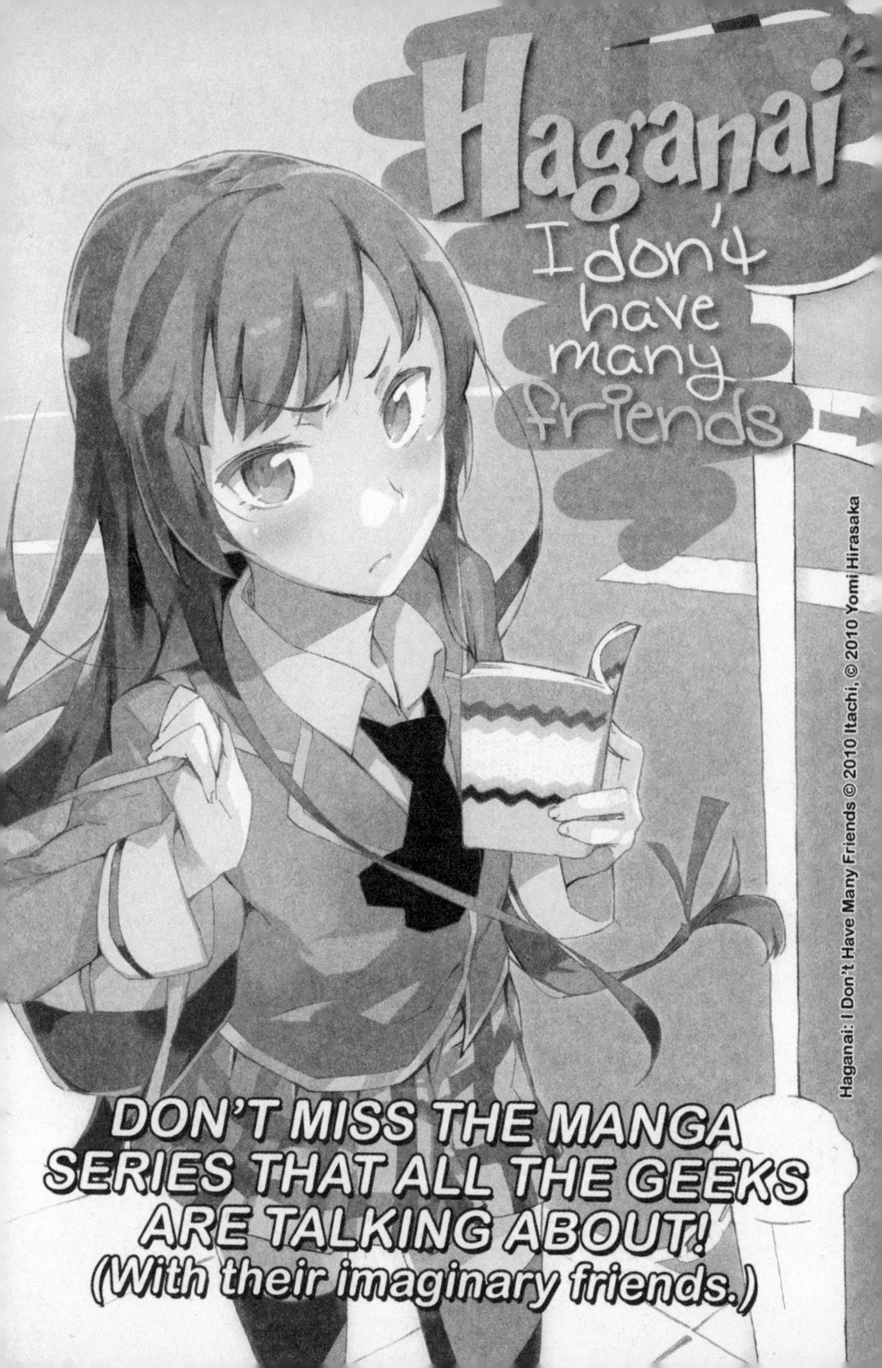
Haganai
I don't have many friends
DON'T MISS THE MANGA SERIES THAT ALL THE GEEKS ARE TALKING ABOUT!
(With their imaginary friends.)
Haganai: I Don't Have Many Friends © 2010 Itachi, © 2010 Yomi Hirasaka

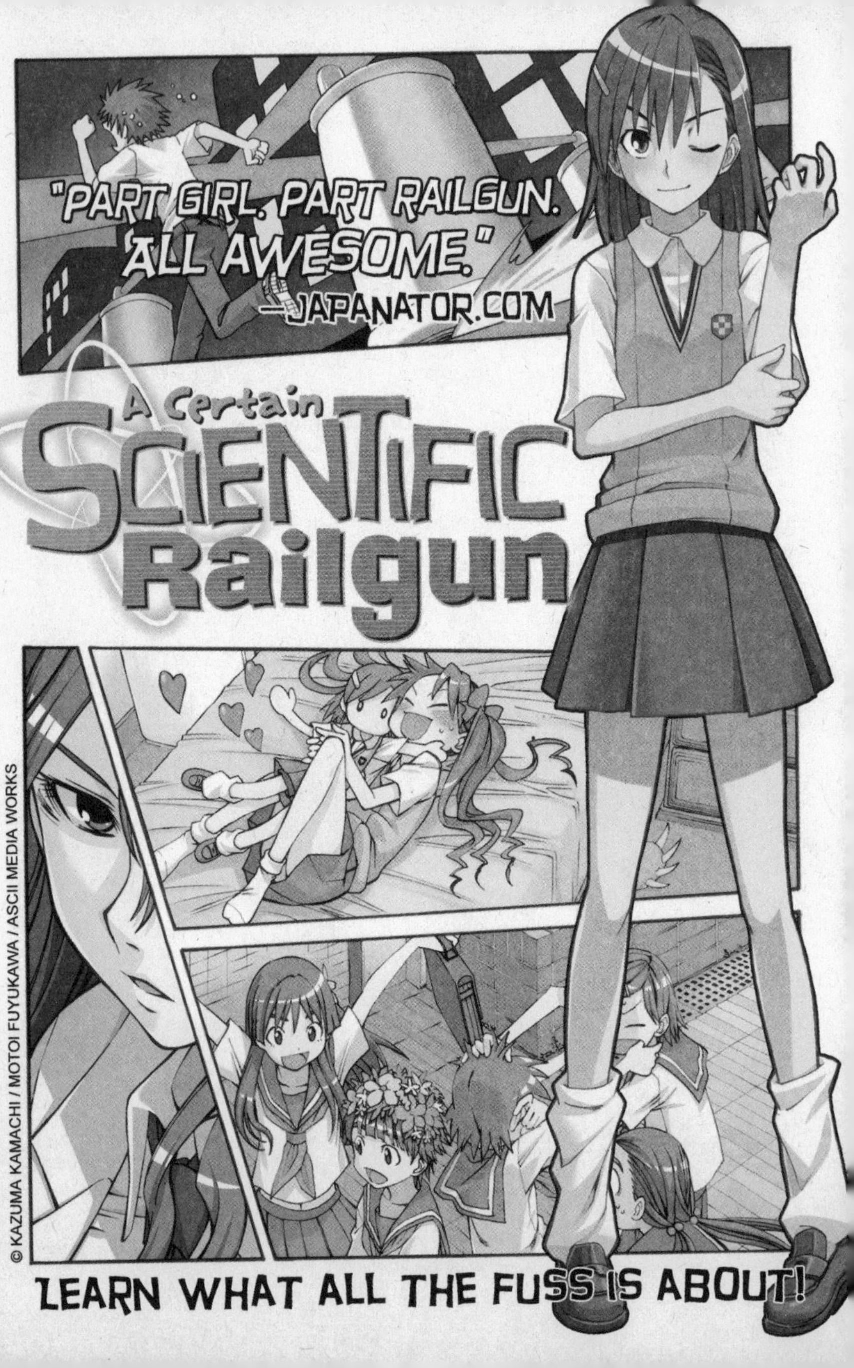
"PART GIRL. PART RAILGUN.
ALL AWESOME."
—JAPANATOR.COM
A Certain SCIENTIFIC Railgun
LEARN WHAT ALL THE FUSS IS ABOUT!
© KAZUMA KAMACHI / MOTOI FUYUKAWA / ASCII MEDIA WORKS

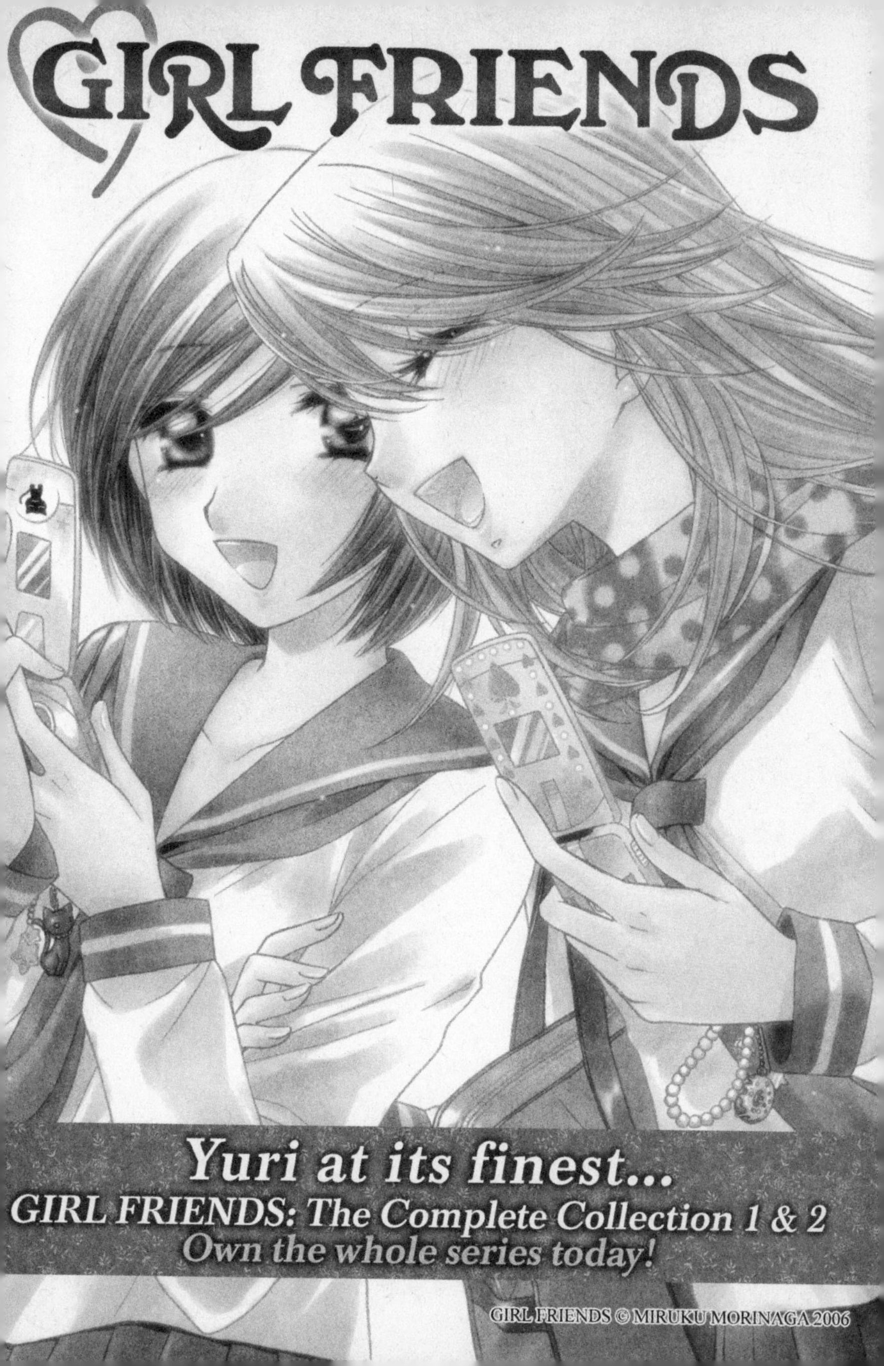

GIRL FRIENDS
Yuri at its finest...
GIRL FRIENDS: The Complete Collection 1 & 2
Own the whole series today!
GIRL FRIENDS © MIRUKU MORINAGA 2006

Kisses, Sighs, and Cherry Blossom Pink

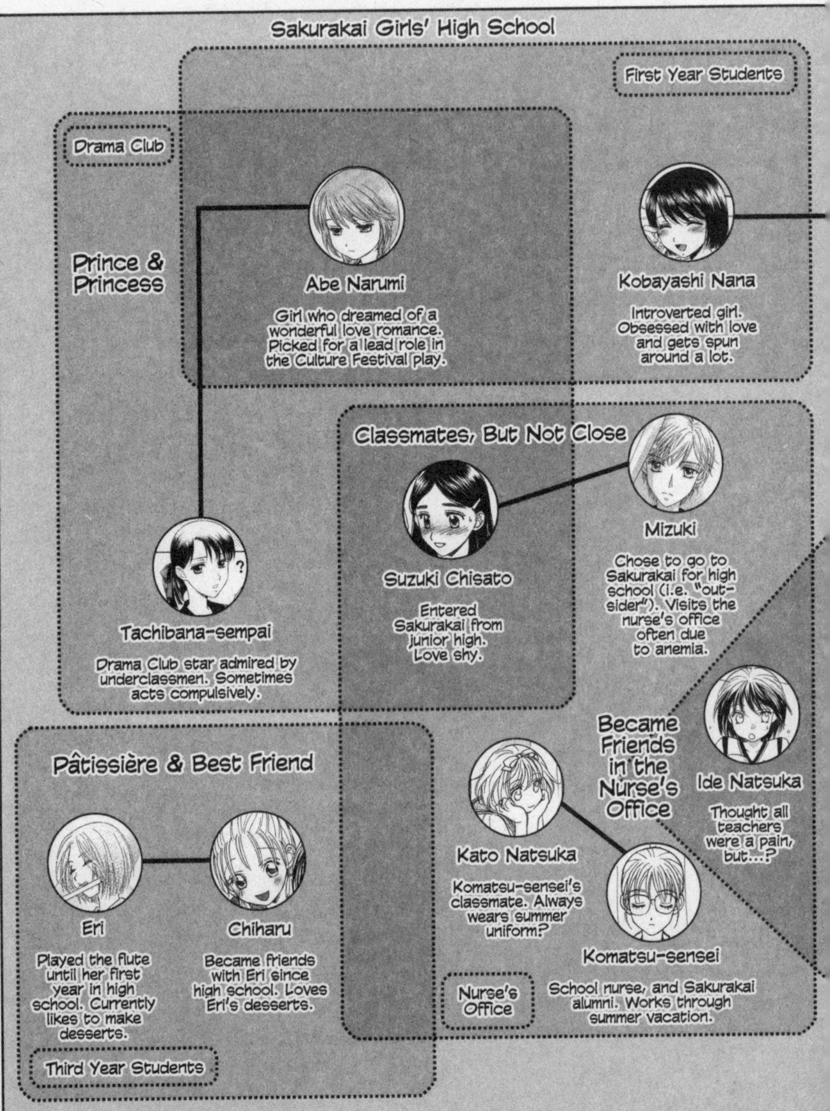
Sakurakai Girls' High School
First Year Students
Drama Club
Prince & Princess
Abe Narumi
Girl who dreamed of a wonderful love romance. Picked for a lead role in the Culture Festival play.
Kobayashi Nana
Introverted girl. Obsessed with love and gets spun around a lot.
Classmates, But Not Close
Mizuki
Chose to go to Sakurakai for high school (i.e. "outsider"). Visits the nurse's office often due to anemia.
Suzuki Chisato
Entered Sakurakai from junior high. Love shy.
Tachibana-sempai
Drama Club star admired by underclassmen. Sometimes acts compulsively.
Pâtissière & Best Friend
Eri
Played the flute until her first year in high school. Currently likes to make desserts.
Chiharu
Became friends with Eri since high school. Loves Eri's desserts.
Third Year Students
Became Friends in the Nurse's Office
Ide Natsuka
Thought all teachers were a pain, but...?
Kato Natsuka
Komatsu-sensei's classmate. Always wears summer uniform?
Komatsu-sensei
School nurse, and Sakurakai alumni. Works through summer vacation.
Nurse's Office

CHARACTER RELATIONSHIP CHART

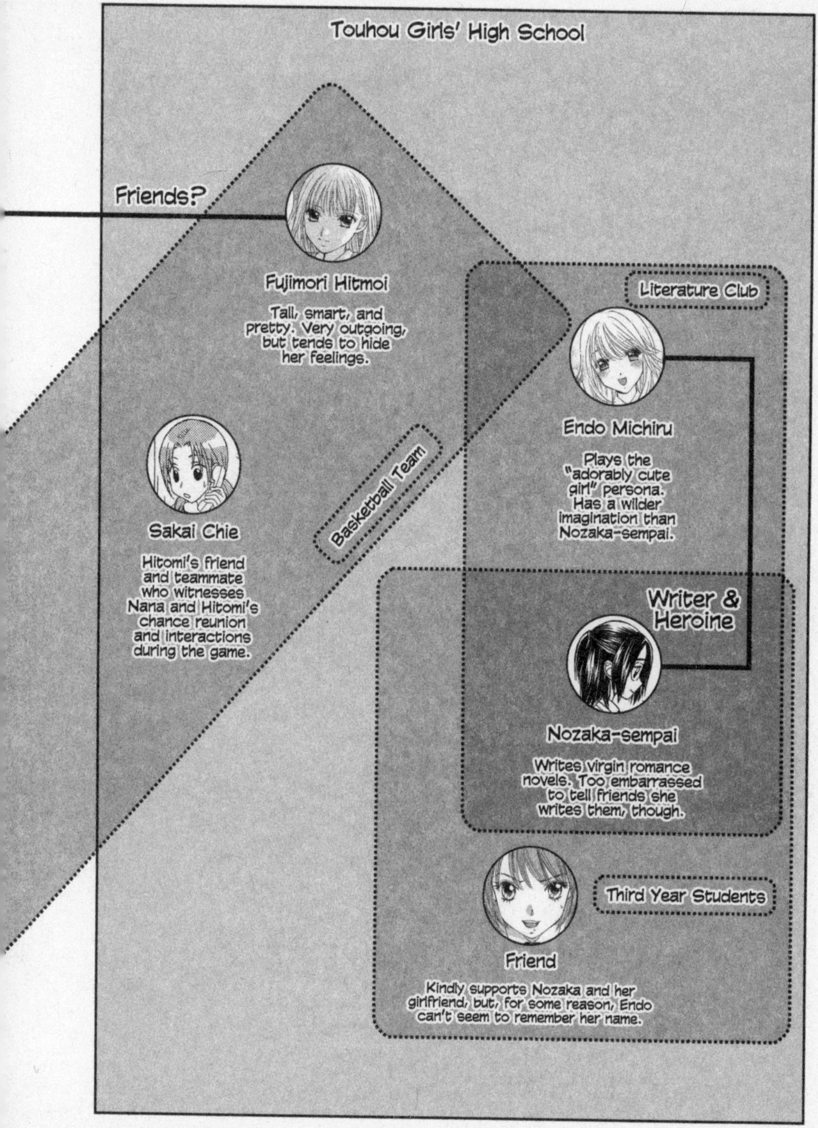

Touhou Girls' High School
Friends?
Fujimori Hitmoi
Tall, smart, and pretty. Very outgoing, but tends to hide her feelings.
Literature Club
Endo Michiru
Plays the "adorably cute girl" persona. Has a wilder imagination than Nozaka-sempai.
Sakai Chie
Hitomi's friend and teammate who witnesses Nana and Hitomi's chance reunion and interactions during the game.
Basketball Team
Writer & Heroine
Nozaka-sempai
Writes virgin romance novels. Too embarrassed to tell friends she writes them, though.
Third Year Students
Friend
Kindly supports Nozaka and her girlfriend, but, for some reason, Endo can't seem to remember her name.

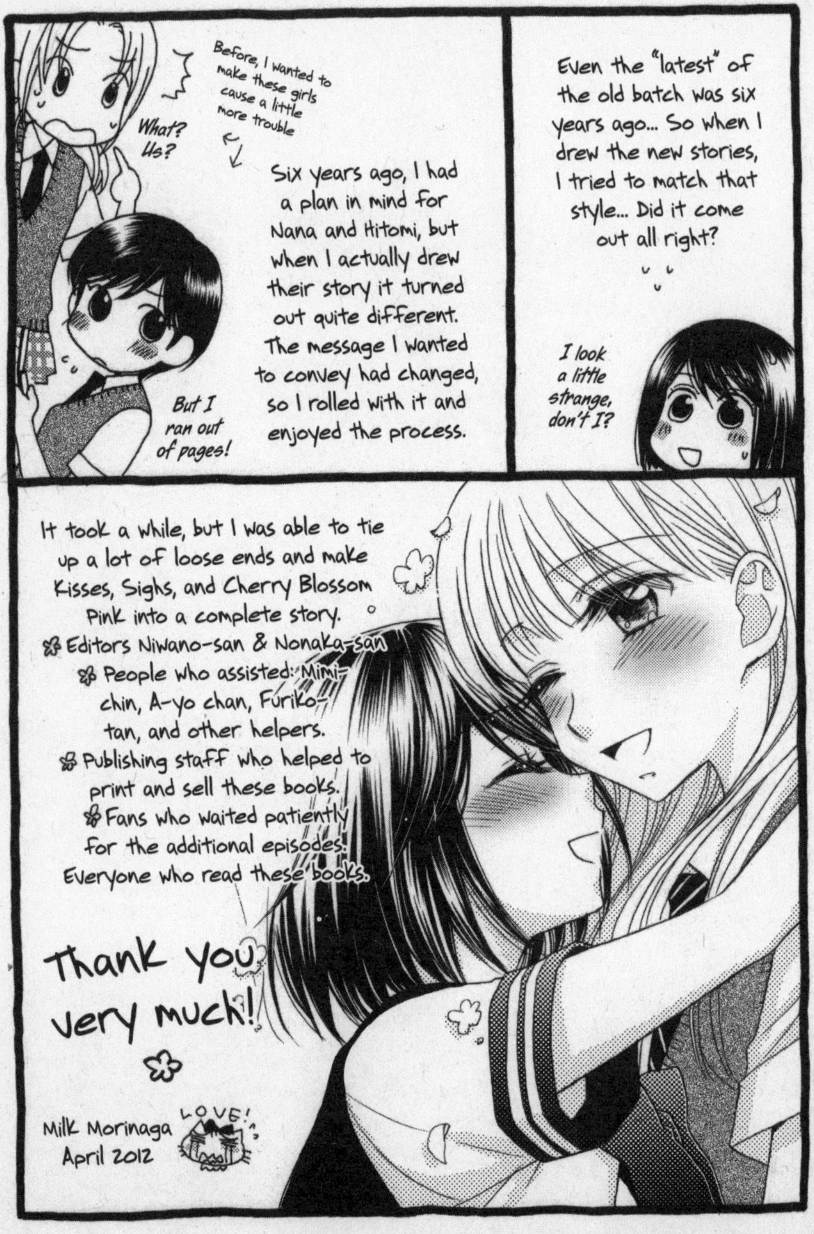
Even the "latest" of the old batch was six years ago... So when I drew the new stories, I tried to match that style... Did it come out all right?
I look a little strange, don't I?
Before, I wanted to make these girls cause a little more trouble
What? Us?
Six years ago, I had a plan in mind for Nana and Hitomi, but when I actually drew their story it turned out quite different. The message I wanted to convey had changed, so I rolled with it and enjoyed the process.
But I ran out of pages!
It took a while, but I was able to tie up a lot of loose ends and make Kisses, Sighs, and Cherry Blossom Pink into a complete story.
Editors Niwano-san & Nonaka-san
People who assisted: Mimi-chin, A-yo chan, Furiko-tan, and other helpers.
Publishing staff who helped to print and sell these books.
Fans who waited patiently for the additional episodes.
Everyone who read these books.
Thank you very much!
Milk Morinaga
April 2012
LOVE!

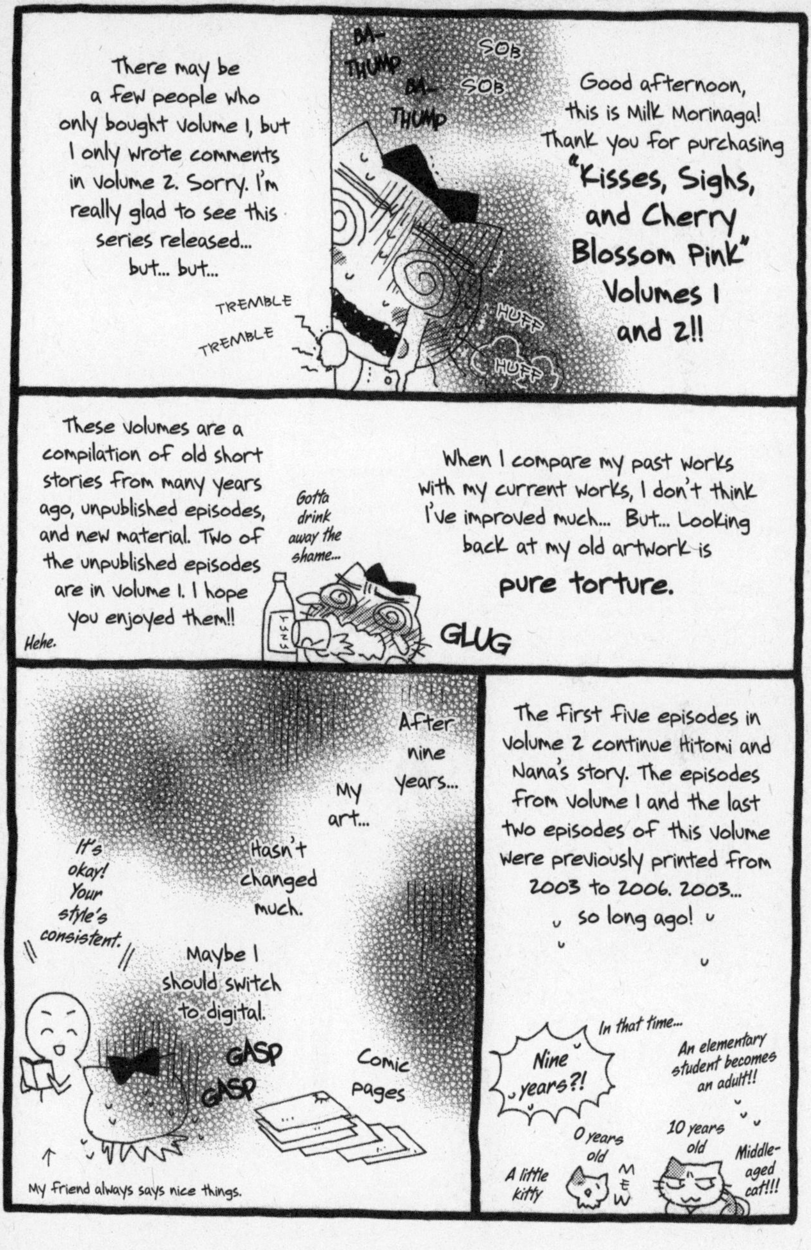
Good afternoon, this is Milk Morinaga! Thank you for purchasing "Kisses, Sighs, and Cherry Blossom Pink" Volumes 1 and 2!!
SOB
SOB
BA-THUMP
BA-THUMP
HUFF
HUFF
There may be a few people who only bought volume 1, but I only wrote comments in volume 2. Sorry. I'm really glad to see this series released... but... but...
TREMBLE
TREMBLE
When I compare my past works with my current works, I don't think I've improved much... But... Looking back at my old artwork is pure torture.
GLUG
Gotta drink away the shame...
These volumes are a compilation of old short stories from many years ago, unpublished episodes, and new material. Two of the unpublished episodes are in volume 1. I hope you enjoyed them!!
Hehe.
The first five episodes in volume 2 continue Hitomi and Nana's story. The episodes from volume 1 and the last two episodes of this volume were previously printed from 2003 to 2006. 2003... so long ago!
In that time...
An elementary student becomes an adult!!
Nine years?!
10 years old
Middle-aged cat!!!
0 years old
MEW
A little kitty
After nine years...
My art...
Hasn't changed much.
It's okay! Your style's consistent.
Maybe I should switch to digital.
GASP
GASP
Comic pages
My friend always says nice things.

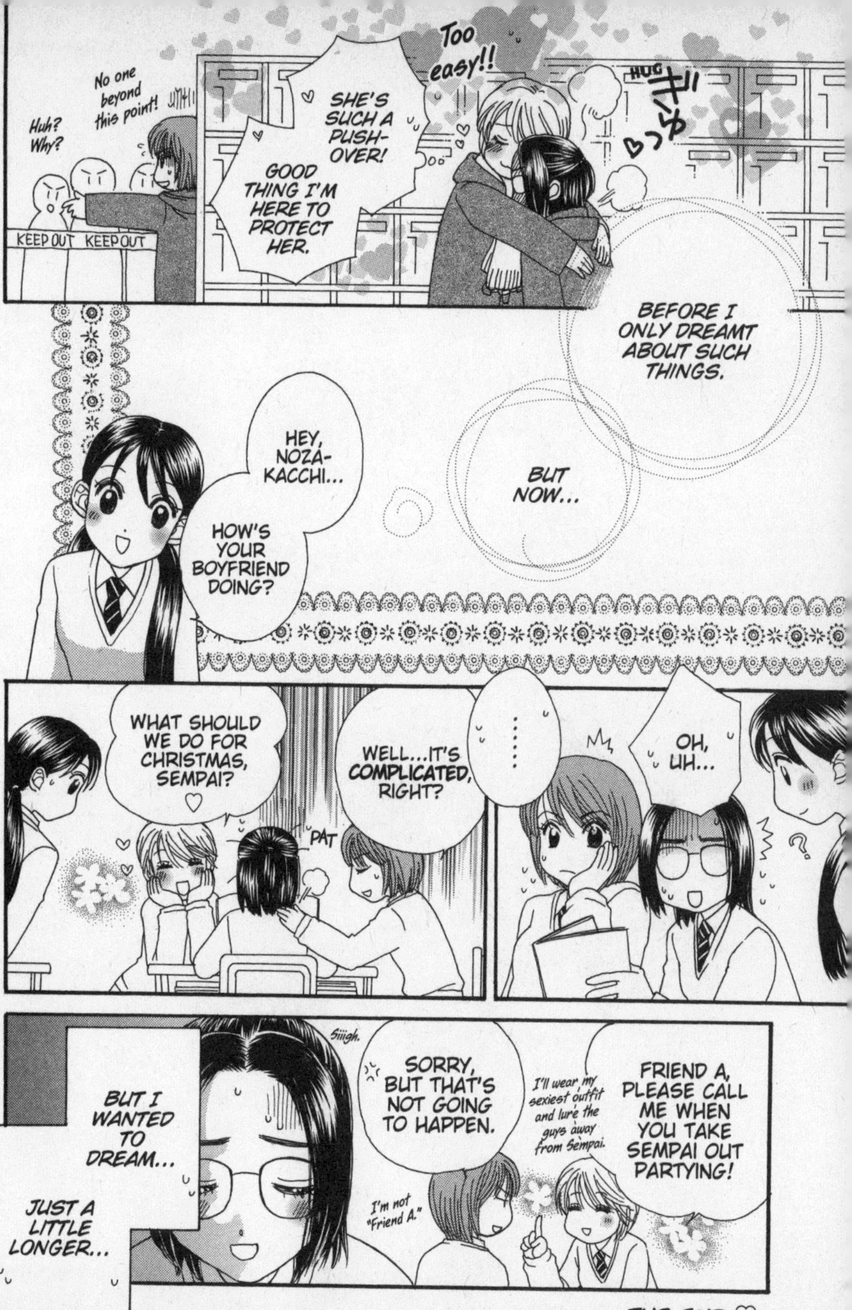
HUG
Too easy!!
SHE'S SUCH A PUSH-OVER!
GOOD THING I'M HERE TO PROTECT HER.
No one beyond this point!
Huh? Why?
KEEP OUT KEEP OUT
BEFORE I ONLY DREAMT ABOUT SUCH THINGS.
BUT NOW...
HEY, NOZA-KACCHI...
HOW'S YOUR BOYFRIEND DOING?
OH, UH...
......
WELL...IT'S COMPLICATED, RIGHT?
WHAT SHOULD WE DO FOR CHRISTMAS, SEMPAI?
PAT
FRIEND A, PLEASE CALL ME WHEN YOU TAKE SEMPAI OUT PARTYING!
I'll wear my sexiest outfit and lure the guys away from Sempai.
SORRY, BUT THAT'S NOT GOING TO HAPPEN.
Siiigh.
I'm not "Friend A."
BUT I WANTED TO DREAM...
JUST A LITTLE LONGER...

THE END ♡

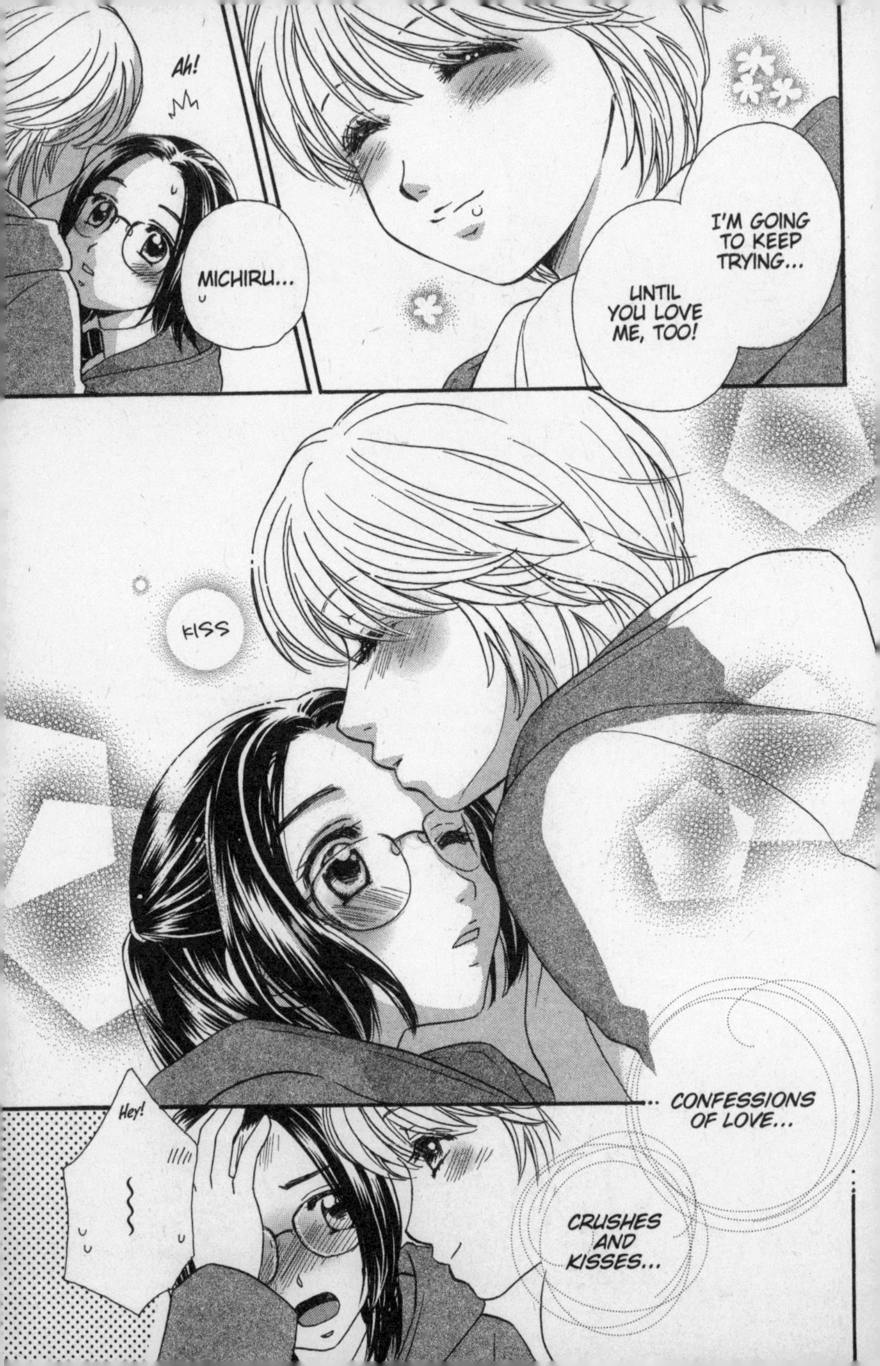
I'M GOING TO KEEP TRYING...
UNTIL YOU LOVE ME, TOO!
Ah!
MICHIRU...
KISS
...CONFESSIONS OF LOVE...
CRUSHES AND KISSES...
Hey!

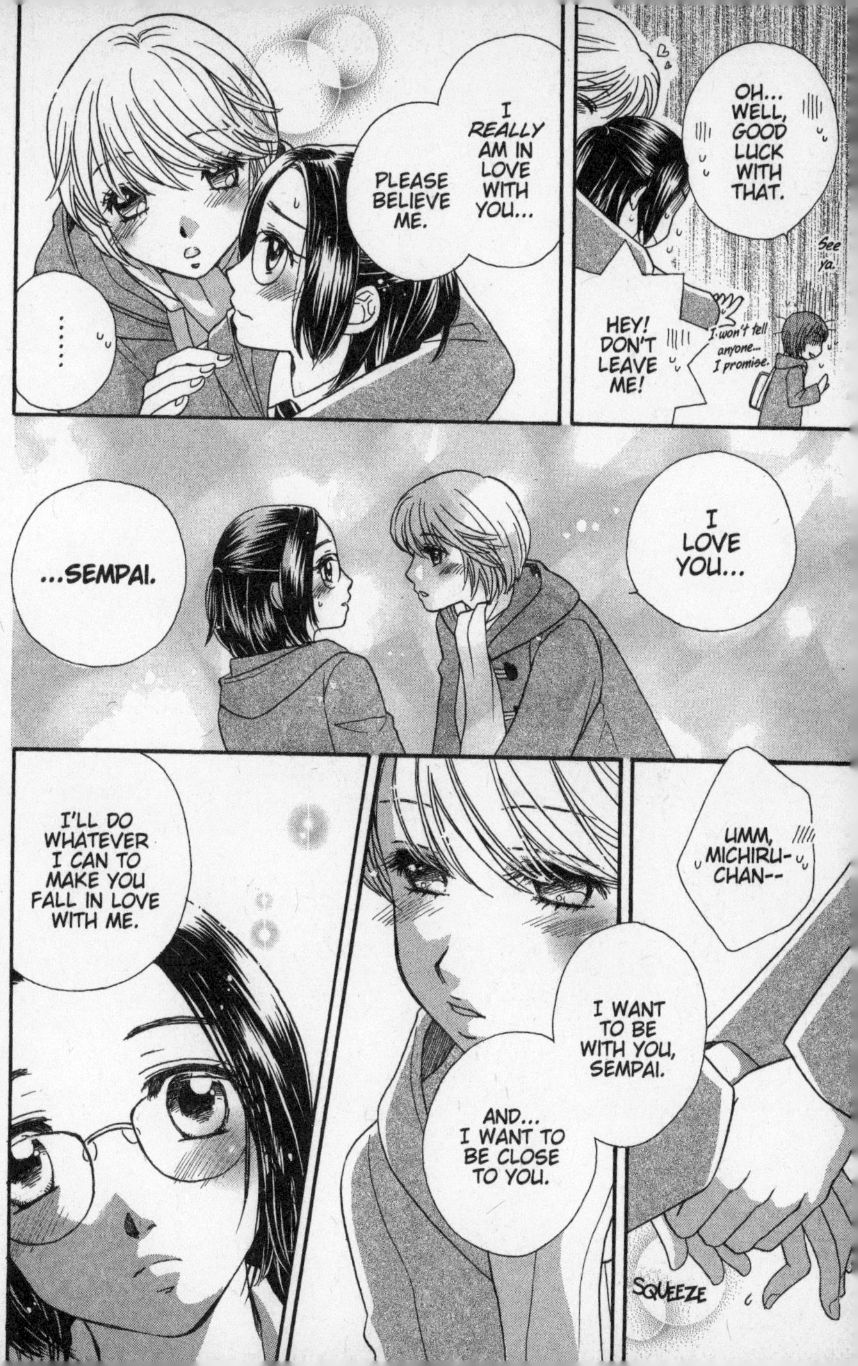
OH... WELL, GOOD LUCK WITH THAT.
See ya.
I won't tell anyone... I promise.
HEY! DON'T LEAVE ME!
I REALLY AM IN LOVE WITH YOU...
PLEASE BELIEVE ME.
......
I LOVE YOU...
...SEMPAI.
UMM, MICHIRU-CHAN--
I WANT TO BE WITH YOU, SEMPAI.
AND... I WANT TO BE CLOSE TO YOU.
SQUEEZE
I'LL DO WHATEVER I CAN TO MAKE YOU FALL IN LOVE WITH ME.

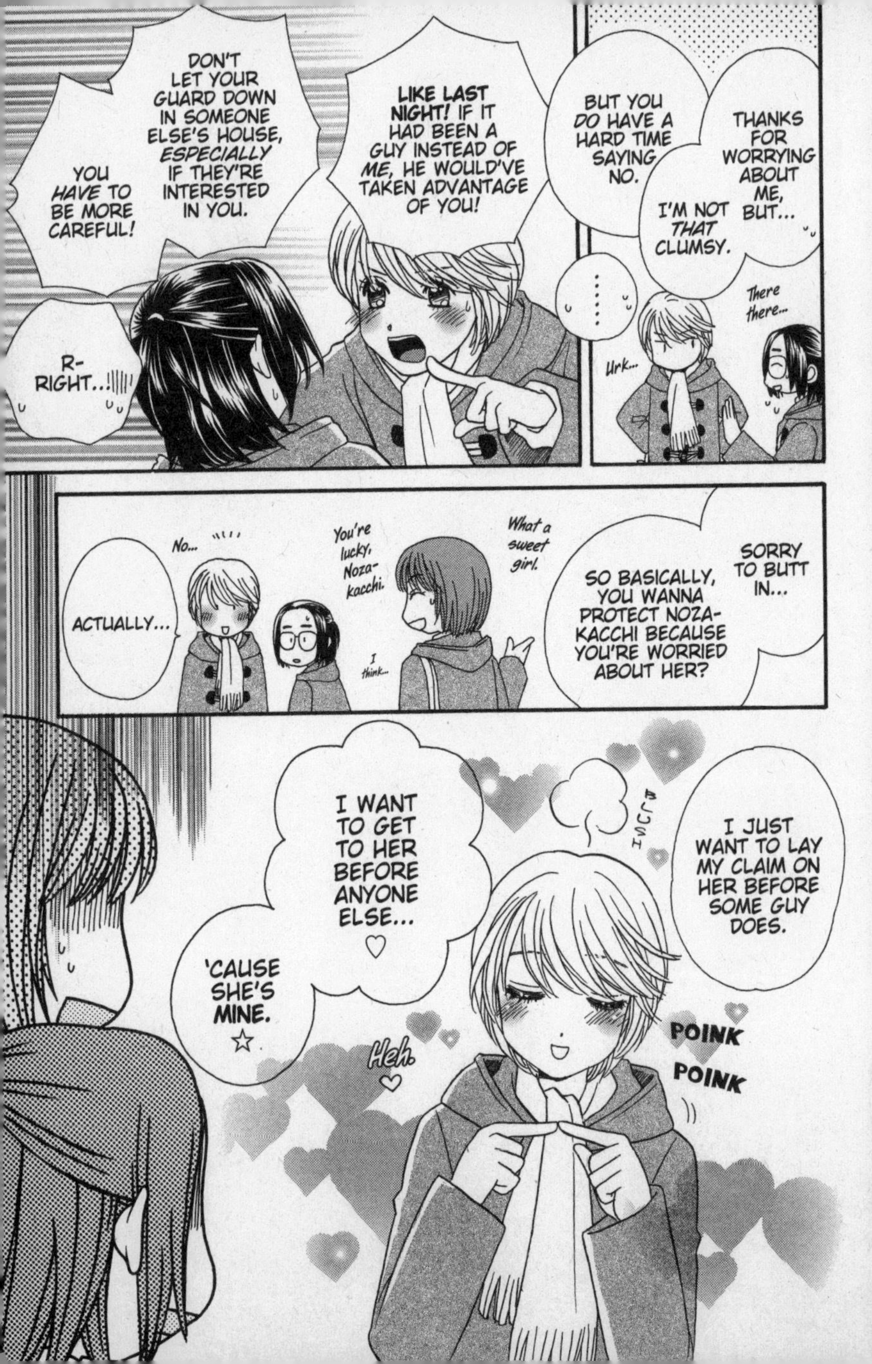
THANKS FOR WORRYING ABOUT ME, BUT...
BUT YOU DO HAVE A HARD TIME SAYING NO.
I'M NOT THAT CLUMSY.
There there...
......
Urk...
LIKE LAST NIGHT! IF IT HAD BEEN A GUY INSTEAD OF ME, HE WOULD'VE TAKEN ADVANTAGE OF YOU!
DON'T LET YOUR GUARD DOWN IN SOMEONE ELSE'S HOUSE, ESPECIALLY IF THEY'RE INTERESTED IN YOU.
YOU HAVE TO BE MORE CAREFUL!
R-RIGHT...!
SORRY TO BUTT IN...
SO BASICALLY, YOU WANNA PROTECT NOZA-KACCHI BECAUSE YOU'RE WORRIED ABOUT HER?
What a sweet girl.
You're lucky, Noza-kacchi.
I think...
No...
ACTUALLY...
I JUST WANT TO LAY MY CLAIM ON HER BEFORE SOME GUY DOES.
BLUSH
POINK
POINK
I WANT TO GET TO HER BEFORE ANYONE ELSE... ♡
'CAUSE SHE'S MINE. ☆
Heh. ♡

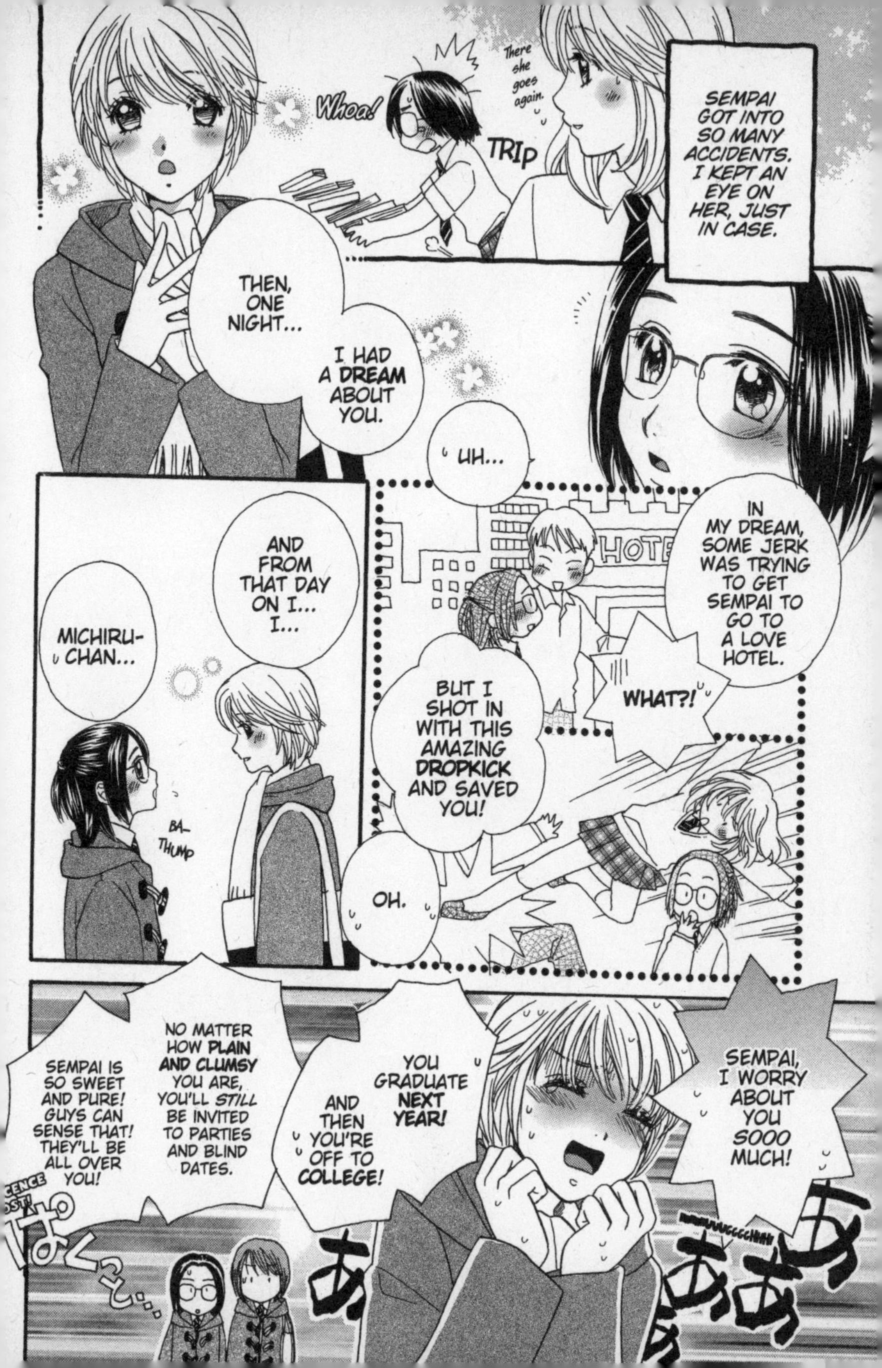
SEMPAI GOT INTO SO MANY ACCIDENTS. I KEPT AN EYE ON HER, JUST IN CASE.
There she goes again.
TRIP
Whoa!
THEN, ONE NIGHT...
I HAD A DREAM ABOUT YOU.
UH...
IN MY DREAM, SOME JERK WAS TRYING TO GET SEMPAI TO GO TO A LOVE HOTEL.
HOTE
WHAT?!
BUT I SHOT IN WITH THIS AMAZING DROPKICK AND SAVED YOU!
OH.
AND FROM THAT DAY ON I... I...
MICHIRU-CHAN...
BA-THUMP
SEMPAI, I WORRY ABOUT YOU SOOO MUCH!
NNNNUUUGGGCHHH
あああ
YOU GRADUATE NEXT YEAR!
AND THEN YOU'RE OFF TO COLLEGE!
NO MATTER HOW PLAIN AND CLUMSY YOU ARE, YOU'LL STILL BE INVITED TO PARTIES AND BLIND DATES.
SEMPAI IS SO SWEET AND PURE! GUYS CAN SENSE THAT! THEY'LL BE ALL OVER YOU!
ぱくっと...

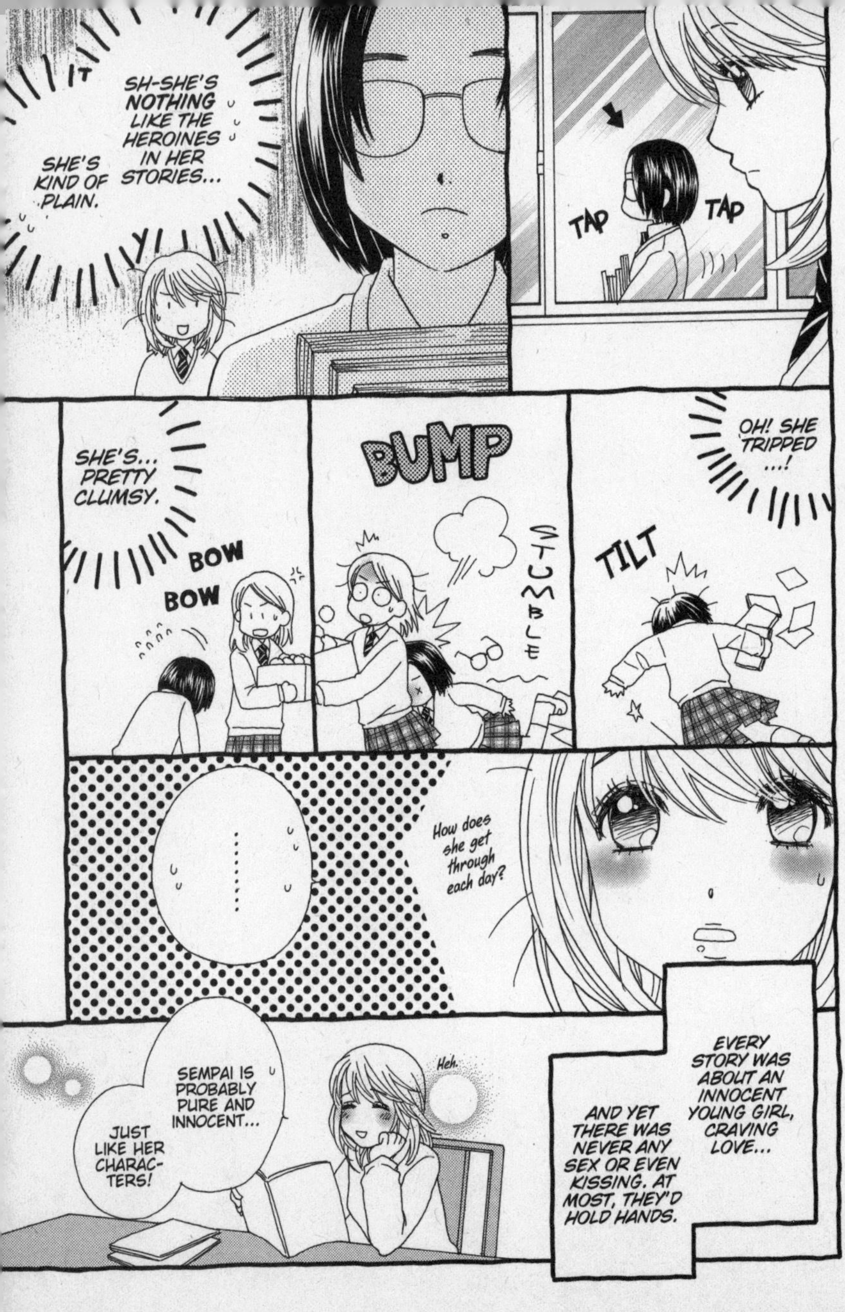
TAP
TAP
SH-SHE'S NOTHING LIKE THE HEROINES IN HER STORIES...
SHE'S KIND OF PLAIN.
OH! SHE TRIPPED ...!
TILT
BUMP
STUMBLE
SHE'S... PRETTY CLUMSY.
BOW
BOW
How does she get through each day?
......
EVERY STORY WAS ABOUT AN INNOCENT YOUNG GIRL, CRAVING LOVE...
AND YET THERE WAS NEVER ANY SEX OR EVEN KISSING. AT MOST, THEY'D HOLD HANDS.
Heh.
SEMPAI IS PROBABLY PURE AND INNOCENT...
JUST LIKE HER CHARAC-TERS!

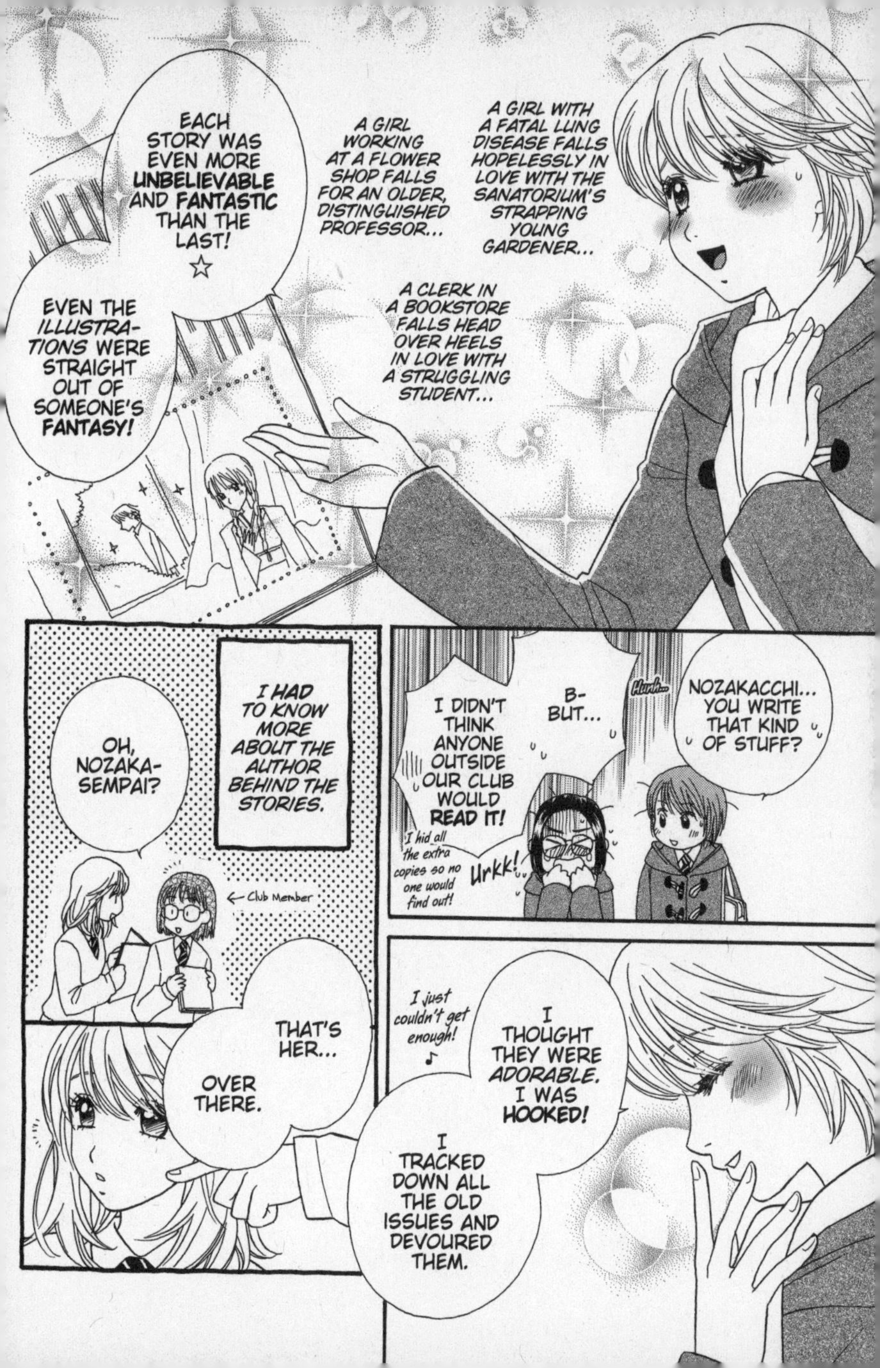
A GIRL WITH A FATAL LUNG DISEASE FALLS HOPELESSLY IN LOVE WITH THE SANATORIUM'S STRAPPING YOUNG GARDENER...
A GIRL WORKING AT A FLOWER SHOP FALLS FOR AN OLDER, DISTINGUISHED PROFESSOR...
A CLERK IN A BOOKSTORE FALLS HEAD OVER HEELS IN LOVE WITH A STRUGGLING STUDENT...
EACH STORY WAS EVEN MORE UNBELIEVABLE AND FANTASTIC THAN THE LAST! ☆
EVEN THE ILLUSTRATIONS WERE STRAIGHT OUT OF SOMEONE'S FANTASY!
NOZAKACCHI... YOU WRITE THAT KIND OF STUFF?
B-BUT...
I DIDN'T THINK ANYONE OUTSIDE OUR CLUB WOULD READ IT!
Urkk!
I hid all the extra copies so no one would find out!
I HAD TO KNOW MORE ABOUT THE AUTHOR BEHIND THE STORIES.
OH, NOZAKA-SEMPAI?
← Club Member
I THOUGHT THEY WERE ADORABLE. I WAS HOOKED!
I just couldn't get enough! ♪
I TRACKED DOWN ALL THE OLD ISSUES AND DEVOURED THEM.
THAT'S HER...
OVER THERE.

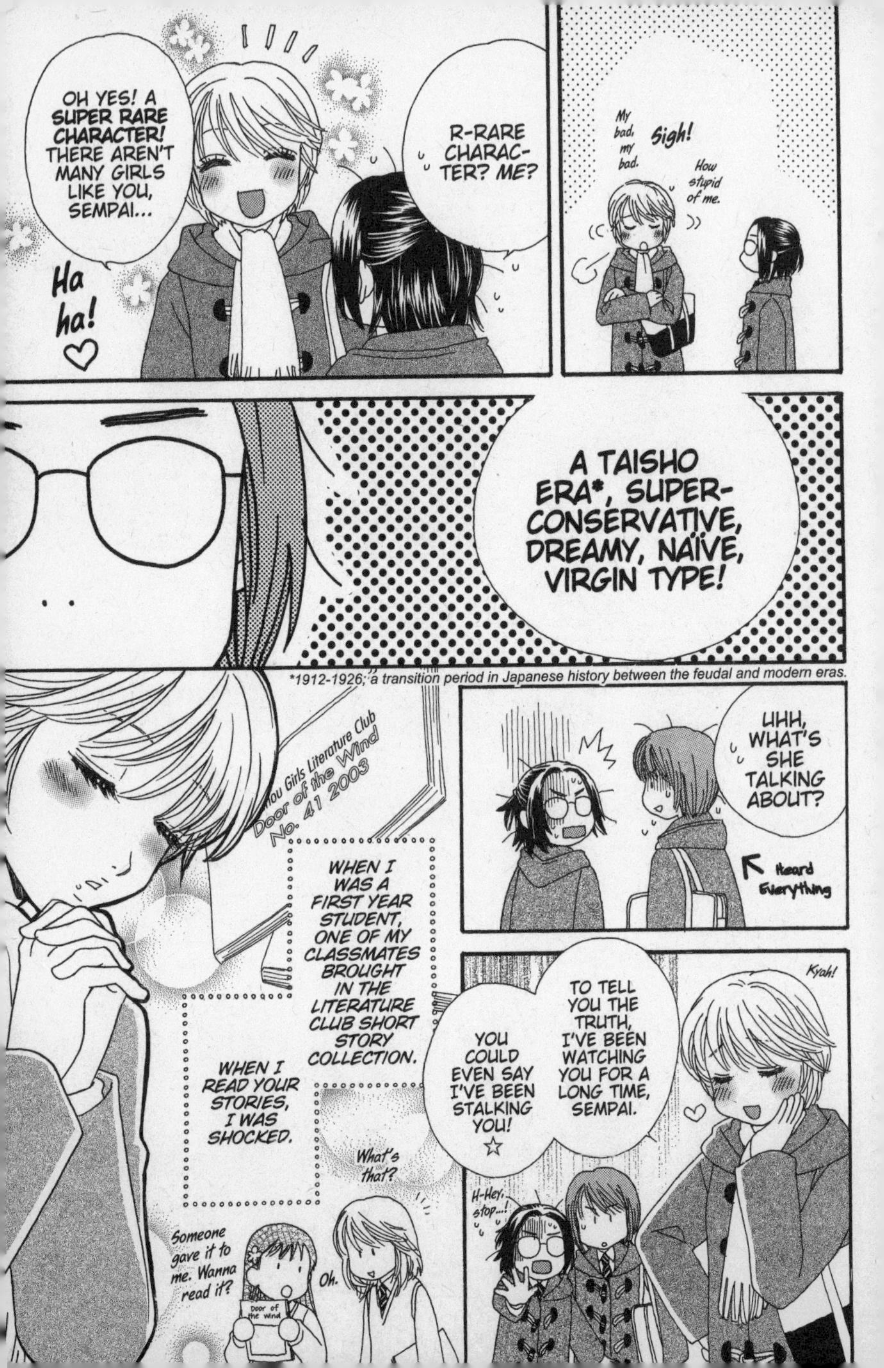
My bad, my bad.
Sigh!
How stupid of me.
OH YES! A SUPER RARE CHARACTER! THERE AREN'T MANY GIRLS LIKE YOU, SEMPAI...
R-RARE CHARAC-TER? ME?
Ha ha! ♡
A TAISHO ERA*, SUPER-CONSERVATIVE, DREAMY, NAÏVE, VIRGIN TYPE!
...
UHH, WHAT'S SHE TALKING ABOUT?
Heard Everything
Kyah!
TO TELL YOU THE TRUTH, I'VE BEEN WATCHING YOU FOR A LONG TIME, SEMPAI.
YOU COULD EVEN SAY I'VE BEEN STALKING YOU! ☆
H-Hey, stop...!
...ihou Girls Literature Club Door of the Wind No. 41 2003
WHEN I WAS A FIRST YEAR STUDENT, ONE OF MY CLASSMATES BROUGHT IN THE LITERATURE CLUB SHORT STORY COLLECTION.
WHEN I READ YOUR STORIES, I WAS SHOCKED.
What's that?
Someone gave it to me. Wanna read it?
Oh.
Door of the Wind

*1912-1926; a transition period in Japanese history between the feudal and modern eras.

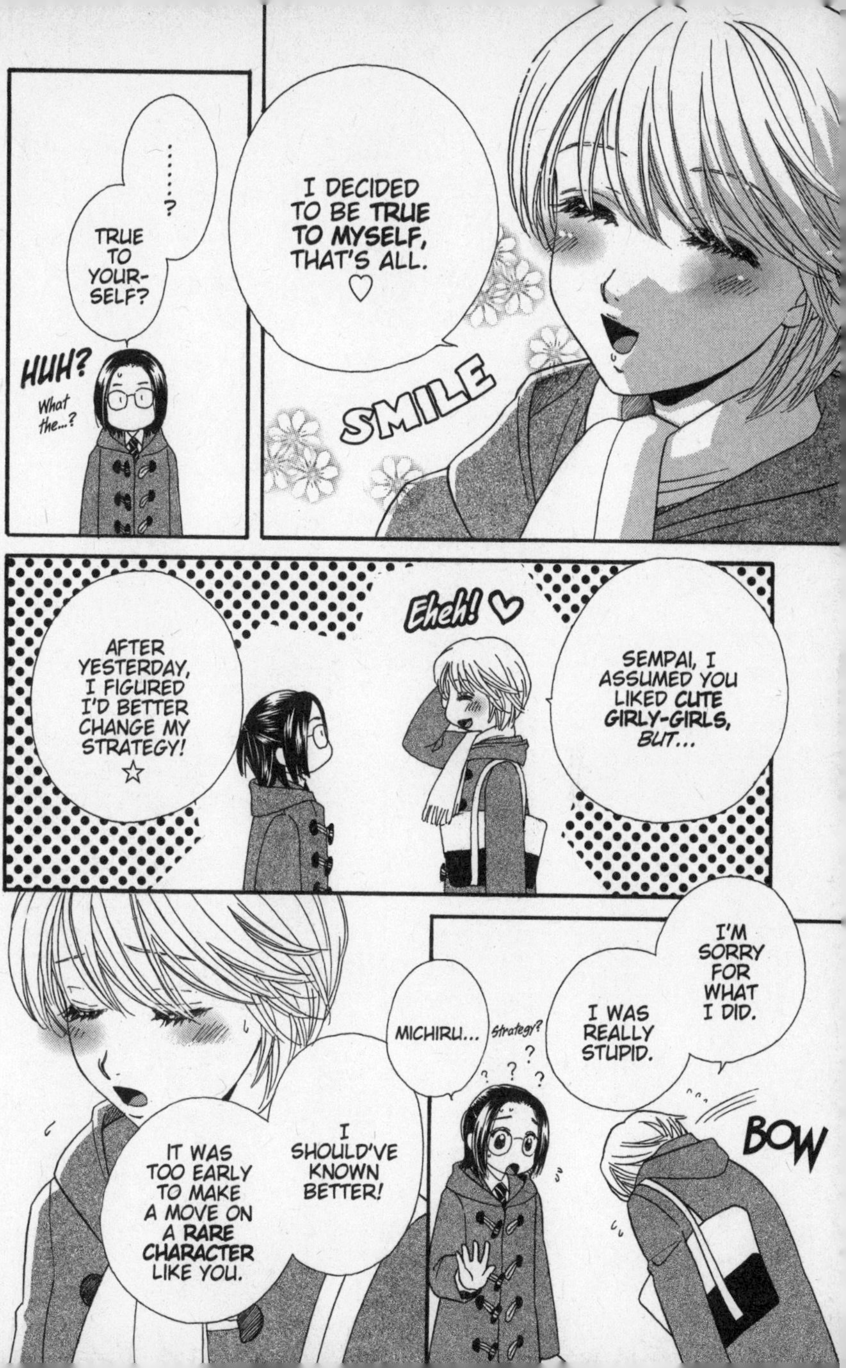
I DECIDED TO BE TRUE TO MYSELF, THAT'S ALL. ♡
SMILE
......?
TRUE TO YOURSELF?
HUH?
What the...?
SEMPAI, I ASSUMED YOU LIKED CUTE GIRLY-GIRLS, BUT...
Eheh! ♡
AFTER YESTERDAY, I FIGURED I'D BETTER CHANGE MY STRATEGY! ☆
BOW
I'M SORRY FOR WHAT I DID.
I WAS REALLY STUPID.
MICHIRU...
Strategy?
I SHOULD'VE KNOWN BETTER!
IT WAS TOO EARLY TO MAKE A MOVE ON A RARE CHARACTER LIKE YOU.

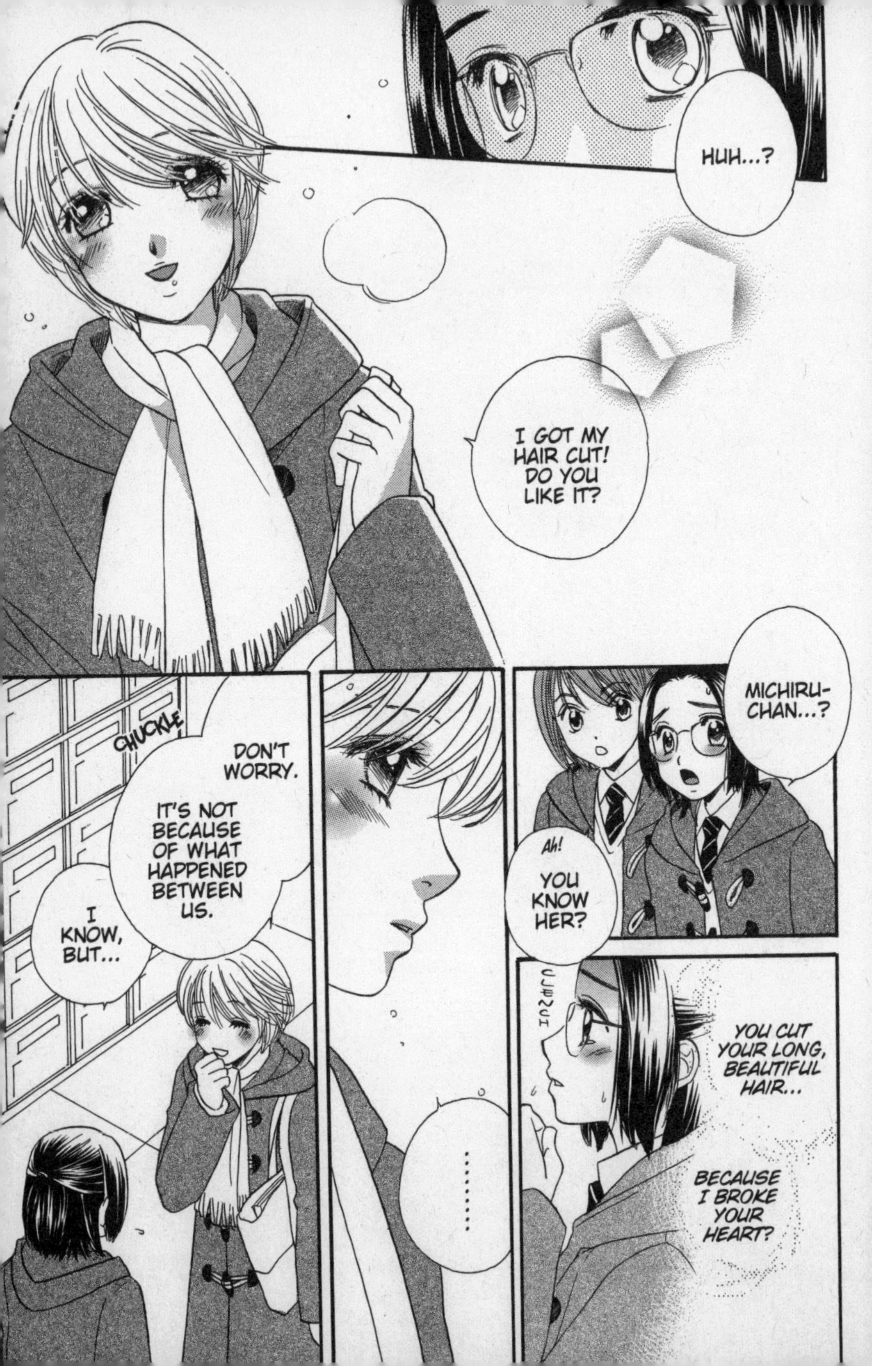
HUH...?
I GOT MY HAIR CUT! DO YOU LIKE IT?
MICHIRU-CHAN...?
Ah!
YOU KNOW HER?
YOU CUT YOUR LONG, BEAUTIFUL HAIR...
BECAUSE I BROKE YOUR HEART?
......
CHUCKLE
DON'T WORRY.
IT'S NOT BECAUSE OF WHAT HAPPENED BETWEEN US.
I KNOW, BUT...

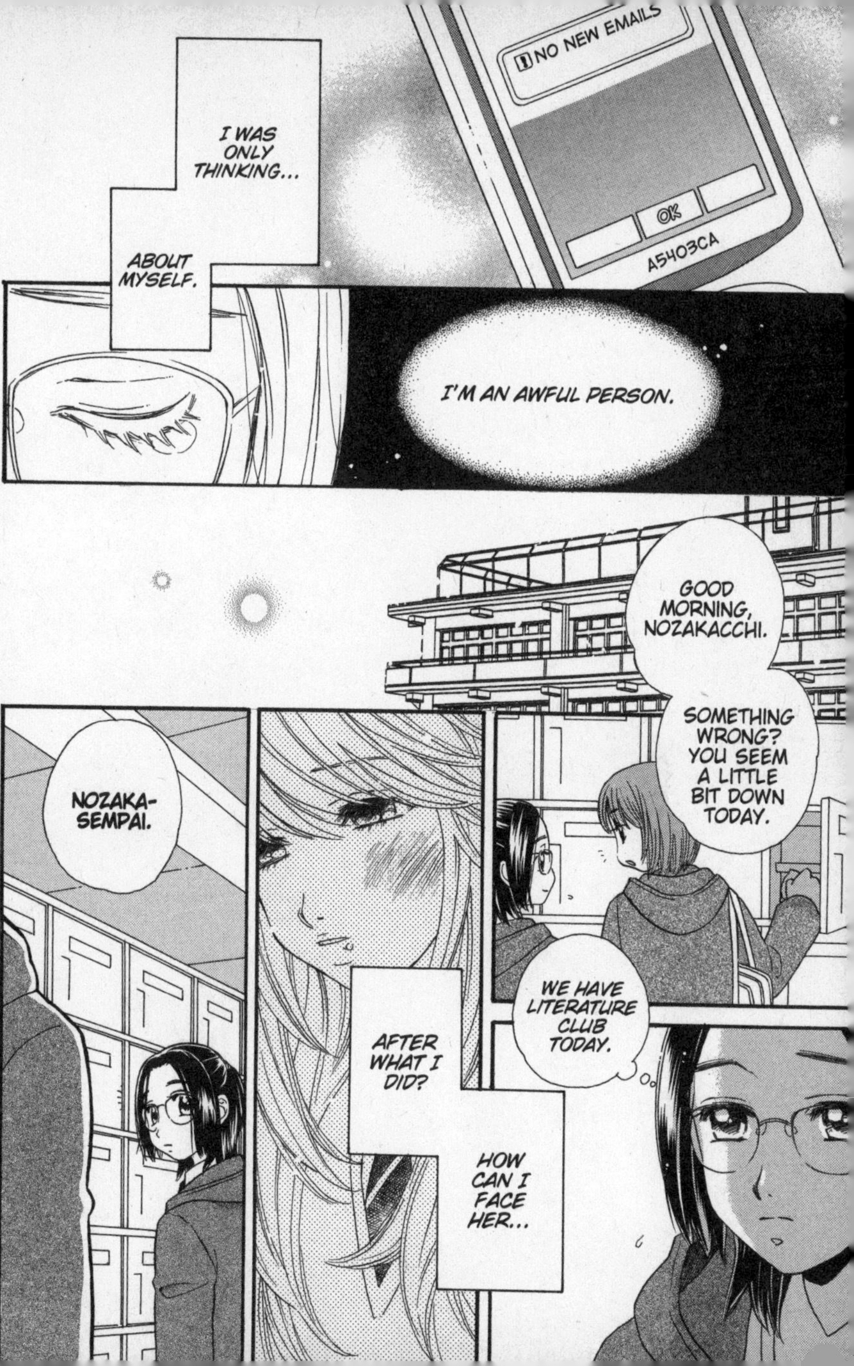
NO NEW EMAILS
OK
A5403CA
I WAS ONLY THINKING...
ABOUT MYSELF.
I'M AN AWFUL PERSON.
GOOD MORNING, NOZAKACCHI.
SOMETHING WRONG? YOU SEEM A LITTLE BIT DOWN TODAY.
WE HAVE LITERATURE CLUB TODAY.
AFTER WHAT I DID?
HOW CAN I FACE HER...
NOZAKA-SEMPAI.

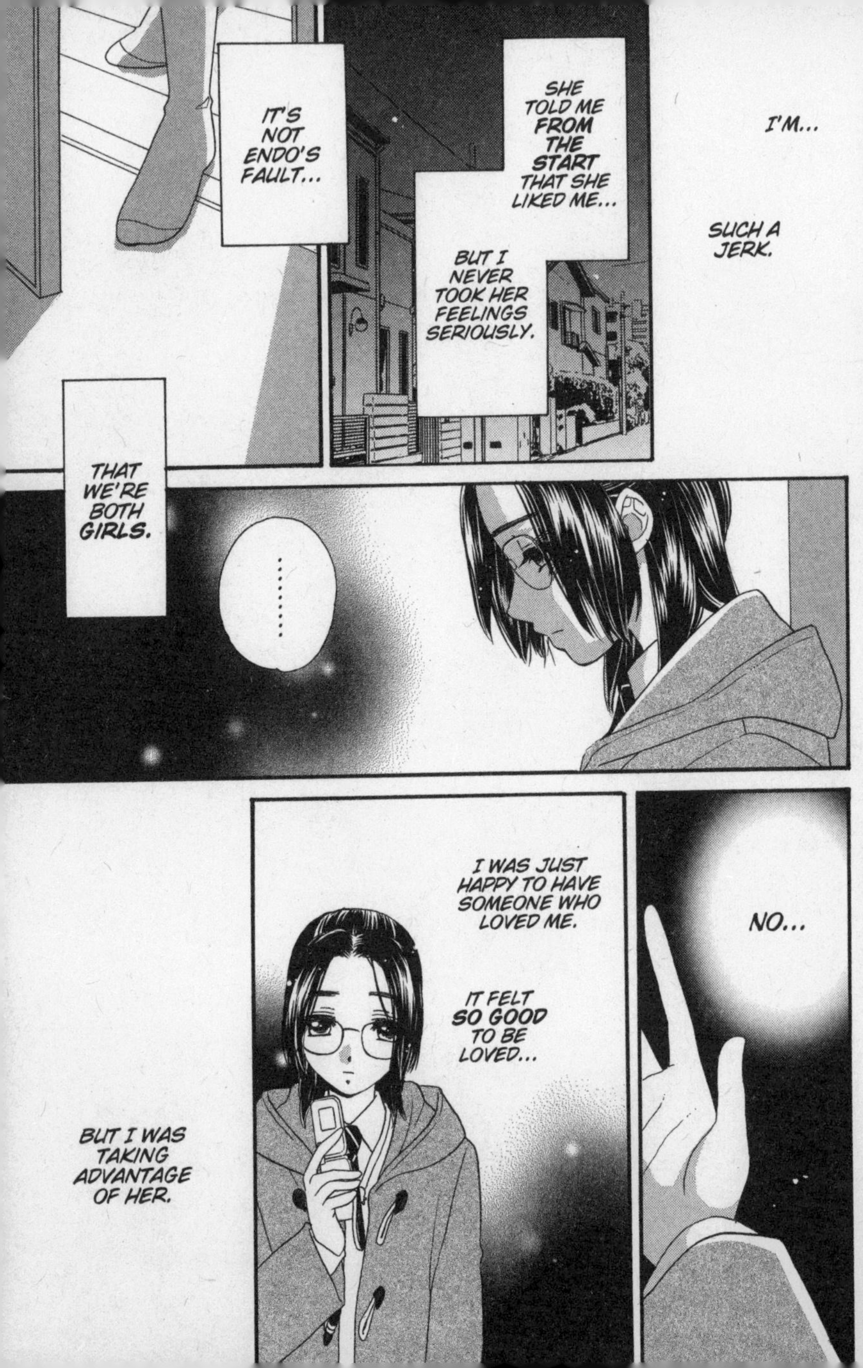
I'M...
SUCH A JERK.
SHE TOLD ME FROM THE START THAT SHE LIKED ME...
BUT I NEVER TOOK HER FEELINGS SERIOUSLY.
IT'S NOT ENDO'S FAULT...
THAT WE'RE BOTH GIRLS.
......
NO...
I WAS JUST HAPPY TO HAVE SOMEONE WHO LOVED ME.
IT FELT SO GOOD TO BE LOVED...
BUT I WAS TAKING ADVANTAGE OF HER.

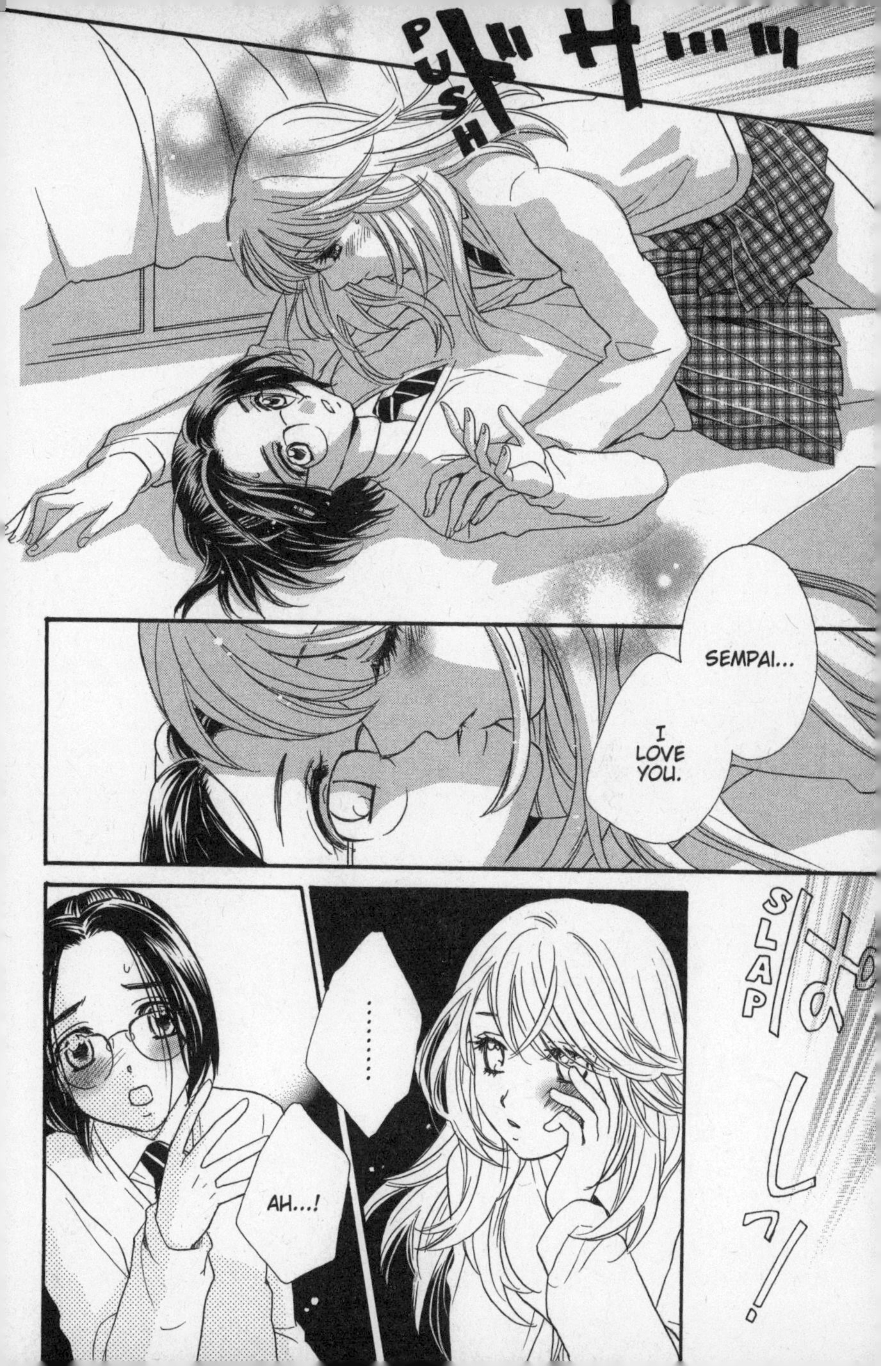
PUSH
SEMPAI...
I LOVE YOU.
SLAP
......
AH...!

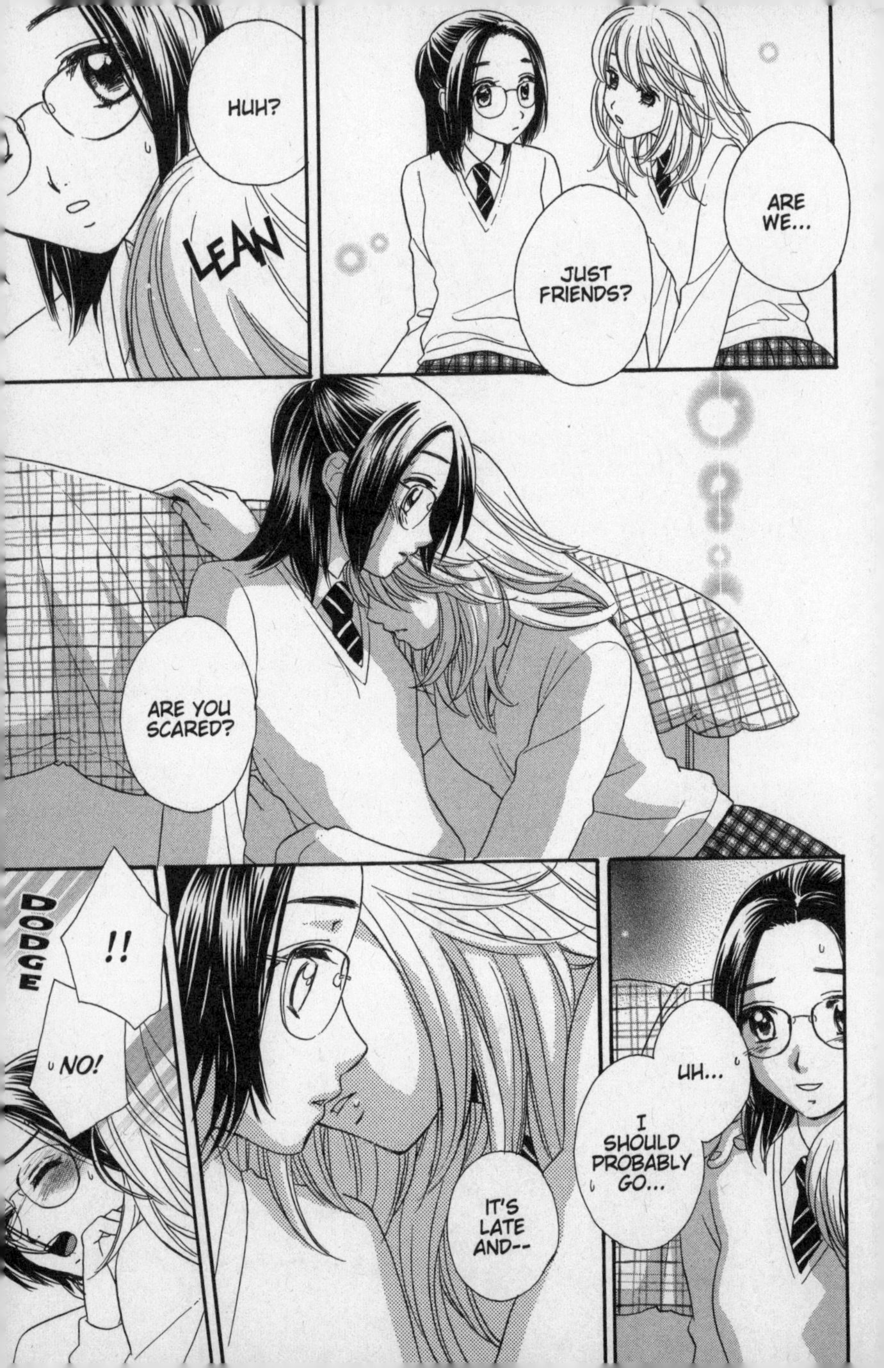
ARE WE...
JUST FRIENDS?
HUH?
LEAN
ARE YOU SCARED?
UH...
I SHOULD PROBABLY GO...
IT'S LATE AND--
!!
DODGE
NO!

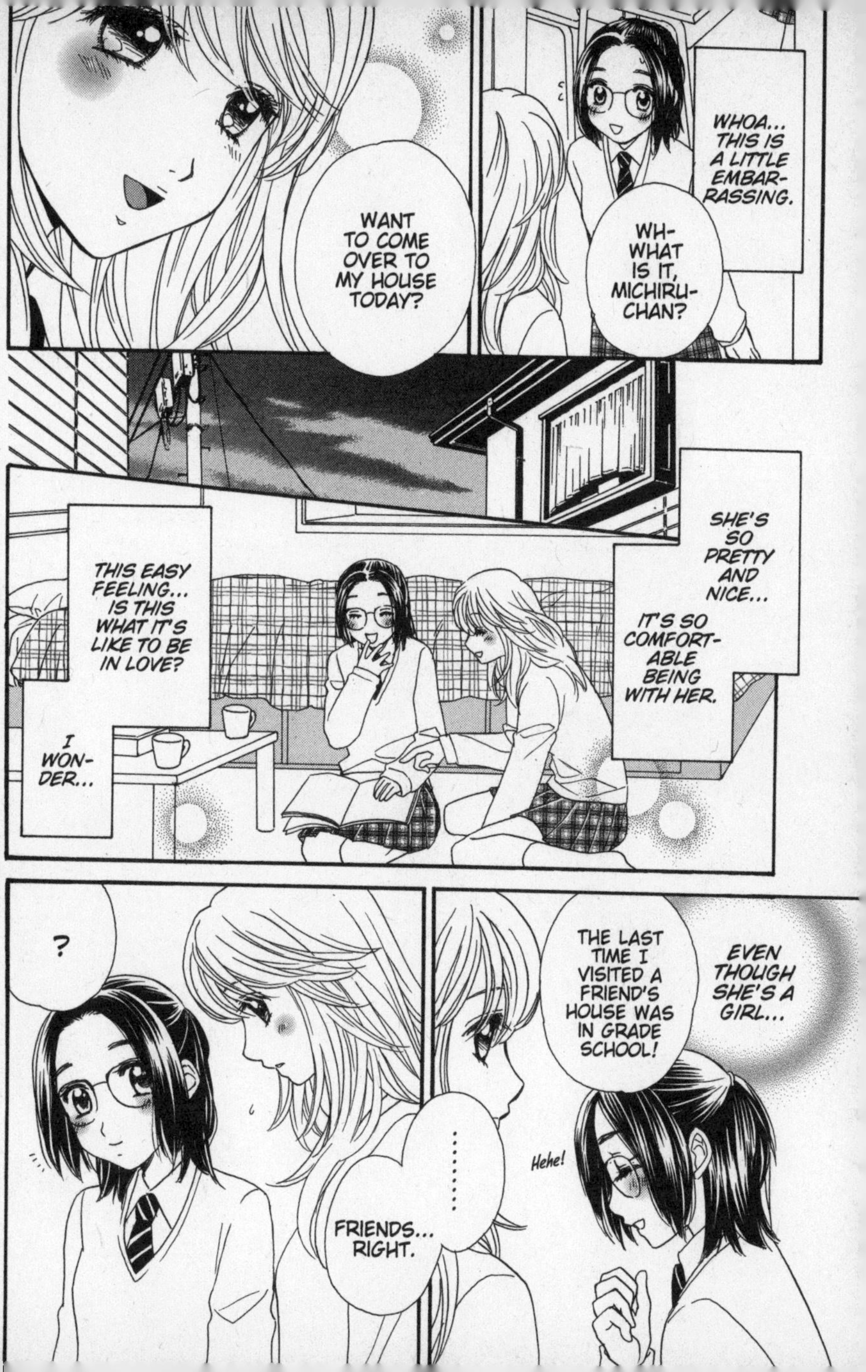
WHOA... THIS IS A LITTLE EMBARRASSING.
WH-WHAT IS IT, MICHIRU-CHAN?
WANT TO COME OVER TO MY HOUSE TODAY?
SHE'S SO PRETTY AND NICE...
IT'S SO COMFORTABLE BEING WITH HER.
THIS EASY FEELING... IS THIS WHAT IT'S LIKE TO BE IN LOVE?
I WONDER...
EVEN THOUGH SHE'S A GIRL...
THE LAST TIME I VISITED A FRIEND'S HOUSE WAS IN GRADE SCHOOL!
Hehe!
......
FRIENDS... RIGHT.
?

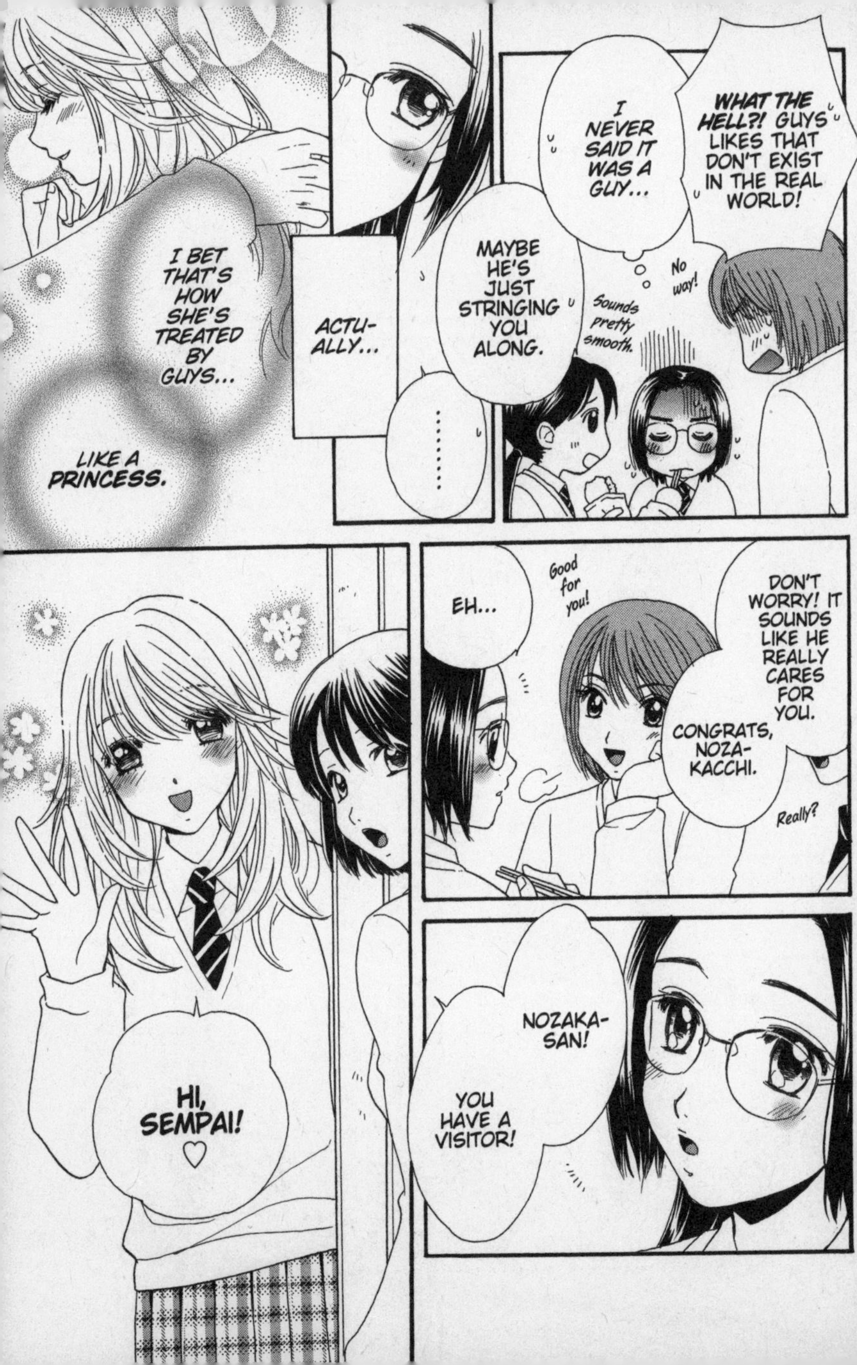
WHAT THE HELL?! GUYS LIKES THAT DON'T EXIST IN THE REAL WORLD!
I NEVER SAID IT WAS A GUY...
No way!
Sounds pretty smooth.
MAYBE HE'S JUST STRINGING YOU ALONG.
ACTU-ALLY...
......
I BET THAT'S HOW SHE'S TREATED BY GUYS...
LIKE A PRINCESS.
DON'T WORRY! IT SOUNDS LIKE HE REALLY CARES FOR YOU.
CONGRATS, NOZA-KACCHI.
Really?
Good for you!
EH...
NOZAKA-SAN!
YOU HAVE A VISITOR!
HI, SEMPAI! ♡

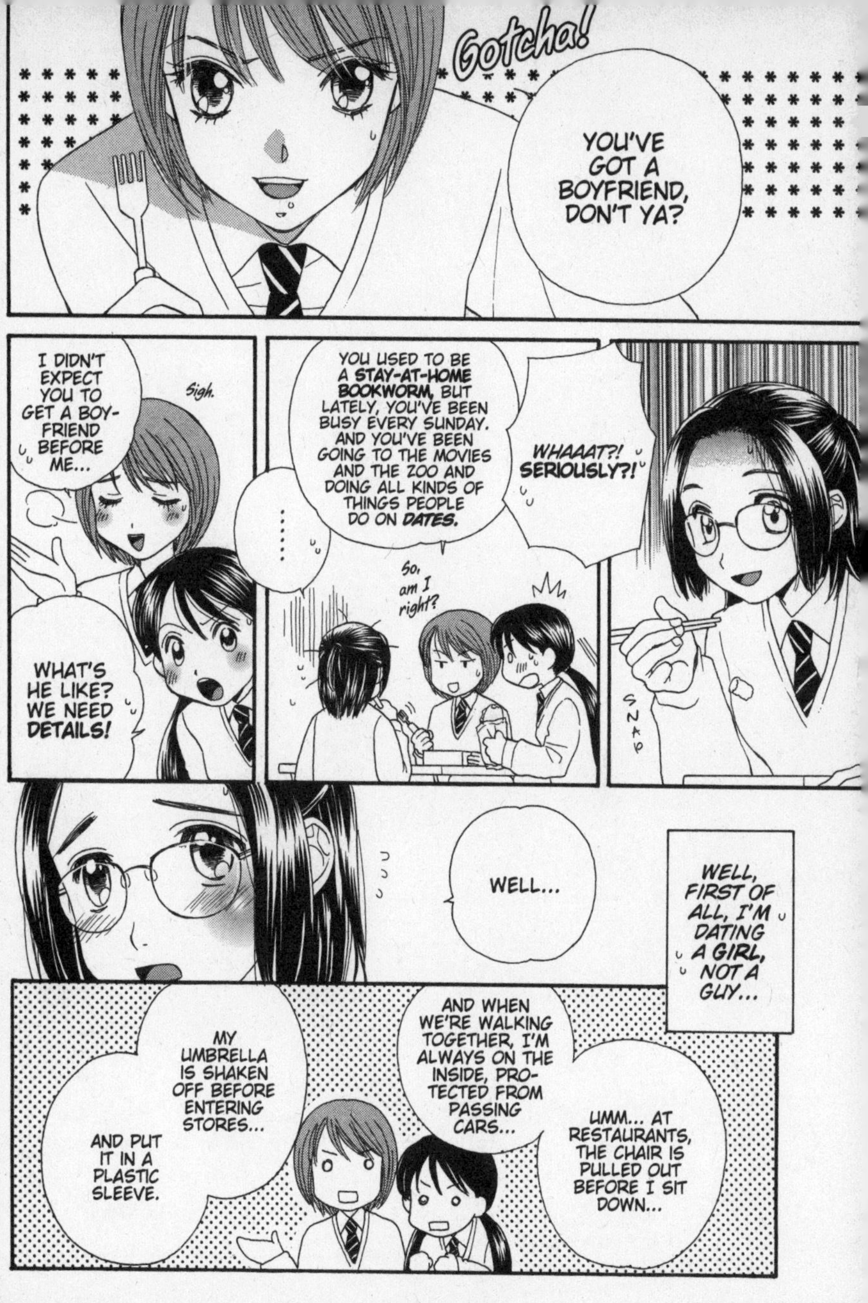
Gotcha!
YOU'VE GOT A BOYFRIEND, DON'T YA?
WHAAAT?! SERIOUSLY?!
SNAP
YOU USED TO BE A STAY-AT-HOME BOOKWORM, BUT LATELY, YOU'VE BEEN BUSY EVERY SUNDAY. AND YOU'VE BEEN GOING TO THE MOVIES AND THE ZOO AND DOING ALL KINDS OF THINGS PEOPLE DO ON DATES.
......
So, am I right?
I DIDN'T EXPECT YOU TO GET A BOY-FRIEND BEFORE ME...
Sigh.
WHAT'S HE LIKE? WE NEED DETAILS!
WELL...
WELL, FIRST OF ALL, I'M DATING A GIRL, NOT A GUY...
UMM... AT RESTAURANTS, THE CHAIR IS PULLED OUT BEFORE I SIT DOWN...
AND WHEN WE'RE WALKING TOGETHER, I'M ALWAYS ON THE INSIDE, PRO-TECTED FROM PASSING CARS...
MY UMBRELLA IS SHAKEN OFF BEFORE ENTERING STORES...
AND PUT IT IN A PLASTIC SLEEVE.

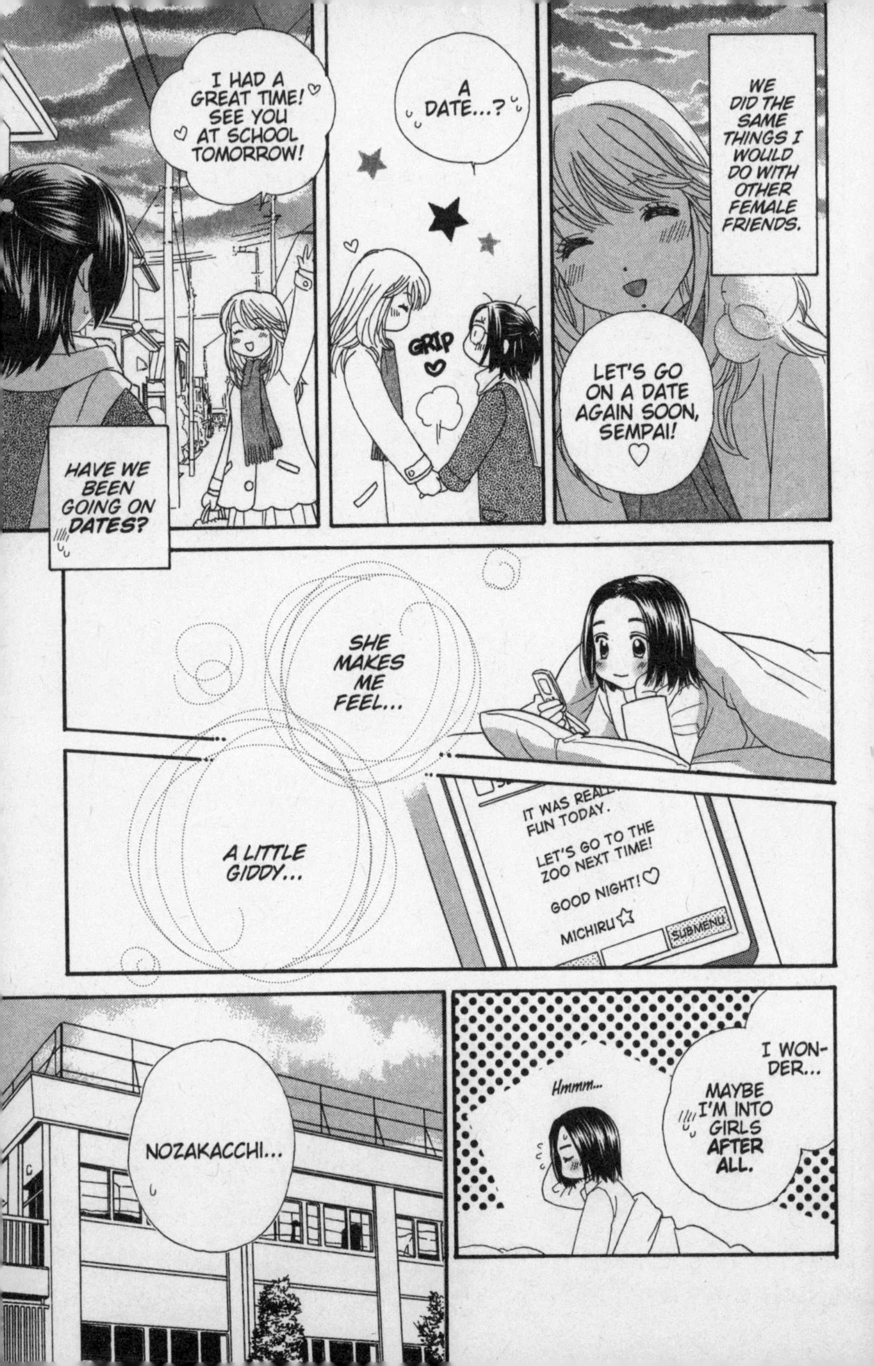
WE DID THE SAME THINGS I WOULD DO WITH OTHER FEMALE FRIENDS.
LET'S GO ON A DATE AGAIN SOON, SEMPAI! ♡
A DATE...?
GRIP ♡
I HAD A GREAT TIME! ♡ SEE YOU AT SCHOOL TOMORROW! ♡
HAVE WE BEEN GOING ON DATES?
SHE MAKES ME FEEL...
IT WAS REALL
FUN TODAY.
LET'S GO TO THE ZOO NEXT TIME!
GOOD NIGHT! ♡
MICHIRU ☆
SUBMENU
A LITTLE GIDDY...
I WON-DER...
MAYBE I'M INTO GIRLS AFTER ALL.
Hmmm...
NOZAKACCHI...

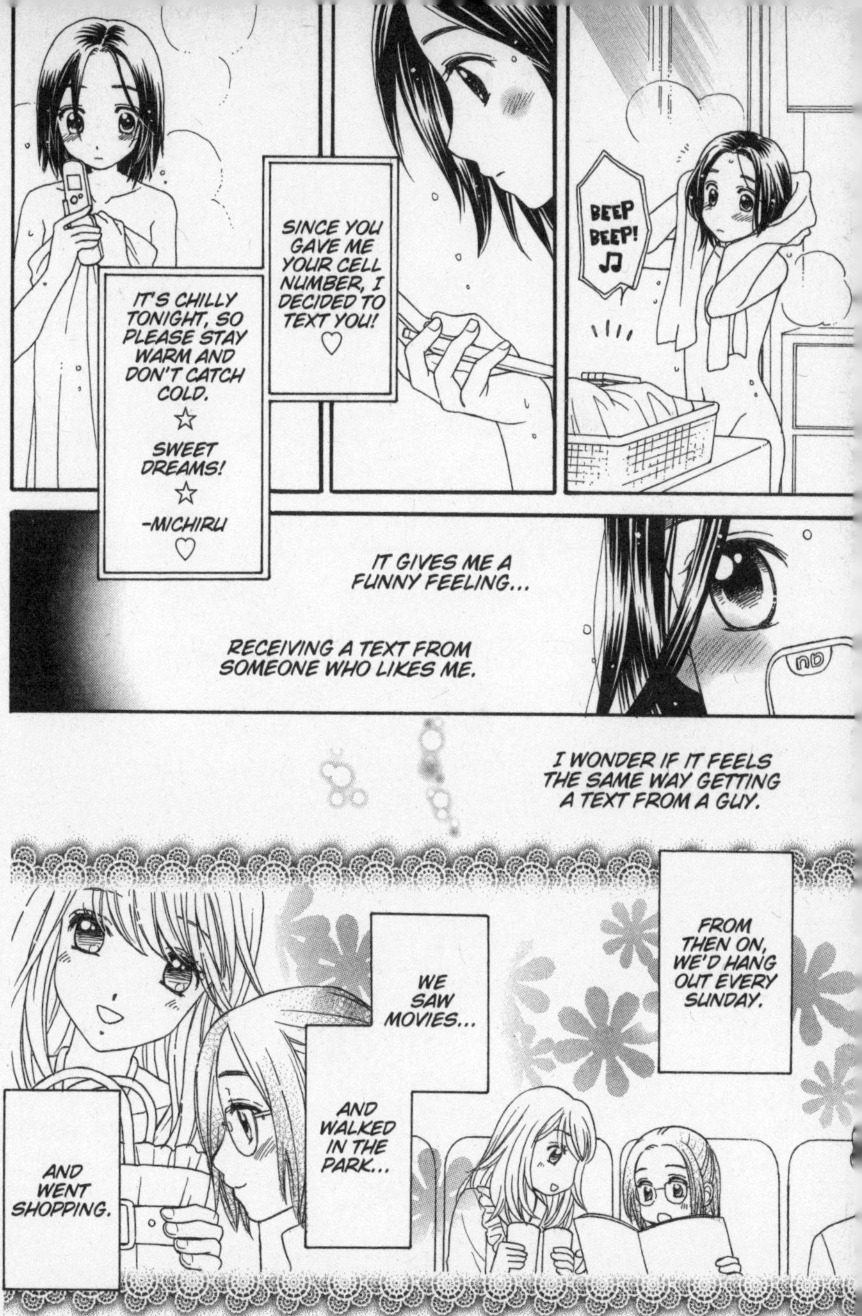
BEEP BEEP! ♫
SINCE YOU GAVE ME YOUR CELL NUMBER, I DECIDED TO TEXT YOU! ♡
IT'S CHILLY TONIGHT, SO PLEASE STAY WARM AND DON'T CATCH COLD. ☆ SWEET DREAMS! ☆ -MICHIRU ♡
IT GIVES ME A FUNNY FEELING...
RECEIVING A TEXT FROM SOMEONE WHO LIKES ME.
I WONDER IF IT FEELS THE SAME WAY GETTING A TEXT FROM A GUY.
FROM THEN ON, WE'D HANG OUT EVERY SUNDAY.
WE SAW MOVIES...
AND WALKED IN THE PARK...
AND WENT SHOPPING.

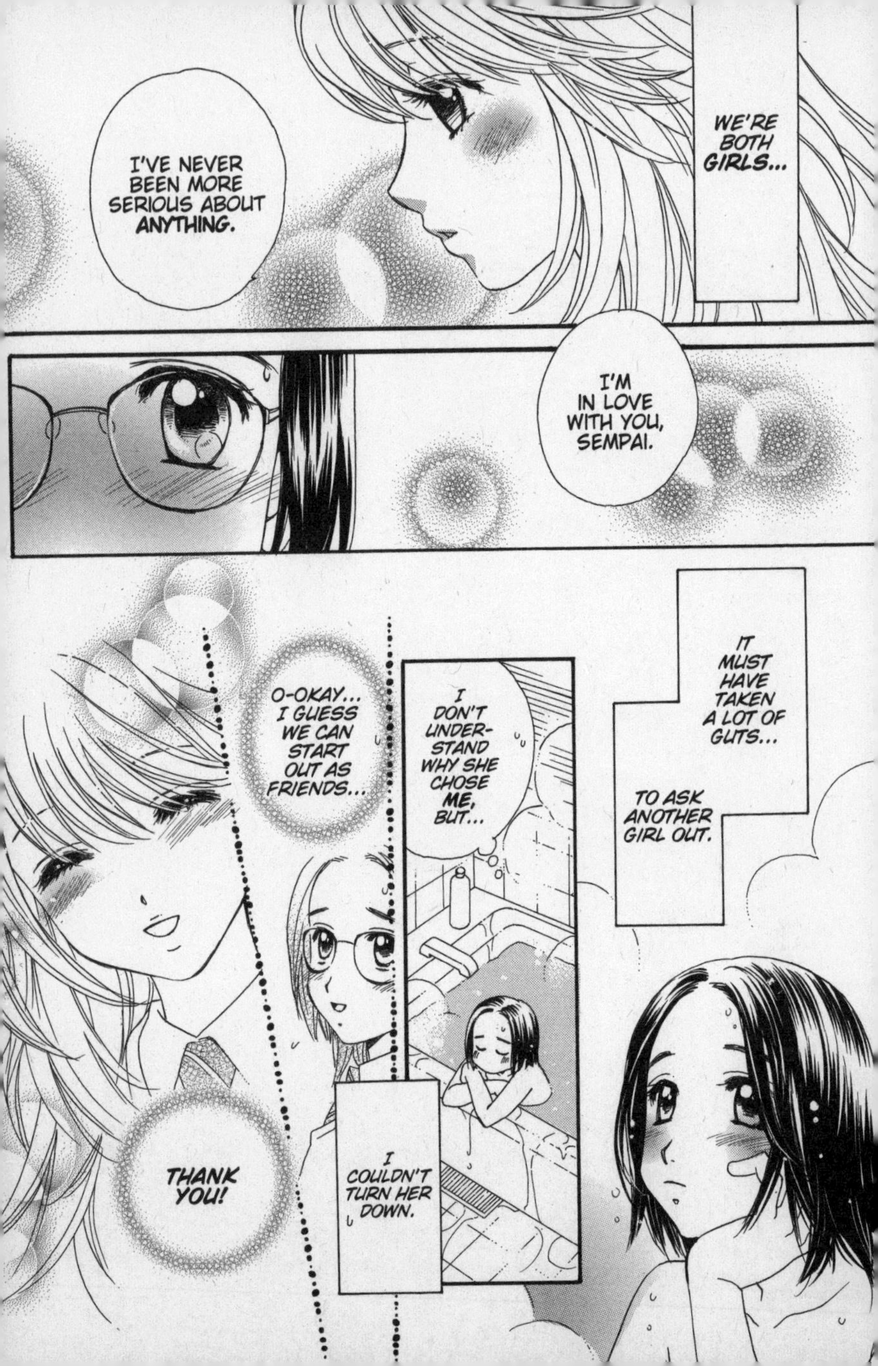
WE'RE BOTH GIRLS...
I'VE NEVER BEEN MORE SERIOUS ABOUT ANYTHING.
I'M IN LOVE WITH YOU, SEMPAI.
IT MUST HAVE TAKEN A LOT OF GUTS...
TO ASK ANOTHER GIRL OUT.
I DON'T UNDER-STAND WHY SHE CHOSE ME, BUT...
I COULDN'T TURN HER DOWN.
O-OKAY... I GUESS WE CAN START OUT AS FRIENDS...
THANK YOU!

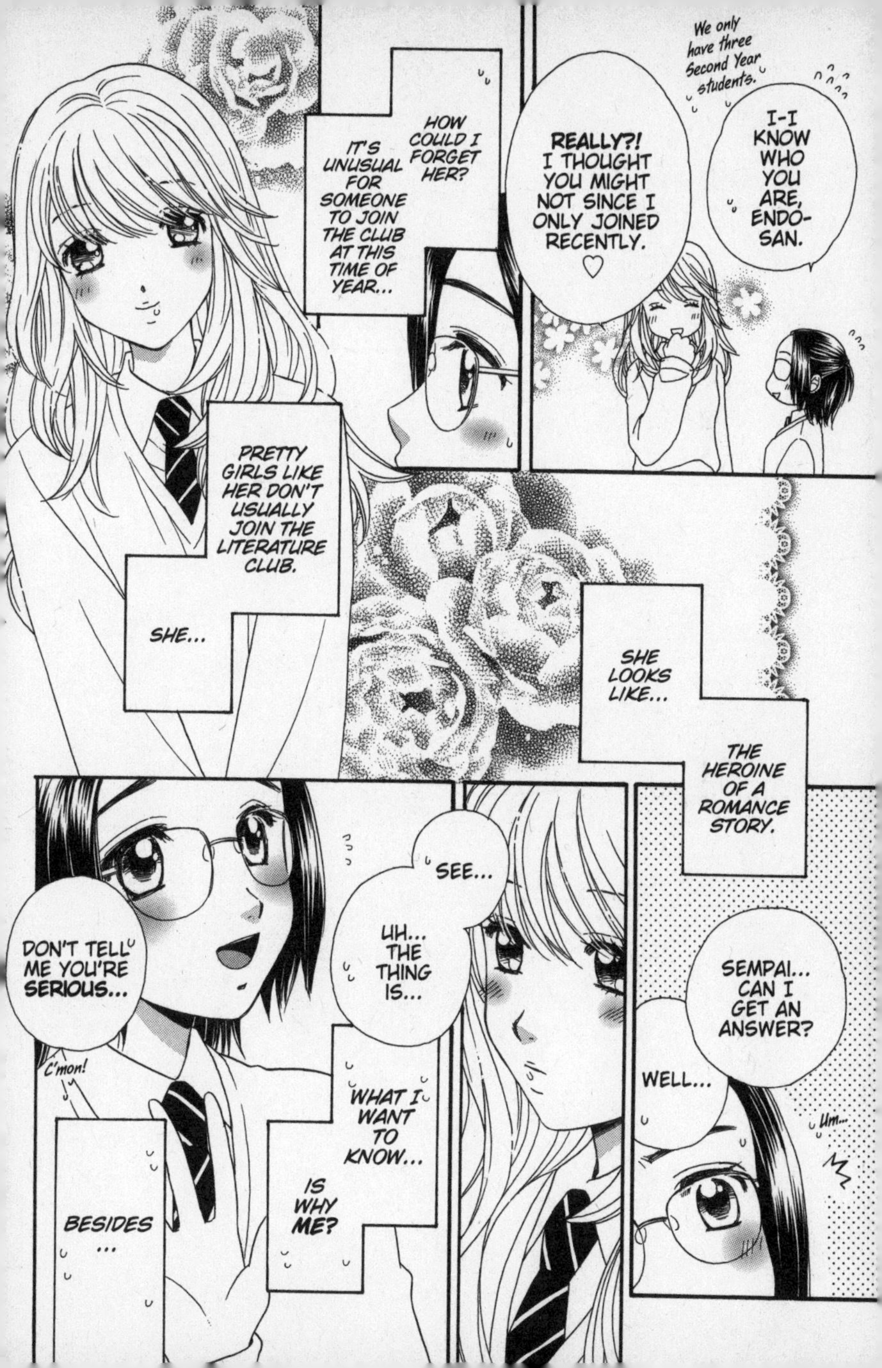
We only have three Second Year students.
I-I KNOW WHO YOU ARE, ENDO-SAN.
REALLY?! I THOUGHT YOU MIGHT NOT SINCE I ONLY JOINED RECENTLY. ♡
HOW COULD I FORGET HER?
IT'S UNUSUAL FOR SOMEONE TO JOIN THE CLUB AT THIS TIME OF YEAR...
PRETTY GIRLS LIKE HER DON'T USUALLY JOIN THE LITERATURE CLUB.
SHE...
SHE LOOKS LIKE...
THE HEROINE OF A ROMANCE STORY.
SEMPAI... CAN I GET AN ANSWER?
WELL...
Um...
SEE...
UH... THE THING IS...
WHAT I WANT TO KNOW...
IS WHY ME?
DON'T TELL ME YOU'RE SERIOUS...
C'mon!
BESIDES...

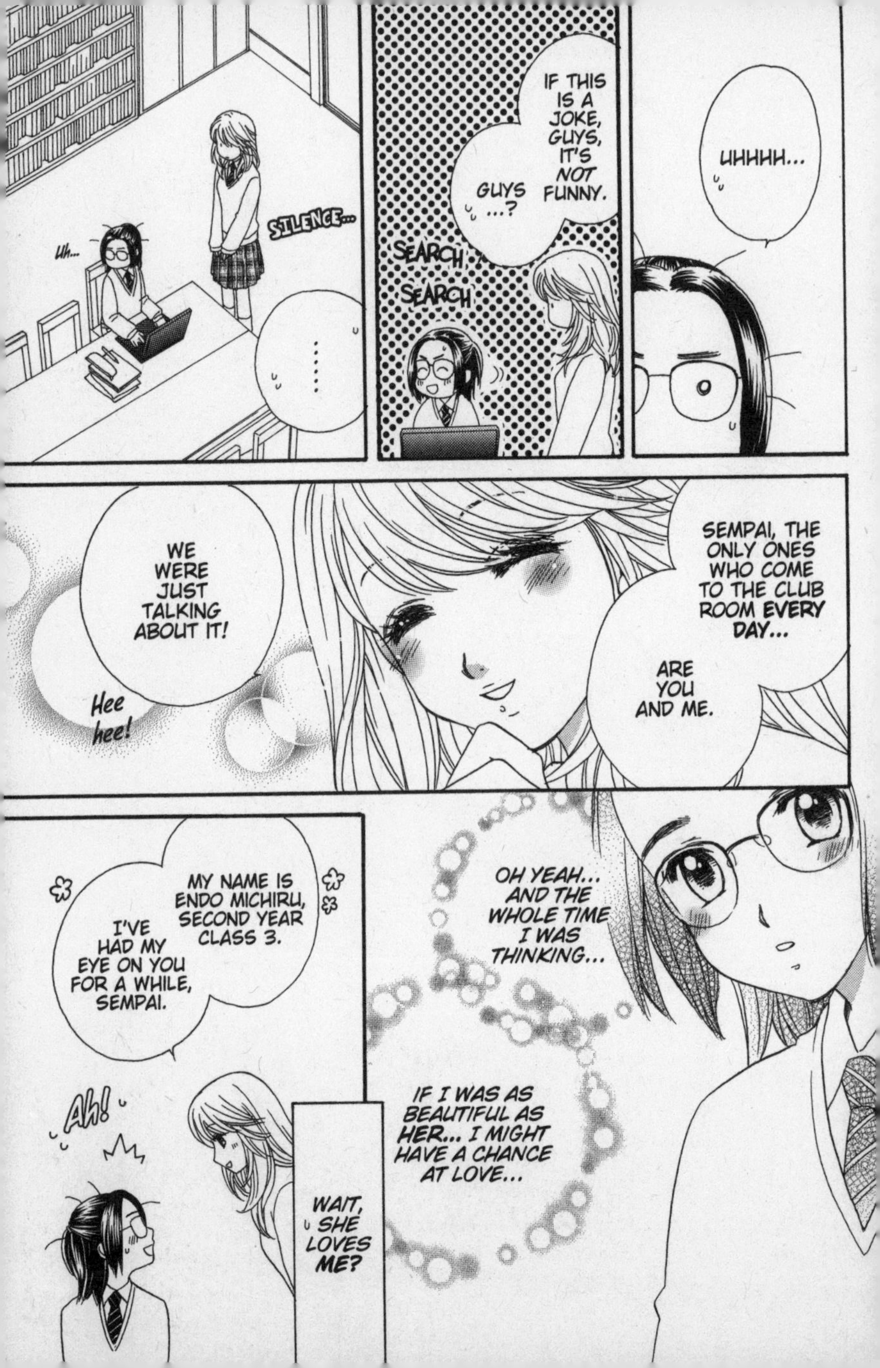
UHHHH...
IF THIS IS A JOKE, GUYS, IT'S NOT FUNNY.
GUYS ...?
SEARCH SEARCH
SILENCE...
Uh...
......
SEMPAI, THE ONLY ONES WHO COME TO THE CLUB ROOM EVERY DAY...
ARE YOU AND ME.
WE WERE JUST TALKING ABOUT IT!
Hee hee!
OH YEAH... AND THE WHOLE TIME I WAS THINKING...
IF I WAS AS BEAUTIFUL AS HER... I MIGHT HAVE A CHANCE AT LOVE...
WAIT, SHE LOVES ME?
MY NAME IS ENDO MICHIRU, SECOND YEAR CLASS 3.
I'VE HAD MY EYE ON YOU FOR A WHILE, SEMPAI.
Ah!

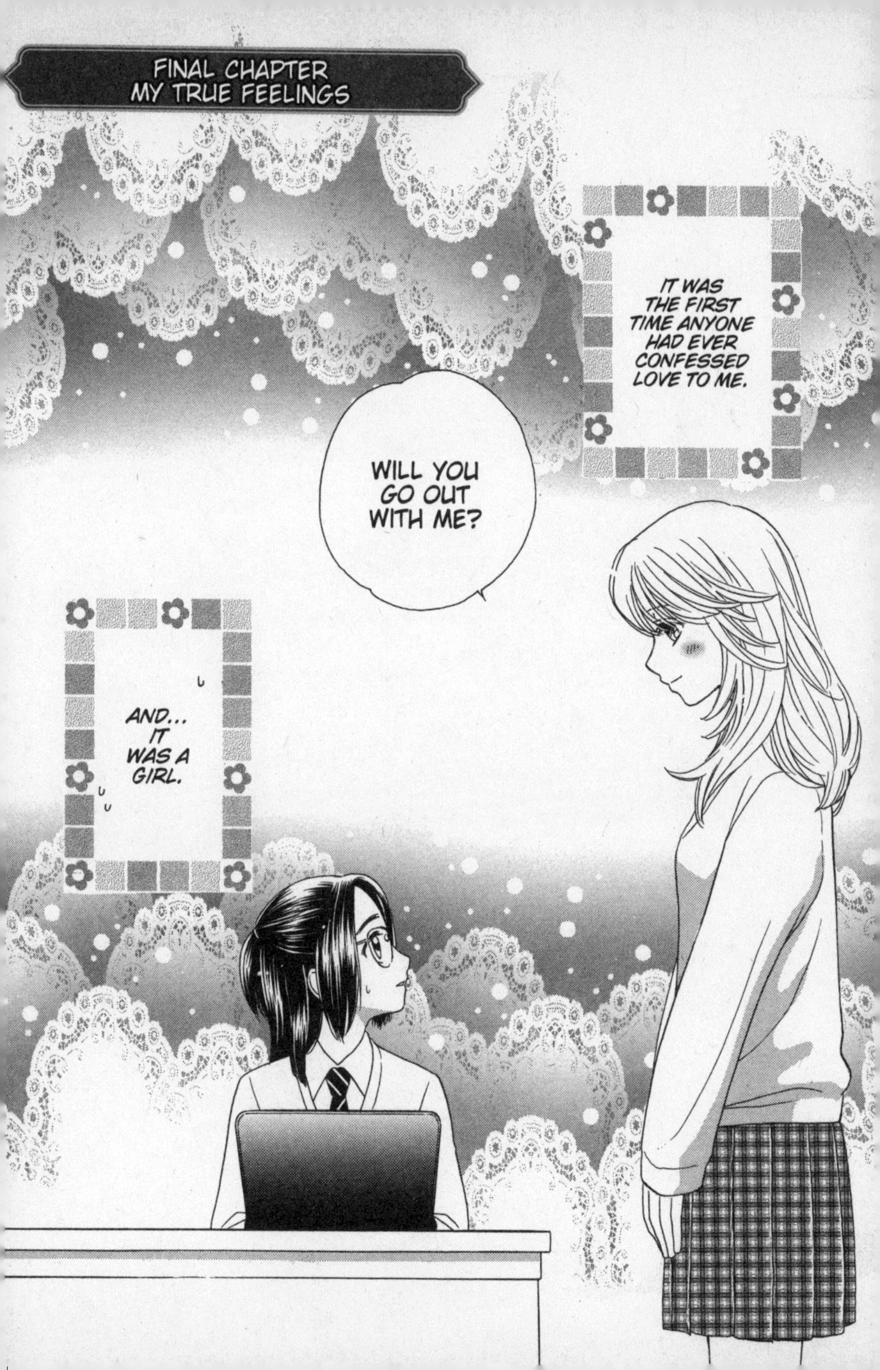
FINAL CHAPTER MY TRUE FEELINGS
IT WAS THE FIRST TIME ANYONE HAD EVER CONFESSED LOVE TO ME.
WILL YOU GO OUT WITH ME?
AND... IT WAS A GIRL.

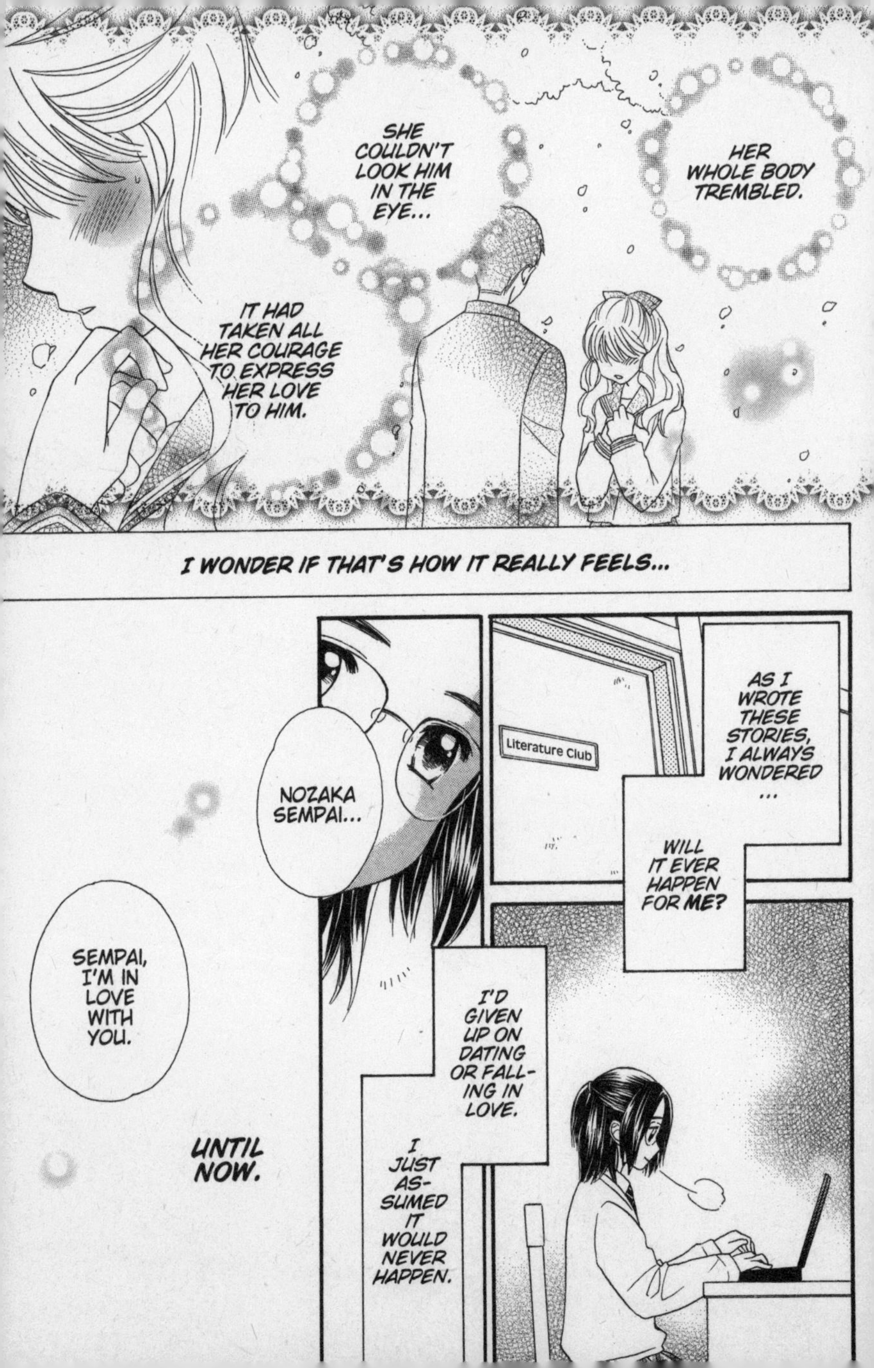
HER WHOLE BODY TREMBLED.
SHE COULDN'T LOOK HIM IN THE EYE...
IT HAD TAKEN ALL HER COURAGE TO EXPRESS HER LOVE TO HIM.
I WONDER IF THAT'S HOW IT REALLY FEELS...
Literature Club
AS I WROTE THESE STORIES, I ALWAYS WONDERED...
WILL IT EVER HAPPEN FOR ME?
NOZAKA SEMPAI...
I'D GIVEN UP ON DATING OR FALLING IN LOVE.
I JUST AS-SUMED IT WOULD NEVER HAPPEN.
SEMPAI, I'M IN LOVE WITH YOU.
UNTIL NOW.

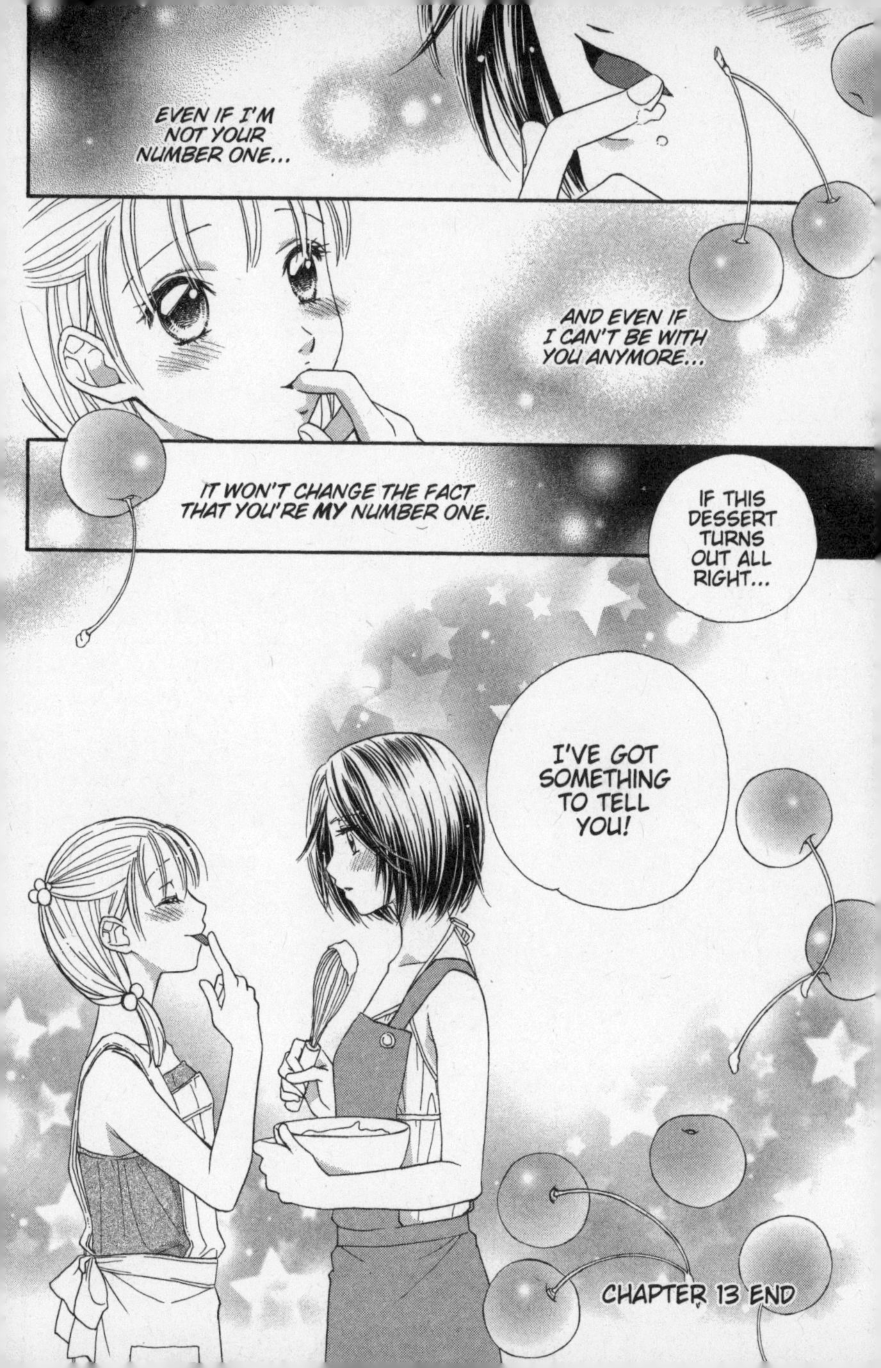
EVEN IF I'M NOT YOUR NUMBER ONE...
AND EVEN IF I CAN'T BE WITH YOU ANYMORE...
IT WON'T CHANGE THE FACT THAT YOU'RE MY NUMBER ONE.
IF THIS DESSERT TURNS OUT ALL RIGHT...
I'VE GOT SOMETHING TO TELL YOU!
CHAPTER 13 END

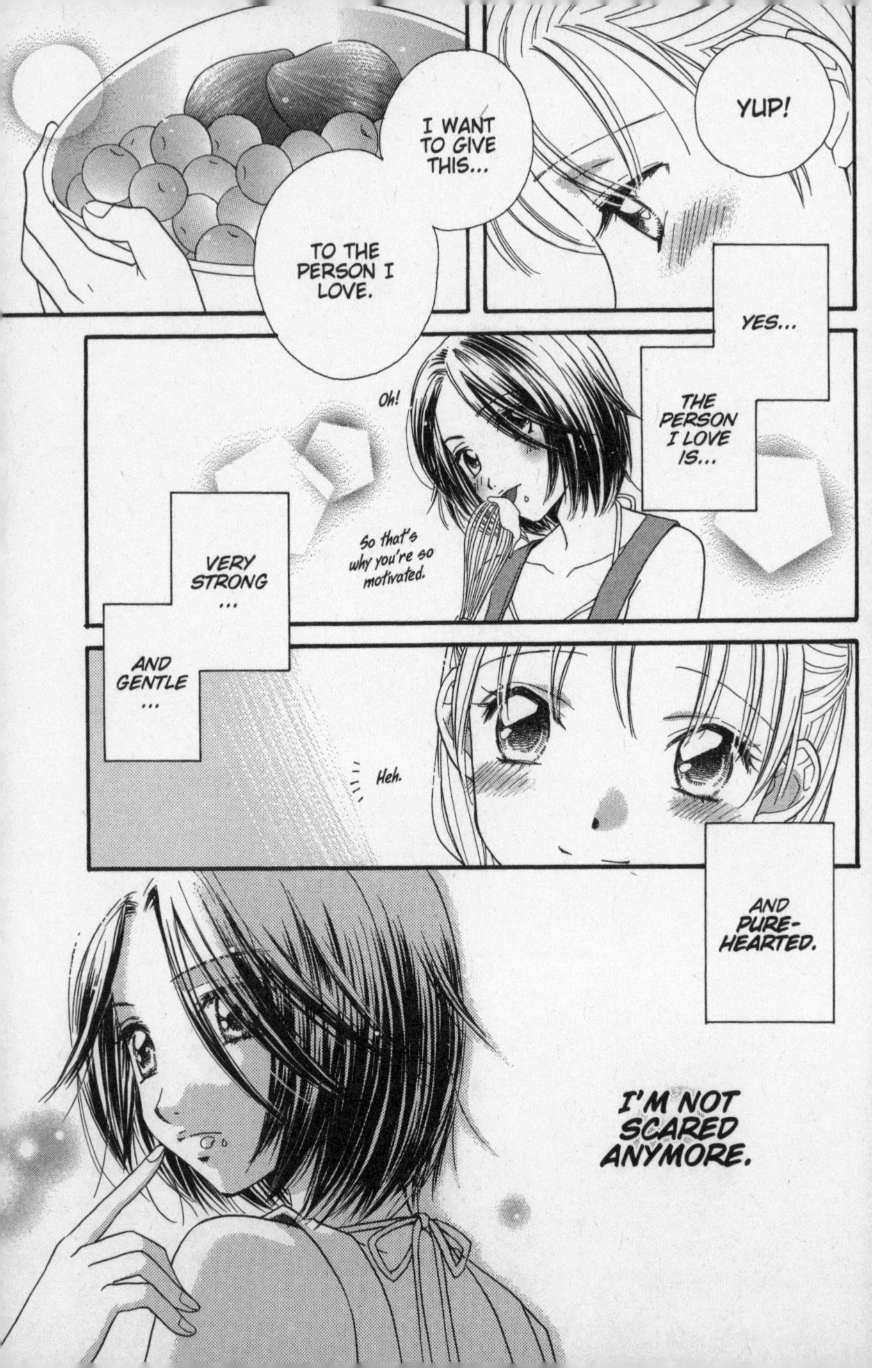
YUP!
I WANT TO GIVE THIS...
TO THE PERSON I LOVE.
YES...
THE PERSON I LOVE IS...
Oh!
So that's why you're so motivated.
VERY STRONG ...
AND GENTLE ...
Heh.
AND PURE-HEARTED.
I'M NOT SCARED ANYMORE.

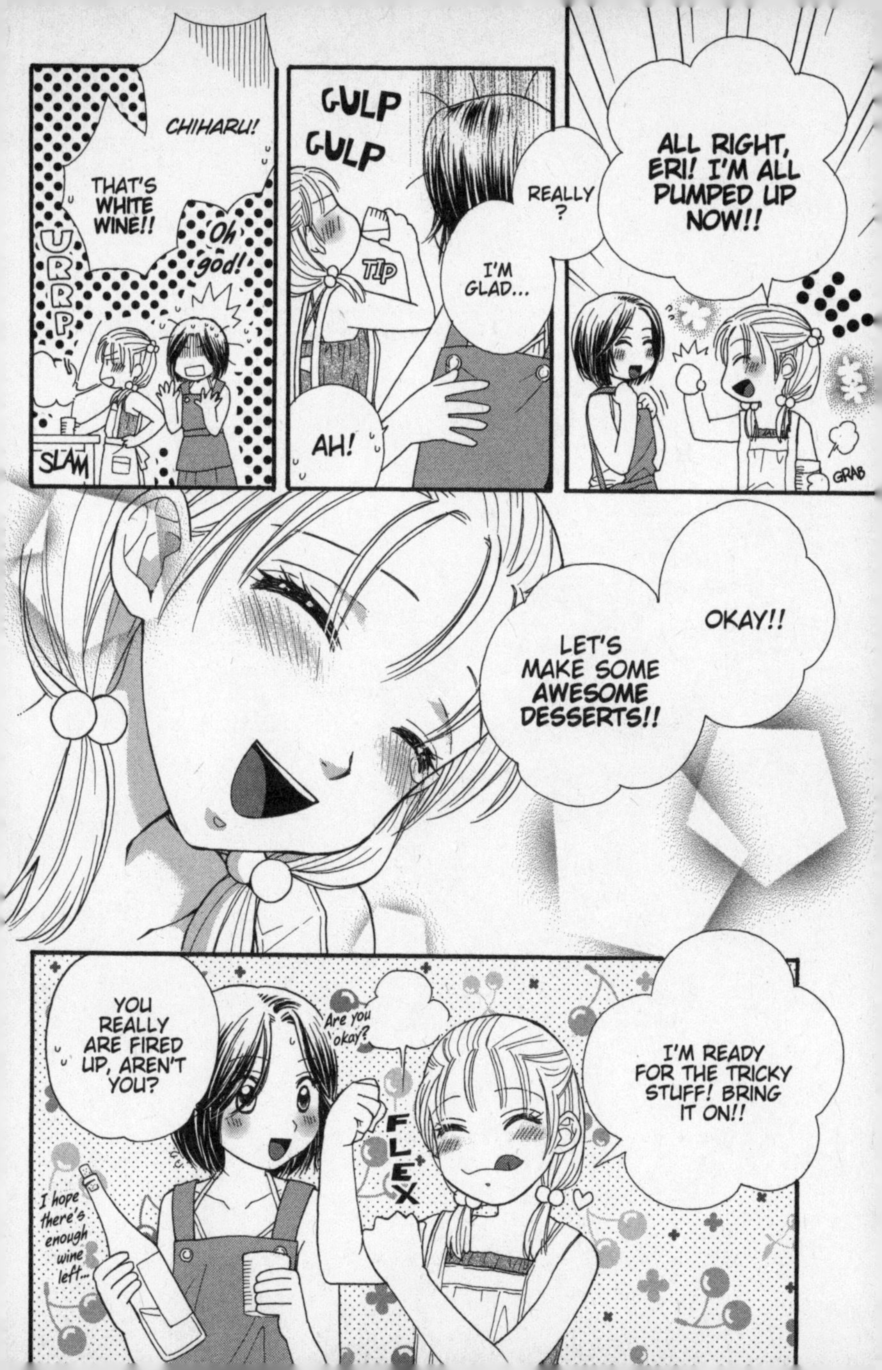
ALL RIGHT, ERI! I'M ALL PUMPED UP NOW!!
REALLY ?
I'M GLAD...
GRAB
GULP
GULP
TIP
AH!
CHIHARU!
THAT'S WHITE WINE!!
Oh god!
URRP
SLAM
OKAY!!
LET'S MAKE SOME AWESOME DESSERTS!!
I'M READY FOR THE TRICKY STUFF! BRING IT ON!!
FLEX
Are you okay?
YOU REALLY ARE FIRED UP, AREN'T YOU?
I hope there's enough wine left...

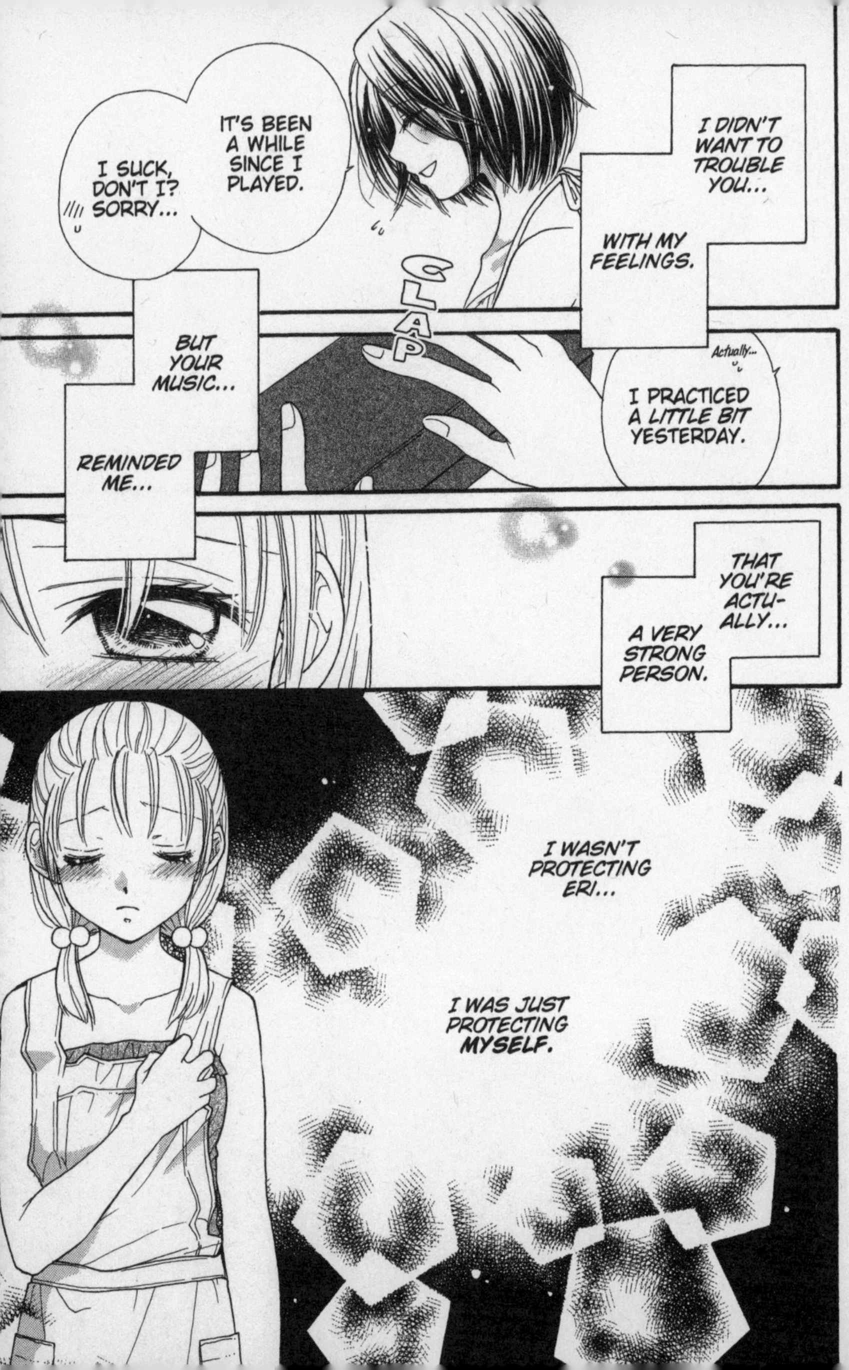
I DIDN'T WANT TO TROUBLE YOU...
WITH MY FEELINGS.
IT'S BEEN A WHILE SINCE I PLAYED.
I SUCK, DON'T I? SORRY...
CLAP
Actually...
I PRACTICED A LITTLE BIT YESTERDAY.
BUT YOUR MUSIC...
REMINDED ME...
THAT YOU'RE ACTU-ALLY...
A VERY STRONG PERSON.
I WASN'T PROTECTING ERI...
I WAS JUST PROTECTING MYSELF.

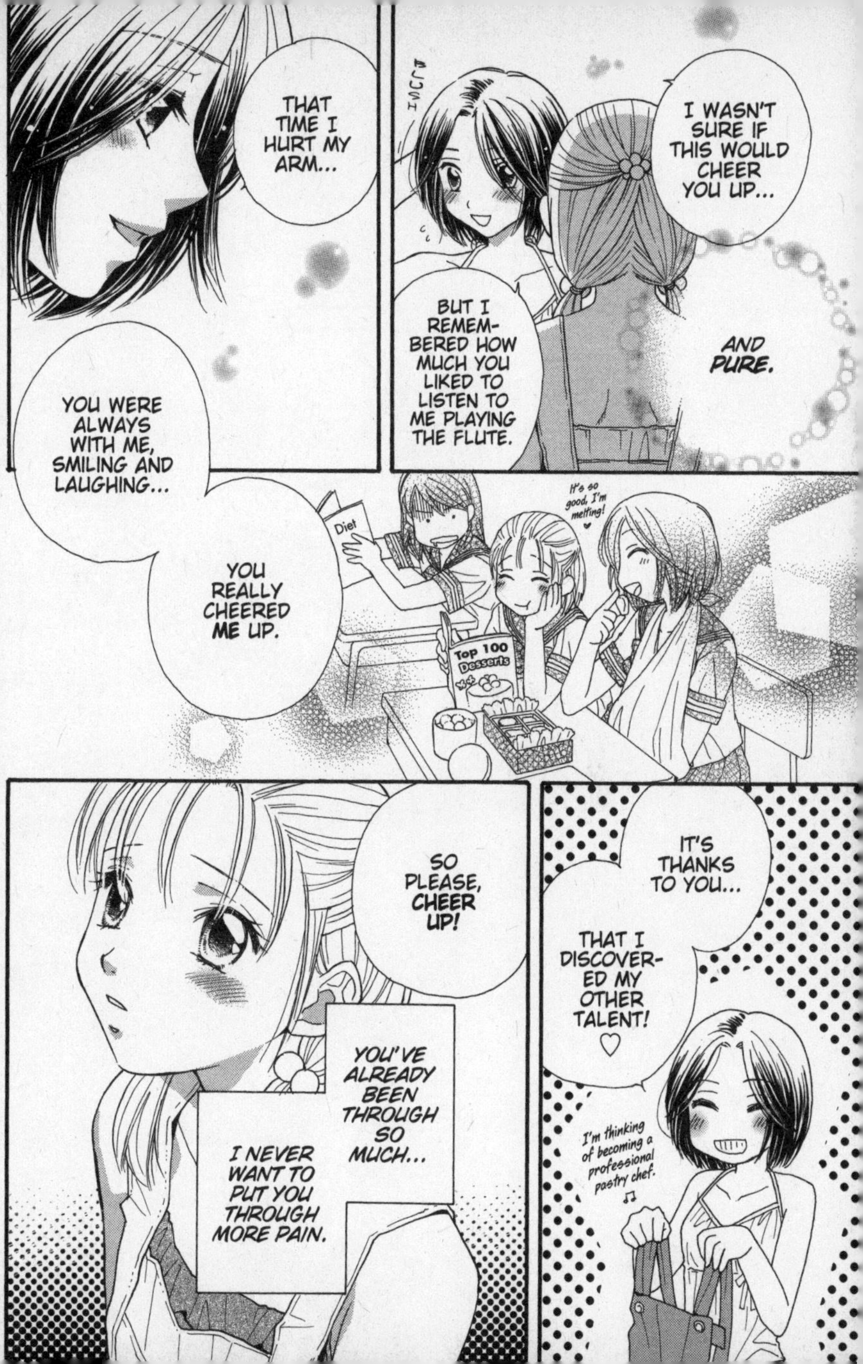
BLUSH
I WASN'T SURE IF THIS WOULD CHEER YOU UP...
BUT I REMEMBERED HOW MUCH YOU LIKED TO LISTEN TO ME PLAYING THE FLUTE.
AND PURE.
THAT TIME I HURT MY ARM...
YOU WERE ALWAYS WITH ME, SMILING AND LAUGHING...
It's so good, I'm melting! ♥
Diet
Top 100 Desserts
YOU REALLY CHEERED ME UP.
IT'S THANKS TO YOU...
THAT I DISCOVERED MY OTHER TALENT! ♡
I'm thinking of becoming a professional pastry chef. ♫
SO PLEASE, CHEER UP!
YOU'VE ALREADY BEEN THROUGH SO MUCH...
I NEVER WANT TO PUT YOU THROUGH MORE PAIN.

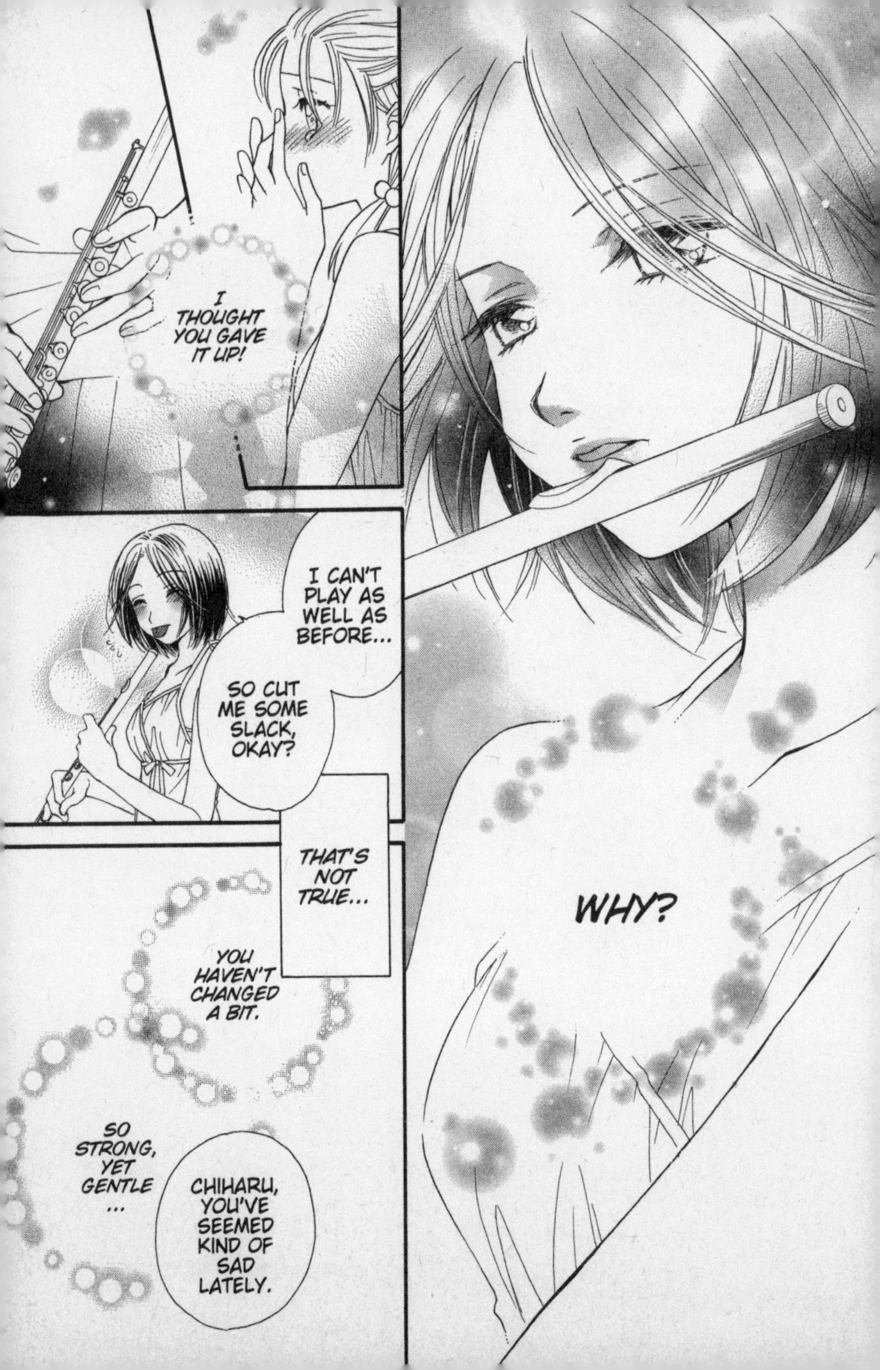
WHY?
I THOUGHT YOU GAVE IT UP!
I CAN'T PLAY AS WELL AS BEFORE...
SO CUT ME SOME SLACK, OKAY?
THAT'S NOT TRUE...
YOU HAVEN'T CHANGED A BIT.
SO STRONG, YET GENTLE ...
CHIHARU, YOU'VE SEEMED KIND OF SAD LATELY.

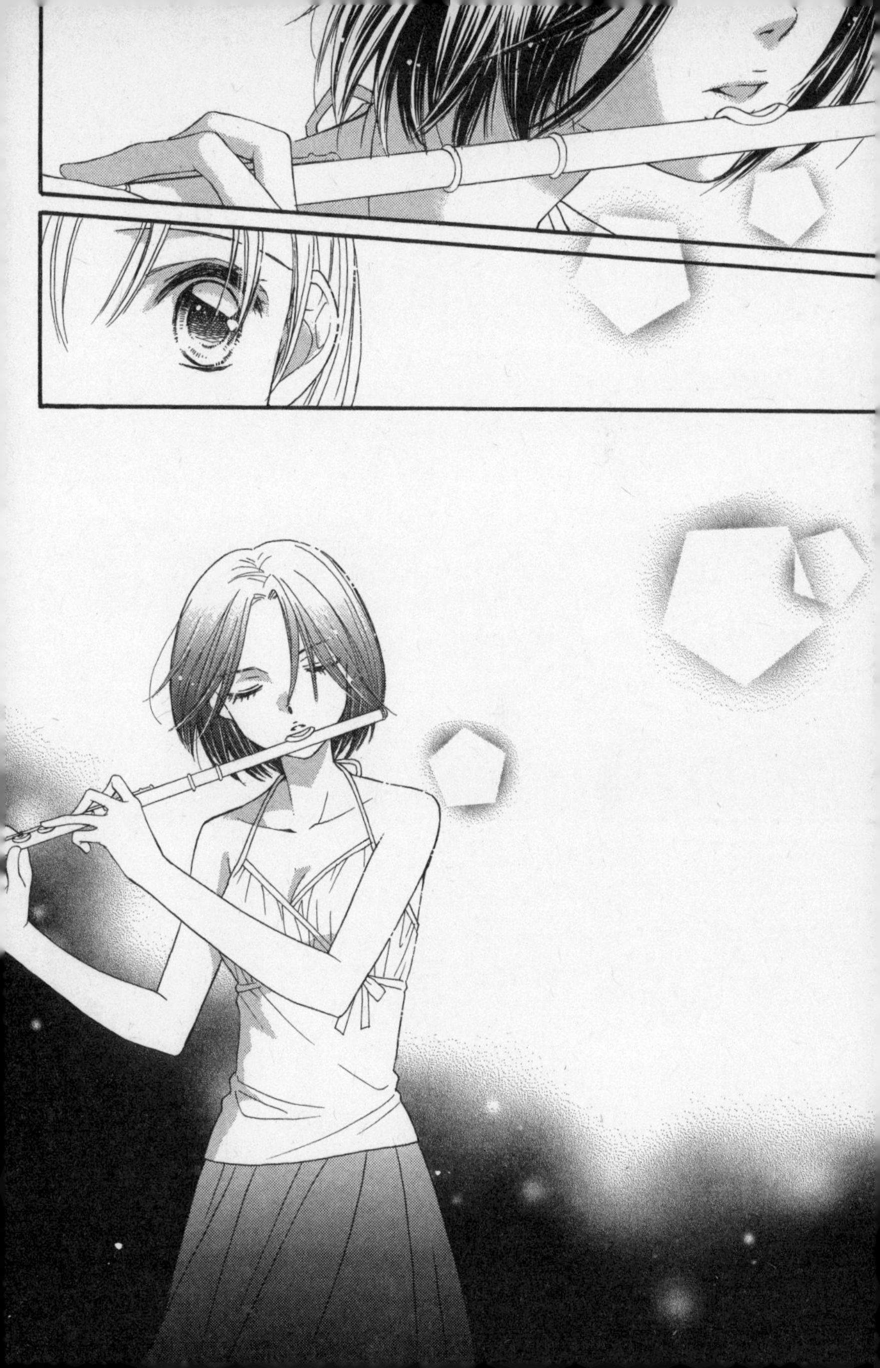

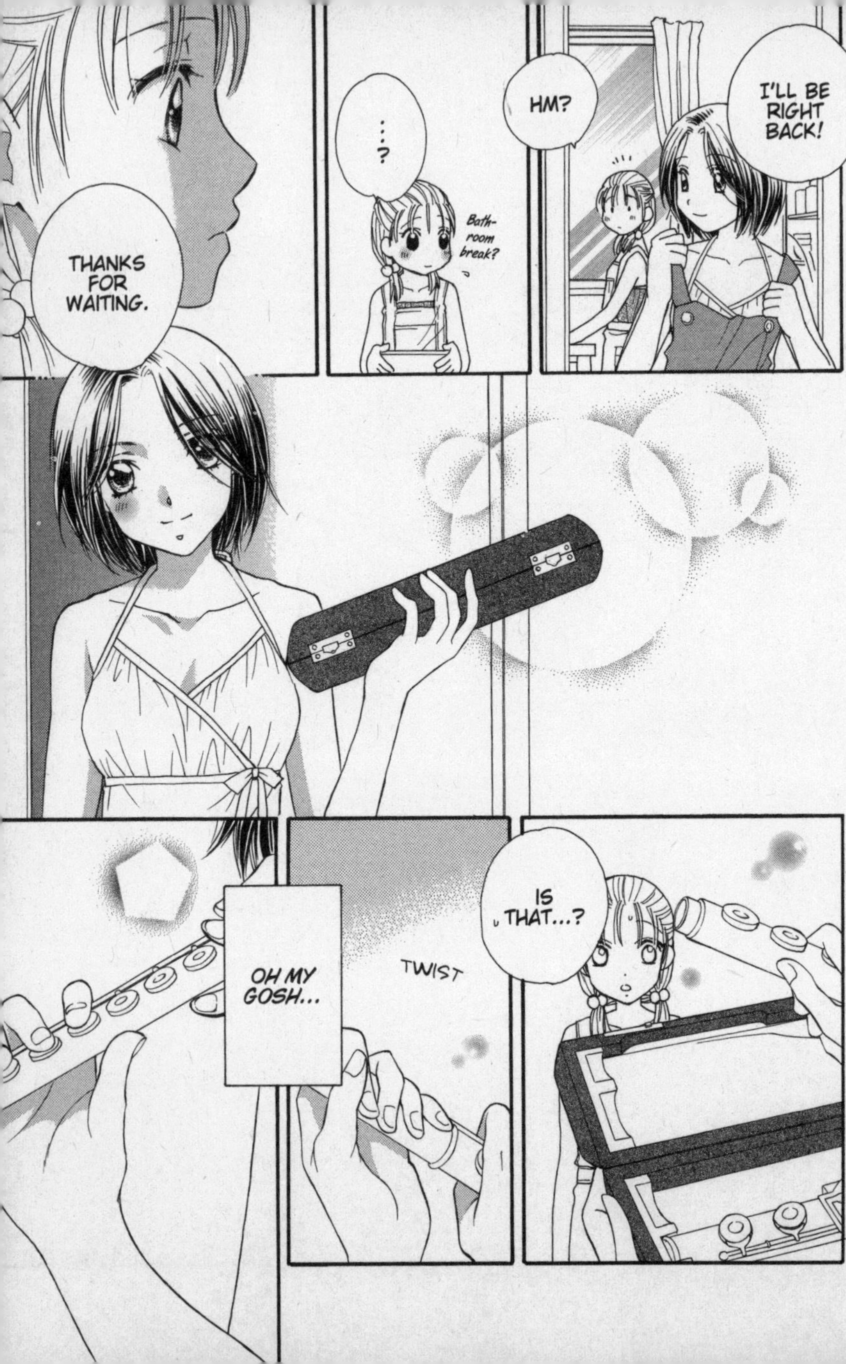
I'LL BE RIGHT BACK!
HM?
...?
Bath-room break?
THANKS FOR WAITING.
IS THAT...?
TWIST
OH MY GOSH...

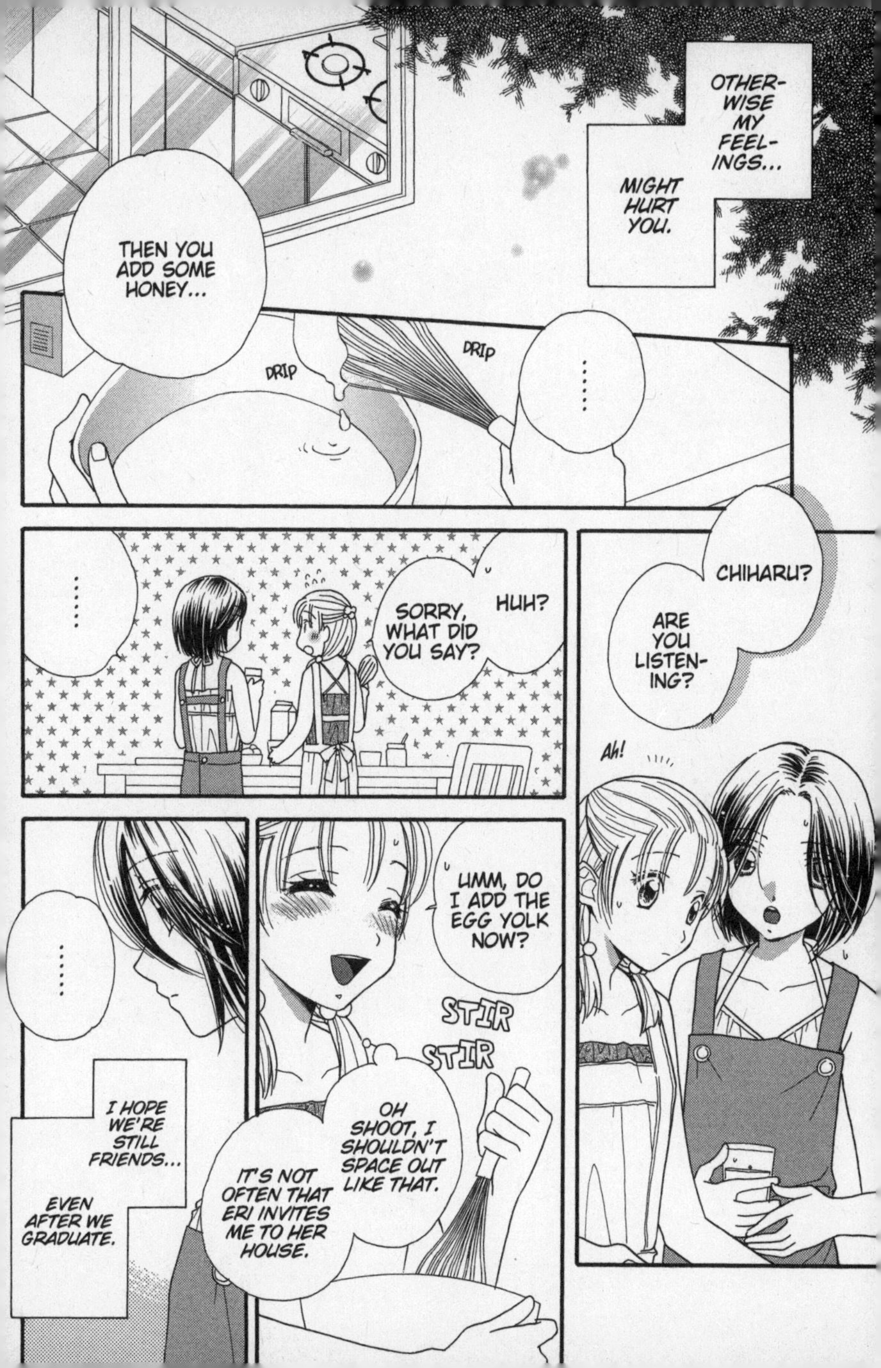
OTHER-WISE MY FEEL-INGS...
MIGHT HURT YOU.
THEN YOU ADD SOME HONEY...
......
DRIP
DRIP
CHIHARU?
ARE YOU LISTEN-ING?
Ah!
HUH?
SORRY, WHAT DID YOU SAY?
......
UMM, DO I ADD THE EGG YOLK NOW?
STIR
STIR
OH SHOOT, I SHOULDN'T SPACE OUT LIKE THAT.
IT'S NOT OFTEN THAT ERI INVITES ME TO HER HOUSE.
......
I HOPE WE'RE STILL FRIENDS...
EVEN AFTER WE GRADUATE.

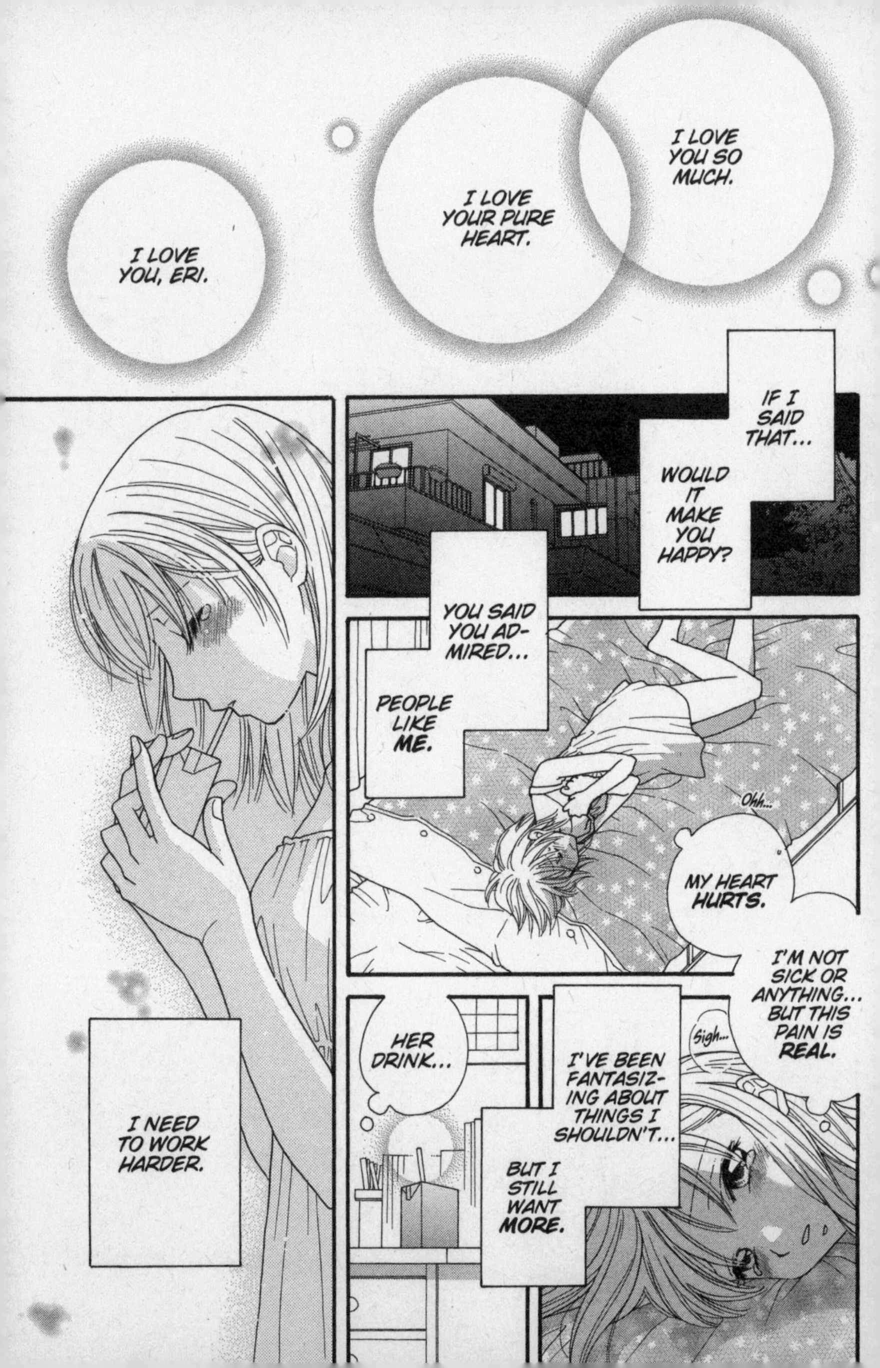
I LOVE YOU SO MUCH.
I LOVE YOUR PURE HEART.
I LOVE YOU, ERI.
IF I SAID THAT...
WOULD IT MAKE YOU HAPPY?
YOU SAID YOU ADMIRED...
PEOPLE LIKE ME.
Ohh...
MY HEART HURTS.
I'M NOT SICK OR ANYTHING... BUT THIS PAIN IS REAL.
Sigh...
I'VE BEEN FANTASIZING ABOUT THINGS I SHOULDN'T...
BUT I STILL WANT MORE.
HER DRINK...
I NEED TO WORK HARDER.

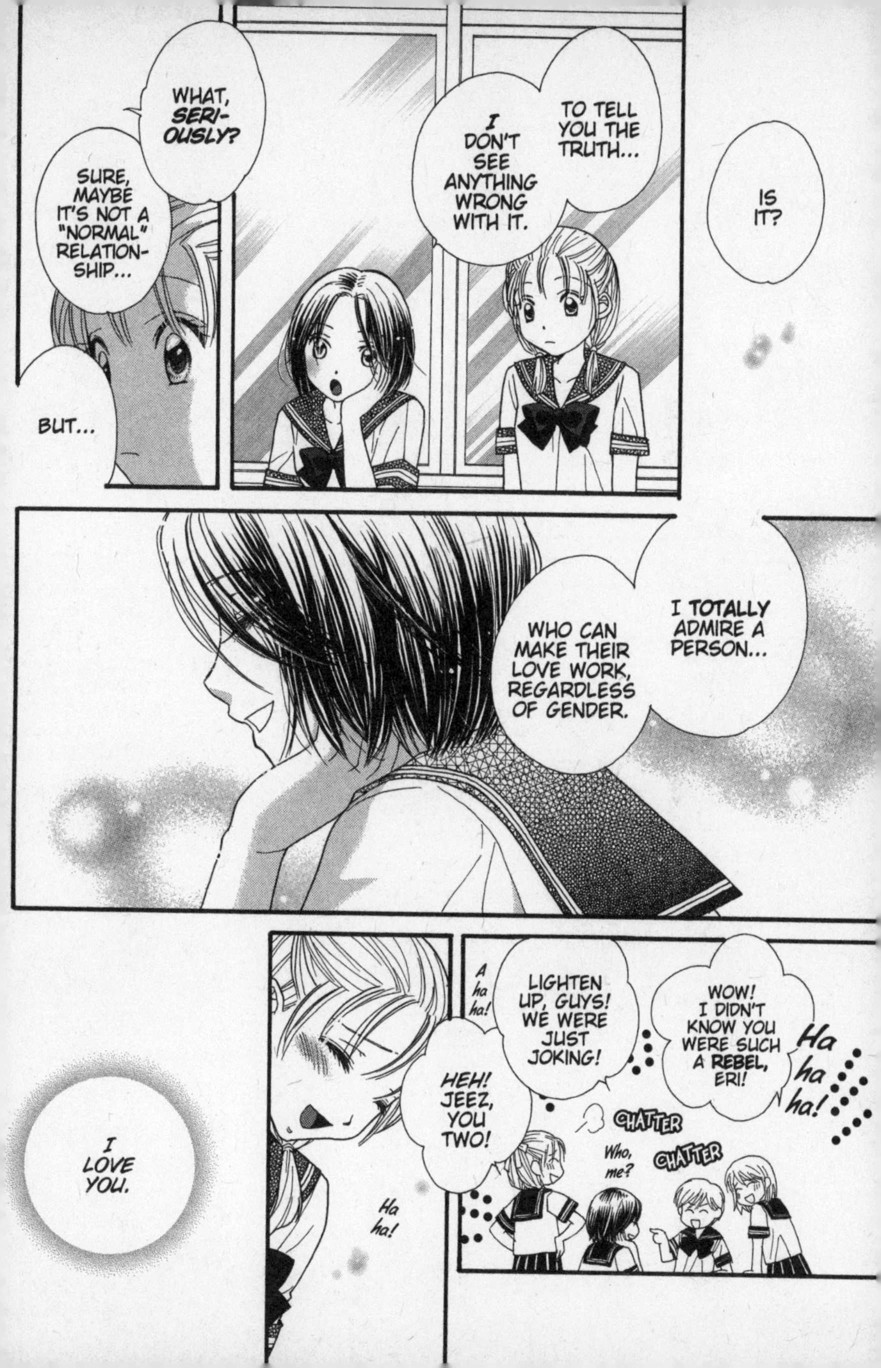

IS IT?
TO TELL YOU THE TRUTH...
I DON'T SEE ANYTHING WRONG WITH IT.
WHAT, SERIOUSLY?
SURE, MAYBE IT'S NOT A "NORMAL" RELATIONSHIP...
BUT...
I TOTALLY ADMIRE A PERSON...
WHO CAN MAKE THEIR LOVE WORK, REGARDLESS OF GENDER.
Ha ha ha!
WOW! I DIDN'T KNOW YOU WERE SUCH A REBEL, ERI!
LIGHTEN UP, GUYS! WE WERE JUST JOKING!
A ha ha!
CHATTER
CHATTER
Who, me?
HEH! JEEZ, YOU TWO!
Ha ha!
I LOVE YOU.

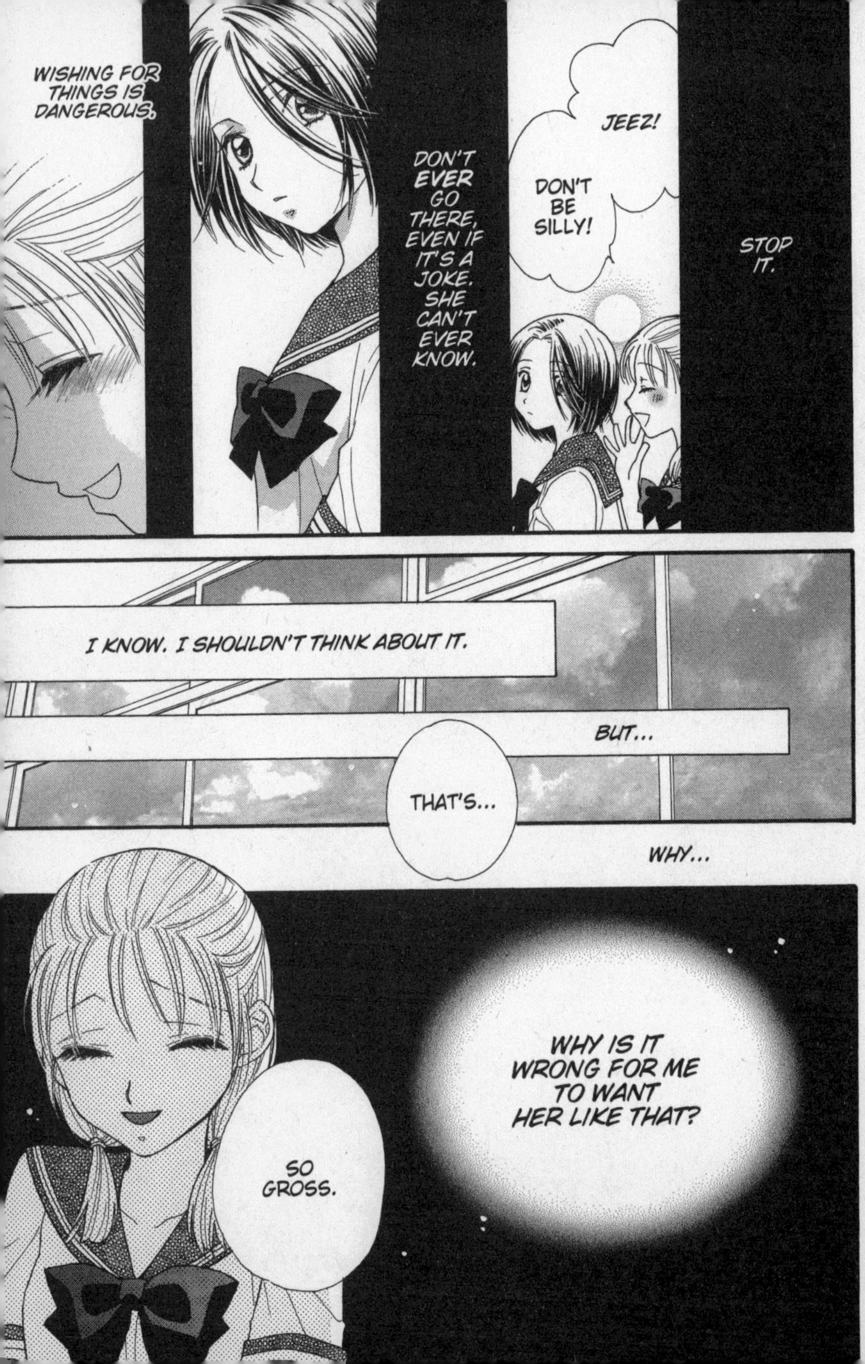
STOP IT.
JEEZ!
DON'T BE SILLY!
DON'T EVER GO THERE, EVEN IF IT'S A JOKE. SHE CAN'T EVER KNOW.
WISHING FOR THINGS IS DANGEROUS.
I KNOW. I SHOULDN'T THINK ABOUT IT.
BUT...
THAT'S...
WHY...
WHY IS IT WRONG FOR ME TO WANT HER LIKE THAT?
SO GROSS.

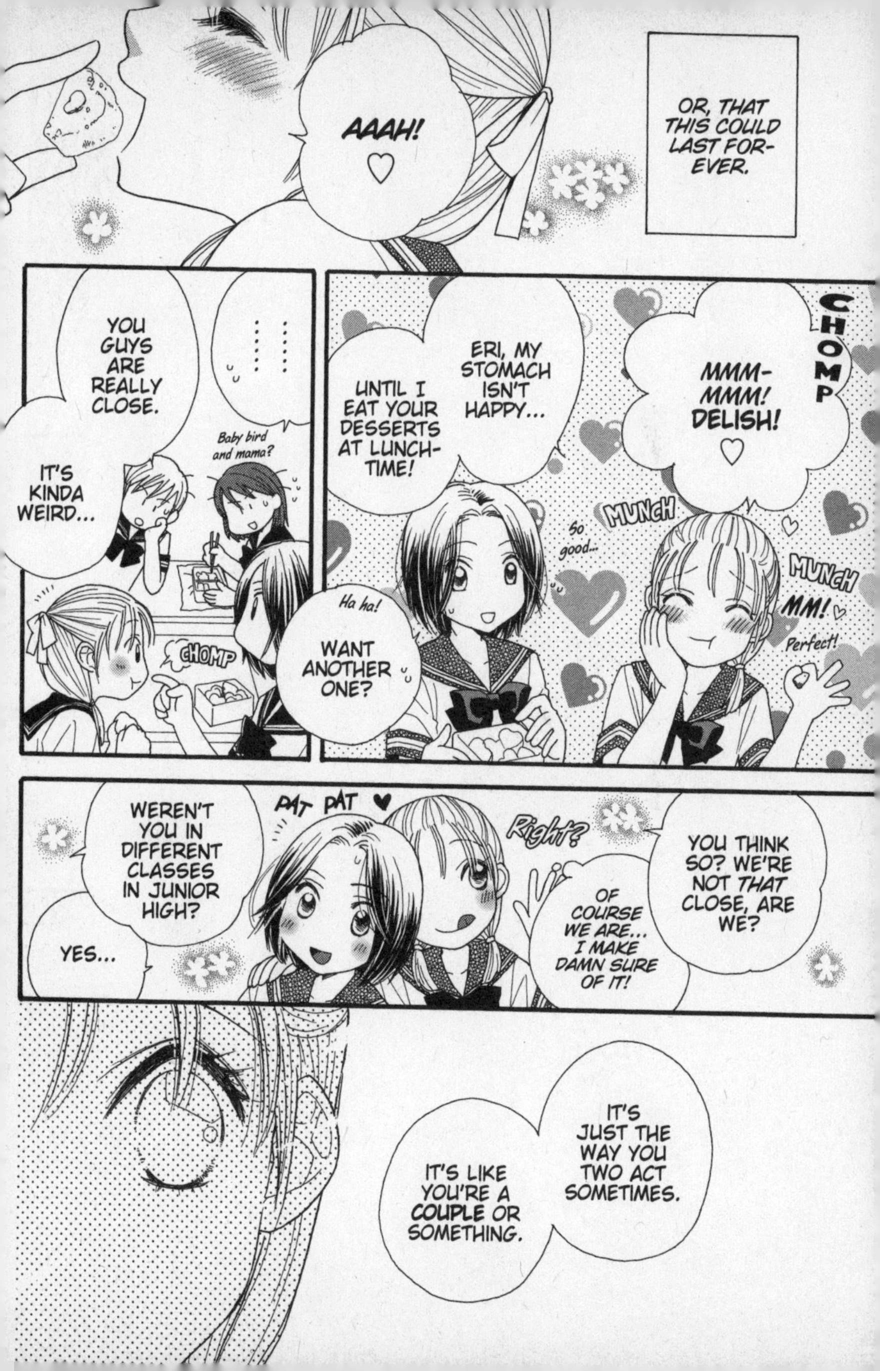
OR, THAT THIS COULD LAST FOREVER.
AAAH! ♡
CHOMP
MMM-MMM! DELISH! ♡
ERI, MY STOMACH ISN'T HAPPY...
UNTIL I EAT YOUR DESSERTS AT LUNCHTIME!
MUNCH
So good...
MUNCH
MM! ♡
Perfect!
Ha ha!
WANT ANOTHER ONE?
......
YOU GUYS ARE REALLY CLOSE.
Baby bird and mama?
IT'S KINDA WEIRD...
CHOMP
YOU THINK SO? WE'RE NOT *THAT* CLOSE, ARE WE?
Right?
OF COURSE WE ARE... I MAKE DAMN SURE OF IT!
PAT PAT ♥
WEREN'T YOU IN DIFFERENT CLASSES IN JUNIOR HIGH?
YES...
IT'S JUST THE WAY YOU TWO ACT SOMETIMES.
IT'S LIKE YOU'RE A COUPLE OR SOMETHING.

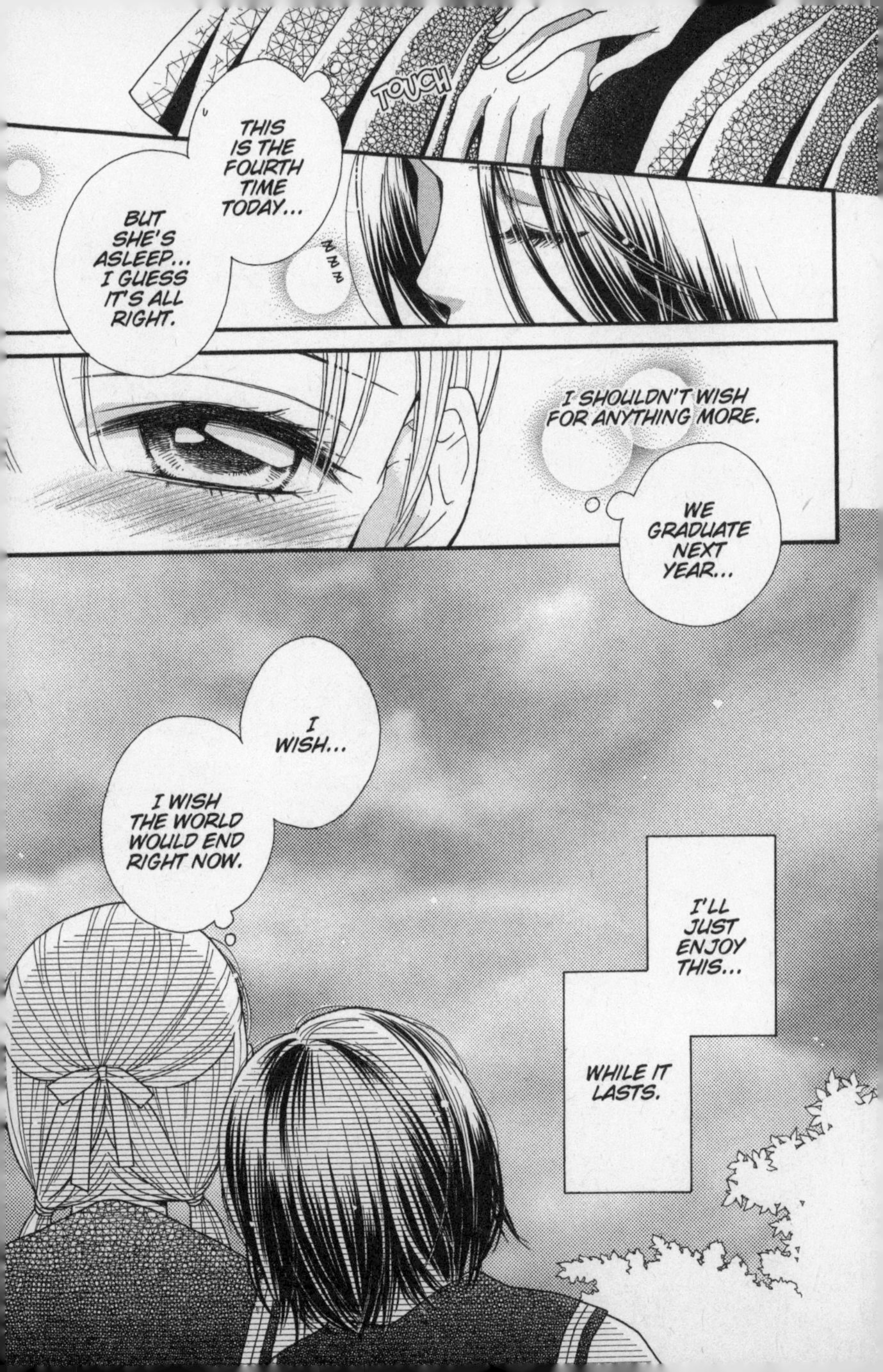
TOUCH
THIS IS THE FOURTH TIME TODAY...
ZZZ
BUT SHE'S ASLEEP... I GUESS IT'S ALL RIGHT.
I SHOULDN'T WISH FOR ANYTHING MORE.
WE GRADUATE NEXT YEAR...
I WISH...
I WISH THE WORLD WOULD END RIGHT NOW.
I'LL JUST ENJOY THIS...
WHILE IT LASTS.

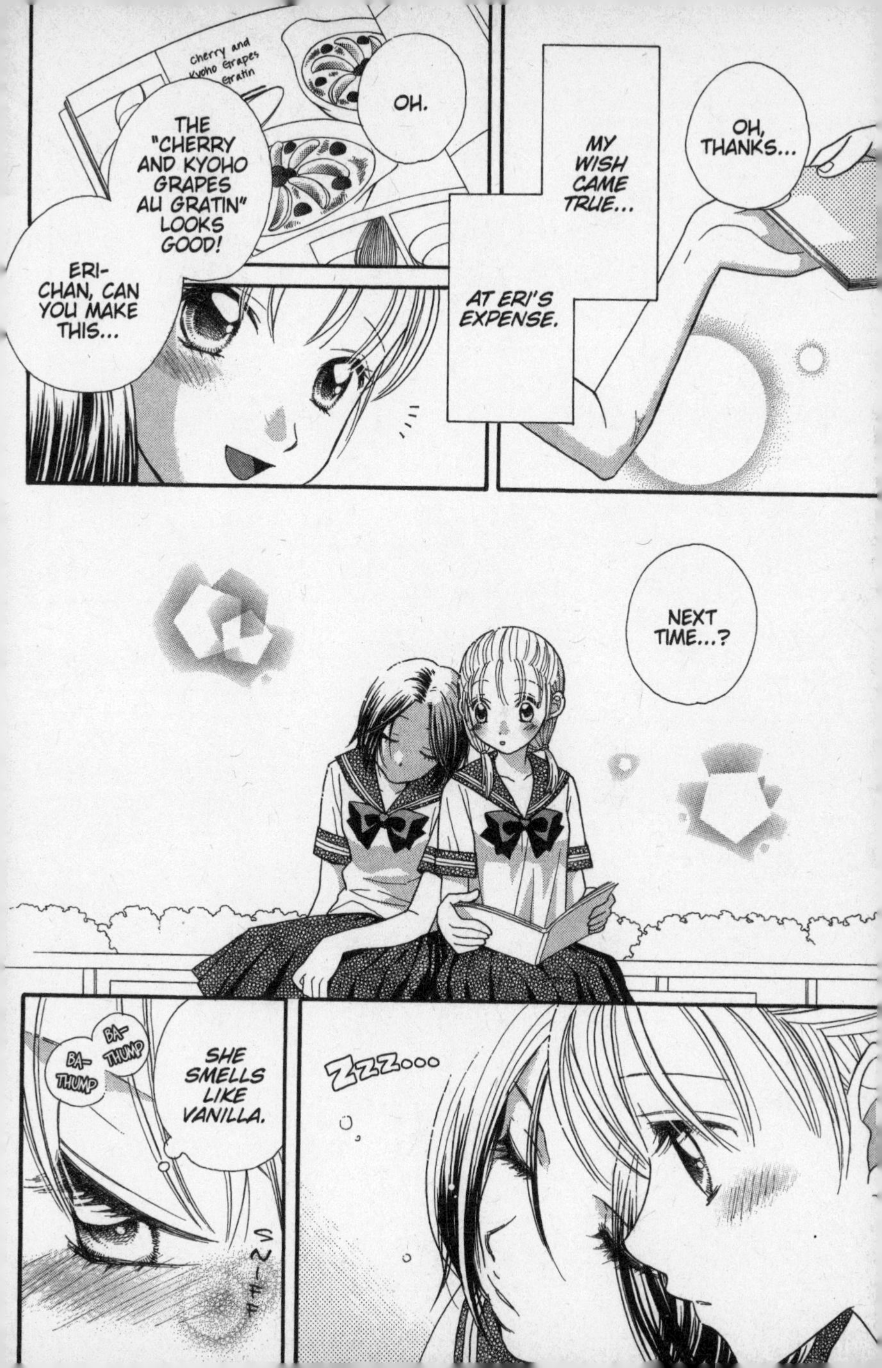
OH, THANKS...
MY WISH CAME TRUE...
AT ERI'S EXPENSE.
Cherry and Kyoho Grapes Gratin
OH.
THE "CHERRY AND KYOHO GRAPES AU GRATIN" LOOKS GOOD!
ERI-CHAN, CAN YOU MAKE THIS...
NEXT TIME...?
ZZZooo
BA-THUMP
BA-THUMP
SHE SMELLS LIKE VANILLA.
SNIFF

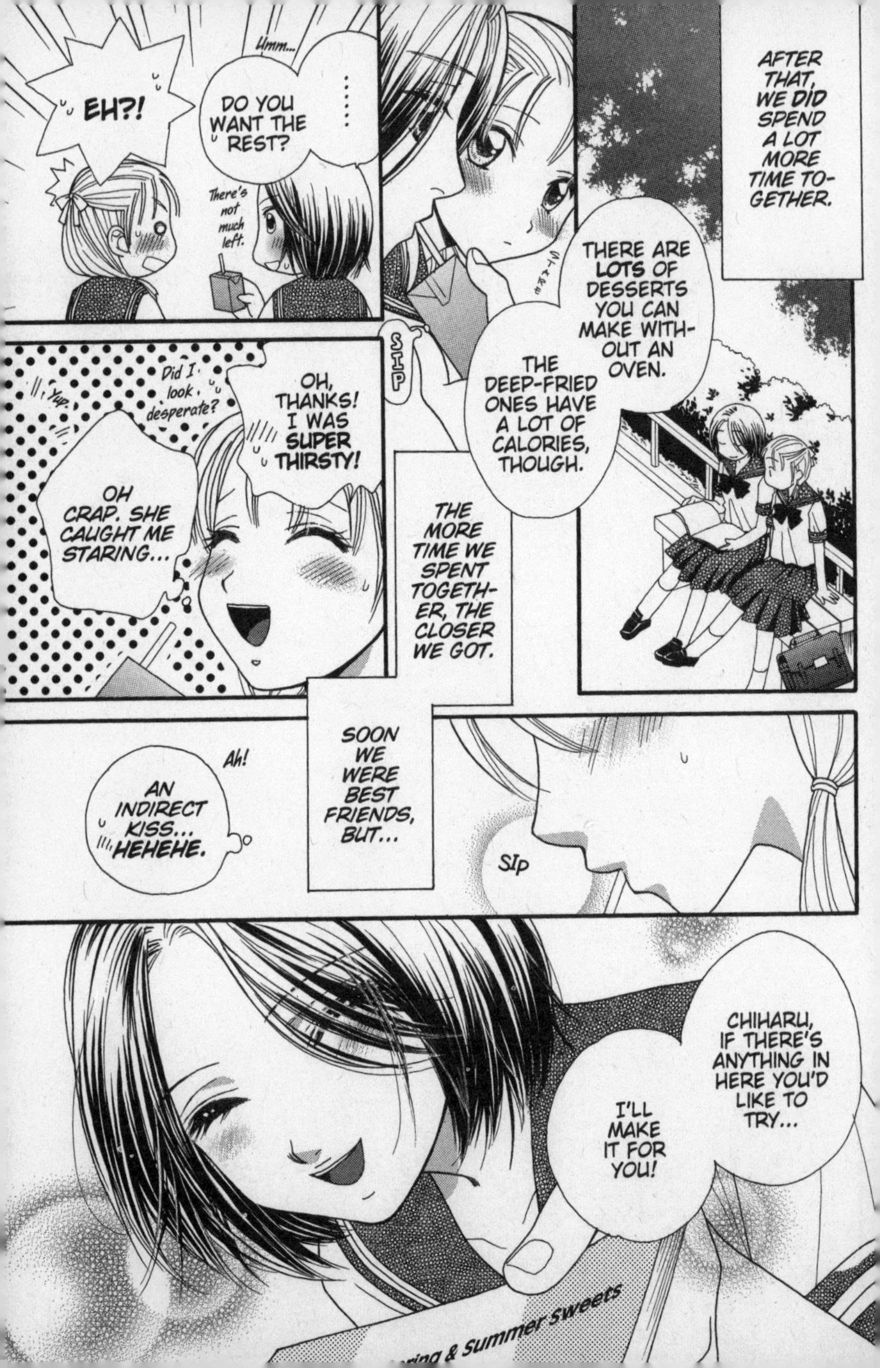
AFTER THAT, WE DID SPEND A LOT MORE TIME TOGETHER.
THERE ARE LOTS OF DESSERTS YOU CAN MAKE WITHOUT AN OVEN.
THE DEEP-FRIED ONES HAVE A LOT OF CALORIES, THOUGH.
STARE
SIP
Umm...
......
DO YOU WANT THE REST?
There's not much left.
EH?!
THE MORE TIME WE SPENT TOGETHER, THE CLOSER WE GOT.
OH, THANKS! I WAS SUPER THIRSTY!
Did I look desperate?
Yup.
OH CRAP. SHE CAUGHT ME STARING...
Sip
SOON WE WERE BEST FRIENDS, BUT...
Ah!
AN INDIRECT KISS... HEHEHE.
CHIHARU, IF THERE'S ANYTHING IN HERE YOU'D LIKE TO TRY...
I'LL MAKE IT FOR YOU!

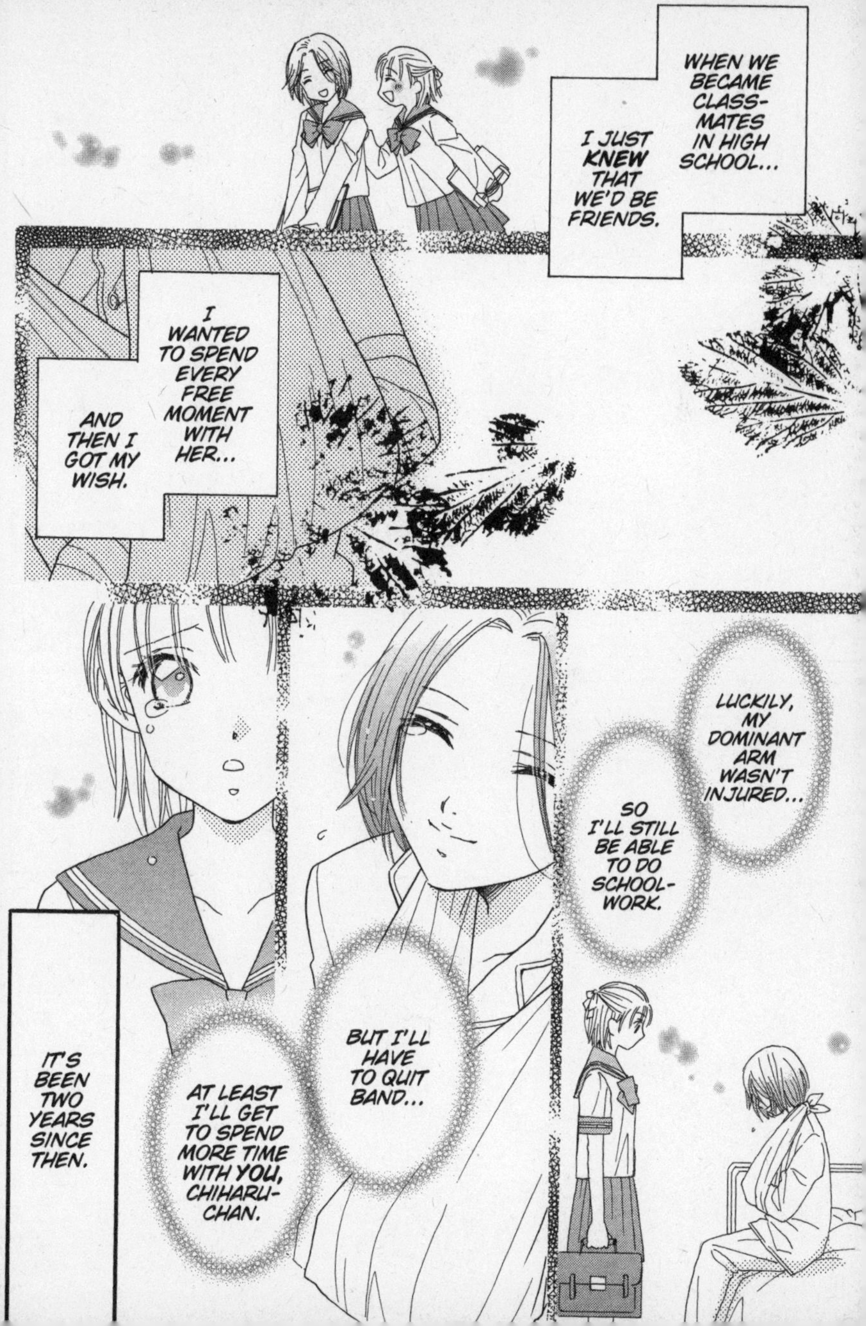
WHEN WE BECAME CLASS-MATES IN HIGH SCHOOL...
I JUST KNEW THAT WE'D BE FRIENDS.
I WANTED TO SPEND EVERY FREE MOMENT WITH HER...
AND THEN I GOT MY WISH.
LUCKILY, MY DOMINANT ARM WASN'T INJURED...
SO I'LL STILL BE ABLE TO DO SCHOOL-WORK.
BUT I'LL HAVE TO QUIT BAND...
AT LEAST I'LL GET TO SPEND MORE TIME WITH YOU, CHIHARU-CHAN.
IT'S BEEN TWO YEARS SINCE THEN.

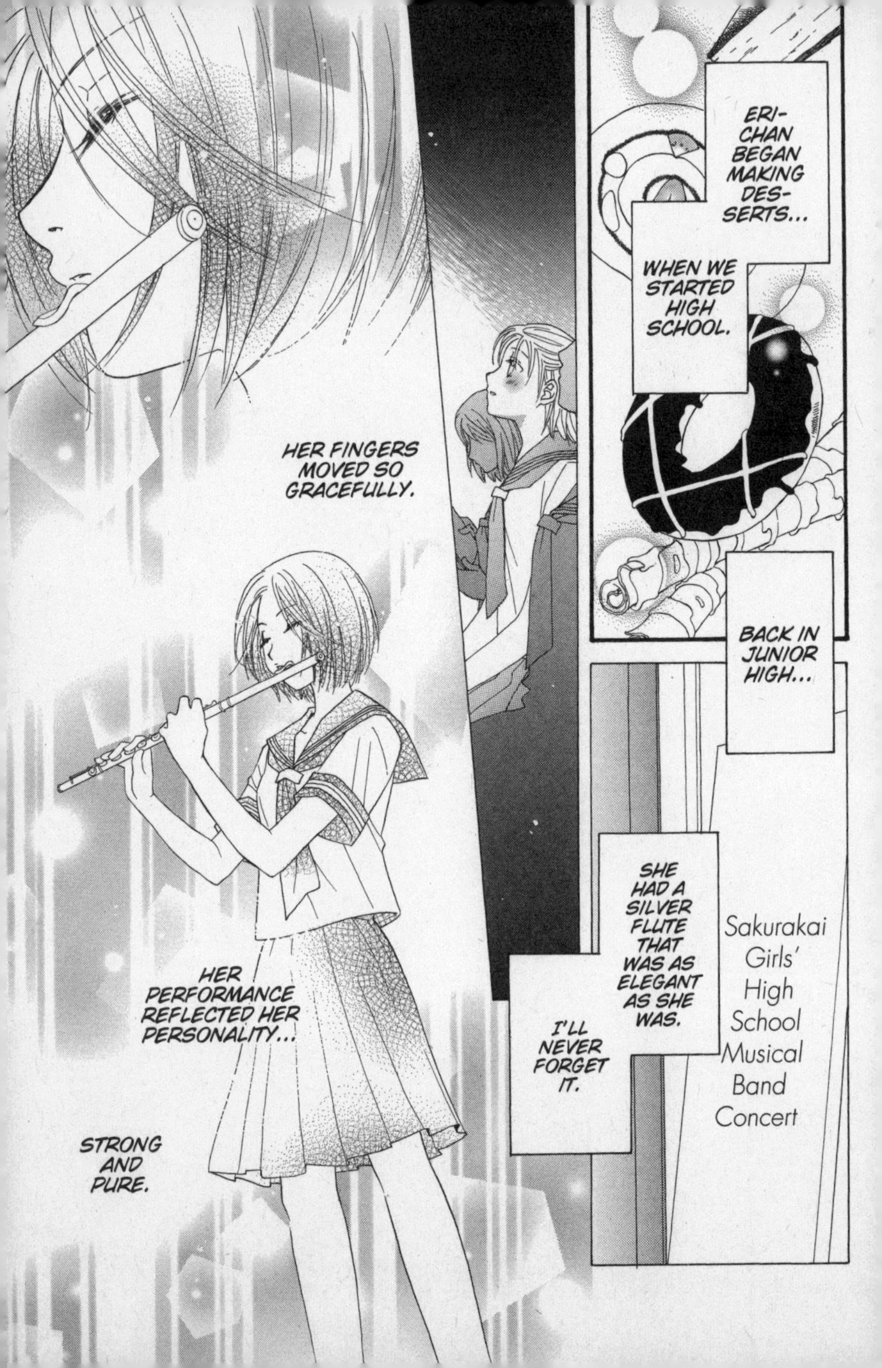
ERI-CHAN BEGAN MAKING DES-SERTS...
WHEN WE STARTED HIGH SCHOOL.
BACK IN JUNIOR HIGH...
Sakurakai Girls' High School Musical Band Concert
SHE HAD A SILVER FLUTE THAT WAS AS ELEGANT AS SHE WAS.
I'LL NEVER FORGET IT.
HER FINGERS MOVED SO GRACEFULLY.
HER PERFORMANCE REFLECTED HER PERSONALITY...
STRONG AND PURE.

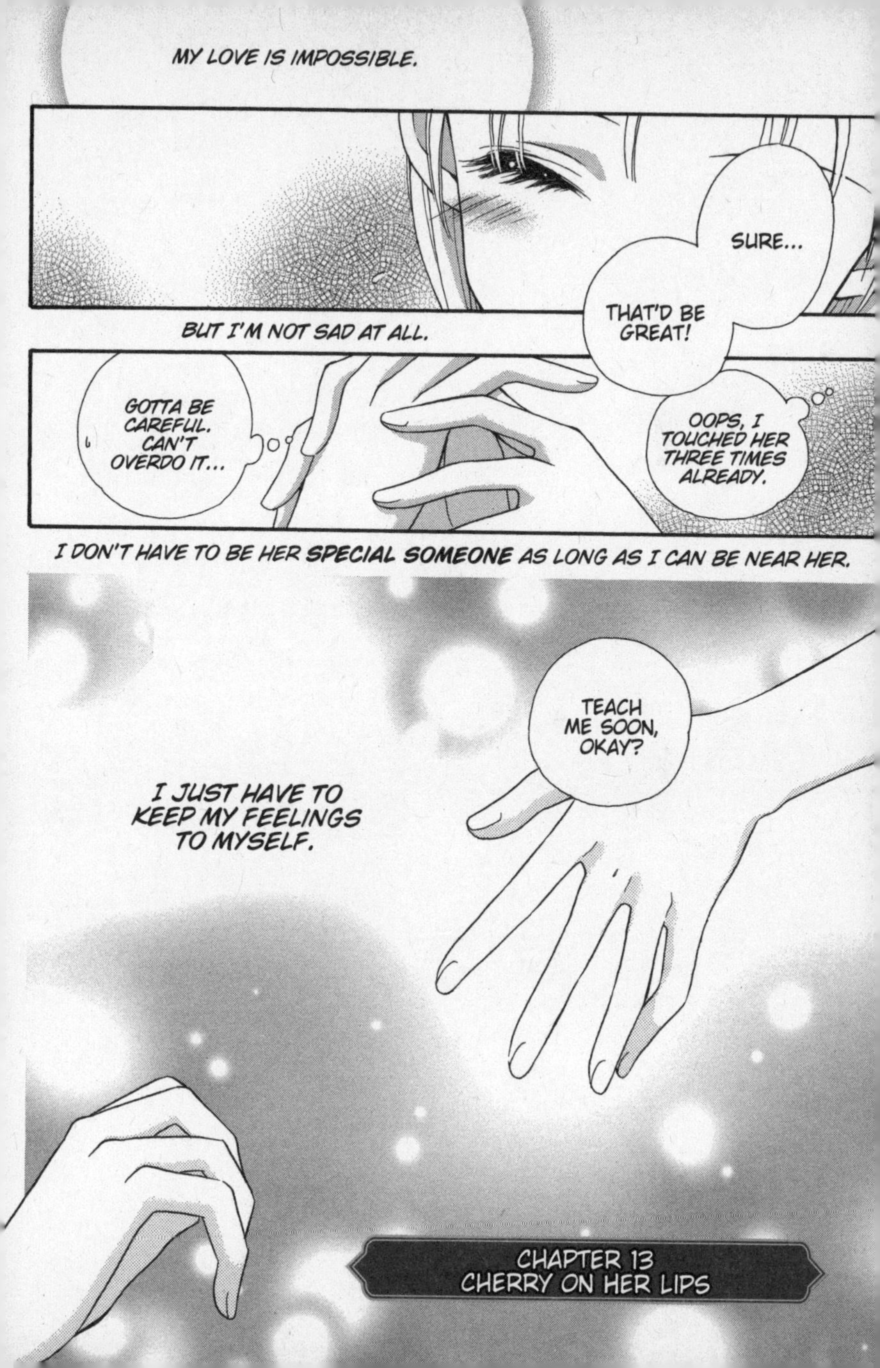
MY LOVE IS IMPOSSIBLE.
SURE...
THAT'D BE GREAT!
BUT I'M NOT SAD AT ALL.
OOPS, I TOUCHED HER THREE TIMES ALREADY.
GOTTA BE CAREFUL. CAN'T OVERDO IT...
I DON'T HAVE TO BE HER SPECIAL SOMEONE AS LONG AS I CAN BE NEAR HER.
TEACH ME SOON, OKAY?
I JUST HAVE TO KEEP MY FEELINGS TO MYSELF.
CHAPTER 13
CHERRY ON HER LIPS

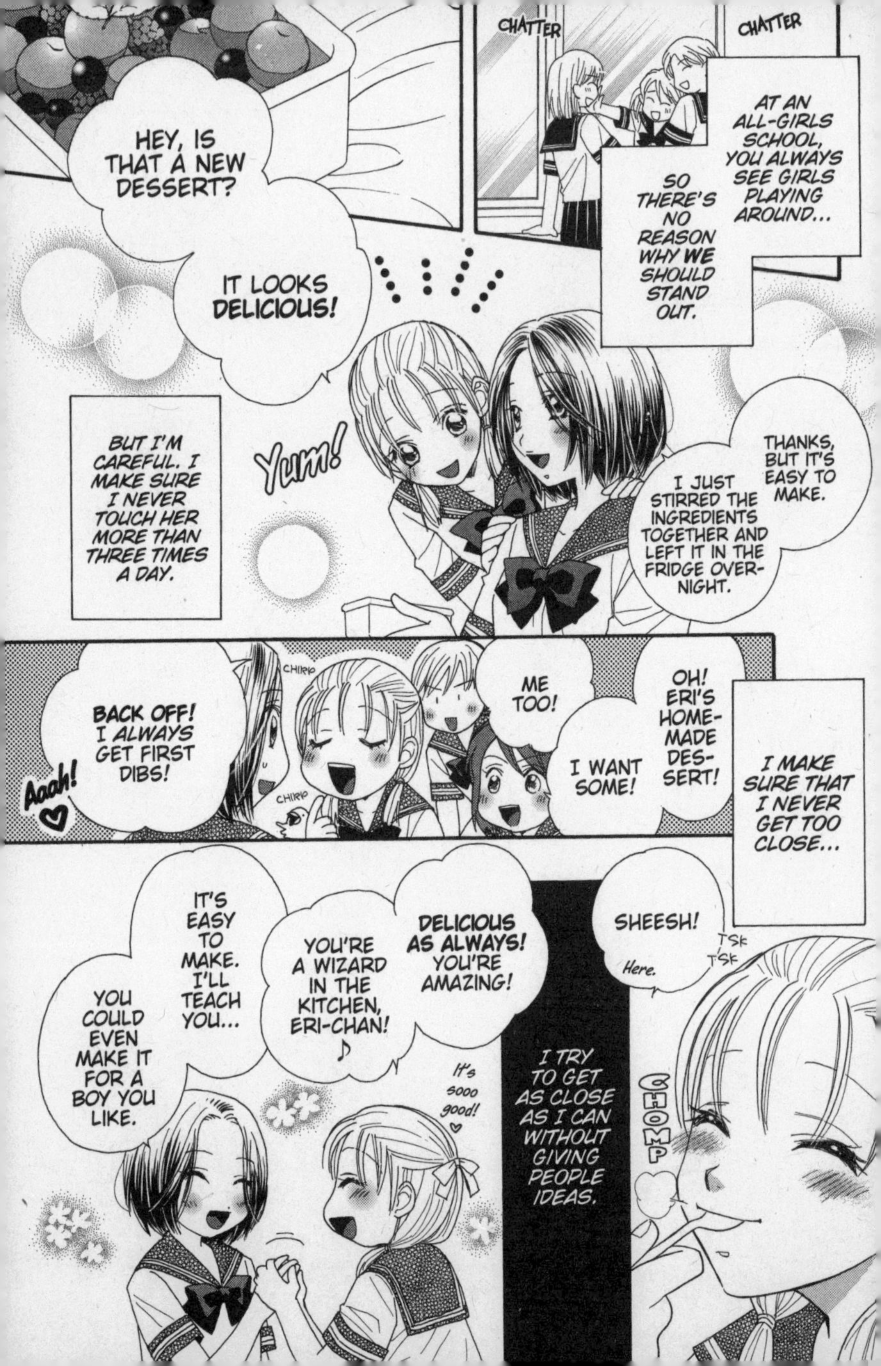
CHATTER
CHATTER
AT AN ALL-GIRLS SCHOOL, YOU ALWAYS SEE GIRLS PLAYING AROUND...
SO THERE'S NO REASON WHY WE SHOULD STAND OUT.
HEY, IS THAT A NEW DESSERT?
IT LOOKS DELICIOUS!
THANKS, BUT IT'S EASY TO MAKE.
I JUST STIRRED THE INGREDIENTS TOGETHER AND LEFT IT IN THE FRIDGE OVER-NIGHT.
Yum!
BUT I'M CAREFUL. I MAKE SURE I NEVER TOUCH HER MORE THAN THREE TIMES A DAY.
I MAKE SURE THAT I NEVER GET TOO CLOSE...
OH! ERI'S HOME-MADE DES-SERT!
I WANT SOME!
ME TOO!
CHIRP
BACK OFF! I ALWAYS GET FIRST DIBS!
Aaah! ♥
CHIRP
SHEESH!
TSK TSK
Here.
CHOMP
I TRY TO GET AS CLOSE AS I CAN WITHOUT GIVING PEOPLE IDEAS.
DELICIOUS AS ALWAYS! YOU'RE AMAZING!
YOU'RE A WIZARD IN THE KITCHEN, ERI-CHAN! ♪
It's sooo good! ♡
IT'S EASY TO MAKE. I'LL TEACH YOU...
YOU COULD EVEN MAKE IT FOR A BOY YOU LIKE.

くちびるためいきさくらいろ

Kuchibiru Tameiki Sakurairo

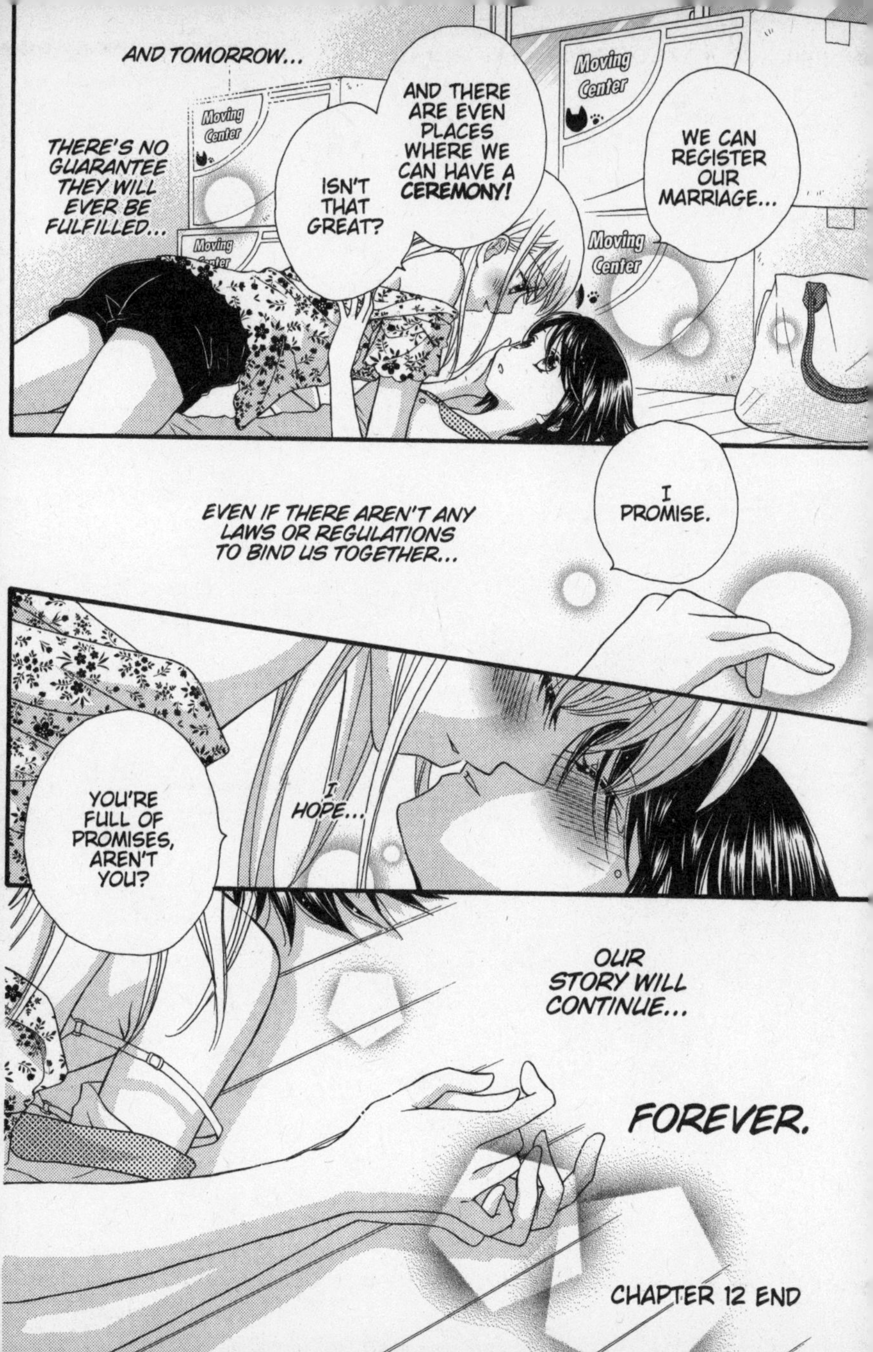
WE CAN REGISTER OUR MARRIAGE...
AND THERE ARE EVEN PLACES WHERE WE CAN HAVE A CEREMONY!
ISN'T THAT GREAT?
AND TOMORROW...
THERE'S NO GUARANTEE THEY WILL EVER BE FULFILLED...
I PROMISE.
EVEN IF THERE AREN'T ANY LAWS OR REGULATIONS TO BIND US TOGETHER...
I HOPE...
YOU'RE FULL OF PROMISES, AREN'T YOU?
OUR STORY WILL CONTINUE...
FOREVER.
CHAPTER 12 END

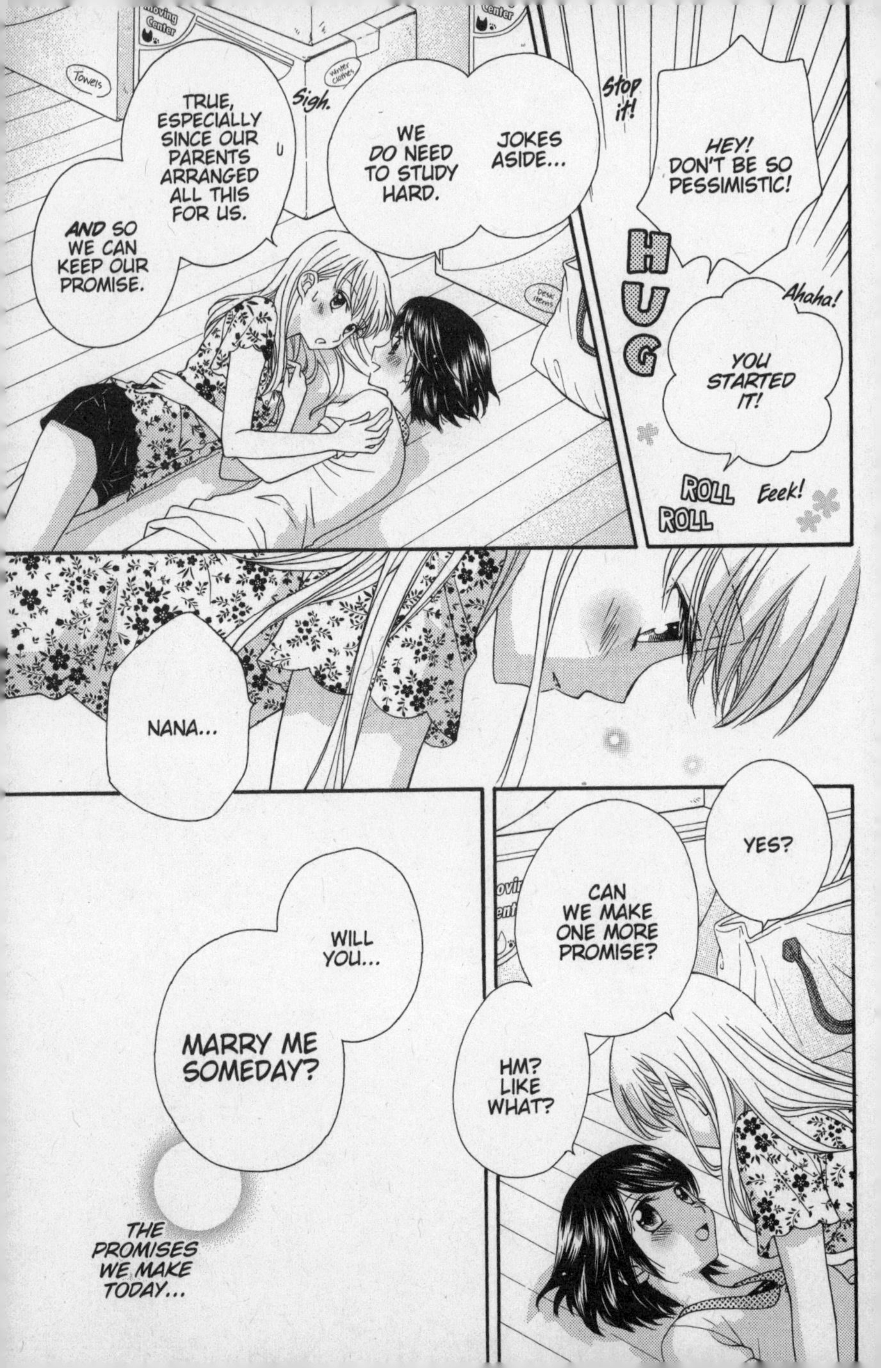
Moving Center
Towels
Winter clothes
HEY! DON'T BE SO PESSIMISTIC!
Stop it!
HUG
Ahaha!
YOU STARTED IT!
ROLL ROLL
Eeek!
JOKES ASIDE...
WE DO NEED TO STUDY HARD.
Sigh.
TRUE, ESPECIALLY SINCE OUR PARENTS ARRANGED ALL THIS FOR US.
AND SO WE CAN KEEP OUR PROMISE.
NANA...
YES?
CAN WE MAKE ONE MORE PROMISE?
HM? LIKE WHAT?
WILL YOU...
MARRY ME SOMEDAY?
THE PROMISES WE MAKE TODAY...

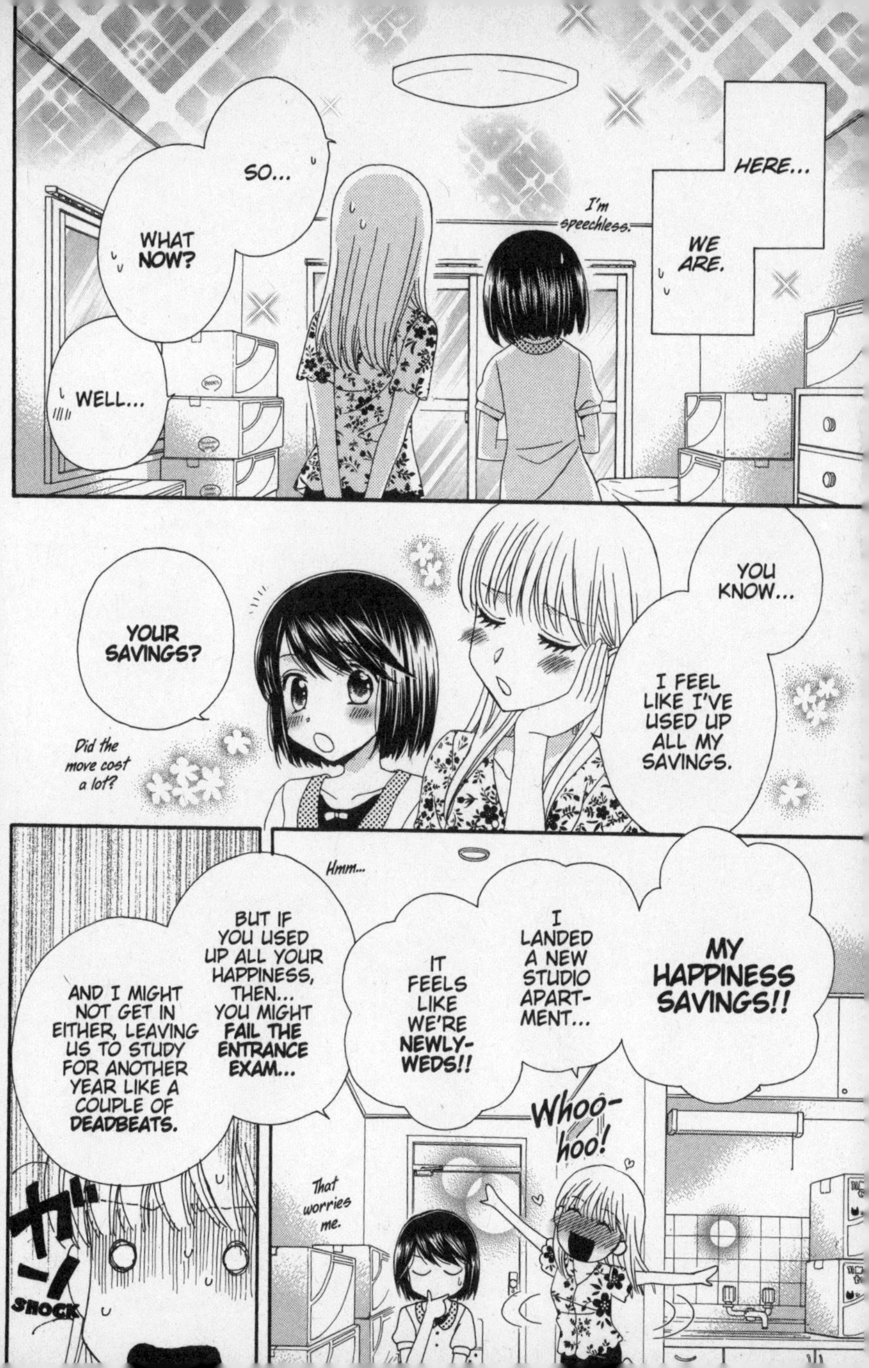
HERE... WE ARE.
I'm speechless.
SO... WHAT NOW?
WELL...
YOU KNOW... I FEEL LIKE I'VE USED UP ALL MY SAVINGS.
YOUR SAVINGS?
Did the move cost a lot?
MY HAPPINESS SAVINGS!!
I LANDED A NEW STUDIO APARTMENT...
IT FEELS LIKE WE'RE NEWLYWEDS!!
Whoo-hoo!
Hmm...
BUT IF YOU USED UP ALL YOUR HAPPINESS, THEN... YOU MIGHT FAIL THE ENTRANCE EXAM...
That worries me.
AND I MIGHT NOT GET IN EITHER, LEAVING US TO STUDY FOR ANOTHER YEAR LIKE A COUPLE OF DEADBEATS.
SHOCK

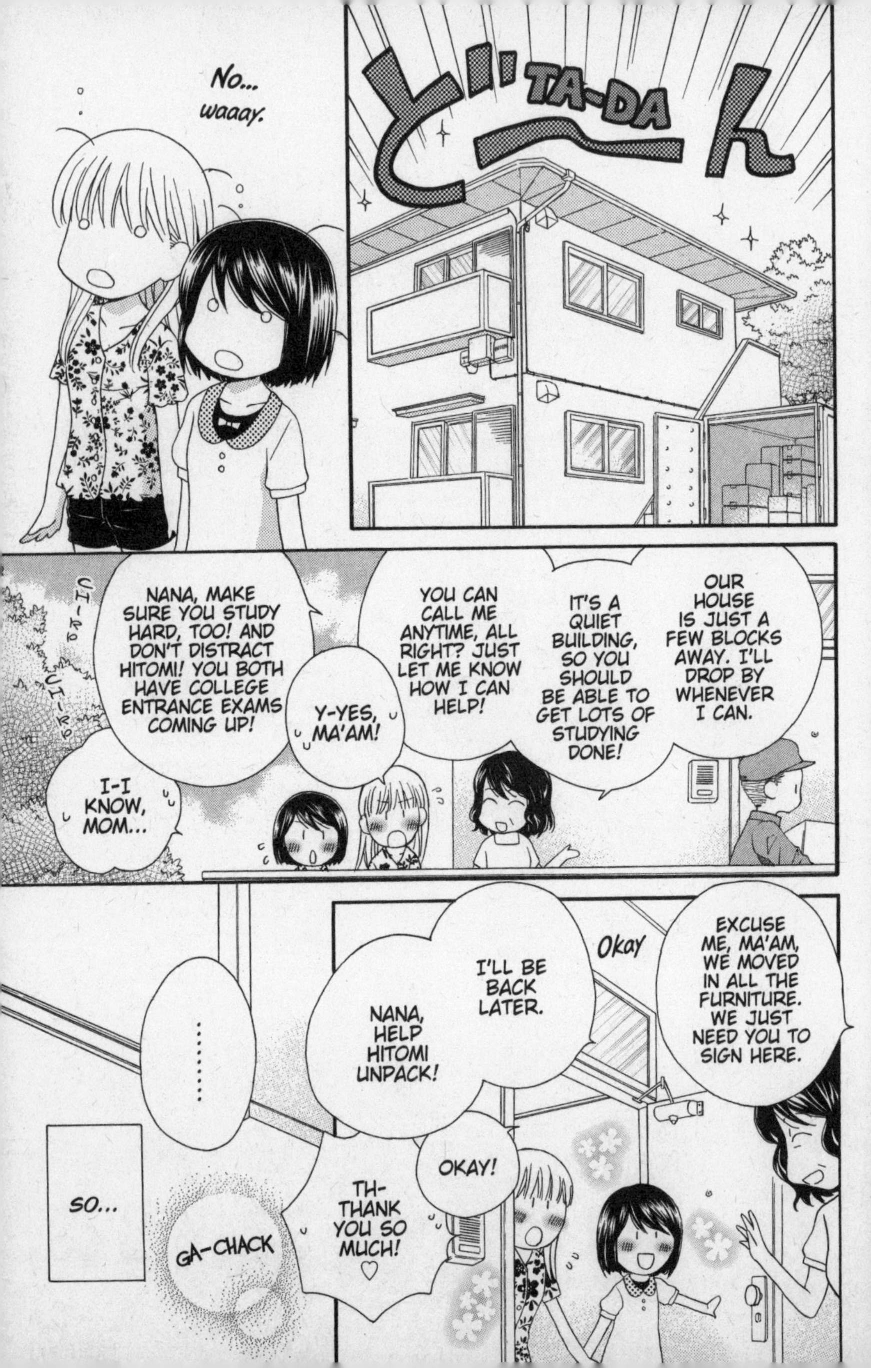
TA-DA
No... waaay.
OUR HOUSE IS JUST A FEW BLOCKS AWAY. I'LL DROP BY WHENEVER I CAN.
IT'S A QUIET BUILDING, SO YOU SHOULD BE ABLE TO GET LOTS OF STUDYING DONE!
YOU CAN CALL ME ANYTIME, ALL RIGHT? JUST LET ME KNOW HOW I CAN HELP!
NANA, MAKE SURE YOU STUDY HARD, TOO! AND DON'T DISTRACT HITOMI! YOU BOTH HAVE COLLEGE ENTRANCE EXAMS COMING UP!
Y-YES, MA'AM!
CHIRP
CHIRP
I-I KNOW, MOM...
EXCUSE ME, MA'AM, WE MOVED IN ALL THE FURNITURE. WE JUST NEED YOU TO SIGN HERE.
Okay
I'LL BE BACK LATER.
NANA, HELP HITOMI UNPACK!
OKAY!
TH-THANK YOU SO MUCH! ♡
GA-CHACK
......
SO...

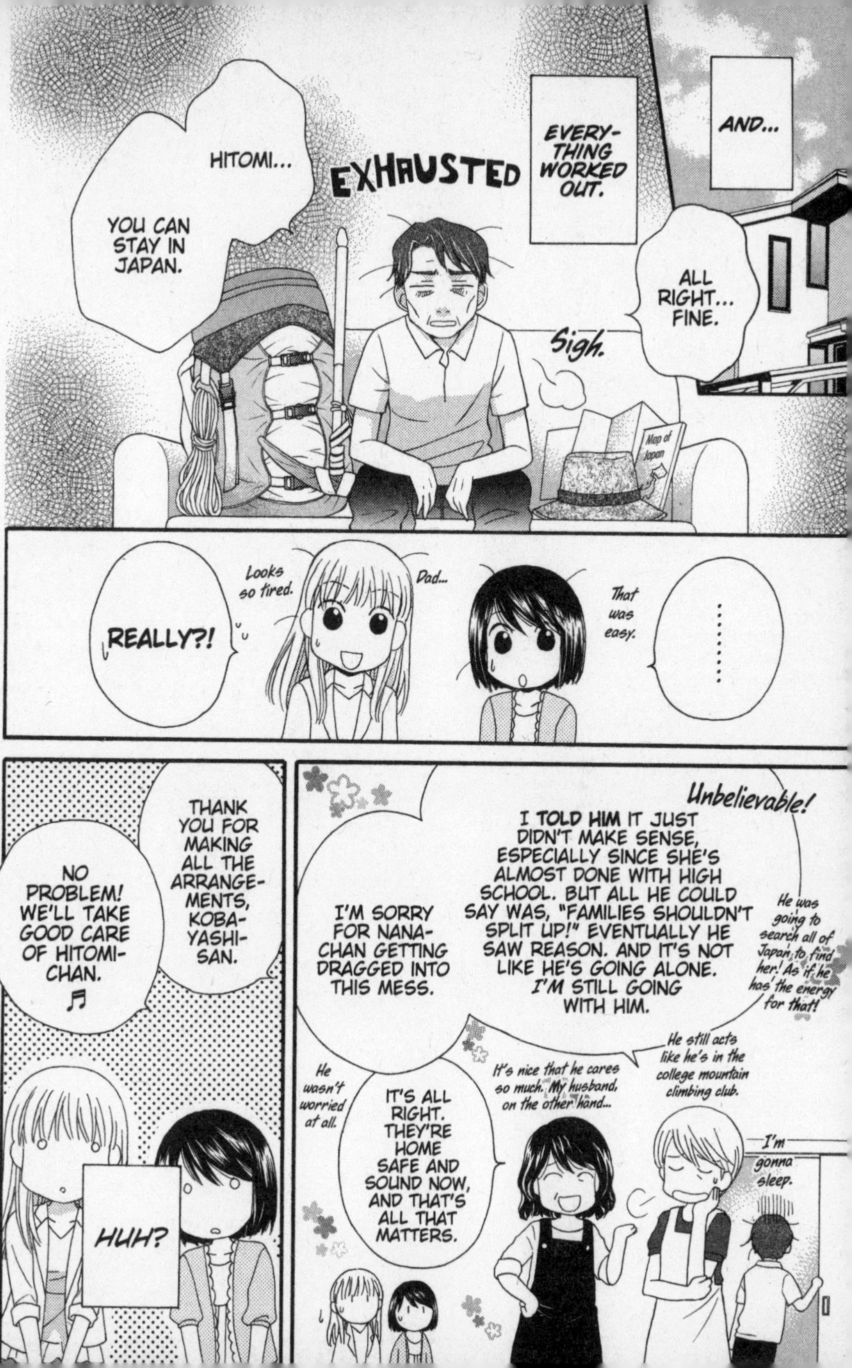
AND...
EVERY-THING WORKED OUT.
ALL RIGHT... FINE.
Sigh.
Map of Japan
EXHAUSTED
HITOMI... YOU CAN STAY IN JAPAN.
......
That was easy.
Dad...
Looks so tired.
REALLY?!
Unbelievable!
I TOLD HIM IT JUST DIDN'T MAKE SENSE, ESPECIALLY SINCE SHE'S ALMOST DONE WITH HIGH SCHOOL. BUT ALL HE COULD SAY WAS, "FAMILIES SHOULDN'T SPLIT UP!" EVENTUALLY HE SAW REASON. AND IT'S NOT LIKE HE'S GOING ALONE. I'M STILL GOING WITH HIM.
He was going to search all of Japan to find her! As if he has the energy for that!
I'M SORRY FOR NANA-CHAN GETTING DRAGGED INTO THIS MESS.
He still acts like he's in the college mountain climbing club.
I'm gonna sleep.
It's nice that he cares so much. My husband, on the other hand...
IT'S ALL RIGHT. THEY'RE HOME SAFE AND SOUND NOW, AND THAT'S ALL THAT MATTERS.
He wasn't worried at all.
THANK YOU FOR MAKING ALL THE ARRANGE-MENTS, KOBA-YASHI-SAN.
NO PROBLEM! WE'LL TAKE GOOD CARE OF HITOMI-CHAN. ♬
HUH?

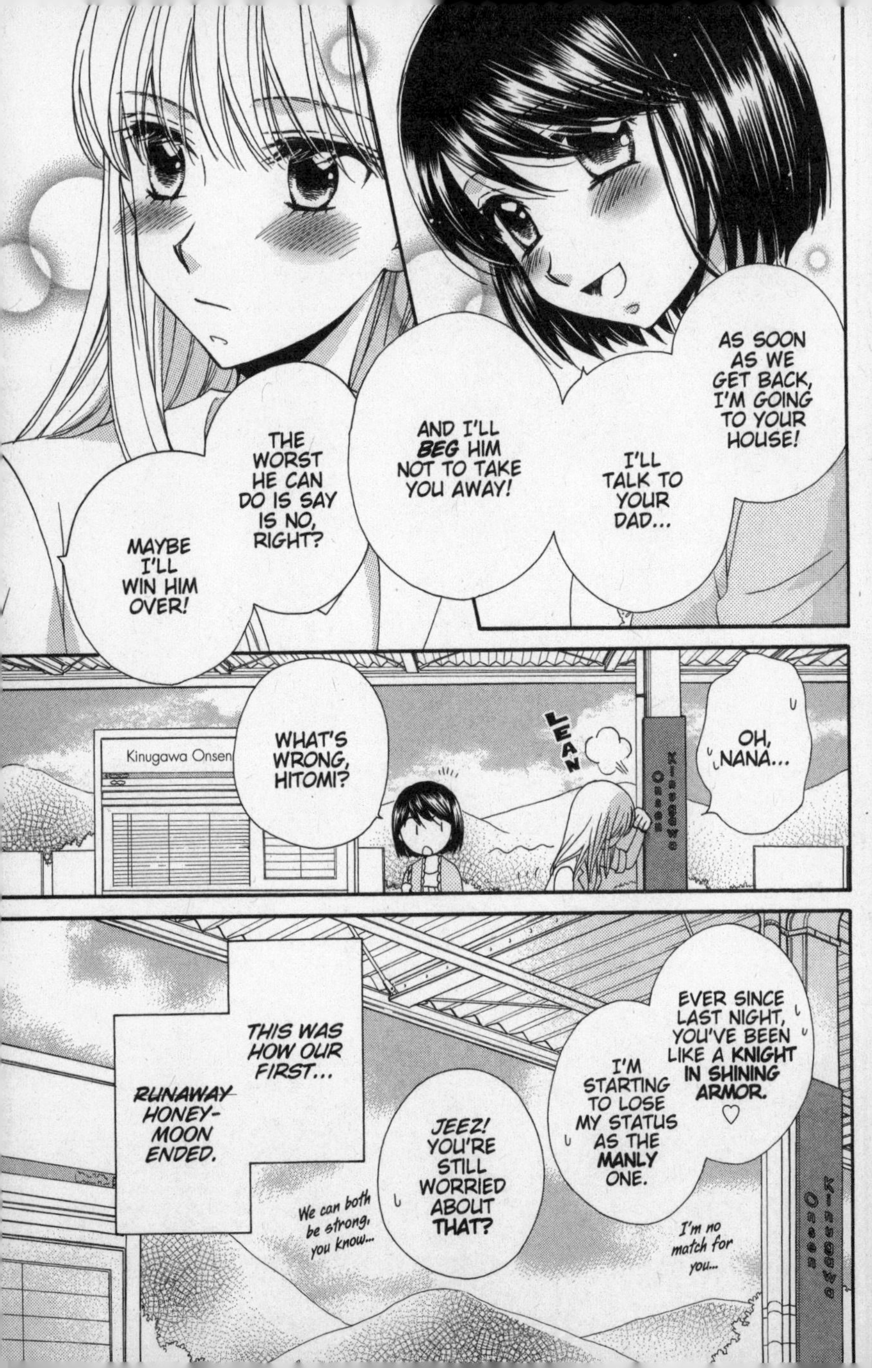
AS SOON AS WE GET BACK, I'M GOING TO YOUR HOUSE!
I'LL TALK TO YOUR DAD...
AND I'LL BEG HIM NOT TO TAKE YOU AWAY!
THE WORST HE CAN DO IS SAY IS NO, RIGHT?
MAYBE I'LL WIN HIM OVER!
OH, NANA...
LEAN
Kinugawa Onsen
WHAT'S WRONG, HITOMI?
Kinugawa Onsen
EVER SINCE LAST NIGHT, YOU'VE BEEN LIKE A KNIGHT IN SHINING ARMOR. ♡
I'M STARTING TO LOSE MY STATUS AS THE MANLY ONE.
I'm no match for you...
JEEZ! YOU'RE STILL WORRIED ABOUT THAT?
We can both be strong, you know...
THIS WAS HOW OUR FIRST...
~~RUNAWAY~~ HONEY-MOON ENDED.
Kinugawa Onsen

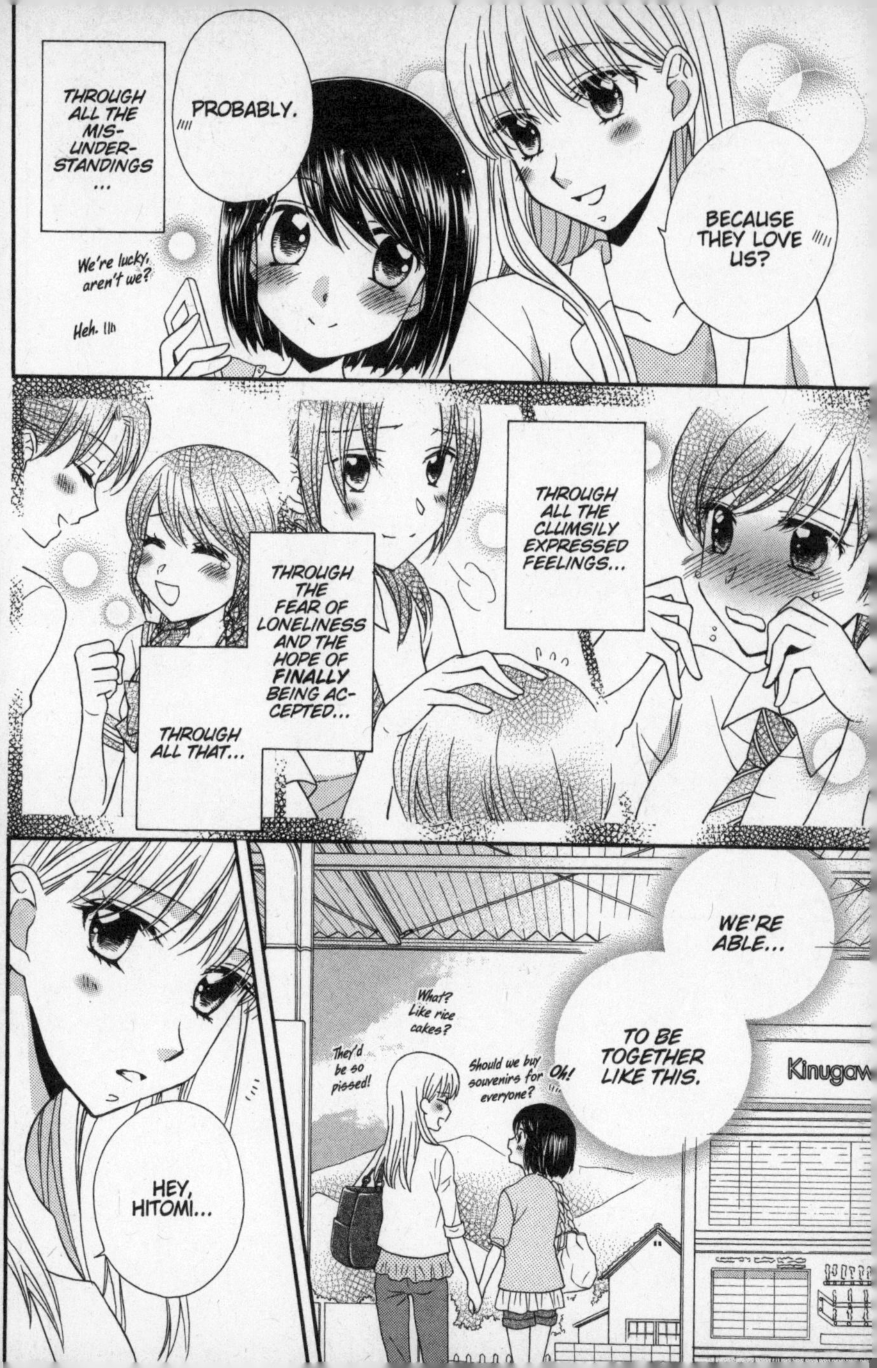
BECAUSE THEY LOVE US?
PROBABLY.
THROUGH ALL THE MIS-UNDER-STANDINGS...
We're lucky, aren't we?
Heh.
THROUGH ALL THE CLUMSILY EXPRESSED FEELINGS...
THROUGH THE FEAR OF LONELINESS AND THE HOPE OF FINALLY BEING AC-CEPTED...
THROUGH ALL THAT...
WE'RE ABLE...
TO BE TOGETHER LIKE THIS.
Oh!
Should we buy souvenirs for everyone?
What? Like rice cakes?
They'd be so pissed!
HEY, HITOMI...

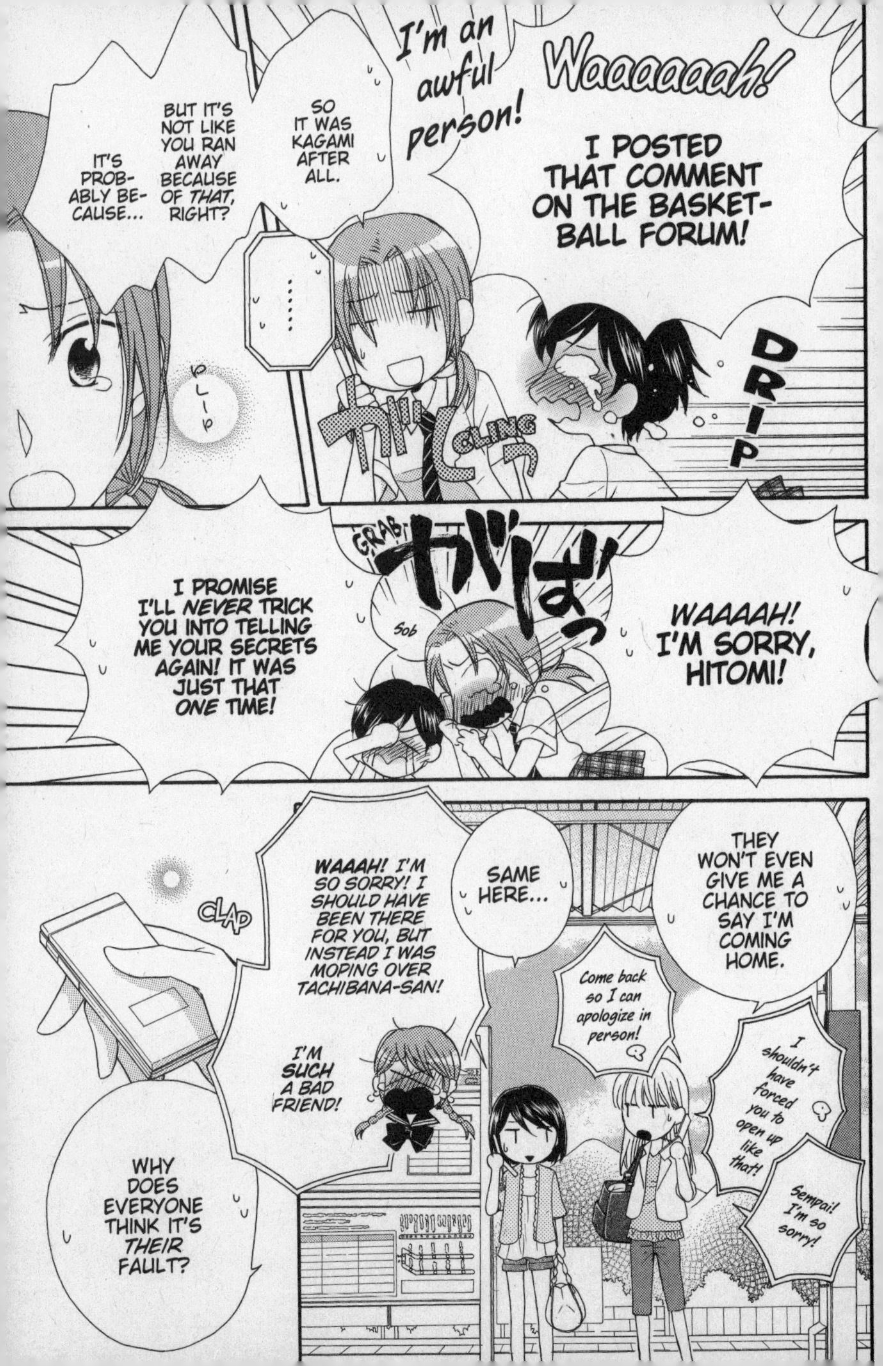
Waaaaaah!
I'm an awful person!
I POSTED THAT COMMENT ON THE BASKET-BALL FORUM!
DRIP
SO IT WAS KAGAMI AFTER ALL.
......
CLING
BUT IT'S NOT LIKE YOU RAN AWAY BECAUSE OF *THAT*, RIGHT?
IT'S PROB-ABLY BE-CAUSE...
WAAAAH! I'M SORRY, HITOMI!
GRAB
Sob
I PROMISE I'LL *NEVER* TRICK YOU INTO TELLING ME YOUR SECRETS AGAIN! IT WAS JUST THAT *ONE* TIME!
THEY WON'T EVEN GIVE ME A CHANCE TO SAY I'M COMING HOME.
Sempai! I'm so sorry!
I shouldn't have forced you to open up like that!
Come back so I can apologize in person!
SAME HERE...
WAAAH! I'M SO SORRY! I SHOULD HAVE BEEN THERE FOR YOU, BUT INSTEAD I WAS MOPING OVER TACHIBANA-SAN!
I'M SUCH A BAD FRIEND!
CLAP
WHY DOES EVERYONE THINK IT'S *THEIR* FAULT?

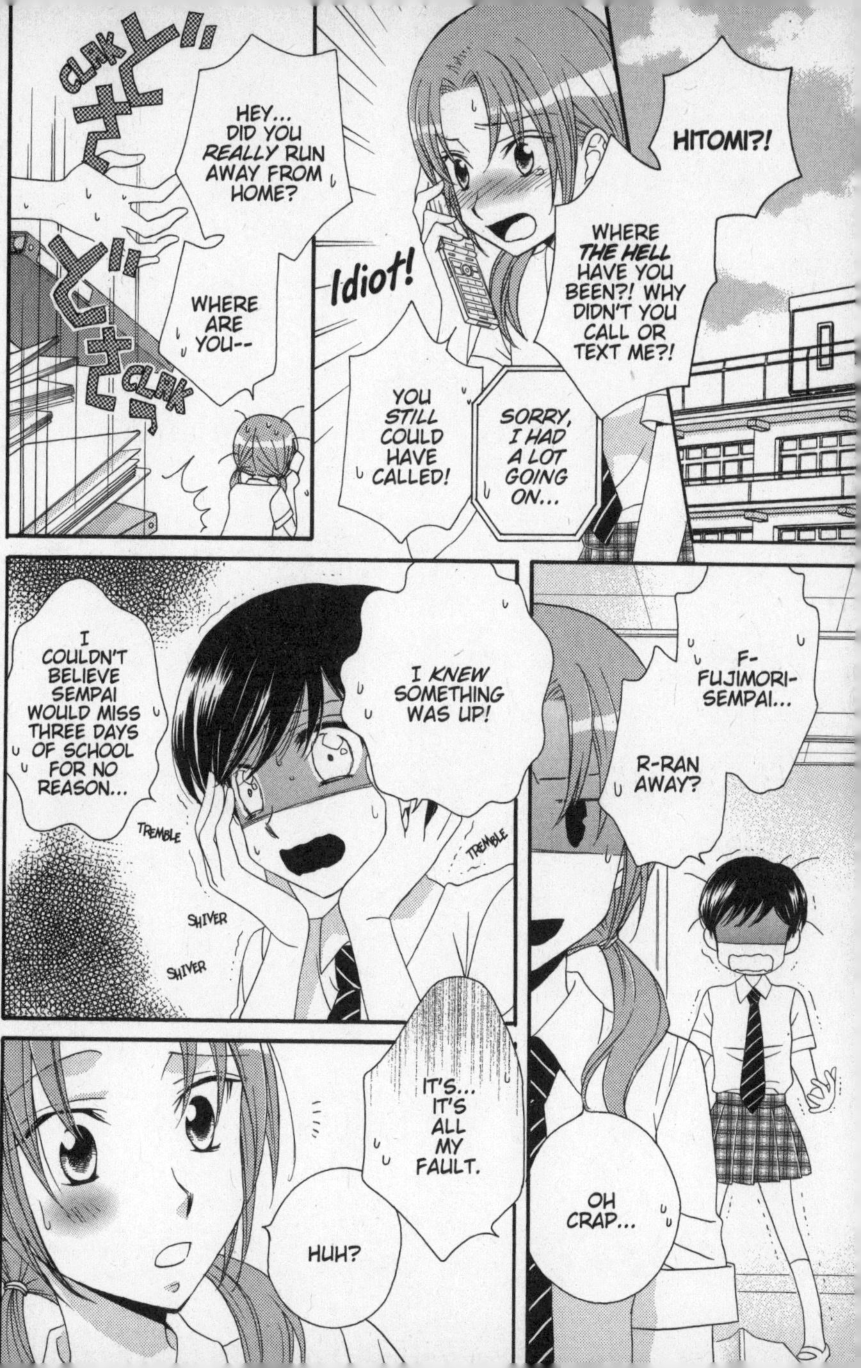
HITOMI?!
WHERE *THE HELL* HAVE YOU BEEN?! WHY DIDN'T YOU CALL OR TEXT ME?!
Idiot!
SORRY, I HAD A LOT GOING ON...
YOU *STILL* COULD HAVE CALLED!
CLAK
HEY... DID YOU *REALLY* RUN AWAY FROM HOME?
WHERE ARE YOU--
CLAK
F-FUJIMORI-SEMPAI...
R-RAN AWAY?
I *KNEW* SOMETHING WAS UP!
TREMBLE
I COULDN'T BELIEVE SEMPAI WOULD MISS THREE DAYS OF SCHOOL FOR NO REASON...
TREMBLE
SHIVER
SHIVER
OH CRAP...
IT'S... IT'S ALL MY FAULT.
HUH?

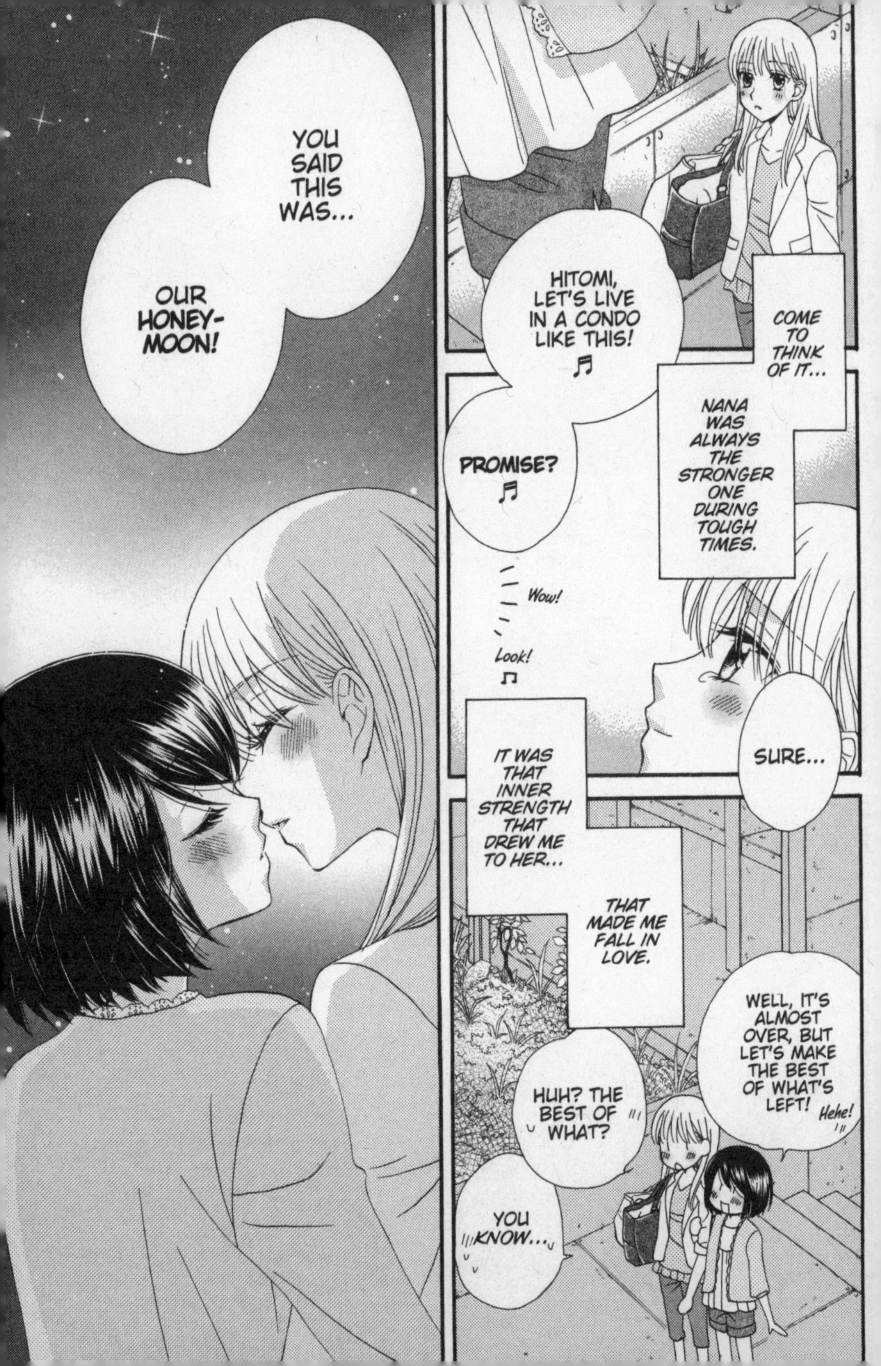

HITOMI, LET'S LIVE IN A CONDO LIKE THIS! ♬
PROMISE? ♬
COME TO THINK OF IT...
NANA WAS ALWAYS THE STRONGER ONE DURING TOUGH TIMES.
Wow!
Look! ♫
SURE...
IT WAS THAT INNER STRENGTH THAT DREW ME TO HER...
THAT MADE ME FALL IN LOVE.
WELL, IT'S ALMOST OVER, BUT LET'S MAKE THE BEST OF WHAT'S LEFT!
Hehe!
HUH? THE BEST OF WHAT?
YOU KNOW...
YOU SAID THIS WAS...
OUR HONEYMOON!

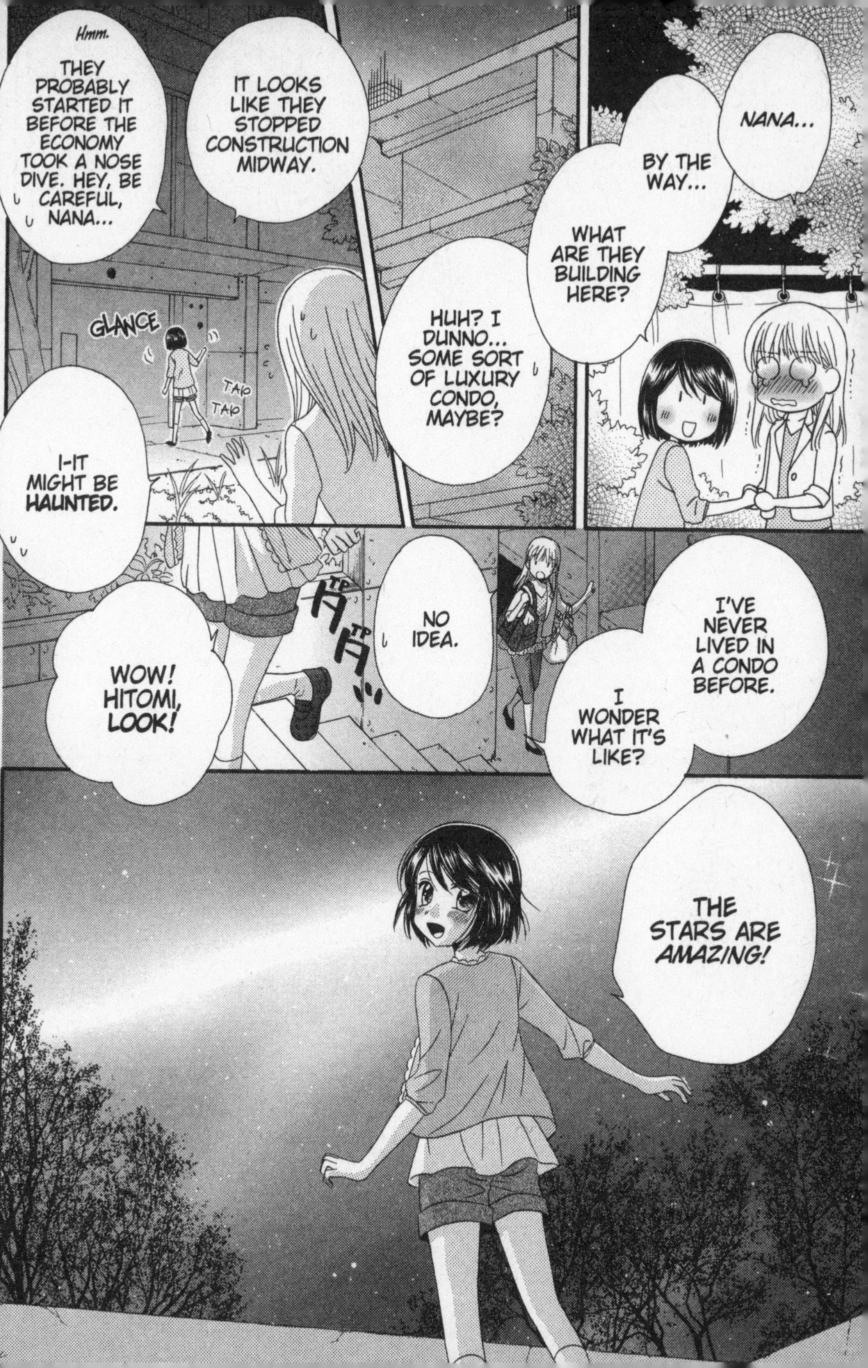
NANA...
BY THE WAY...
WHAT ARE THEY BUILDING HERE?
HUH? I DUNNO... SOME SORT OF LUXURY CONDO, MAYBE?
IT LOOKS LIKE THEY STOPPED CONSTRUCTION MIDWAY.
Hmm.
THEY PROBABLY STARTED IT BEFORE THE ECONOMY TOOK A NOSE DIVE. HEY, BE CAREFUL, NANA...
GLANCE
TAP
TAP
I-IT MIGHT BE HAUNTED.
I'VE NEVER LIVED IN A CONDO BEFORE.
I WONDER WHAT IT'S LIKE?
NO IDEA.
TP
TP
WOW! HITOMI, LOOK!
THE STARS ARE AMAZING!

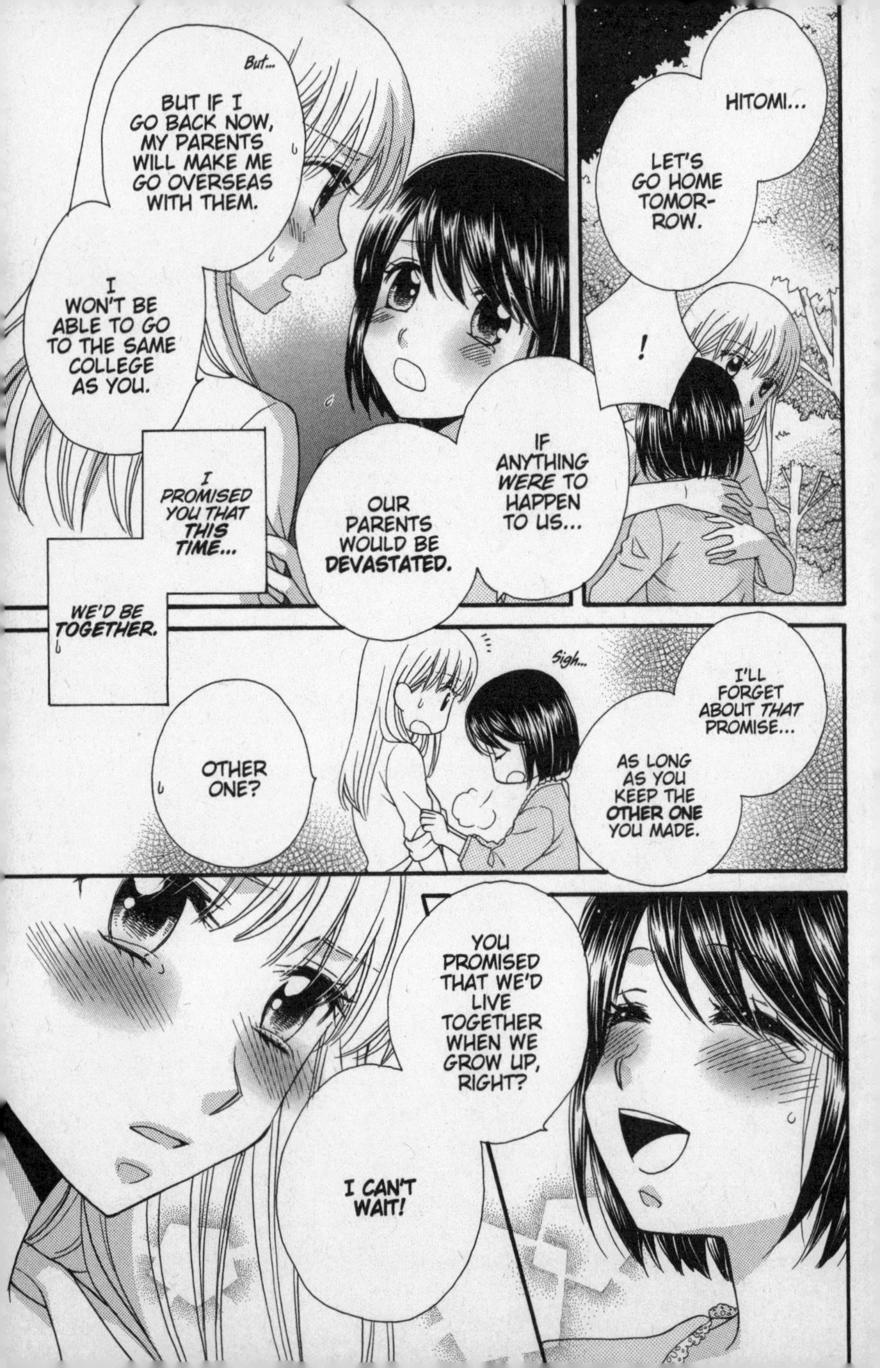
HITOMI...
LET'S GO HOME TOMORROW.
!
But...
BUT IF I GO BACK NOW, MY PARENTS WILL MAKE ME GO OVERSEAS WITH THEM.
I WON'T BE ABLE TO GO TO THE SAME COLLEGE AS YOU.
I PROMISED YOU THAT *THIS TIME*...
WE'D BE TOGETHER.
IF ANYTHING *WERE* TO HAPPEN TO US...
OUR PARENTS WOULD BE **DEVASTATED.**
Sigh...
I'LL FORGET ABOUT *THAT* PROMISE...
AS LONG AS YOU KEEP THE **OTHER ONE** YOU MADE.
OTHER ONE?
YOU PROMISED THAT WE'D LIVE TOGETHER WHEN WE GROW UP, RIGHT?
I CAN'T WAIT!

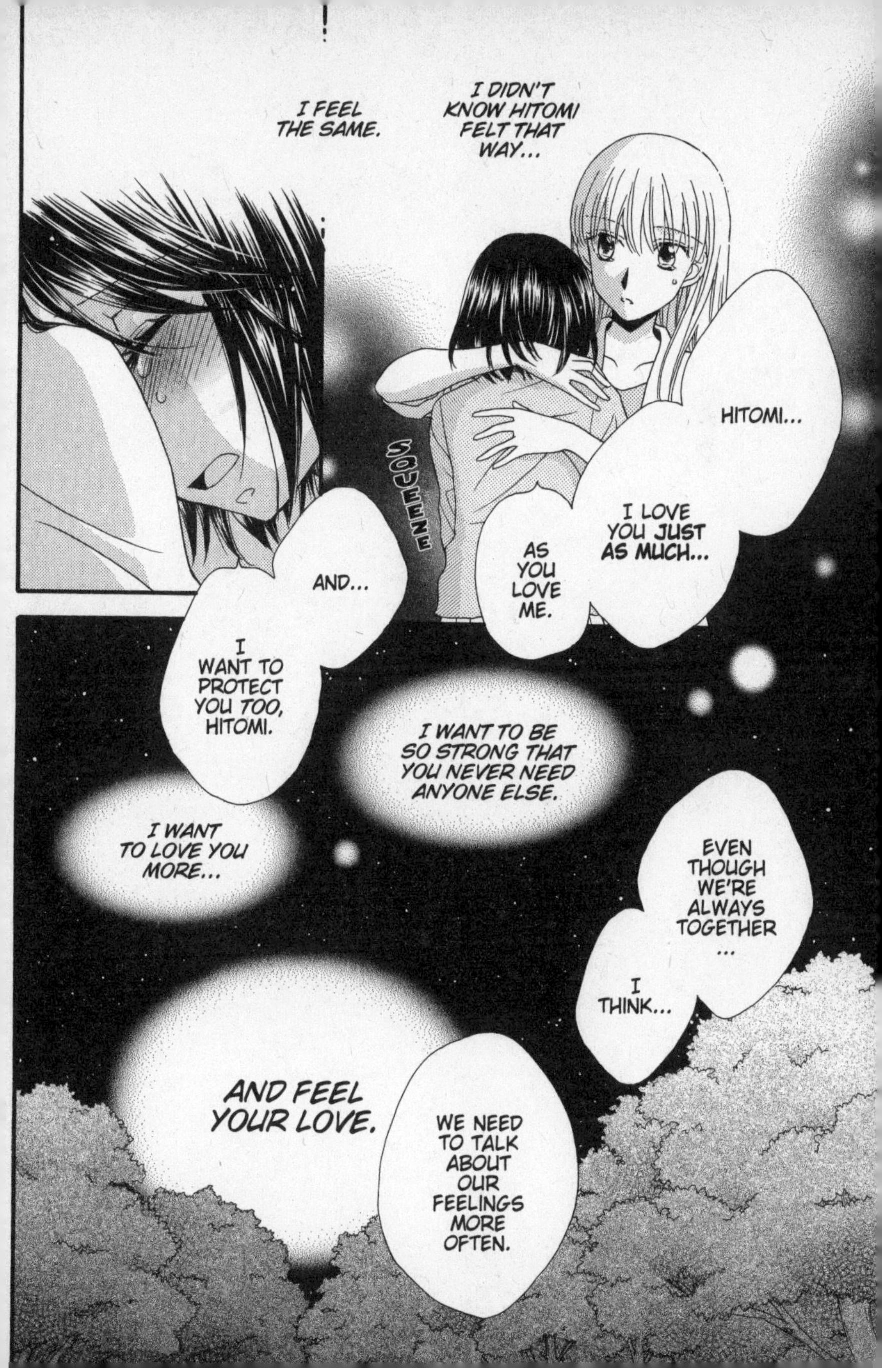
I DIDN'T KNOW HITOMI FELT THAT WAY...
I FEEL THE SAME.
HITOMI...
I LOVE YOU JUST AS MUCH...
AS YOU LOVE ME.
SQUEEZE
AND...
I WANT TO PROTECT YOU TOO, HITOMI.
I WANT TO BE SO STRONG THAT YOU NEVER NEED ANYONE ELSE.
I WANT TO LOVE YOU MORE...
EVEN THOUGH WE'RE ALWAYS TOGETHER...
I THINK...
WE NEED TO TALK ABOUT OUR FEELINGS MORE OFTEN.
AND FEEL YOUR LOVE.

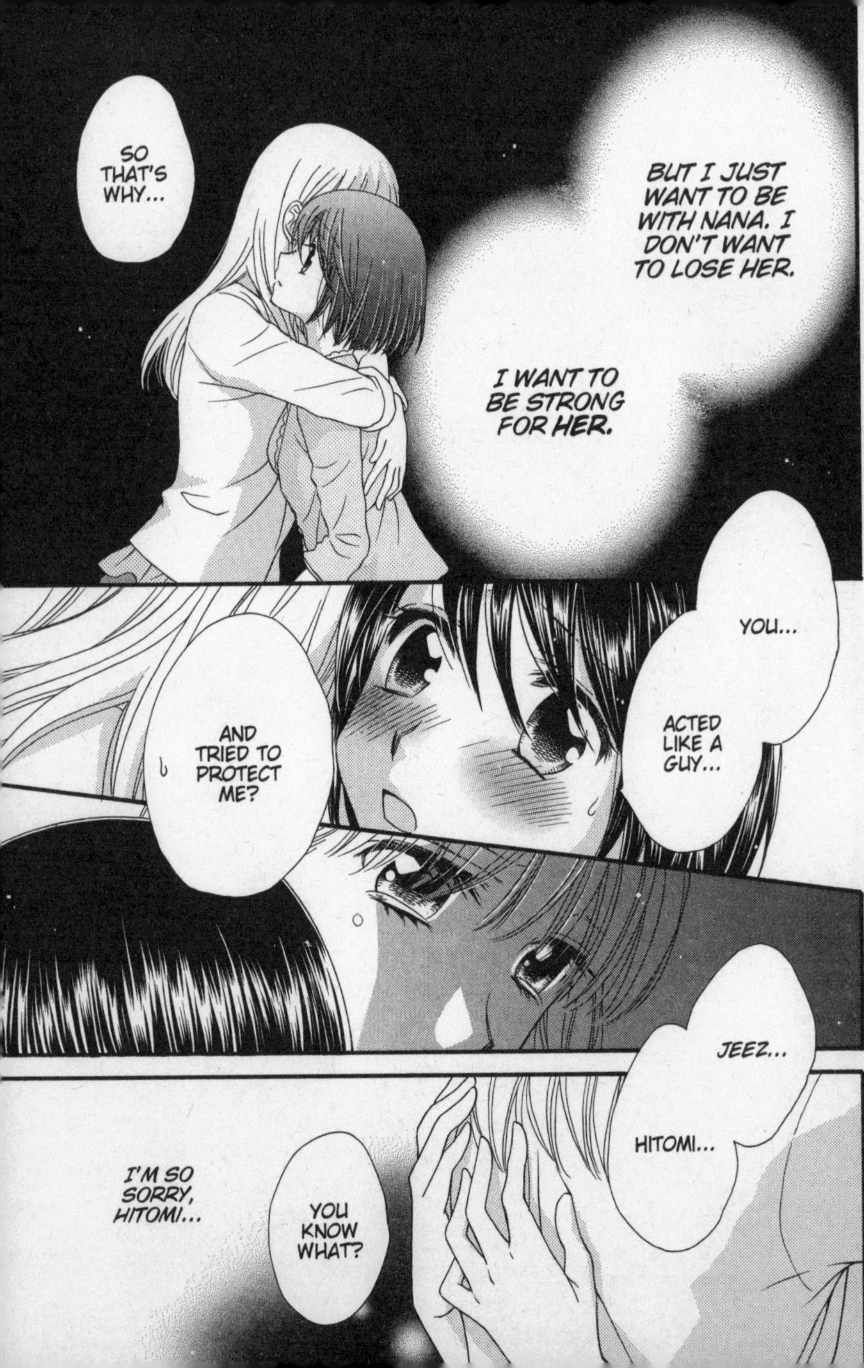
BUT I JUST WANT TO BE WITH NANA. I DON'T WANT TO LOSE HER.
I WANT TO BE STRONG FOR HER.
SO THAT'S WHY...
YOU...
ACTED LIKE A GUY...
AND TRIED TO PROTECT ME?
JEEZ...
HITOMI...
YOU KNOW WHAT?
I'M SO SORRY, HITOMI...

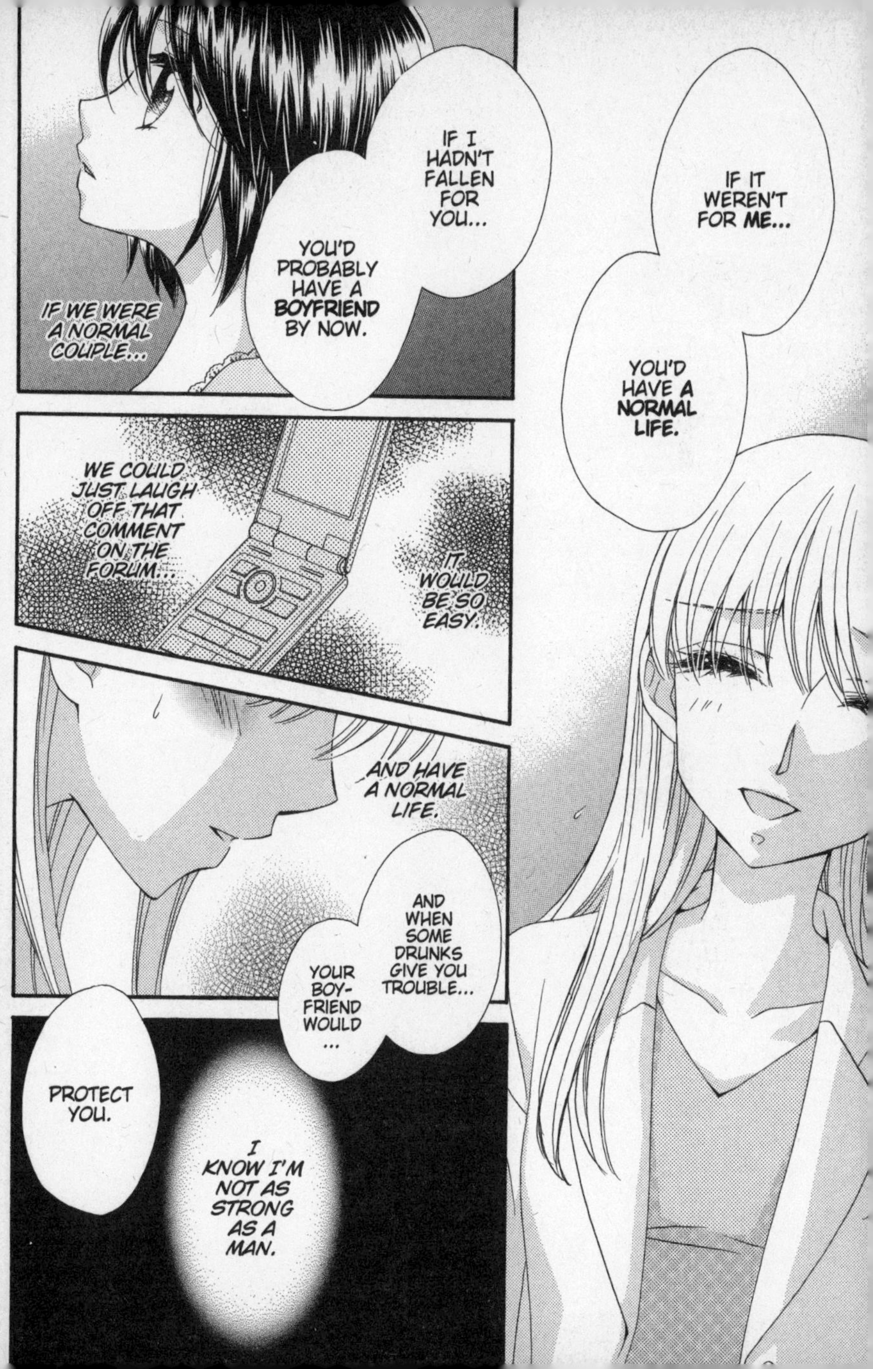
IF IT WEREN'T FOR ME...
YOU'D HAVE A NORMAL LIFE.
IF I HADN'T FALLEN FOR YOU...
YOU'D PROBABLY HAVE A BOYFRIEND BY NOW.
IF WE WERE A NORMAL COUPLE...
WE COULD JUST LAUGH OFF THAT COMMENT ON THE FORUM...
IT WOULD BE SO EASY.
AND HAVE A NORMAL LIFE.
AND WHEN SOME DRUNKS GIVE YOU TROUBLE...
YOUR BOY-FRIEND WOULD ...
PROTECT YOU.
I KNOW I'M NOT AS STRONG AS A MAN.

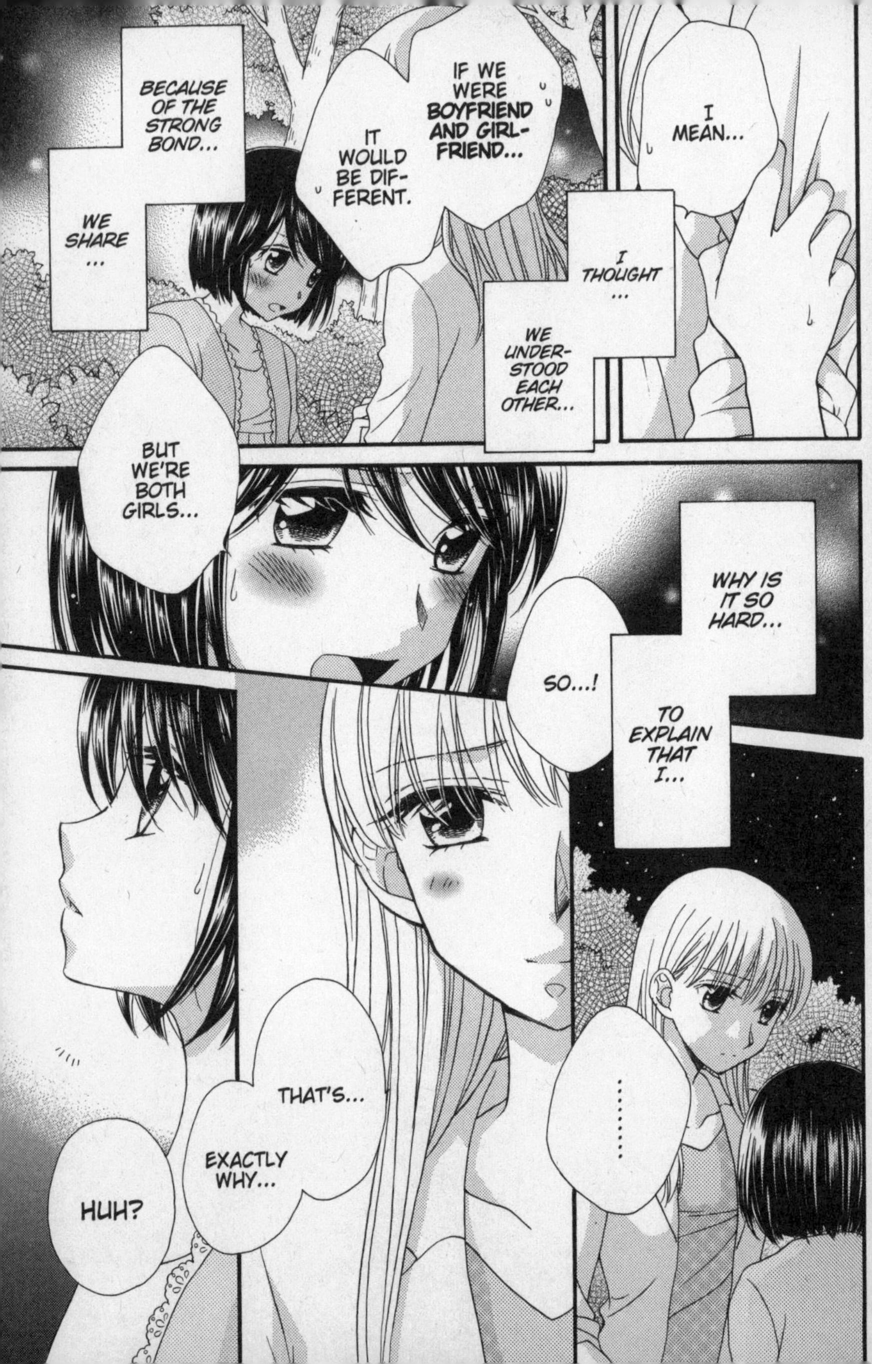
I MEAN...
I THOUGHT ...
WE UNDERSTOOD EACH OTHER...
IF WE WERE BOYFRIEND AND GIRL-FRIEND...
IT WOULD BE DIF-FERENT.
BECAUSE OF THE STRONG BOND...
WE SHARE ...
BUT WE'RE BOTH GIRLS...
WHY IS IT SO HARD...
TO EXPLAIN THAT I...
SO...!
......
THAT'S...
EXACTLY WHY...
HUH?

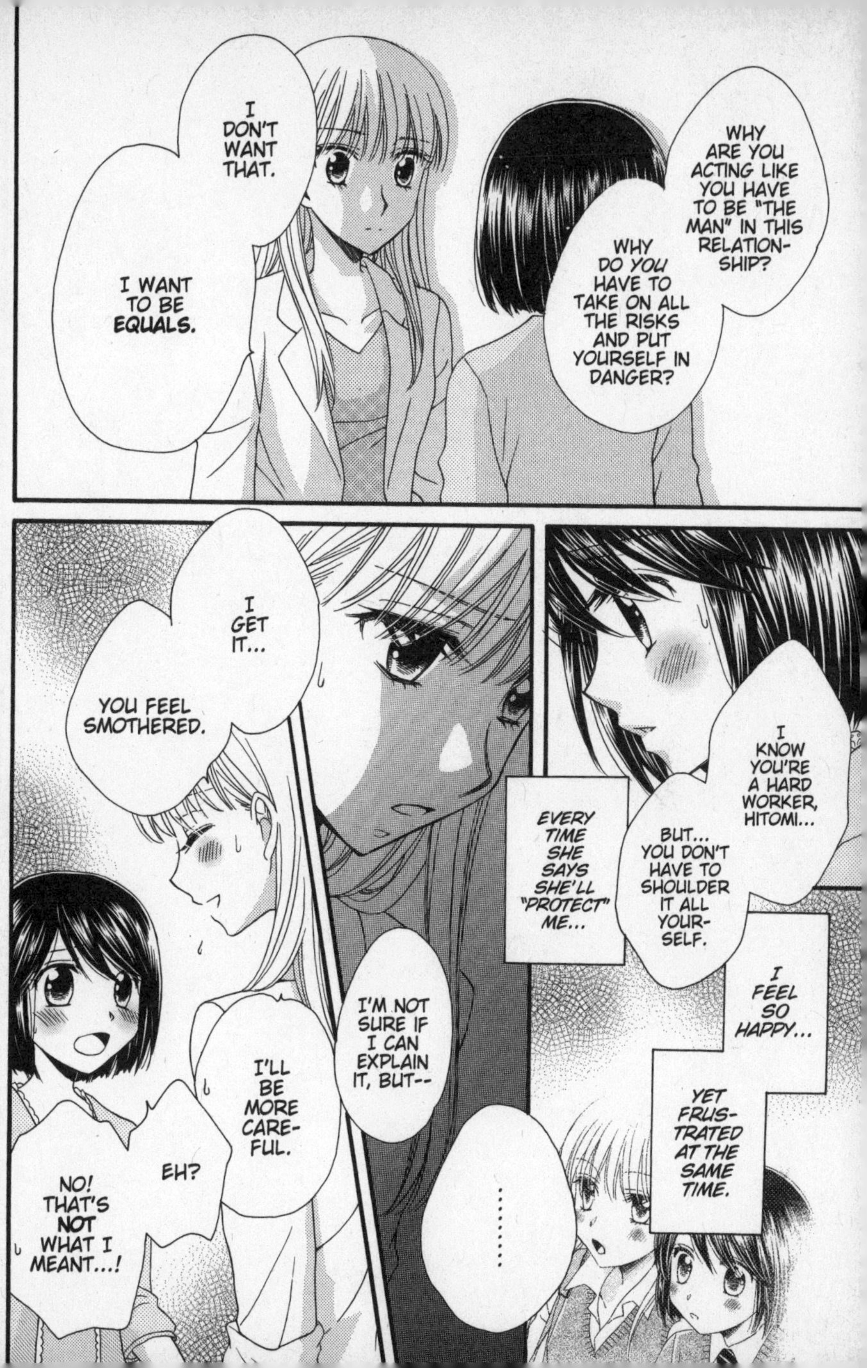
WHY ARE YOU ACTING LIKE YOU HAVE TO BE "THE MAN" IN THIS RELATION-SHIP?
WHY DO YOU HAVE TO TAKE ON ALL THE RISKS AND PUT YOURSELF IN DANGER?
I DON'T WANT THAT.
I WANT TO BE EQUALS.
I KNOW YOU'RE A HARD WORKER, HITOMI...
BUT... YOU DON'T HAVE TO SHOULDER IT ALL YOUR-SELF.
EVERY TIME SHE SAYS SHE'LL "PROTECT" ME...
I FEEL SO HAPPY...
YET FRUS-TRATED AT THE SAME TIME.
......
I GET IT...
YOU FEEL SMOTHERED.
I'M NOT SURE IF I CAN EXPLAIN IT, BUT--
I'LL BE MORE CARE-FUL.
EH?
NO! THAT'S NOT WHAT I MEANT...!

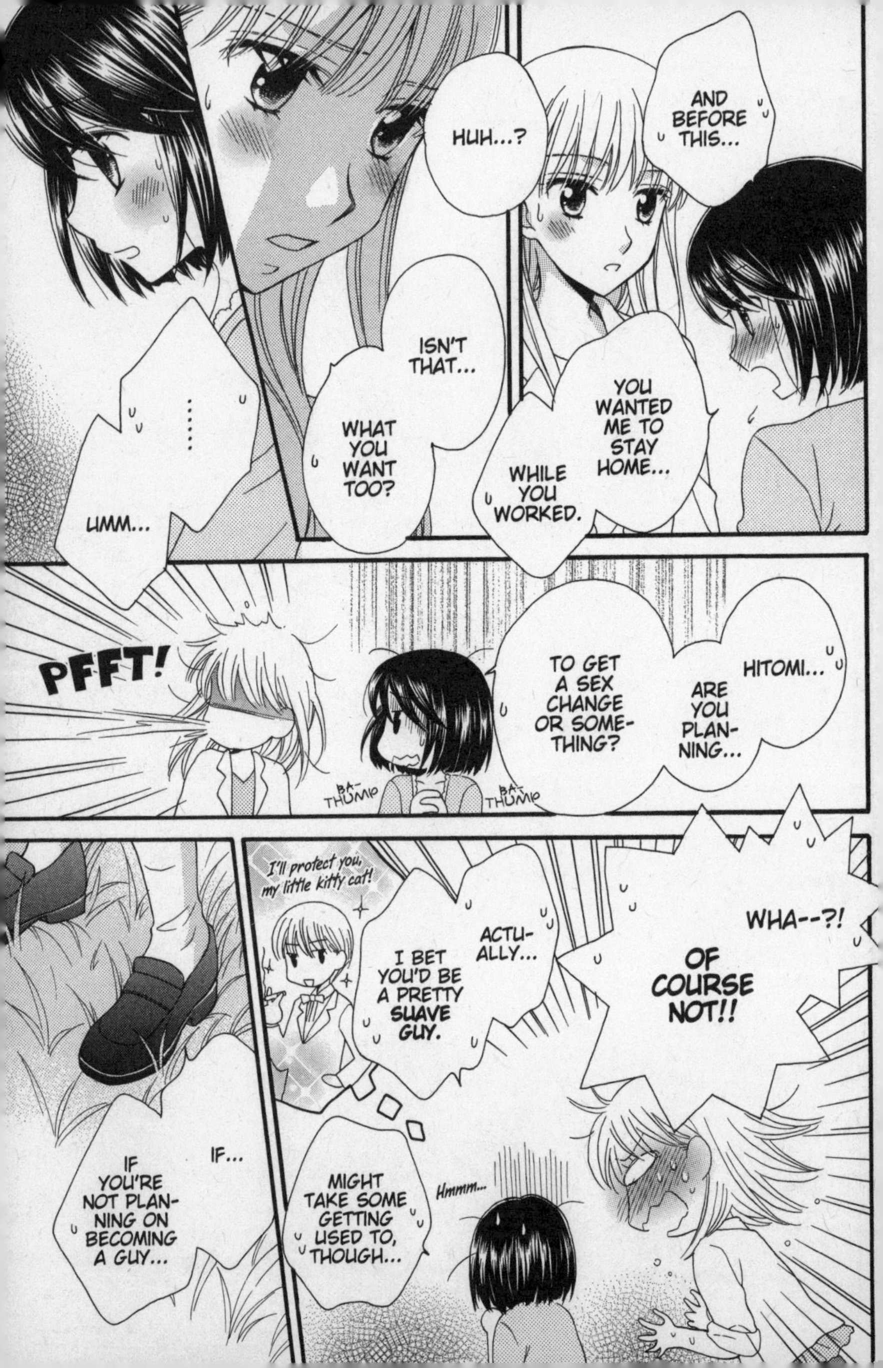
AND BEFORE THIS...
YOU WANTED ME TO STAY HOME... WHILE YOU WORKED.
HUH...?
ISN'T THAT... WHAT YOU WANT TOO?
......
UMM...
HITOMI...
ARE YOU PLANNING...
TO GET A SEX CHANGE OR SOMETHING?
BA-THUMP
BA-THUMP
PFFT!
WHA--?!
OF COURSE NOT!!
ACTUALLY...
I BET YOU'D BE A PRETTY SUAVE GUY.
I'll protect you, my little kitty cat!
MIGHT TAKE SOME GETTING USED TO, THOUGH...
Hmmm...
IF...
IF YOU'RE NOT PLANNING ON BECOMING A GUY...

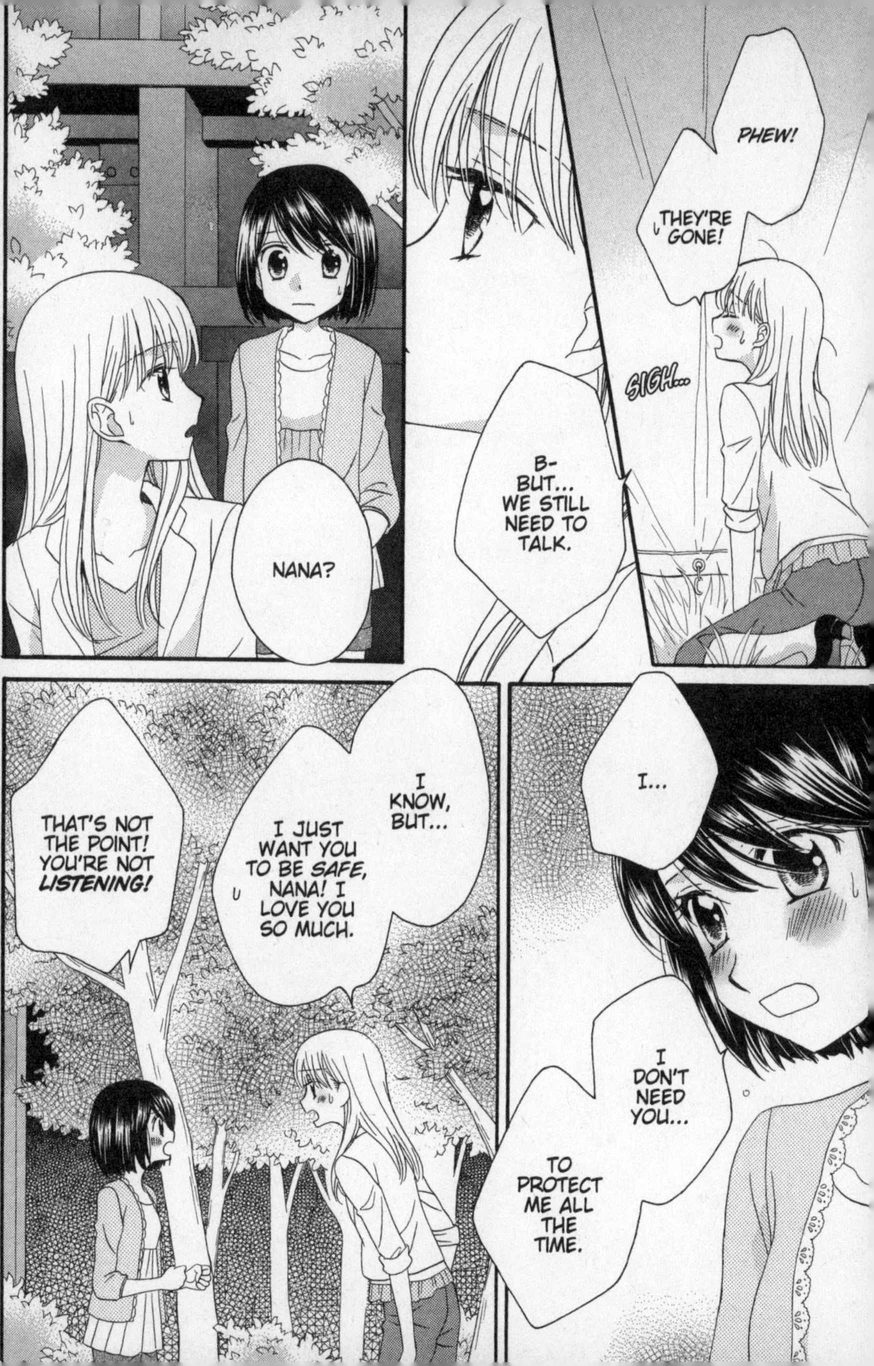
PHEW!
THEY'RE GONE!
SIGH...
B-BUT... WE STILL NEED TO TALK.
NANA?
I...
I DON'T NEED YOU...
TO PROTECT ME ALL THE TIME.
I KNOW, BUT...
I JUST WANT YOU TO BE *SAFE*, NANA! I LOVE YOU SO MUCH.
THAT'S NOT THE POINT! YOU'RE NOT ***LISTENING!***

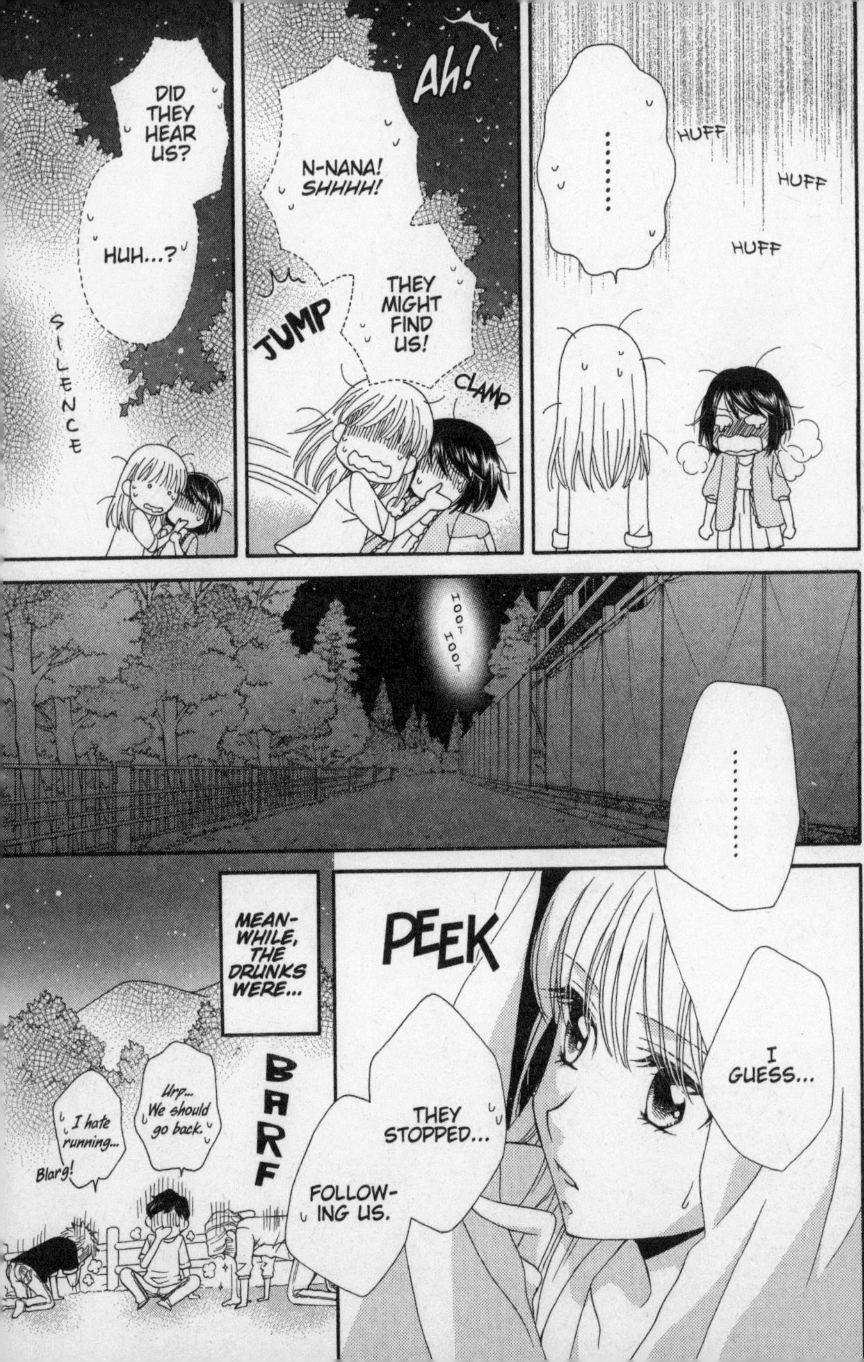
......
HUFF
HUFF
HUFF
Ah!
N-NANA! SHHHH!
THEY MIGHT FIND US!
JUMP
CLAMP
DID THEY HEAR US?
HUH...?
SILENCE
HOOT HOOT
......
PEEK
THEY STOPPED... FOLLOWING US.
I GUESS...
MEAN-WHILE, THE DRUNKS WERE...
BARF
Urp... We should go back.
I hate running...
Blarg!

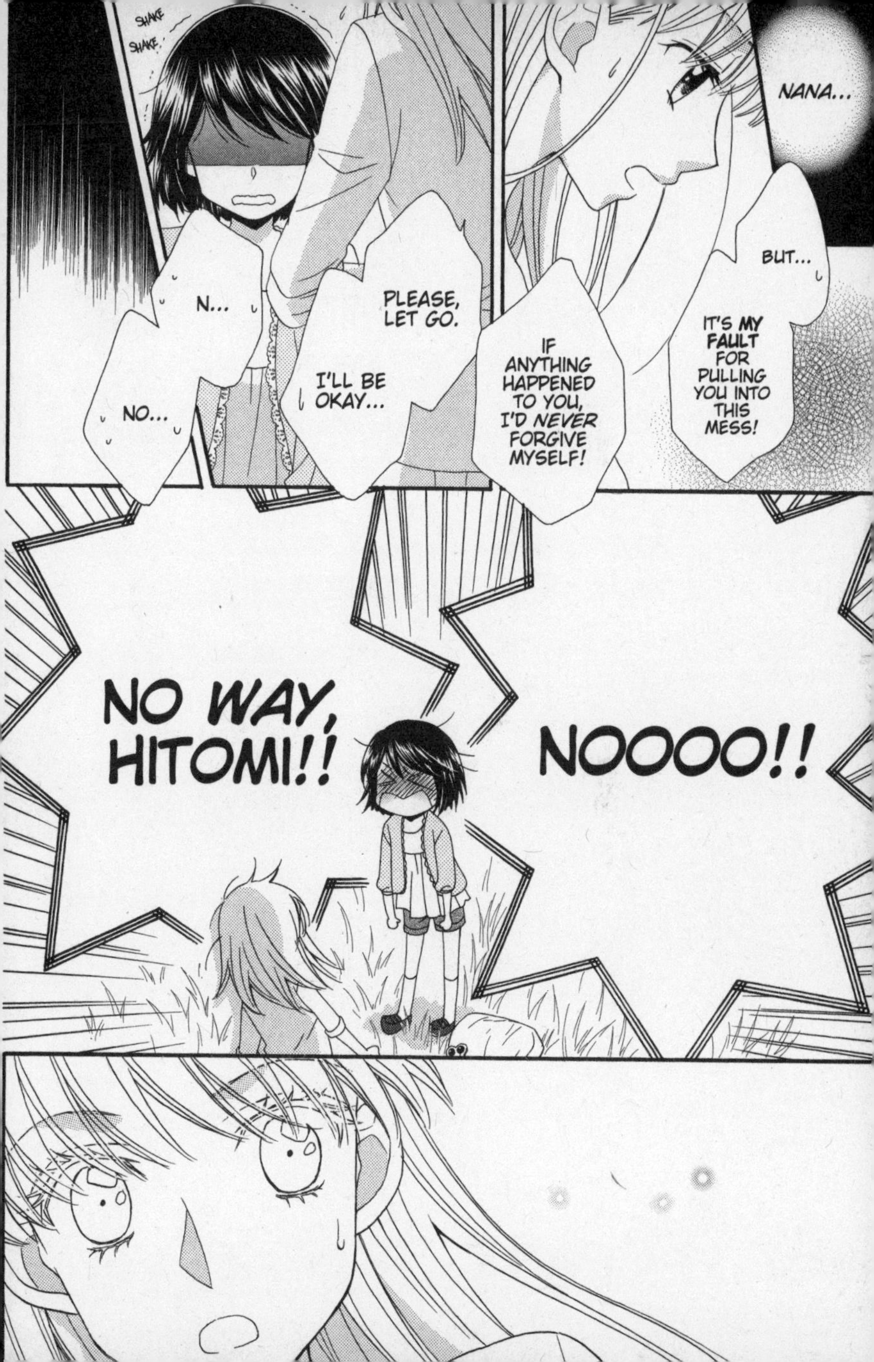
NANA...
BUT...
IT'S MY FAULT FOR PULLING YOU INTO THIS MESS!
IF ANYTHING HAPPENED TO YOU, I'D NEVER FORGIVE MYSELF!
SHAKE SHAKE
PLEASE, LET GO.
N...
I'LL BE OKAY...
NO...
NOOOO!!
NO WAY, HITOMI!!

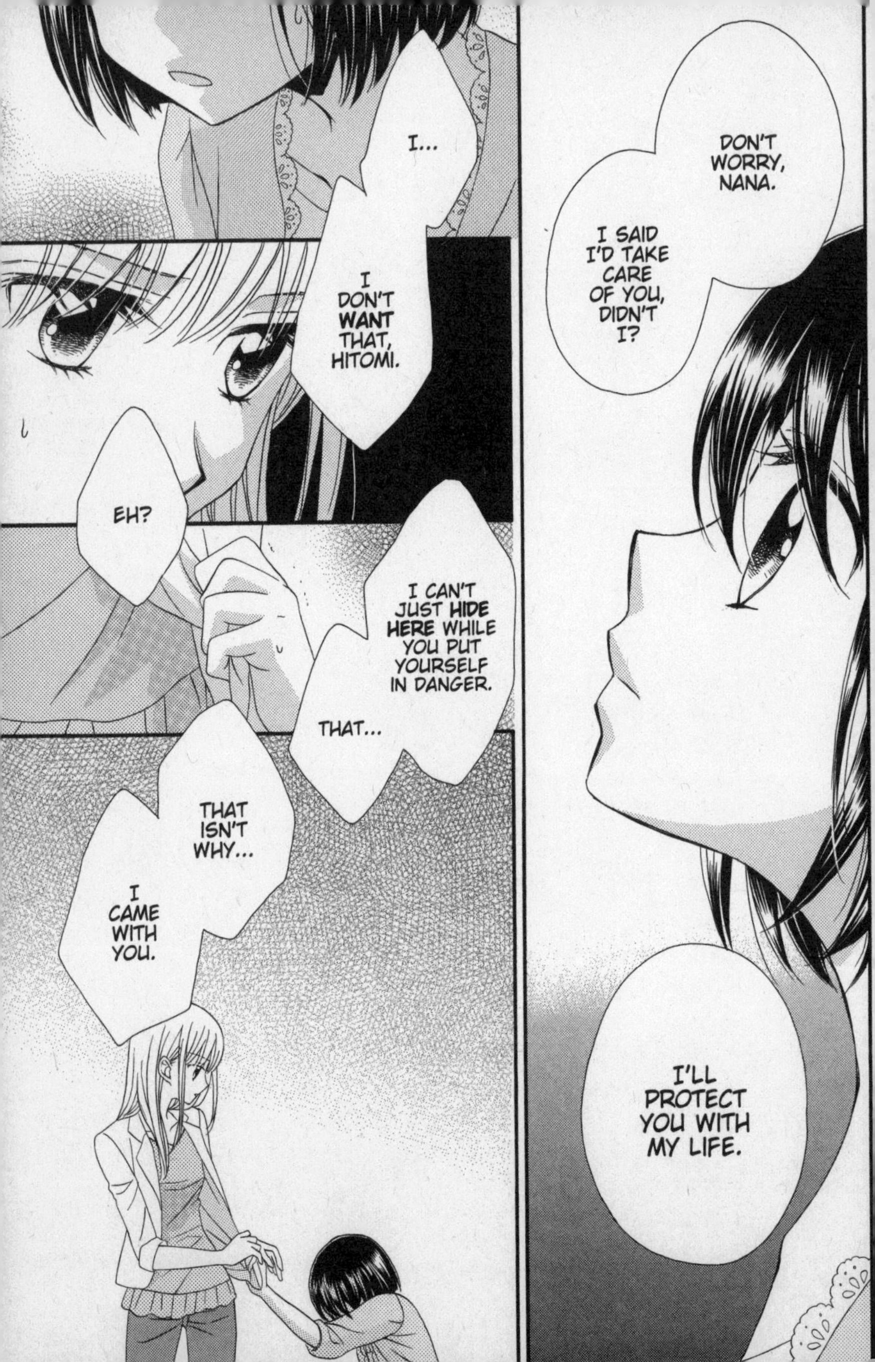
DON'T WORRY, NANA.
I SAID I'D TAKE CARE OF YOU, DIDN'T I?
I'LL PROTECT YOU WITH MY LIFE.
I...
I DON'T WANT THAT, HITOMI.
EH?
I CAN'T JUST HIDE HERE WHILE YOU PUT YOURSELF IN DANGER.
THAT...
THAT ISN'T WHY...
I CAME WITH YOU.

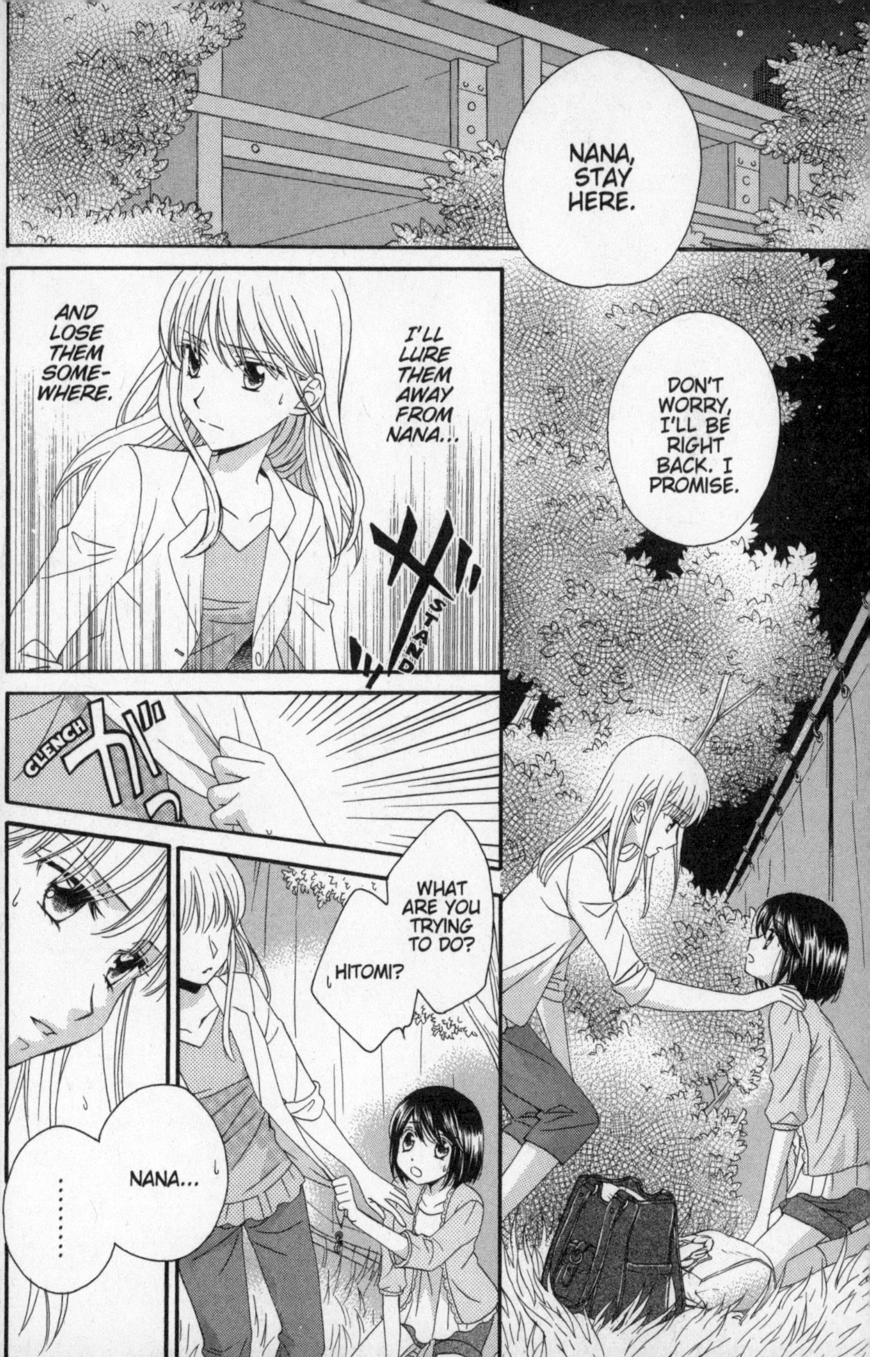
NANA, STAY HERE.
DON'T WORRY, I'LL BE RIGHT BACK. I PROMISE.
I'LL LURE THEM AWAY FROM NANA...
AND LOSE THEM SOME-WHERE.
STAND
CLENCH
WHAT ARE YOU TRYING TO DO?
HITOMI?
NANA...
......

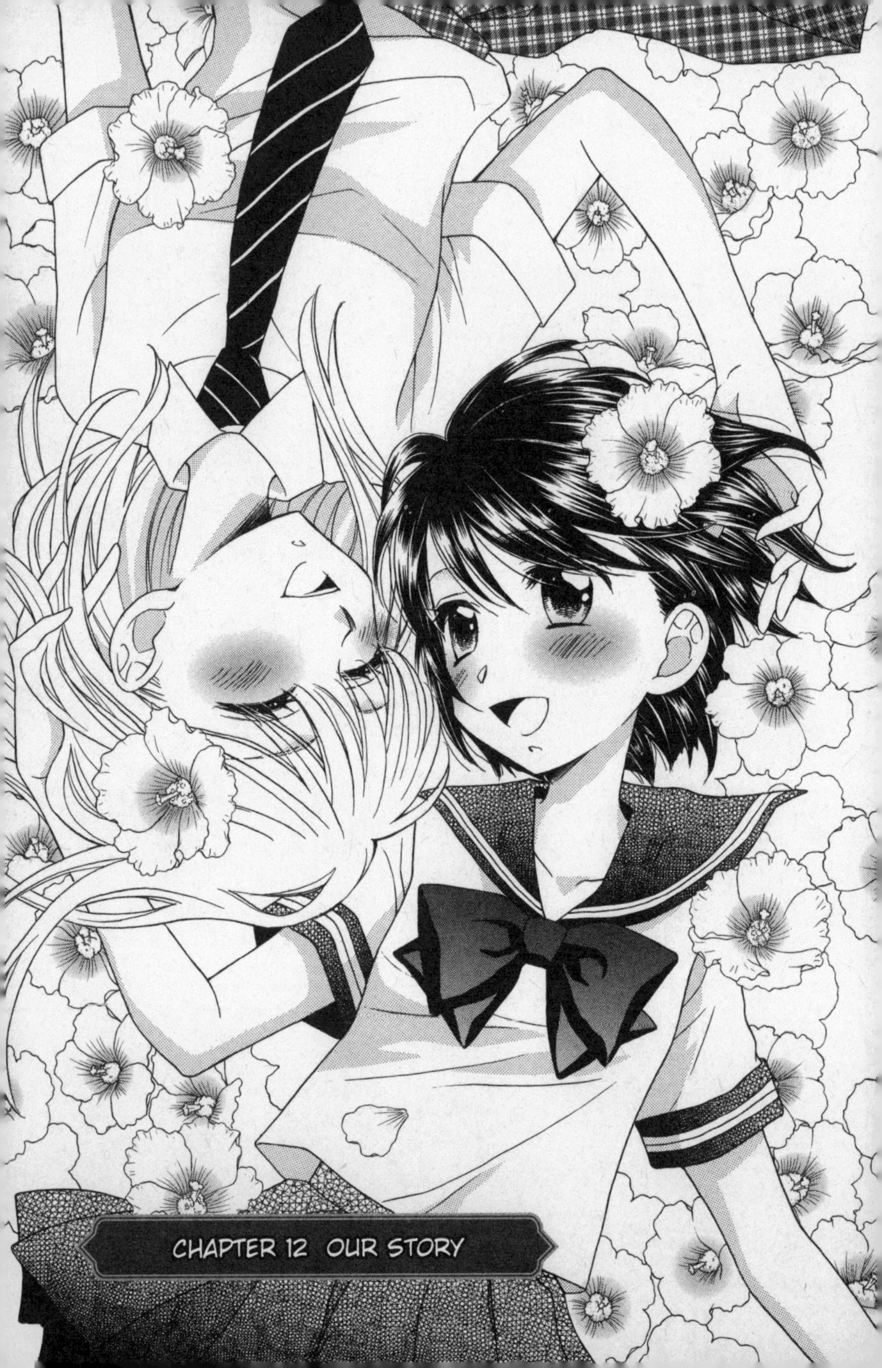
CHAPTER 12 OUR STORY

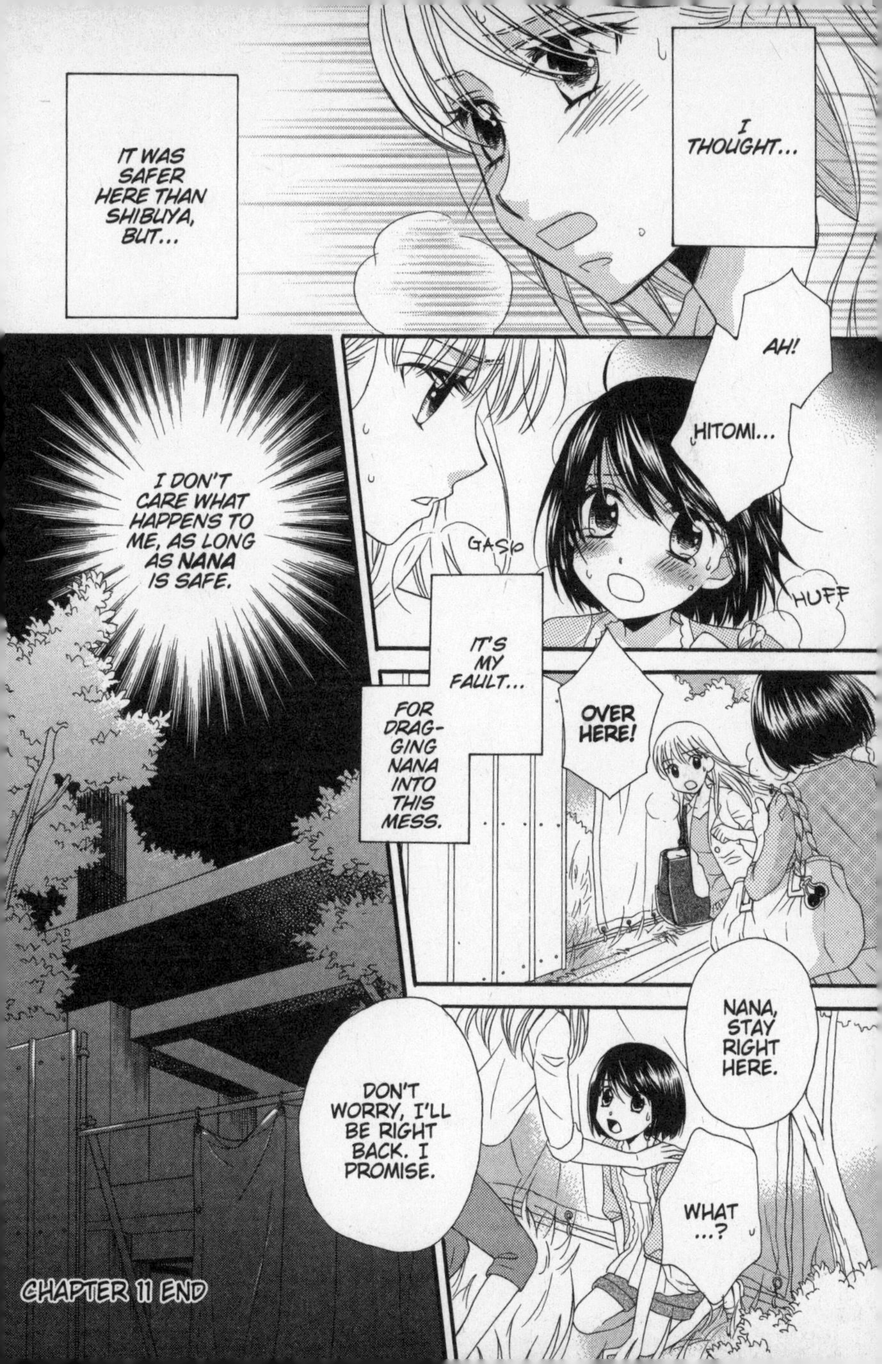
I THOUGHT...
IT WAS SAFER HERE THAN SHIBUYA, BUT...
AH!
HITOMI...
GASP
HUFF
OVER HERE!
IT'S MY FAULT...
FOR DRAG-GING NANA INTO THIS MESS.
NANA, STAY RIGHT HERE.
DON'T WORRY, I'LL BE RIGHT BACK. I PROMISE.
WHAT ...?
I DON'T CARE WHAT HAPPENS TO ME, AS LONG AS NANA IS SAFE.
CHAPTER 11 END

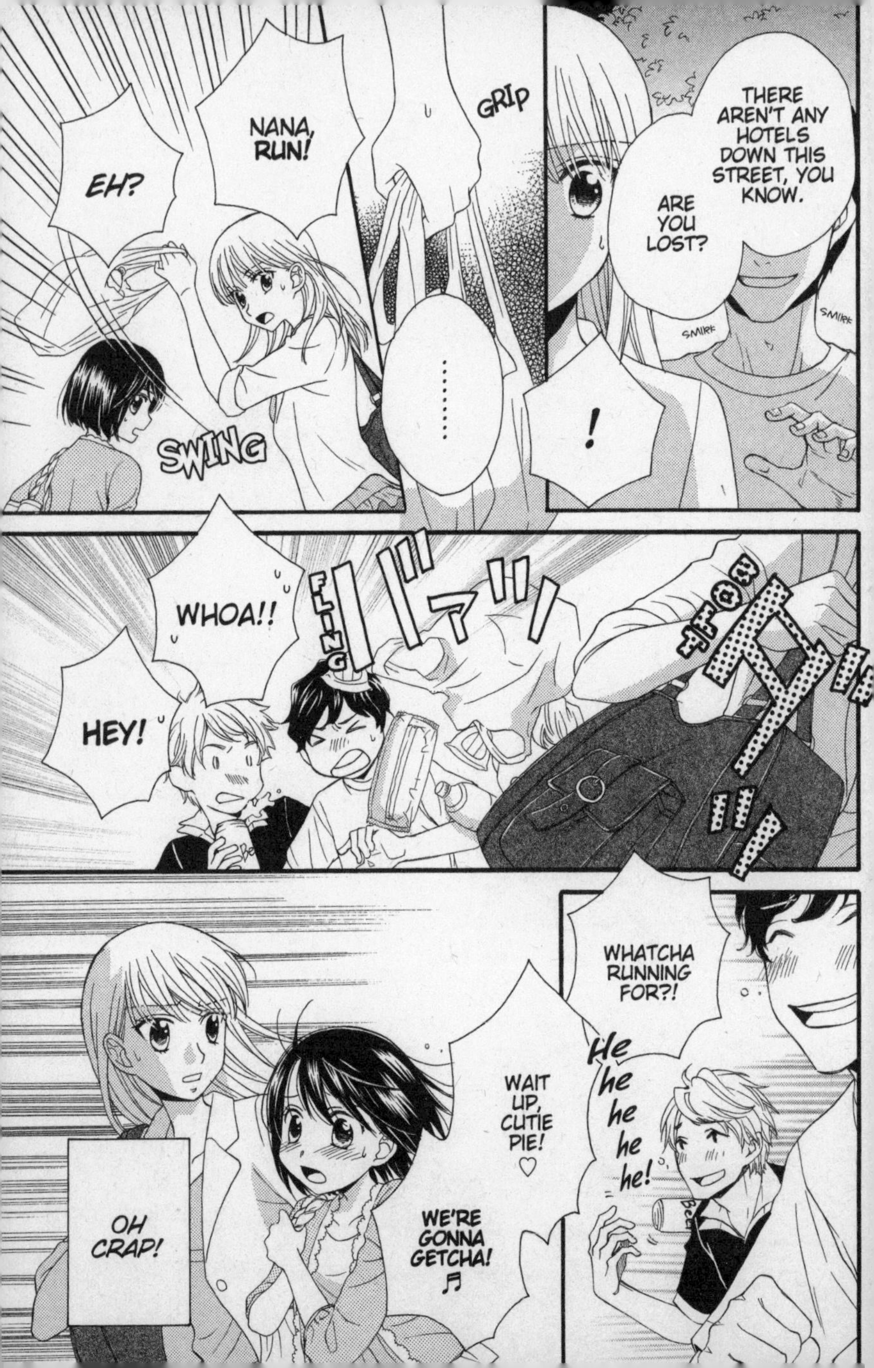
THERE AREN'T ANY HOTELS DOWN THIS STREET, YOU KNOW.
ARE YOU LOST?
SMIRK
SMIRK
!
GRIP
......
NANA, RUN!
EH?
SWING
ダッ!!
GRAB
ドアッ
FLING
WHOA!!
HEY!
WHATCHA RUNNING FOR?!
He he he he he!
WAIT UP, CUTIE PIE! ♡
WE'RE GONNA GETCHA! ♬
OH CRAP!

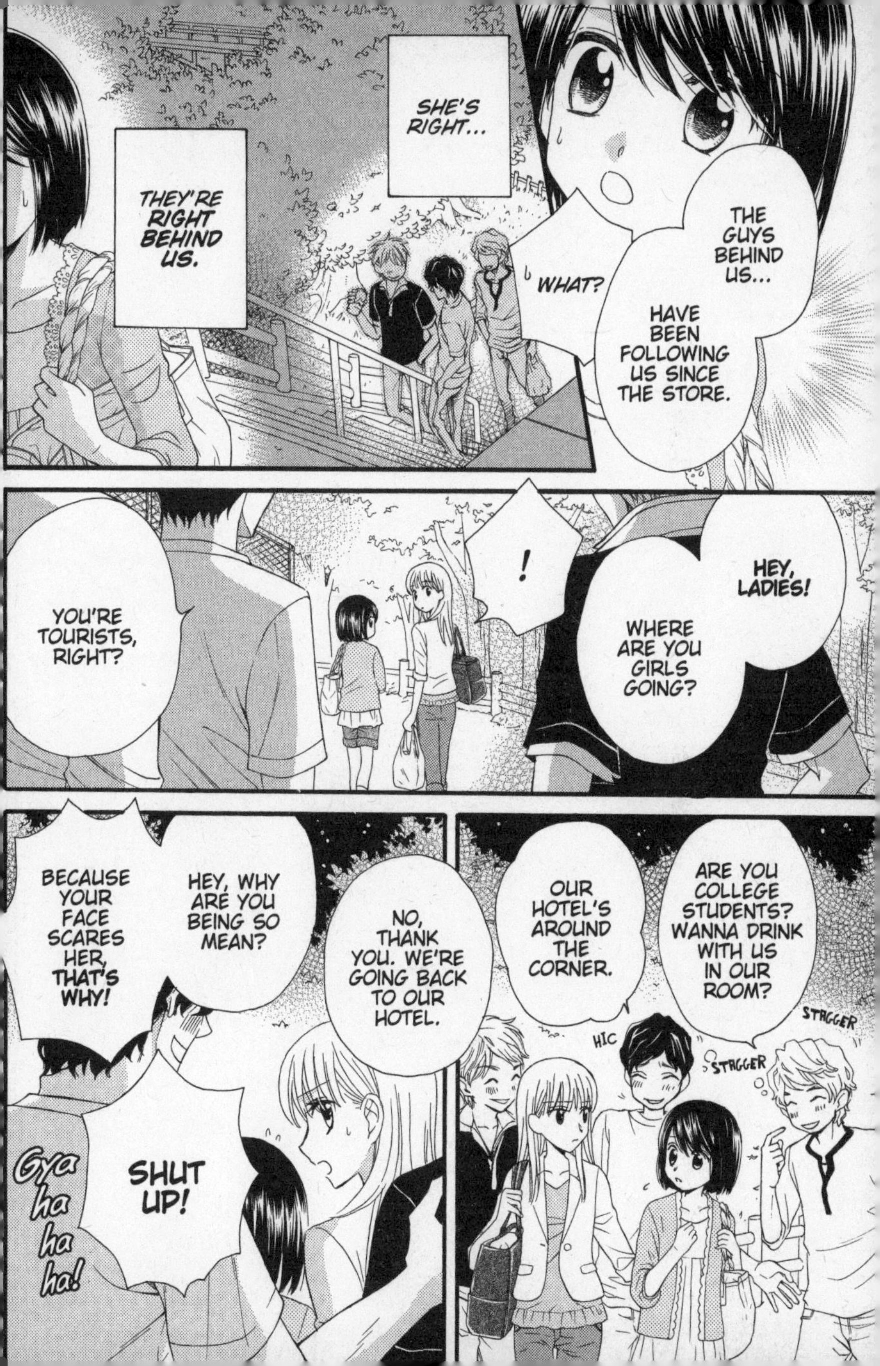
THE GUYS BEHIND US... HAVE BEEN FOLLOWING US SINCE THE STORE.
WHAT?
SHE'S RIGHT...
THEY'RE RIGHT BEHIND US.
HEY, LADIES! WHERE ARE YOU GIRLS GOING?
!
YOU'RE TOURISTS, RIGHT?
ARE YOU COLLEGE STUDENTS? WANNA DRINK WITH US IN OUR ROOM?
STAGGER
STAGGER
HIC
OUR HOTEL'S AROUND THE CORNER.
NO, THANK YOU. WE'RE GOING BACK TO OUR HOTEL.
HEY, WHY ARE YOU BEING SO MEAN?
BECAUSE YOUR FACE SCARES HER, THAT'S WHY!
SHUT UP!
Gya ha ha ha!

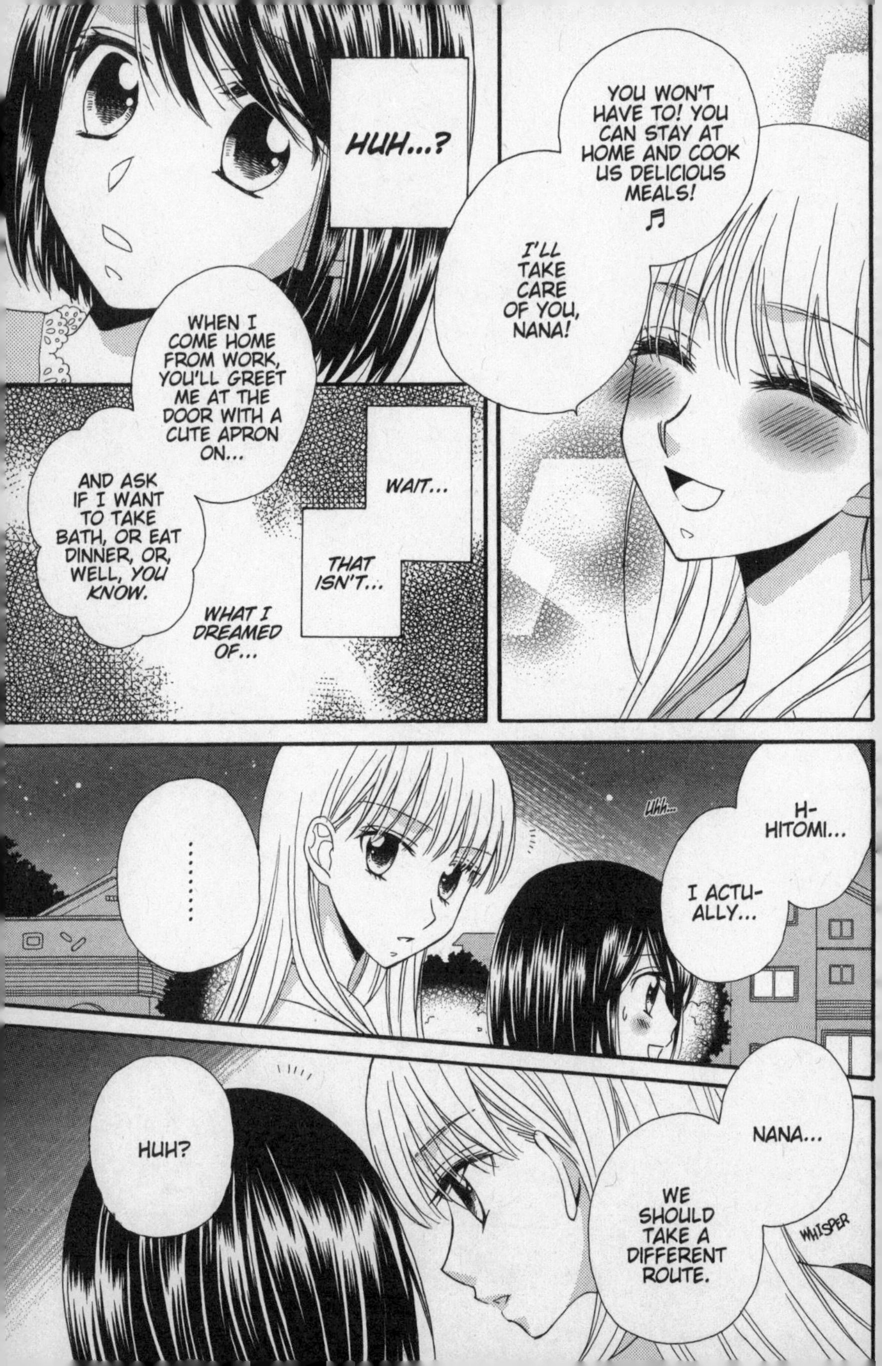
YOU WON'T HAVE TO! YOU CAN STAY AT HOME AND COOK US DELICIOUS MEALS! ♬
I'LL TAKE CARE OF YOU, NANA!
HUH...?
WHEN I COME HOME FROM WORK, YOU'LL GREET ME AT THE DOOR WITH A CUTE APRON ON...
AND ASK IF I WANT TO TAKE BATH, OR EAT DINNER, OR, WELL, YOU KNOW.
WAIT...
THAT ISN'T...
WHAT I DREAMED OF...
H-HITOMI...
I ACTU-ALLY...
UHH...
......
NANA...
WE SHOULD TAKE A DIFFERENT ROUTE.
WHISPER
HUH?

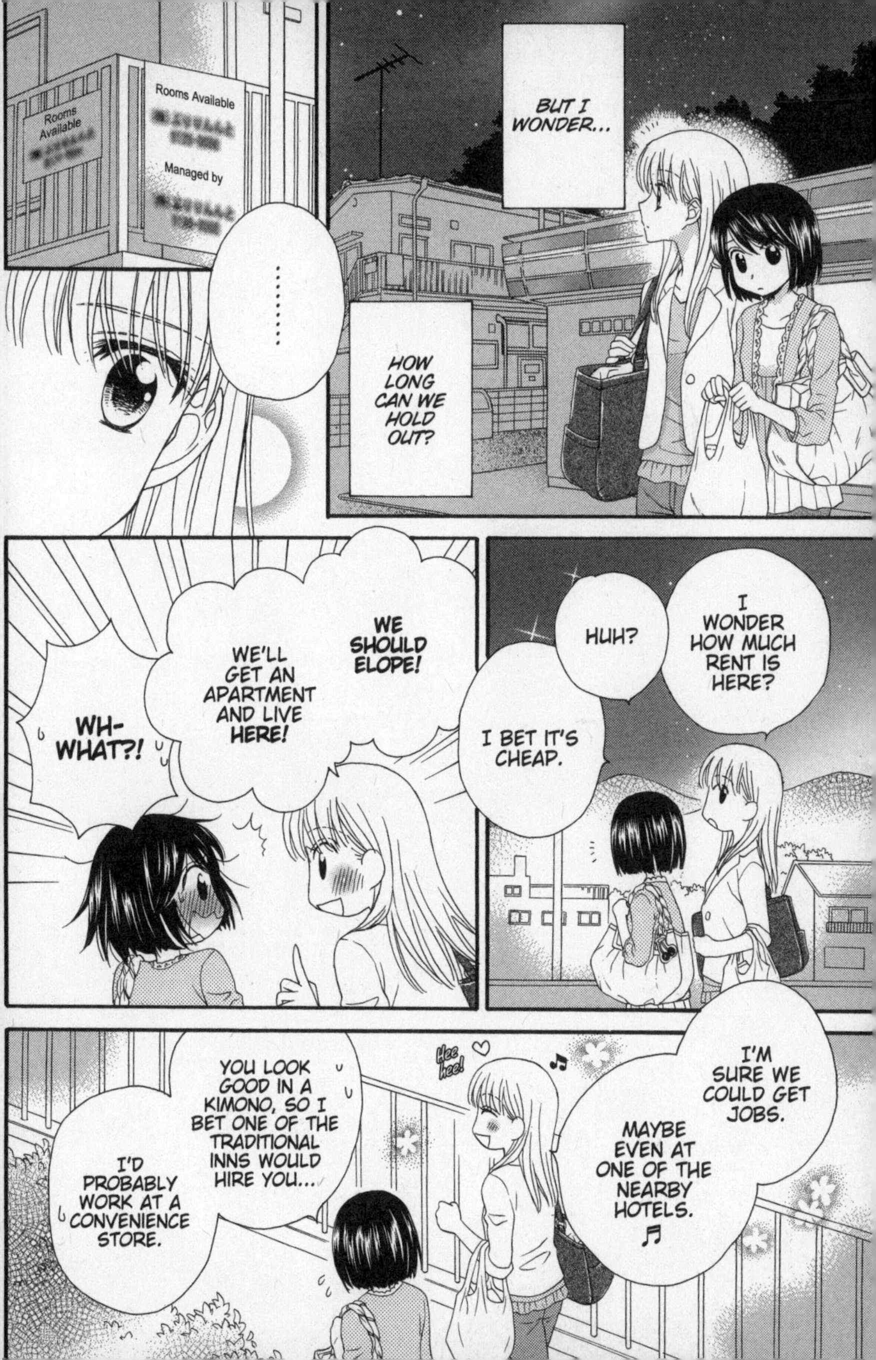
BUT I WONDER...
HOW LONG CAN WE HOLD OUT?
Rooms Available
Managed by
Rooms Available
......
I WONDER HOW MUCH RENT IS HERE?
HUH?
I BET IT'S CHEAP.
WE SHOULD ELOPE!
WE'LL GET AN APARTMENT AND LIVE HERE!
WH- WHAT?!
I'M SURE WE COULD GET JOBS.
MAYBE EVEN AT ONE OF THE NEARBY HOTELS.
Hee hee!
YOU LOOK GOOD IN A KIMONO, SO I BET ONE OF THE TRADITIONAL INNS WOULD HIRE YOU...
I'D PROBABLY WORK AT A CONVENIENCE STORE.

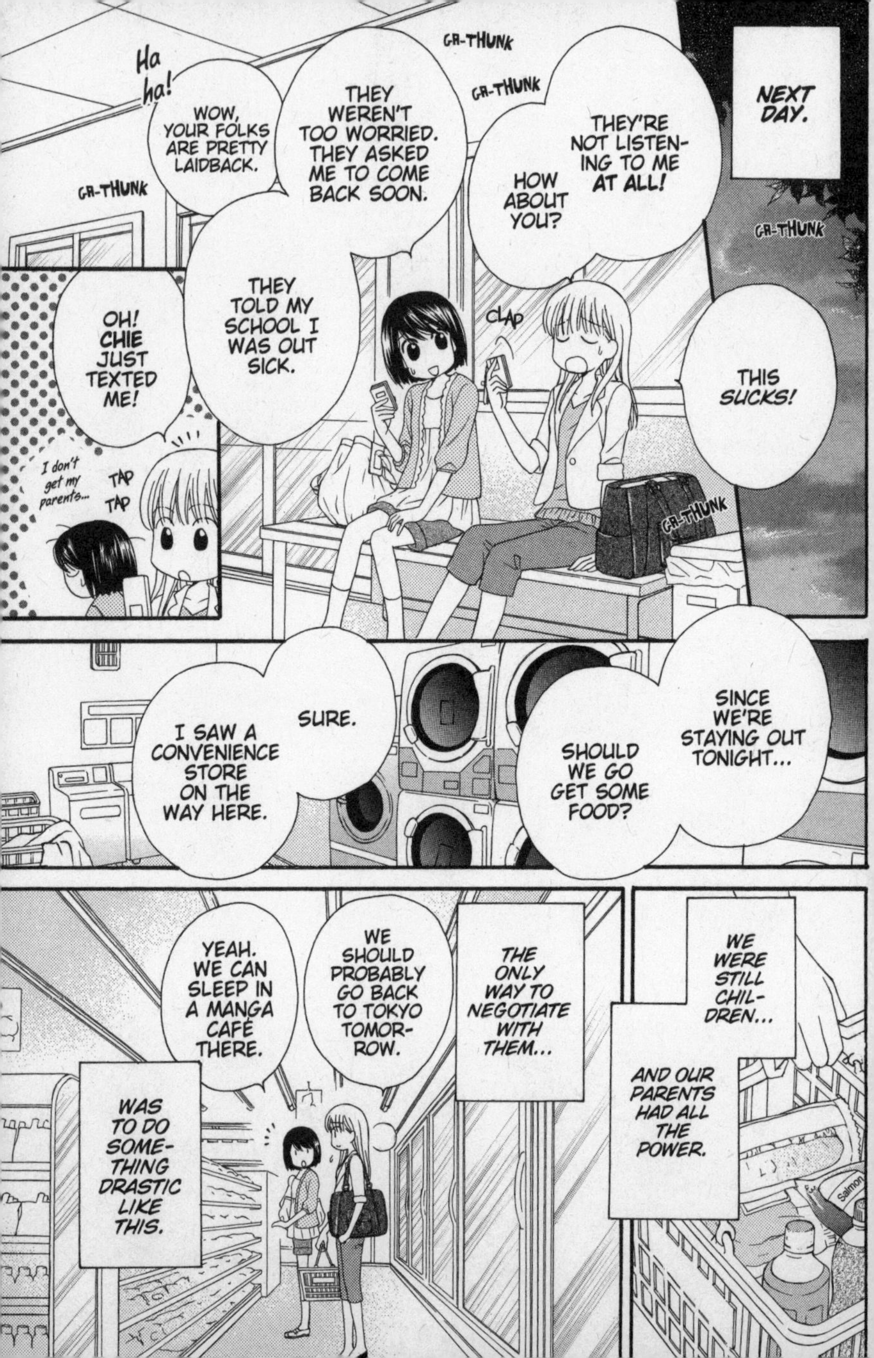
NEXT DAY.
GA-THUNK
THEY'RE NOT LISTENING TO ME AT ALL!
HOW ABOUT YOU?
GA-THUNK
THEY WEREN'T TOO WORRIED. THEY ASKED ME TO COME BACK SOON.
WOW, YOUR FOLKS ARE PRETTY LAIDBACK.
Ha ha!
GA-THUNK
THIS SUCKS!
CLAP
THEY TOLD MY SCHOOL I WAS OUT SICK.
GA-THUNK
OH! CHIE JUST TEXTED ME!
TAP TAP
I don't get my parents...
SINCE WE'RE STAYING OUT TONIGHT...
SHOULD WE GO GET SOME FOOD?
SURE.
I SAW A CONVENIENCE STORE ON THE WAY HERE.
WE WERE STILL CHILDREN...
AND OUR PARENTS HAD ALL THE POWER.
THE ONLY WAY TO NEGOTIATE WITH THEM...
WE SHOULD PROBABLY GO BACK TO TOKYO TOMORROW.
YEAH. WE CAN SLEEP IN A MANGA CAFÉ THERE.
WAS TO DO SOMETHING DRASTIC LIKE THIS.

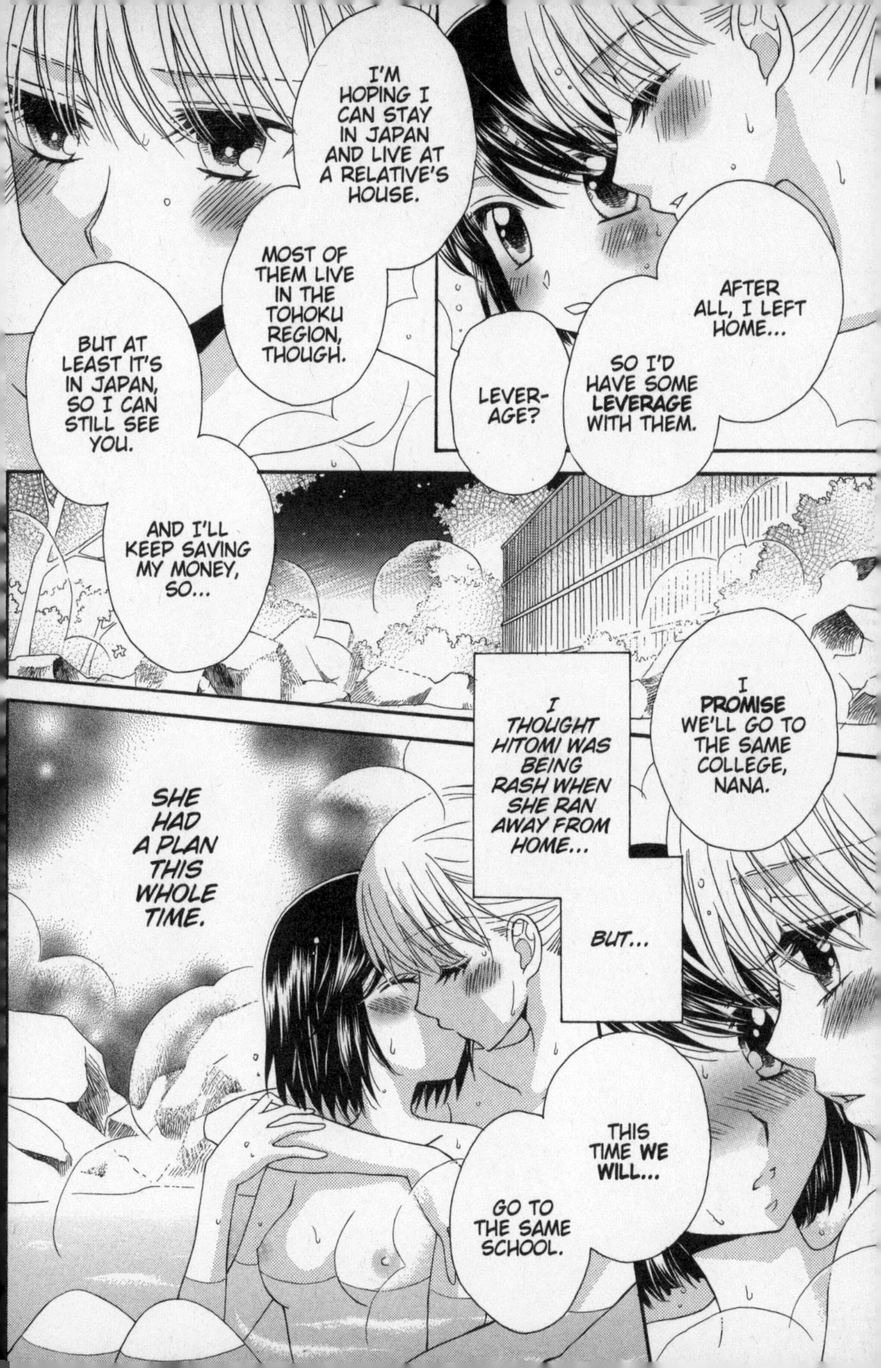
AFTER ALL, I LEFT HOME...
SO I'D HAVE SOME LEVERAGE WITH THEM.
LEVER-AGE?
I'M HOPING I CAN STAY IN JAPAN AND LIVE AT A RELATIVE'S HOUSE.
MOST OF THEM LIVE IN THE TOHOKU REGION, THOUGH.
BUT AT LEAST IT'S IN JAPAN, SO I CAN STILL SEE YOU.
AND I'LL KEEP SAVING MY MONEY, SO...
I PROMISE WE'LL GO TO THE SAME COLLEGE, NANA.
I THOUGHT HITOMI WAS BEING RASH WHEN SHE RAN AWAY FROM HOME...
BUT...
SHE HAD A PLAN THIS WHOLE TIME.
THIS TIME WE WILL...
GO TO THE SAME SCHOOL.

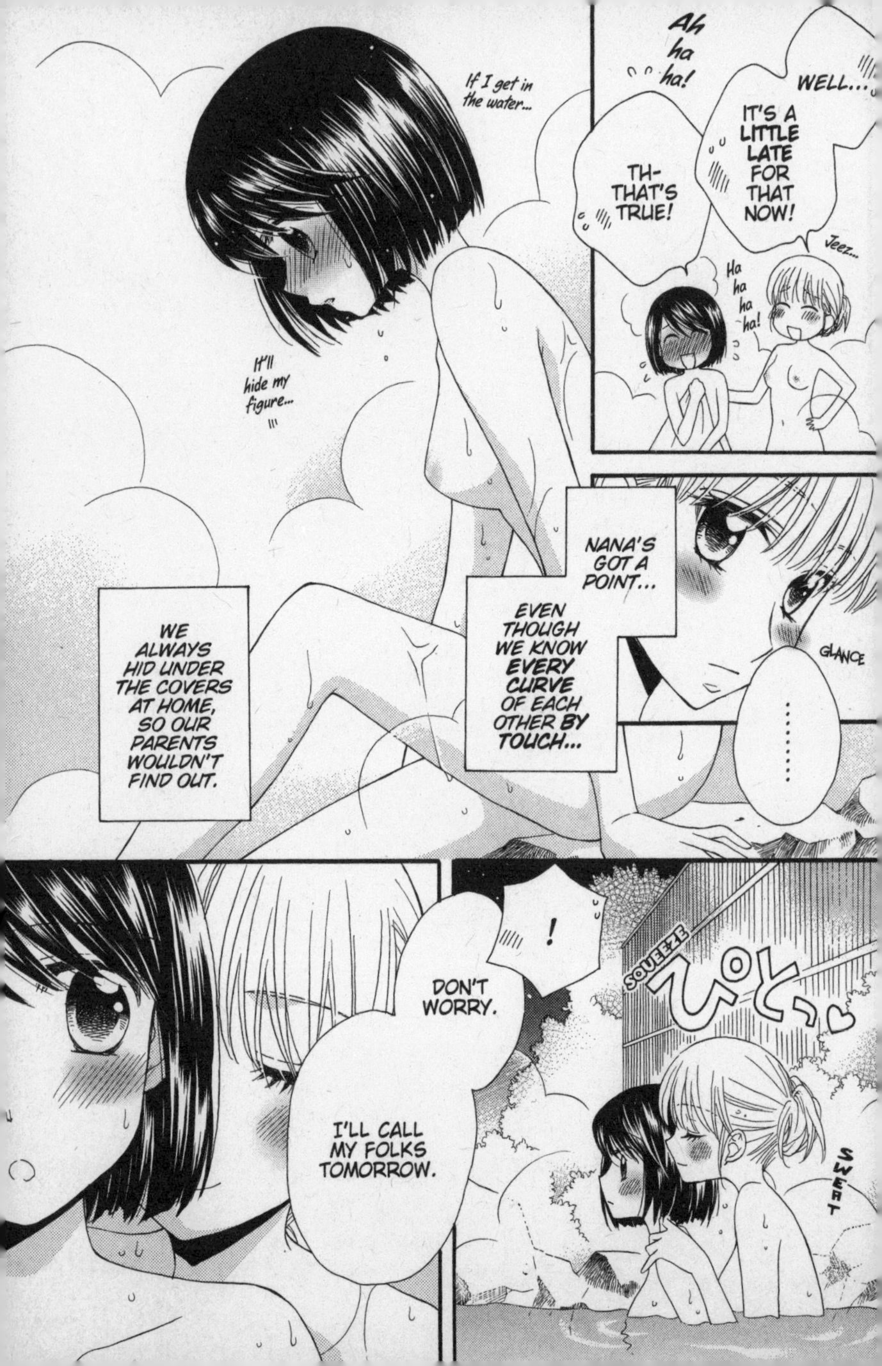
WELL...
IT'S A LITTLE LATE FOR THAT NOW!
Ah ha ha!
TH- THAT'S TRUE!
Jeez...
Ha ha ha ha!
NANA'S GOT A POINT...
EVEN THOUGH WE KNOW EVERY CURVE OF EACH OTHER BY TOUCH...
GLANCE
......
If I get in the water...
It'll hide my figure...
WE ALWAYS HID UNDER THE COVERS AT HOME, SO OUR PARENTS WOULDN'T FIND OUT.
!
SQUEEZE
ぴと
SWEAT
DON'T WORRY.
I'LL CALL MY FOLKS TOMORROW.

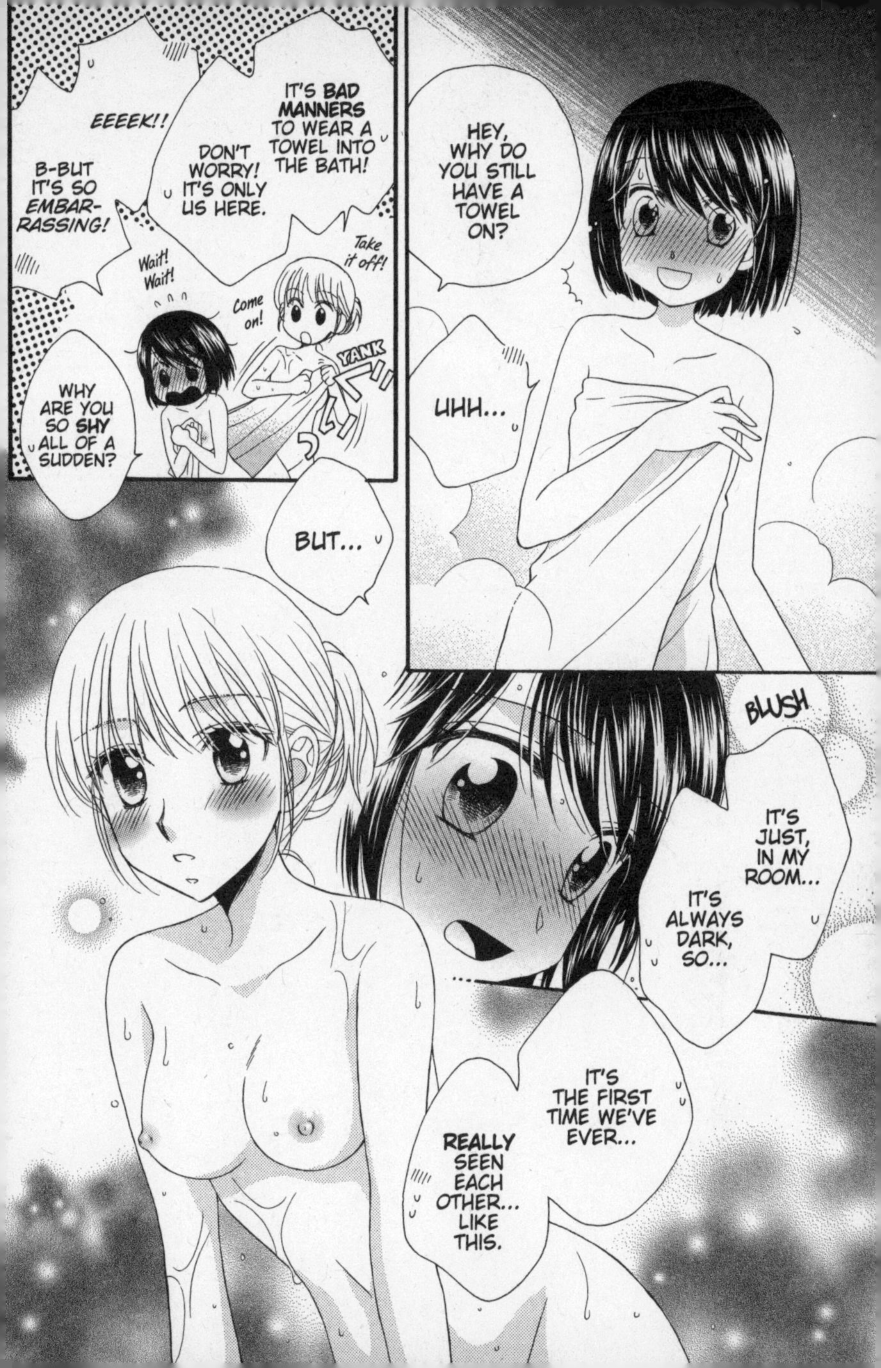
HEY, WHY DO YOU STILL HAVE A TOWEL ON?
UHH...
IT'S BAD MANNERS TO WEAR A TOWEL INTO THE BATH!
DON'T WORRY! IT'S ONLY US HERE.
EEEEK!!
B-BUT IT'S SO EMBARRASSING!
Take it off!
Wait! Wait!
Come on!
YANK
WHY ARE YOU SO SHY ALL OF A SUDDEN?
BUT...
BLUSH
IT'S JUST, IN MY ROOM...
IT'S ALWAYS DARK, SO...
...
IT'S THE FIRST TIME WE'VE EVER...
REALLY SEEN EACH OTHER... LIKE THIS.

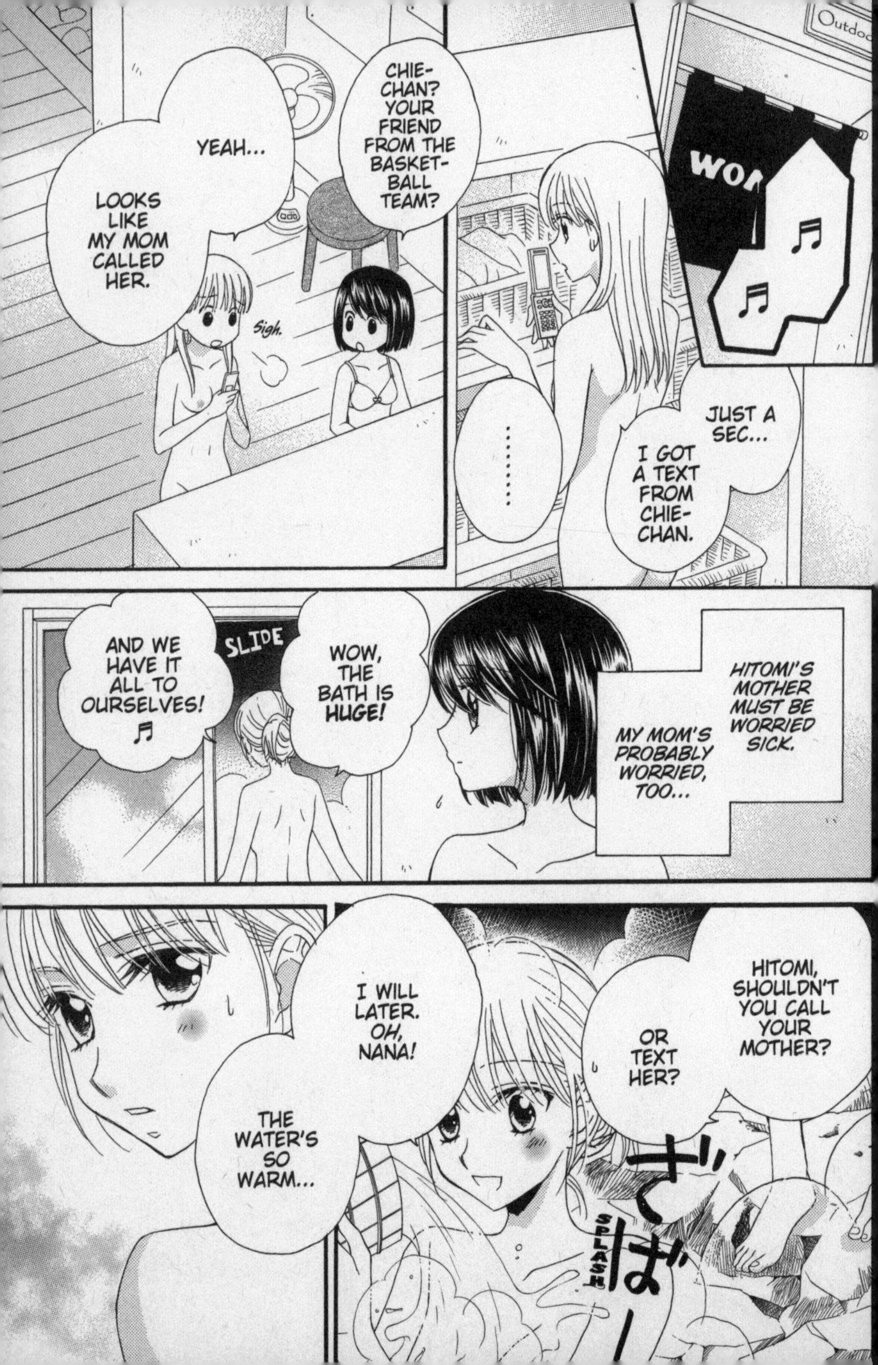
JUST A SEC...
I GOT A TEXT FROM CHIE-CHAN.
......
CHIE-CHAN? YOUR FRIEND FROM THE BASKET-BALL TEAM?
YEAH...
LOOKS LIKE MY MOM CALLED HER.
Sigh.
HITOMI'S MOTHER MUST BE WORRIED SICK.
MY MOM'S PROBABLY WORRIED, TOO...
WOW, THE BATH IS HUGE!
SLIDE
AND WE HAVE IT ALL TO OURSELVES! ♫
HITOMI, SHOULDN'T YOU CALL YOUR MOTHER?
OR TEXT HER?
SPLASH
I WILL LATER. OH, NANA!
THE WATER'S SO WARM...

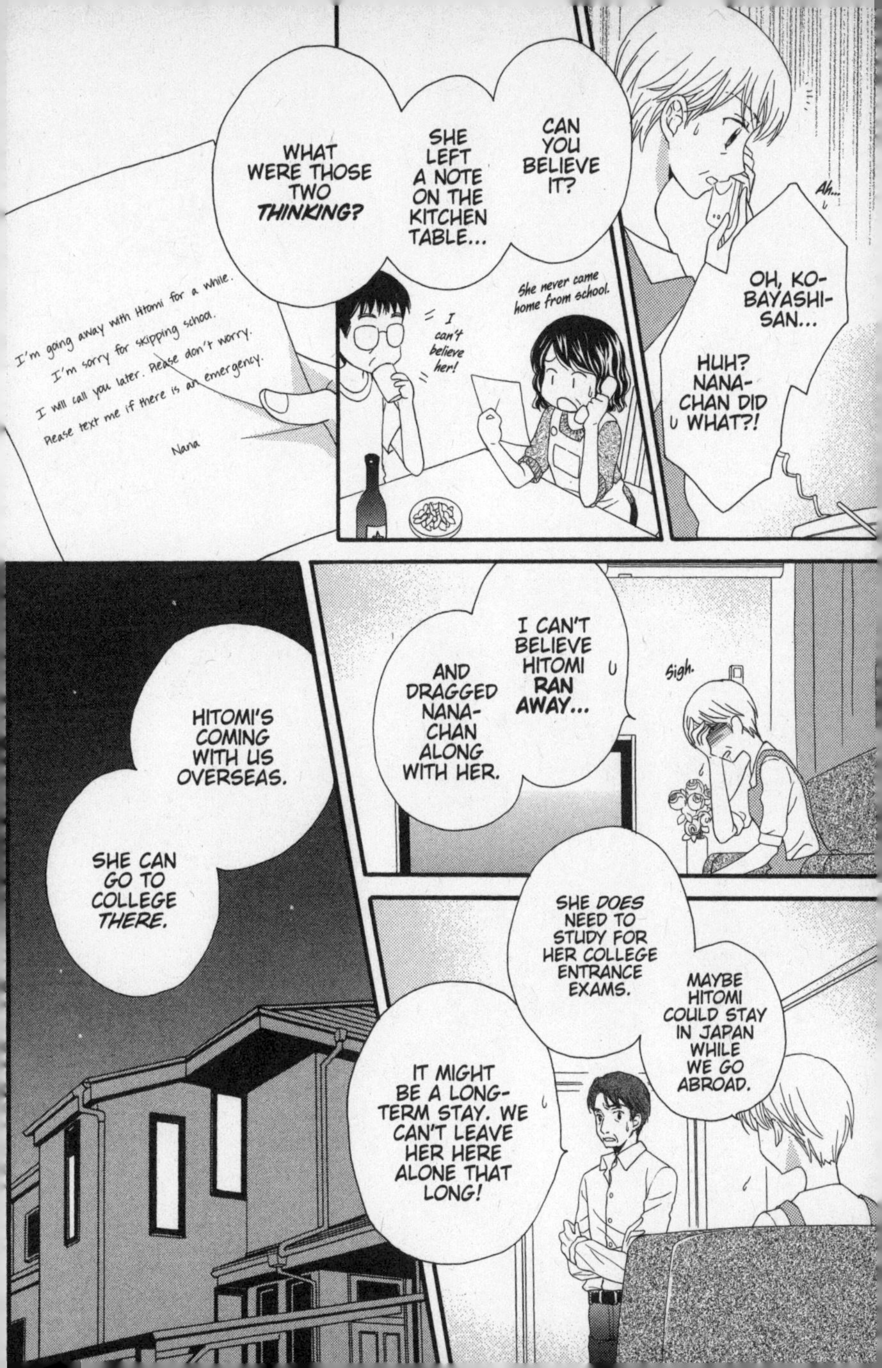

Ah...
OH, KO-BAYASHI-SAN...
HUH? NANA-CHAN DID WHAT?!
CAN YOU BELIEVE IT?
SHE LEFT A NOTE ON THE KITCHEN TABLE...
She never came home from school.
I can't believe her!
WHAT WERE THOSE TWO *THINKING?*
I'm going away with Hitomi for a while.
I'm sorry for skipping school.
I will call you later. Please don't worry.
Please text me if there is an emergency.
Nana
Sigh.
I CAN'T BELIEVE HITOMI RAN AWAY...
AND DRAGGED NANA-CHAN ALONG WITH HER.
MAYBE HITOMI COULD STAY IN JAPAN WHILE WE GO ABROAD.
SHE *DOES* NEED TO STUDY FOR HER COLLEGE ENTRANCE EXAMS.
IT MIGHT BE A LONG-TERM STAY. WE CAN'T LEAVE HER HERE ALONE THAT LONG!
HITOMI'S COMING WITH US OVERSEAS.
SHE CAN GO TO COLLEGE *THERE.*

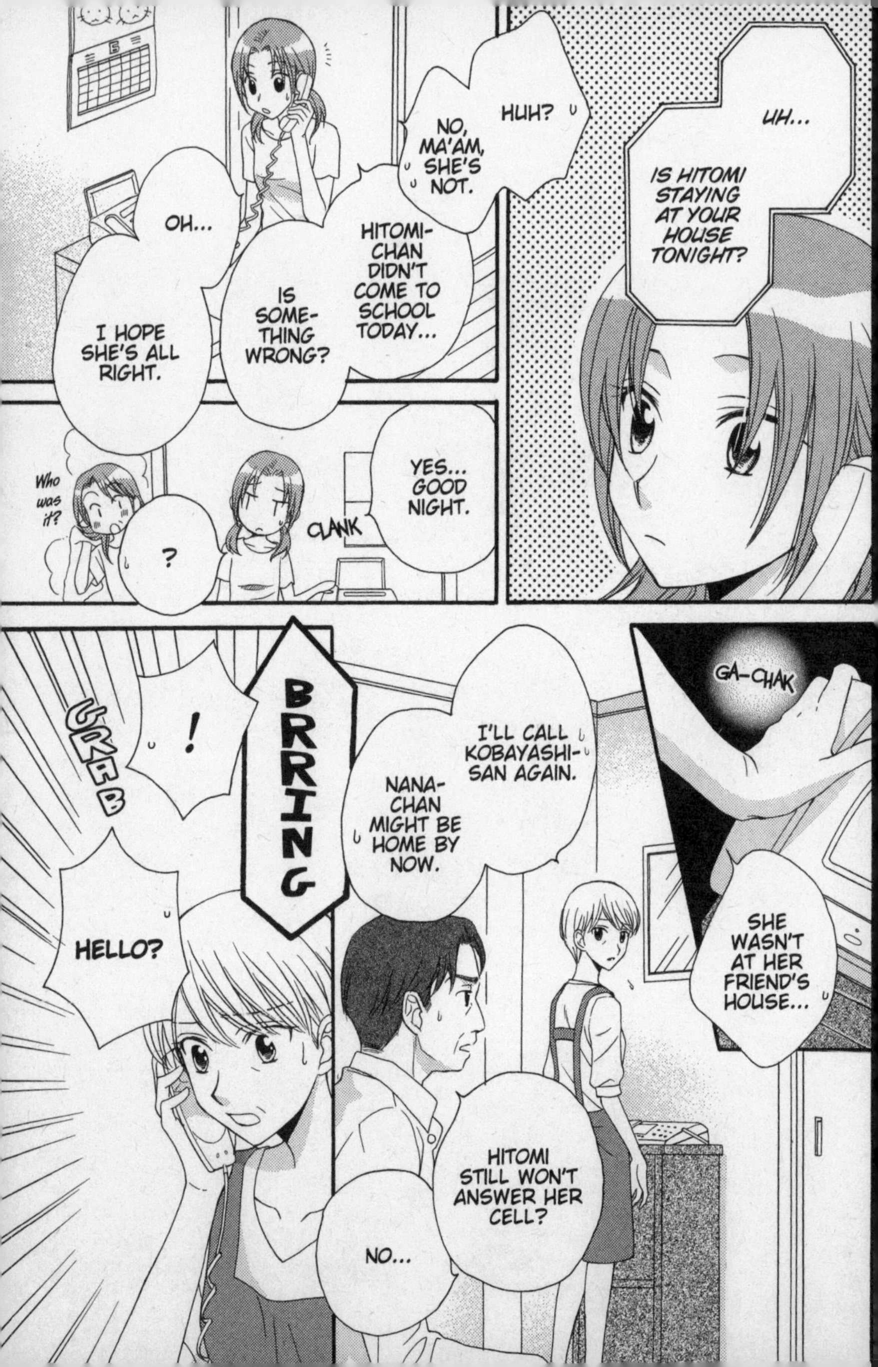
UH...
IS HITOMI STAYING AT YOUR HOUSE TONIGHT?
HUH?
NO, MA'AM, SHE'S NOT.
HITOMI-CHAN DIDN'T COME TO SCHOOL TODAY...
IS SOMETHING WRONG?
OH...
I HOPE SHE'S ALL RIGHT.
YES... GOOD NIGHT.
CLANK
?
Who was it?
GA-CHAK
SHE WASN'T AT HER FRIEND'S HOUSE...
HITOMI STILL WON'T ANSWER HER CELL?
NO...
I'LL CALL KOBAYASHI-SAN AGAIN.
NANA-CHAN MIGHT BE HOME BY NOW.
BRRING
!
GRAB
HELLO?

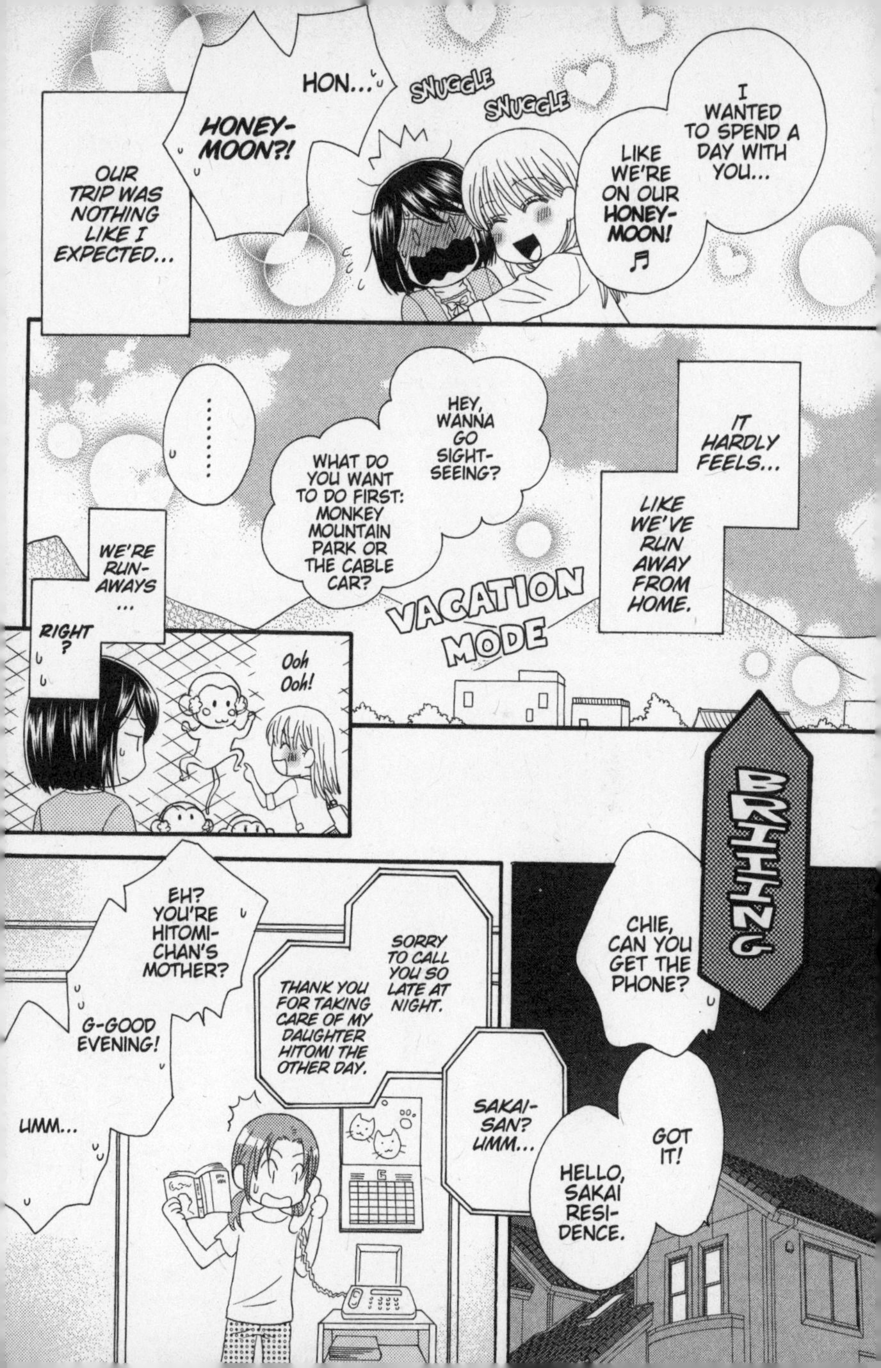
I WANTED TO SPEND A DAY WITH YOU...
LIKE WE'RE ON OUR HONEY-MOON! ♪
SNUGGLE SNUGGLE
HON...
HONEY-MOON?!
OUR TRIP WAS NOTHING LIKE I EXPECTED...
IT HARDLY FEELS...
LIKE WE'VE RUN AWAY FROM HOME.
VACATION MODE
HEY, WANNA GO SIGHT-SEEING?
WHAT DO YOU WANT TO DO FIRST: MONKEY MOUNTAIN PARK OR THE CABLE CAR?
......
WE'RE RUN-AWAYS ...
RIGHT?
Ooh Ooh!
BRIIING
CHIE, CAN YOU GET THE PHONE?
GOT IT!
HELLO, SAKAI RESI-DENCE.
SAKAI-SAN? UMM...
SORRY TO CALL YOU SO LATE AT NIGHT.
THANK YOU FOR TAKING CARE OF MY DAUGHTER HITOMI THE OTHER DAY.
EH? YOU'RE HITOMI-CHAN'S MOTHER?
G-GOOD EVENING!
UMM...

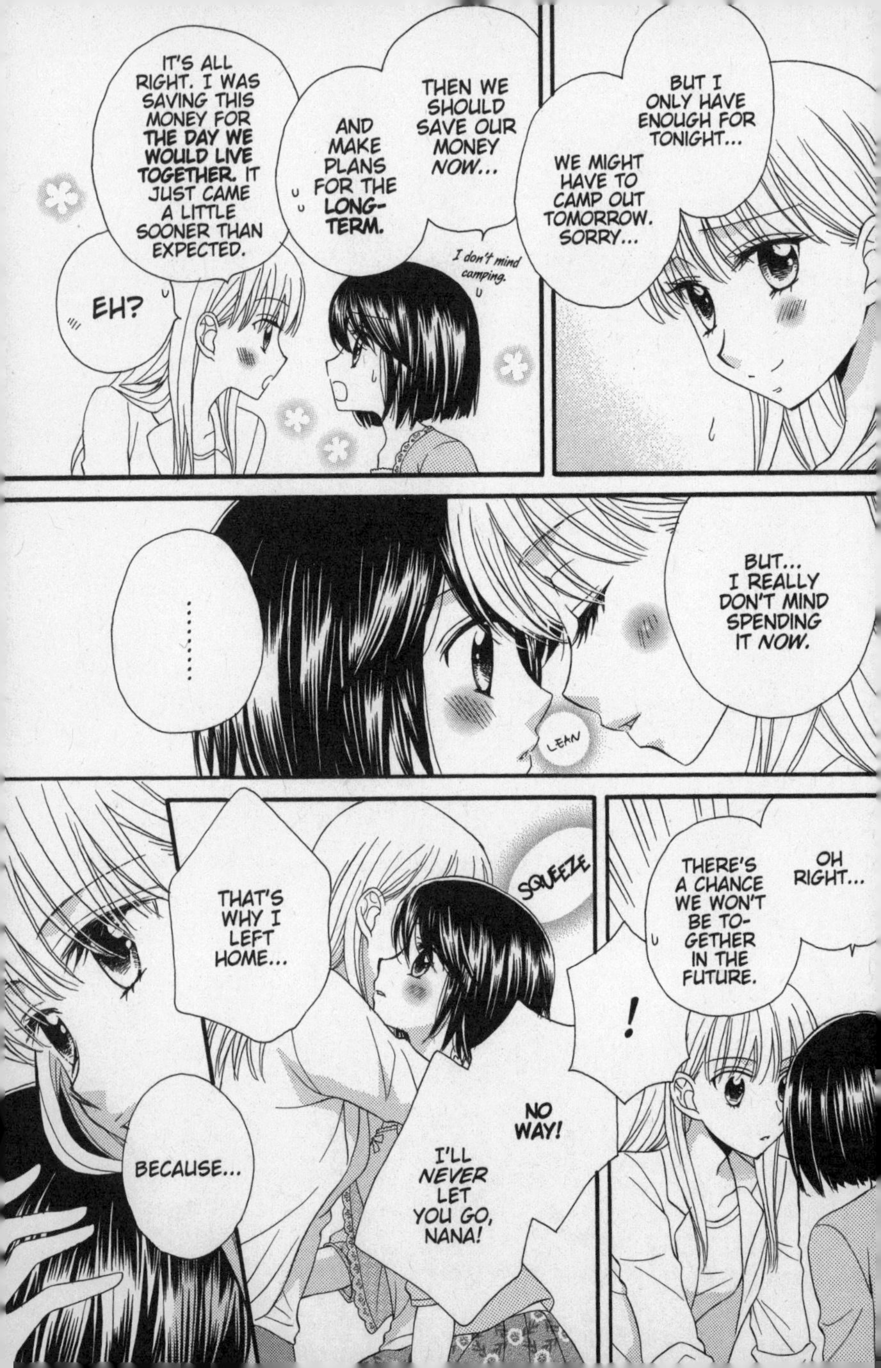

BUT I ONLY HAVE ENOUGH FOR TONIGHT...
WE MIGHT HAVE TO CAMP OUT TOMORROW. SORRY...
THEN WE SHOULD SAVE OUR MONEY NOW...
AND MAKE PLANS FOR THE LONG-TERM.
I don't mind camping.
IT'S ALL RIGHT. I WAS SAVING THIS MONEY FOR THE DAY WE WOULD LIVE TOGETHER. IT JUST CAME A LITTLE SOONER THAN EXPECTED.
EH?
BUT... I REALLY DON'T MIND SPENDING IT NOW.
LEAN
......
OH RIGHT...
THERE'S A CHANCE WE WON'T BE TO-GETHER IN THE FUTURE.
!
SQUEEZE
THAT'S WHY I LEFT HOME...
NO WAY!
I'LL NEVER LET YOU GO, NANA!
BECAUSE...

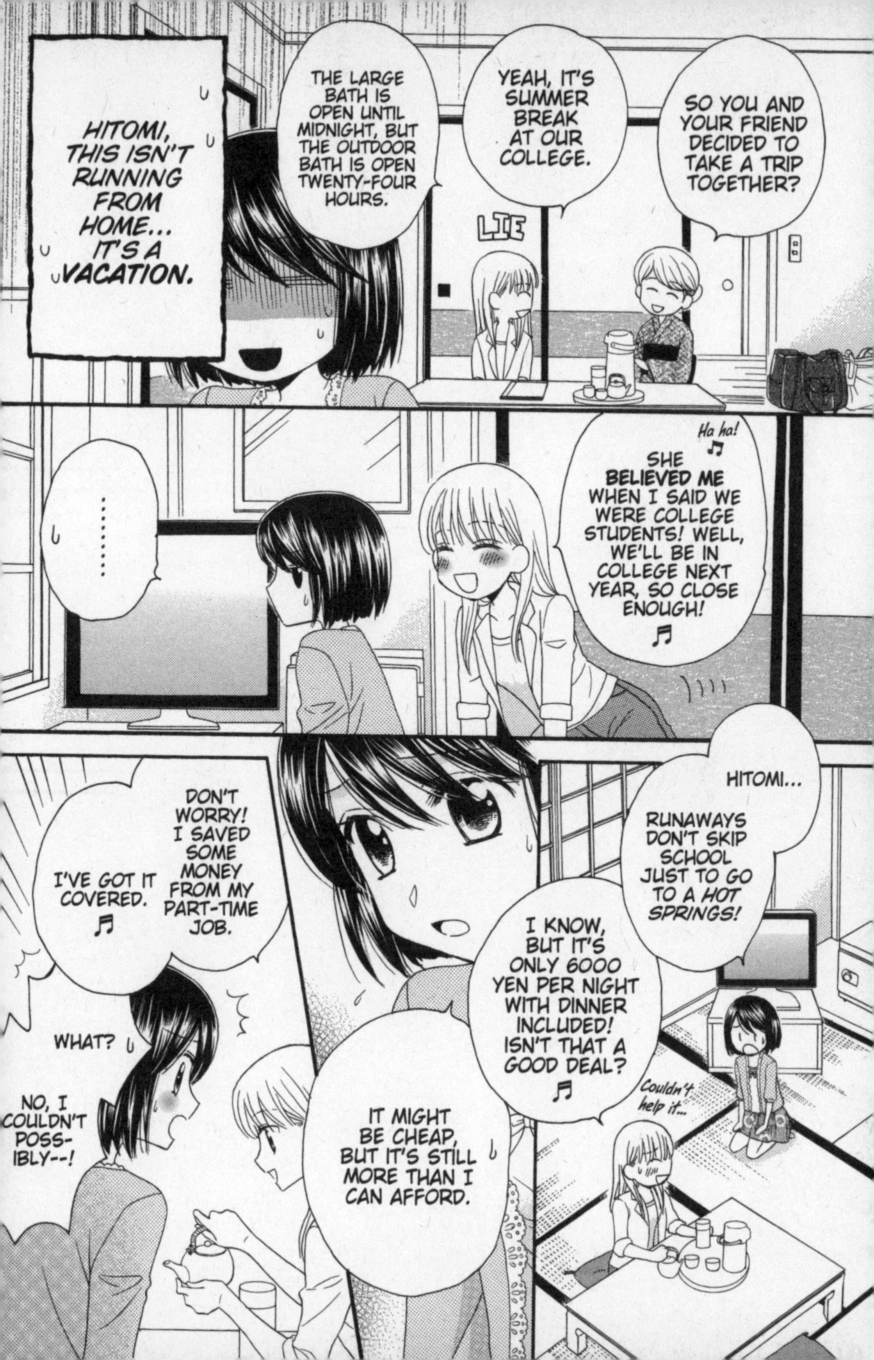
SO YOU AND YOUR FRIEND DECIDED TO TAKE A TRIP TOGETHER?
YEAH, IT'S SUMMER BREAK AT OUR COLLEGE.
LIE
THE LARGE BATH IS OPEN UNTIL MIDNIGHT, BUT THE OUTDOOR BATH IS OPEN TWENTY-FOUR HOURS.
HITOMI, THIS ISN'T RUNNING FROM HOME... IT'S A VACATION.
Ha ha! ♫
SHE BELIEVED ME WHEN I SAID WE WERE COLLEGE STUDENTS! WELL, WE'LL BE IN COLLEGE NEXT YEAR, SO CLOSE ENOUGH! ♫
......
HITOMI... RUNAWAYS DON'T SKIP SCHOOL JUST TO GO TO A HOT SPRINGS!
Couldn't help it...
I KNOW, BUT IT'S ONLY 6000 YEN PER NIGHT WITH DINNER INCLUDED! ISN'T THAT A GOOD DEAL? ♫
IT MIGHT BE CHEAP, BUT IT'S STILL MORE THAN I CAN AFFORD.
DON'T WORRY! I SAVED SOME MONEY FROM MY PART-TIME JOB.
I'VE GOT IT COVERED. ♫
WHAT?
NO, I COULDN'T POSS-IBLY--!

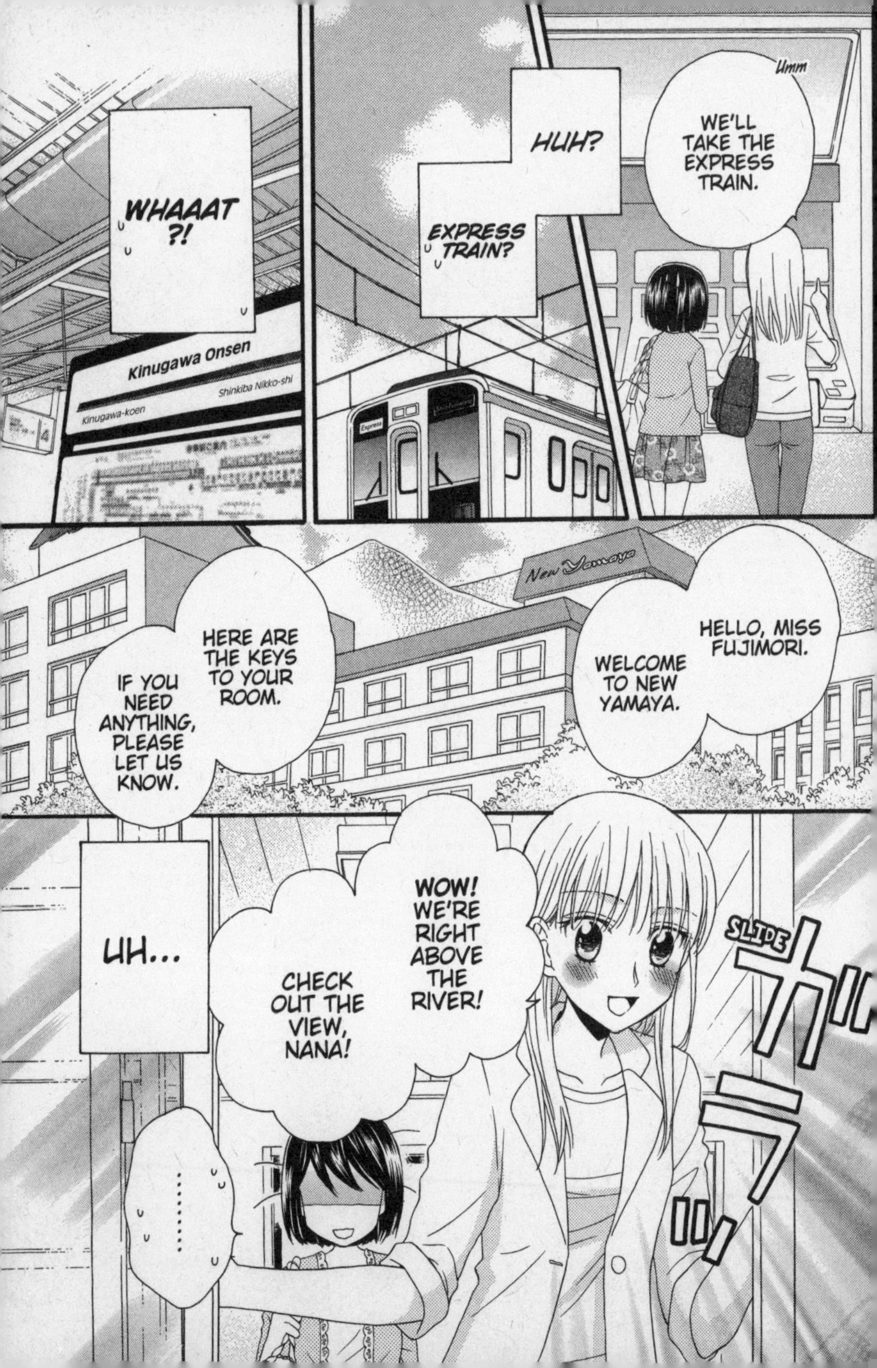
Umm
WE'LL TAKE THE EXPRESS TRAIN.
HUH?
EXPRESS TRAIN?
Express
WHAAAT ?!
Kinugawa Onsen
Shinkiba Nikko-shi
Kinugawa-koen
New Yamaya
HELLO, MISS FUJIMORI.
WELCOME TO NEW YAMAYA.
HERE ARE THE KEYS TO YOUR ROOM.
IF YOU NEED ANYTHING, PLEASE LET US KNOW.
SLIDE
WOW! WE'RE RIGHT ABOVE THE RIVER!
CHECK OUT THE VIEW, NANA!
UH...
......

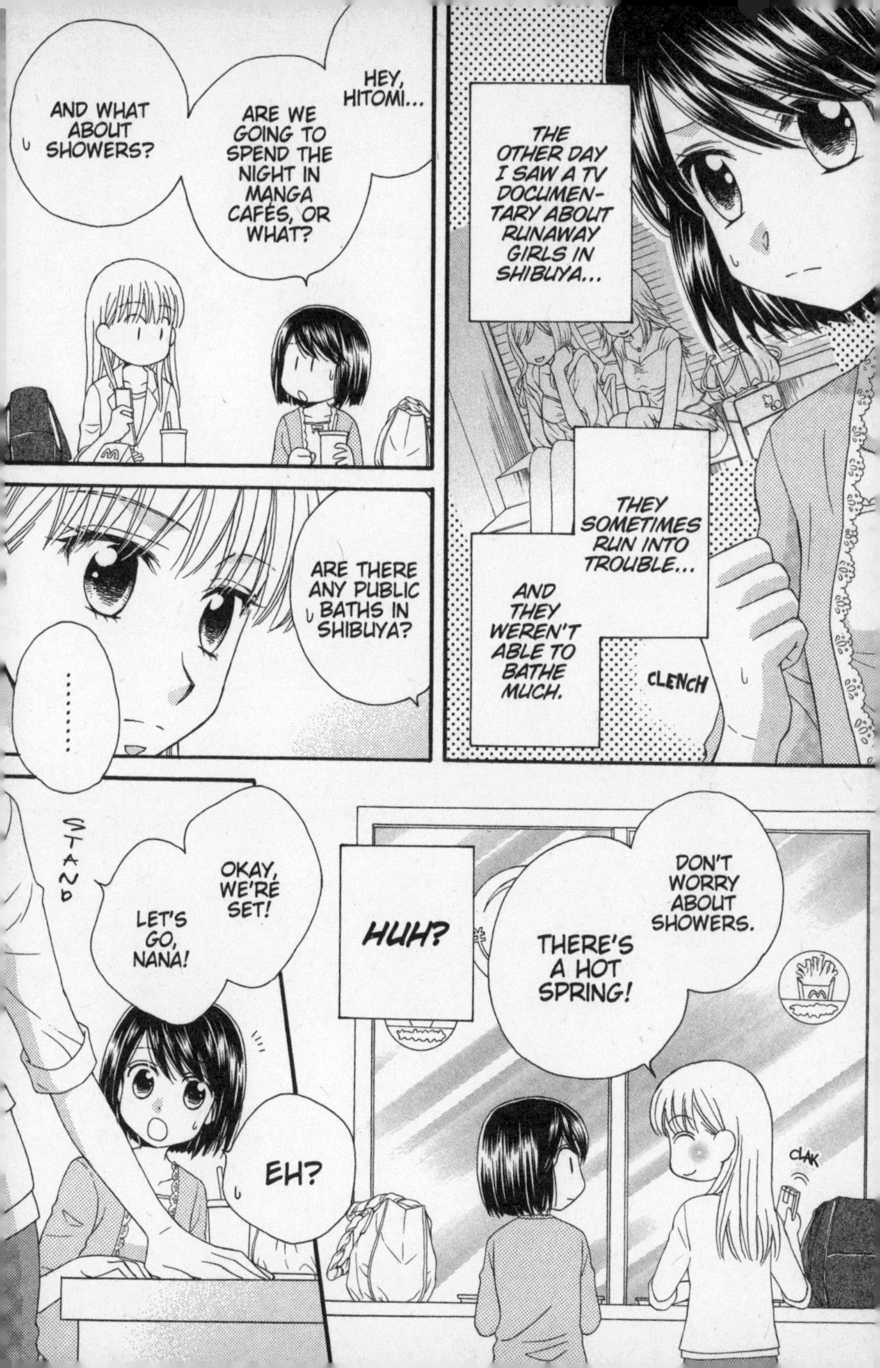
THE OTHER DAY I SAW A TV DOCUMENTARY ABOUT RUNAWAY GIRLS IN SHIBUYA...
THEY SOMETIMES RUN INTO TROUBLE...
AND THEY WEREN'T ABLE TO BATHE MUCH.
CLENCH
HEY, HITOMI...
ARE WE GOING TO SPEND THE NIGHT IN MANGA CAFÉS, OR WHAT?
AND WHAT ABOUT SHOWERS?
ARE THERE ANY PUBLIC BATHS IN SHIBUYA?
......
DON'T WORRY ABOUT SHOWERS.
THERE'S A HOT SPRING!
HUH?
CLAK
STAND
OKAY, WE'RE SET!
LET'S GO, NANA!
EH?

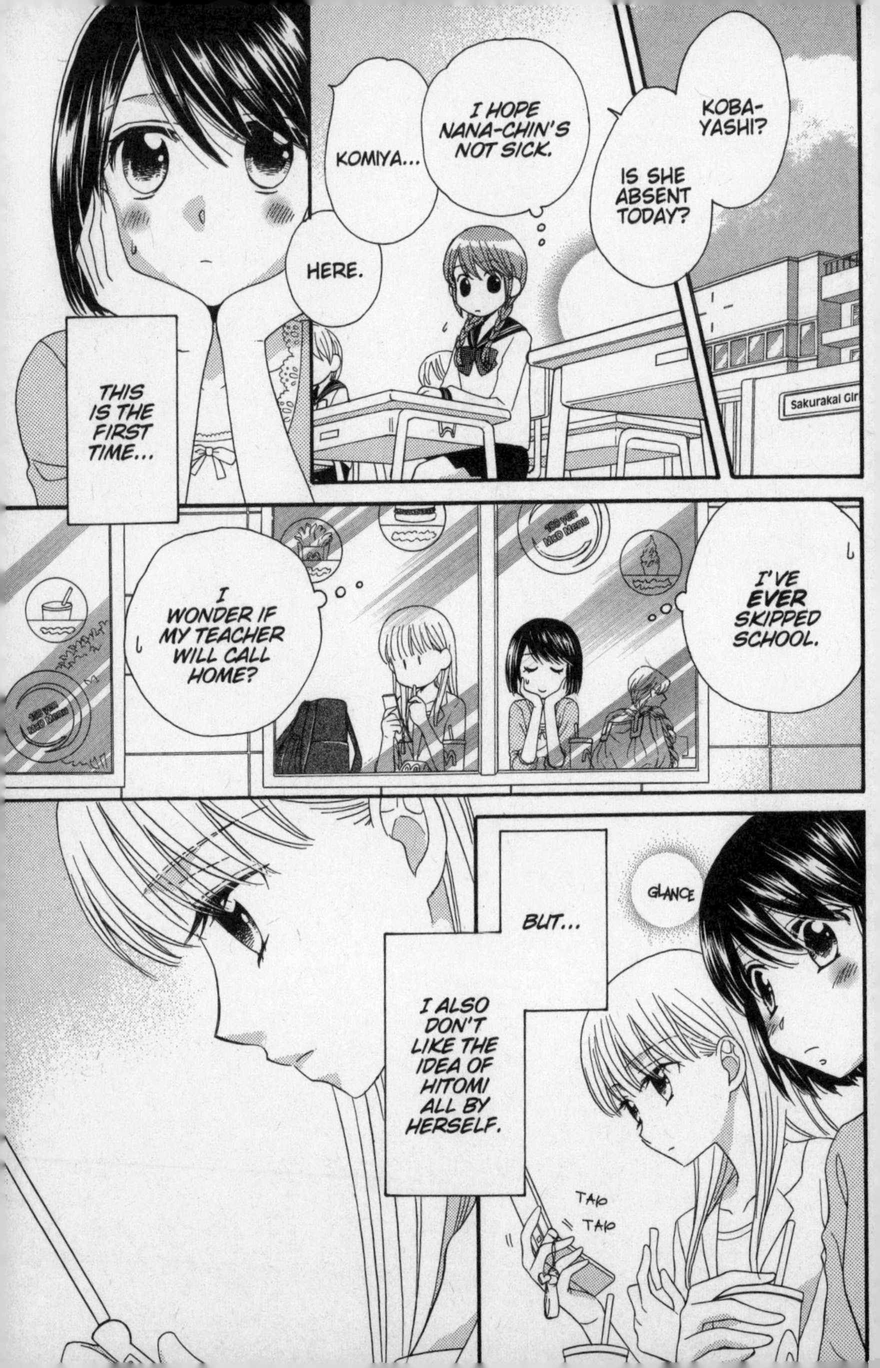
KOBA-YASHI?
IS SHE ABSENT TODAY?
Sakurakai Gir
I HOPE NANA-CHIN'S NOT SICK.
KOMIYA...
HERE.
THIS IS THE FIRST TIME...
I'VE EVER SKIPPED SCHOOL.
I WONDER IF MY TEACHER WILL CALL HOME?
GLANCE
BUT...
I ALSO DON'T LIKE THE IDEA OF HITOMI ALL BY HERSELF.
TAK
TAK

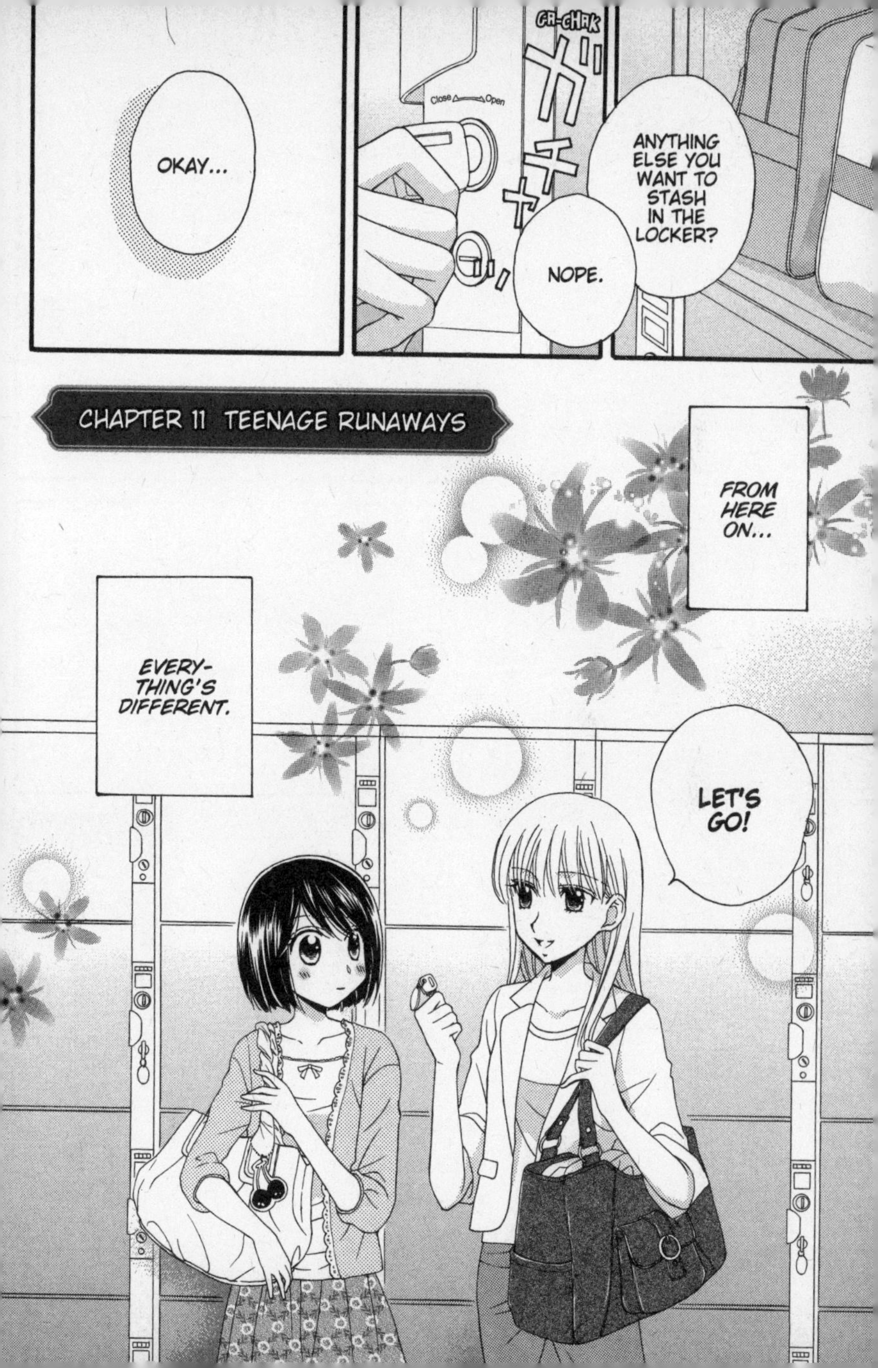
ANYTHING ELSE YOU WANT TO STASH IN THE LOCKER?
NOPE.
GA-CHAK
Close Open
OKAY...
CHAPTER 11 TEENAGE RUNAWAYS
FROM HERE ON...
EVERY-THING'S DIFFERENT.
LET'S GO!

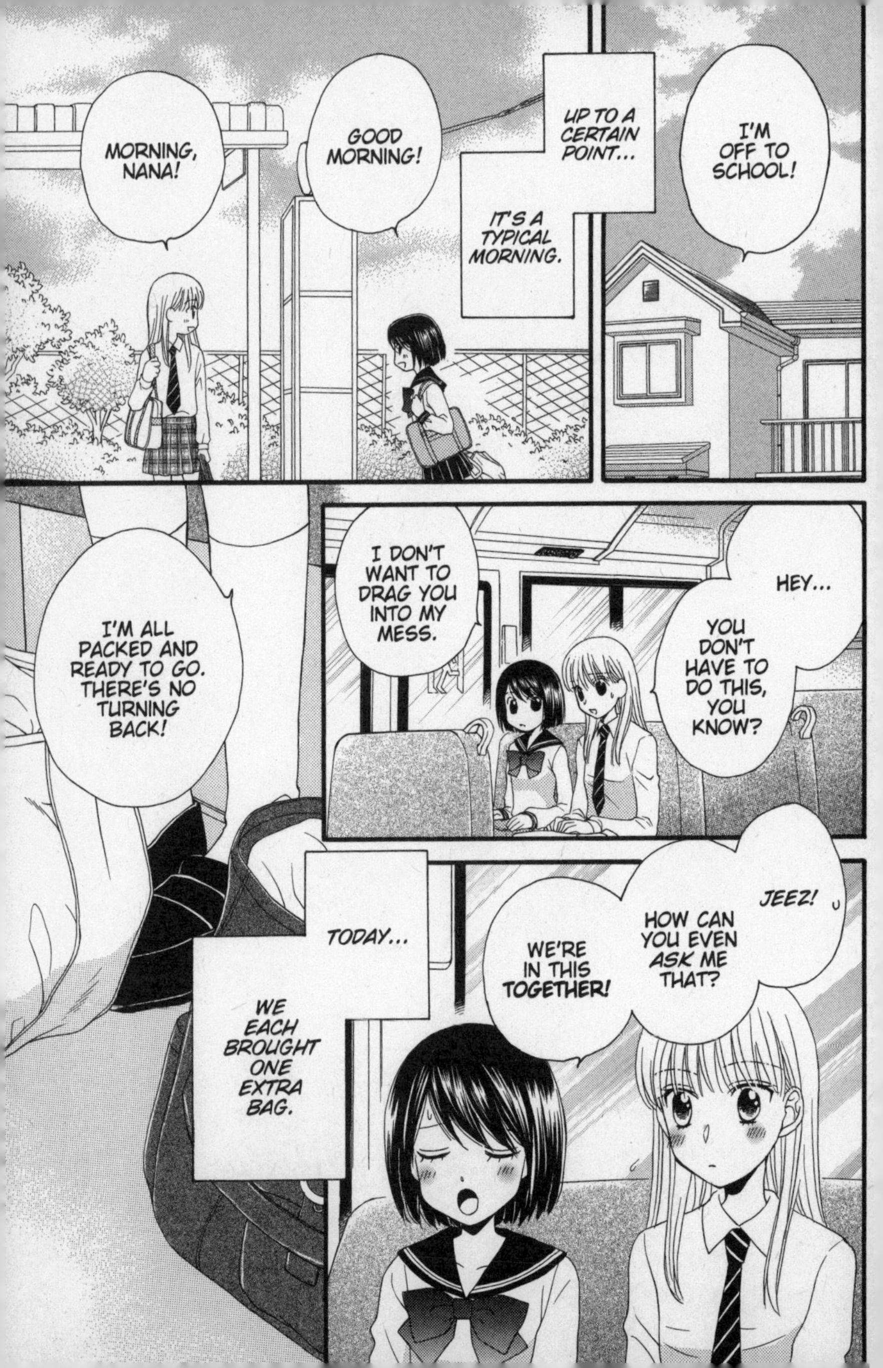
I'M OFF TO SCHOOL!
UP TO A CERTAIN POINT...
IT'S A TYPICAL MORNING.
GOOD MORNING!
MORNING, NANA!
HEY...
YOU DON'T HAVE TO DO THIS, YOU KNOW?
I DON'T WANT TO DRAG YOU INTO MY MESS.
JEEZ!
HOW CAN YOU EVEN ASK ME THAT?
WE'RE IN THIS TOGETHER!
TODAY...
WE EACH BROUGHT ONE EXTRA BAG.
I'M ALL PACKED AND READY TO GO. THERE'S NO TURNING BACK!

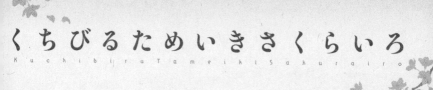

くちびるためいきさくらいろ

KuchibiruTameikiSakurairo.

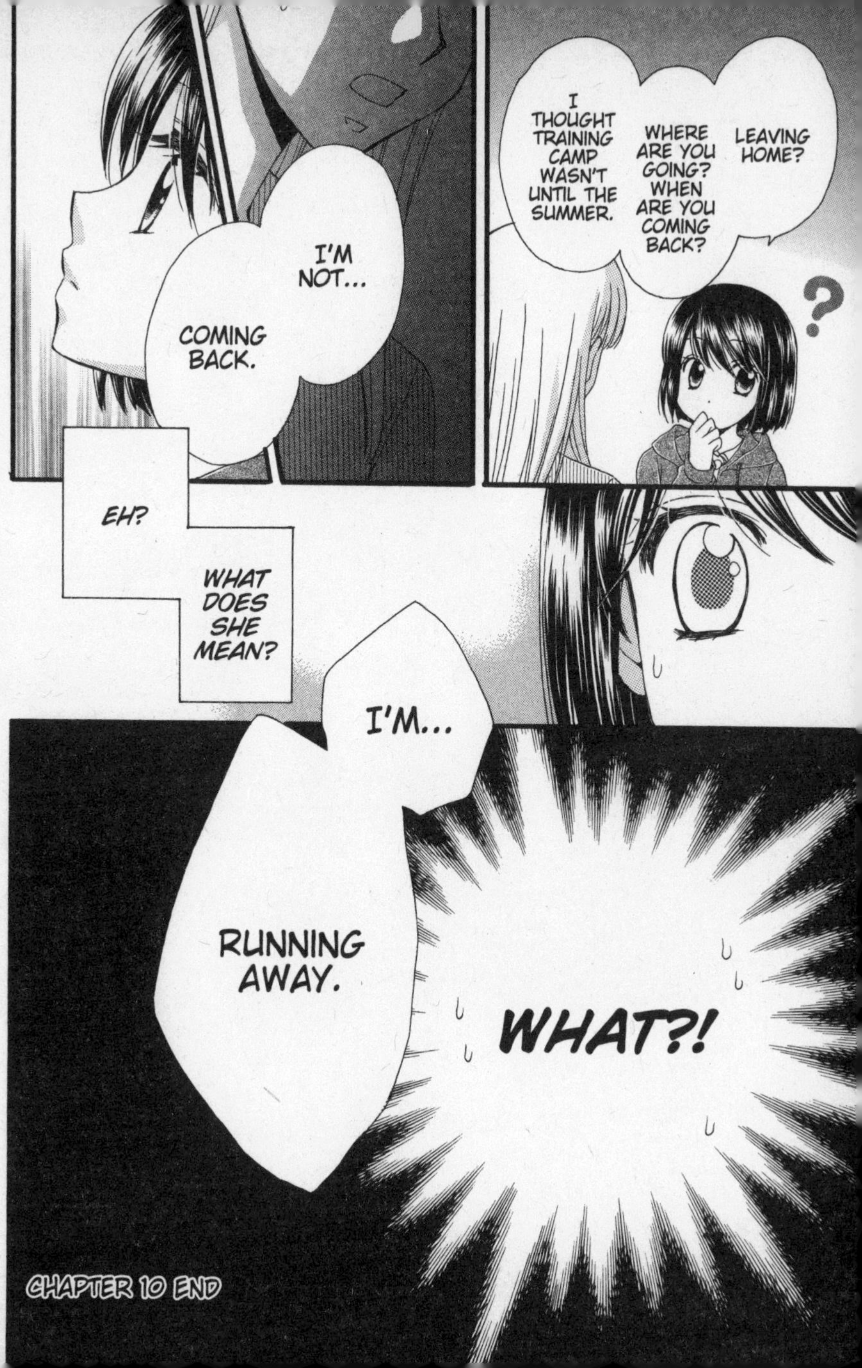
LEAVING HOME?
WHERE ARE YOU GOING? WHEN ARE YOU COMING BACK?
I THOUGHT TRAINING CAMP WASN'T UNTIL THE SUMMER.
?
I'M NOT...
COMING BACK.
EH?
WHAT DOES SHE MEAN?
I'M...
RUNNING AWAY.
WHAT?!
CHAPTER 10 END

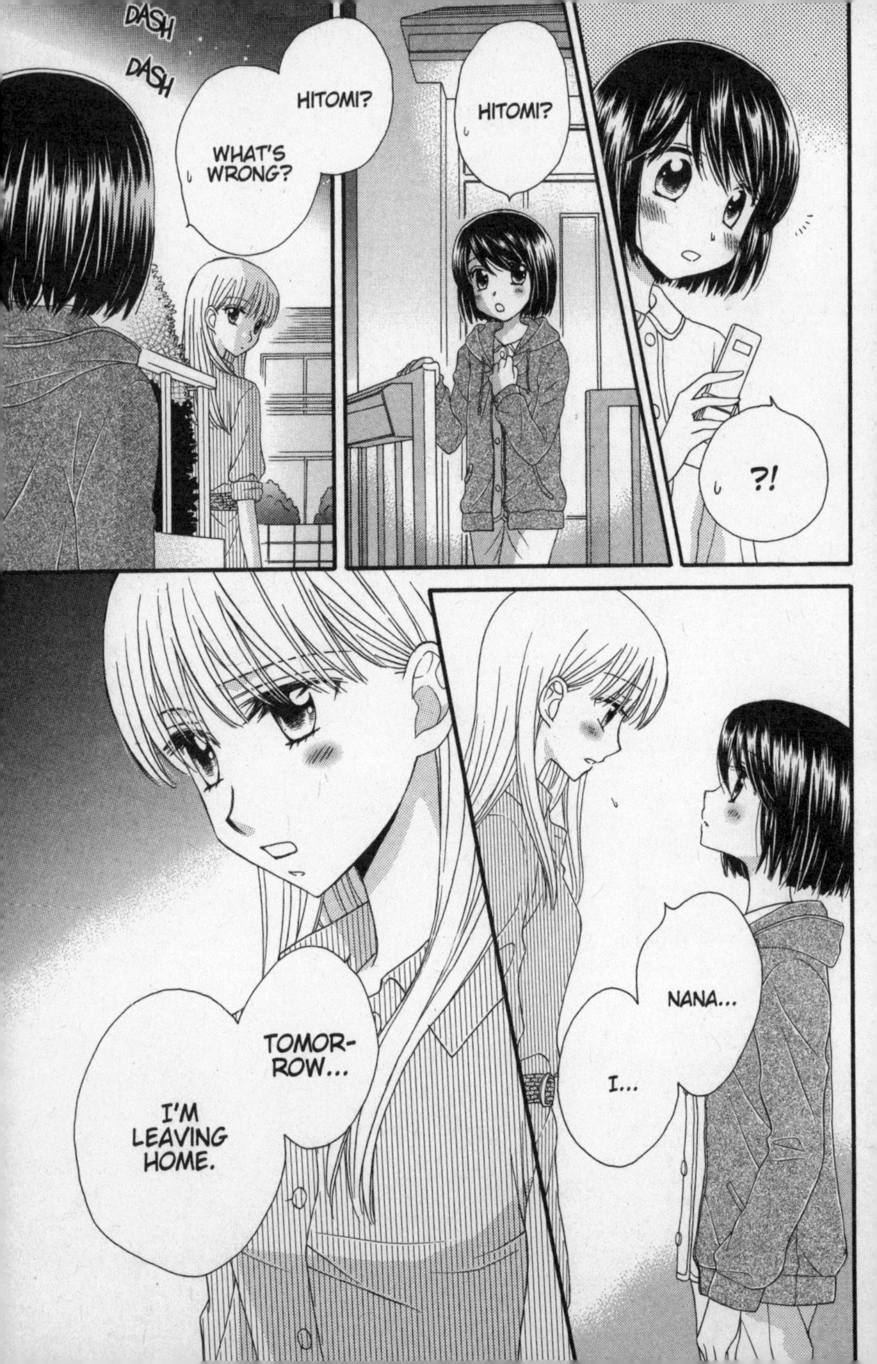
?!
HITOMI?
HITOMI? WHAT'S WRONG?
DASH
DASH
NANA... I...
TOMORROW... I'M LEAVING HOME.

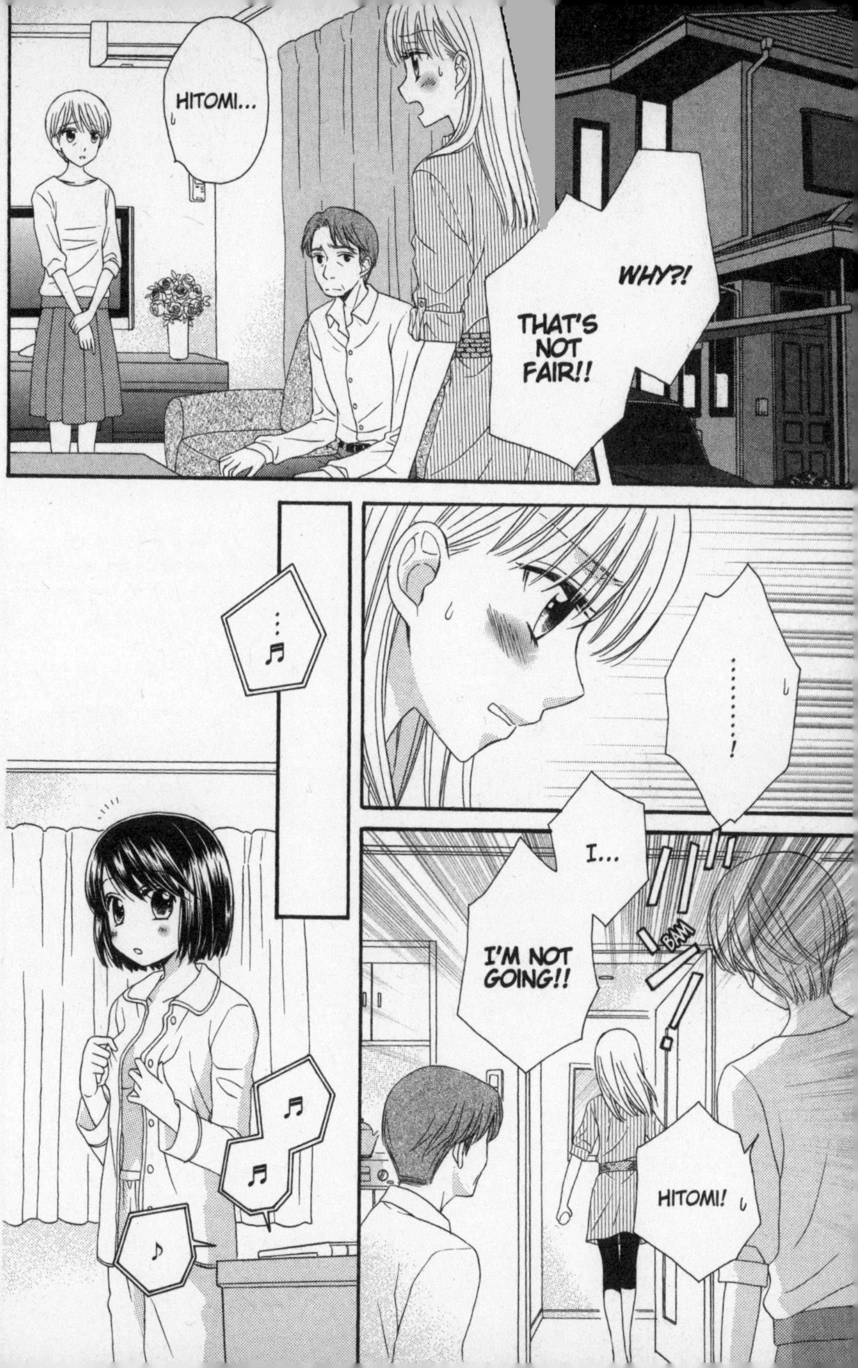
WHY?!
THAT'S NOT FAIR!!
HITOMI...
......!
I...
I'M NOT GOING!!
BAM
HITOMI!
...♬
♬
♬
♪

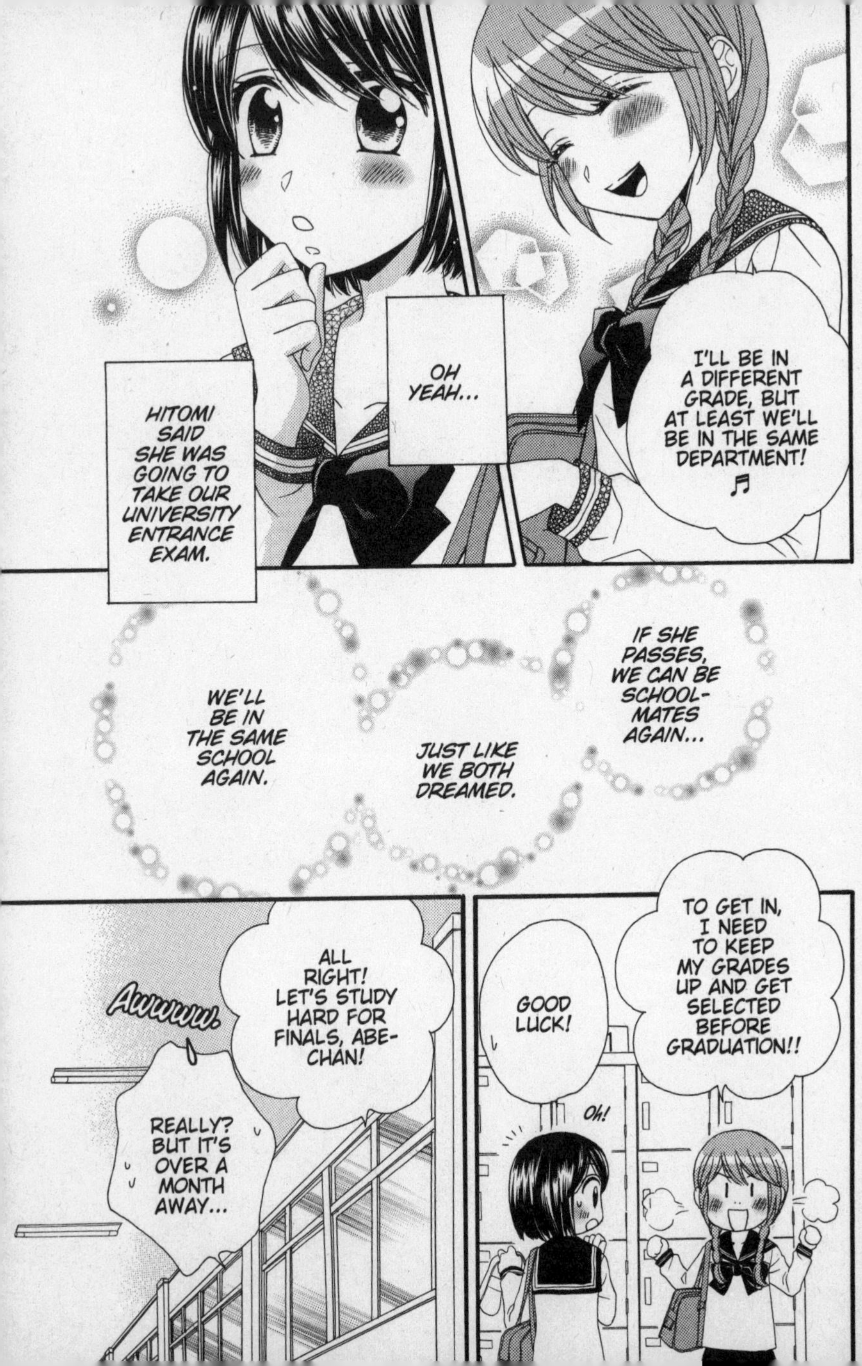
I'LL BE IN A DIFFERENT GRADE, BUT AT LEAST WE'LL BE IN THE SAME DEPARTMENT! ♬
OH YEAH...
HITOMI SAID SHE WAS GOING TO TAKE OUR UNIVERSITY ENTRANCE EXAM.
IF SHE PASSES, WE CAN BE SCHOOL-MATES AGAIN...
WE'LL BE IN THE SAME SCHOOL AGAIN.
JUST LIKE WE BOTH DREAMED.
TO GET IN, I NEED TO KEEP MY GRADES UP AND GET SELECTED BEFORE GRADUATION!!
GOOD LUCK!
Oh!
ALL RIGHT! LET'S STUDY HARD FOR FINALS, ABE-CHAN!
Awwww.
REALLY? BUT IT'S OVER A MONTH AWAY...

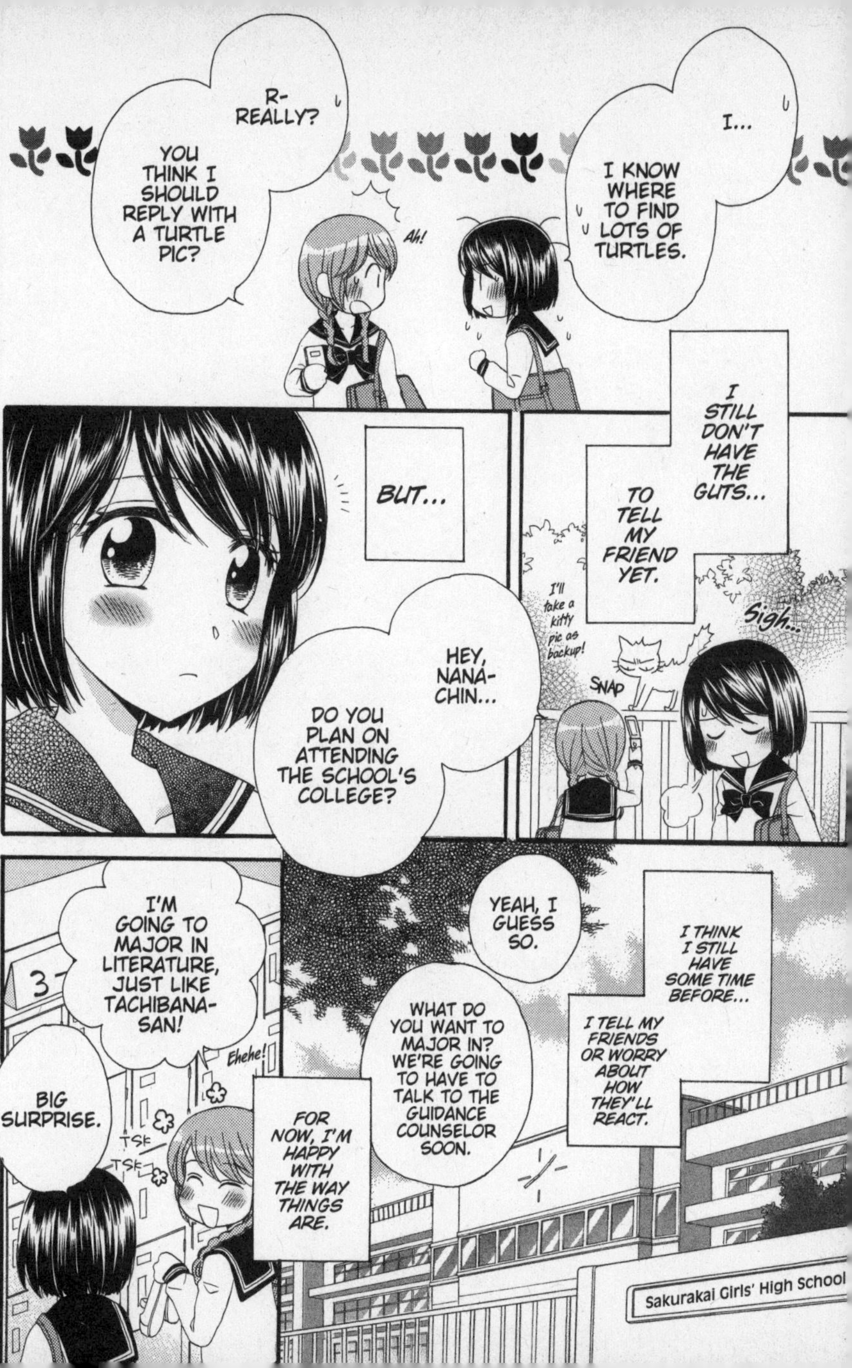
I...
I KNOW WHERE TO FIND LOTS OF TURTLES.
Ah!
R-REALLY?
YOU THINK I SHOULD REPLY WITH A TURTLE PIC?
I STILL DON'T HAVE THE GUTS...
TO TELL MY FRIEND YET.
Sigh...
I'll take a kitty pic as backup!
SNAP
BUT...
HEY, NANA-CHIN...
DO YOU PLAN ON ATTENDING THE SCHOOL'S COLLEGE?
I THINK I STILL HAVE SOME TIME BEFORE...
I TELL MY FRIENDS OR WORRY ABOUT HOW THEY'LL REACT.
YEAH, I GUESS SO.
WHAT DO YOU WANT TO MAJOR IN? WE'RE GOING TO HAVE TO TALK TO THE GUIDANCE COUNSELOR SOON.
FOR NOW, I'M HAPPY WITH THE WAY THINGS ARE.
Sakurakai Girls' High School
I'M GOING TO MAJOR IN LITERATURE, JUST LIKE TACHIBANA-SAN!
Ehehe!
BIG SURPRISE.
TSK
TSK

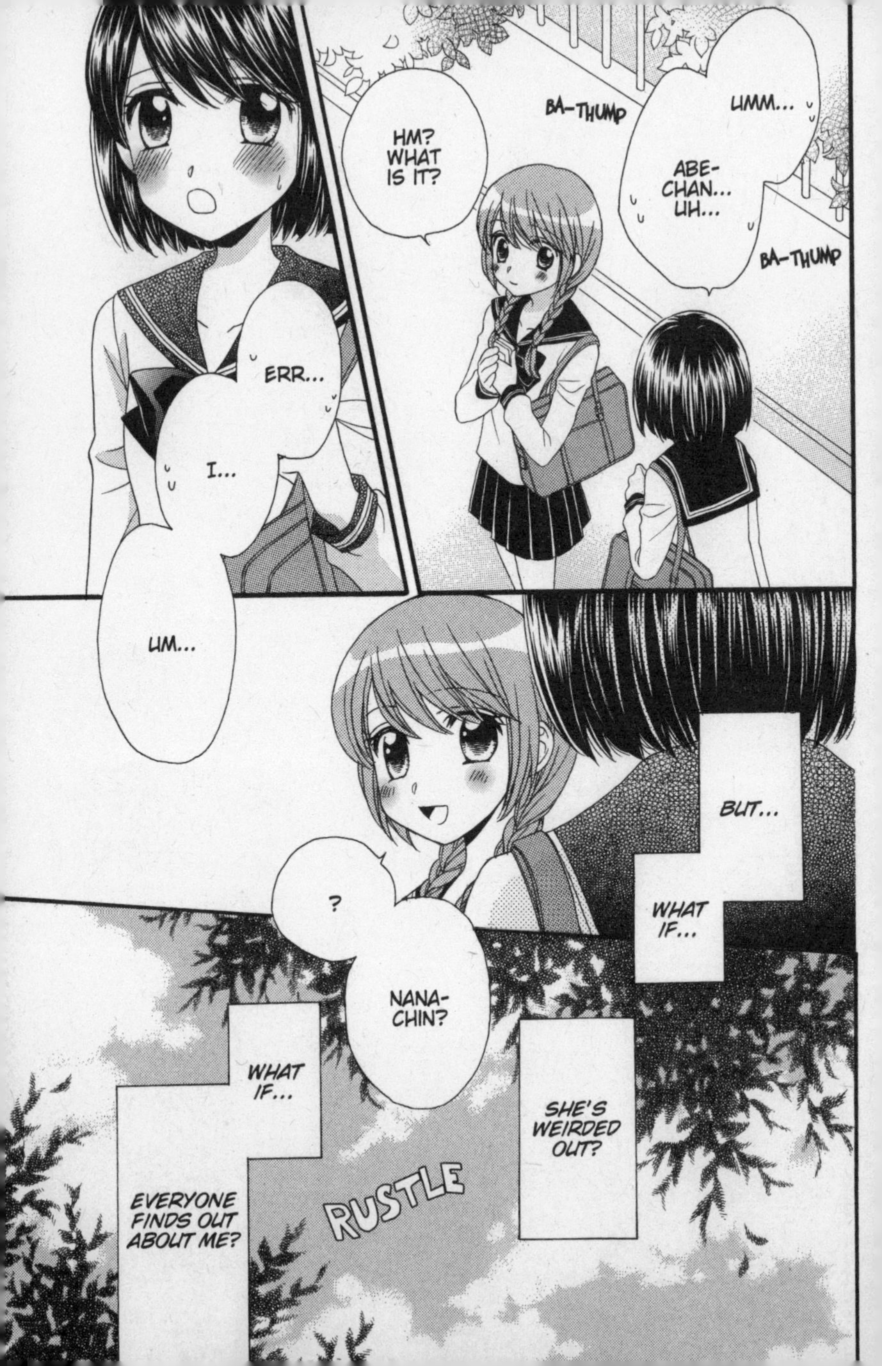
UMM...
ABE-CHAN... UH...
BA-THUMP
BA-THUMP
HM? WHAT IS IT?
ERR...
I...
UM...
BUT...
WHAT IF...
?
NANA-CHIN?
SHE'S WEIRDED OUT?
WHAT IF...
EVERYONE FINDS OUT ABOUT ME?
RUSTLE

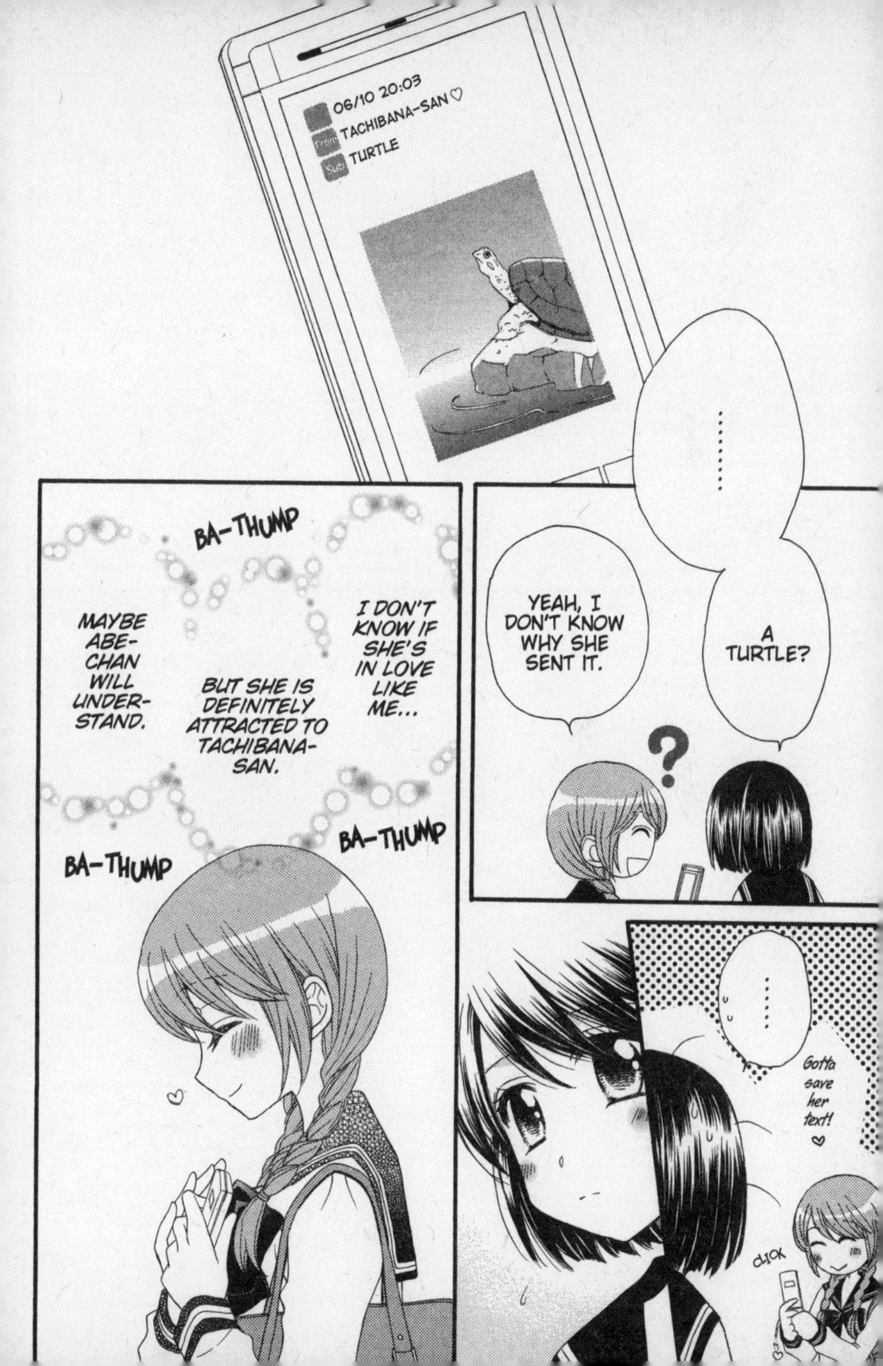
06/10 20:03
TACHIBANA-SAN♡
TURTLE
......
A TURTLE?
YEAH, I DON'T KNOW WHY SHE SENT IT.
......
Gotta save her text! ♡
CLICK
BA-THUMP
I DON'T KNOW IF SHE'S IN LOVE LIKE ME...
BUT SHE IS DEFINITELY ATTRACTED TO TACHIBANA-SAN.
MAYBE ABE-CHAN WILL UNDER-STAND.
BA-THUMP
BA-THUMP

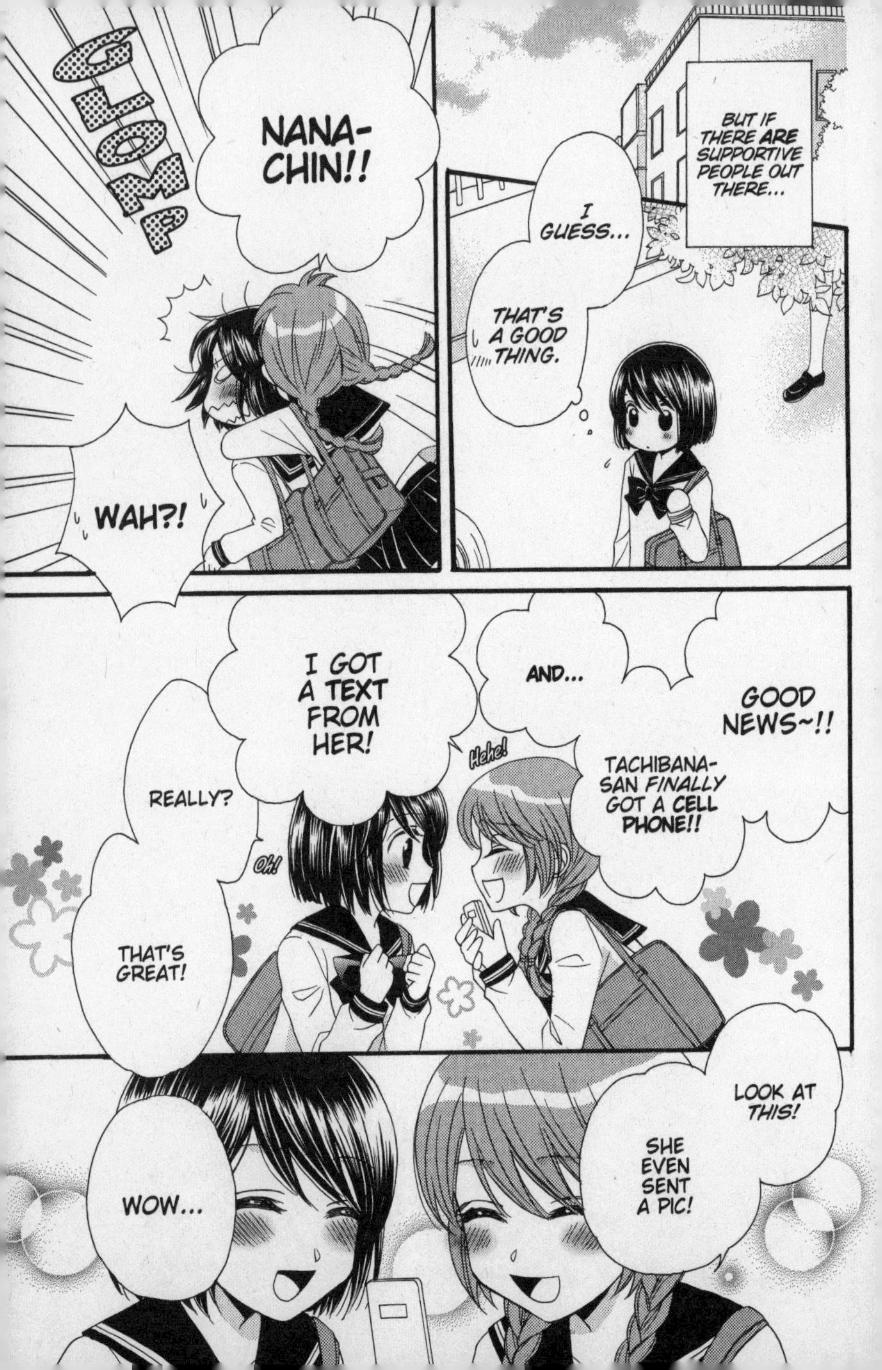

BUT IF THERE ARE SUPPORTIVE PEOPLE OUT THERE...
I GUESS...
THAT'S A GOOD THING.
GLOMP
NANA-CHIN!!
WAH?!
GOOD NEWS~!!
AND...
TACHIBANA-SAN FINALLY GOT A CELL PHONE!!
Hehe!
I GOT A TEXT FROM HER!
Oh!
REALLY?
THAT'S GREAT!
LOOK AT THIS!
SHE EVEN SENT A PIC!
WOW...

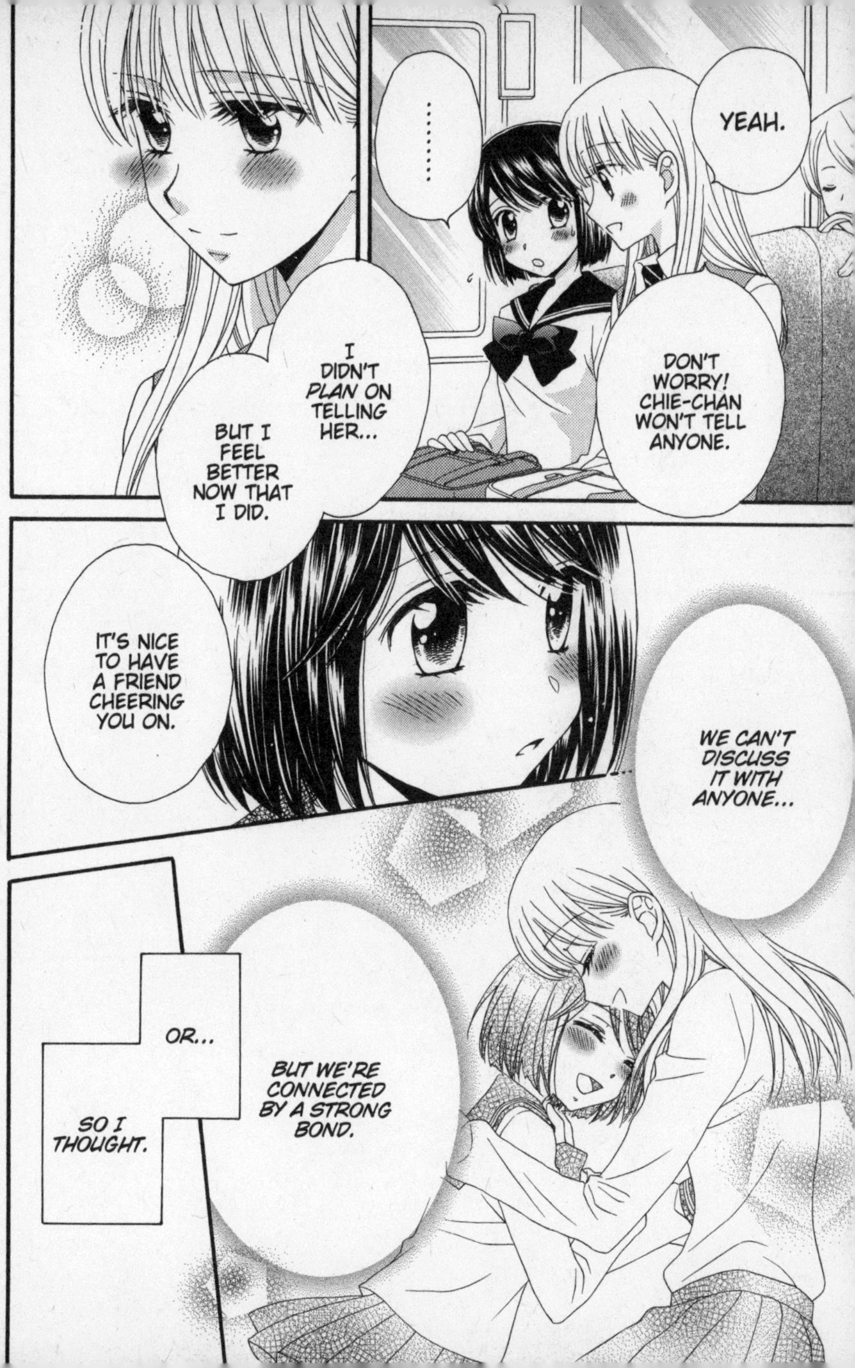
YEAH.
......
DON'T WORRY! CHIE-CHAN WON'T TELL ANYONE.
I DIDN'T *PLAN* ON TELLING HER...
BUT I FEEL BETTER NOW THAT I DID.
IT'S NICE TO HAVE A FRIEND CHEERING YOU ON.
WE CAN'T DISCUSS IT WITH ANYONE...
BUT WE'RE CONNECTED BY A STRONG BOND.
OR...
SO I THOUGHT.

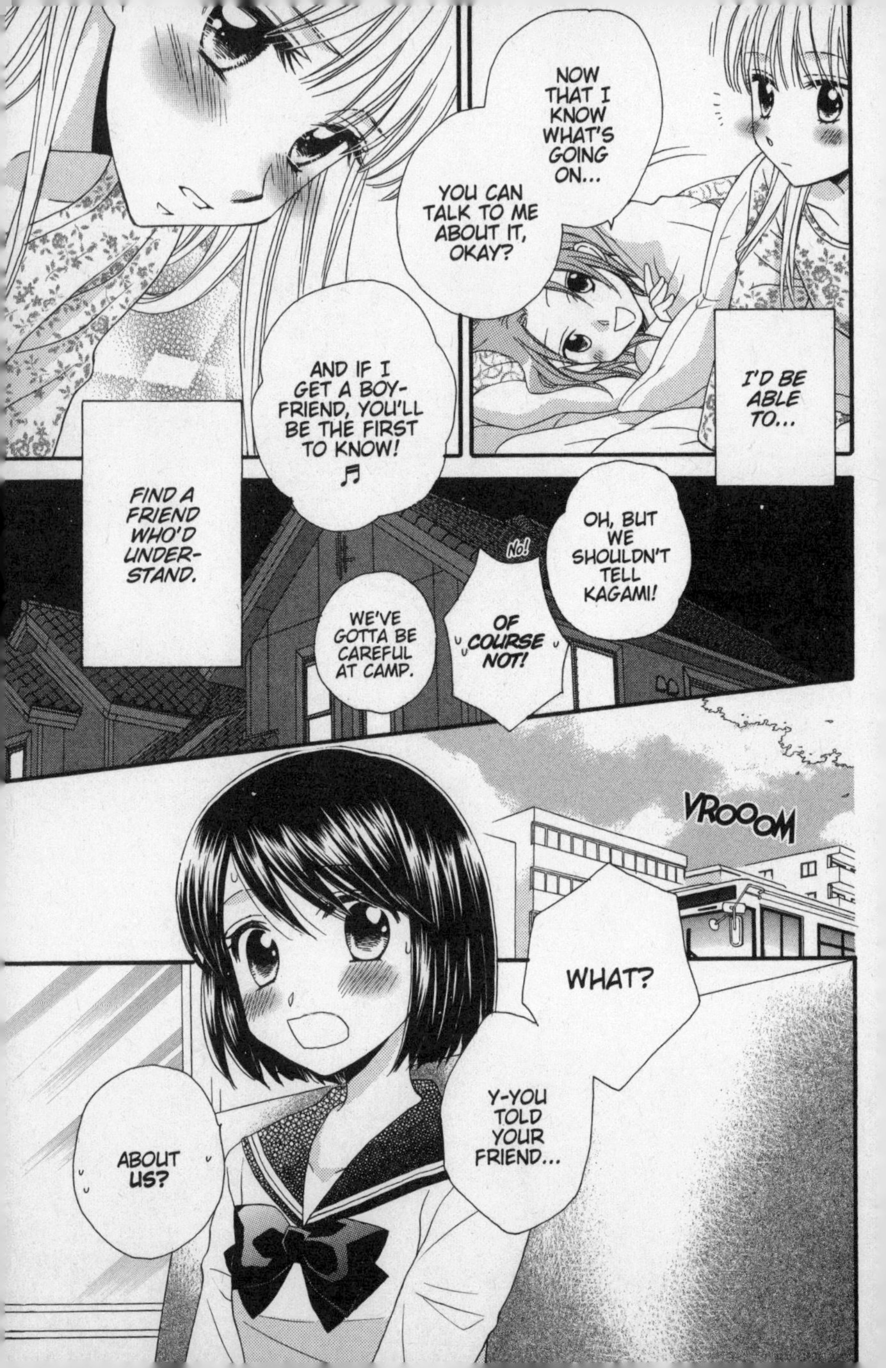

NOW THAT I KNOW WHAT'S GOING ON...
YOU CAN TALK TO ME ABOUT IT, OKAY?
I'D BE ABLE TO...
AND IF I GET A BOY-FRIEND, YOU'LL BE THE FIRST TO KNOW! ♬
FIND A FRIEND WHO'D UNDER-STAND.
OH, BUT WE SHOULDN'T TELL KAGAMI!
No!
OF COURSE NOT!
WE'VE GOTTA BE CAREFUL AT CAMP.
VROOOM
WHAT?
Y-YOU TOLD YOUR FRIEND...
ABOUT US?

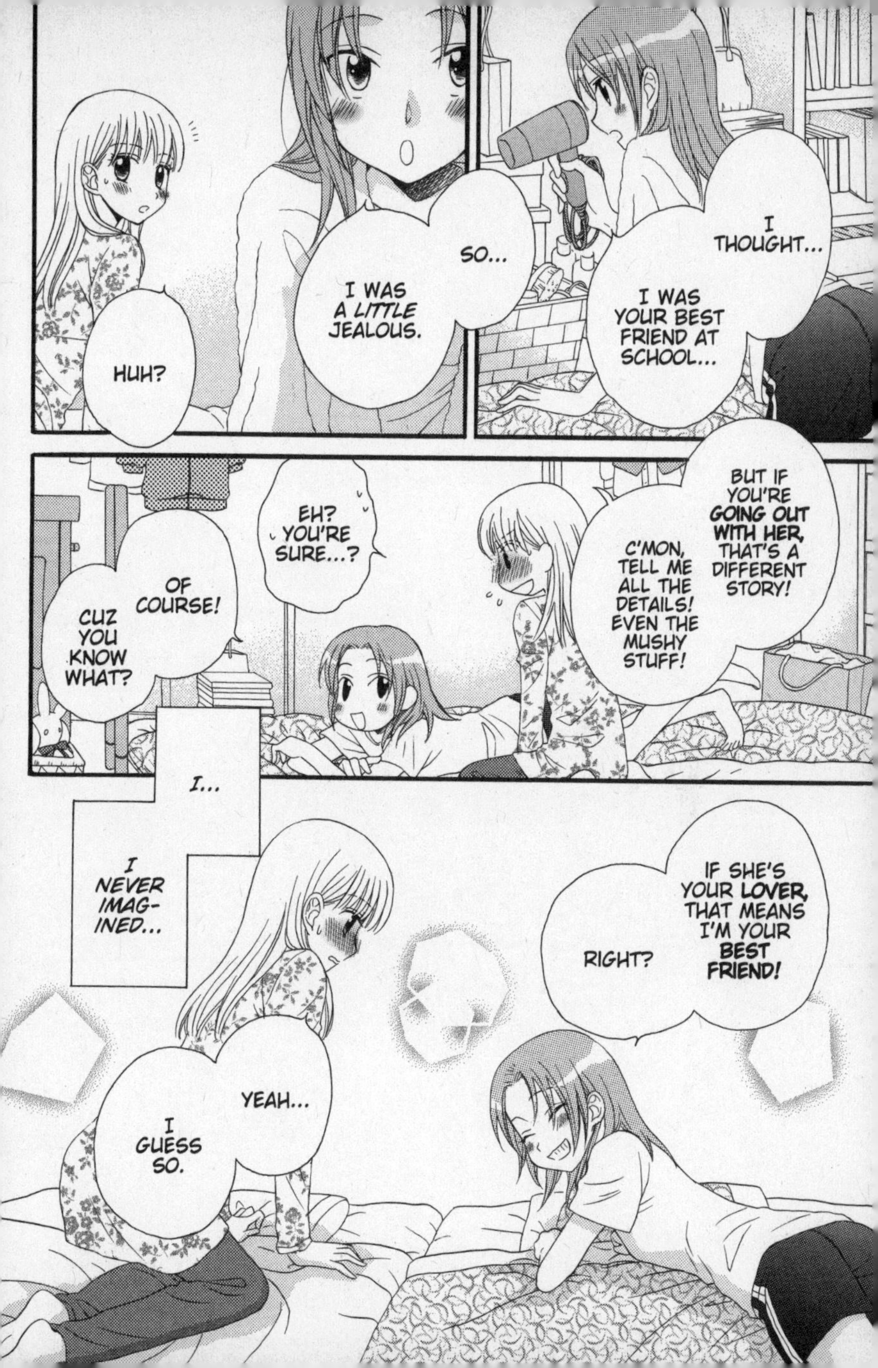
I THOUGHT...
I WAS YOUR BEST FRIEND AT SCHOOL...
SO...
I WAS A *LITTLE* JEALOUS.
HUH?
BUT IF YOU'RE GOING OUT WITH HER, THAT'S A DIFFERENT STORY!
C'MON, TELL ME ALL THE DETAILS! EVEN THE MUSHY STUFF!
EH? YOU'RE SURE...?
OF COURSE!
CUZ YOU KNOW WHAT?
IF SHE'S YOUR LOVER, THAT MEANS I'M YOUR BEST FRIEND!
RIGHT?
I...
I NEVER IMAGINED...
YEAH...
I GUESS SO.

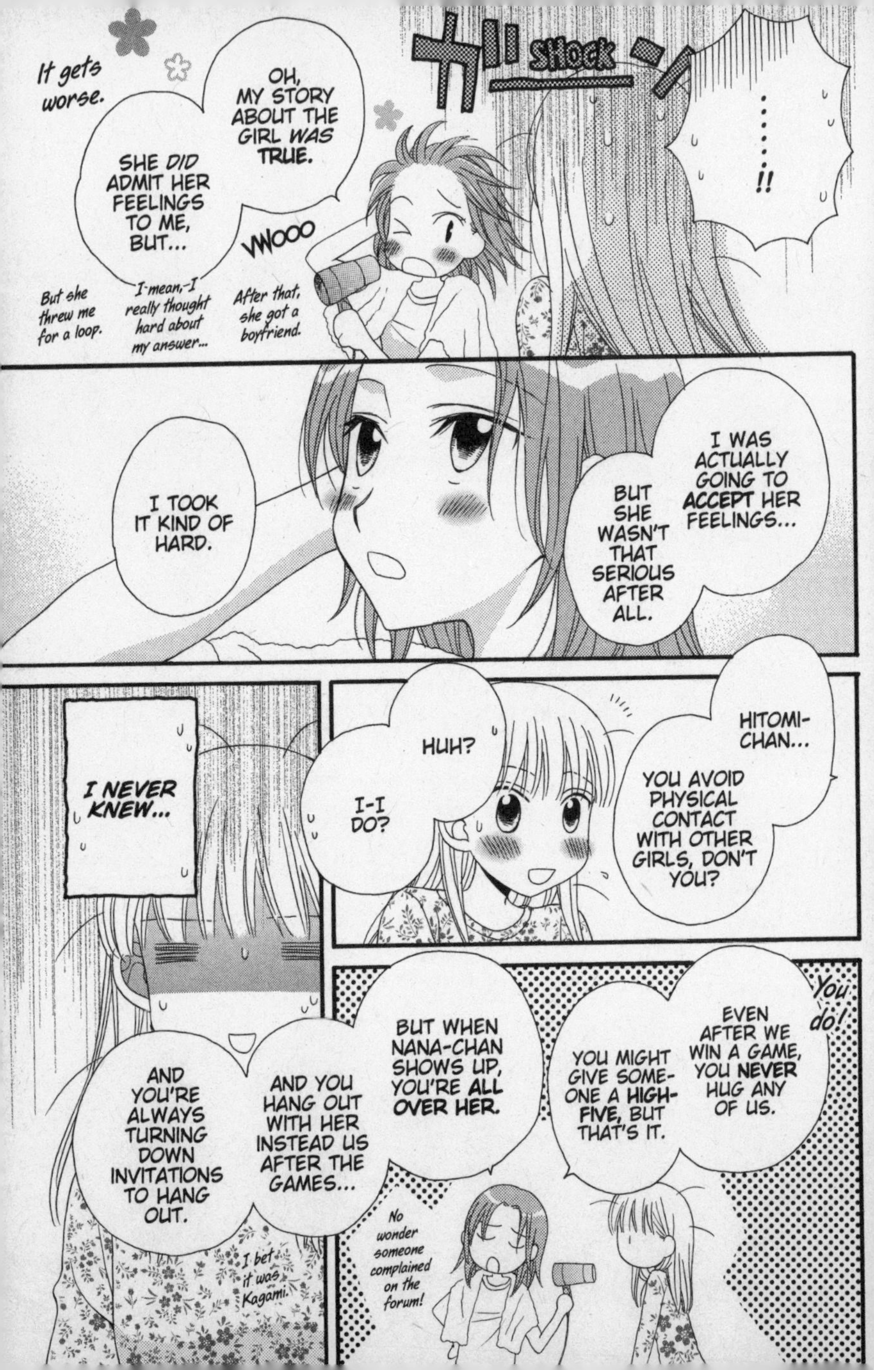
SHOCK
......!!
OH, MY STORY ABOUT THE GIRL WAS TRUE.
SHE DID ADMIT HER FEELINGS TO ME, BUT...
It gets worse.
VWOOO
After that, she got a boyfriend.
I-mean,-I really thought hard about my answer...
But she threw me for a loop.
I WAS ACTUALLY GOING TO ACCEPT HER FEELINGS...
BUT SHE WASN'T THAT SERIOUS AFTER ALL.
I TOOK IT KIND OF HARD.
HITOMI-CHAN...
YOU AVOID PHYSICAL CONTACT WITH OTHER GIRLS, DON'T YOU?
HUH?
I-I DO?
You do!
EVEN AFTER WE WIN A GAME, YOU NEVER HUG ANY OF US.
YOU MIGHT GIVE SOME-ONE A HIGH-FIVE, BUT THAT'S IT.
BUT WHEN NANA-CHAN SHOWS UP, YOU'RE ALL OVER HER.
No wonder someone complained on the forum!
AND YOU HANG OUT WITH HER INSTEAD US AFTER THE GAMES...
AND YOU'RE ALWAYS TURNING DOWN INVITATIONS TO HANG OUT.
I bet it was Kagami.
I NEVER KNEW...

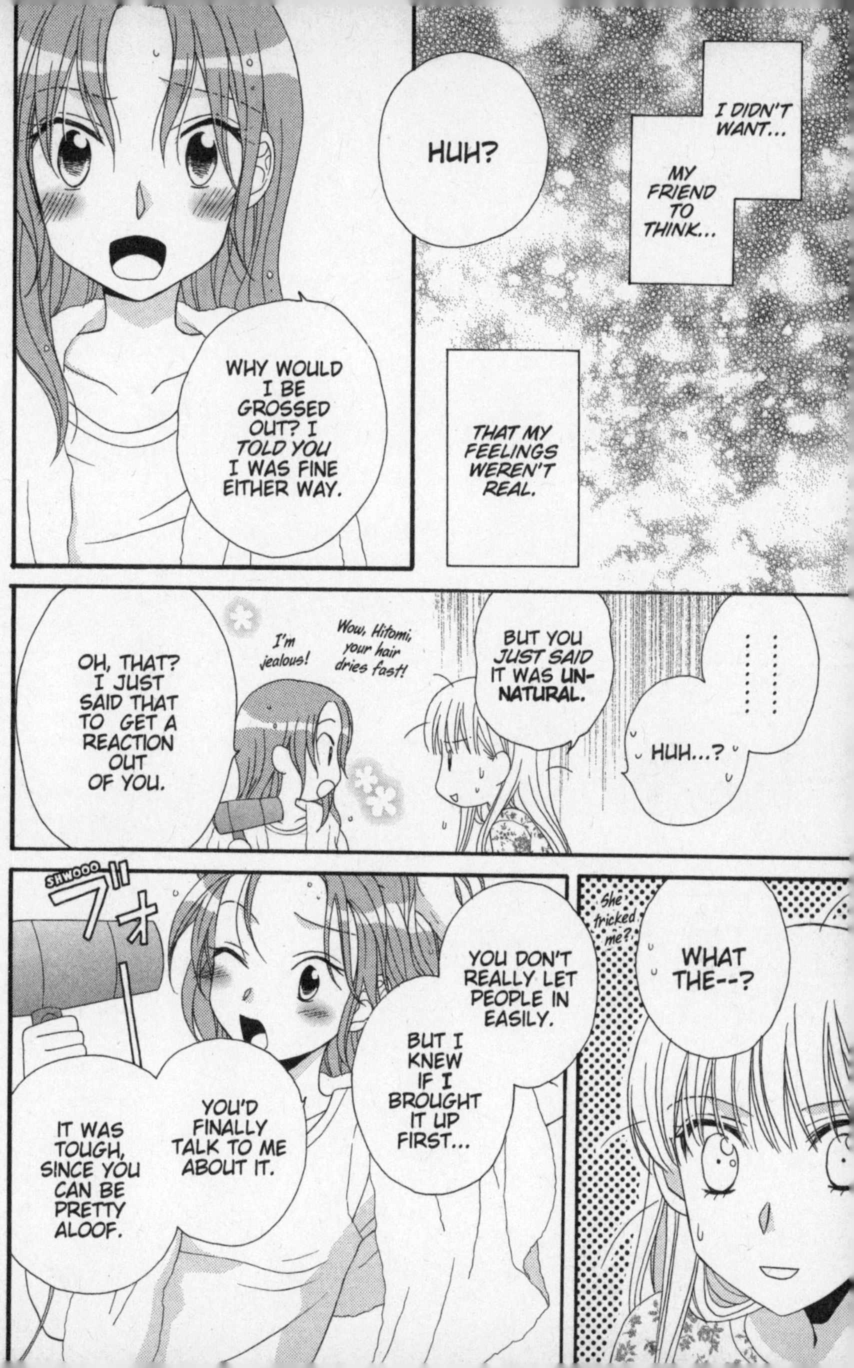
I DIDN'T WANT...
MY FRIEND TO THINK...
THAT MY FEELINGS WEREN'T REAL.
HUH?
WHY WOULD I BE GROSSED OUT? I TOLD YOU I WAS FINE EITHER WAY.
......
HUH...?
BUT YOU JUST SAID IT WAS UNNATURAL.
Wow, Hitomi, your hair dries fast!
I'm jealous!
OH, THAT? I JUST SAID THAT TO GET A REACTION OUT OF YOU.
She tricked me?
WHAT THE--?
SHWOOO
YOU DON'T REALLY LET PEOPLE IN EASILY.
BUT I KNEW IF I BROUGHT IT UP FIRST...
YOU'D FINALLY TALK TO ME ABOUT IT.
IT WAS TOUGH, SINCE YOU CAN BE PRETTY ALOOF.

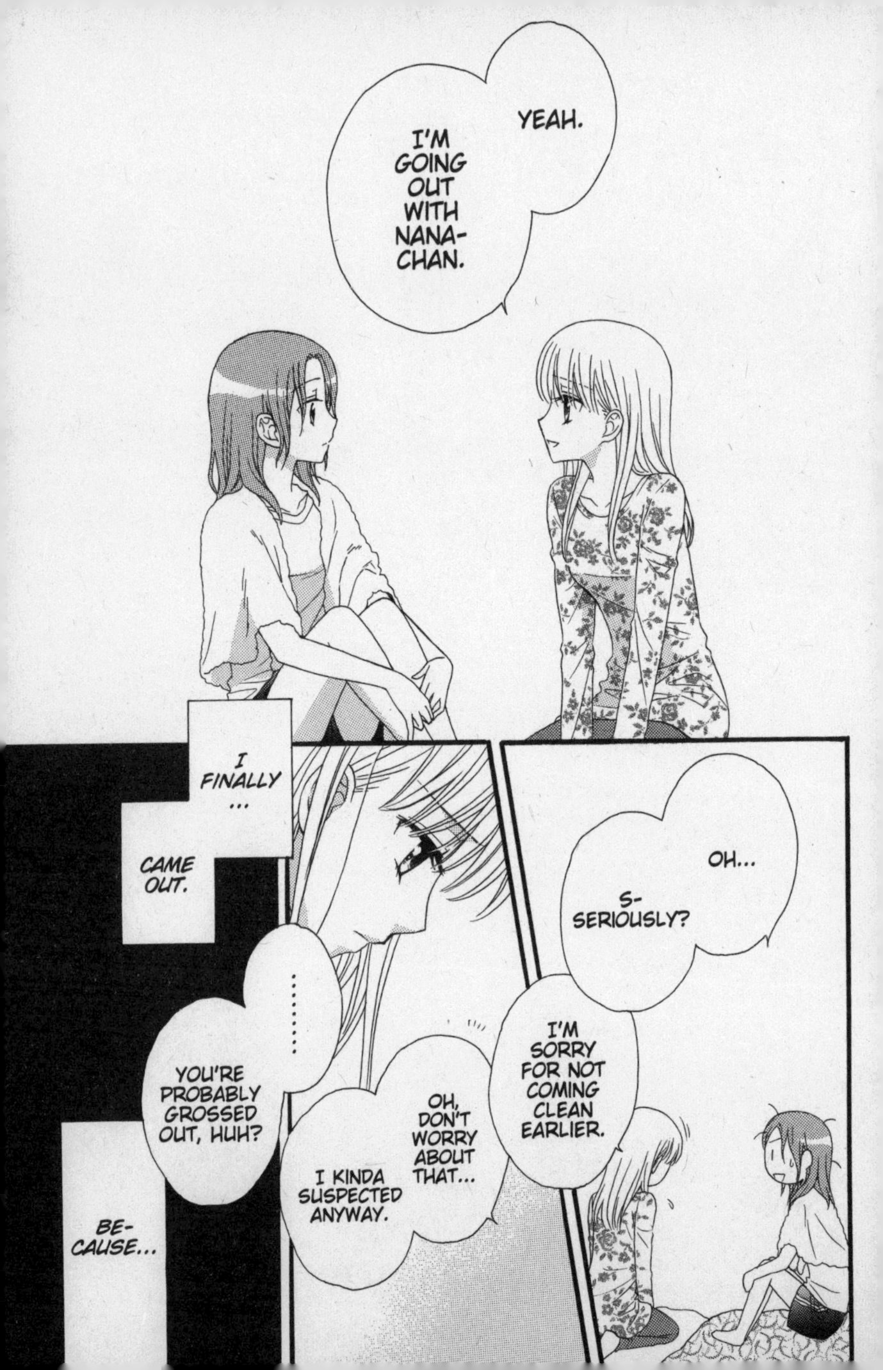
YEAH.
I'M GOING OUT WITH NANA-CHAN.
OH...
S-SERIOUSLY?
I FINALLY ...
CAME OUT.
......
I'M SORRY FOR NOT COMING CLEAN EARLIER.
YOU'RE PROBABLY GROSSED OUT, HUH?
OH, DON'T WORRY ABOUT THAT...
I KINDA SUSPECTED ANYWAY.
BE-CAUSE...

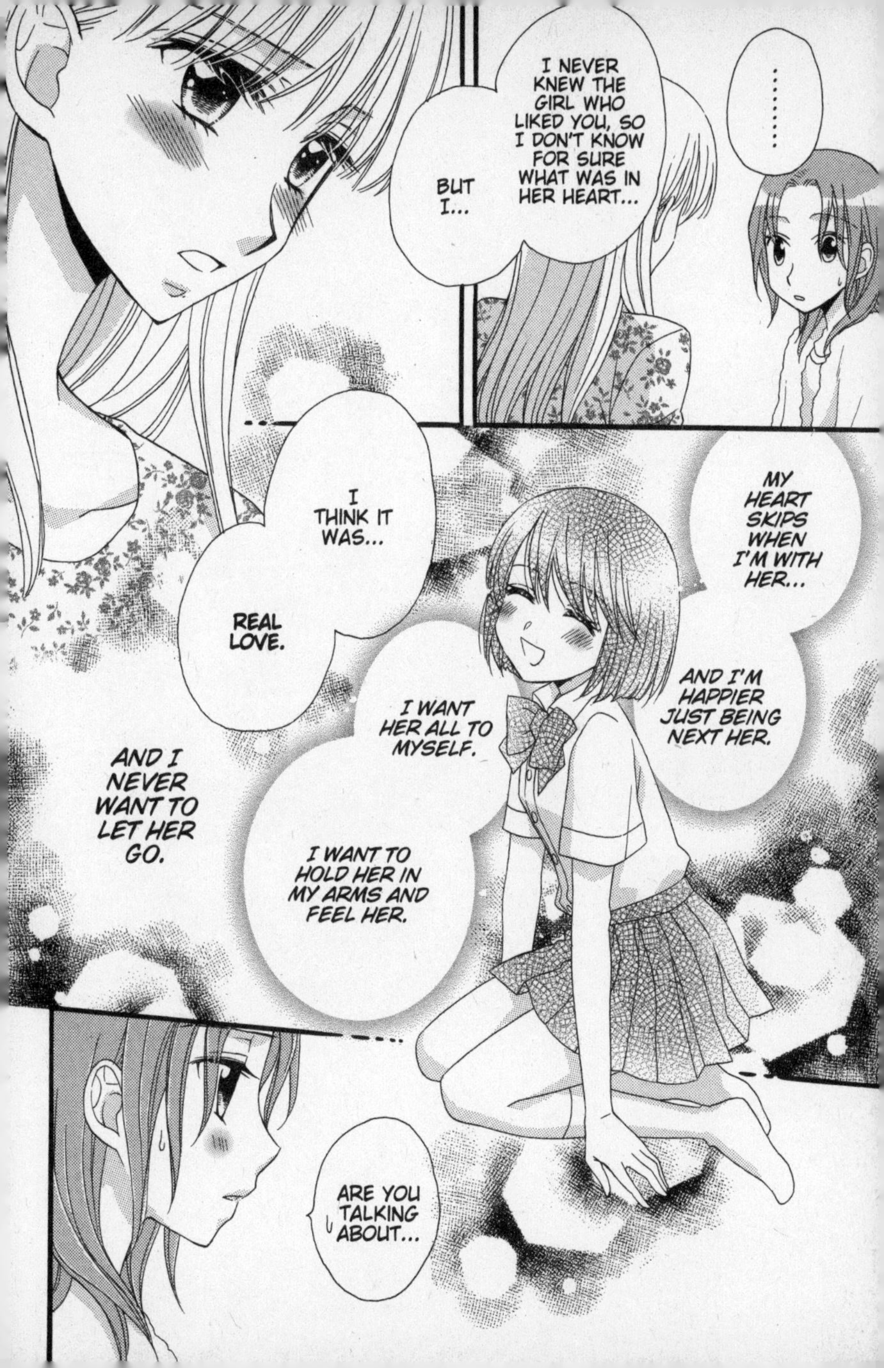
......
I NEVER KNEW THE GIRL WHO LIKED YOU, SO I DON'T KNOW FOR SURE WHAT WAS IN HER HEART...
BUT I...
I THINK IT WAS...
REAL LOVE.
MY HEART SKIPS WHEN I'M WITH HER...
AND I'M HAPPIER JUST BEING NEXT HER.
I WANT HER ALL TO MYSELF.
I WANT TO HOLD HER IN MY ARMS AND FEEL HER.
AND I NEVER WANT TO LET HER GO.
ARE YOU TALKING ABOUT...

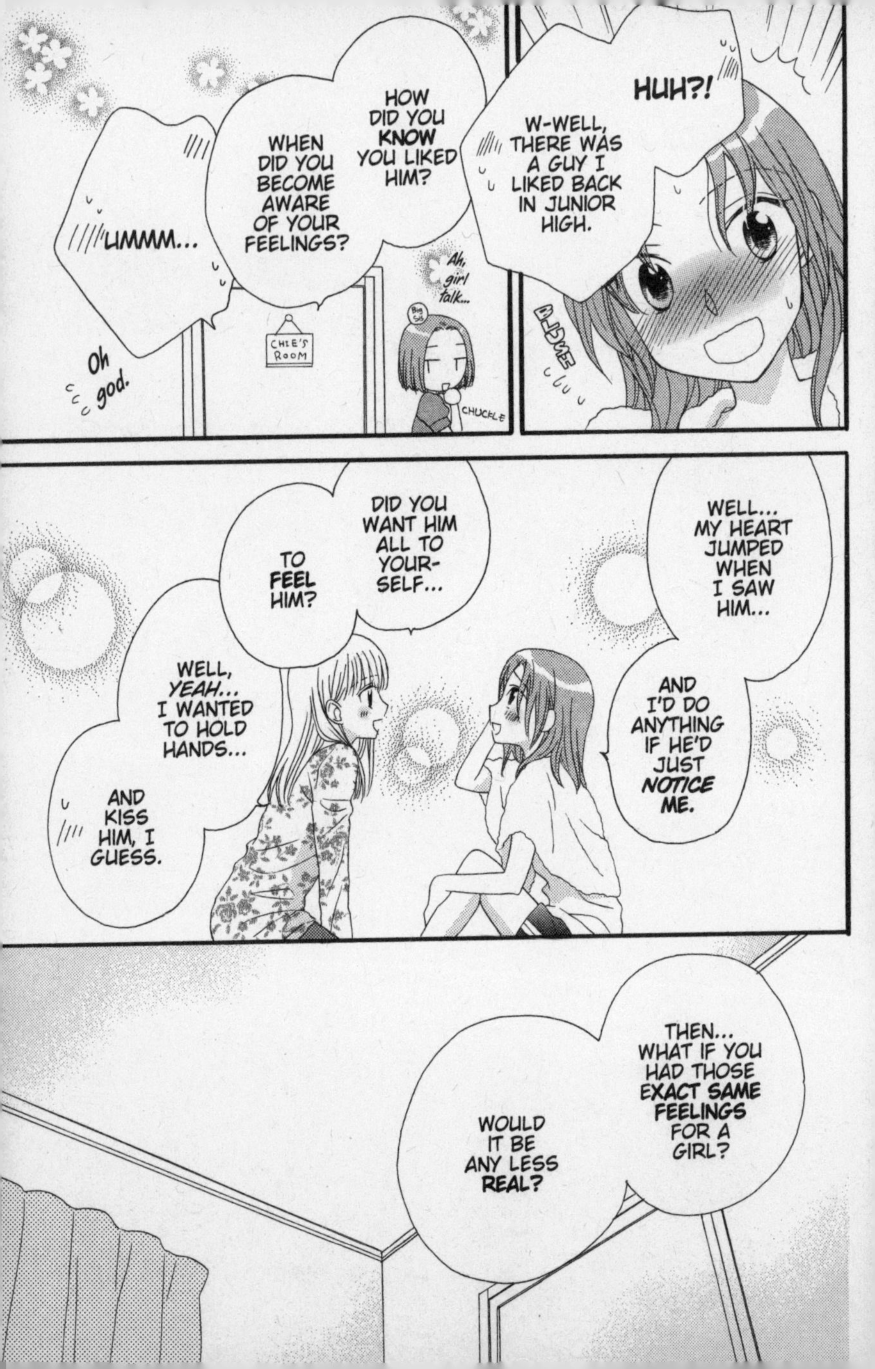
HUH?!
W-WELL, THERE WAS A GUY I LIKED BACK IN JUNIOR HIGH.
BLUSH
HOW DID YOU KNOW YOU LIKED HIM?
WHEN DID YOU BECOME AWARE OF YOUR FEELINGS?
UMMM...
Oh god.
Ah, girl talk...
Big Sis
CHIE'S ROOM
CHUCKLE
WELL... MY HEART JUMPED WHEN I SAW HIM...
AND I'D DO ANYTHING IF HE'D JUST NOTICE ME.
DID YOU WANT HIM ALL TO YOURSELF...
TO FEEL HIM?
WELL, YEAH... I WANTED TO HOLD HANDS...
AND KISS HIM, I GUESS.
THEN... WHAT IF YOU HAD THOSE EXACT SAME FEELINGS FOR A GIRL?
WOULD IT BE ANY LESS REAL?

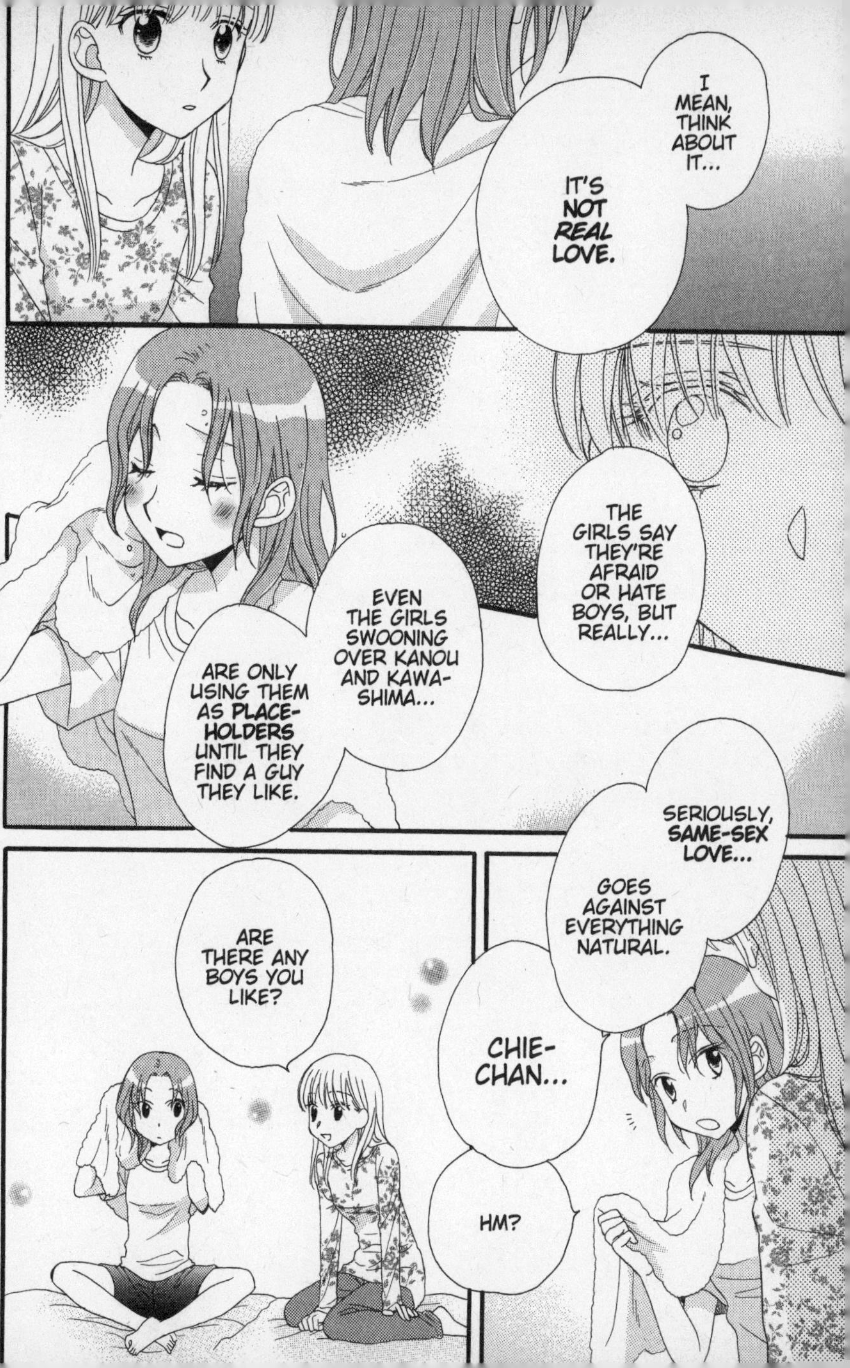
I MEAN, THINK ABOUT IT...
IT'S NOT REAL LOVE.
THE GIRLS SAY THEY'RE AFRAID OR HATE BOYS, BUT REALLY...
EVEN THE GIRLS SWOONING OVER KANOU AND KAWA-SHIMA...
ARE ONLY USING THEM AS PLACE-HOLDERS UNTIL THEY FIND A GUY THEY LIKE.
SERIOUSLY, SAME-SEX LOVE...
GOES AGAINST EVERYTHING NATURAL.
CHIE-CHAN...
HM?
ARE THERE ANY BOYS YOU LIKE?

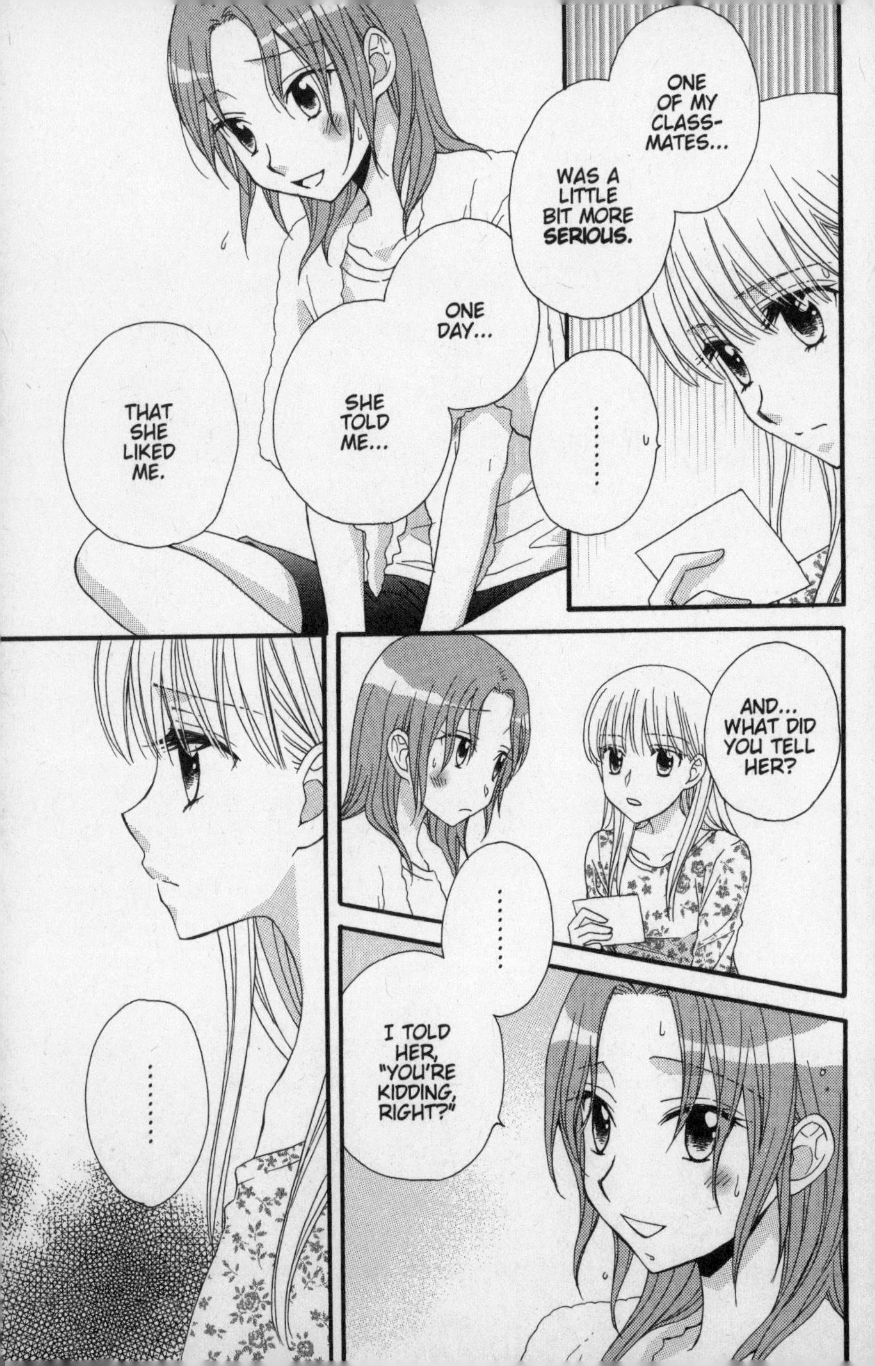
ONE OF MY CLASS-MATES...
WAS A LITTLE BIT MORE SERIOUS.
......
ONE DAY...
SHE TOLD ME...
THAT SHE LIKED ME.
AND... WHAT DID YOU TELL HER?
......
I TOLD HER, "YOU'RE KIDDING, RIGHT?"
......

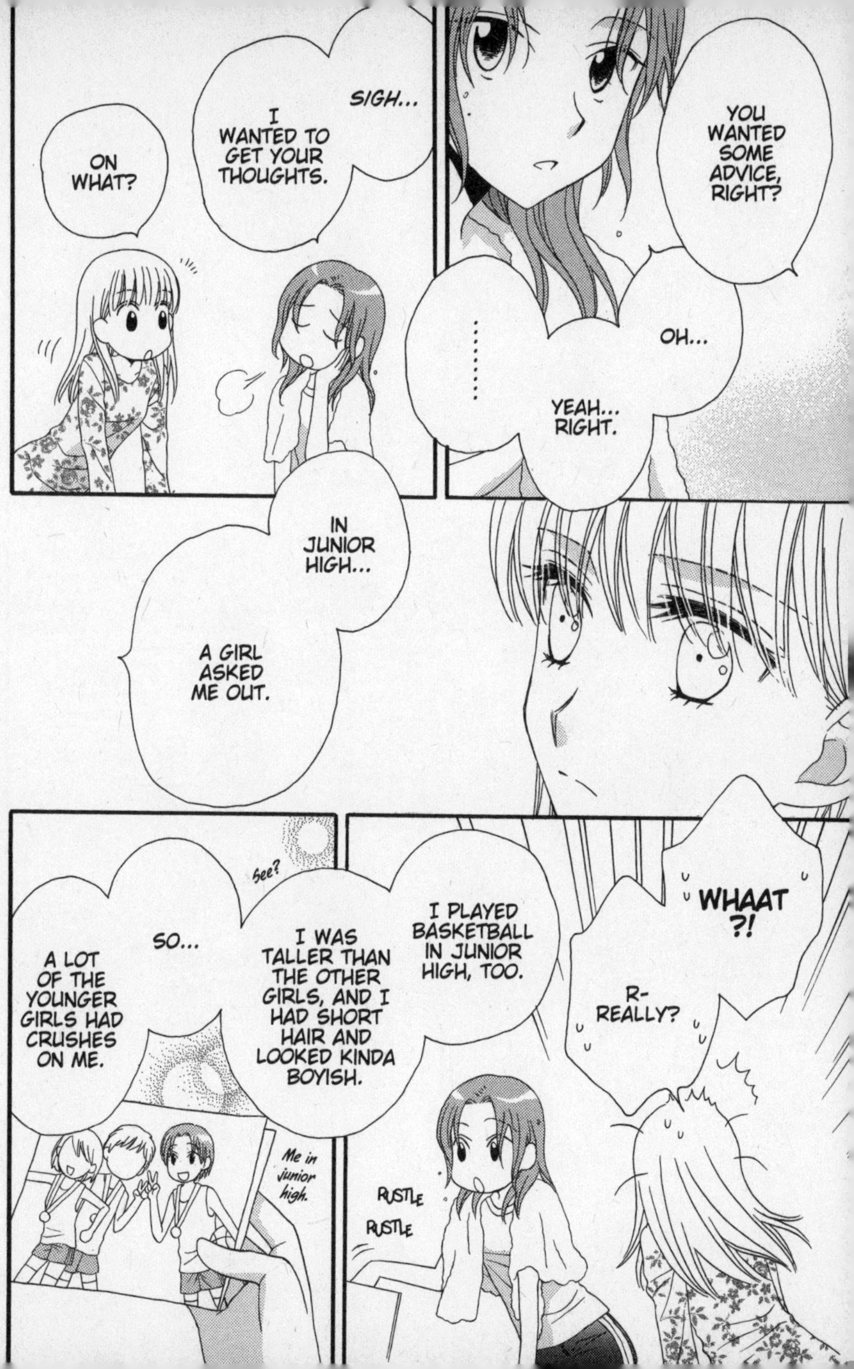
YOU WANTED SOME ADVICE, RIGHT?
OH...
......
YEAH... RIGHT.
SIGH...
I WANTED TO GET YOUR THOUGHTS.
ON WHAT?
IN JUNIOR HIGH...
A GIRL ASKED ME OUT.
WHAAT?!
R-REALLY?
I PLAYED BASKETBALL IN JUNIOR HIGH, TOO.
RUSTLE
RUSTLE
See?
I WAS TALLER THAN THE OTHER GIRLS, AND I HAD SHORT HAIR AND LOOKED KINDA BOYISH.
SO...
A LOT OF THE YOUNGER GIRLS HAD CRUSHES ON ME.
Me in junior high.

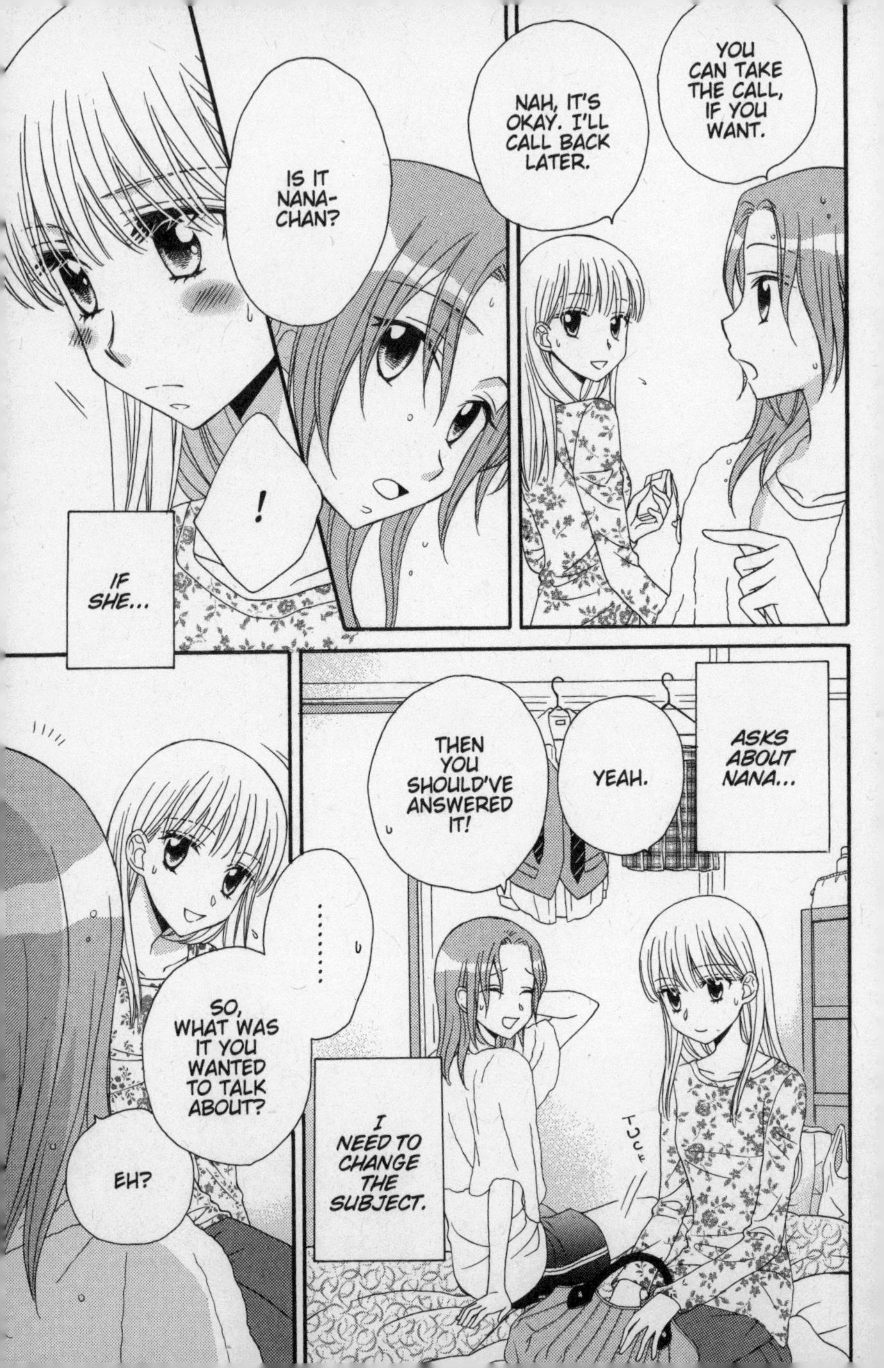
YOU CAN TAKE THE CALL, IF YOU WANT.
NAH, IT'S OKAY. I'LL CALL BACK LATER.
IS IT NANA-CHAN?
!
IF SHE...
ASKS ABOUT NANA...
YEAH.
THEN YOU SHOULD'VE ANSWERED IT!
I NEED TO CHANGE THE SUBJECT.
TUCK
......
SO, WHAT WAS IT YOU WANTED TO TALK ABOUT?
EH?

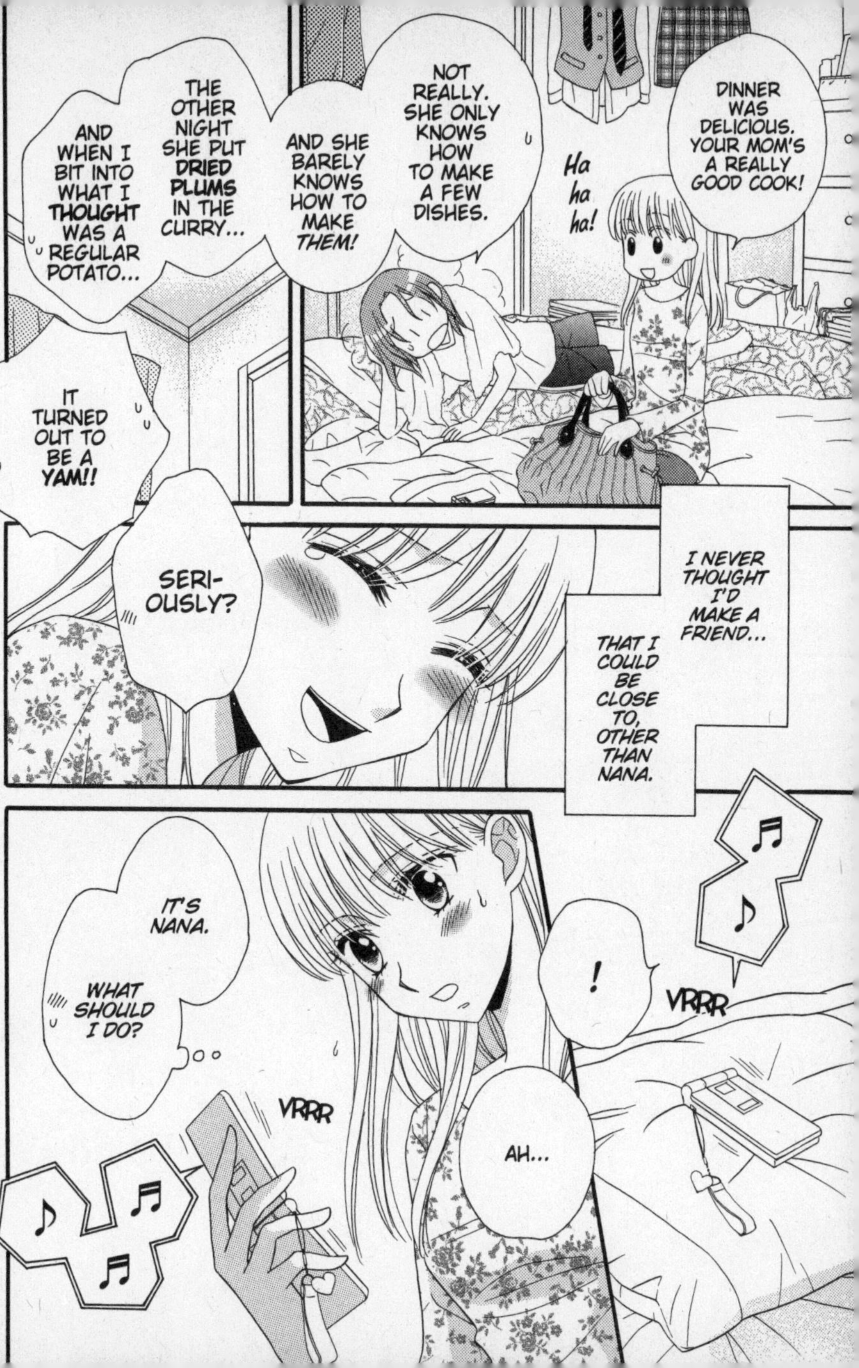
DINNER WAS DELICIOUS. YOUR MOM'S A REALLY GOOD COOK!
Ha ha ha!
NOT REALLY. SHE ONLY KNOWS HOW TO MAKE A FEW DISHES.
AND SHE BARELY KNOWS HOW TO MAKE THEM!
THE OTHER NIGHT SHE PUT DRIED PLUMS IN THE CURRY...
AND WHEN I BIT INTO WHAT I THOUGHT WAS A REGULAR POTATO...
IT TURNED OUT TO BE A YAM!!
I NEVER THOUGHT I'D MAKE A FRIEND...
THAT I COULD BE CLOSE TO, OTHER THAN NANA.
SERI-OUSLY?
♫ ♪
VRRR
!
AH...
IT'S NANA.
WHAT SHOULD I DO?
VRRR
♪ ♫ ♫

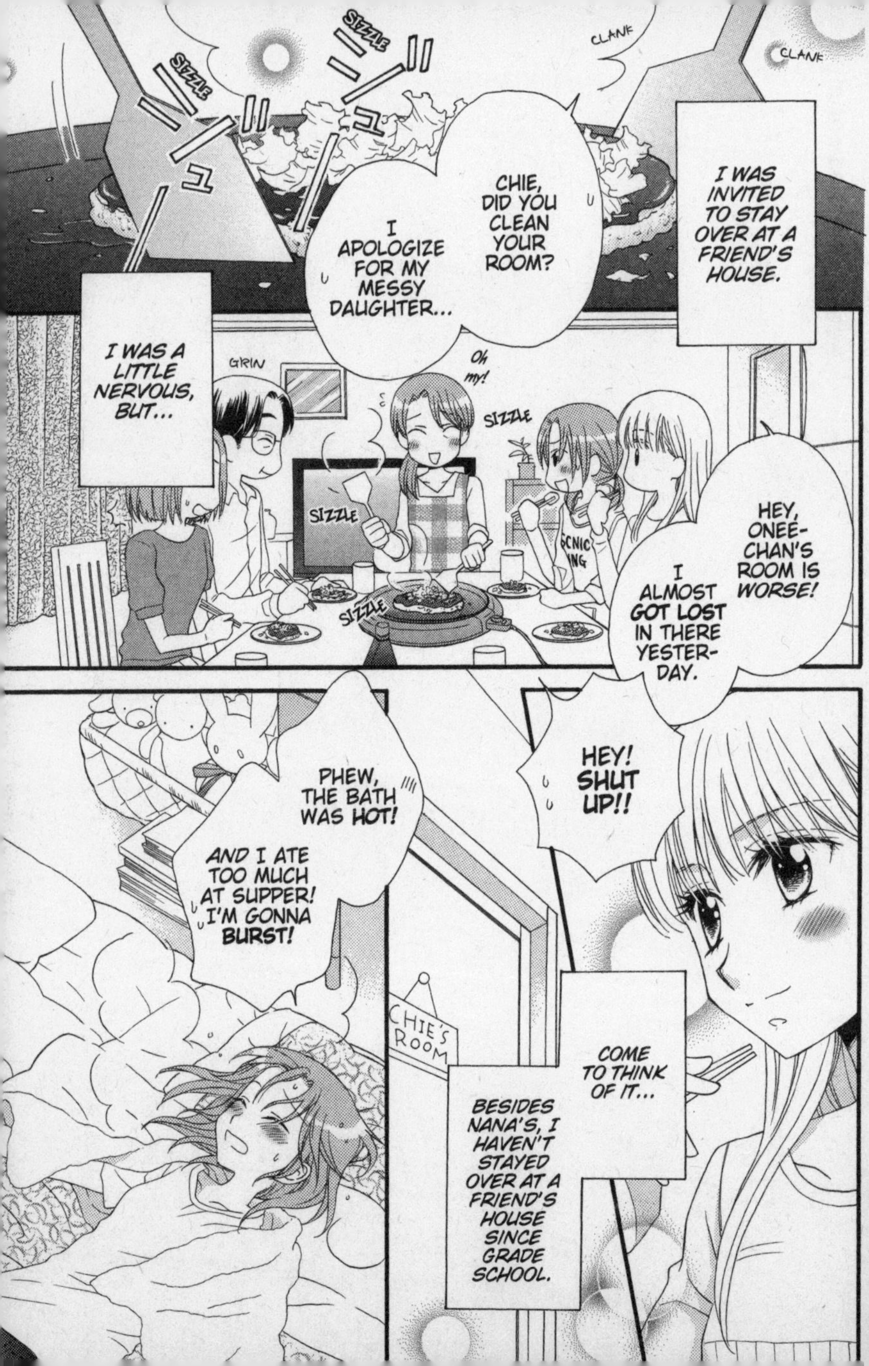
I WAS INVITED TO STAY OVER AT A FRIEND'S HOUSE.
CLANK
CLANK
SIZZLE
SIZZLE
CHIE, DID YOU CLEAN YOUR ROOM?
I APOLOGIZE FOR MY MESSY DAUGHTER...
I WAS A LITTLE NERVOUS, BUT...
HEY, ONEE-CHAN'S ROOM IS WORSE!
I ALMOST GOT LOST IN THERE YESTERDAY.
Oh my!
GRIN
SIZZLE
SIZZLE
SIZZLE
HEY! SHUT UP!!
COME TO THINK OF IT...
BESIDES NANA'S, I HAVEN'T STAYED OVER AT A FRIEND'S HOUSE SINCE GRADE SCHOOL.
PHEW, THE BATH WAS HOT!
AND I ATE TOO MUCH AT SUPPER! I'M GONNA BURST!
CHIE'S ROOM

CHAPTER 10 BEFORE THE STORM

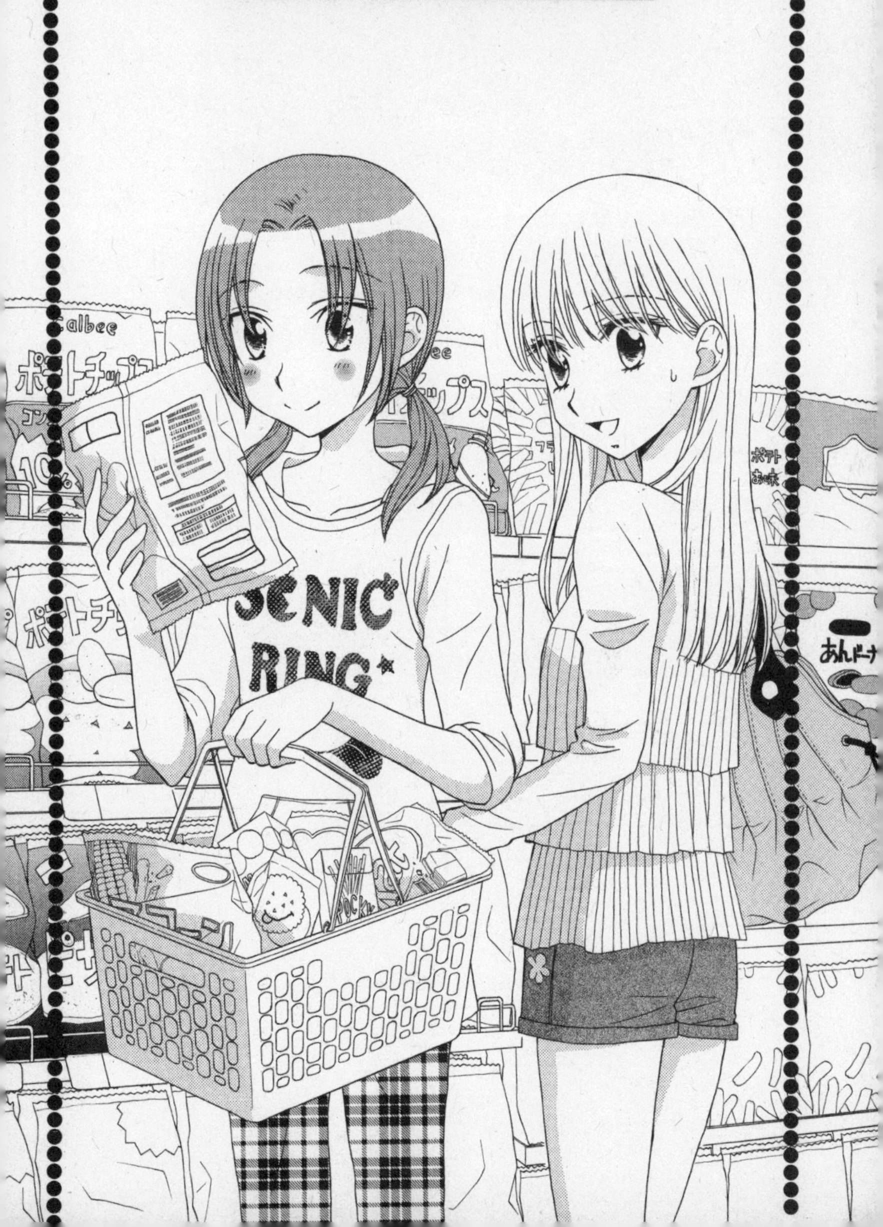
SENIC
RING

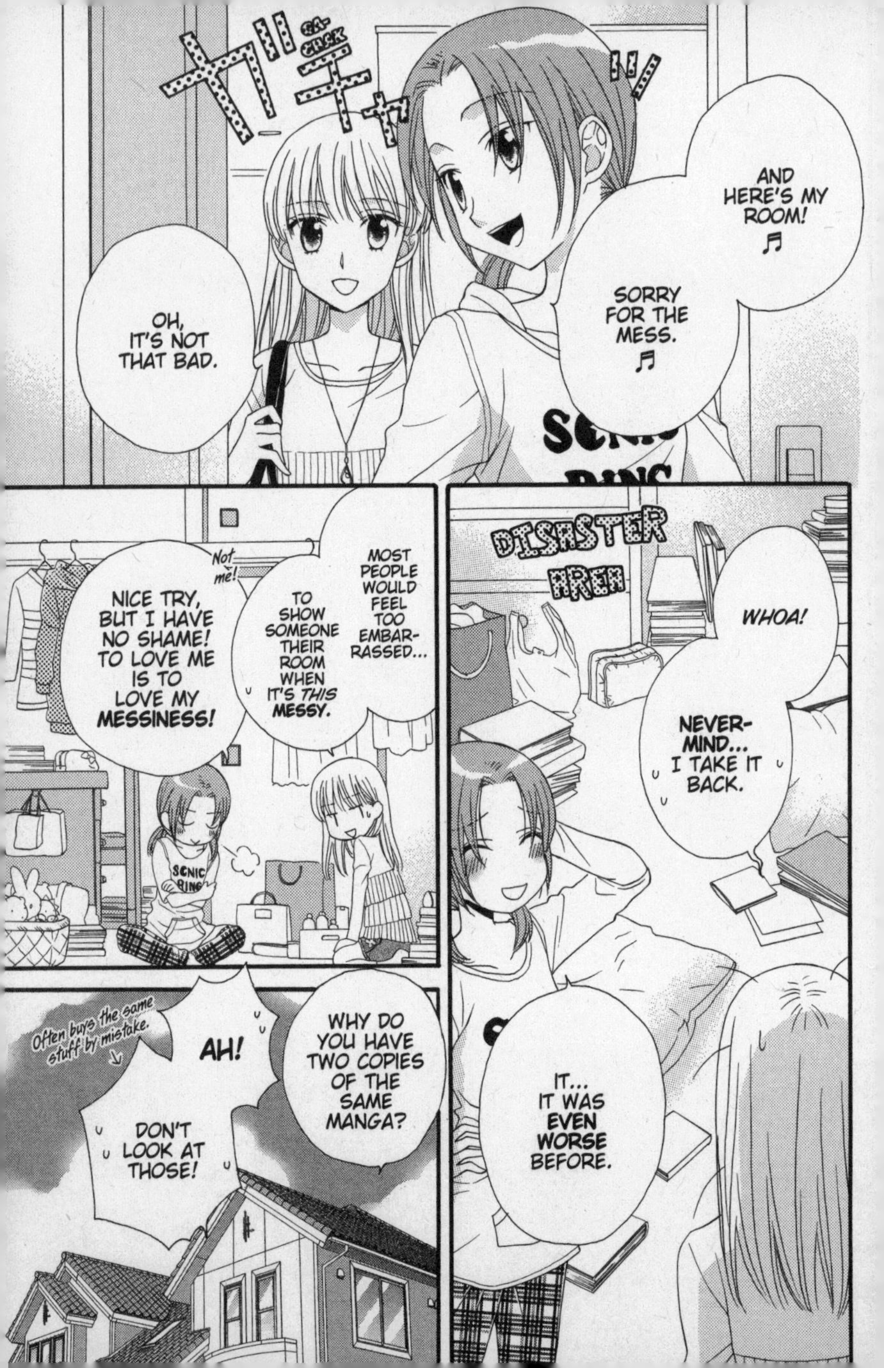
GA-CHICK
AND HERE'S MY ROOM! ♫
SORRY FOR THE MESS. ♫
OH, IT'S NOT THAT BAD.
DISASTER AREA
WHOA!
NEVER-MIND... I TAKE IT BACK.
IT... IT WAS EVEN WORSE BEFORE.
MOST PEOPLE WOULD FEEL TOO EMBARRASSED...
TO SHOW SOMEONE THEIR ROOM WHEN IT'S *THIS* MESSY.
Not me!
NICE TRY, BUT I HAVE NO SHAME! TO LOVE ME IS TO LOVE MY MESSINESS!
WHY DO YOU HAVE TWO COPIES OF THE SAME MANGA?
AH!
DON'T LOOK AT THOSE!
Often buys the same stuff by mistake.

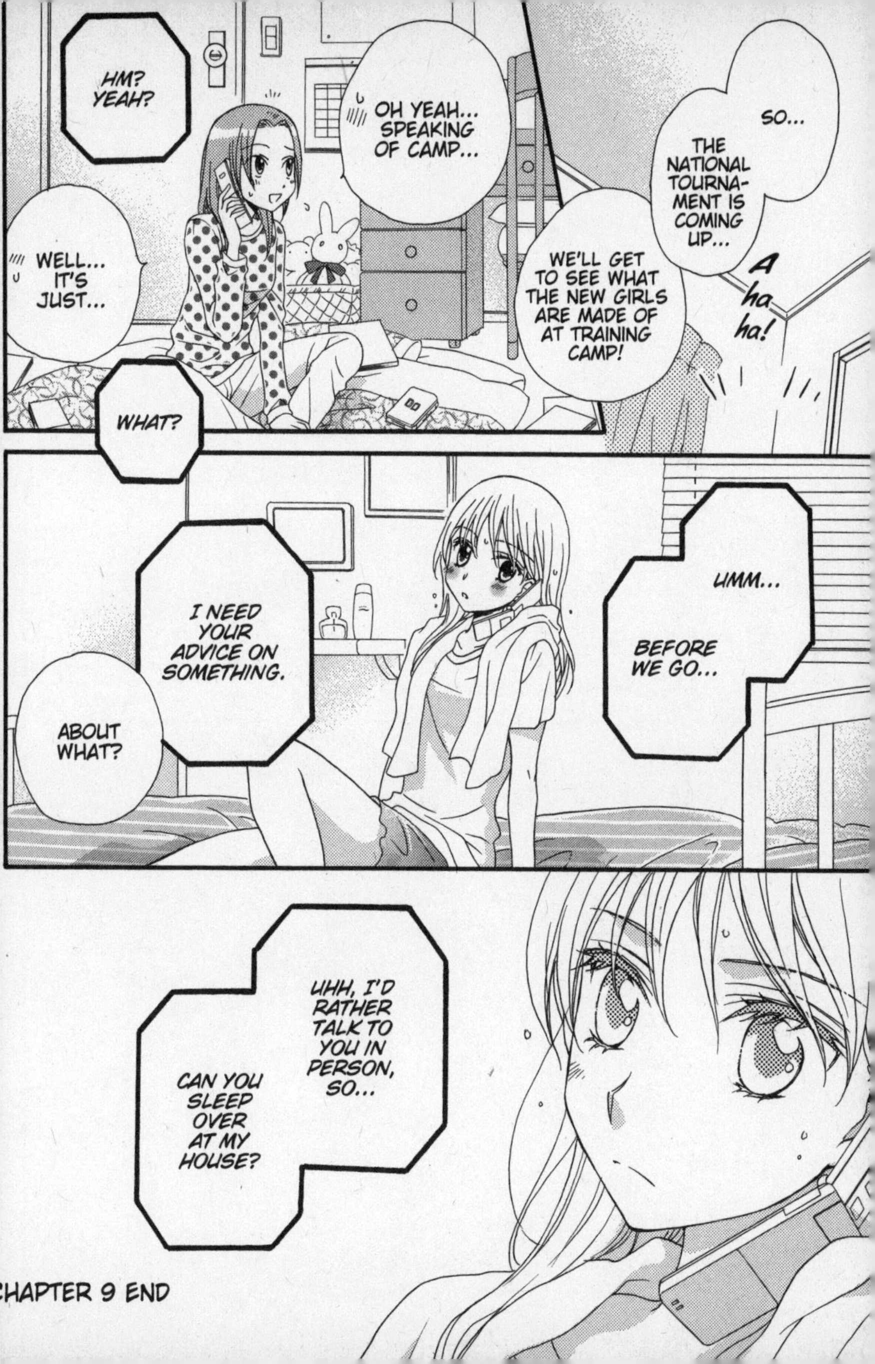
SO...
THE NATIONAL TOURNAMENT IS COMING UP...
WE'LL GET TO SEE WHAT THE NEW GIRLS ARE MADE OF AT TRAINING CAMP!
A ha ha!
OH YEAH... SPEAKING OF CAMP...
HM? YEAH?
WELL... IT'S JUST...
WHAT?
UMM...
BEFORE WE GO...
I NEED YOUR ADVICE ON SOMETHING.
ABOUT WHAT?
UHH, I'D RATHER TALK TO YOU IN PERSON, SO...
CAN YOU SLEEP OVER AT MY HOUSE?

CHAPTER 9 END

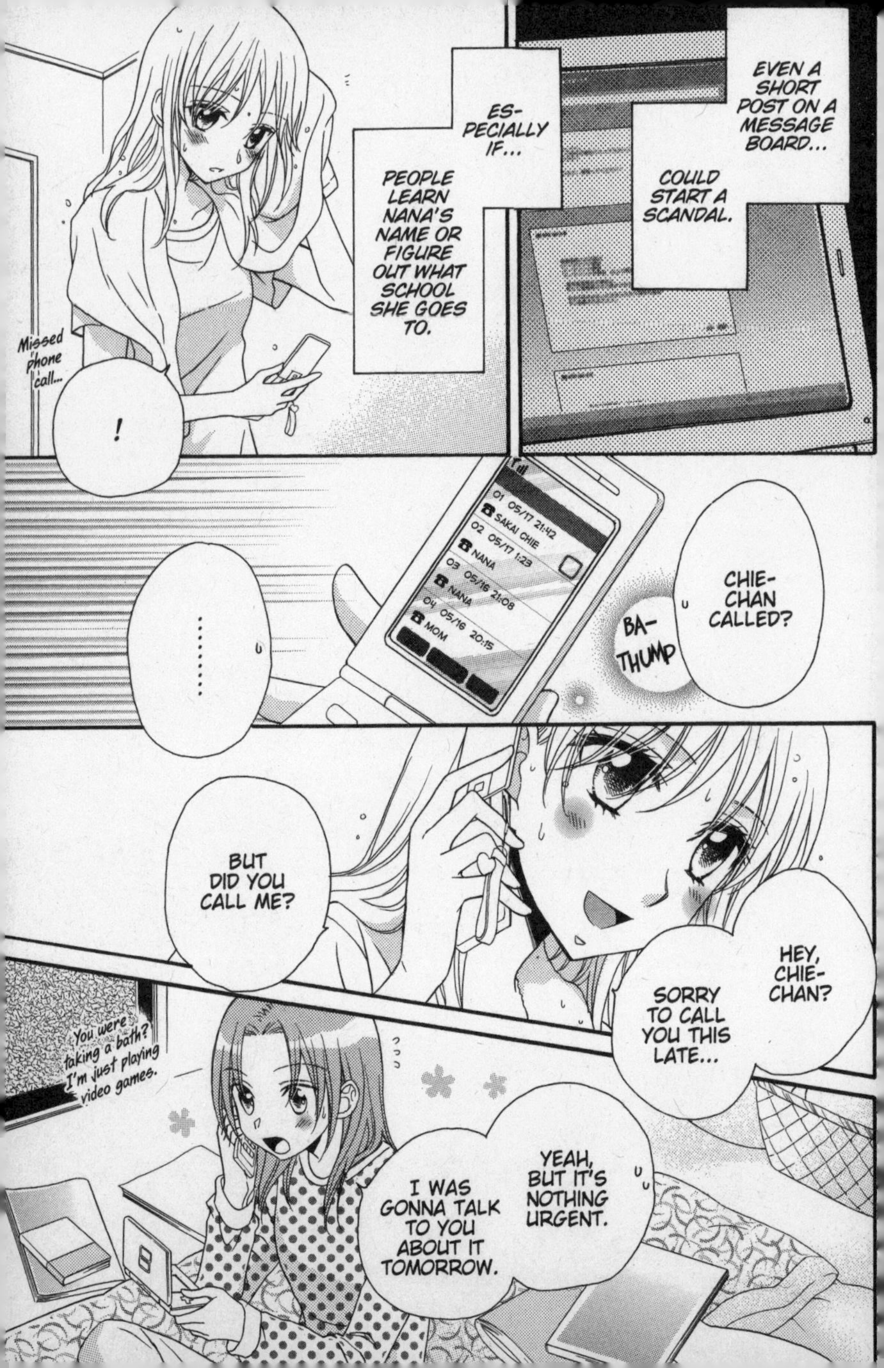
EVEN A SHORT POST ON A MESSAGE BOARD...
COULD START A SCANDAL.
ES-PECIALLY IF...
PEOPLE LEARN NANA'S NAME OR FIGURE OUT WHAT SCHOOL SHE GOES TO.
Missed phone call...
!
01 05/17 21:42
SAKAI CHIE
02 05/17 1:23
NANA
03 05/16 21:08
NANA
04 05/16 20:15
MOM
CHIE-CHAN CALLED?
BA-THUMP
......
HEY, CHIE-CHAN?
SORRY TO CALL YOU THIS LATE...
BUT DID YOU CALL ME?
YEAH, BUT IT'S NOTHING URGENT.
I WAS GONNA TALK TO YOU ABOUT IT TOMORROW.
You were taking a bath? I'm just playing video games.

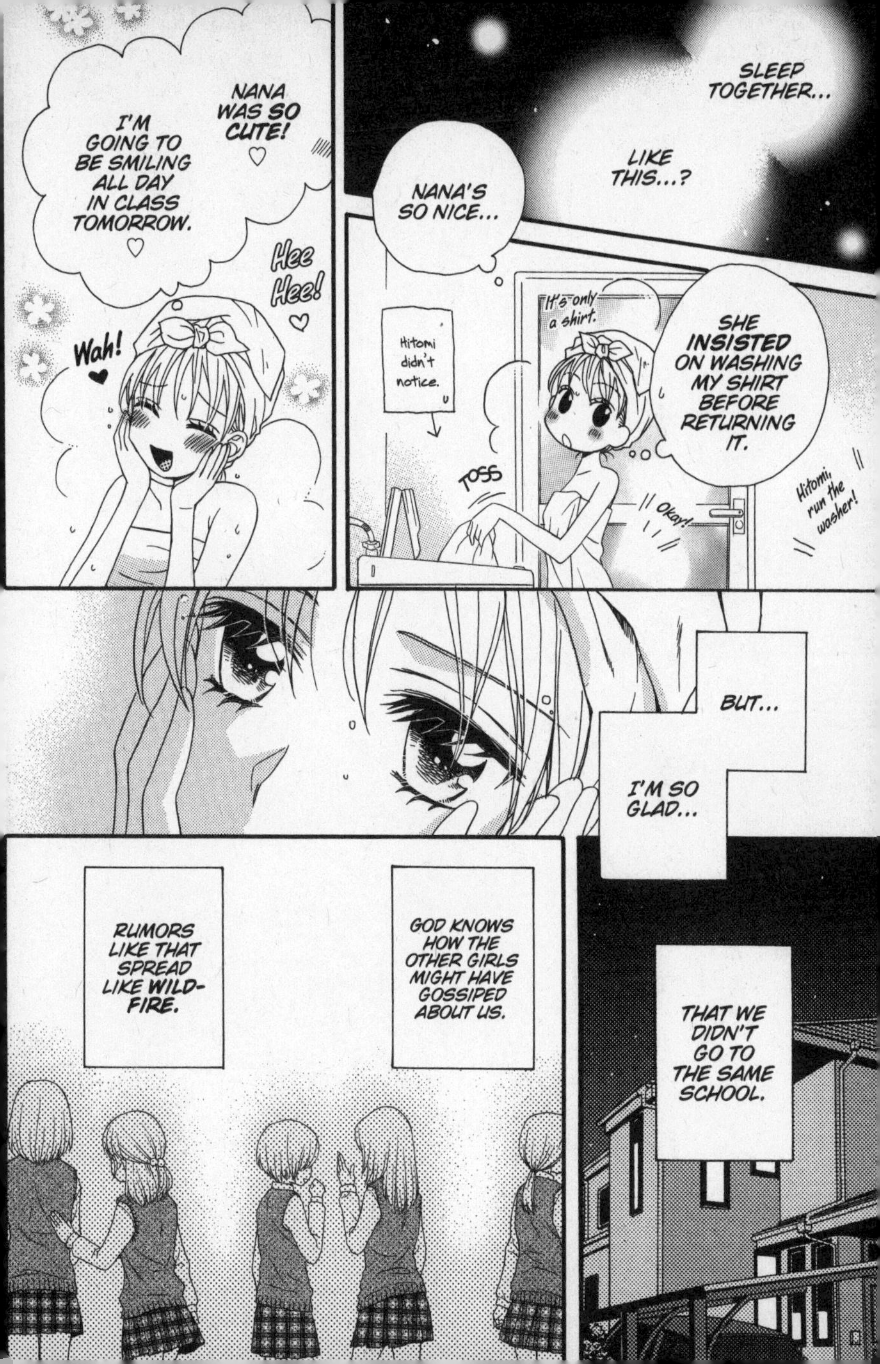
SLEEP TOGETHER...
LIKE THIS...?
NANA'S SO NICE...
SHE INSISTED ON WASHING MY SHIRT BEFORE RETURNING IT.
Hitomi, run the washer!
Okay!
It's only a shirt.
Hitomi didn't notice.
TOSS
NANA WAS SO CUTE!
I'M GOING TO BE SMILING ALL DAY IN CLASS TOMORROW.
Hee Hee!
Wah!
BUT...
I'M SO GLAD...
THAT WE DIDN'T GO TO THE SAME SCHOOL.
GOD KNOWS HOW THE OTHER GIRLS MIGHT HAVE GOSSIPED ABOUT US.
RUMORS LIKE THAT SPREAD LIKE WILD-FIRE.

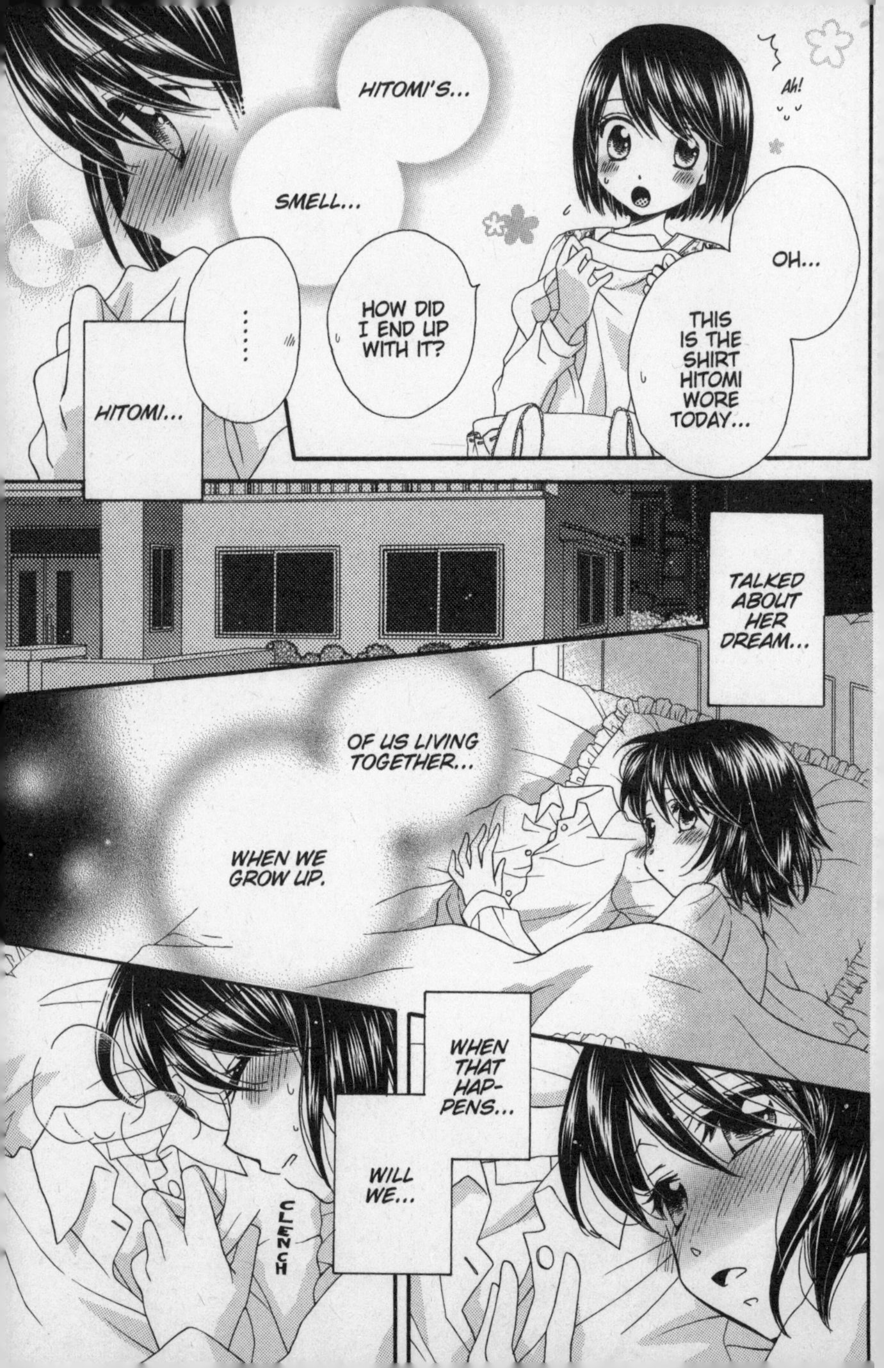

AH!
OH...
THIS IS THE SHIRT HITOMI WORE TODAY...
HOW DID I END UP WITH IT?
......
HITOMI'S...
SMELL...
HITOMI...
TALKED ABOUT HER DREAM...
OF US LIVING TOGETHER...
WHEN WE GROW UP.
WHEN THAT HAP-PENS...
WILL WE...
CLENCH

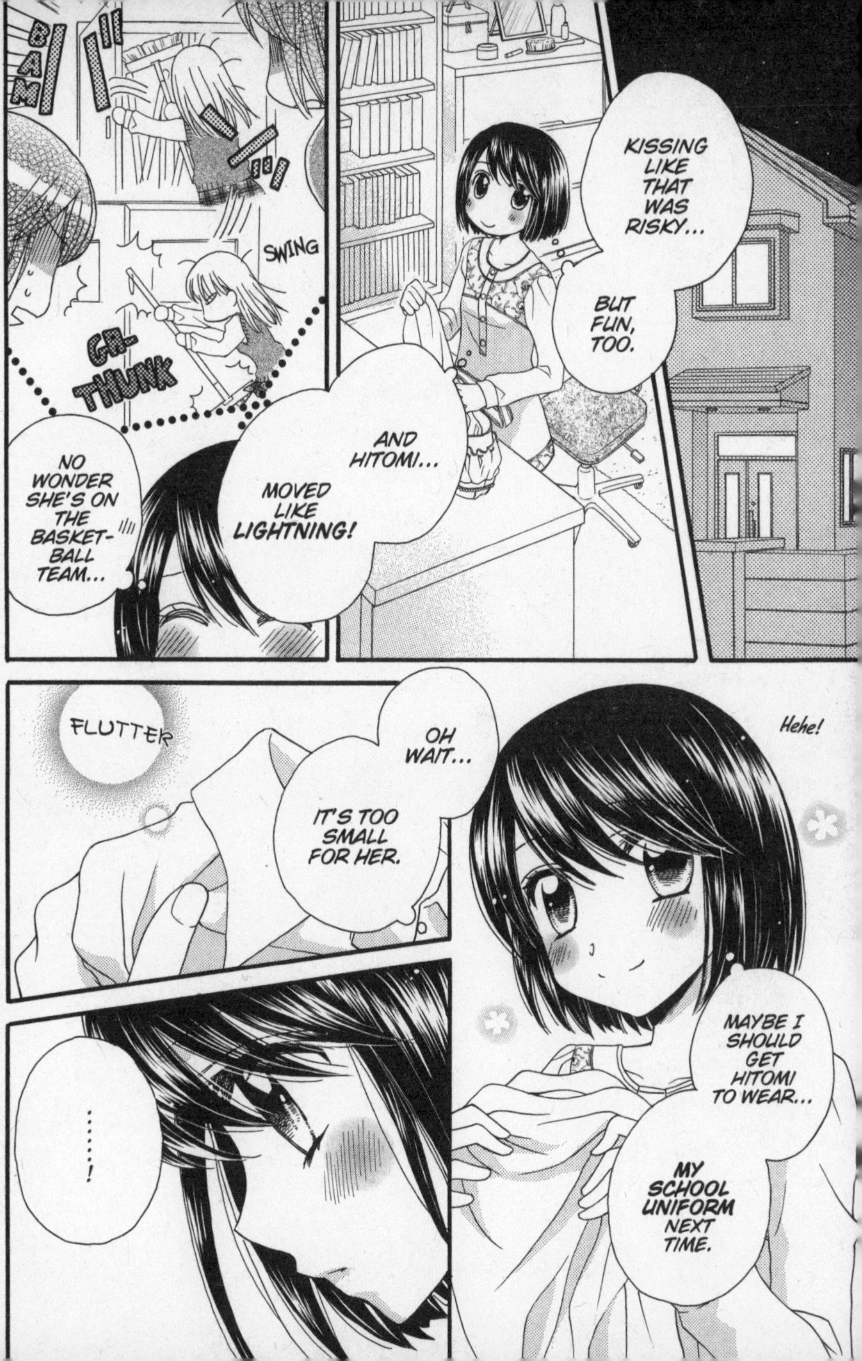
KISSING LIKE THAT WAS RISKY...
BUT FUN, TOO.
AND HITOMI...
MOVED LIKE LIGHTNING!
BAM
SWING
GA-THUNK
NO WONDER SHE'S ON THE BASKET-BALL TEAM...
Hehe!
MAYBE I SHOULD GET HITOMI TO WEAR...
MY SCHOOL UNIFORM NEXT TIME.
FLUTTER
OH WAIT...
IT'S TOO SMALL FOR HER.
......!

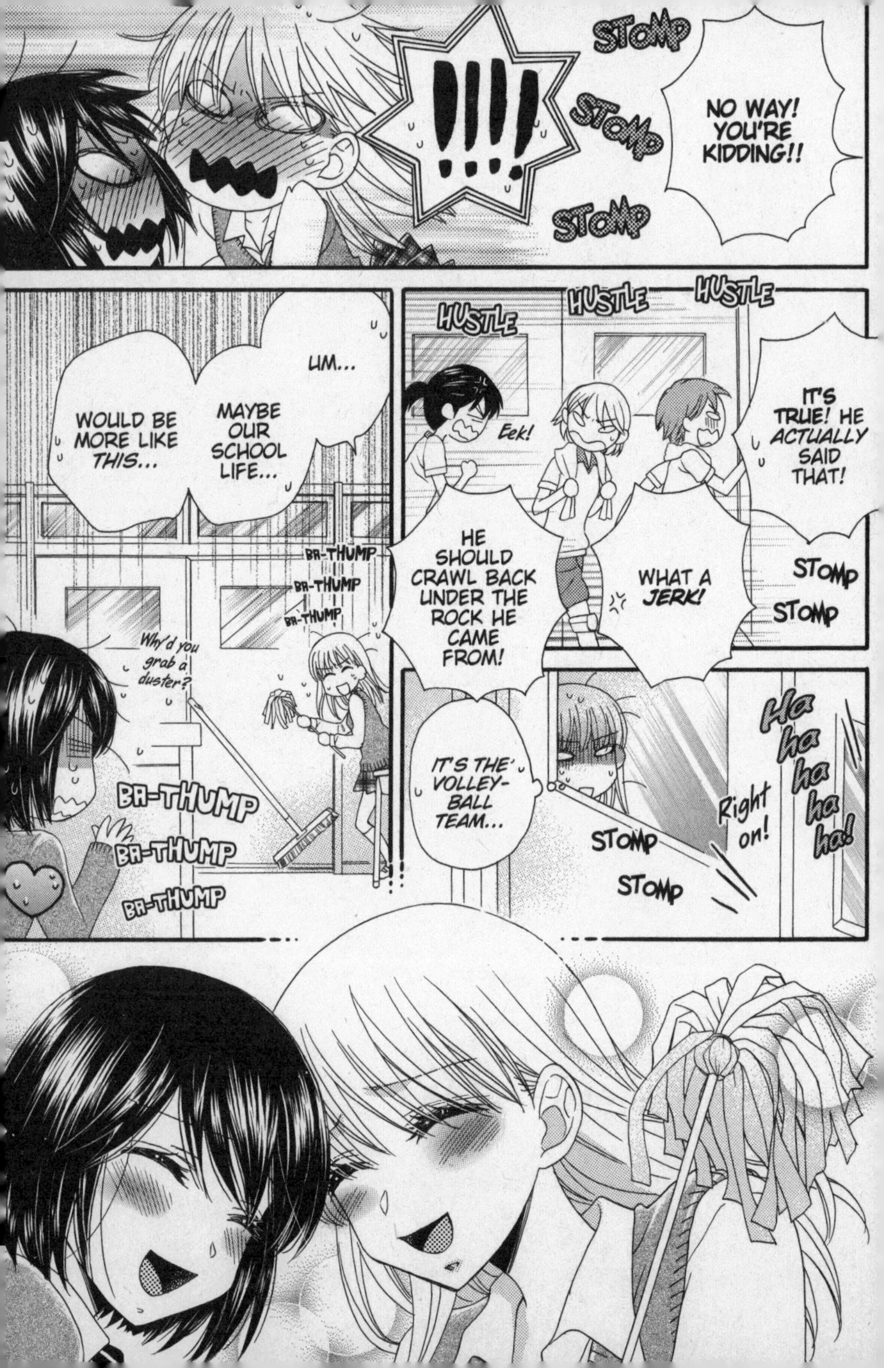
NO WAY! YOU'RE KIDDING!!
STOMP
STOMP
STOMP
!!!!
HUSTLE
HUSTLE
HUSTLE
IT'S TRUE! HE ACTUALLY SAID THAT!
WHAT A JERK!
Eek!
HE SHOULD CRAWL BACK UNDER THE ROCK HE CAME FROM!
STOMP
STOMP
Ha ha ha ha ha!
Right on!
IT'S THE VOLLEY-BALL TEAM...
STOMP
STOMP
UM...
MAYBE OUR SCHOOL LIFE...
WOULD BE MORE LIKE THIS...
BA-THUMP
BA-THUMP
BA-THUMP
Why'd you grab a duster?
BA-THUMP
BA-THUMP
BA-THUMP

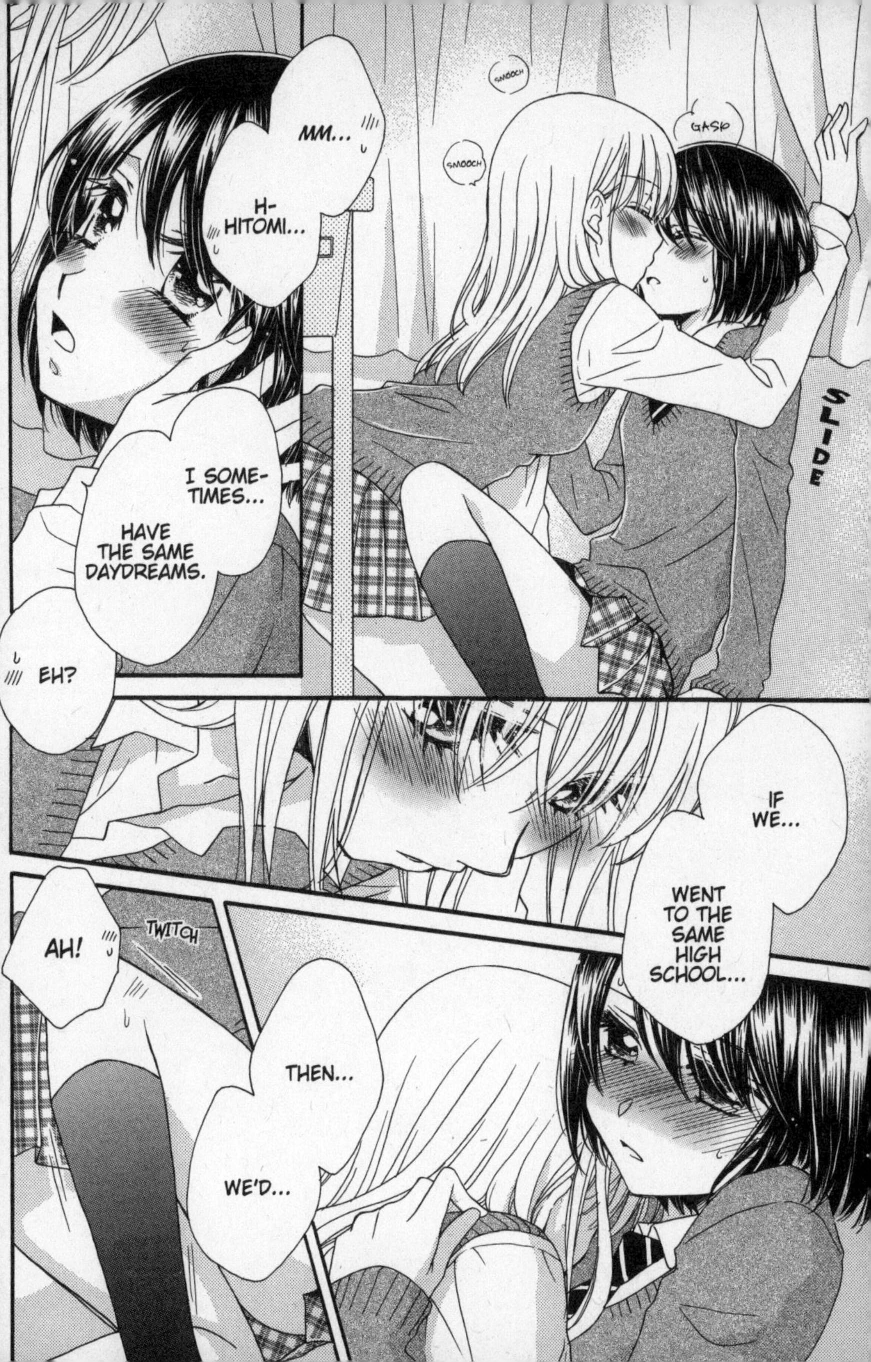
SMOOCH
GASP
SMOOCH
SLIDE
MM...
H-HITOMI...
I SOME-TIMES...
HAVE THE SAME DAYDREAMS.
EH?
IF WE...
WENT TO THE SAME HIGH SCHOOL...
THEN...
WE'D...
AH!
TWITCH

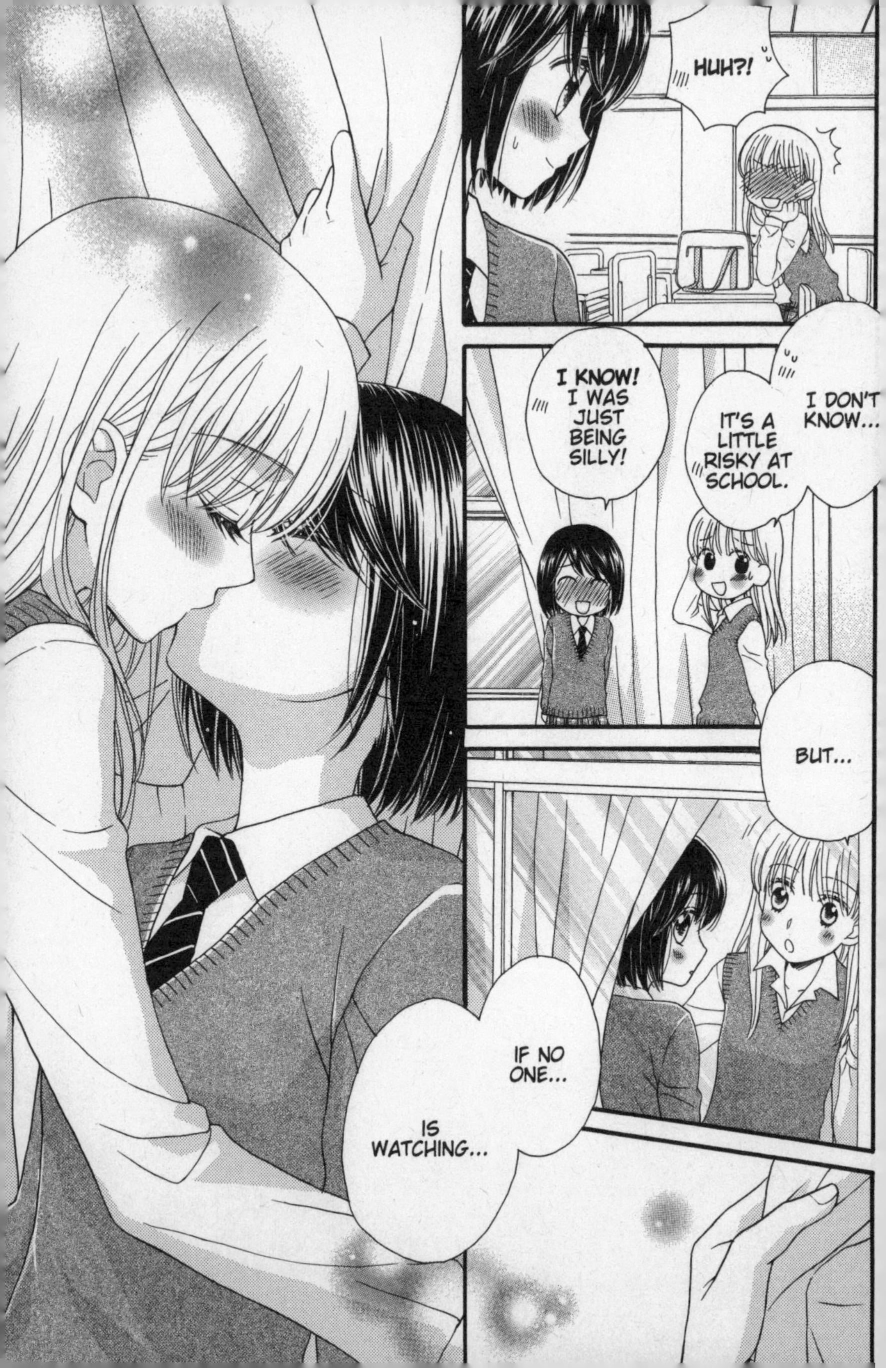
HUH?!
I DON'T KNOW...
IT'S A LITTLE RISKY AT SCHOOL.
I KNOW! I WAS JUST BEING SILLY!
BUT...
IF NO ONE...
IS WATCHING...

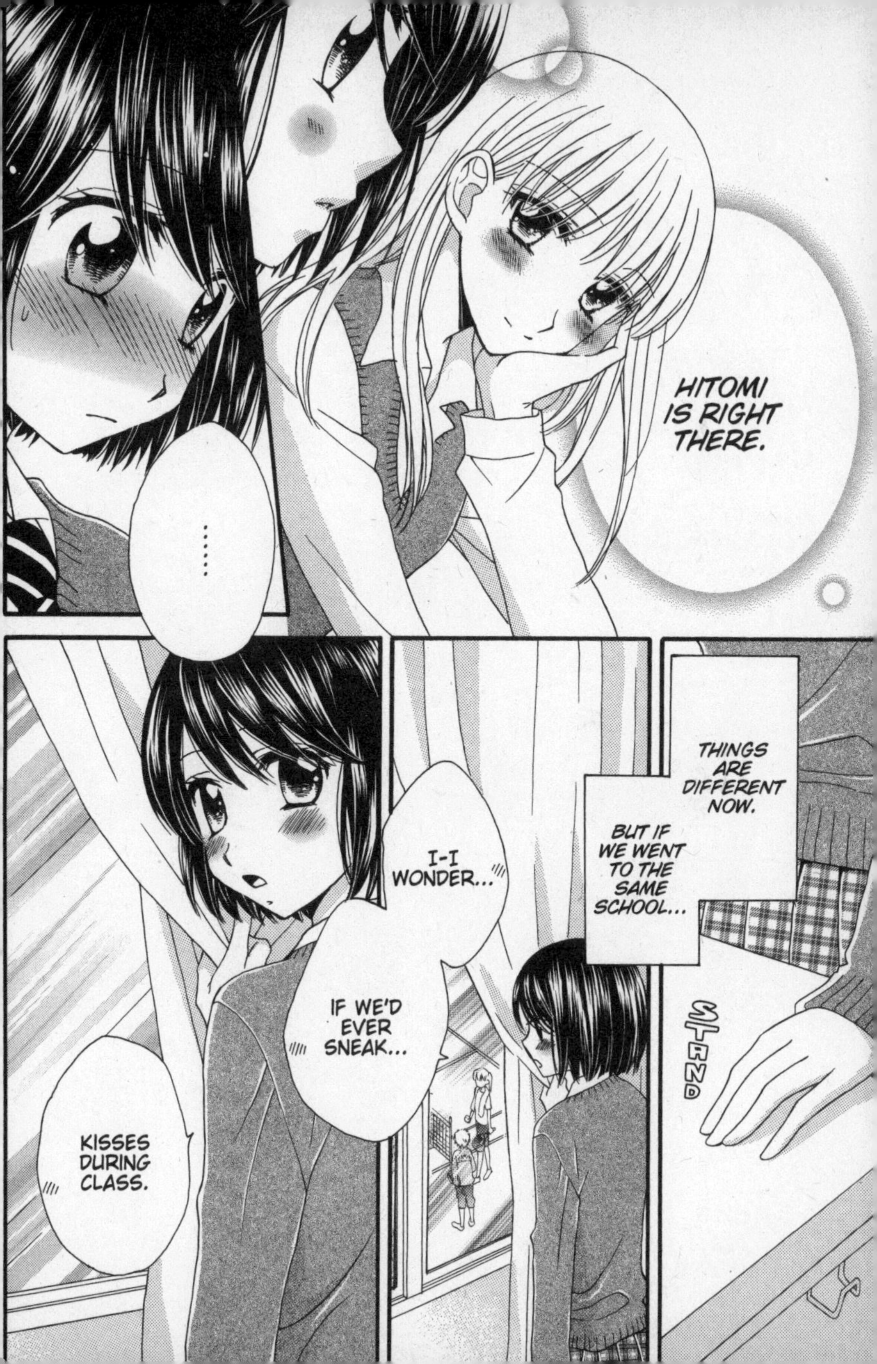
HITOMI IS RIGHT THERE.
......
THINGS ARE DIFFERENT NOW.
BUT IF WE WENT TO THE SAME SCHOOL...
STAND
I-I WONDER...
IF WE'D EVER SNEAK...
KISSES DURING CLASS.

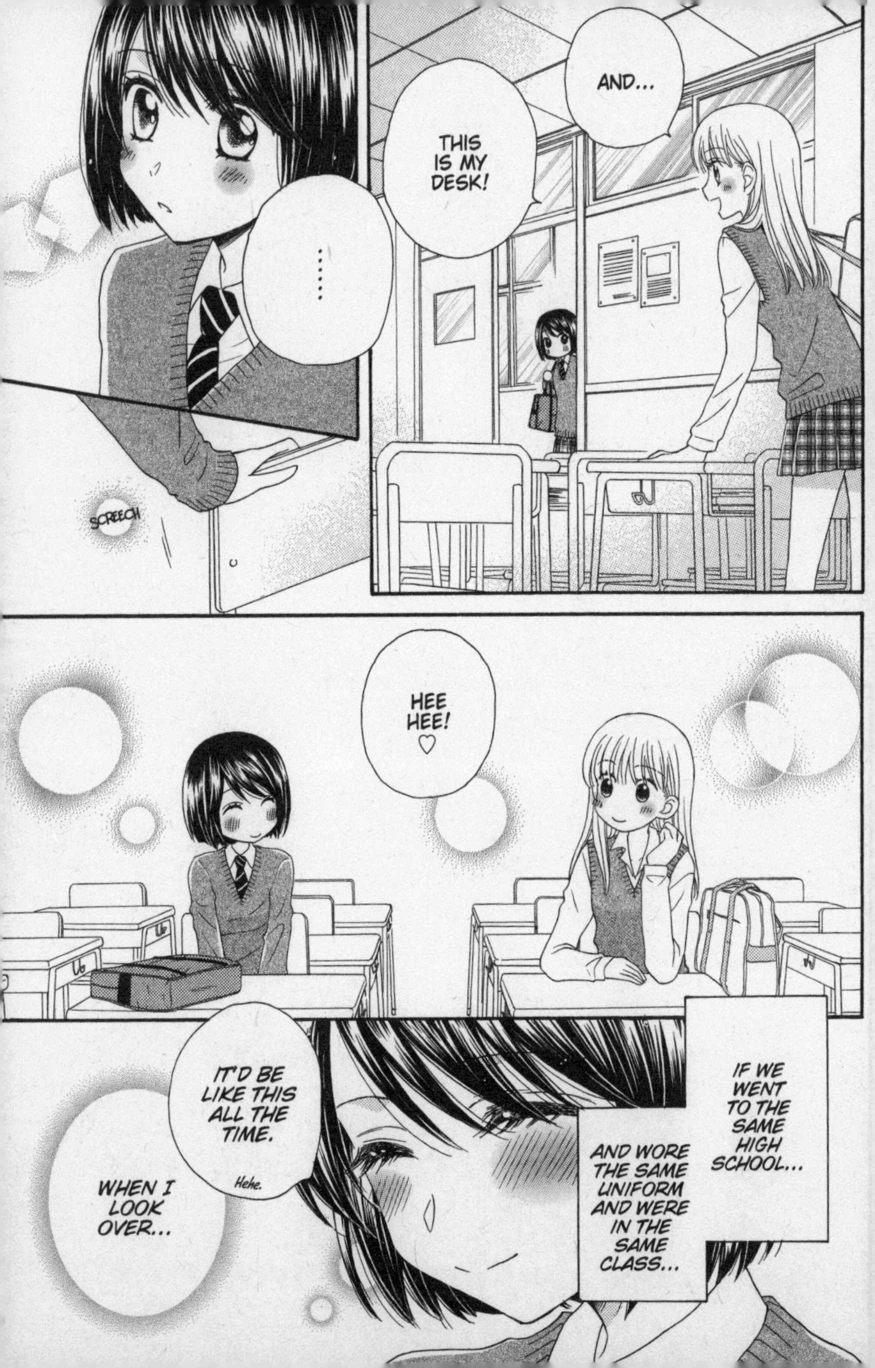
AND...
THIS IS MY DESK!
......
SCREECH
HEE HEE! ♡
IF WE WENT TO THE SAME HIGH SCHOOL...
AND WORE THE SAME UNIFORM AND WERE IN THE SAME CLASS...
WHEN I LOOK OVER...
IT'D BE LIKE THIS ALL THE TIME.
Hehe.

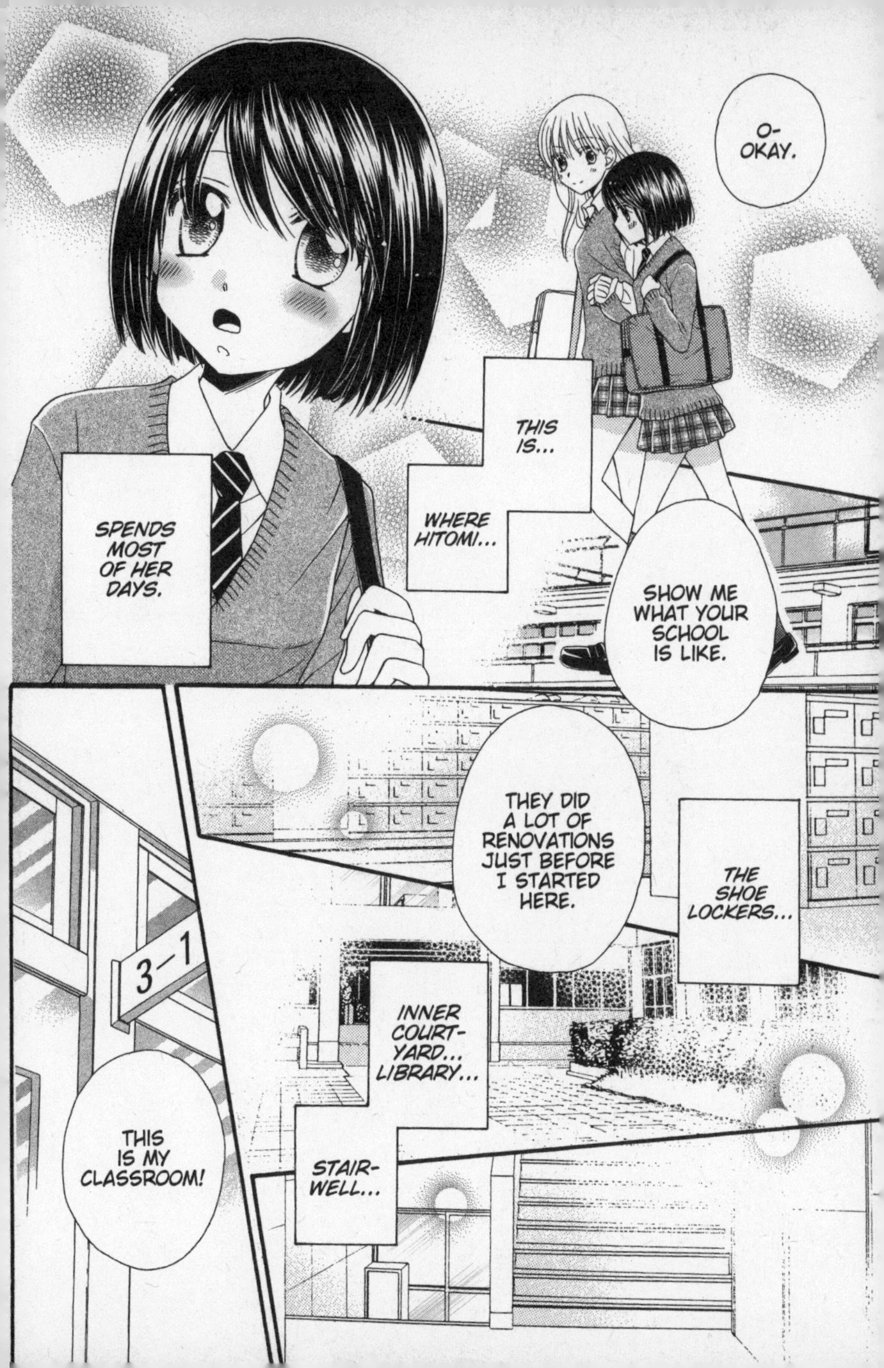
O-OKAY.
SHOW ME WHAT YOUR SCHOOL IS LIKE.
THIS IS...
WHERE HITOMI...
SPENDS MOST OF HER DAYS.
THE SHOE LOCKERS...
THEY DID A LOT OF RENOVATIONS JUST BEFORE I STARTED HERE.
INNER COURT-YARD... LIBRARY...
STAIR-WELL...
3-1
THIS IS MY CLASSROOM!

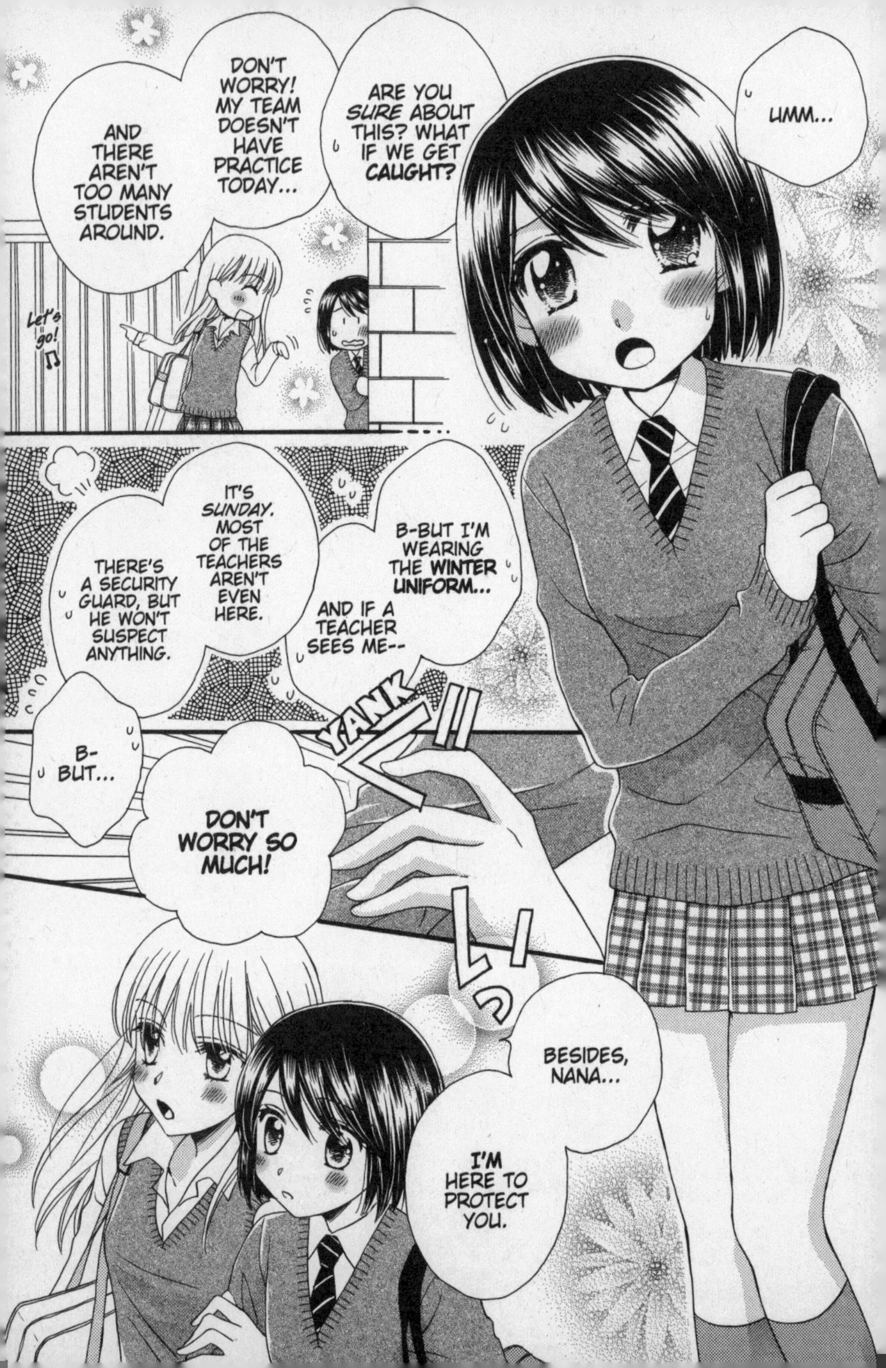
UMM...
ARE YOU SURE ABOUT THIS? WHAT IF WE GET CAUGHT?
DON'T WORRY! MY TEAM DOESN'T HAVE PRACTICE TODAY...
AND THERE AREN'T TOO MANY STUDENTS AROUND.
Let's go! ♫
B-BUT I'M WEARING THE WINTER UNIFORM...
AND IF A TEACHER SEES ME--
IT'S SUNDAY. MOST OF THE TEACHERS AREN'T EVEN HERE.
THERE'S A SECURITY GUARD, BUT HE WON'T SUSPECT ANYTHING.
YANK
DON'T WORRY SO MUCH!
B- BUT...
BESIDES, NANA...
I'M HERE TO PROTECT YOU.

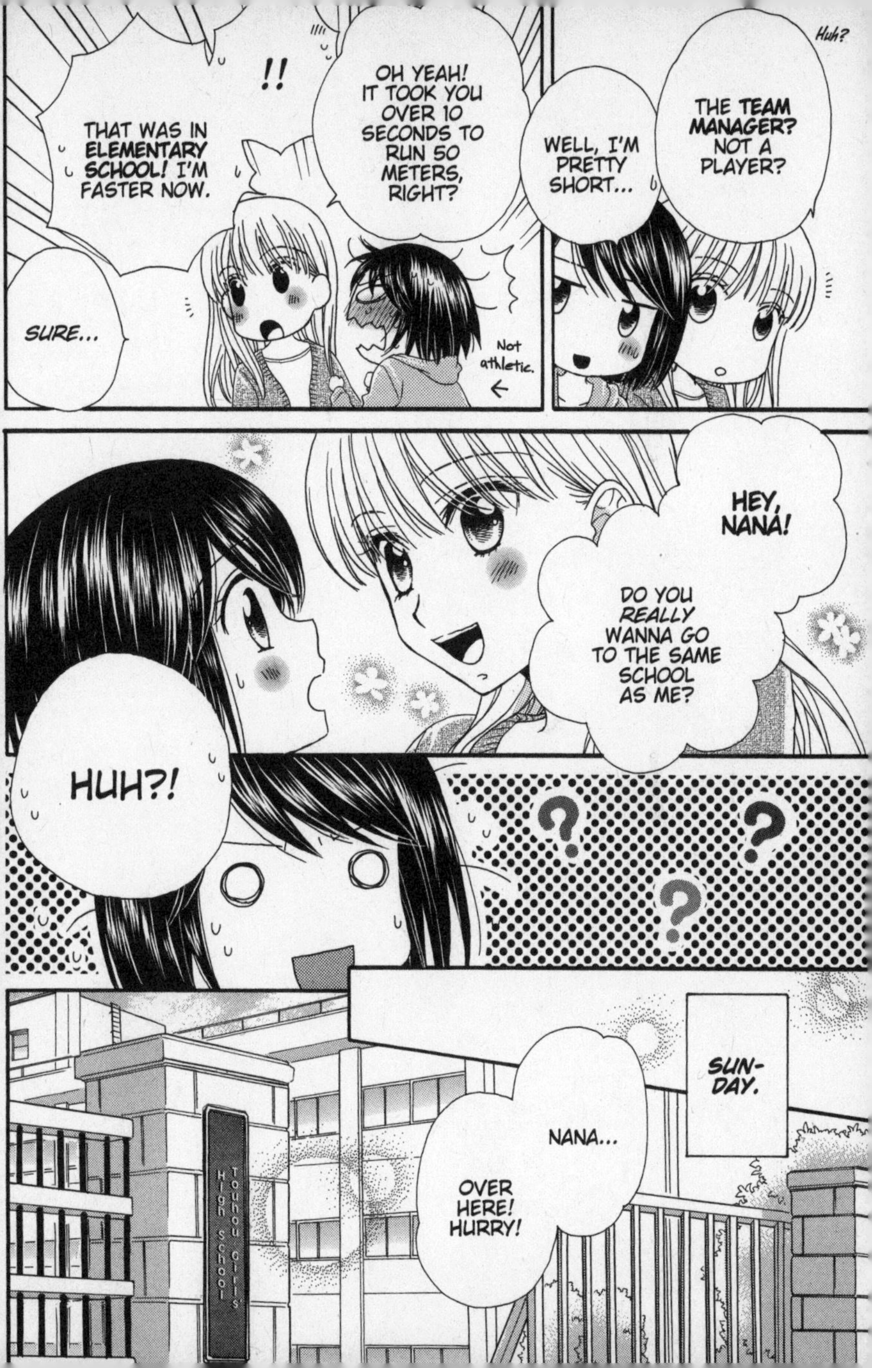
Huh?
THE TEAM MANAGER? NOT A PLAYER?
WELL, I'M PRETTY SHORT...
OH YEAH! IT TOOK YOU OVER 10 SECONDS TO RUN 50 METERS, RIGHT?
!!
THAT WAS IN ELEMENTARY SCHOOL! I'M FASTER NOW.
Not athletic.
SURE...
HEY, NANA!
DO YOU REALLY WANNA GO TO THE SAME SCHOOL AS ME?
HUH?!
SUN-DAY.
NANA...
OVER HERE! HURRY!
Touhou Girls High School

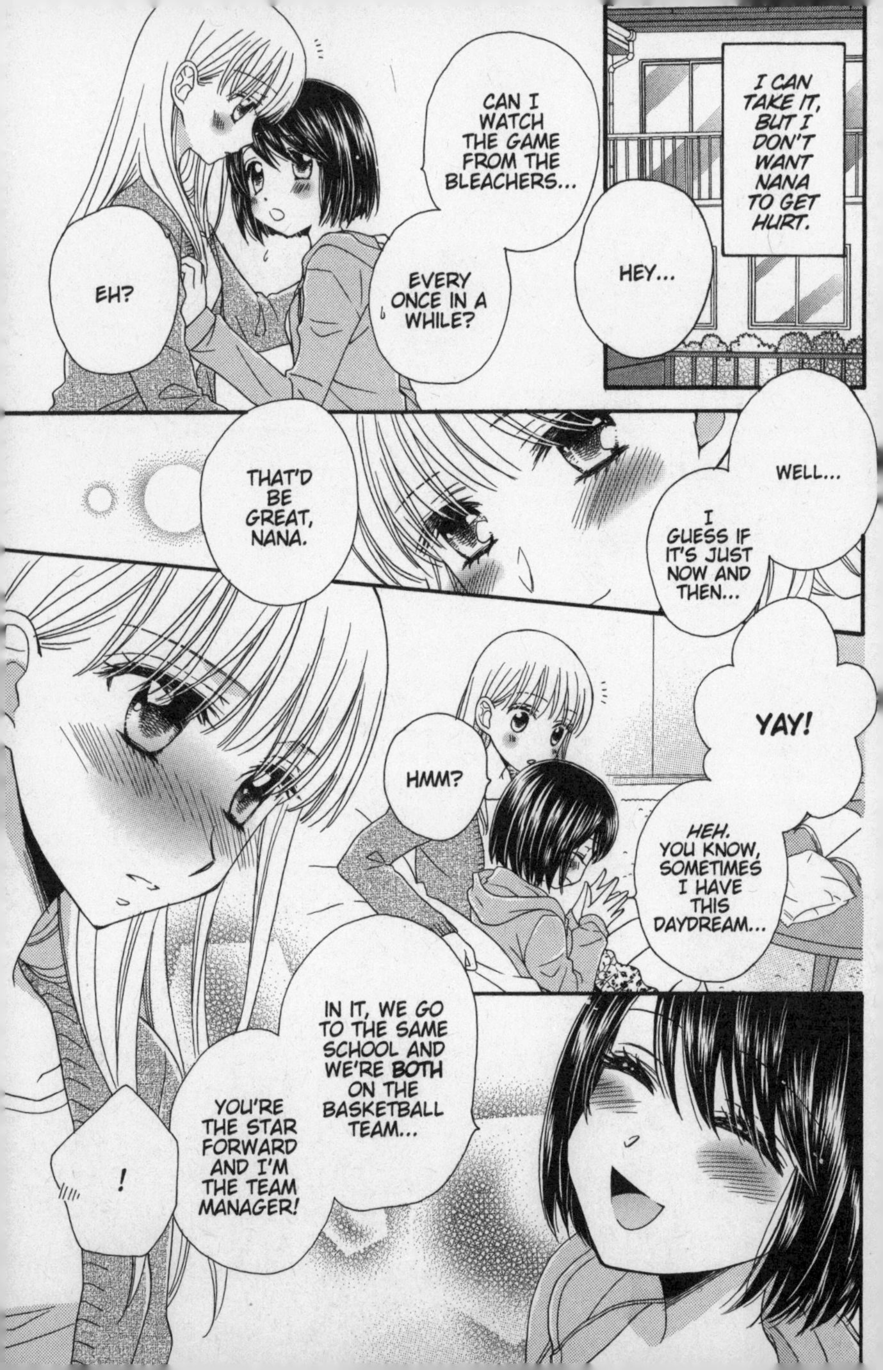
I CAN TAKE IT, BUT I DON'T WANT NANA TO GET HURT.
HEY...
CAN I WATCH THE GAME FROM THE BLEACHERS...
EVERY ONCE IN A WHILE?
EH?
WELL...
I GUESS IF IT'S JUST NOW AND THEN...
THAT'D BE GREAT, NANA.
YAY!
HMM?
HEH. YOU KNOW, SOMETIMES I HAVE THIS DAYDREAM...
IN IT, WE GO TO THE SAME SCHOOL AND WE'RE BOTH ON THE BASKETBALL TEAM...
YOU'RE THE STAR FORWARD AND I'M THE TEAM MANAGER!
!

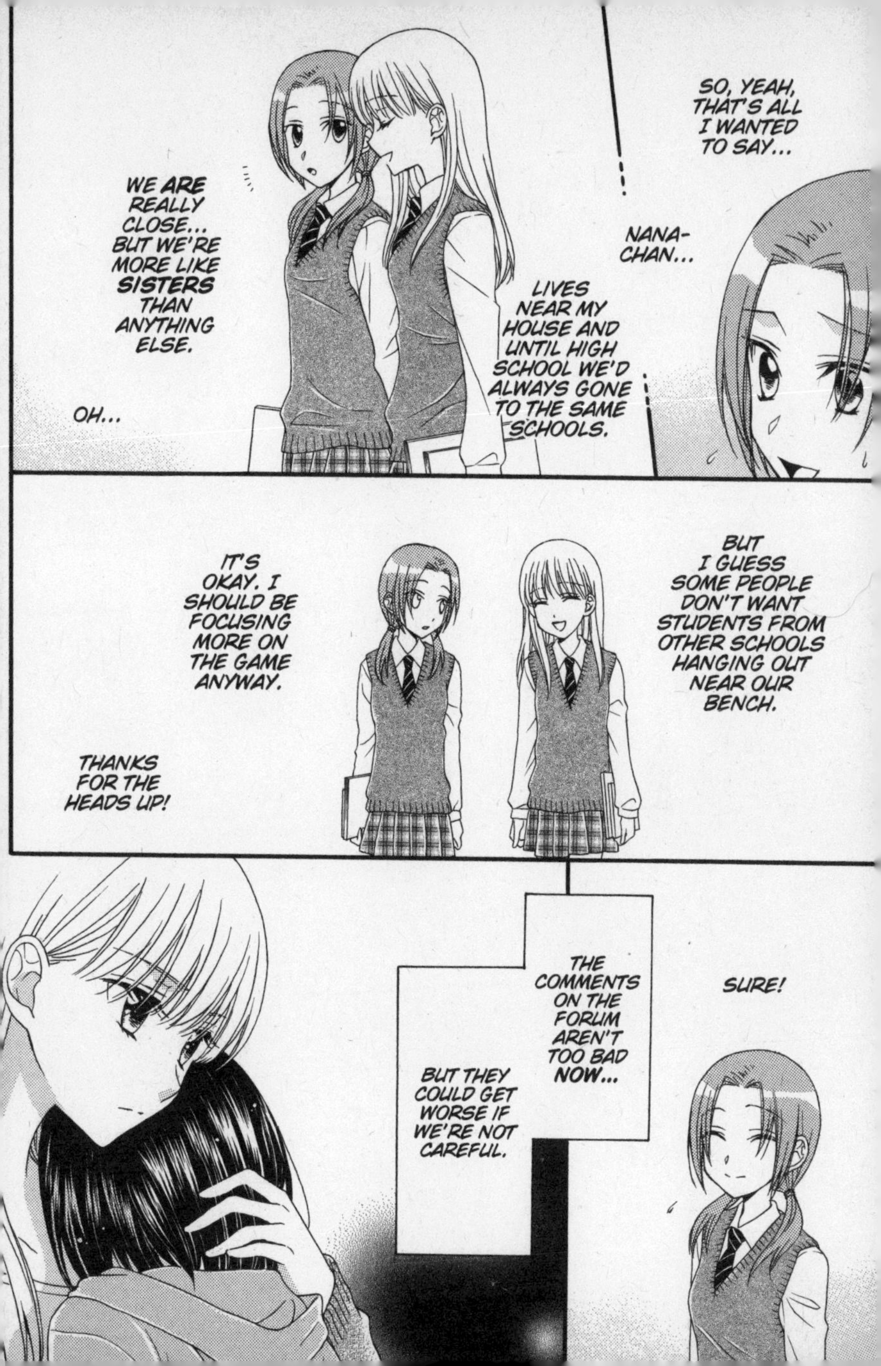
SO, YEAH, THAT'S ALL I WANTED TO SAY...
NANA-CHAN...
LIVES NEAR MY HOUSE AND UNTIL HIGH SCHOOL WE'D ALWAYS GONE TO THE SAME SCHOOLS.
WE ARE REALLY CLOSE... BUT WE'RE MORE LIKE SISTERS THAN ANYTHING ELSE.
OH...
BUT I GUESS SOME PEOPLE DON'T WANT STUDENTS FROM OTHER SCHOOLS HANGING OUT NEAR OUR BENCH.
IT'S OKAY. I SHOULD BE FOCUSING MORE ON THE GAME ANYWAY.
THANKS FOR THE HEADS UP!
SURE!
THE COMMENTS ON THE FORUM AREN'T TOO BAD NOW...
BUT THEY COULD GET WORSE IF WE'RE NOT CAREFUL.

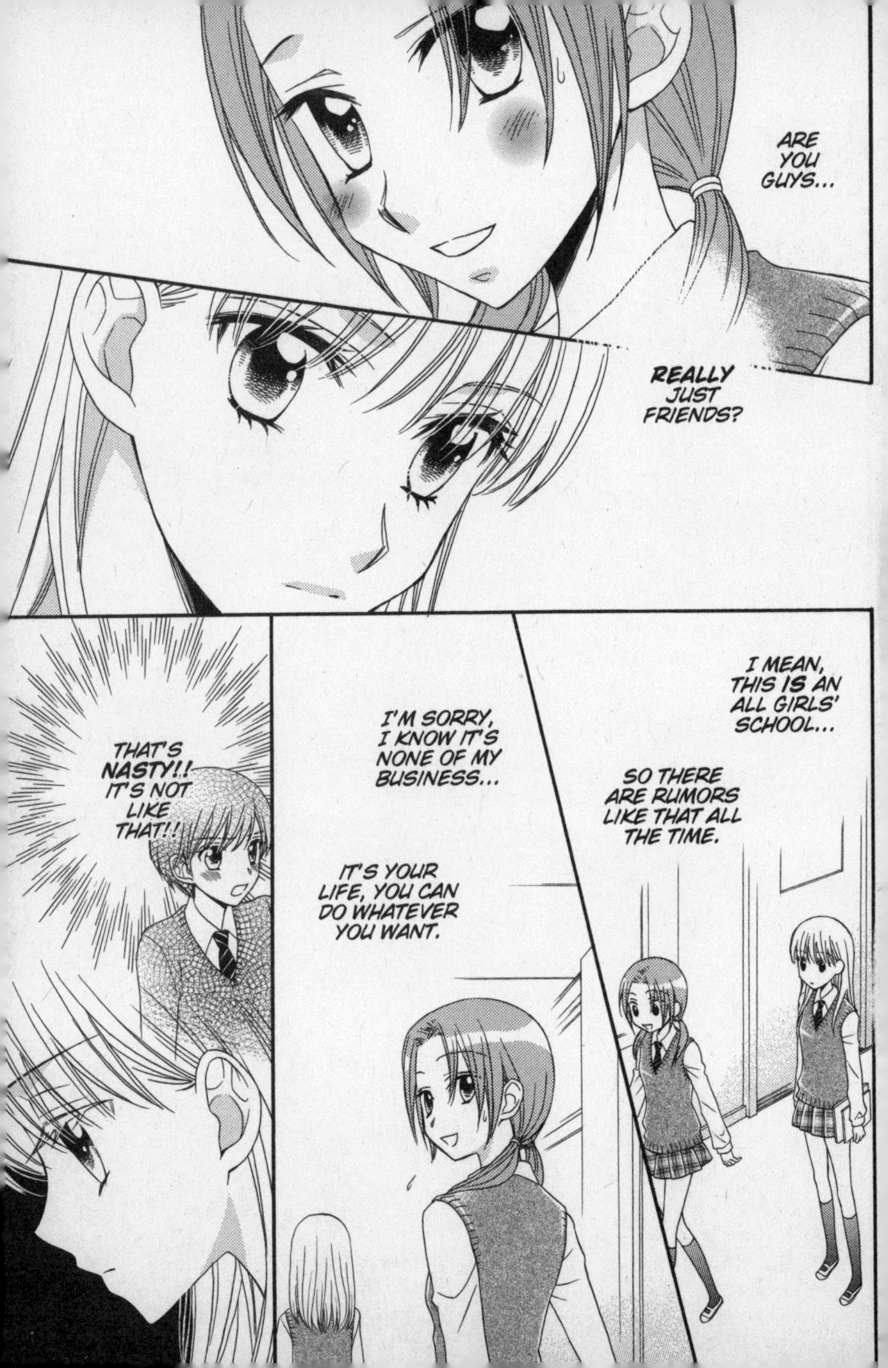
ARE YOU GUYS...
...REALLY JUST FRIENDS?
I MEAN, THIS **IS** AN ALL GIRLS' SCHOOL...
SO THERE ARE RUMORS LIKE THAT ALL THE TIME.
I'M SORRY, I KNOW IT'S NONE OF MY BUSINESS...
IT'S YOUR LIFE, YOU CAN DO WHATEVER YOU WANT.
THAT'S **NASTY!!** IT'S NOT LIKE THAT!!

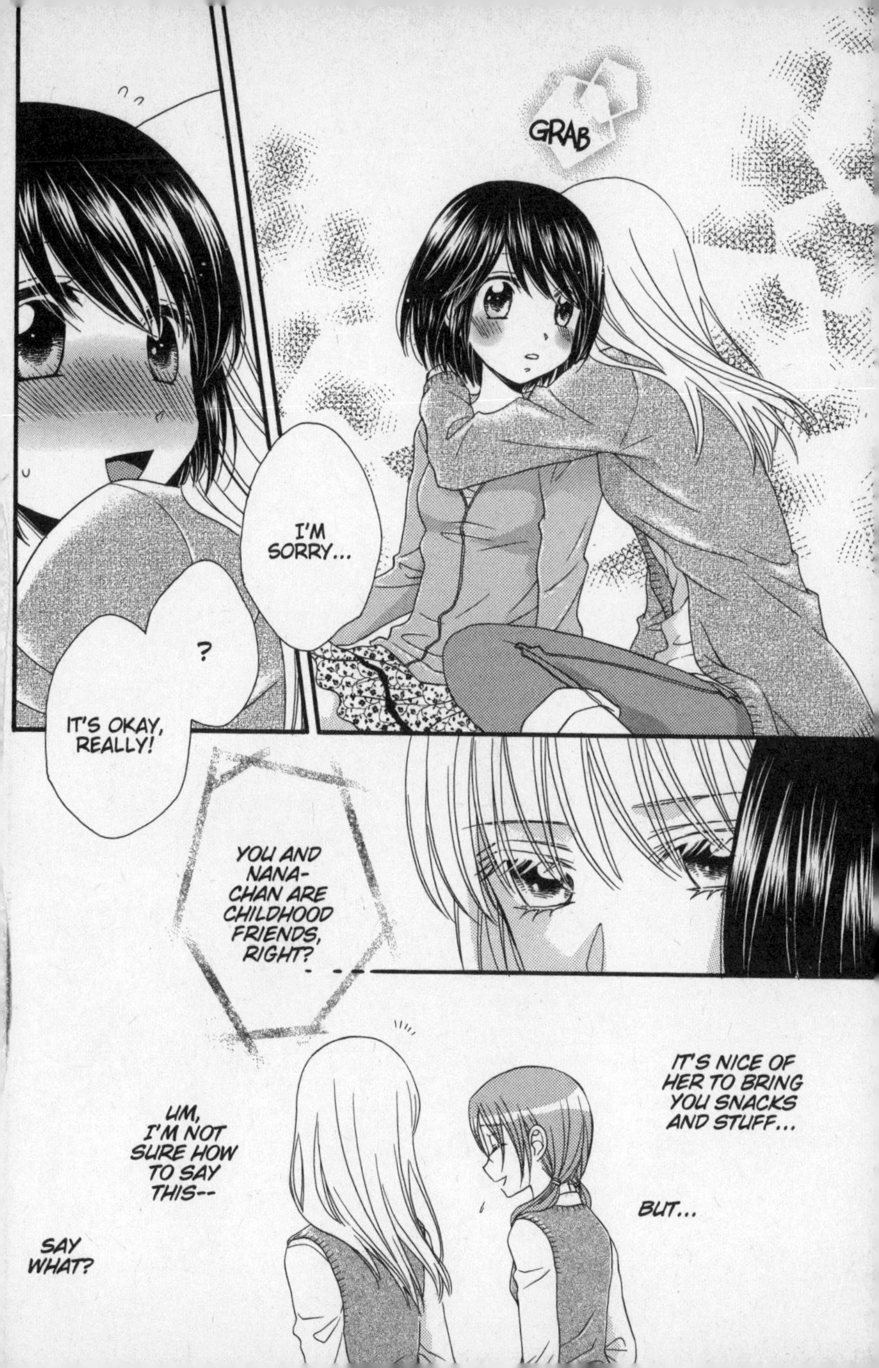
GRAB
I'M SORRY...
?
IT'S OKAY, REALLY!
YOU AND NANA-CHAN ARE CHILDHOOD FRIENDS, RIGHT?
IT'S NICE OF HER TO BRING YOU SNACKS AND STUFF...
BUT...
UM, I'M NOT SURE HOW TO SAY THIS--
SAY WHAT?

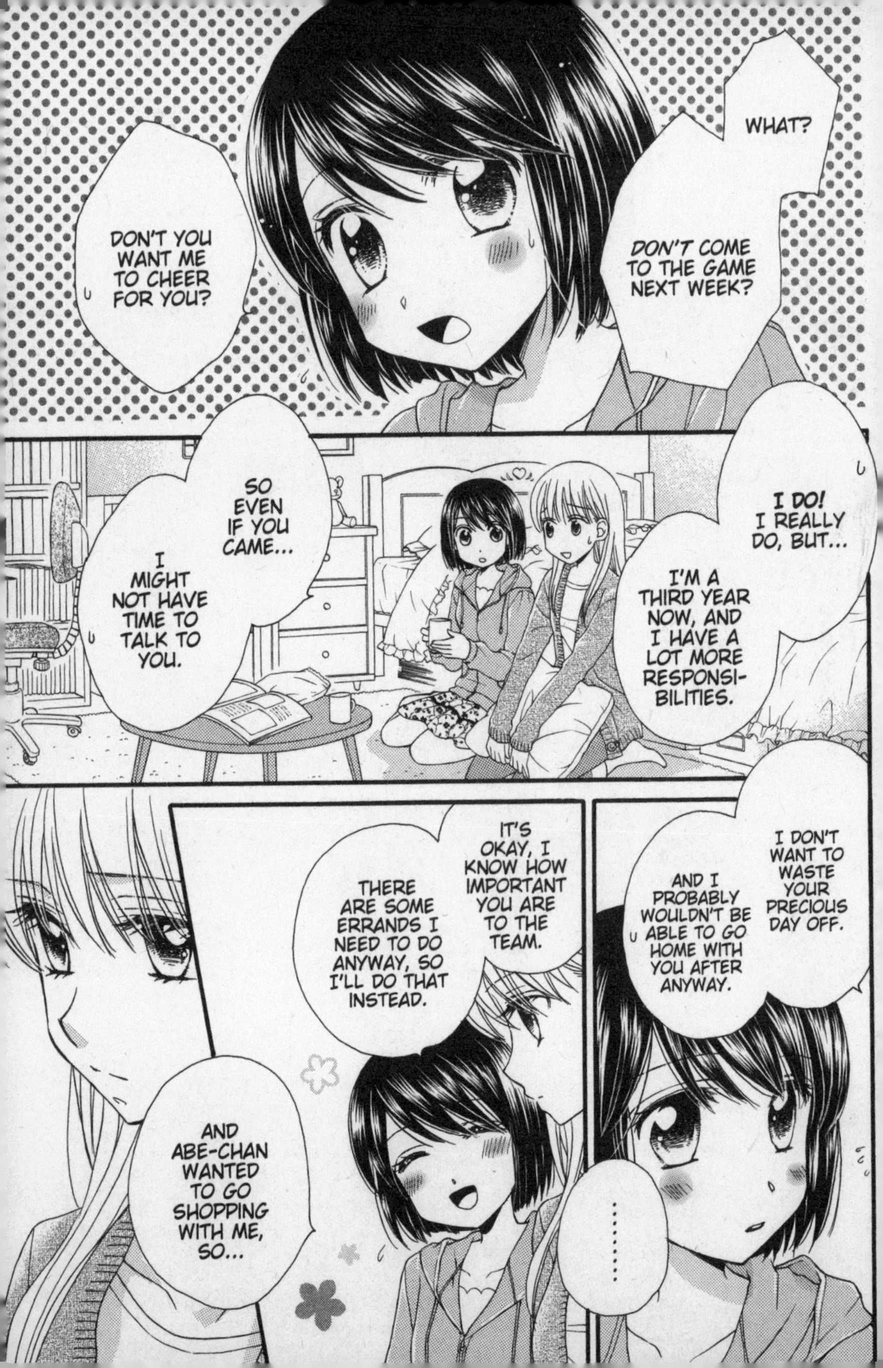
WHAT?
DON'T COME TO THE GAME NEXT WEEK?
DON'T YOU WANT ME TO CHEER FOR YOU?
I DO! I REALLY DO, BUT...
I'M A THIRD YEAR NOW, AND I HAVE A LOT MORE RESPONSIBILITIES.
SO EVEN IF YOU CAME...
I MIGHT NOT HAVE TIME TO TALK TO YOU.
I DON'T WANT TO WASTE YOUR PRECIOUS DAY OFF.
AND I PROBABLY WOULDN'T BE ABLE TO GO HOME WITH YOU AFTER ANYWAY.
......
IT'S OKAY, I KNOW HOW IMPORTANT YOU ARE TO THE TEAM.
THERE ARE SOME ERRANDS I NEED TO DO ANYWAY, SO I'LL DO THAT INSTEAD.
AND ABE-CHAN WANTED TO GO SHOPPING WITH ME, SO...

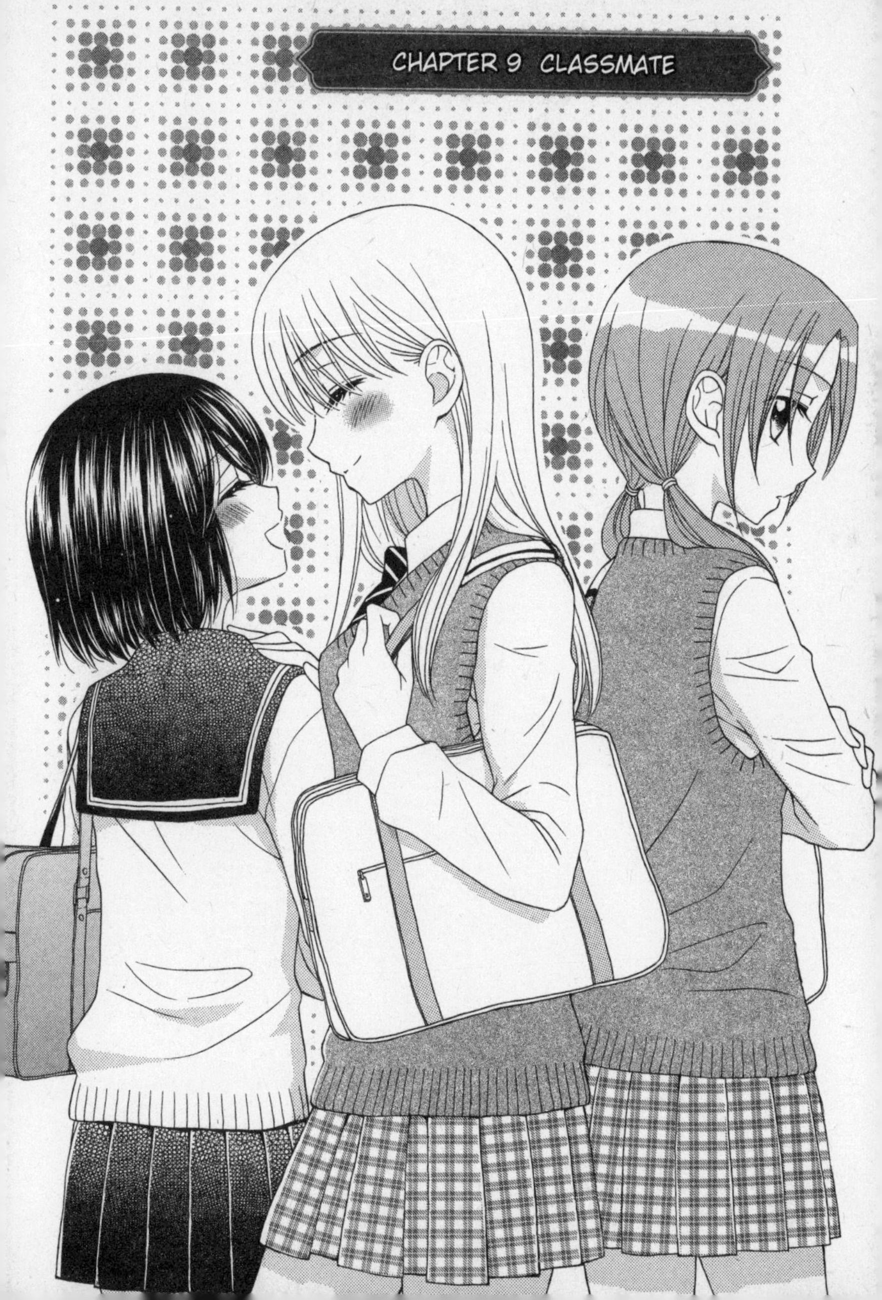
CHAPTER 9 CLASSMATE

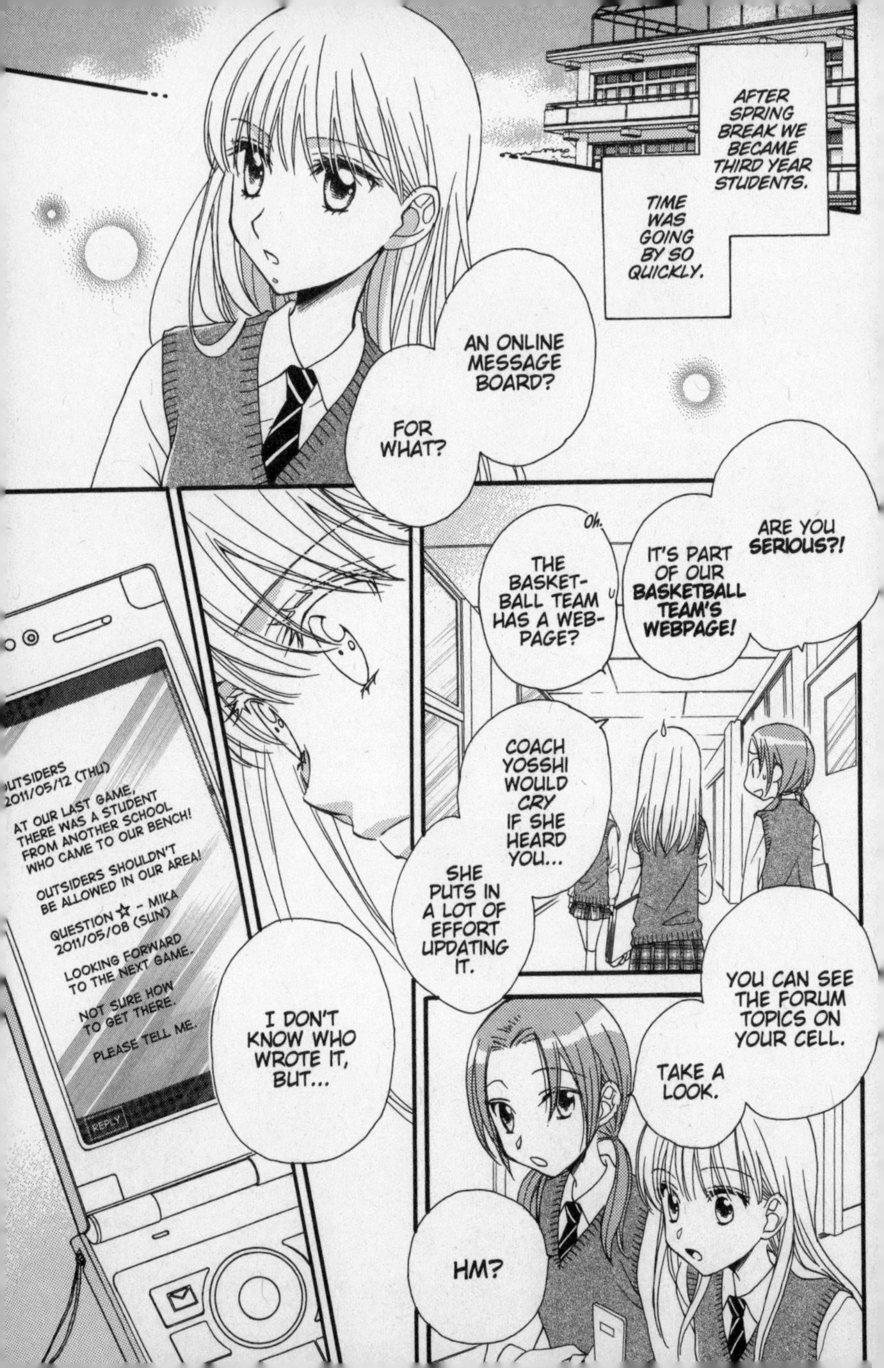
—...
AFTER SPRING BREAK WE BECAME THIRD YEAR STUDENTS.
TIME WAS GOING BY SO QUICKLY.
AN ONLINE MESSAGE BOARD?
FOR WHAT?
ARE YOU SERIOUS?!
IT'S PART OF OUR BASKETBALL TEAM'S WEBPAGE!
Oh.
THE BASKETBALL TEAM HAS A WEBPAGE?
COACH YOSSHI WOULD CRY IF SHE HEARD YOU...
SHE PUTS IN A LOT OF EFFORT UPDATING IT.
YOU CAN SEE THE FORUM TOPICS ON YOUR CELL.
TAKE A LOOK.
HM?
I DON'T KNOW WHO WROTE IT, BUT...
OUTSIDERS
2011/05/12 (THU)
AT OUR LAST GAME, THERE WAS A STUDENT FROM ANOTHER SCHOOL WHO CAME TO OUR BENCH!
OUTSIDERS SHOULDN'T BE ALLOWED IN OUR AREA!
QUESTION ☆ - MIKA
2011/05/08 (SUN)
LOOKING FORWARD TO THE NEXT GAME.
NOT SURE HOW TO GET THERE.
PLEASE TELL ME.
REPLY

くちびるためいきさくらいろ

KuchibiruTameikiSakurairo.

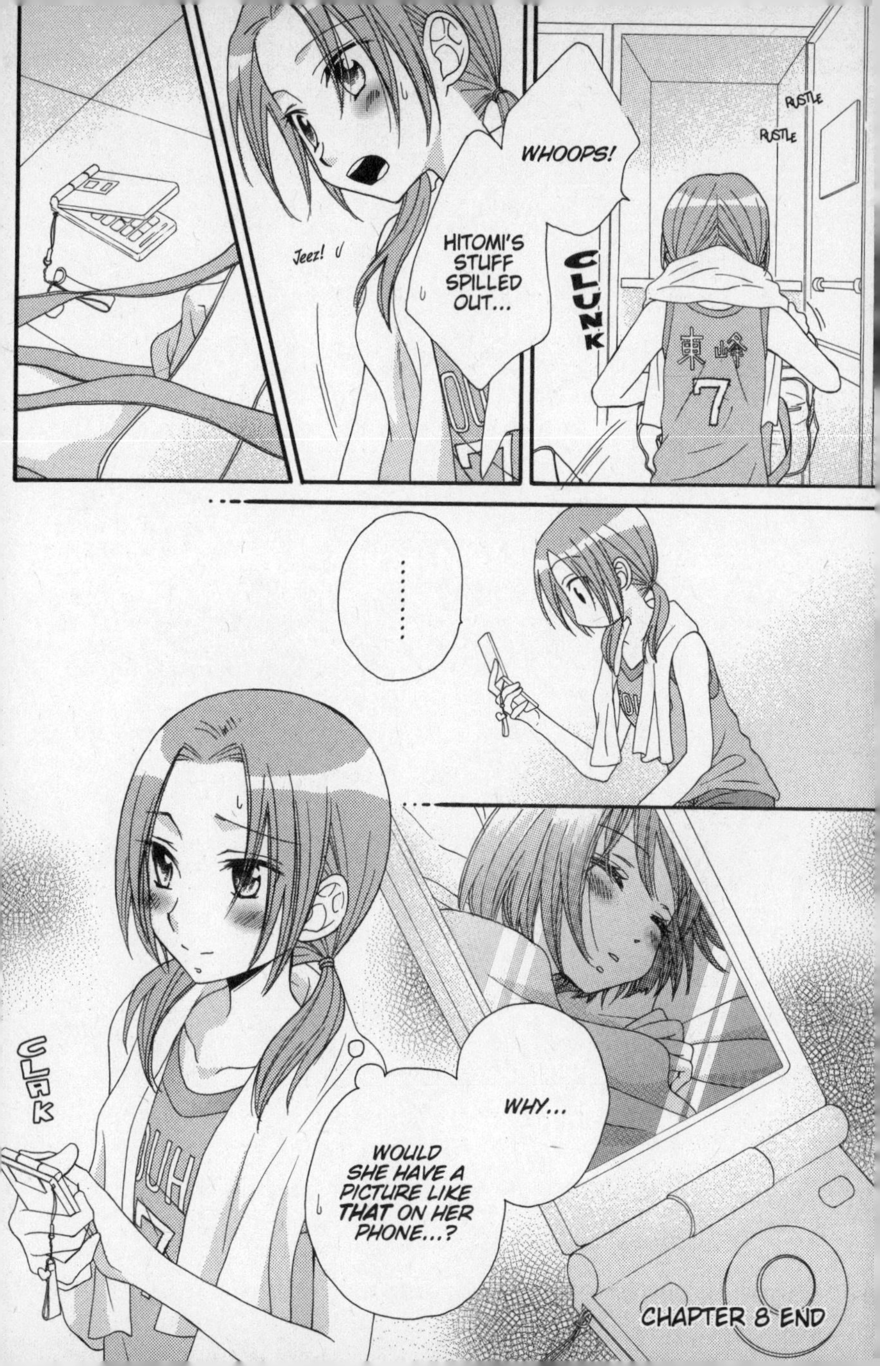
RUSTLE
RUSTLE
CLUNK
東峰
7
WHOOPS!
HITOMI'S STUFF SPILLED OUT...
Jeez!
......
WHY...
WOULD SHE HAVE A PICTURE LIKE THAT ON HER PHONE...?
CLAK
CHAPTER 8 END

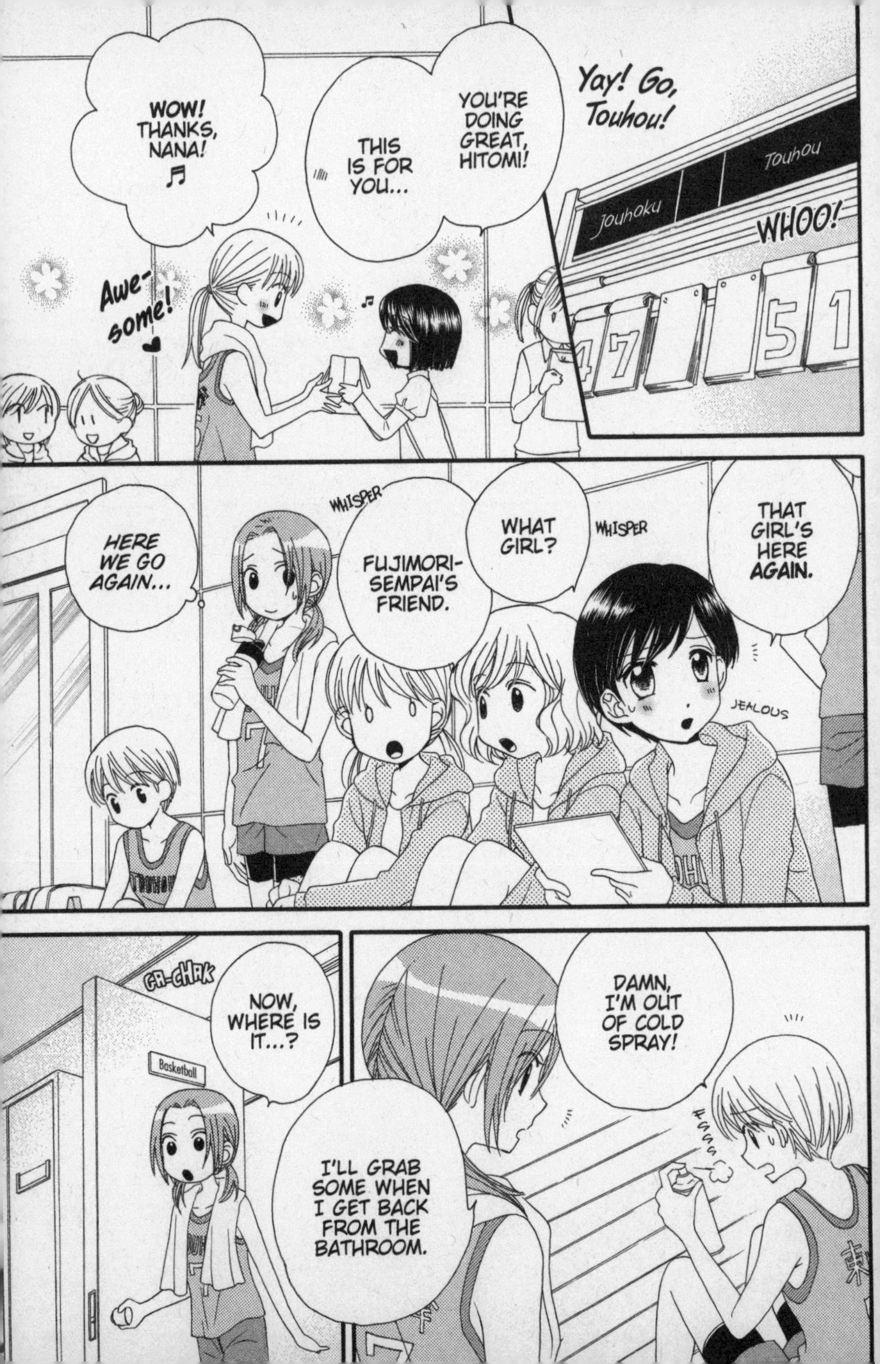
Yay! Go, Touhou!
Touhou
Jouhoku
WHOO!
47
51
YOU'RE DOING GREAT, HITOMI!
THIS IS FOR YOU...
WOW! THANKS, NANA! ♬
Awe-some!
THAT GIRL'S HERE AGAIN.
JEALOUS
WHISPER
WHAT GIRL?
WHISPER
FUJIMORI-SEMPAI'S FRIEND.
HERE WE GO AGAIN...
DAMN, I'M OUT OF COLD SPRAY!
FSSS
I'LL GRAB SOME WHEN I GET BACK FROM THE BATHROOM.
GA-CHAK
NOW, WHERE IS IT...?
Basketball

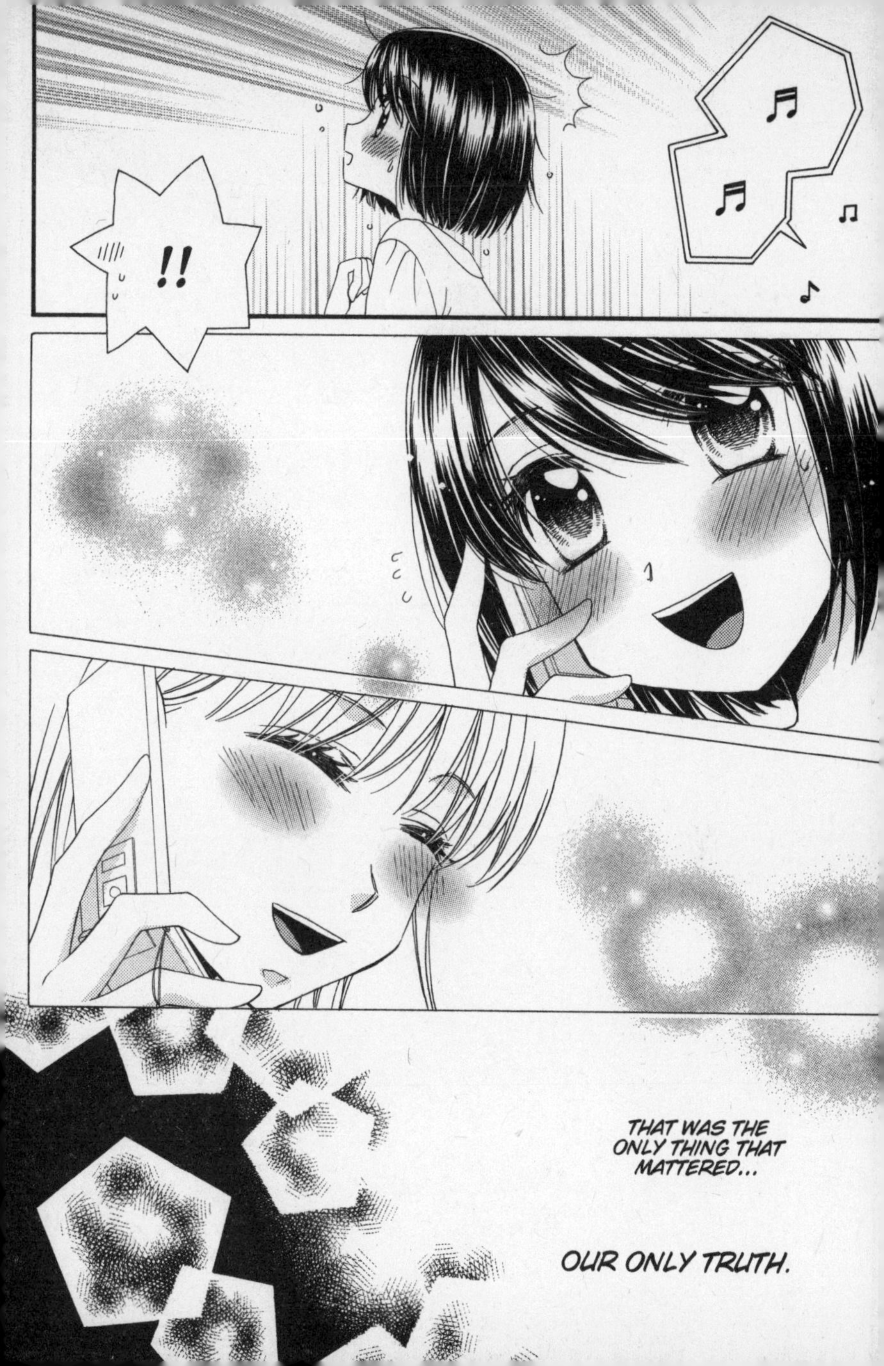
!!
THAT WAS THE ONLY THING THAT MATTERED...
OUR ONLY TRUTH.

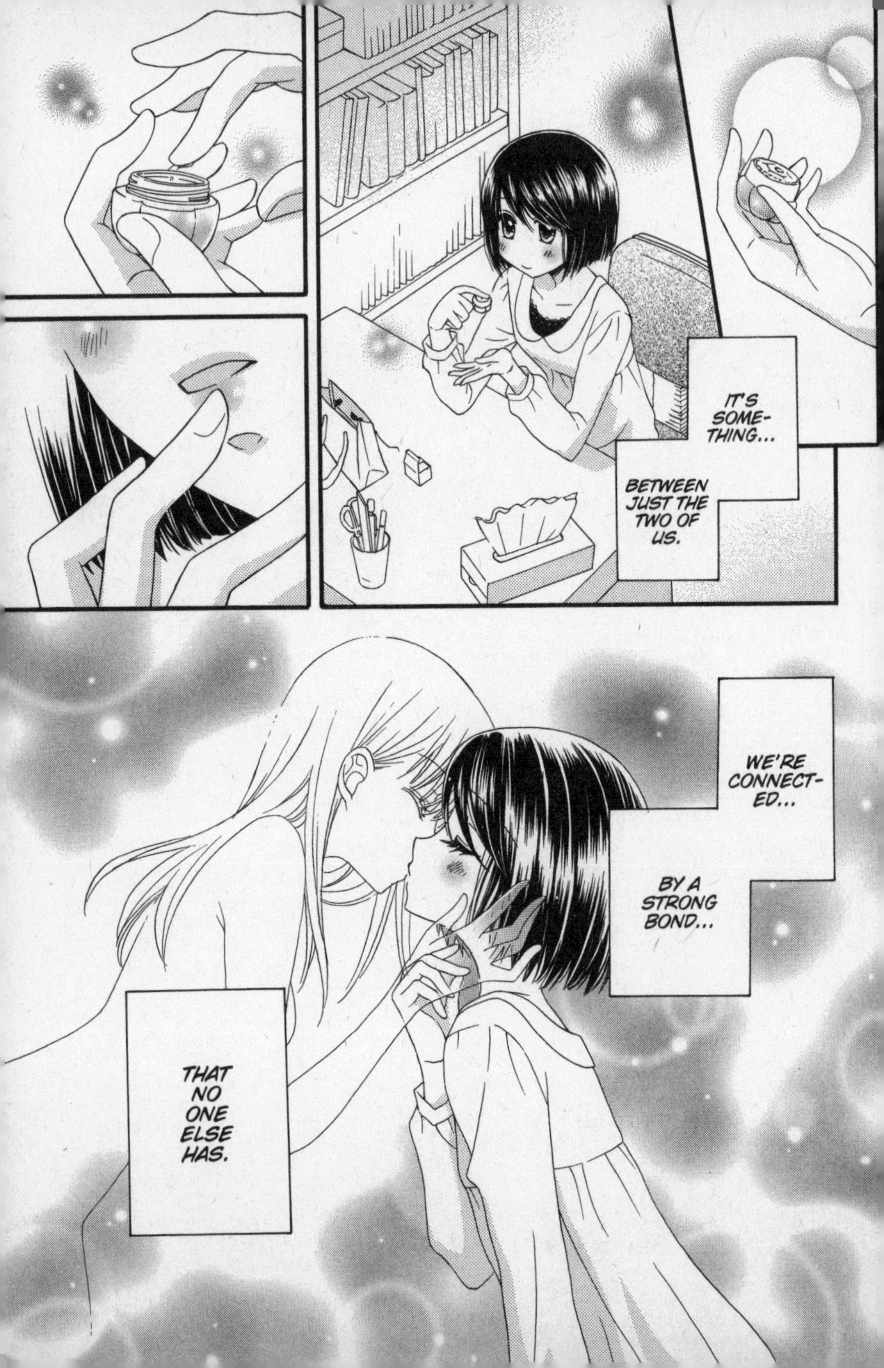
IT'S SOMETHING...
BETWEEN JUST THE TWO OF US.
WE'RE CONNECTED...
BY A STRONG BOND...
THAT NO ONE ELSE HAS.

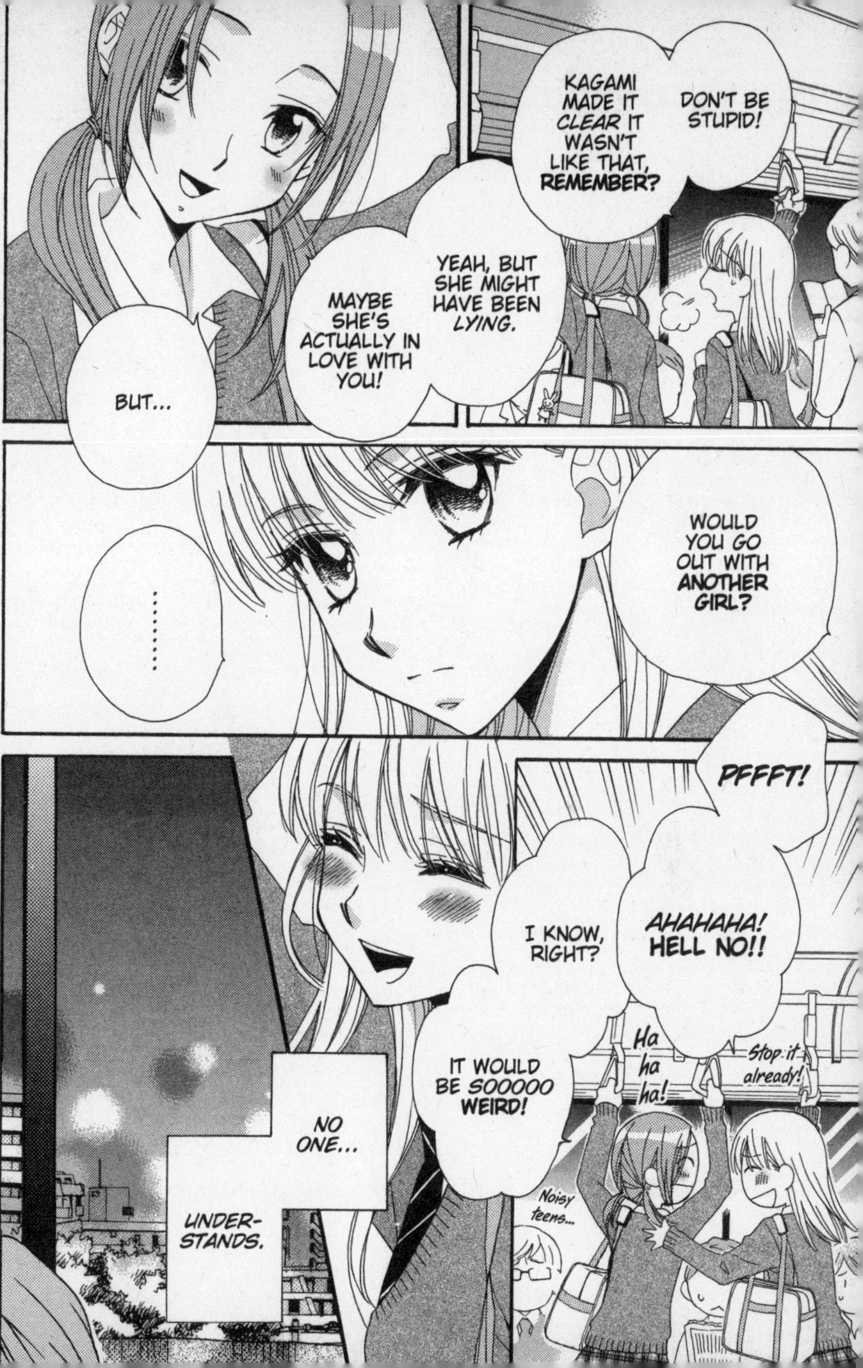
DON'T BE STUPID!
KAGAMI MADE IT CLEAR IT WASN'T LIKE THAT, REMEMBER?
YEAH, BUT SHE MIGHT HAVE BEEN LYING.
MAYBE SHE'S ACTUALLY IN LOVE WITH YOU!
BUT...
WOULD YOU GO OUT WITH ANOTHER GIRL?
......
PFFFT!
AHAHAHA! HELL NO!!
Stop it already!
Ha ha ha!
Noisy teens...
I KNOW, RIGHT?
IT WOULD BE SOOOOO WEIRD!
NO ONE...
UNDER-STANDS.

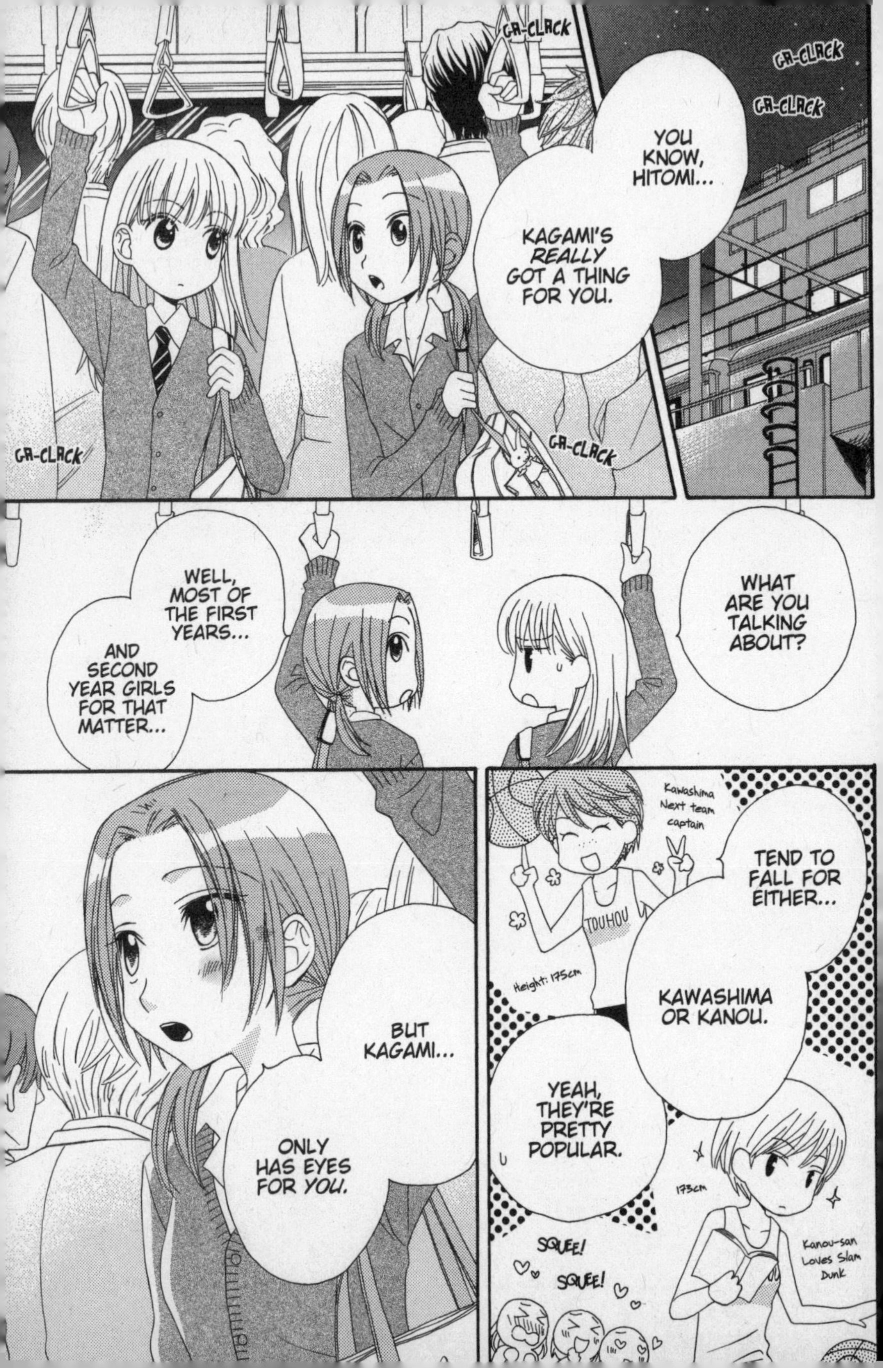
GA-CLACK
GA-CLACK
GA-CLACK
YOU KNOW, HITOMI...
KAGAMI'S REALLY GOT A THING FOR YOU.
GA-CLACK
GA-CLACK
WHAT ARE YOU TALKING ABOUT?
WELL, MOST OF THE FIRST YEARS...
AND SECOND YEAR GIRLS FOR THAT MATTER...
Kawashima Next team captain
TEND TO FALL FOR EITHER...
KAWASHIMA OR KANOU.
TOUHOU
Height: 175cm
YEAH, THEY'RE PRETTY POPULAR.
173cm
Kanou-san Loves Slam Dunk
SQUEE!
SQUEE!
BUT KAGAMI...
ONLY HAS EYES FOR YOU.

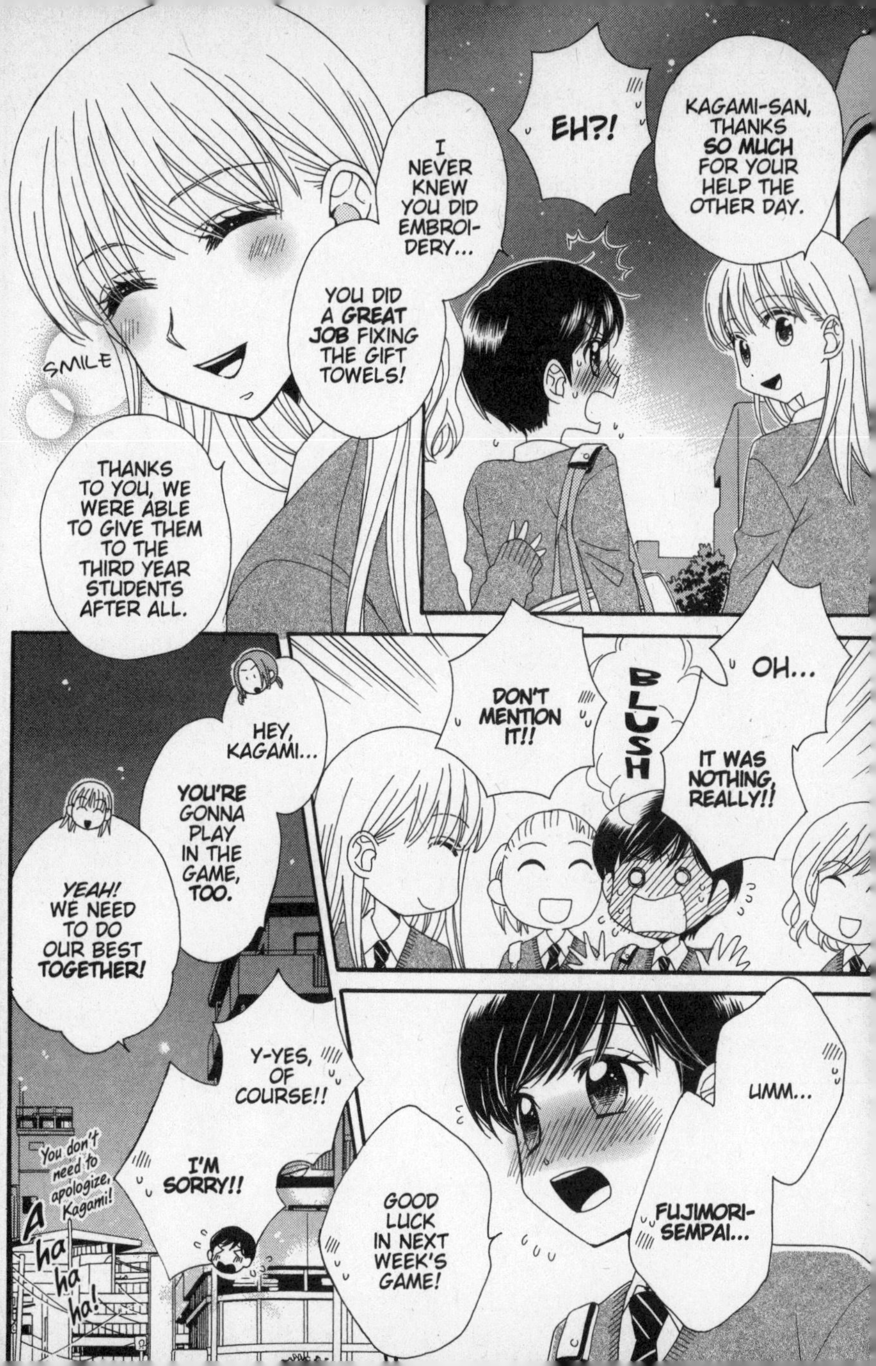
KAGAMI-SAN, THANKS SO MUCH FOR YOUR HELP THE OTHER DAY.
EH?!
I NEVER KNEW YOU DID EMBROIDERY...
YOU DID A GREAT JOB FIXING THE GIFT TOWELS!
SMILE
THANKS TO YOU, WE WERE ABLE TO GIVE THEM TO THE THIRD YEAR STUDENTS AFTER ALL.
OH...
IT WAS NOTHING, REALLY!!
BLUSH
DON'T MENTION IT!!
UMM...
FUJIMORI-SEMPAI...
GOOD LUCK IN NEXT WEEK'S GAME!
HEY, KAGAMI...
YOU'RE GONNA PLAY IN THE GAME, TOO.
YEAH! WE NEED TO DO OUR BEST TOGETHER!
Y-YES, OF COURSE!!
I'M SORRY!!
You don't need to apologize, Kagami!
A ha ha ha!

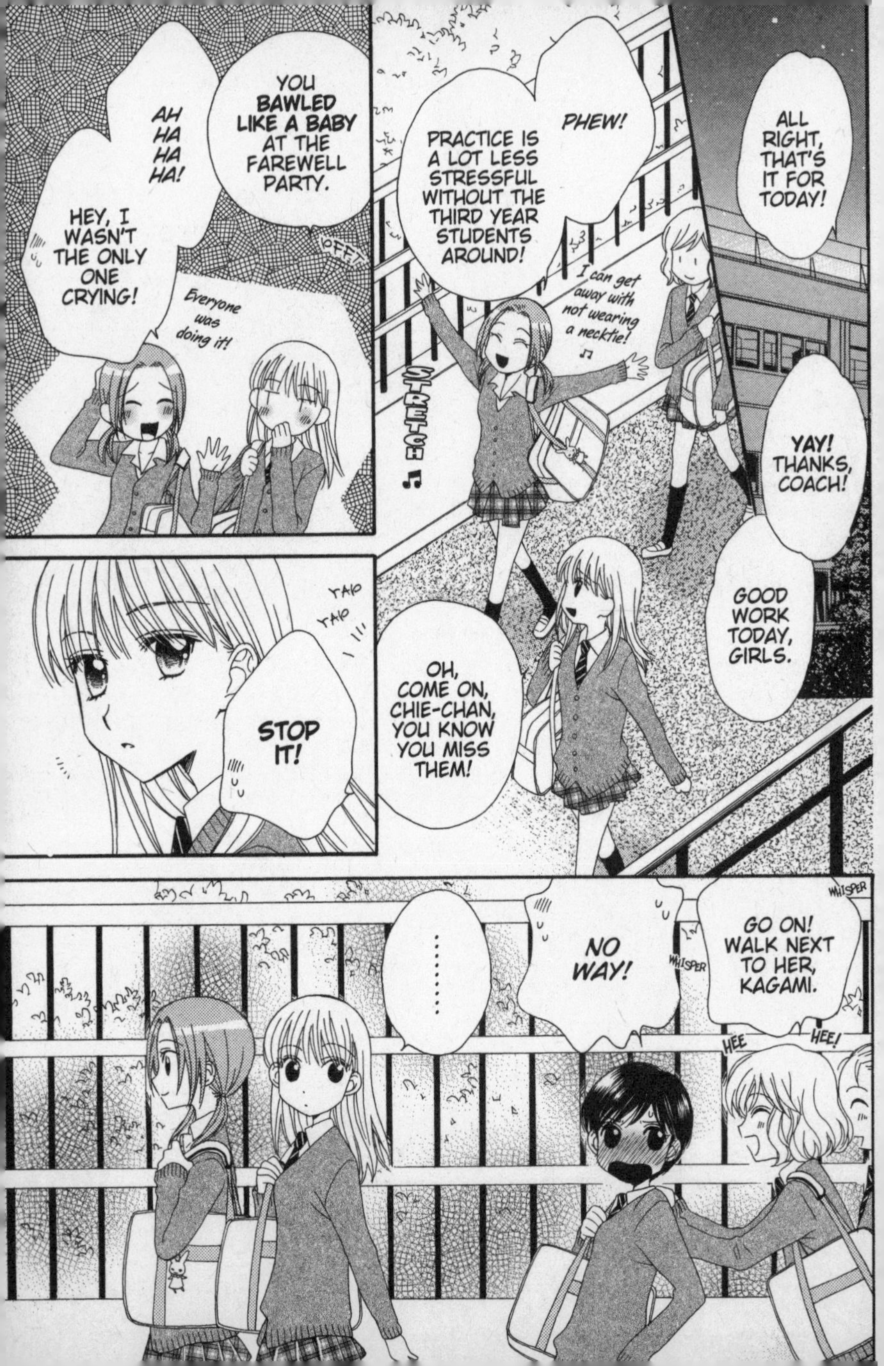
ALL RIGHT, THAT'S IT FOR TODAY!
YAY! THANKS, COACH!
GOOD WORK TODAY, GIRLS.
PHEW!
PRACTICE IS A LOT LESS STRESSFUL WITHOUT THE THIRD YEAR STUDENTS AROUND!
I can get away with not wearing a necktie! ♫
STRETCH ♫
OH, COME ON, CHIE-CHAN, YOU KNOW YOU MISS THEM!
YOU BAWLED LIKE A BABY AT THE FAREWELL PARTY.
AH HA HA HA!
HEY, I WASN'T THE ONLY ONE CRYING!
Everyone was doing it!
STOP IT!
WHISPER
GO ON! WALK NEXT TO HER, KAGAMI.
WHISPER
HEE HEE!
NO WAY!
....

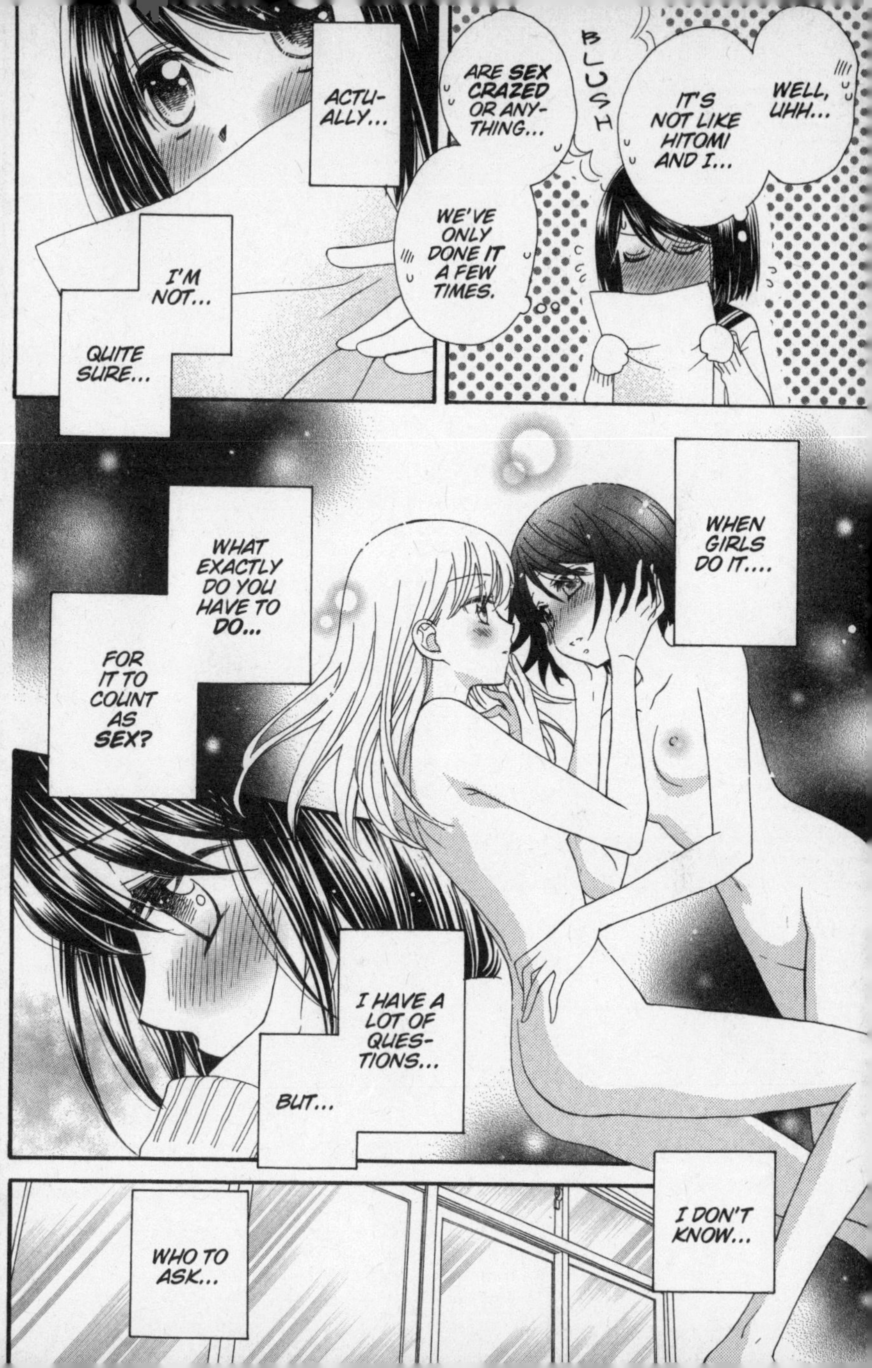
WELL, UHH...
IT'S NOT LIKE HITOMI AND I...
BLUSH
ARE SEX CRAZED OR ANYTHING...
WE'VE ONLY DONE IT A FEW TIMES.
ACTU-ALLY...
I'M NOT...
QUITE SURE...
WHEN GIRLS DO IT....
WHAT EXACTLY DO YOU HAVE TO DO...
FOR IT TO COUNT AS SEX?
I HAVE A LOT OF QUES-TIONS...
BUT...
I DON'T KNOW...
WHO TO ASK...

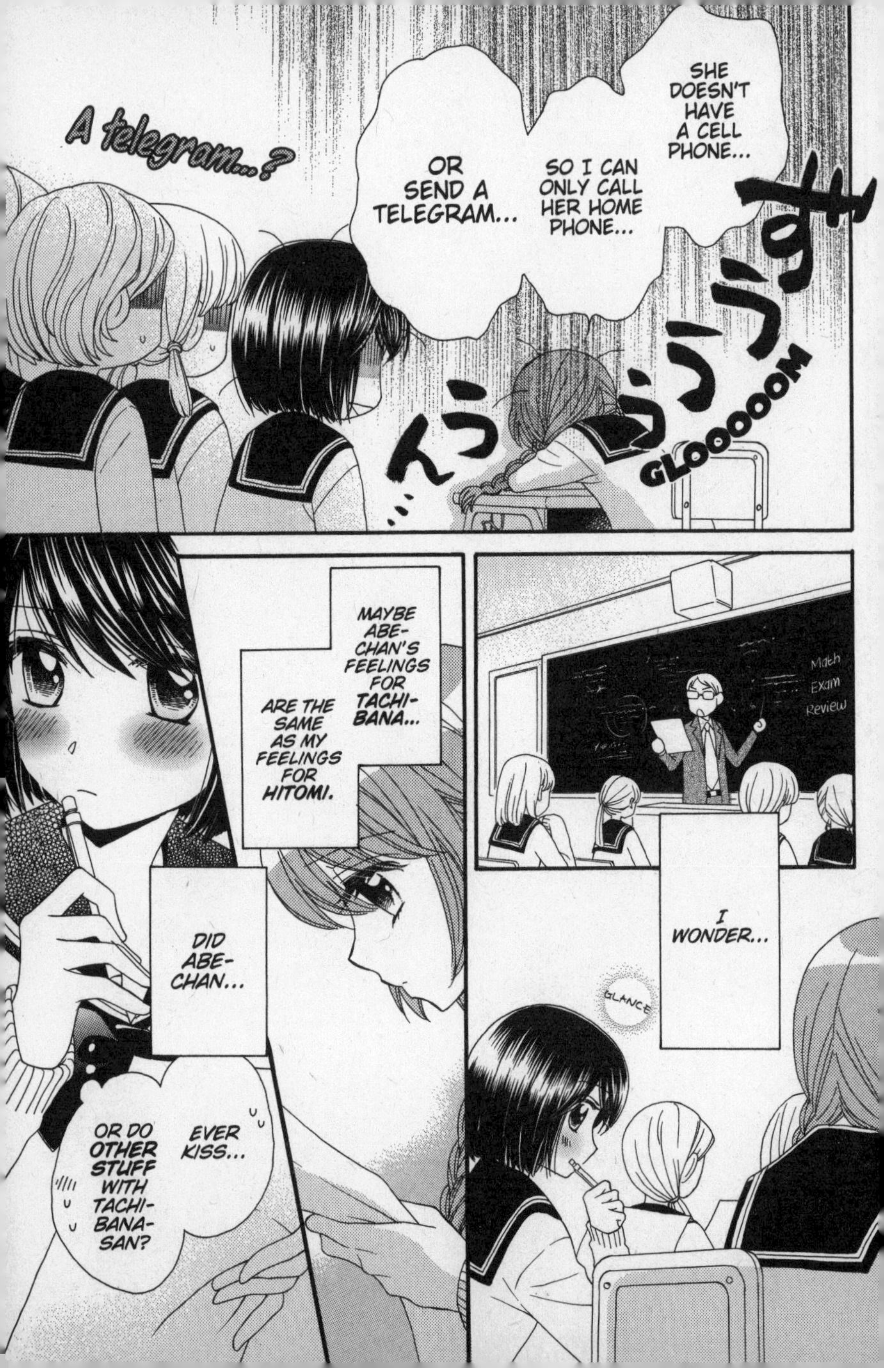

SHE DOESN'T HAVE A CELL PHONE...
SO I CAN ONLY CALL HER HOME PHONE...
OR SEND A TELEGRAM...
GLOOOOOOM
A telegram...?
Math Exam Review
I WONDER...
GLANCE
MAYBE ABE-CHAN'S FEELINGS FOR TACHIBANA...
ARE THE SAME AS MY FEELINGS FOR HITOMI.
DID ABE-CHAN...
EVER KISS...
OR DO OTHER STUFF WITH TACHIBANA-SAN?

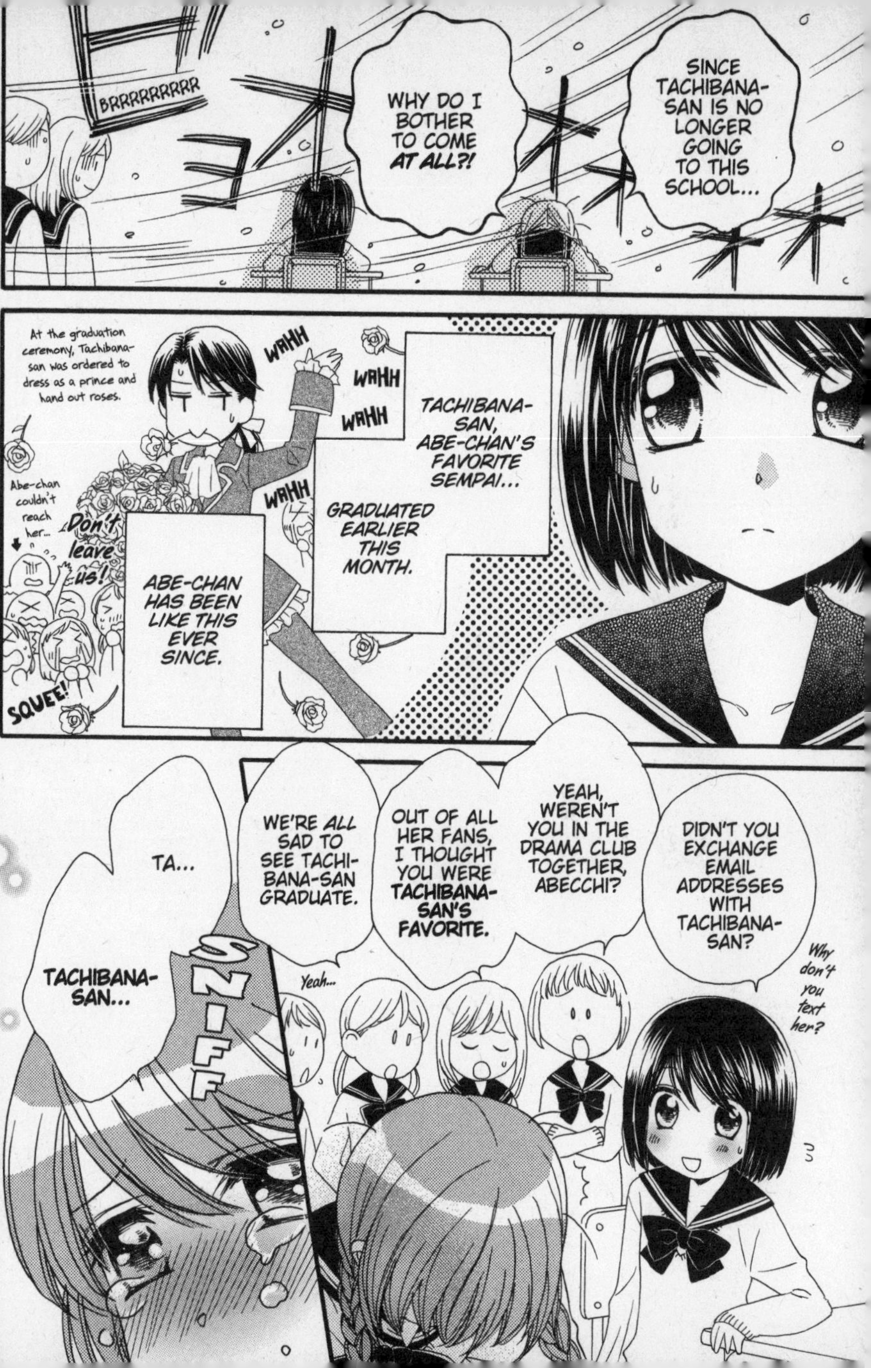
SINCE TACHIBANA-SAN IS NO LONGER GOING TO THIS SCHOOL...
WHY DO I BOTHER TO COME AT ALL?!
BRRRRRRRRR
TACHIBANA-SAN, ABE-CHAN'S FAVORITE SEMPAI...
GRADUATED EARLIER THIS MONTH.
ABE-CHAN HAS BEEN LIKE THIS EVER SINCE.
At the graduation ceremony, Tachibana-san was ordered to dress as a prince and hand out roses.
WAHH
WAHH
WAHH
WAHH
Abe-chan couldn't reach her...
Don't leave us!
SQUEE!
DIDN'T YOU EXCHANGE EMAIL ADDRESSES WITH TACHIBANA-SAN?
Why don't you text her?
YEAH, WEREN'T YOU IN THE DRAMA CLUB TOGETHER, ABECCHI?
OUT OF ALL HER FANS, I THOUGHT YOU WERE TACHIBANA-SAN'S FAVORITE.
WE'RE ALL SAD TO SEE TACHI-BANA-SAN GRADUATE.
Yeah...
TA...
TACHIBANA-SAN...
SNIFF

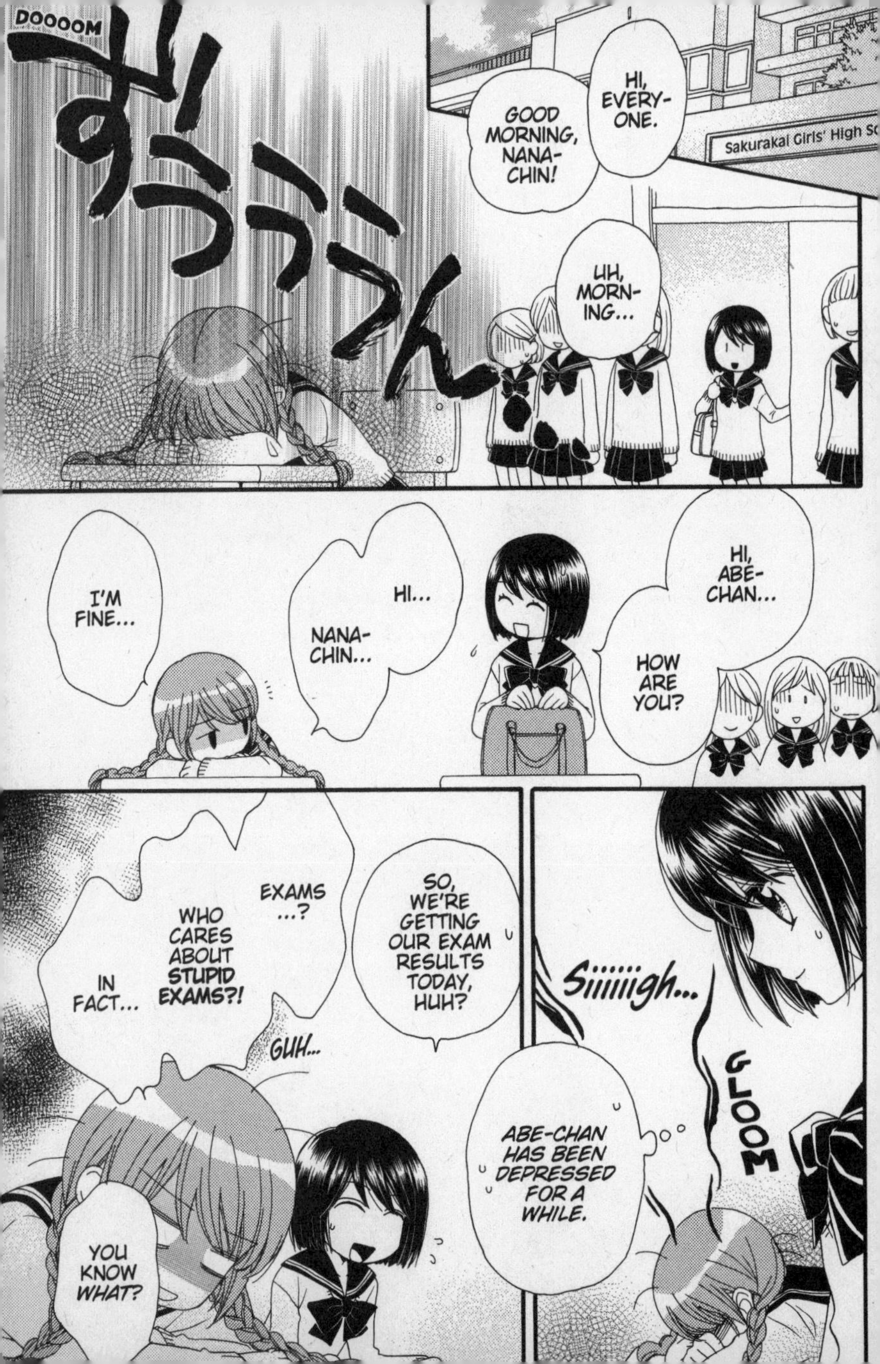
Sakurakai Girls' High Sc
HI, EVERY-ONE.
GOOD MORNING, NANA-CHIN!
UH, MORN-ING...
DOOOOM
ずううん
HI, ABE-CHAN...
HOW ARE YOU?
HI...
NANA-CHIN...
I'M FINE...
Siiiiigh...
GLOOM
ABE-CHAN HAS BEEN DEPRESSED FOR A WHILE.
SO, WE'RE GETTING OUR EXAM RESULTS TODAY, HUH?
GUH...
EXAMS ...?
WHO CARES ABOUT STUPID EXAMS?!
IN FACT...
YOU KNOW WHAT?

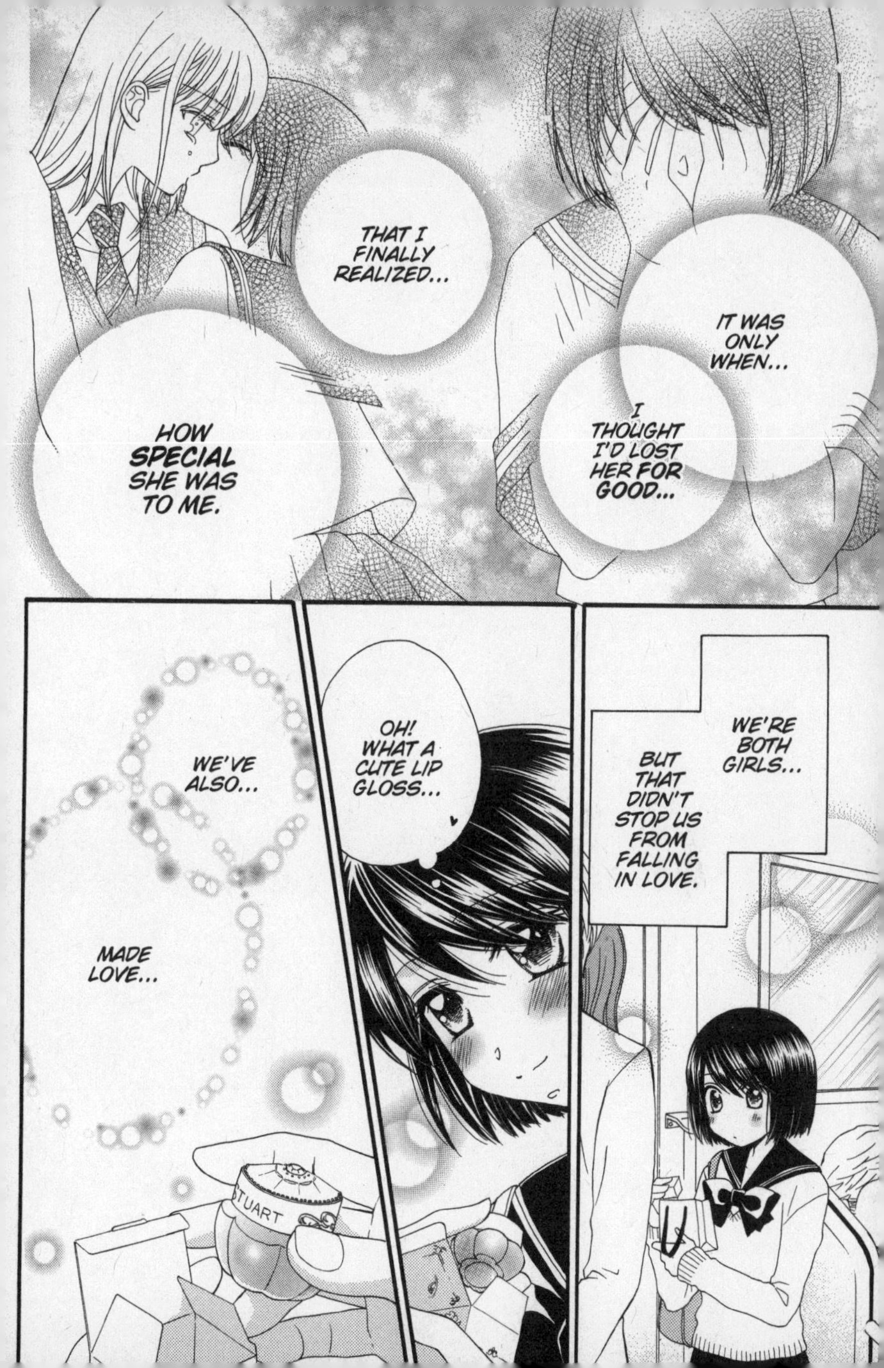
IT WAS ONLY WHEN...
I THOUGHT I'D LOST HER FOR GOOD...
THAT I FINALLY REALIZED...
HOW **SPECIAL** SHE WAS TO ME.
WE'RE BOTH GIRLS...
BUT THAT DIDN'T STOP US FROM FALLING IN LOVE.
OH! WHAT A CUTE LIP GLOSS...
WE'VE ALSO...
MADE LOVE...
STUART

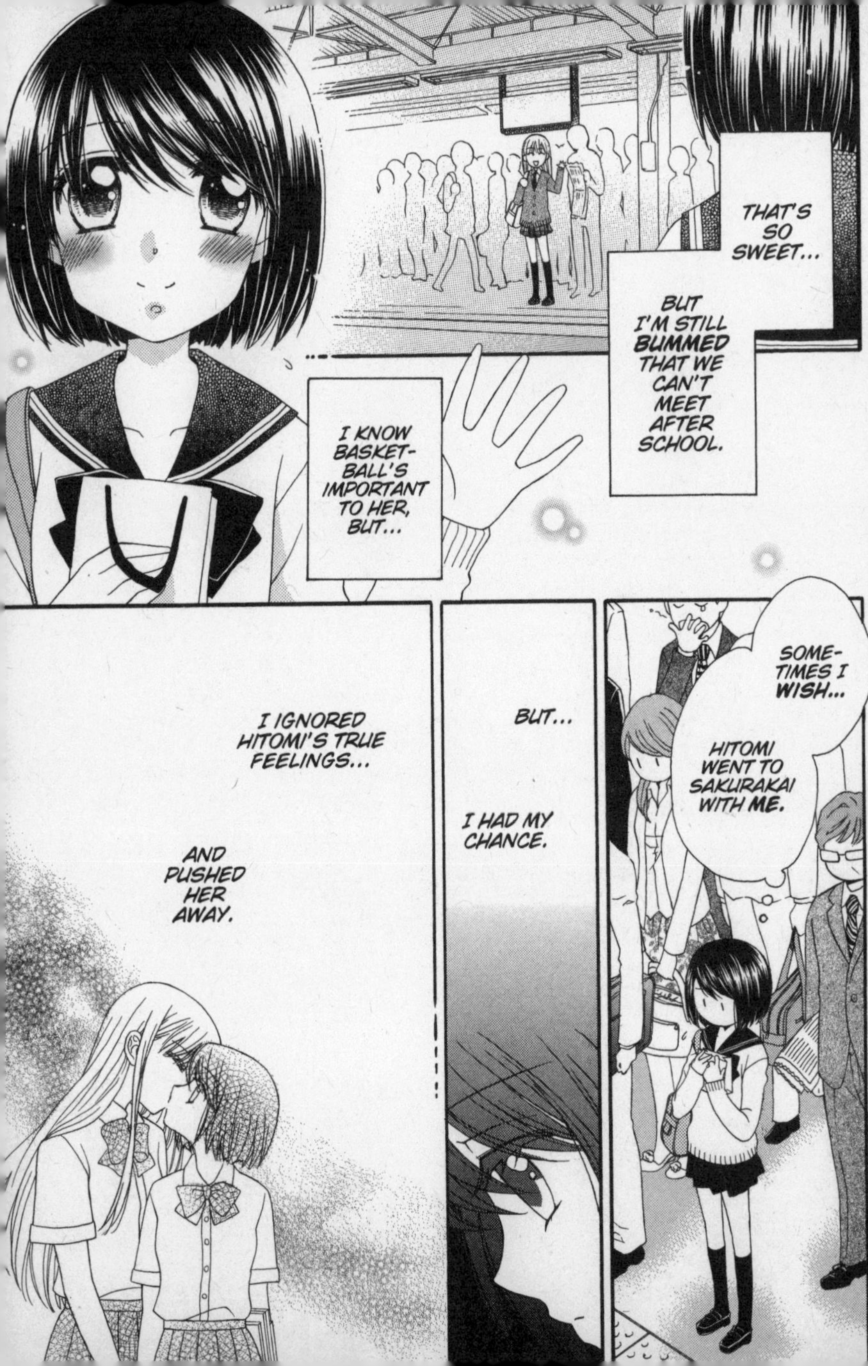
THAT'S SO SWEET...
BUT I'M STILL BUMMED THAT WE CAN'T MEET AFTER SCHOOL.
I KNOW BASKET-BALL'S IMPORTANT TO HER, BUT...
SOME-TIMES I WISH...
HITOMI WENT TO SAKURAKAI WITH ME.
BUT...
I HAD MY CHANCE.
I IGNORED HITOMI'S TRUE FEELINGS...
AND PUSHED HER AWAY.

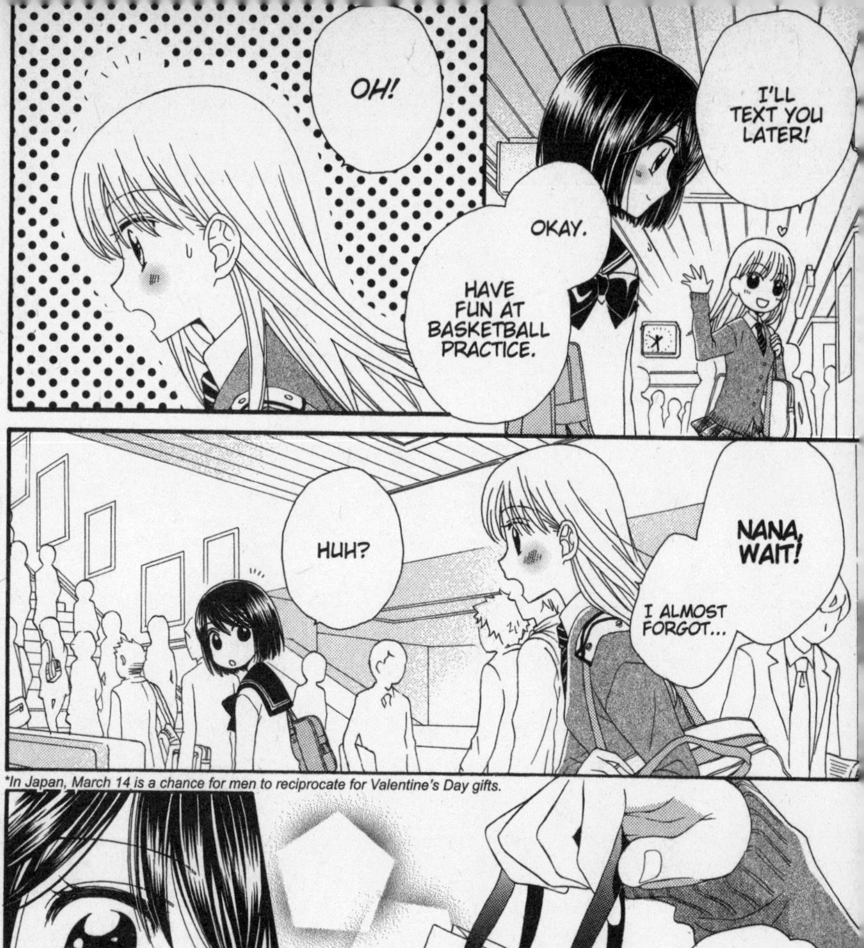
I'LL TEXT YOU LATER!
OKAY.
HAVE FUN AT BASKETBALL PRACTICE.
OH!
NANA, WAIT!
I ALMOST FORGOT...
HUH?

*In Japan, March 14 is a chance for men to reciprocate for Valentine's Day gifts.

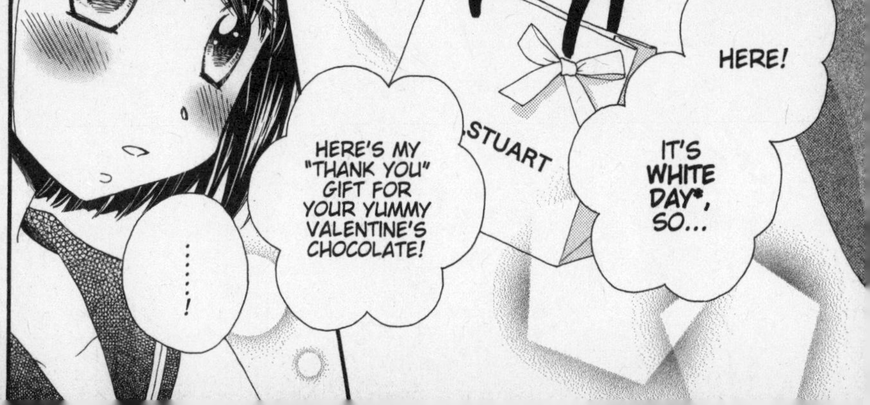
HERE!
IT'S WHITE DAY*, SO...
STUART
HERE'S MY "THANK YOU" GIFT FOR YOUR YUMMY VALENTINE'S CHOCOLATE!
......!

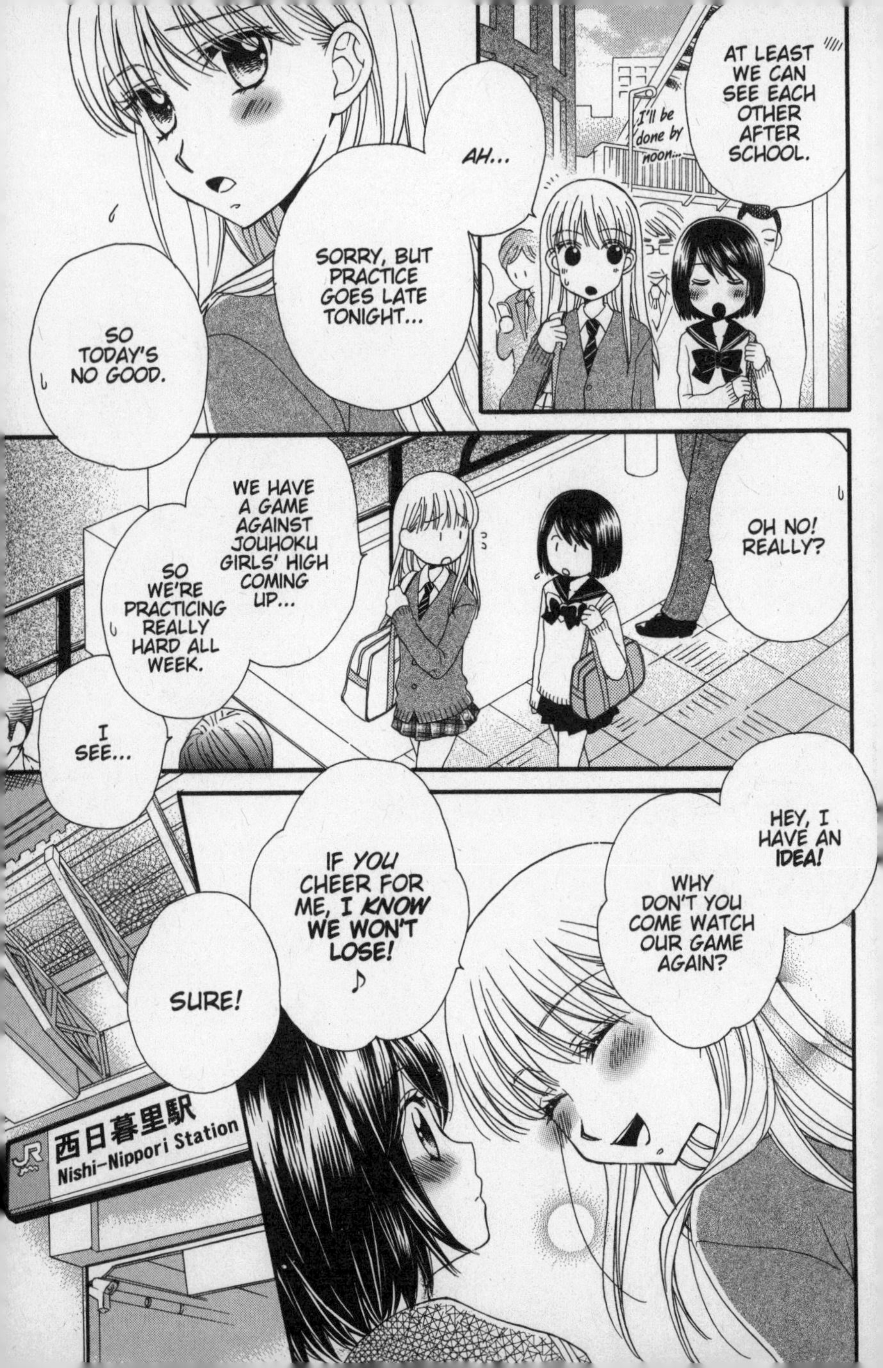
AT LEAST WE CAN SEE EACH OTHER AFTER SCHOOL.
I'll be done by noon...
AH...
SORRY, BUT PRACTICE GOES LATE TONIGHT...
SO TODAY'S NO GOOD.
OH NO! REALLY?
WE HAVE A GAME AGAINST JOUHOKU GIRLS' HIGH COMING UP...
SO WE'RE PRACTICING REALLY HARD ALL WEEK.
I SEE...
HEY, I HAVE AN IDEA!
WHY DON'T YOU COME WATCH OUR GAME AGAIN?
IF YOU CHEER FOR ME, I KNOW WE WON'T LOSE! ♪
SURE!
JR
西日暮里駅
Nishi-Nippori Station

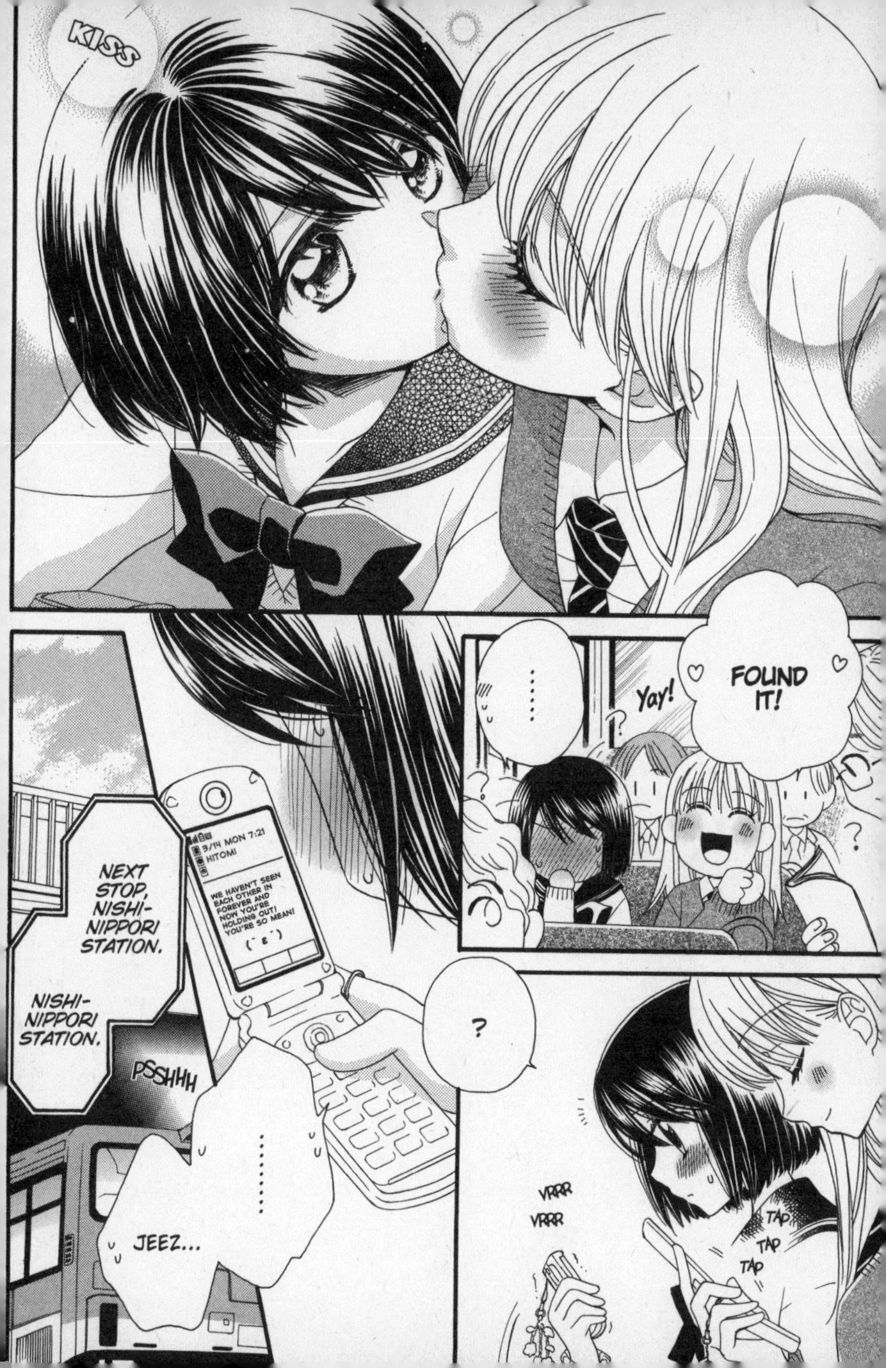
KISS
FOUND IT!
Yay!
......
VRRR
VRRR
TAP
TAP
TAP
3/14 MON 7:21
HITOMI
WE HAVEN'T SEEN EACH OTHER IN FOREVER AND NOW YOU'RE HOLDING OUT! YOU'RE SO MEAN!
(ˇεˇ)
NEXT STOP, NISHI-NIPPORI STATION.
NISHI-NIPPORI STATION.
PSSHHH
?
......
JEEZ...

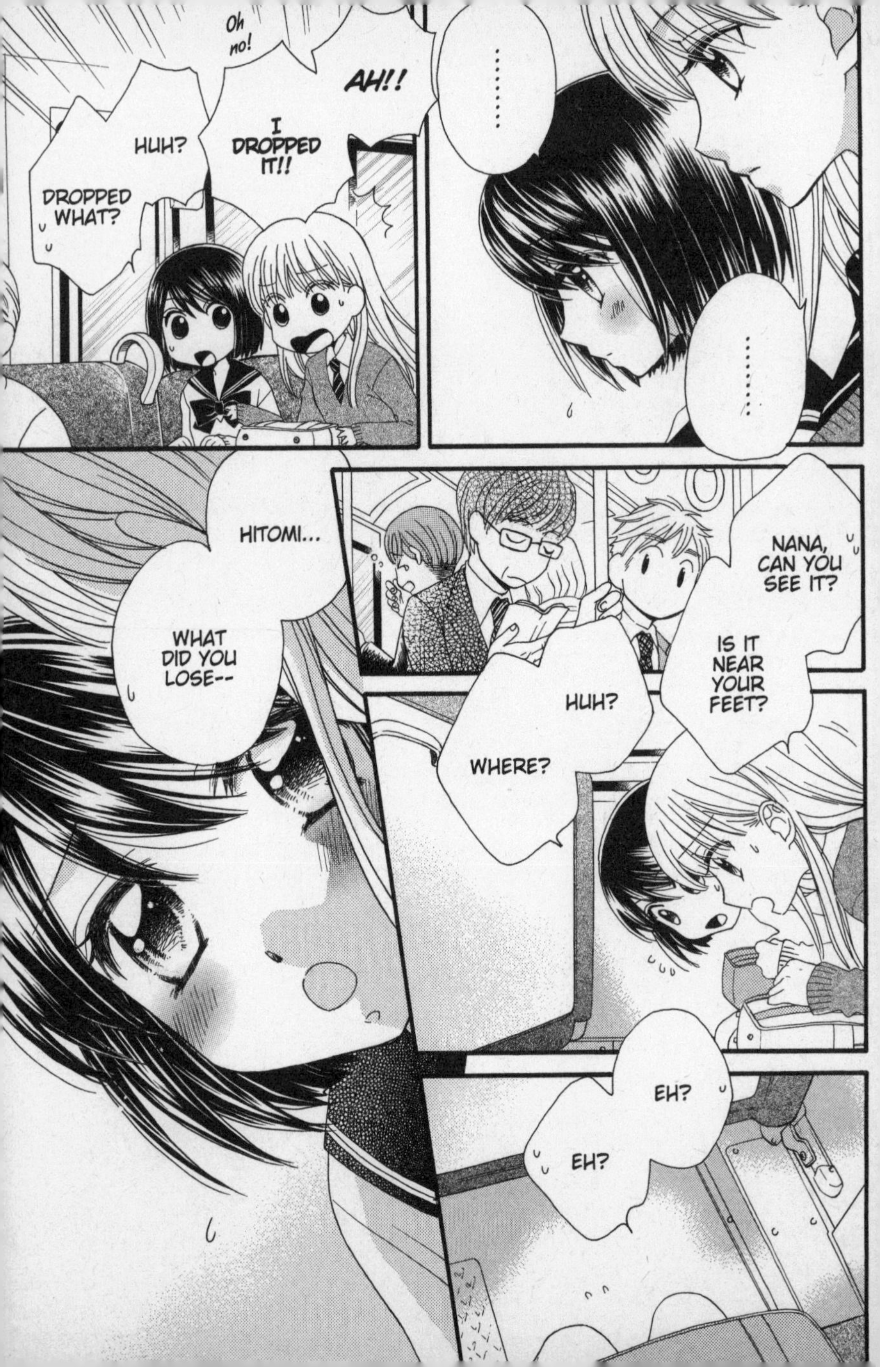

......
......
AH!!
Oh no!
I DROPPED IT!!
HUH?
DROPPED WHAT?
NANA, CAN YOU SEE IT?
IS IT NEAR YOUR FEET?
HUH?
WHERE?
EH?
EH?
HITOMI...
WHAT DID YOU LOSE--

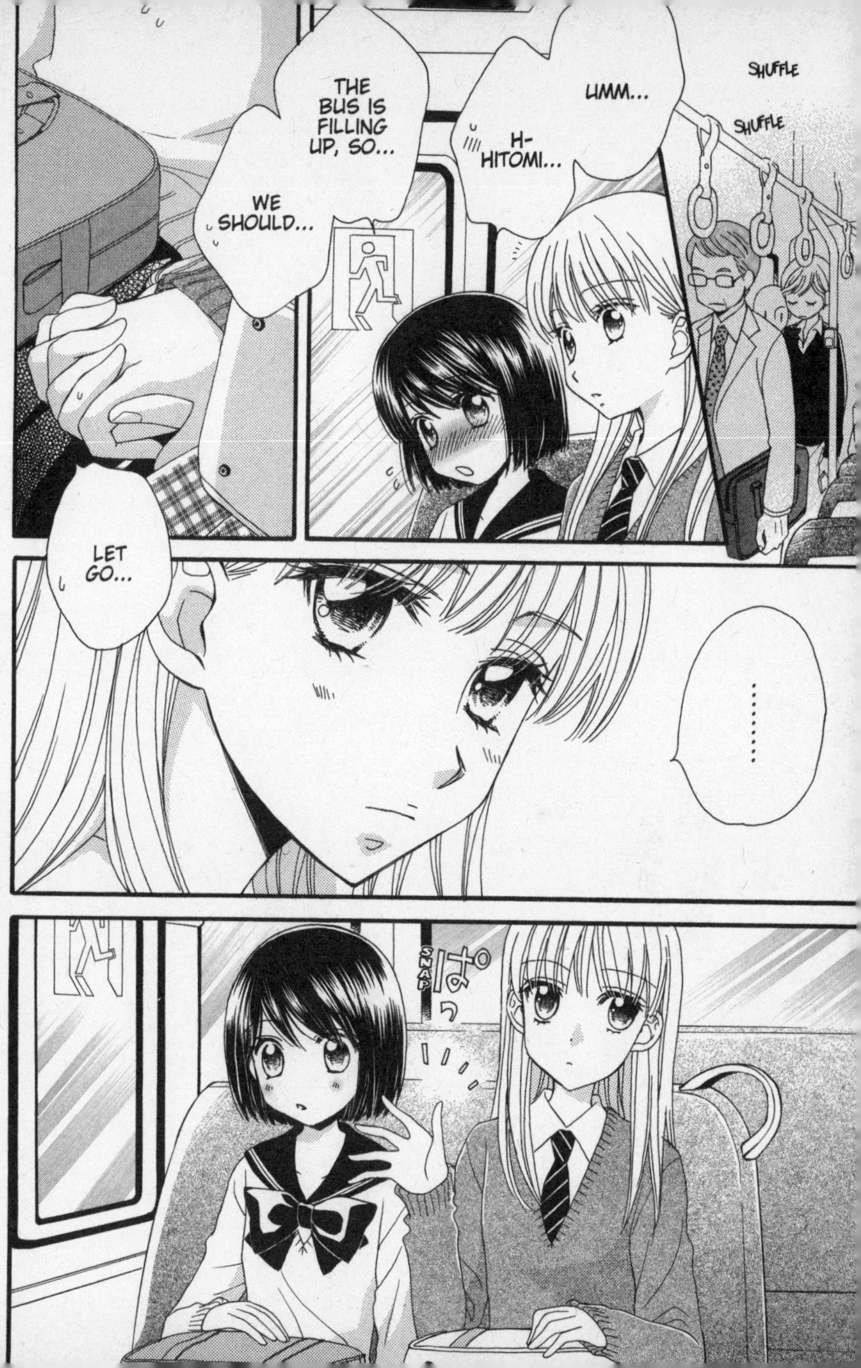
SHUFFLE
SHUFFLE
UMM...
H-HITOMI...
THE BUS IS FILLING UP, SO...
WE SHOULD...
LET GO...
......
SNAP
ぱっ

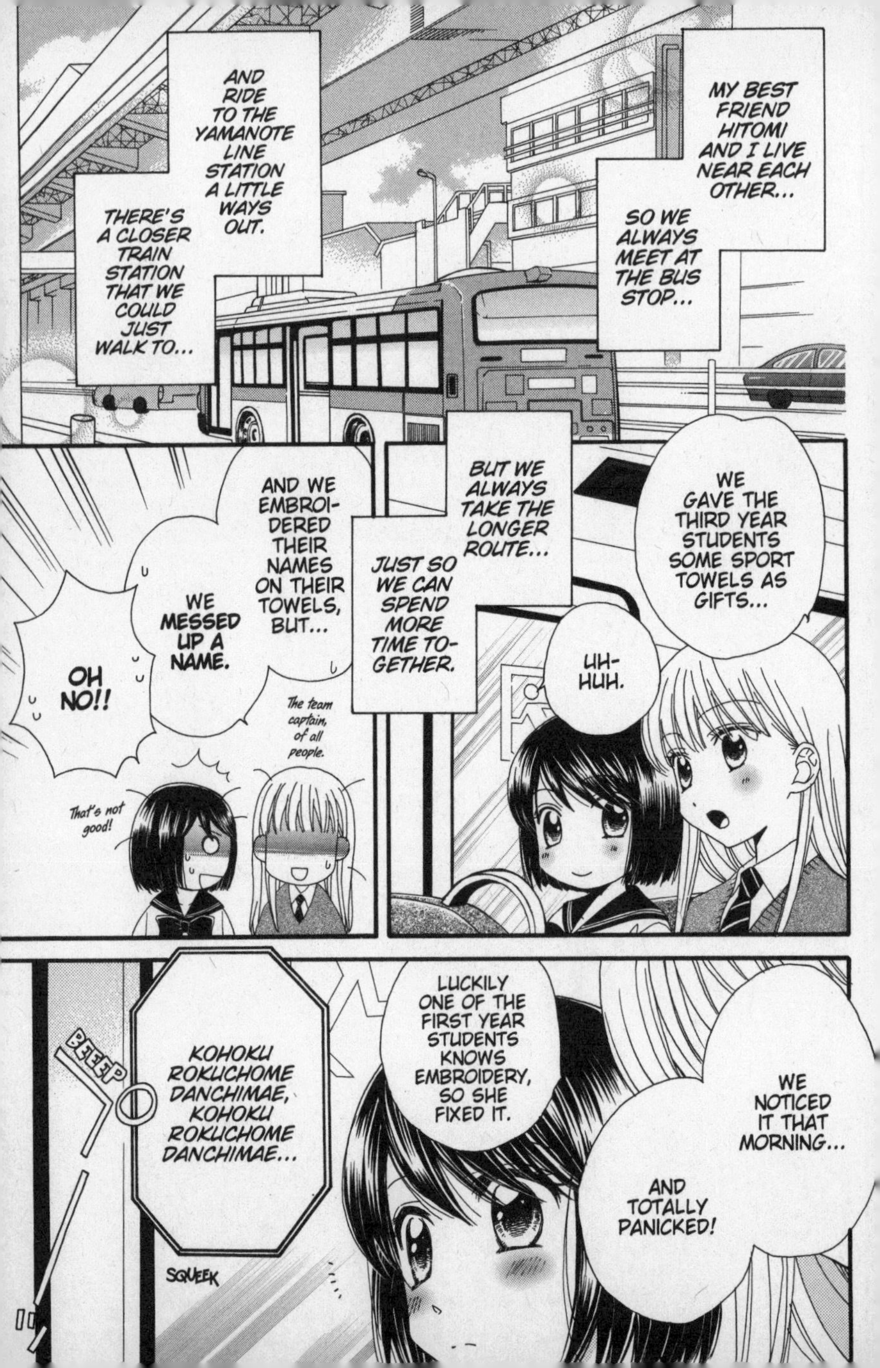
MY BEST FRIEND HITOMI AND I LIVE NEAR EACH OTHER...
SO WE ALWAYS MEET AT THE BUS STOP...
AND RIDE TO THE YAMANOTE LINE STATION A LITTLE WAYS OUT.
THERE'S A CLOSER TRAIN STATION THAT WE COULD JUST WALK TO...
BUT WE ALWAYS TAKE THE LONGER ROUTE...
JUST SO WE CAN SPEND MORE TIME TO-GETHER.
WE GAVE THE THIRD YEAR STUDENTS SOME SPORT TOWELS AS GIFTS...
UH-HUH.
AND WE EMBROI-DERED THEIR NAMES ON THEIR TOWELS, BUT...
WE MESSED UP A NAME.
OH NO!!
The team captain, of all people.
That's not good!
WE NOTICED IT THAT MORNING...
AND TOTALLY PANICKED!
LUCKILY ONE OF THE FIRST YEAR STUDENTS KNOWS EMBROIDERY, SO SHE FIXED IT.
KOHOKU ROKUCHOME DANCHIMAE, KOHOKU ROKUCHOME DANCHIMAE...
BEEEP
SQUEEK

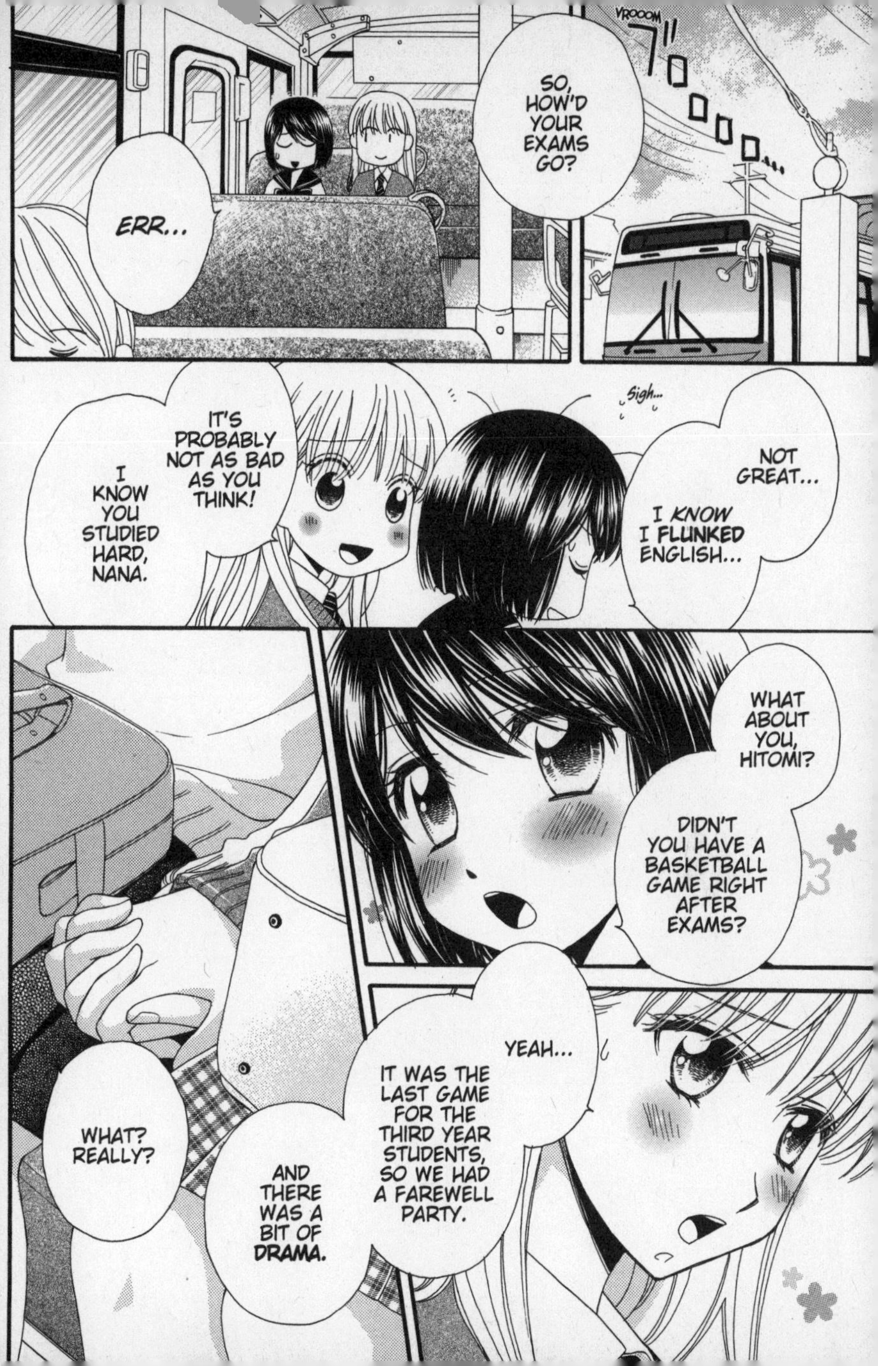
VROOOM
SO, HOW'D YOUR EXAMS GO?
ERR...
Sigh...
NOT GREAT...
I *KNOW* I FLUNKED ENGLISH...
IT'S PROBABLY NOT AS BAD AS YOU THINK!
I KNOW YOU STUDIED HARD, NANA.
WHAT ABOUT YOU, HITOMI?
DIDN'T YOU HAVE A BASKETBALL GAME RIGHT AFTER EXAMS?
YEAH...
IT WAS THE LAST GAME FOR THE THIRD YEAR STUDENTS, SO WE HAD A FAREWELL PARTY.
AND THERE WAS A BIT OF **DRAMA.**
WHAT? REALLY?

CHAPTER 8 SECRET LOVERS

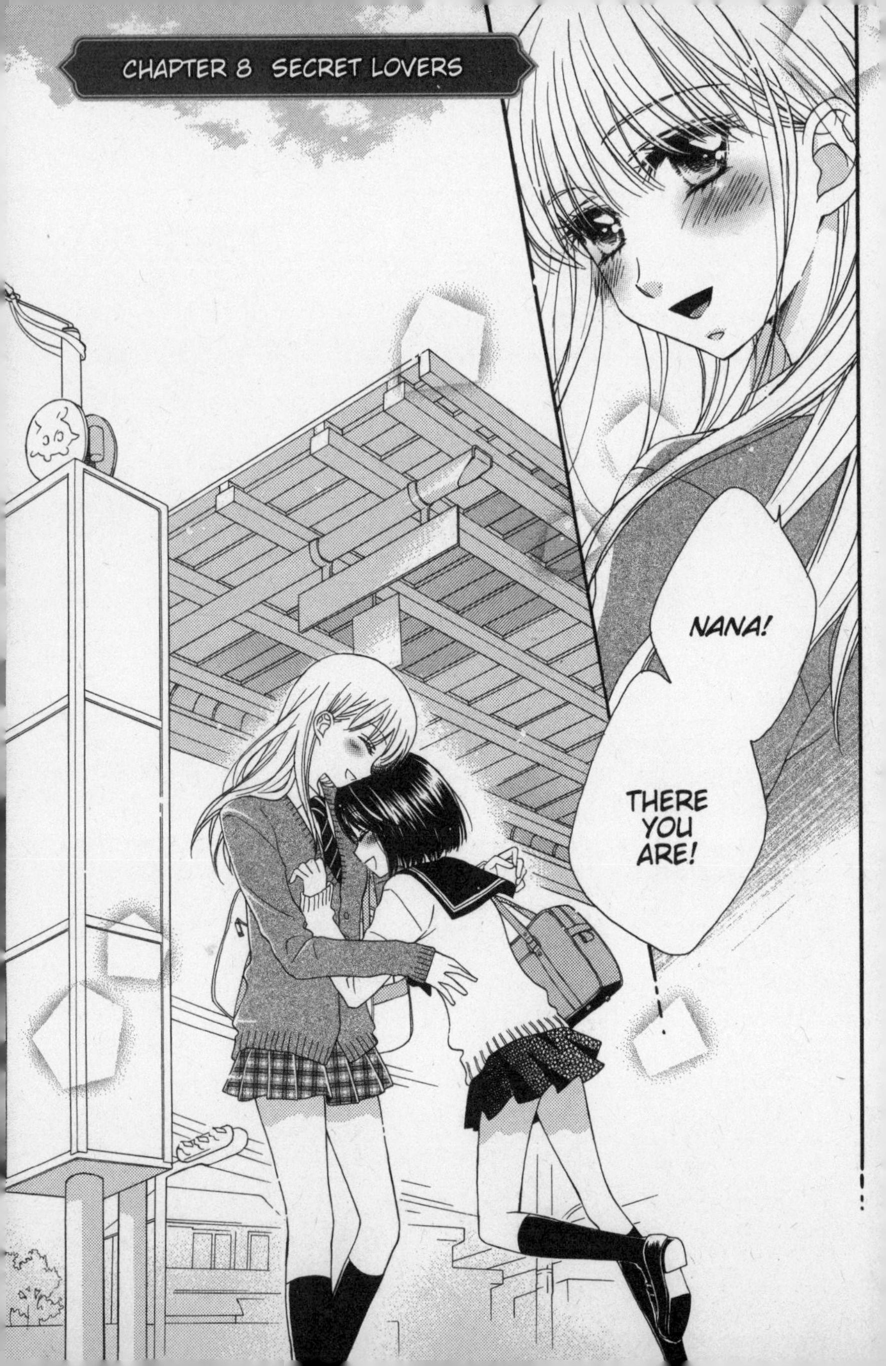
NANA!
THERE YOU ARE!

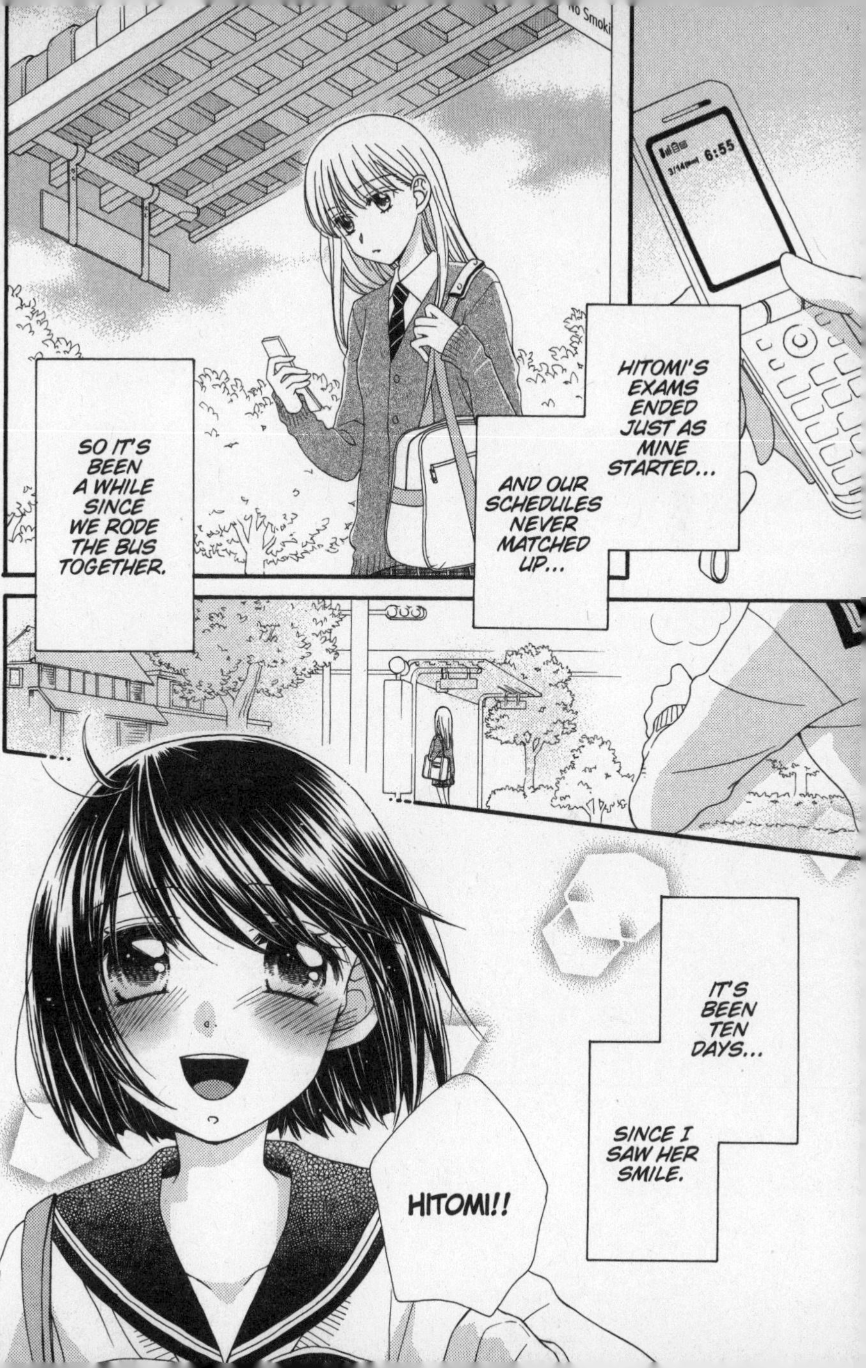
6:55
HITOMI'S EXAMS ENDED JUST AS MINE STARTED...
AND OUR SCHEDULES NEVER MATCHED UP...
SO IT'S BEEN A WHILE SINCE WE RODE THE BUS TOGETHER.
...
IT'S BEEN TEN DAYS...
SINCE I SAW HER SMILE.
HITOMI!!

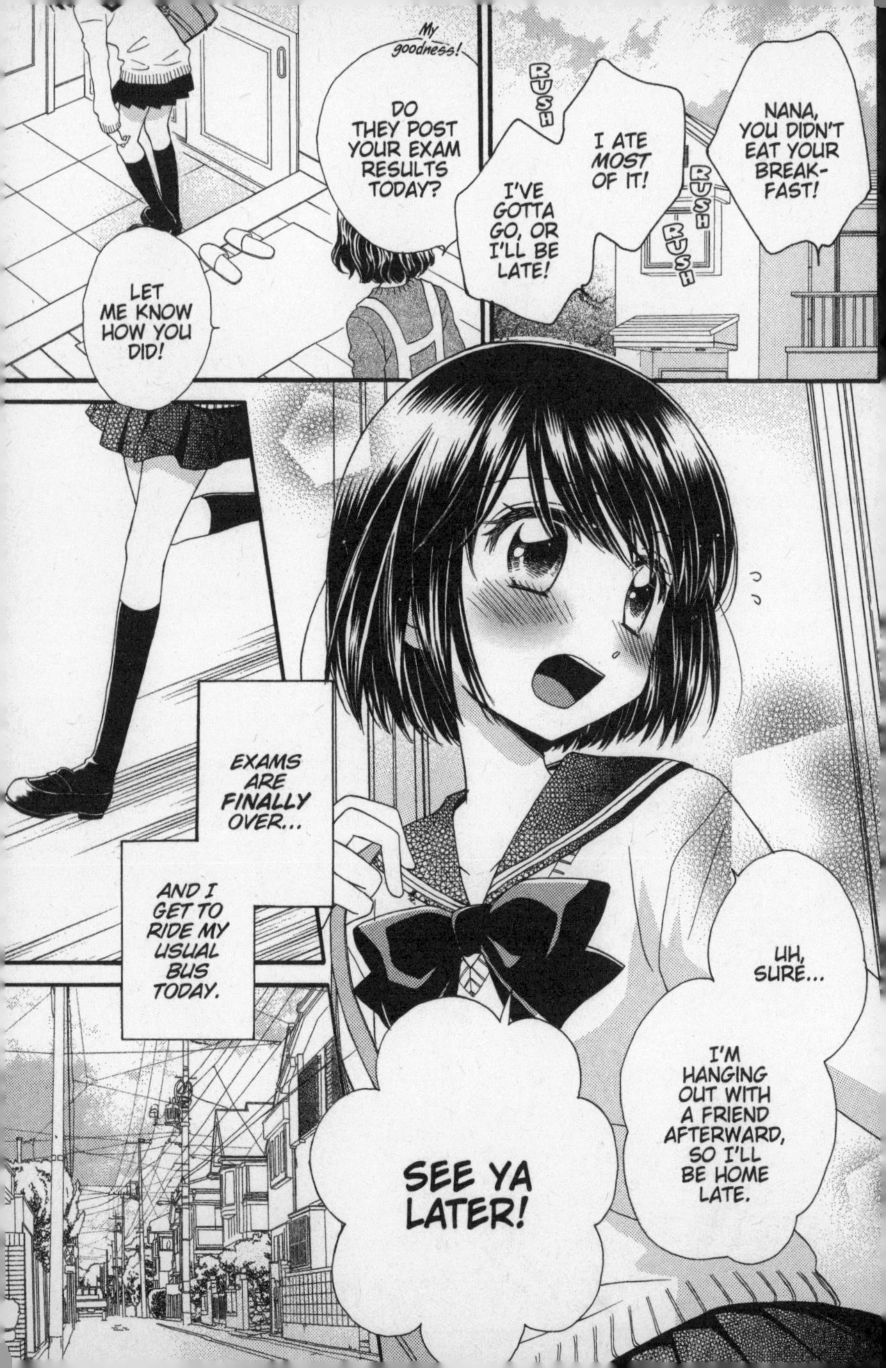
NANA, YOU DIDN'T EAT YOUR BREAK-FAST!
RUSH
RUSH
RUSH
I ATE MOST OF IT!
I'VE GOTTA GO, OR I'LL BE LATE!
My goodness!
DO THEY POST YOUR EXAM RESULTS TODAY?
LET ME KNOW HOW YOU DID!
UH, SURE...
I'M HANGING OUT WITH A FRIEND AFTERWARD, SO I'LL BE HOME LATE.
SEE YA LATER!
EXAMS ARE FINALLY OVER...
AND I GET TO RIDE MY USUAL BUS TODAY.

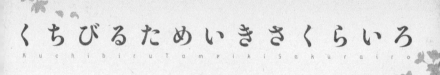

くちびるためいきさくらいろ

Kuchibiru Tameiki Sakurairo.

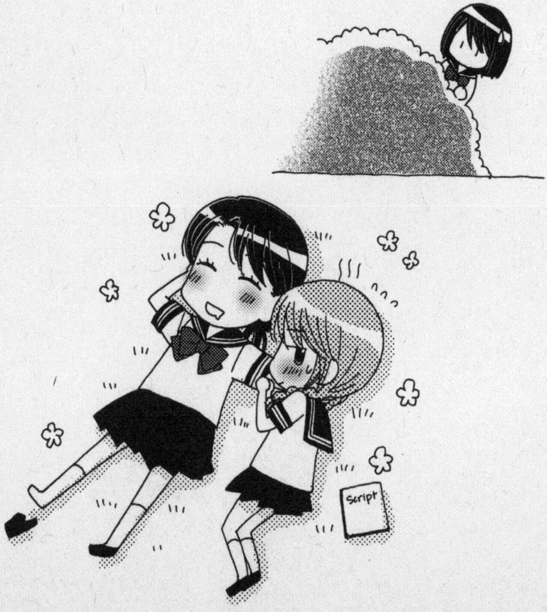
Script

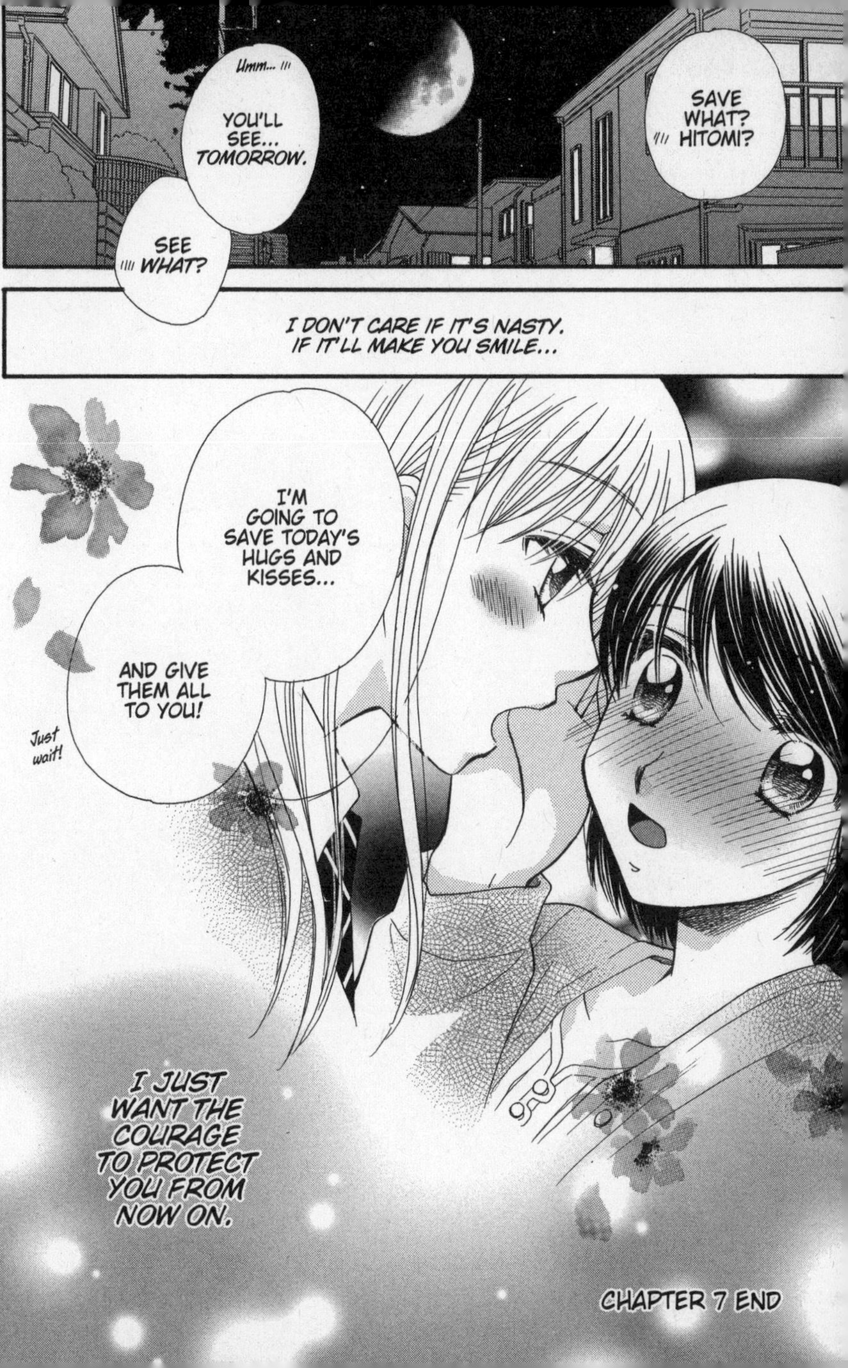
SAVE WHAT? HITOMI?
Umm...
YOU'LL SEE... TOMORROW.
SEE WHAT?
I DON'T CARE IF IT'S NASTY. IF IT'LL MAKE YOU SMILE...
I'M GOING TO SAVE TODAY'S HUGS AND KISSES...
AND GIVE THEM ALL TO YOU!
Just wait!
I JUST WANT THE COURAGE TO PROTECT YOU FROM NOW ON.
CHAPTER 7 END

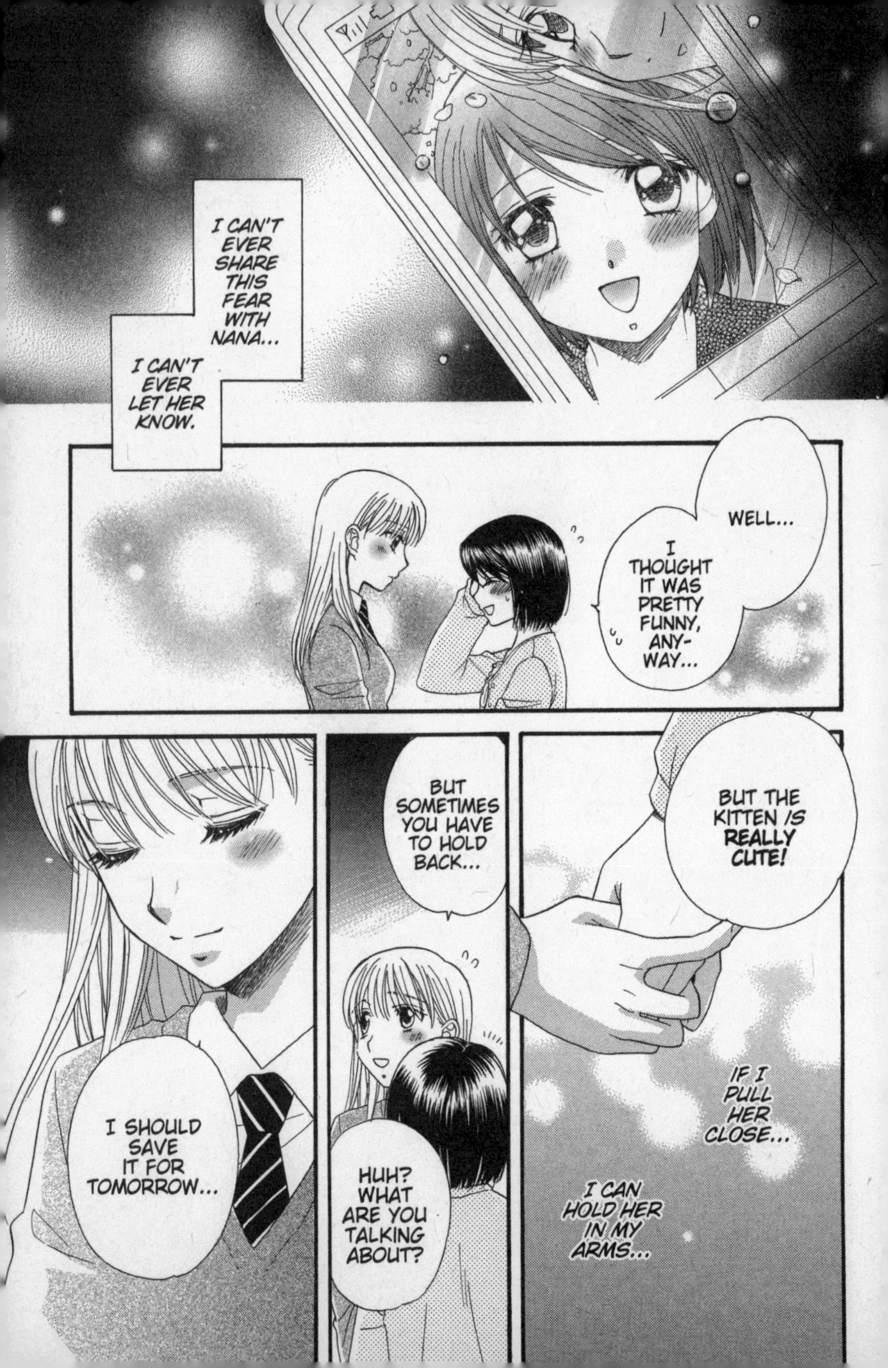
I CAN'T EVER SHARE THIS FEAR WITH NANA...
I CAN'T EVER LET HER KNOW.
WELL... I THOUGHT IT WAS PRETTY FUNNY, ANY-WAY...
BUT THE KITTEN *IS* **REALLY CUTE!**
IF I PULL HER CLOSE...
I CAN HOLD HER IN MY ARMS...
BUT SOMETIMES YOU HAVE TO HOLD BACK...
HUH? WHAT ARE YOU TALKING ABOUT?
I SHOULD SAVE IT FOR TOMORROW...

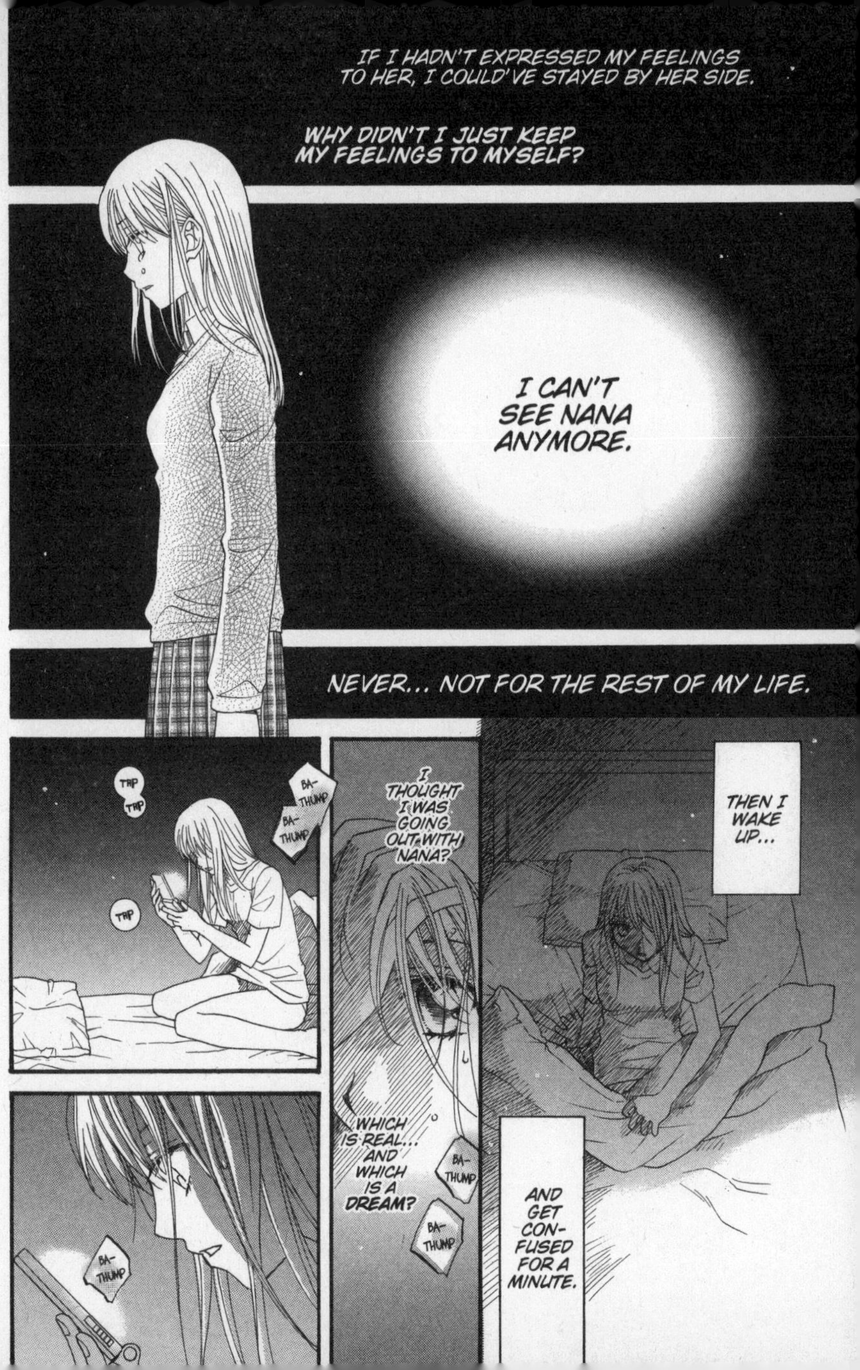
IF I HADN'T EXPRESSED MY FEELINGS TO HER, I COULD'VE STAYED BY HER SIDE.
WHY DIDN'T I JUST KEEP MY FEELINGS TO MYSELF?
I CAN'T SEE NANA ANYMORE.
NEVER... NOT FOR THE REST OF MY LIFE.
THEN I WAKE UP...
AND GET CONFUSED FOR A MINUTE.
I THOUGHT I WAS GOING OUT WITH NANA?
WHICH IS REAL... AND WHICH IS A DREAM?
BA-THUMP
BA-THUMP
TAP
TAP
BA-THUMP
BA-THUMP
TAP
BA-THUMP

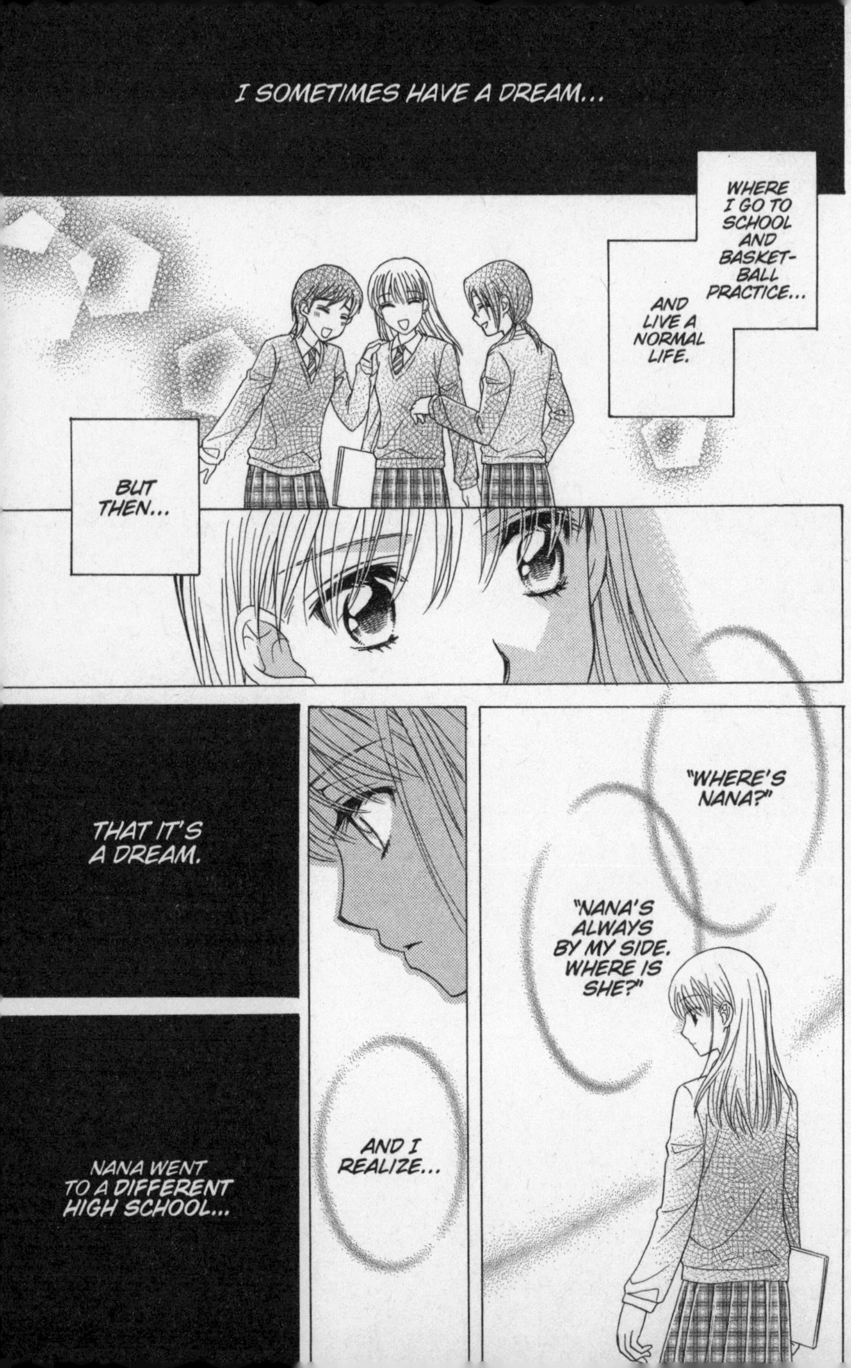
I SOMETIMES HAVE A DREAM...
WHERE I GO TO SCHOOL AND BASKET-BALL PRACTICE...
AND LIVE A NORMAL LIFE.
BUT THEN...
"WHERE'S NANA?"
"NANA'S ALWAYS BY MY SIDE. WHERE IS SHE?"
AND I REALIZE...
THAT IT'S A DREAM.
NANA WENT TO A DIFFERENT HIGH SCHOOL...

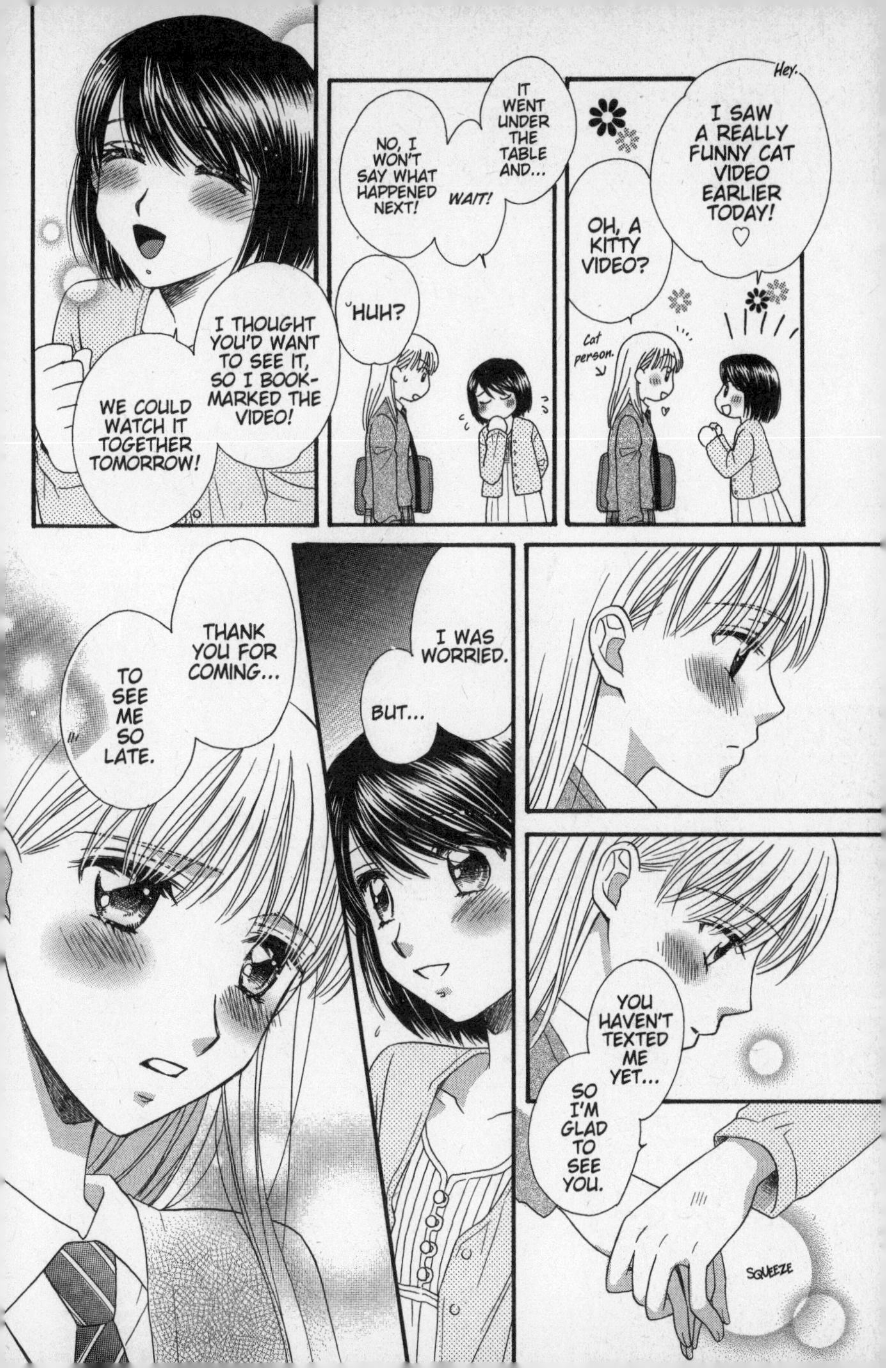

Hey.
I SAW A REALLY FUNNY CAT VIDEO EARLIER TODAY! ♡
OH, A KITTY VIDEO?
Cat person.
IT WENT UNDER THE TABLE AND...
WAIT!
NO, I WON'T SAY WHAT HAPPENED NEXT!
HUH?
I THOUGHT YOU'D WANT TO SEE IT, SO I BOOK-MARKED THE VIDEO!
WE COULD WATCH IT TOGETHER TOMORROW!
YOU HAVEN'T TEXTED ME YET...
SO I'M GLAD TO SEE YOU.
SQUEEZE
I WAS WORRIED.
BUT...
THANK YOU FOR COMING...
TO SEE ME SO LATE.

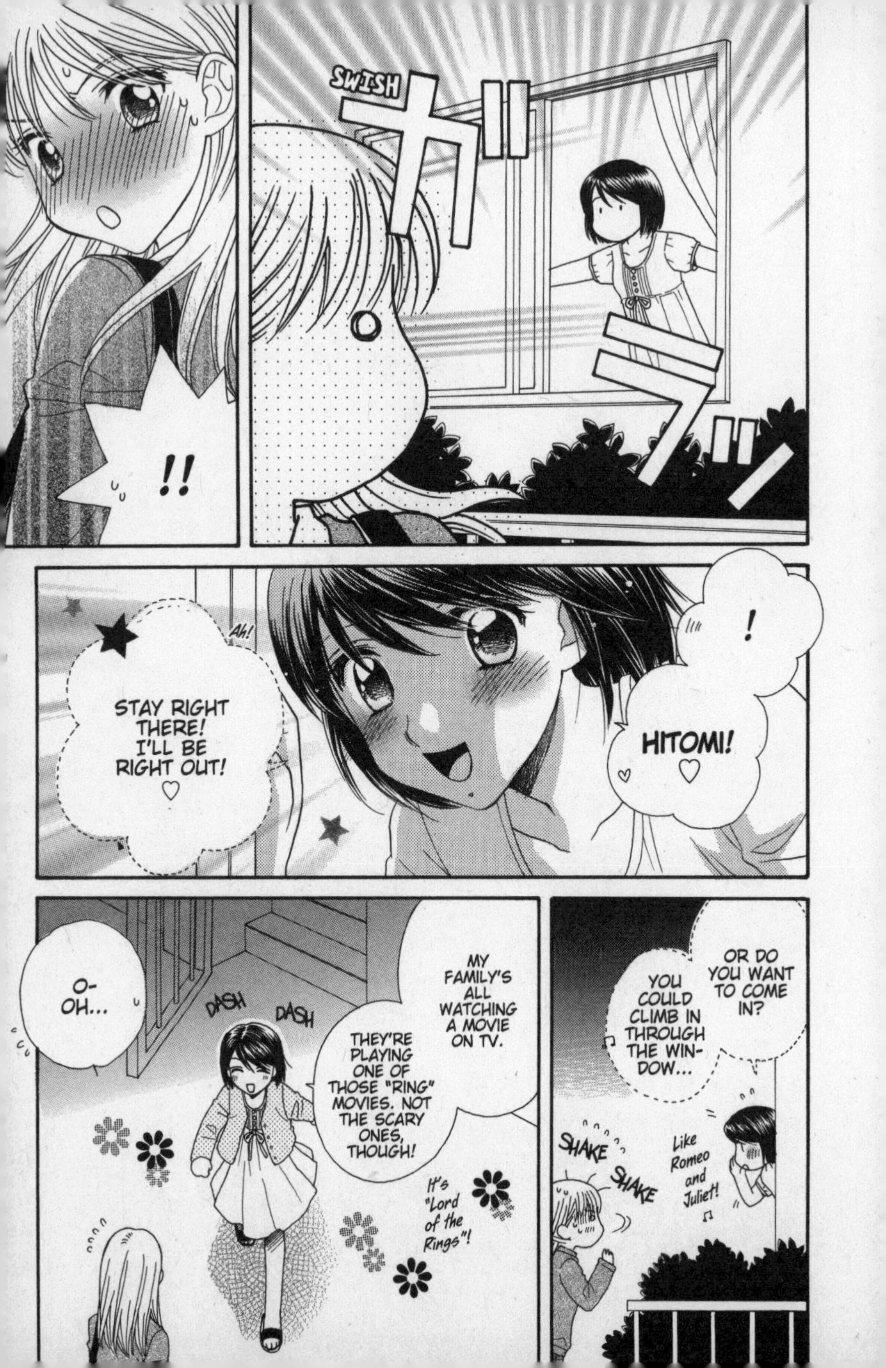
SWISH
!!
!
HITOMI!
Ah!
STAY RIGHT THERE! I'LL BE RIGHT OUT!
OR DO YOU WANT TO COME IN?
YOU COULD CLIMB IN THROUGH THE WINDOW...
Like Romeo and Juliet!
SHAKE
SHAKE
MY FAMILY'S ALL WATCHING A MOVIE ON TV.
THEY'RE PLAYING ONE OF THOSE "RING" MOVIES. NOT THE SCARY ONES, THOUGH!
DASH
DASH
It's "Lord of the Rings"!
O-OH...

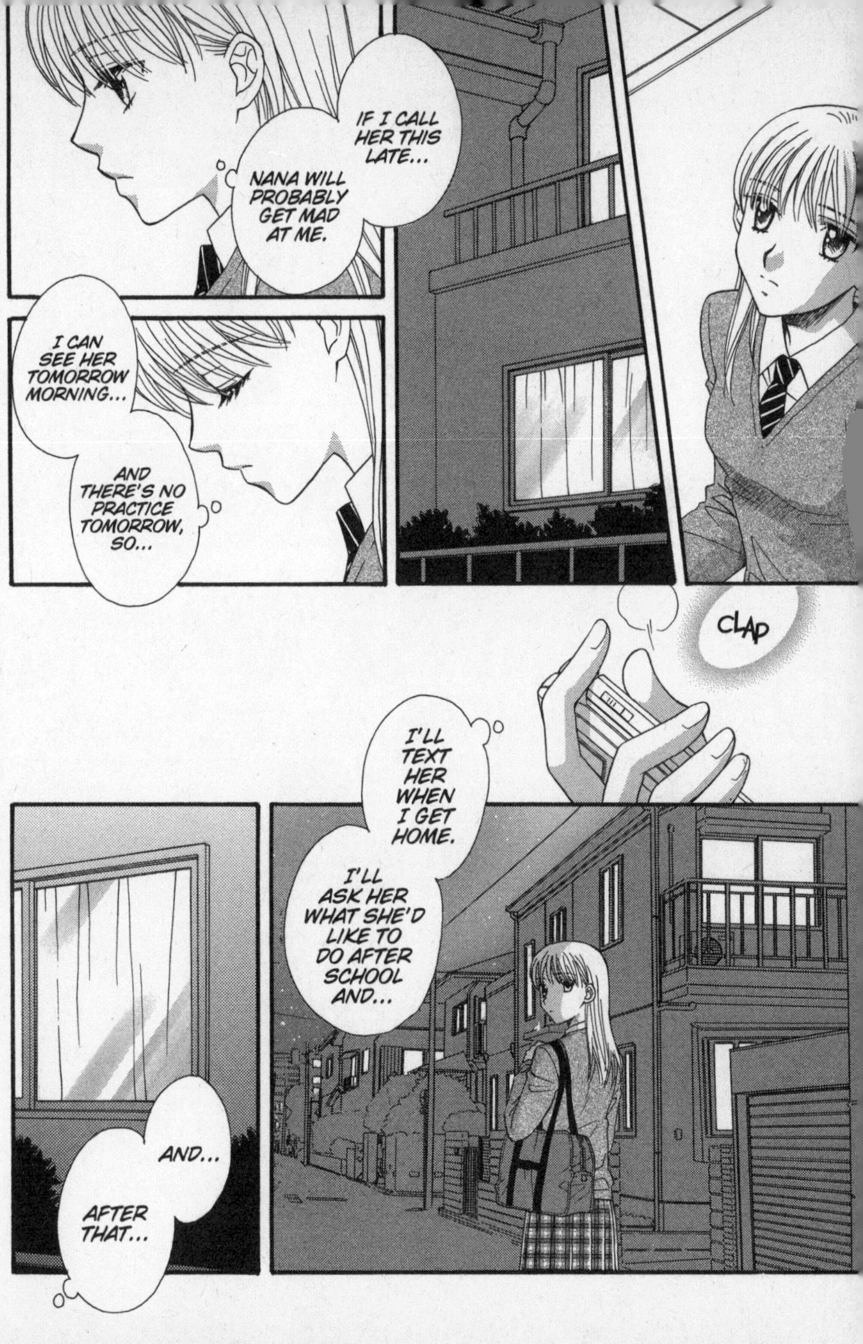
IF I CALL HER THIS LATE...
NANA WILL PROBABLY GET MAD AT ME.
I CAN SEE HER TOMORROW MORNING...
AND THERE'S NO PRACTICE TOMORROW, SO...
CLAP
I'LL TEXT HER WHEN I GET HOME.
I'LL ASK HER WHAT SHE'D LIKE TO DO AFTER SCHOOL AND...
AND...
AFTER THAT...

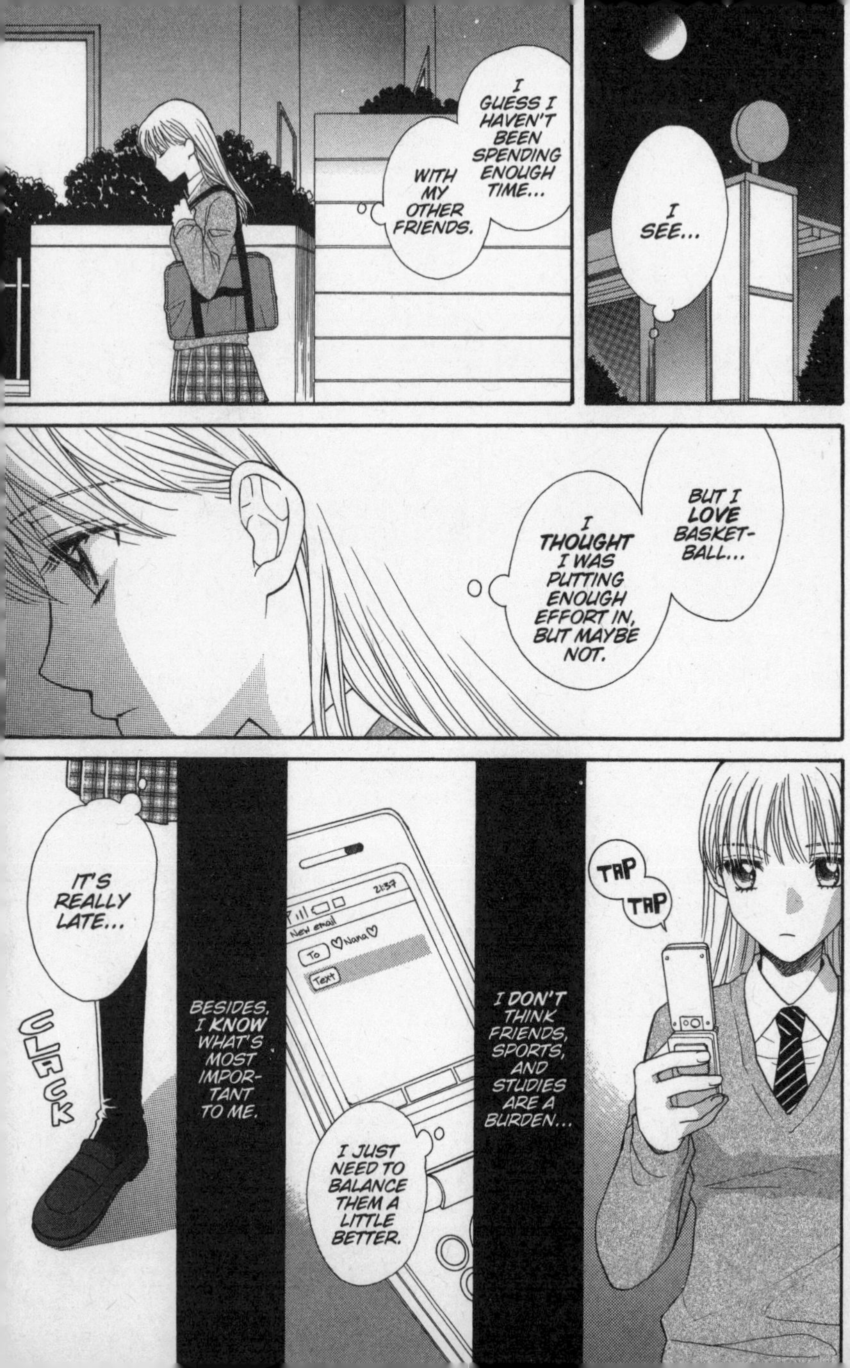
I SEE...
I GUESS I HAVEN'T BEEN SPENDING ENOUGH TIME...
WITH MY OTHER FRIENDS.
BUT I LOVE BASKET-BALL...
I THOUGHT I WAS PUTTING ENOUGH EFFORT IN, BUT MAYBE NOT.
TAP
TAP
I DON'T THINK FRIENDS, SPORTS, AND STUDIES ARE A BURDEN...
21:37
New email
To ♡Nana♡
Text
I JUST NEED TO BALANCE THEM A LITTLE BETTER.
BESIDES, I KNOW WHAT'S MOST IMPOR-TANT TO ME.
IT'S REALLY LATE...
CLACK

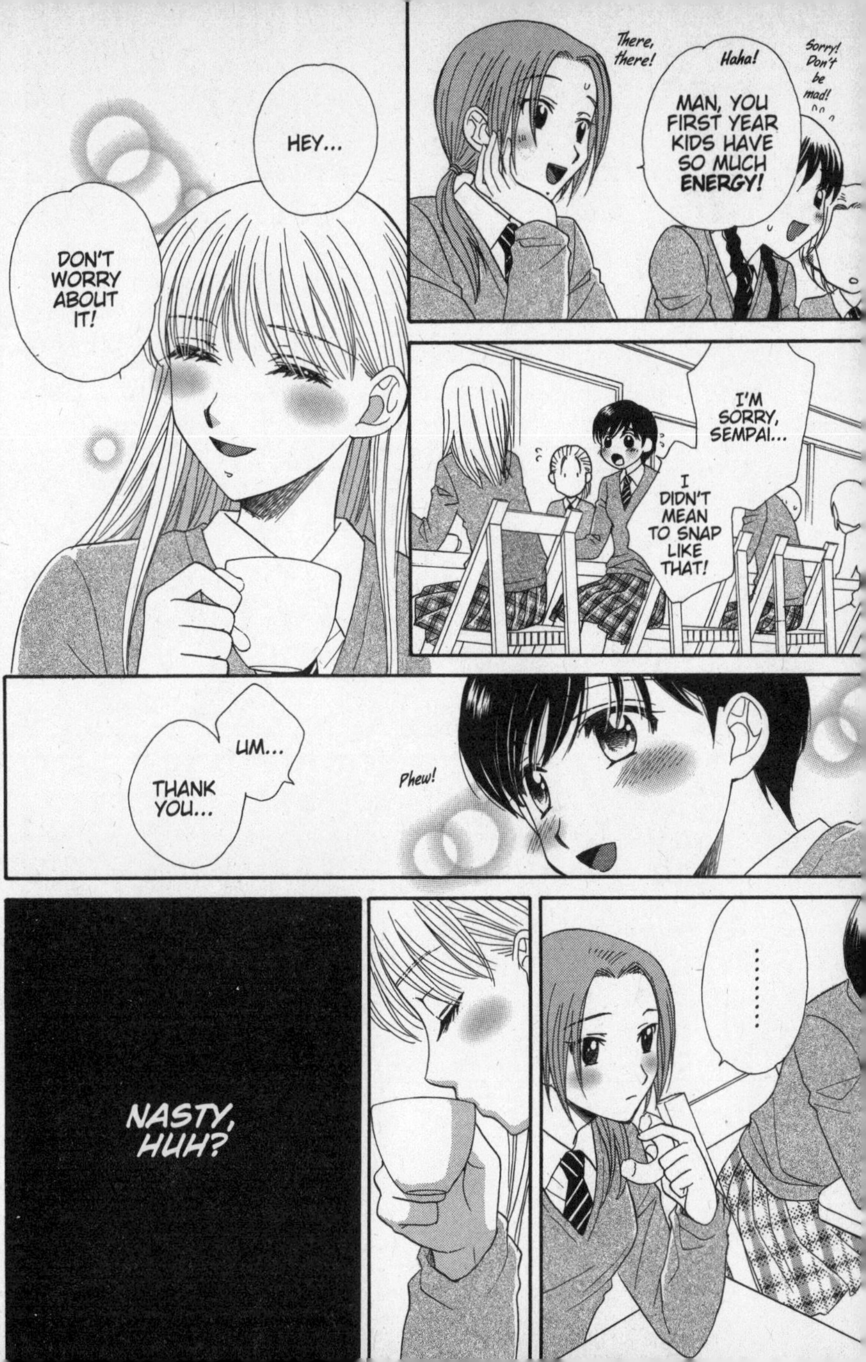
Sorry! Don't be mad!
Haha!
MAN, YOU FIRST YEAR KIDS HAVE SO MUCH ENERGY!
There, there!
I'M SORRY, SEMPAI...
I DIDN'T MEAN TO SNAP LIKE THAT!
HEY...
DON'T WORRY ABOUT IT!
Phew!
UM...
THANK YOU...
......
NASTY, HUH?

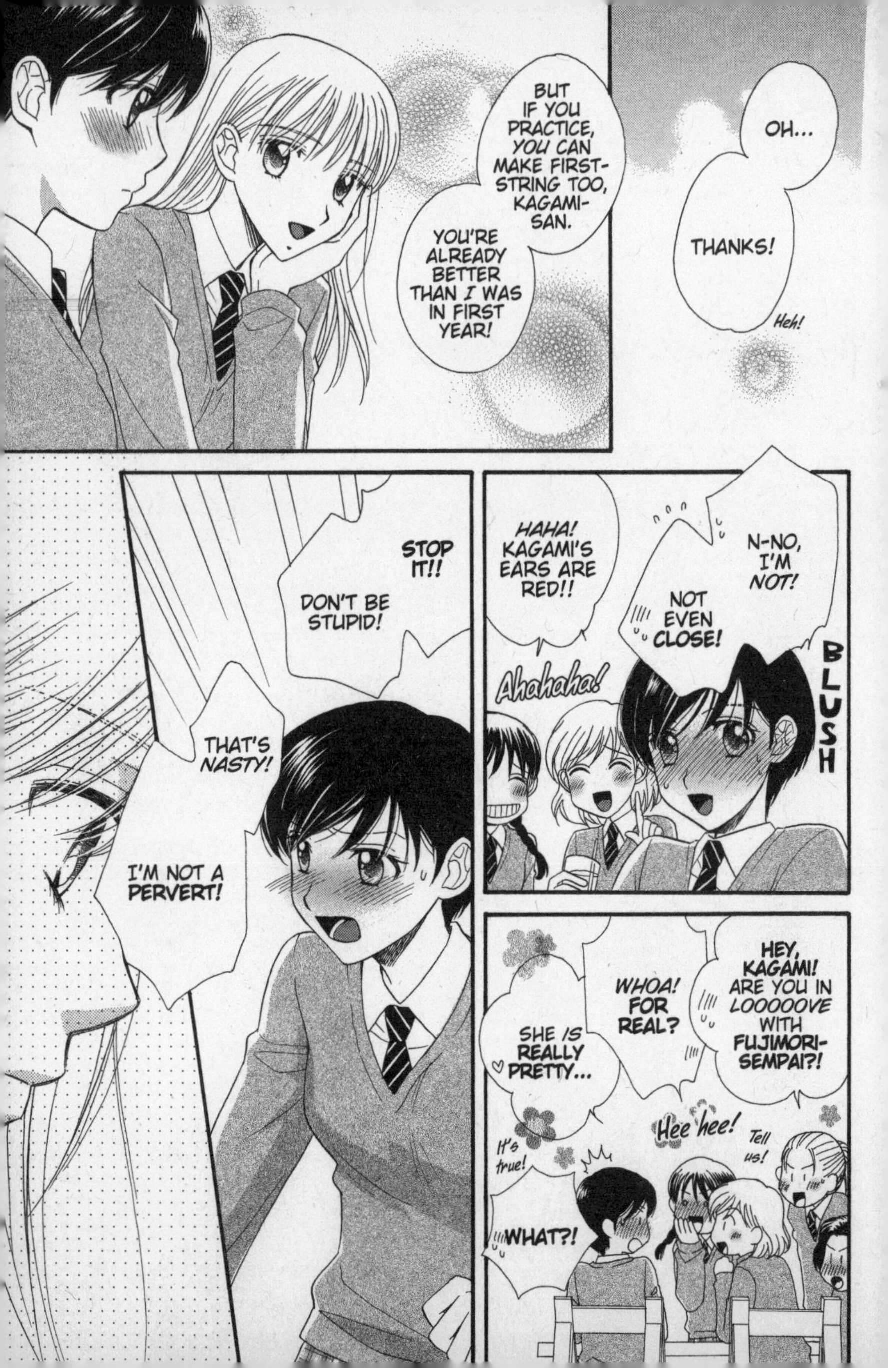
OH...
THANKS!
Heh!
BUT IF YOU PRACTICE, YOU CAN MAKE FIRST-STRING TOO, KAGAMI-SAN.
YOU'RE ALREADY BETTER THAN I WAS IN FIRST YEAR!
N-NO, I'M NOT!
NOT EVEN CLOSE!
BLUSH
HAHA! KAGAMI'S EARS ARE RED!!
Ahahaha!
HEY, KAGAMI! ARE YOU IN LOOOOOVE WITH FUJIMORI-SEMPAI?!
WHOA! FOR REAL?
SHE IS REALLY PRETTY...
Tell us!
Hee hee!
It's true!
WHAT?!
STOP IT!!
DON'T BE STUPID!
THAT'S NASTY!
I'M NOT A PERVERT!

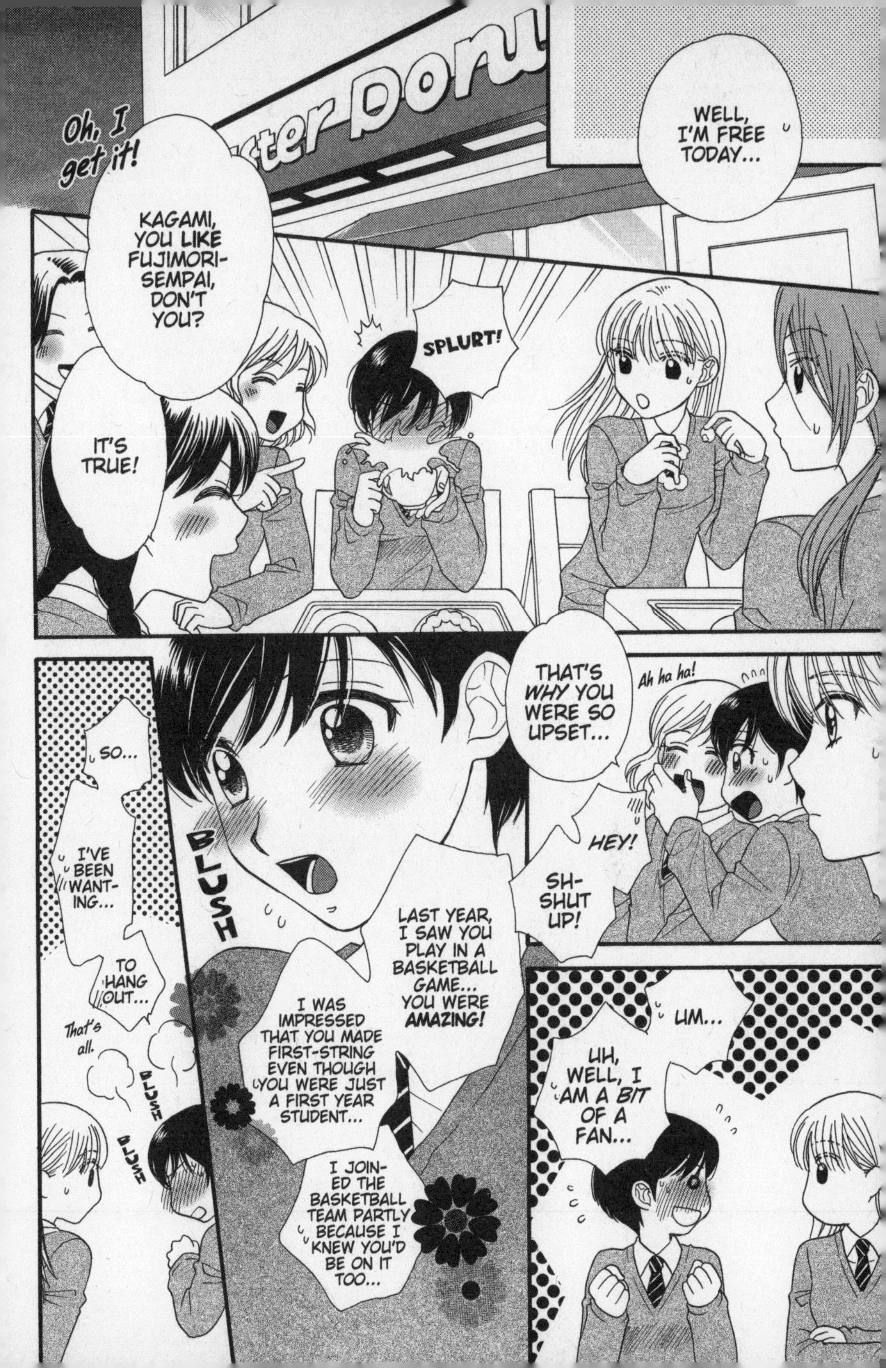
WELL, I'M FREE TODAY...
Oh, I get it!
KAGAMI, YOU LIKE FUJIMORI-SEMPAI, DON'T YOU?
SPLURT!
IT'S TRUE!
THAT'S *WHY* YOU WERE SO UPSET...
Ah ha ha!
HEY!
SH-SHUT UP!
UM...
UH, WELL, I AM A *BIT* OF A FAN...
BLUSH
LAST YEAR, I SAW YOU PLAY IN A BASKETBALL GAME... YOU WERE **AMAZING!**
I WAS IMPRESSED THAT YOU MADE FIRST-STRING EVEN THOUGH YOU WERE JUST A FIRST YEAR STUDENT...
I JOIN-ED THE BASKETBALL TEAM PARTLY BECAUSE I KNEW YOU'D BE ON IT TOO...
SO...
I'VE BEEN WANT-ING...
TO HANG OUT...
That's all.
BLUSH
BLUSH

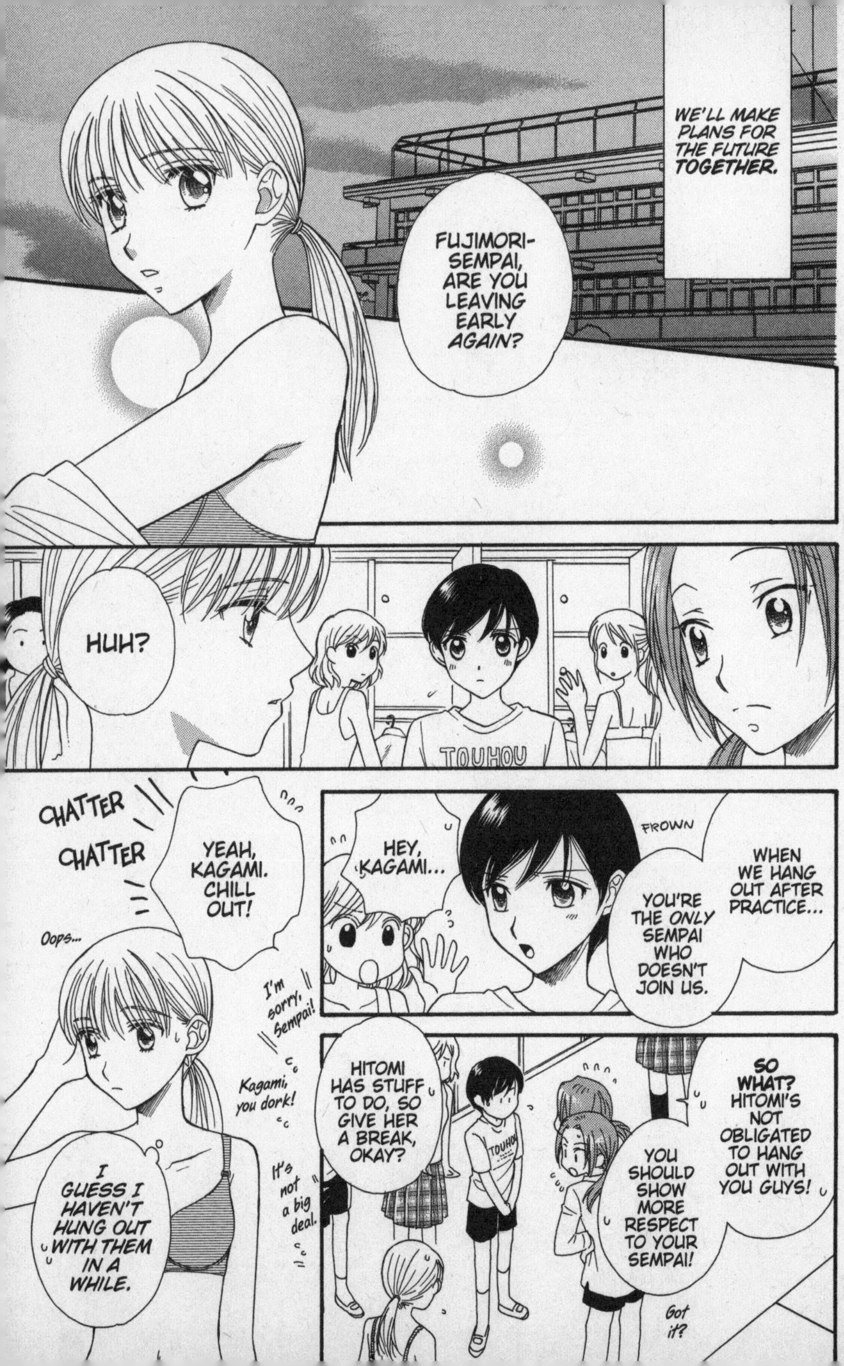
WE'LL MAKE PLANS FOR THE FUTURE TOGETHER.
FUJIMORI-SEMPAI, ARE YOU LEAVING EARLY AGAIN?
HUH?
WHEN WE HANG OUT AFTER PRACTICE...
YOU'RE THE ONLY SEMPAI WHO DOESN'T JOIN US.
FROWN
HEY, KAGAMI...
SO WHAT? HITOMI'S NOT OBLIGATED TO HANG OUT WITH YOU GUYS!
YOU SHOULD SHOW MORE RESPECT TO YOUR SEMPAI!
Got it?
HITOMI HAS STUFF TO DO, SO GIVE HER A BREAK, OKAY?
YEAH, KAGAMI. CHILL OUT!
CHATTER
CHATTER
Oops...
I'm sorry, Sempai!
Kagami, you dork!
It's not a big deal.
I GUESS I HAVEN'T HUNG OUT WITH THEM IN A WHILE.

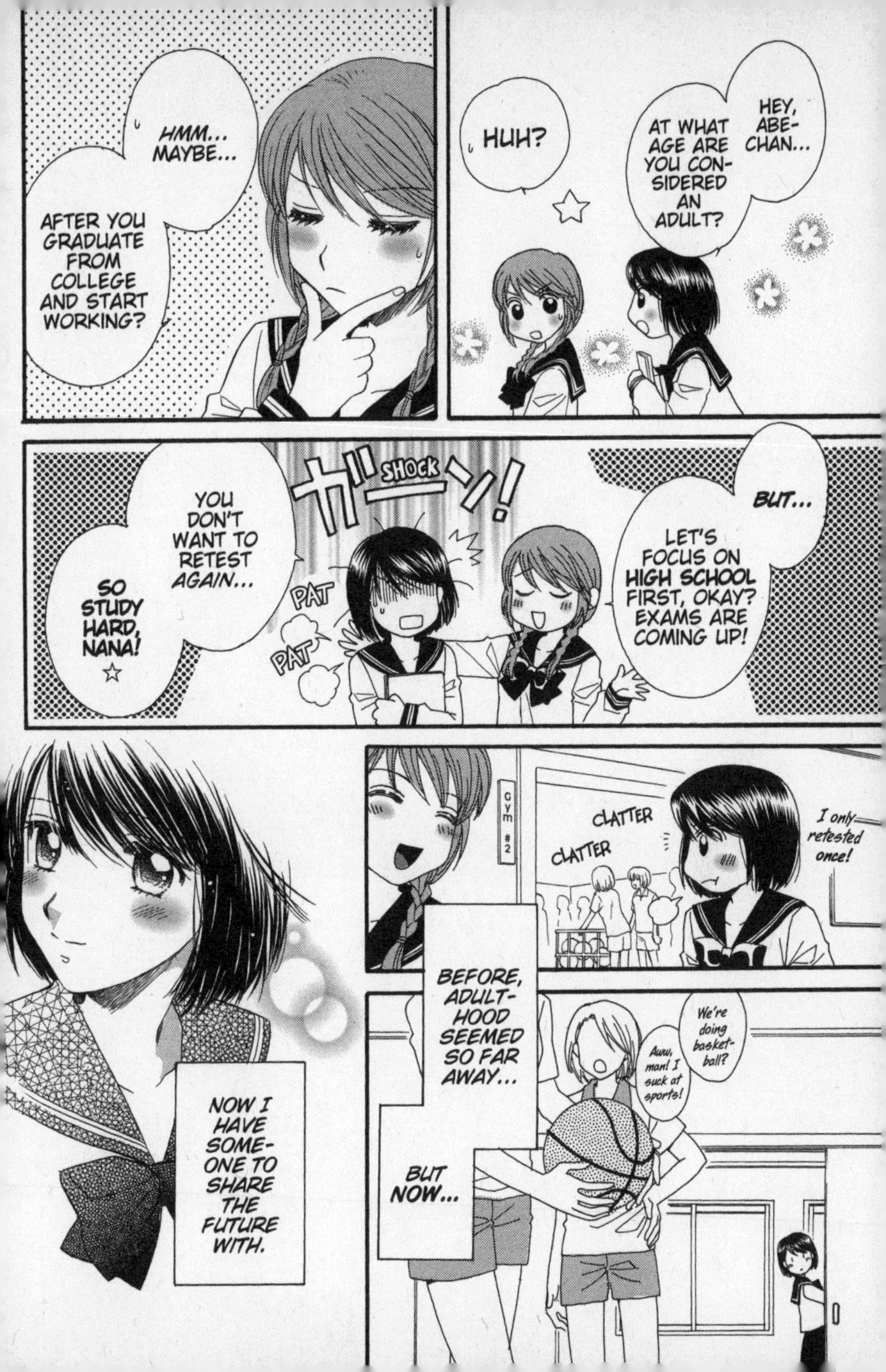
HEY, ABE-CHAN...
AT WHAT AGE ARE YOU CONSIDERED AN ADULT?
HUH?
HMM... MAYBE...
AFTER YOU GRADUATE FROM COLLEGE AND START WORKING?
BUT...
LET'S FOCUS ON HIGH SCHOOL FIRST, OKAY? EXAMS ARE COMING UP!
SHOCK
PAT
PAT
YOU DON'T WANT TO RETEST AGAIN...
SO STUDY HARD, NANA! ☆
I only retested once!
CLATTER
CLATTER
GYM #2
We're doing basketball?
Aww, man! I suck at sports!
BEFORE, ADULTHOOD SEEMED SO FAR AWAY...
BUT NOW...
NOW I HAVE SOMEONE TO SHARE THE FUTURE WITH.

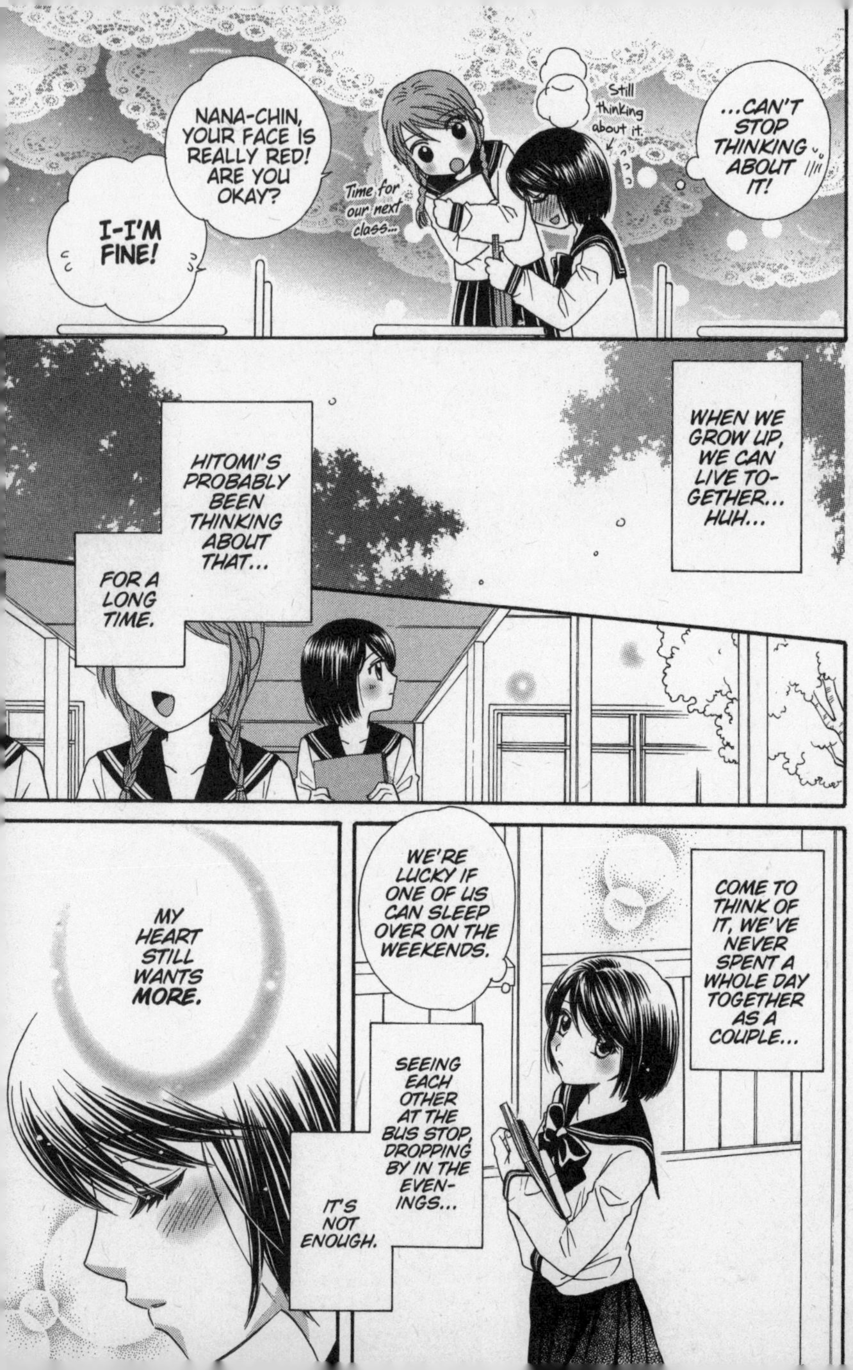
...CAN'T STOP THINKING ABOUT IT!
Still thinking about it.
NANA-CHIN, YOUR FACE IS REALLY RED! ARE YOU OKAY?
Time for our next class...
I-I'M FINE!
WHEN WE GROW UP, WE CAN LIVE TOGETHER... HUH...
HITOMI'S PROBABLY BEEN THINKING ABOUT THAT...
FOR A LONG TIME.
COME TO THINK OF IT, WE'VE NEVER SPENT A WHOLE DAY TOGETHER AS A COUPLE...
WE'RE LUCKY IF ONE OF US CAN SLEEP OVER ON THE WEEKENDS.
SEEING EACH OTHER AT THE BUS STOP, DROPPING BY IN THE EVENINGS...
IT'S NOT ENOUGH.
MY HEART STILL WANTS MORE.

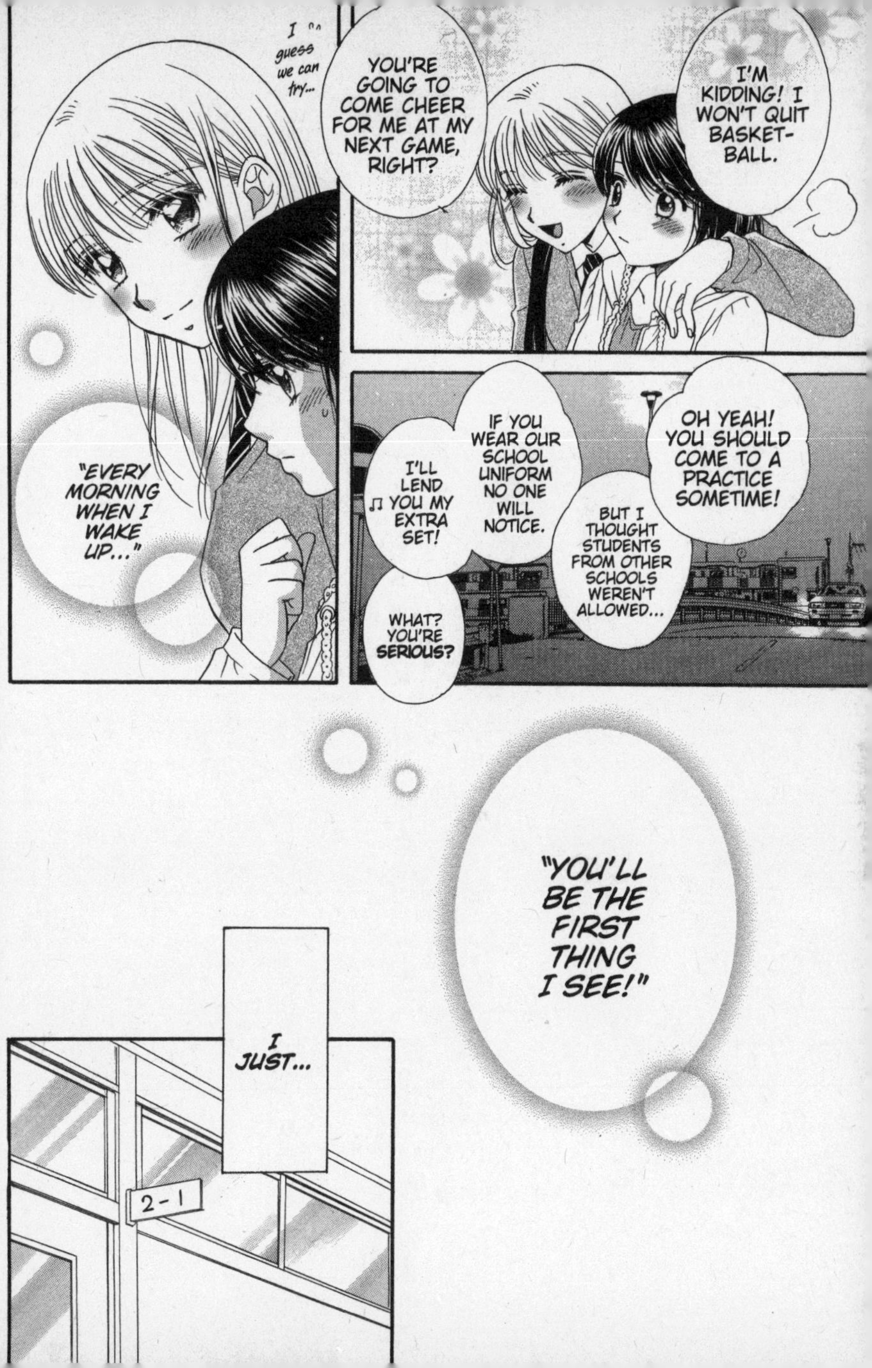
I'M KIDDING! I WON'T QUIT BASKET-BALL.
YOU'RE GOING TO COME CHEER FOR ME AT MY NEXT GAME, RIGHT?
OH YEAH! YOU SHOULD COME TO A PRACTICE SOMETIME!
BUT I THOUGHT STUDENTS FROM OTHER SCHOOLS WEREN'T ALLOWED...
IF YOU WEAR OUR SCHOOL UNIFORM NO ONE WILL NOTICE.
I'LL LEND ♫ YOU MY EXTRA SET!
WHAT? YOU'RE SERIOUS?
I guess we can try...
"EVERY MORNING WHEN I WAKE UP..."
"YOU'LL BE THE FIRST THING I SEE!"
I JUST...

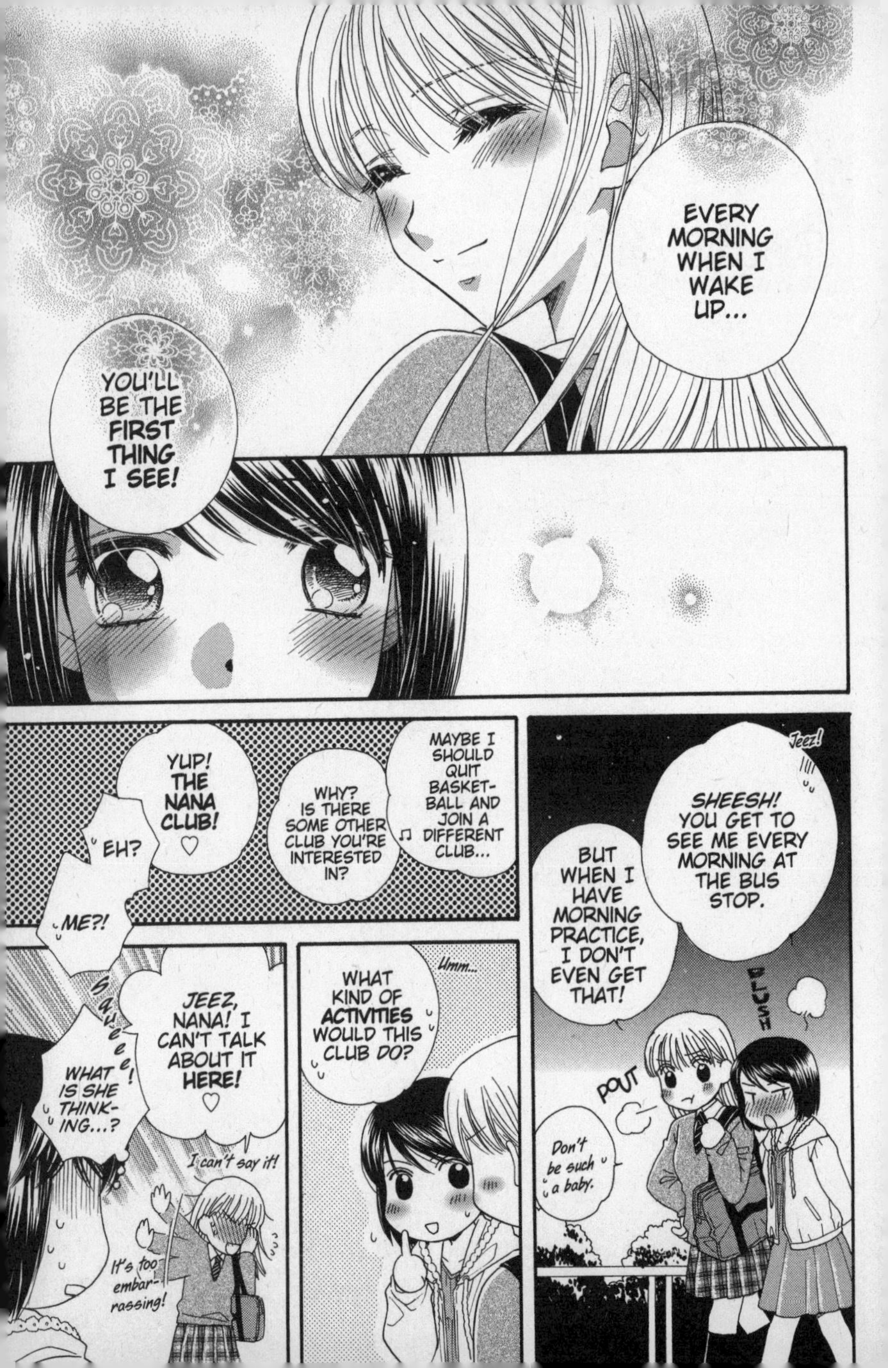
EVERY MORNING WHEN I WAKE UP...
YOU'LL BE THE FIRST THING I SEE!
Jeez!
SHEESH! YOU GET TO SEE ME EVERY MORNING AT THE BUS STOP.
BUT WHEN I HAVE MORNING PRACTICE, I DON'T EVEN GET THAT!
BLUSH
POUT
Don't be such a baby.
MAYBE I SHOULD QUIT BASKET-BALL AND JOIN A DIFFERENT CLUB... ♫
WHY? IS THERE SOME OTHER CLUB YOU'RE INTERESTED IN?
YUP! THE NANA CLUB! ♡
EH?
ME?!
Umm...
WHAT KIND OF ACTIVITIES WOULD THIS CLUB DO?
JEEZ, NANA! I CAN'T TALK ABOUT IT HERE! ♡
Squeeee!
WHAT IS SHE THINKING...?
I can't say it!
It's too embar-rassing!

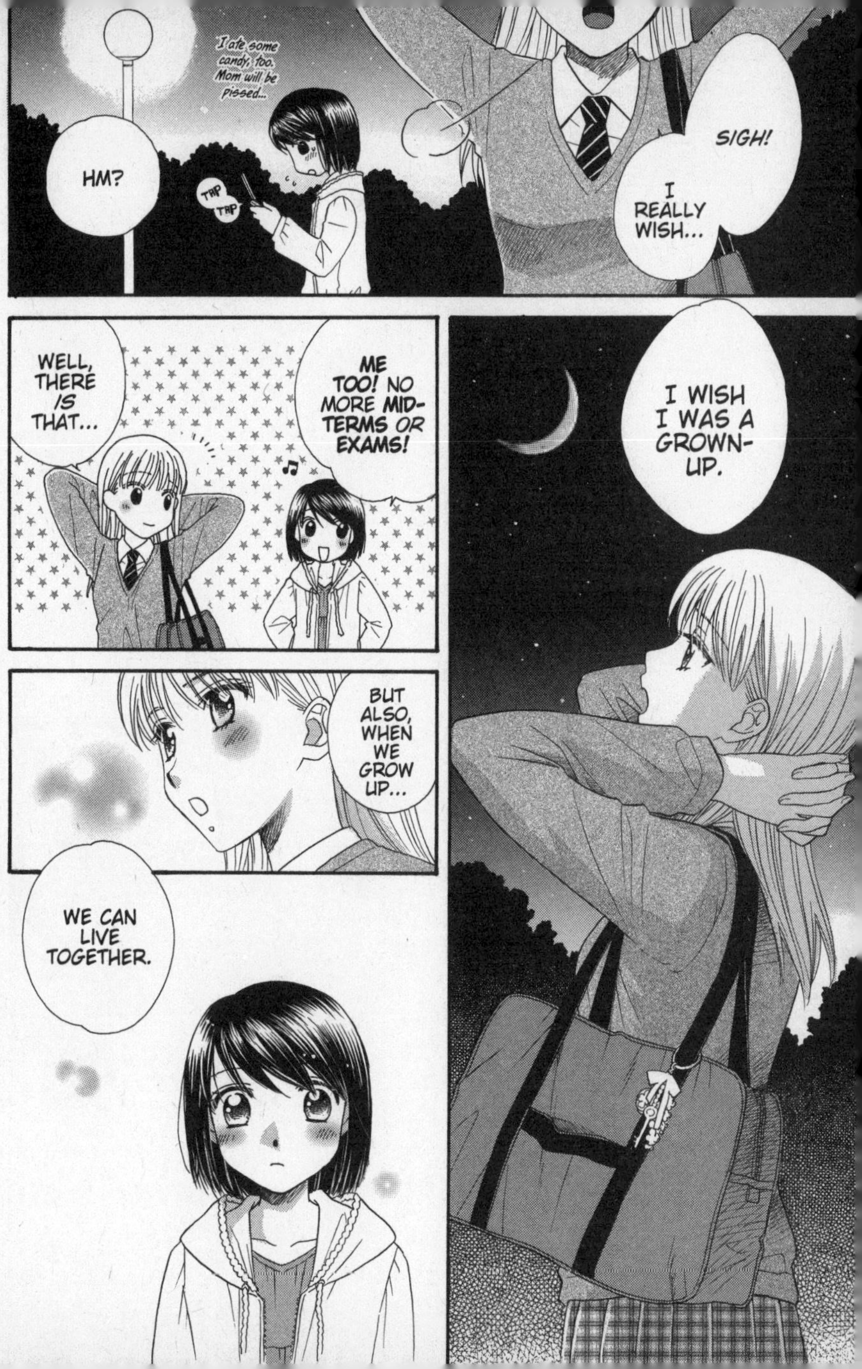
SIGH!
I REALLY WISH...
I ate some candy, too. Mom will be pissed...
HM?
TAP TAP
I WISH I WAS A GROWN-UP.
ME TOO! NO MORE MID-TERMS OR EXAMS!
WELL, THERE IS THAT...
BUT ALSO, WHEN WE GROW UP...
WE CAN LIVE TOGETHER.

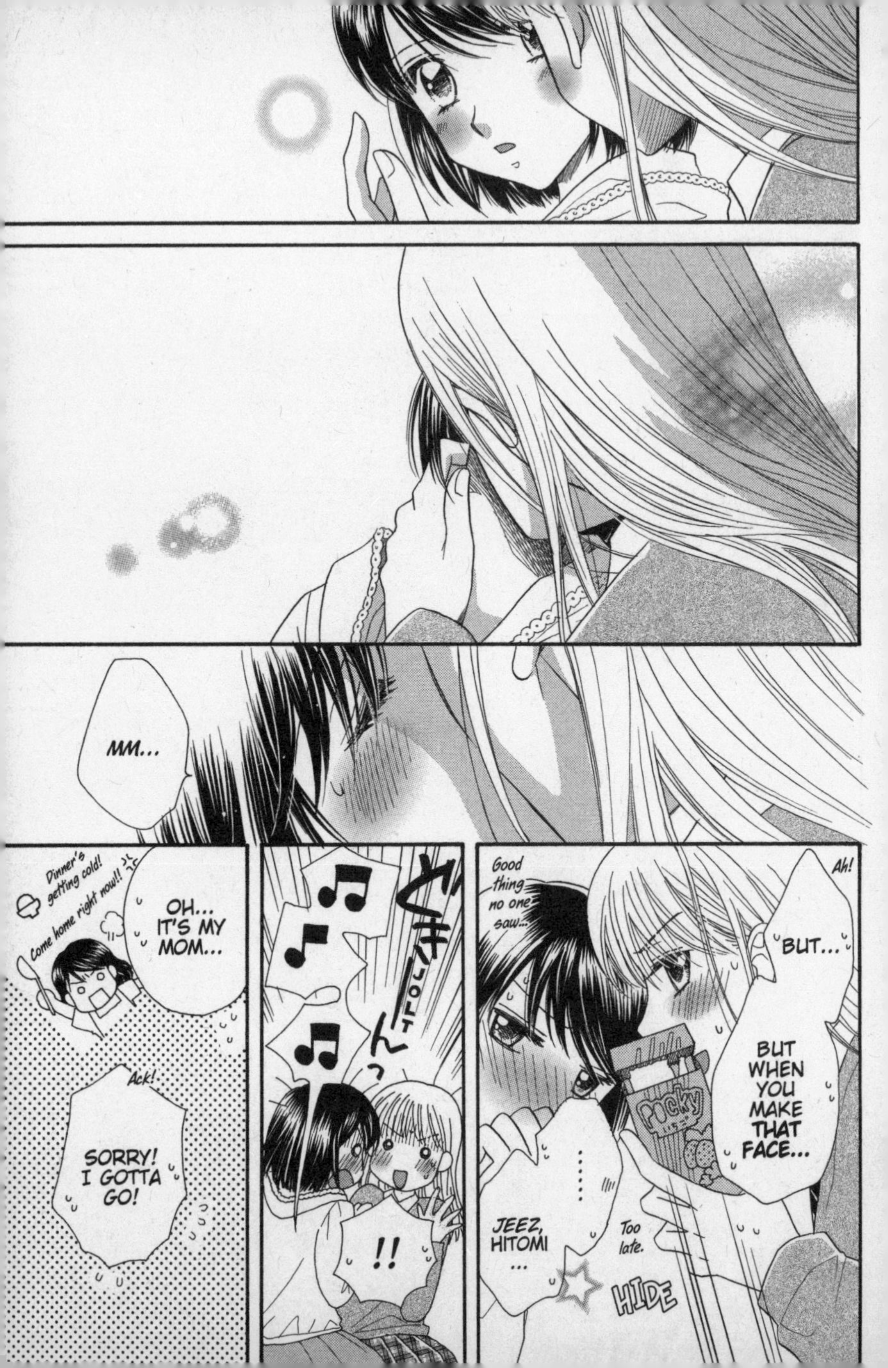
MM...
Ah!
BUT...
BUT WHEN YOU MAKE THAT FACE...
Good thing no one saw...
......
Too late.
JEEZ, HITOMI ...
HIDE
JOLT
!!
OH... IT'S MY MOM...
Dinner's getting cold! Come home right now!!
Ack!
SORRY! I GOTTA GO!

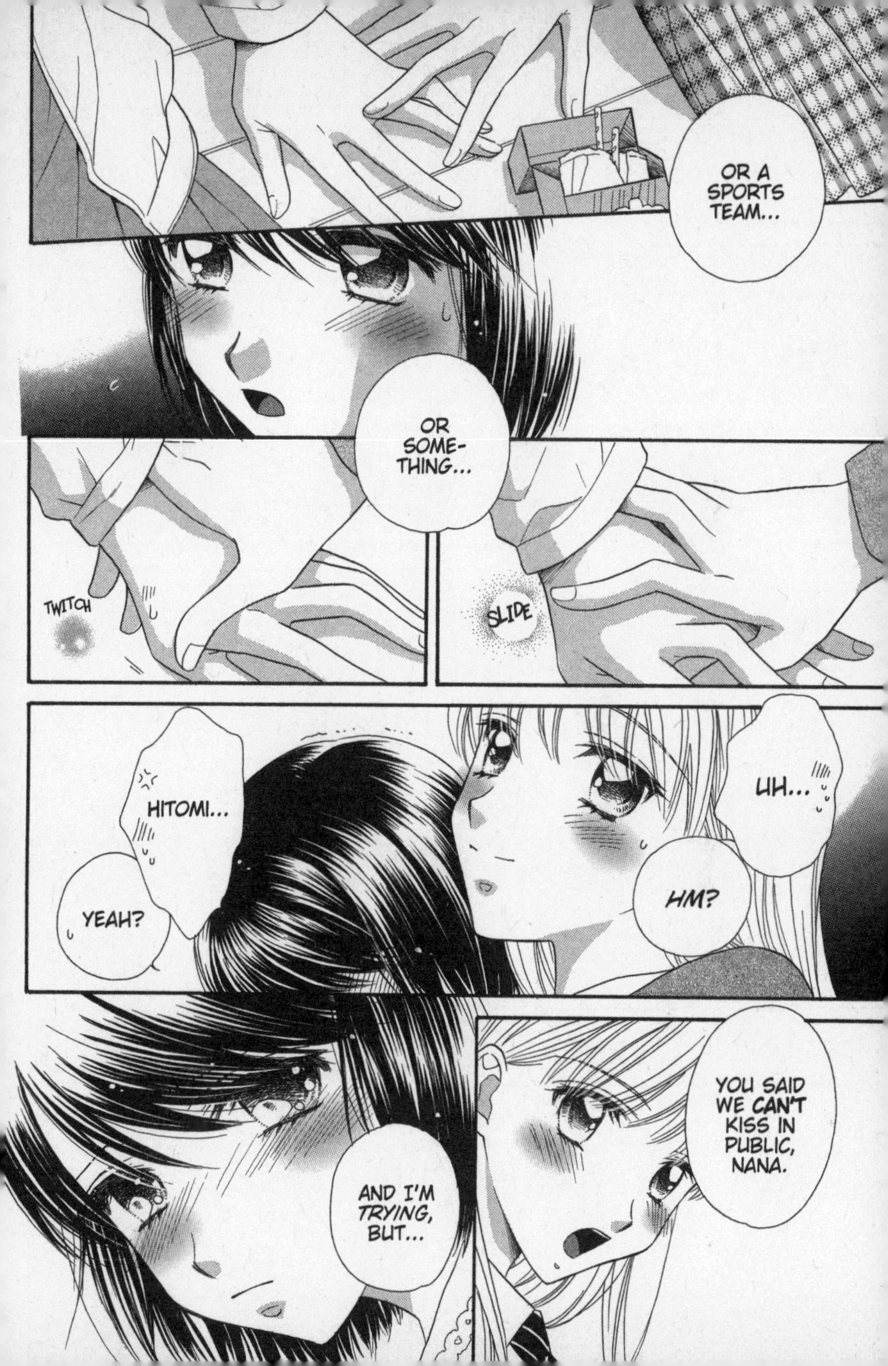

OR A SPORTS TEAM...
OR SOME- THING...
SLIDE
TWITCH
UH...
HM?
HITOMI...
YEAH?
YOU SAID WE CAN'T KISS IN PUBLIC, NANA.
AND I'M *TRYING,* BUT...

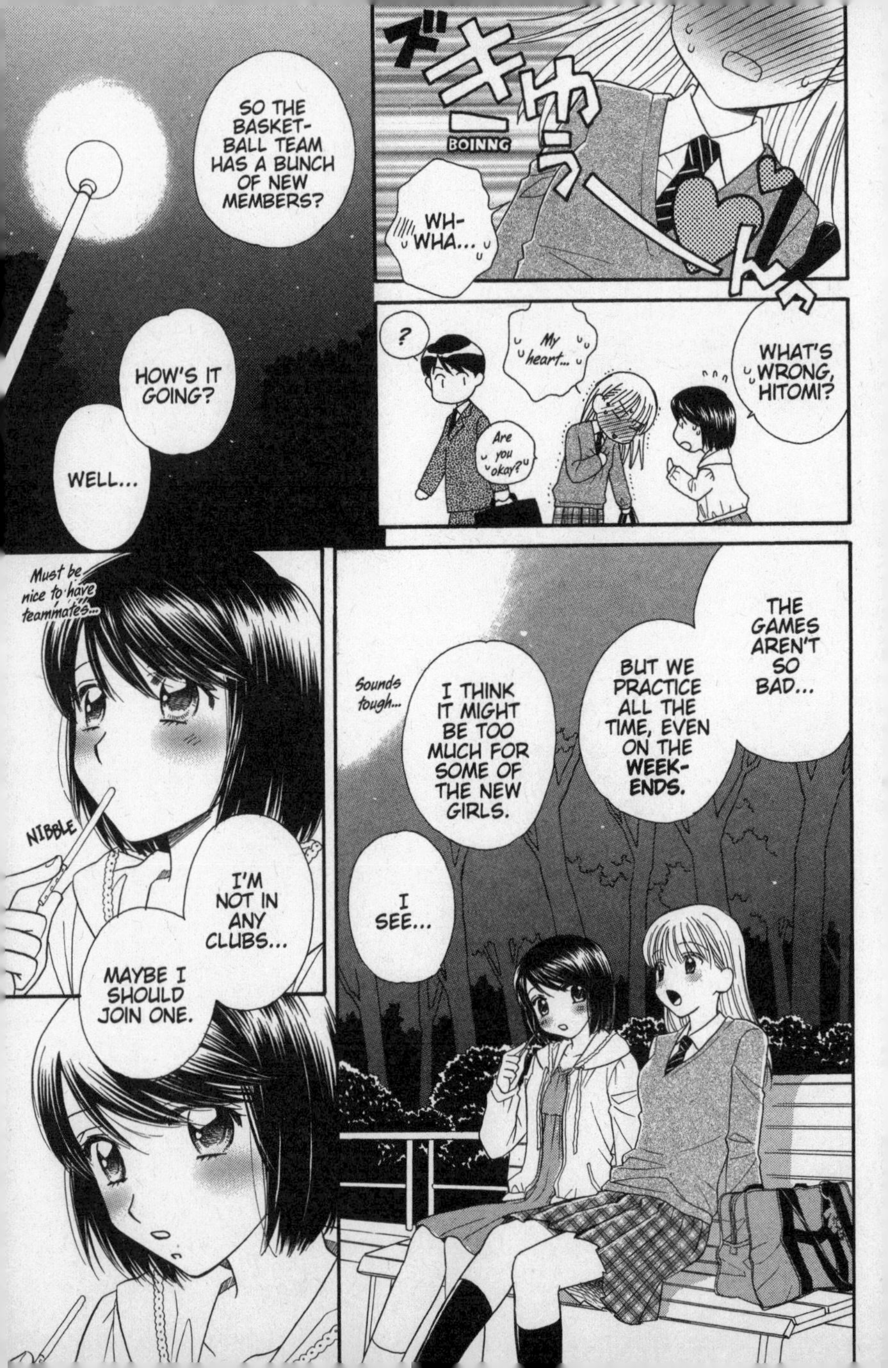
ズキゅうーん
BOINNG
WH-WHA...
WHAT'S WRONG, HITOMI?
My heart...
?
Are you okay?
SO THE BASKET-BALL TEAM HAS A BUNCH OF NEW MEMBERS?
HOW'S IT GOING?
WELL...
THE GAMES AREN'T SO BAD...
BUT WE PRACTICE ALL THE TIME, EVEN ON THE WEEK-ENDS.
I THINK IT MIGHT BE TOO MUCH FOR SOME OF THE NEW GIRLS.
Sounds tough...
I SEE...
Must be nice to have teammates...
NIBBLE
I'M NOT IN ANY CLUBS...
MAYBE I SHOULD JOIN ONE.

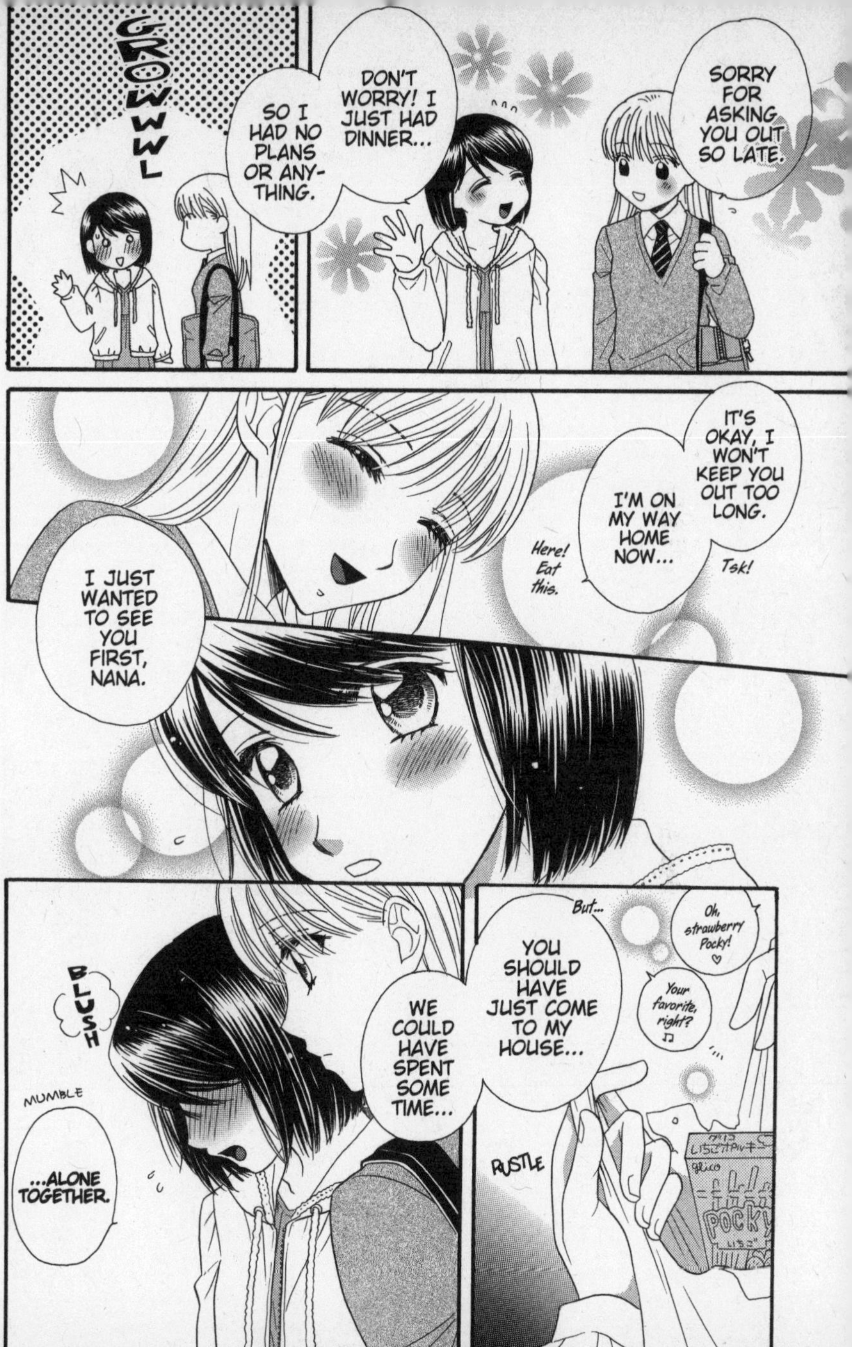
SORRY FOR ASKING YOU OUT SO LATE.
DON'T WORRY! I JUST HAD DINNER...
SO I HAD NO PLANS OR ANY-THING.
GROWWWL
IT'S OKAY, I WON'T KEEP YOU OUT TOO LONG.
Tsk!
I'M ON MY WAY HOME NOW...
Here! Eat this.
I JUST WANTED TO SEE YOU FIRST, NANA.
Oh, strawberry Pocky! ♡
Your favorite, right? ♫
But...
YOU SHOULD HAVE JUST COME TO MY HOUSE...
WE COULD HAVE SPENT SOME TIME...
RUSTLE
POCKY
BLUSH
MUMBLE
...ALONE TOGETHER.

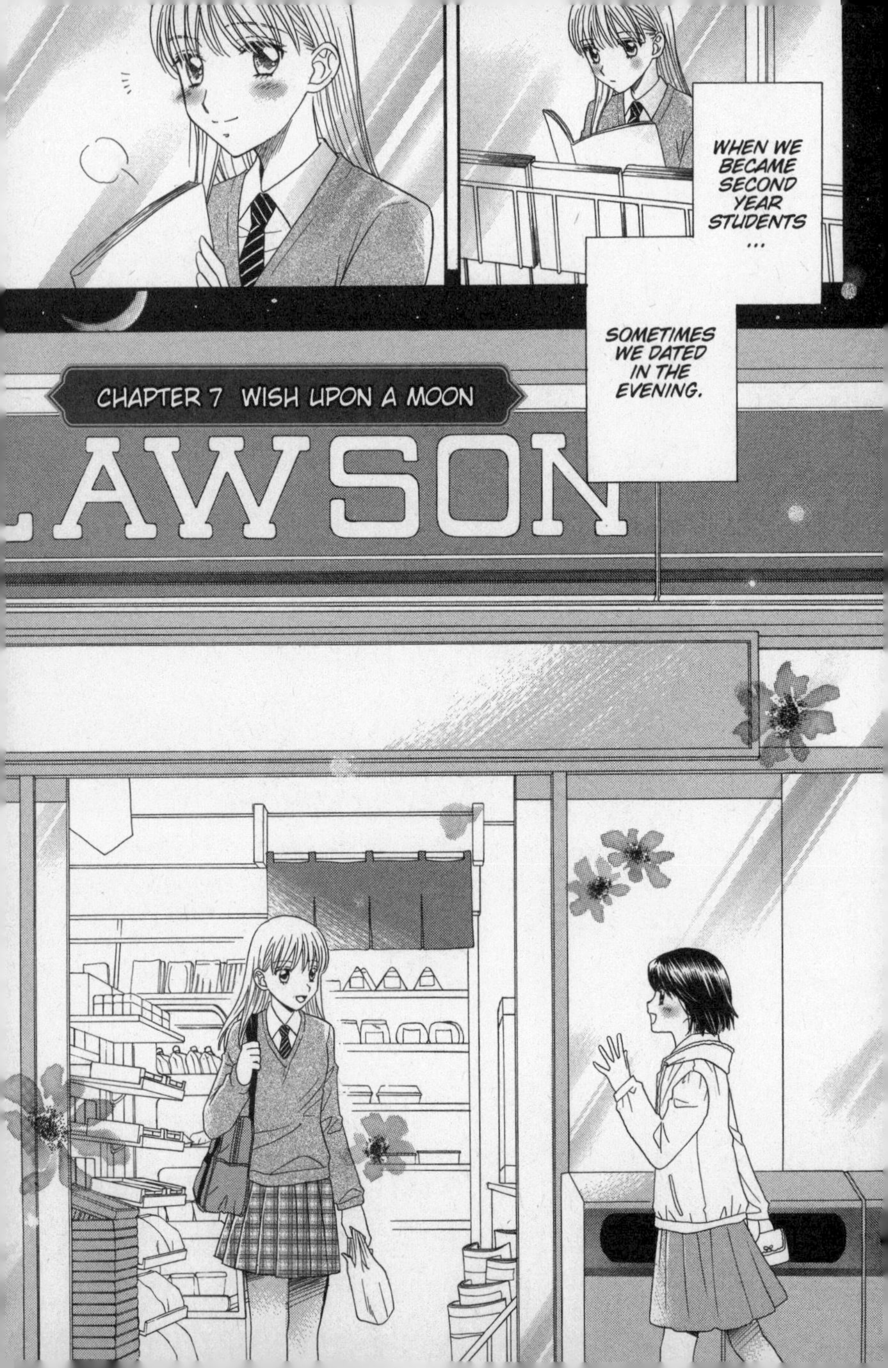
WHEN WE BECAME SECOND YEAR STUDENTS ...
SOMETIMES WE DATED IN THE EVENING.
CHAPTER 7 WISH UPON A MOON

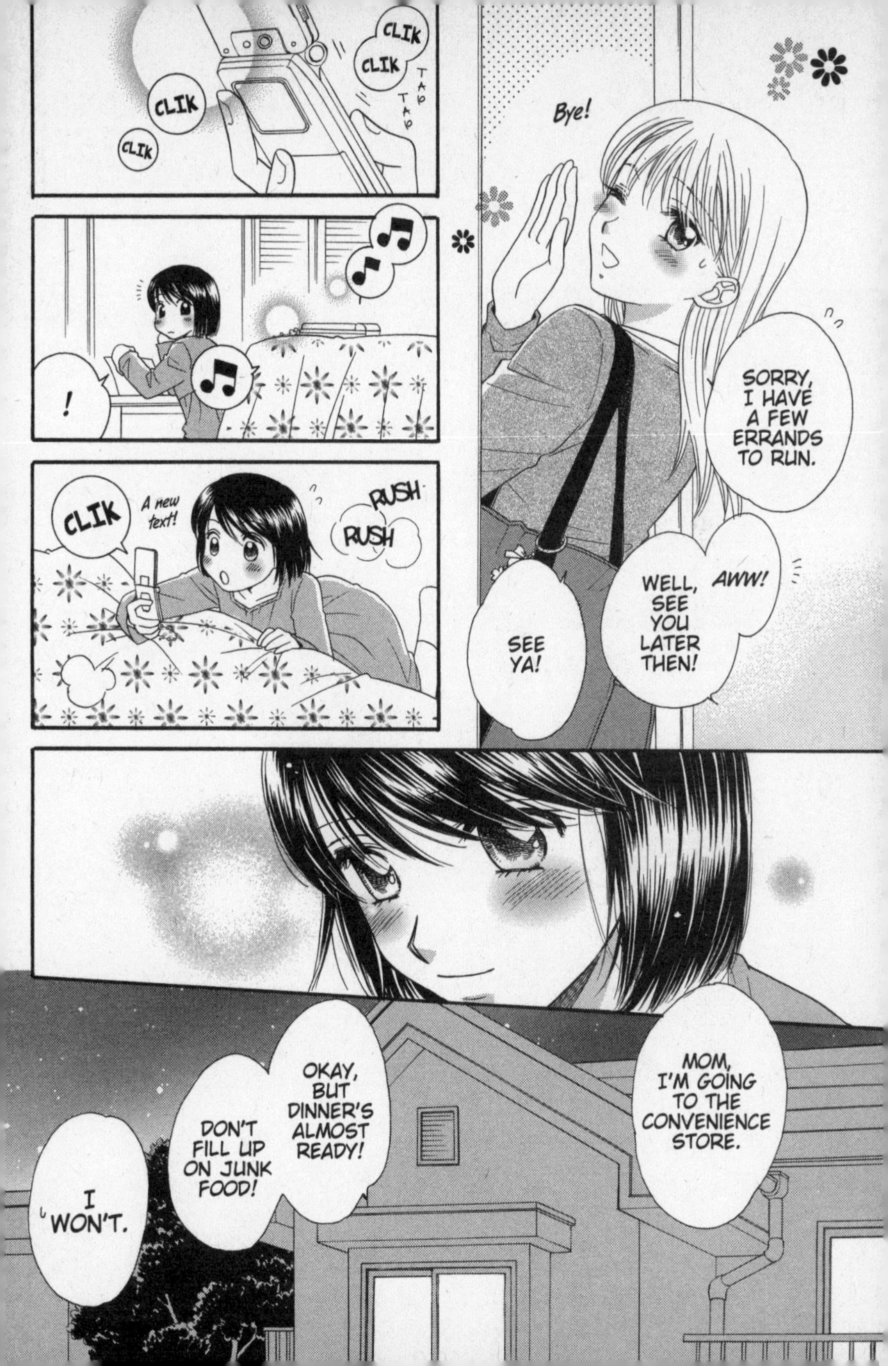
SORRY, I HAVE A FEW ERRANDS TO RUN.
Bye!
AWW!
WELL, SEE YOU LATER THEN!
SEE YA!
CLIK
CLIK
TAP TAP
CLIK
CLIK
!
RUSH
RUSH
A new text!
CLIK
MOM, I'M GOING TO THE CONVENIENCE STORE.
OKAY, BUT DINNER'S ALMOST READY!
DON'T FILL UP ON JUNK FOOD!
I WON'T.

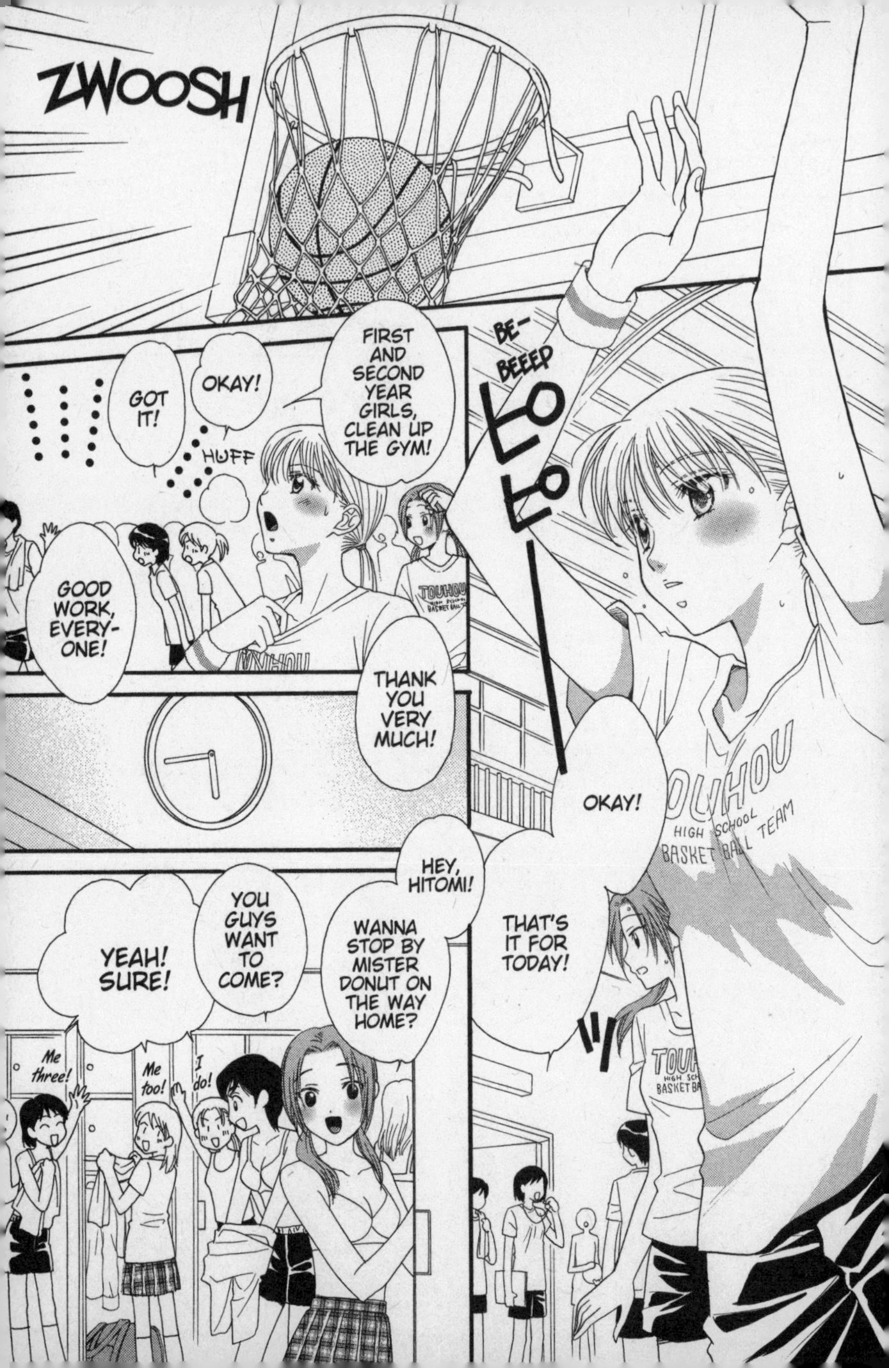
ZWOOSH
BE-BEEEP
OKAY!
THAT'S IT FOR TODAY!
FIRST AND SECOND YEAR GIRLS, CLEAN UP THE GYM!
OKAY!
GOT IT!
HUFF
GOOD WORK, EVERY-ONE!
THANK YOU VERY MUCH!
HEY, HITOMI!
WANNA STOP BY MISTER DONUT ON THE WAY HOME?
YOU GUYS WANT TO COME?
YEAH! SURE!
I do!
Me too!
Me three!

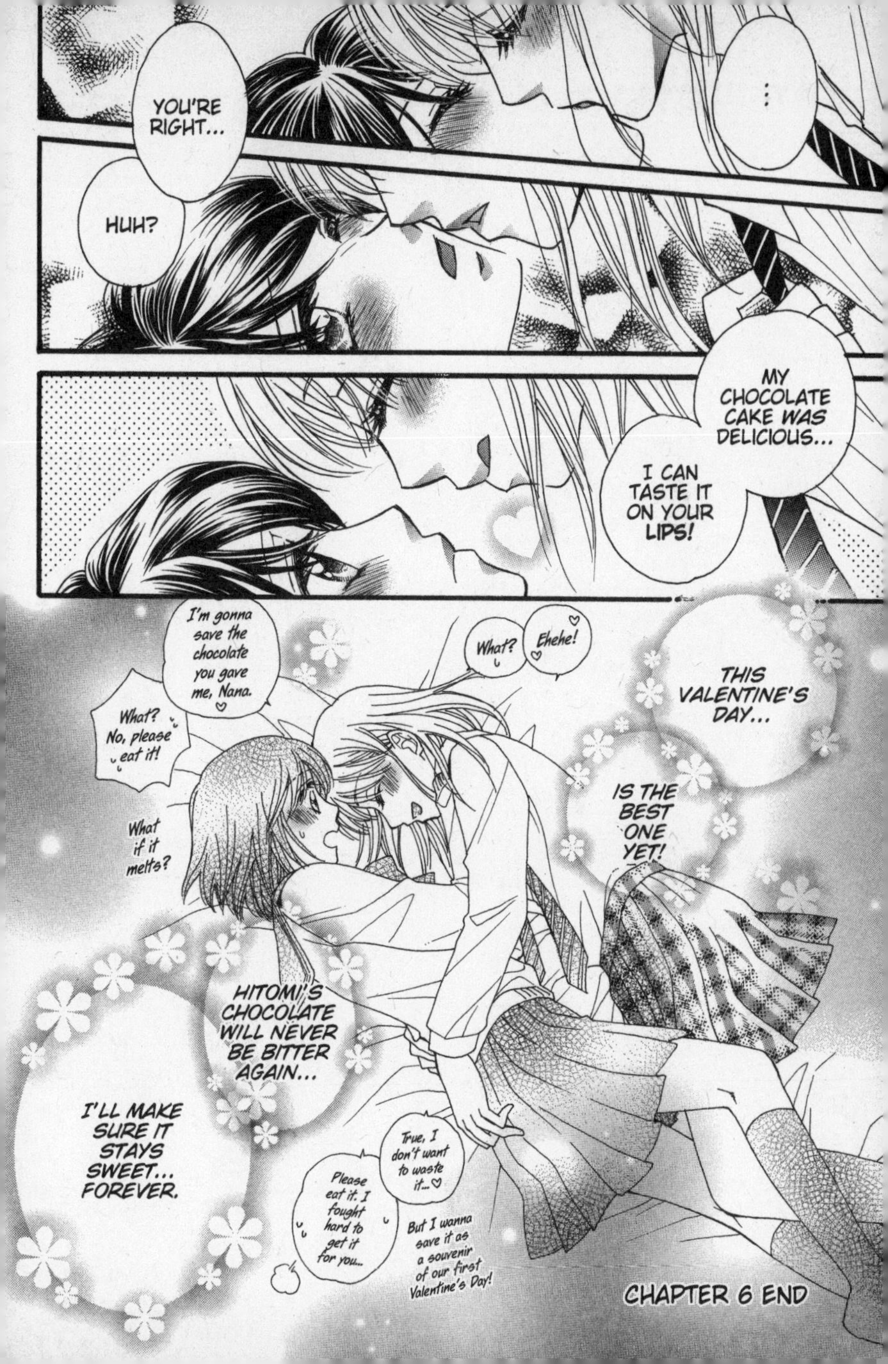
...
YOU'RE RIGHT...
HUH?
MY CHOCOLATE CAKE WAS DELICIOUS...
I CAN TASTE IT ON YOUR LIPS!
THIS VALENTINE'S DAY...
IS THE BEST ONE YET!
Ehehe!
What?
I'm gonna save the chocolate you gave me, Nana.
What? No, please eat it!
What if it melts?
HITOMI'S CHOCOLATE WILL NEVER BE BITTER AGAIN...
I'LL MAKE SURE IT STAYS SWEET... FOREVER.
True, I don't want to waste it...
But I wanna save it as a souvenir of our first Valentine's Day!
Please eat it. I fought hard to get it for you...
CHAPTER 6 END

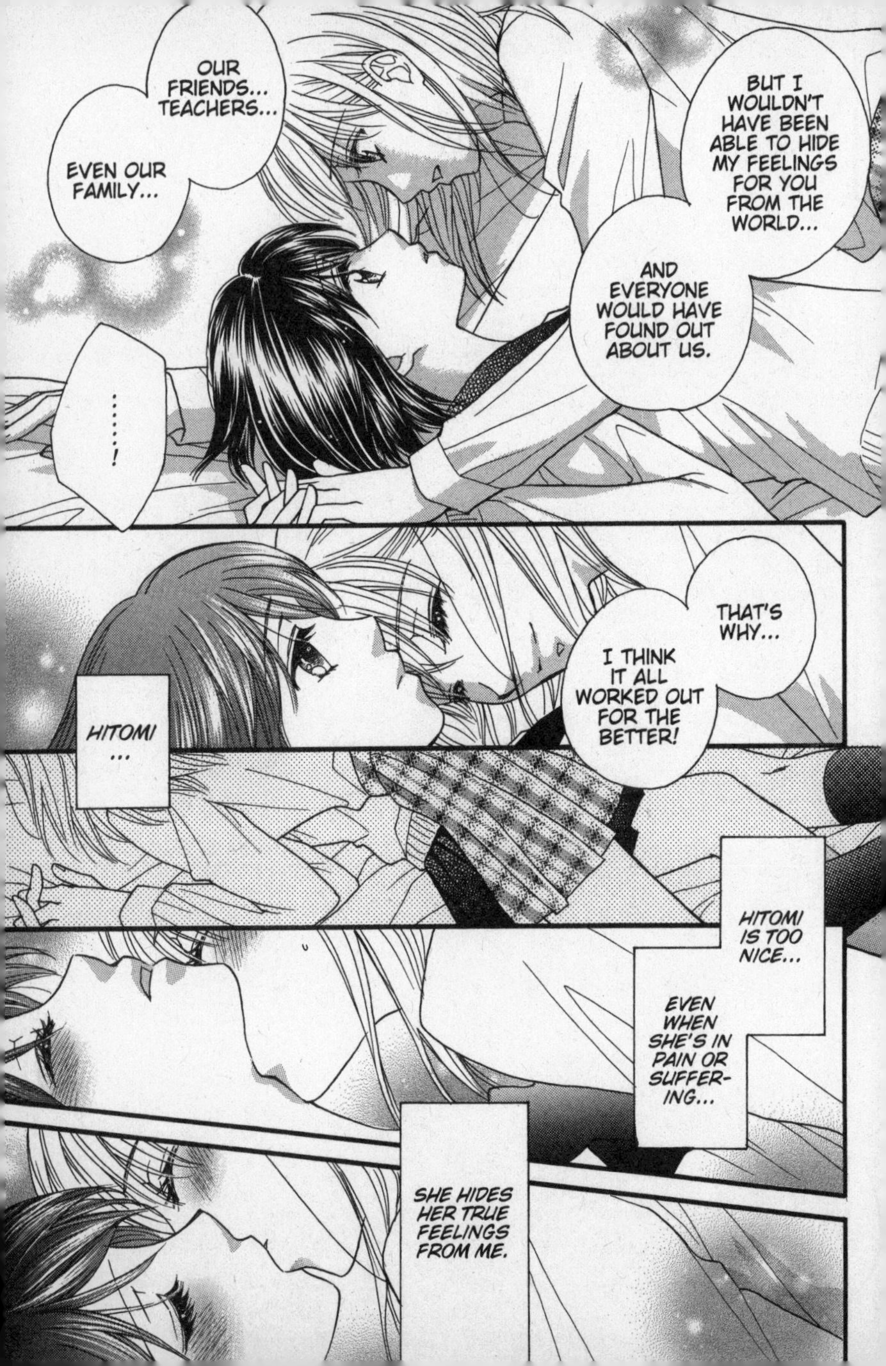
BUT I WOULDN'T HAVE BEEN ABLE TO HIDE MY FEELINGS FOR YOU FROM THE WORLD...
AND EVERYONE WOULD HAVE FOUND OUT ABOUT US.
OUR FRIENDS... TEACHERS...
EVEN OUR FAMILY...
......!
THAT'S WHY...
I THINK IT ALL WORKED OUT FOR THE BETTER!
HITOMI ...
HITOMI IS TOO NICE...
EVEN WHEN SHE'S IN PAIN OR SUFFER-ING...
SHE HIDES HER TRUE FEELINGS FROM ME.

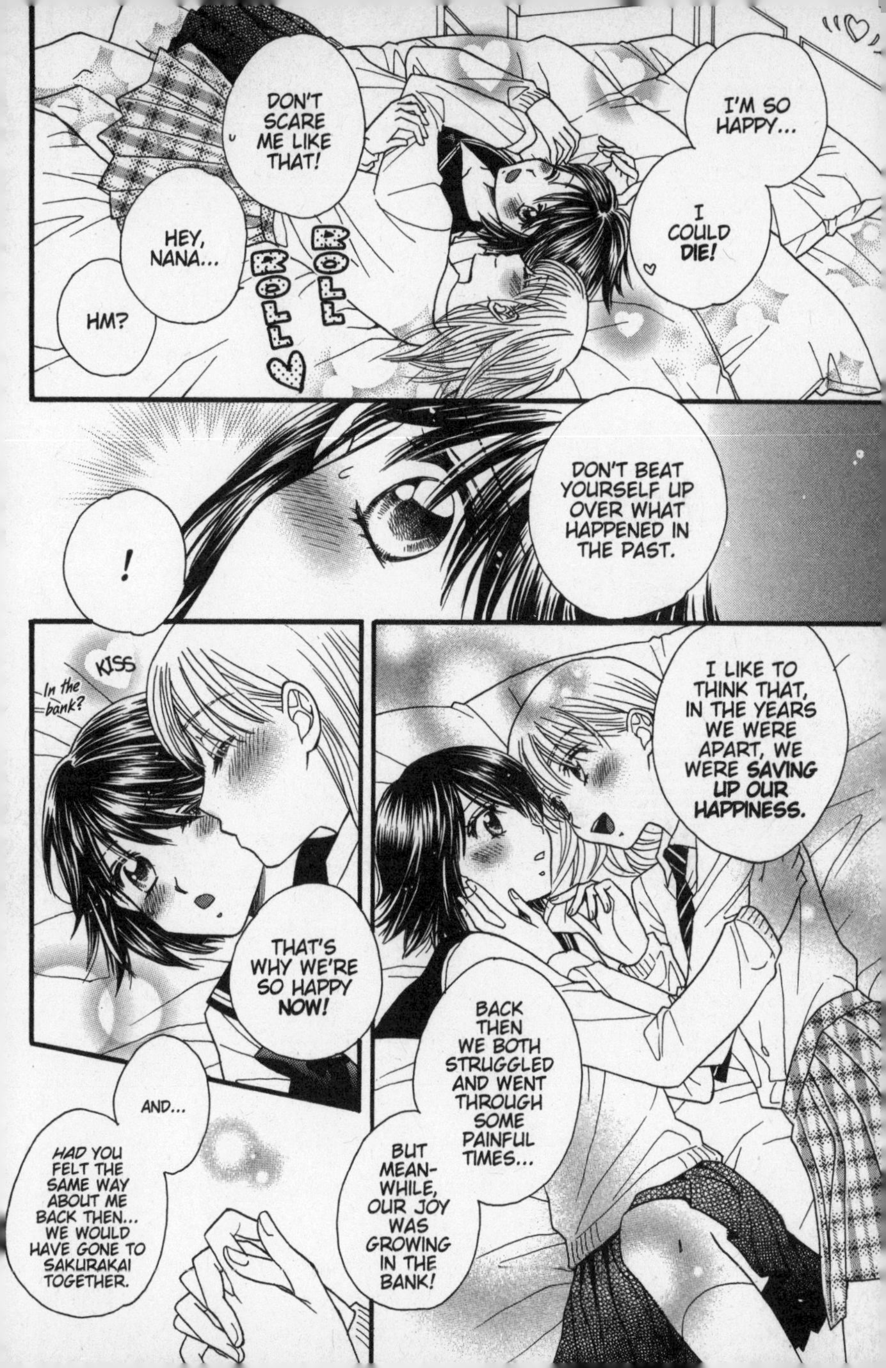
I'M SO HAPPY...
I COULD DIE!
DON'T SCARE ME LIKE THAT!
ROLL ROLL
HEY, NANA...
HM?
DON'T BEAT YOURSELF UP OVER WHAT HAPPENED IN THE PAST.
!
I LIKE TO THINK THAT, IN THE YEARS WE WERE APART, WE WERE SAVING UP OUR HAPPINESS.
BACK THEN WE BOTH STRUGGLED AND WENT THROUGH SOME PAINFUL TIMES...
BUT MEAN-WHILE, OUR JOY WAS GROWING IN THE BANK!
KISS
In the bank?
THAT'S WHY WE'RE SO HAPPY NOW!
AND...
HAD YOU FELT THE SAME WAY ABOUT ME BACK THEN... WE WOULD HAVE GONE TO SAKURAKAI TOGETHER.

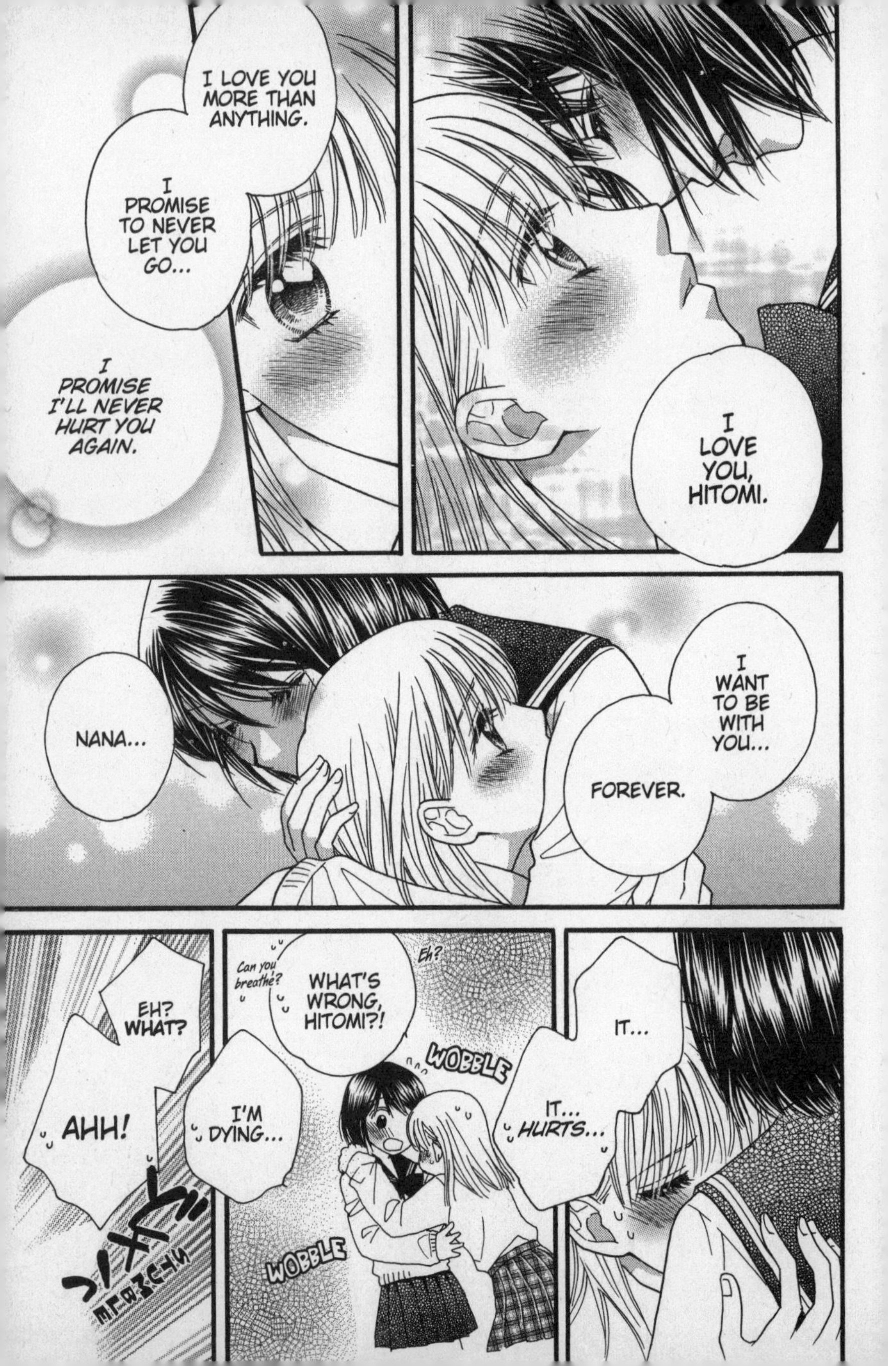
I LOVE YOU, HITOMI.
I LOVE YOU MORE THAN ANYTHING.
I PROMISE TO NEVER LET YOU GO...
I PROMISE I'LL NEVER HURT YOU AGAIN.
I WANT TO BE WITH YOU...
FOREVER.
NANA...
IT...
IT... HURTS...
Eh?
WHAT'S WRONG, HITOMI?!
Can you breathe?
WOBBLE
I'M DYING...
WOBBLE
EH? WHAT?
AHH!

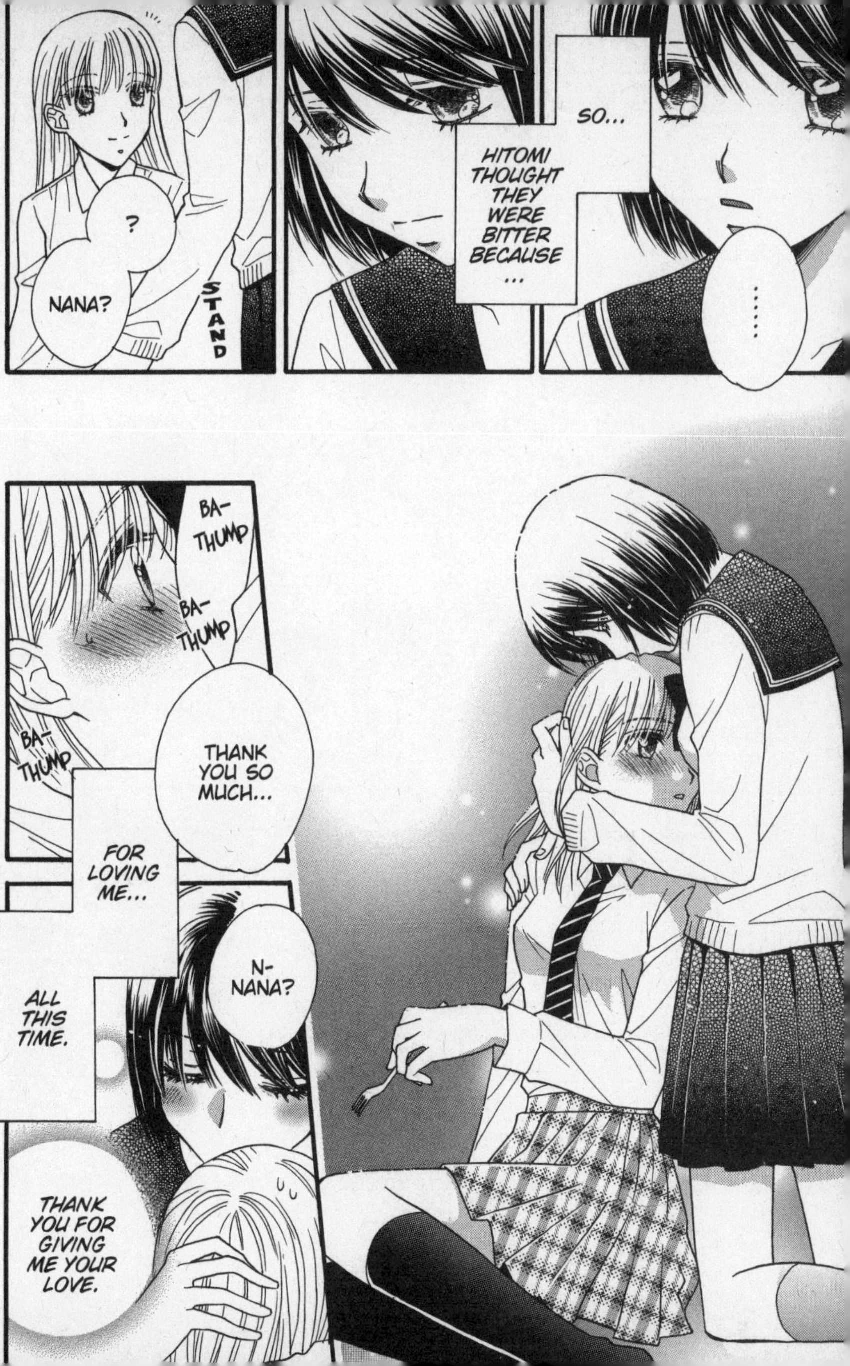
SO...
HITOMI THOUGHT THEY WERE BITTER BECAUSE ...
......
STAND
?
NANA?
BA-THUMP
BA-THUMP
BA-THUMP
THANK YOU SO MUCH...
FOR LOVING ME...
N-NANA?
ALL THIS TIME.
THANK YOU FOR GIVING ME YOUR LOVE.

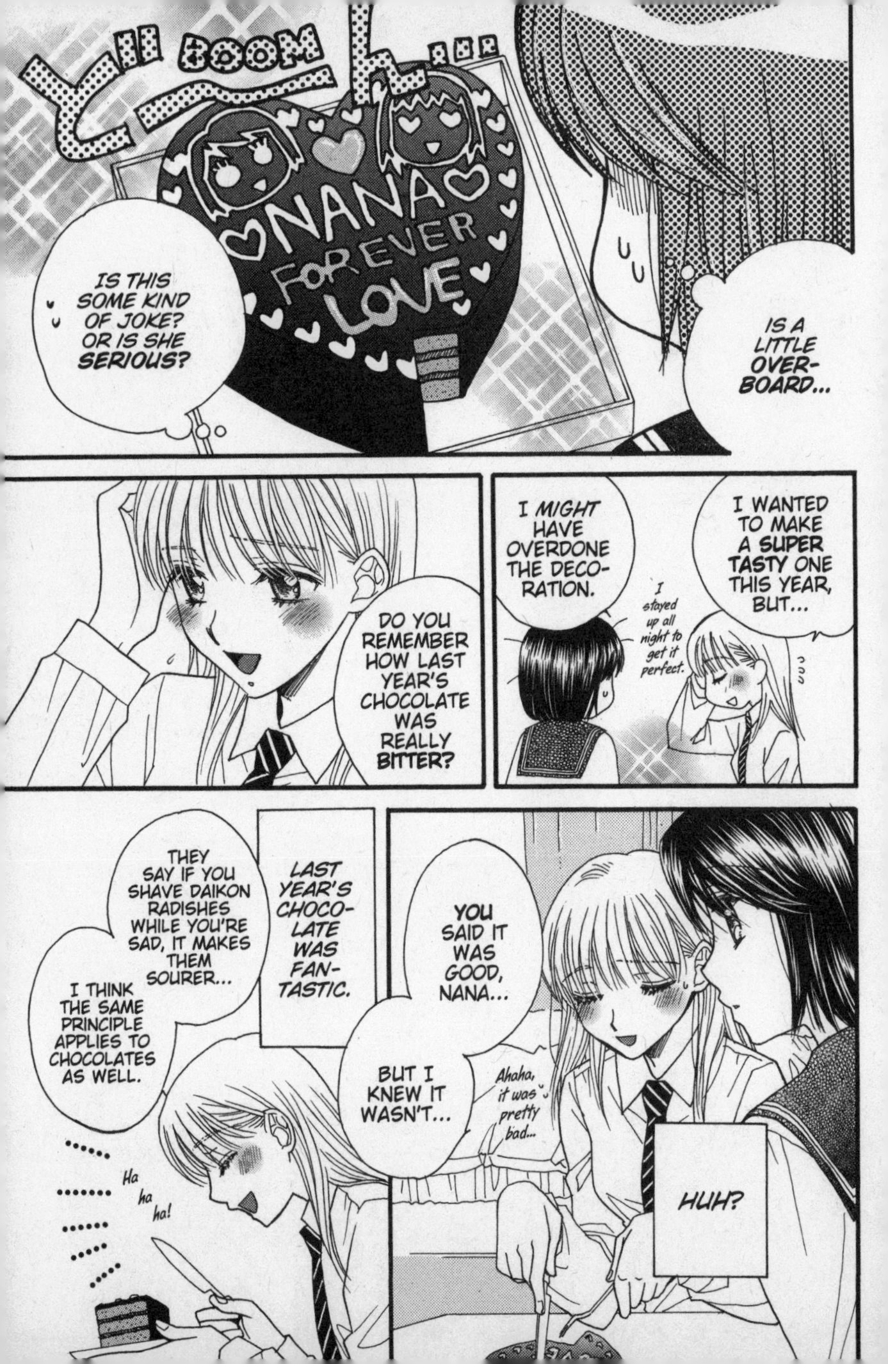
BOOM
NANA FOREVER LOVE
IS A LITTLE OVER-BOARD...
IS THIS SOME KIND OF JOKE? OR IS SHE SERIOUS?
I WANTED TO MAKE A SUPER TASTY ONE THIS YEAR, BUT...
I stayed up all night to get it perfect.
I MIGHT HAVE OVERDONE THE DECO-RATION.
DO YOU REMEMBER HOW LAST YEAR'S CHOCOLATE WAS REALLY BITTER?
YOU SAID IT WAS GOOD, NANA...
Ahaha, it was pretty bad...
BUT I KNEW IT WASN'T...
HUH?
LAST YEAR'S CHOCO-LATE WAS FAN-TASTIC.
THEY SAY IF YOU SHAVE DAIKON RADISHES WHILE YOU'RE SAD, IT MAKES THEM SOURER...
I THINK THE SAME PRINCIPLE APPLIES TO CHOCOLATES AS WELL.
Ha ha ha!

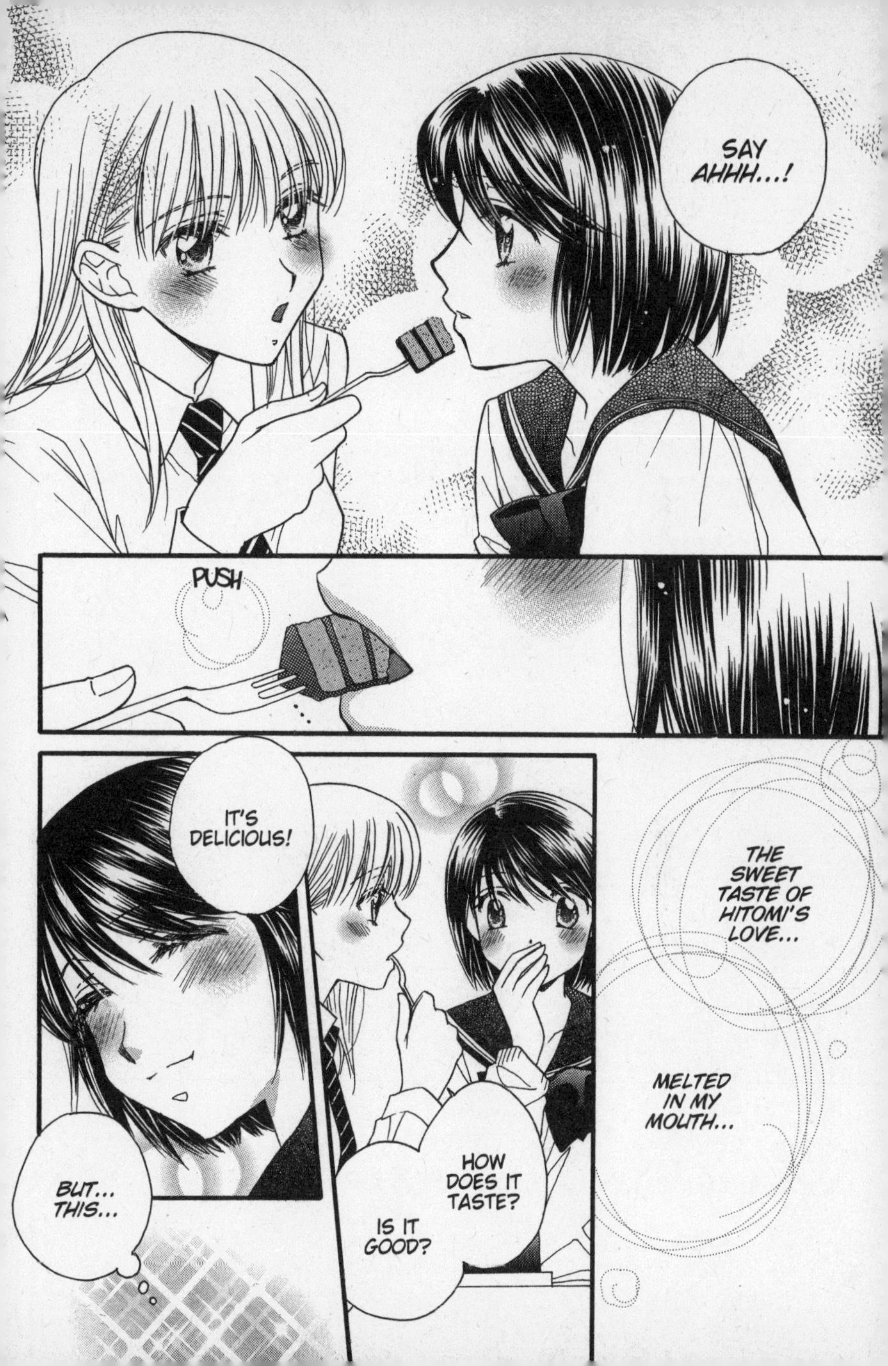
SAY AHHH...!
PUSH
THE SWEET TASTE OF HITOMI'S LOVE...
MELTED IN MY MOUTH...
IT'S DELICIOUS!
HOW DOES IT TASTE?
IS IT GOOD?
BUT... THIS...

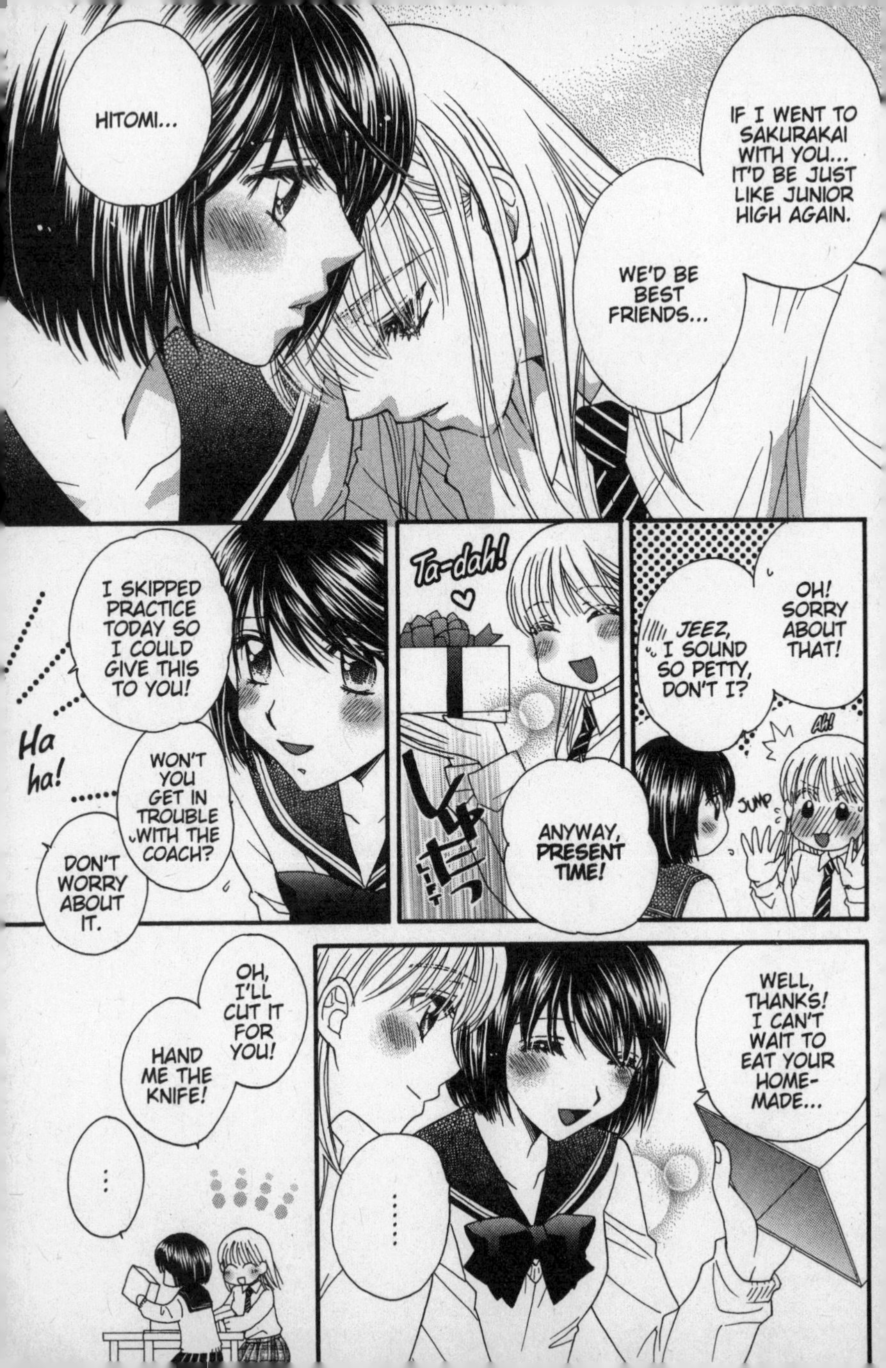
IF I WENT TO SAKURAKAI WITH YOU... IT'D BE JUST LIKE JUNIOR HIGH AGAIN.
WE'D BE BEST FRIENDS...
HITOMI...
OH! SORRY ABOUT THAT!
JEEZ, I SOUND SO PETTY, DON'T I?
Ah!
JUMP
Ta-dah!
ANYWAY, PRESENT TIME!
LIFT
I SKIPPED PRACTICE TODAY SO I COULD GIVE THIS TO YOU!
......
WON'T YOU GET IN TROUBLE WITH THE COACH?
Ha ha!
......
DON'T WORRY ABOUT IT.
WELL, THANKS! I CAN'T WAIT TO EAT YOUR HOME-MADE...
......
OH, I'LL CUT IT FOR YOU!
HAND ME THE KNIFE!
...

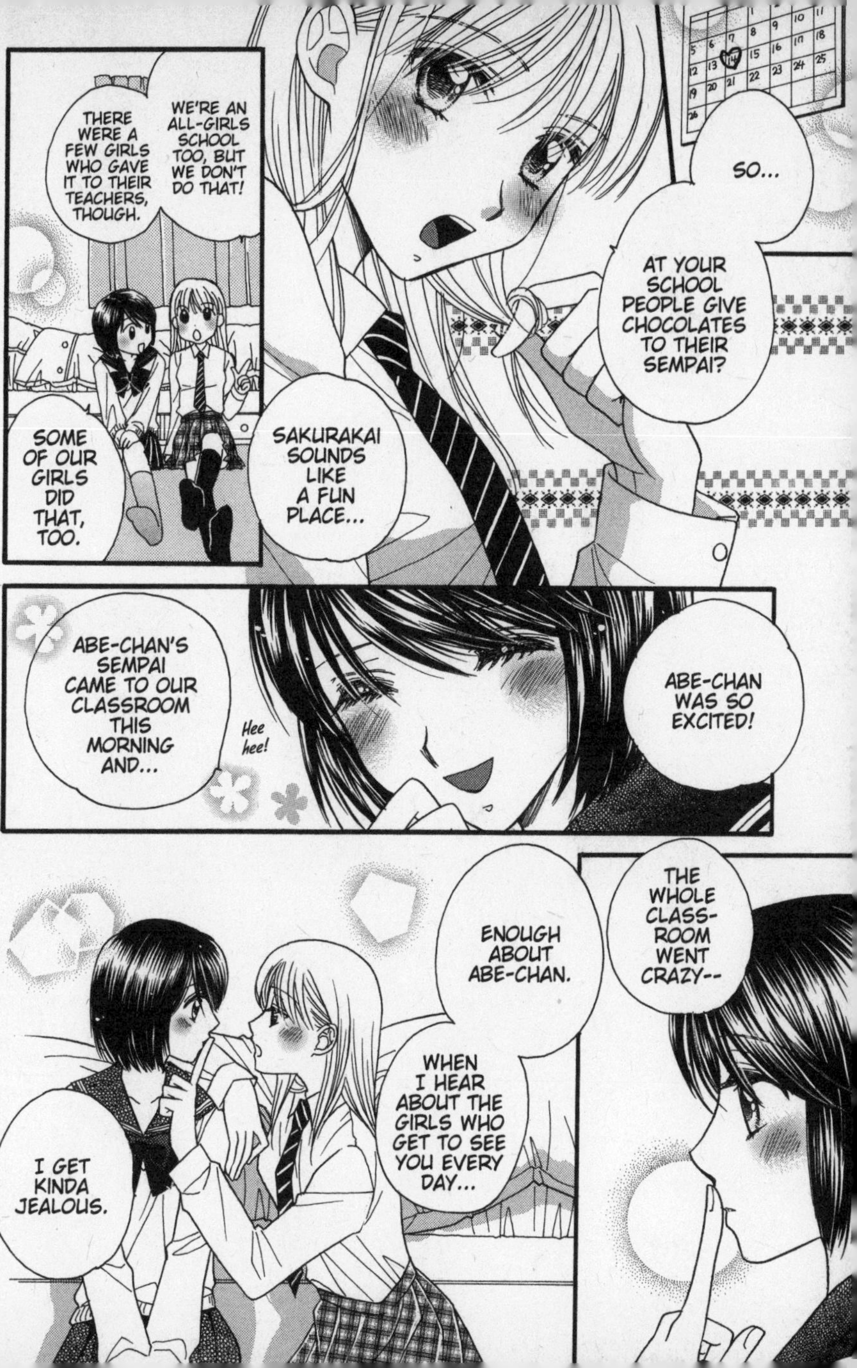
SO...
AT YOUR SCHOOL PEOPLE GIVE CHOCOLATES TO THEIR SEMPAI?
SAKURAKAI SOUNDS LIKE A FUN PLACE...
WE'RE AN ALL-GIRLS SCHOOL TOO, BUT WE DON'T DO THAT!
THERE WERE A FEW GIRLS WHO GAVE IT TO THEIR TEACHERS, THOUGH.
SOME OF OUR GIRLS DID THAT, TOO.
ABE-CHAN WAS SO EXCITED!
Hee hee!
ABE-CHAN'S SEMPAI CAME TO OUR CLASSROOM THIS MORNING AND...
THE WHOLE CLASS-ROOM WENT CRAZY--
ENOUGH ABOUT ABE-CHAN.
WHEN I HEAR ABOUT THE GIRLS WHO GET TO SEE YOU EVERY DAY...
I GET KINDA JEALOUS.

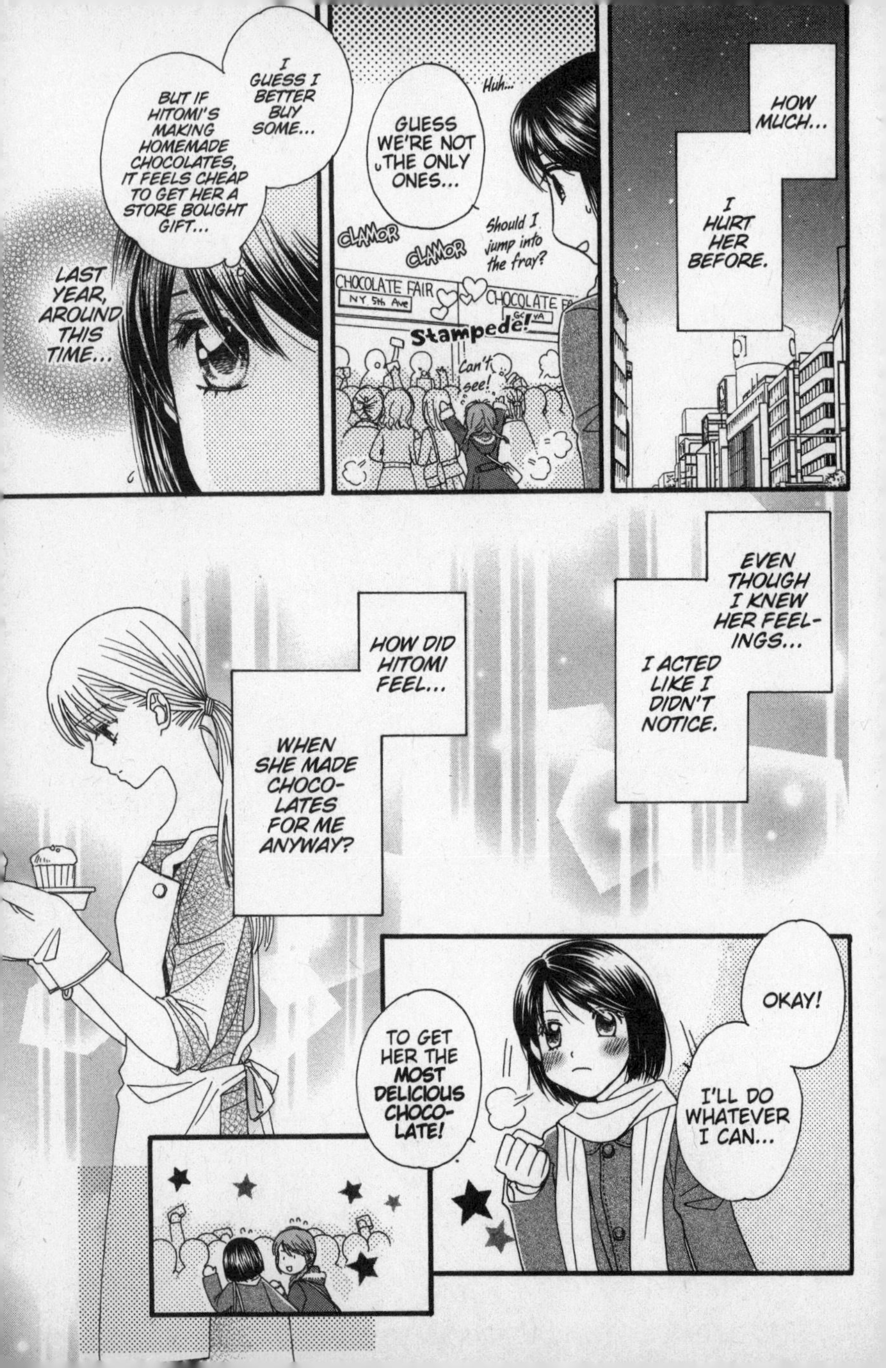
HOW MUCH...
I HURT HER BEFORE.
Huh...
GUESS WE'RE NOT THE ONLY ONES...
Should I jump into the fray?
CLAMOR
CLAMOR
CHOCOLATE FAIR
NY 5th Ave
CHOCOLATE FA
Stampede!
Can't see!
I GUESS I BETTER BUY SOME...
BUT IF HITOMI'S MAKING HOMEMADE CHOCOLATES, IT FEELS CHEAP TO GET HER A STORE BOUGHT GIFT...
LAST YEAR, AROUND THIS TIME...
EVEN THOUGH I KNEW HER FEELINGS...
I ACTED LIKE I DIDN'T NOTICE.
HOW DID HITOMI FEEL...
WHEN SHE MADE CHOCOLATES FOR ME ANYWAY?
OKAY!
I'LL DO WHATEVER I CAN...
TO GET HER THE MOST DELICIOUS CHOCOLATE!

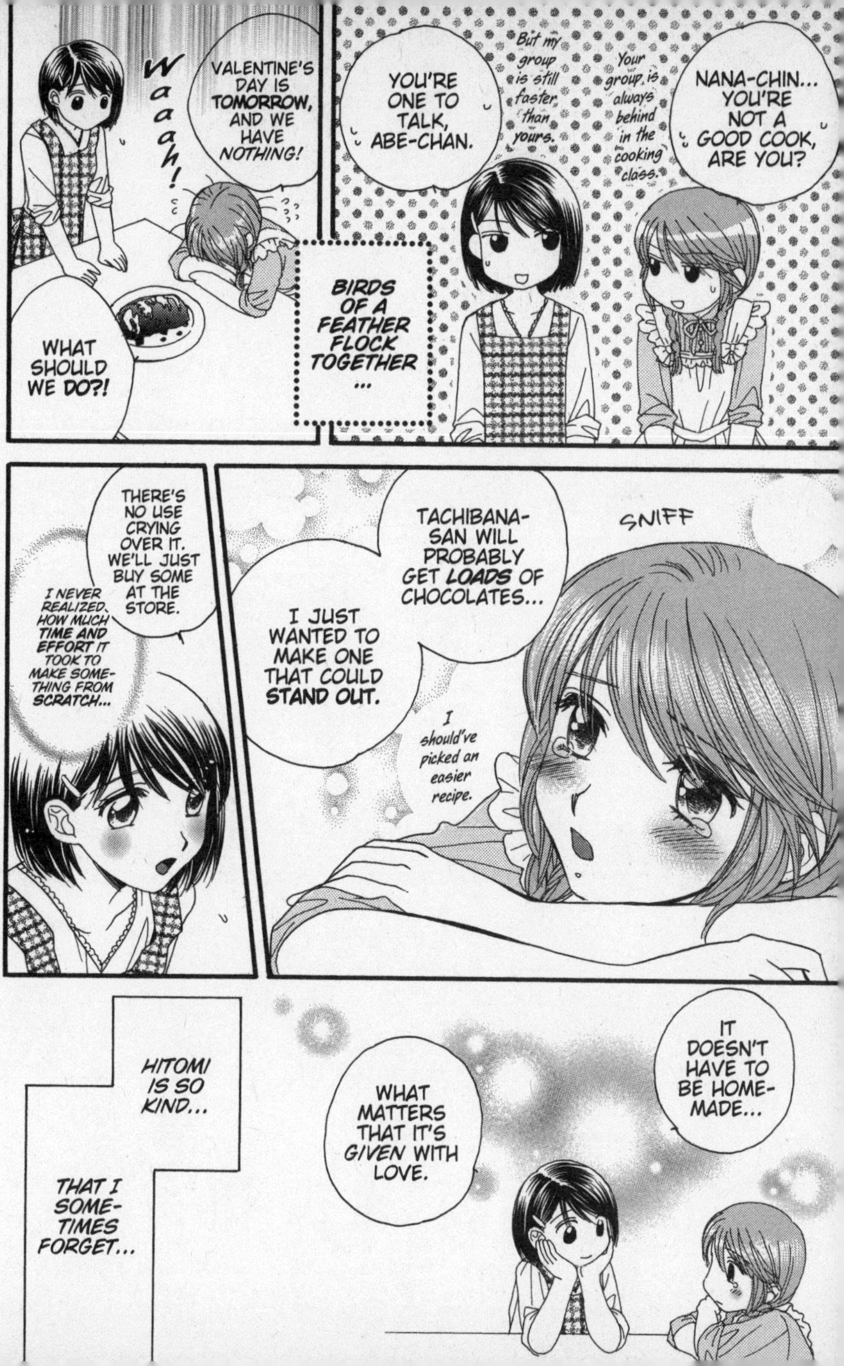

NANA-CHIN... YOU'RE NOT A GOOD COOK, ARE YOU?
Your group is always behind in the cooking class.
But my group is still faster than yours.
YOU'RE ONE TO TALK, ABE-CHAN.
BIRDS OF A FEATHER FLOCK TOGETHER...
Waaah!
VALENTINE'S DAY IS TOMORROW, AND WE HAVE NOTHING!
WHAT SHOULD WE DO?!
SNIFF
TACHIBANA-SAN WILL PROBABLY GET LOADS OF CHOCOLATES...
I JUST WANTED TO MAKE ONE THAT COULD STAND OUT.
I should've picked an easier recipe.
THERE'S NO USE CRYING OVER IT. WE'LL JUST BUY SOME AT THE STORE.
I NEVER REALIZED HOW MUCH TIME AND EFFORT IT TOOK TO MAKE SOME-THING FROM SCRATCH...
IT DOESN'T HAVE TO BE HOME-MADE...
WHAT MATTERS THAT IT'S GIVEN WITH LOVE.
HITOMI IS SO KIND...
THAT I SOME-TIMES FORGET...

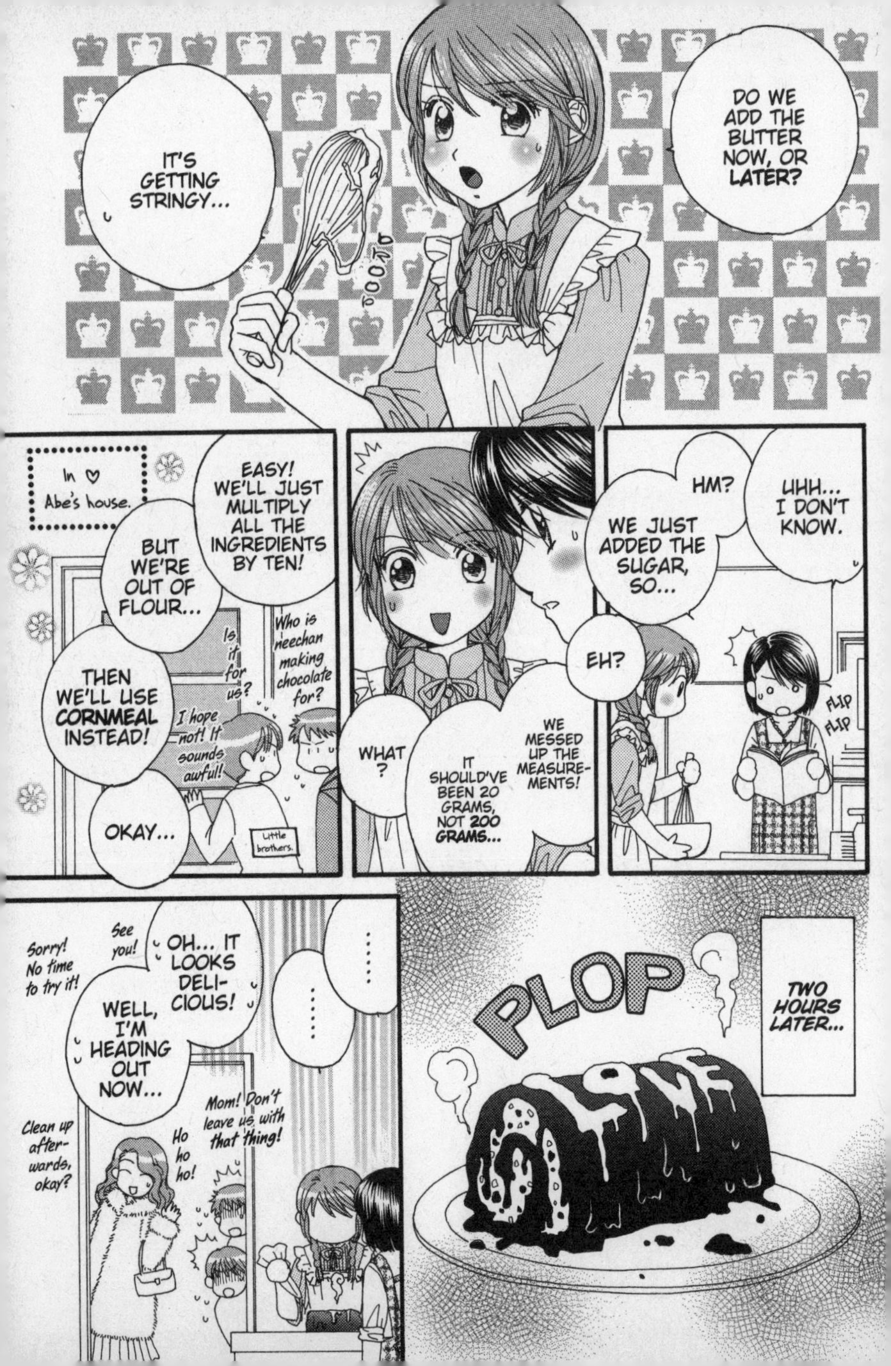
DO WE ADD THE BUTTER NOW, OR LATER?
IT'S GETTING STRINGY...
DROOP
UHHH... I DON'T KNOW.
HM?
WE JUST ADDED THE SUGAR, SO...
EH?
FLIP FLIP
WE MESSED UP THE MEASUREMENTS!
IT SHOULD'VE BEEN 20 GRAMS, NOT 200 GRAMS...
WHAT?
EASY! WE'LL JUST MULTIPLY ALL THE INGREDIENTS BY TEN!
In ♡ Abe's house.
BUT WE'RE OUT OF FLOUR...
Who is neechan making chocolate for?
Is it for us?
THEN WE'LL USE CORNMEAL INSTEAD!
I hope not! It sounds awful!
OKAY...
Little brothers.
TWO HOURS LATER...
PLOP
......
......
OH... IT LOOKS DELICIOUS!
See you!
Sorry! No time to try it!
WELL, I'M HEADING OUT NOW...
Mom! Don't leave us with that thing!
Ho ho ho!
Clean up afterwards, okay?

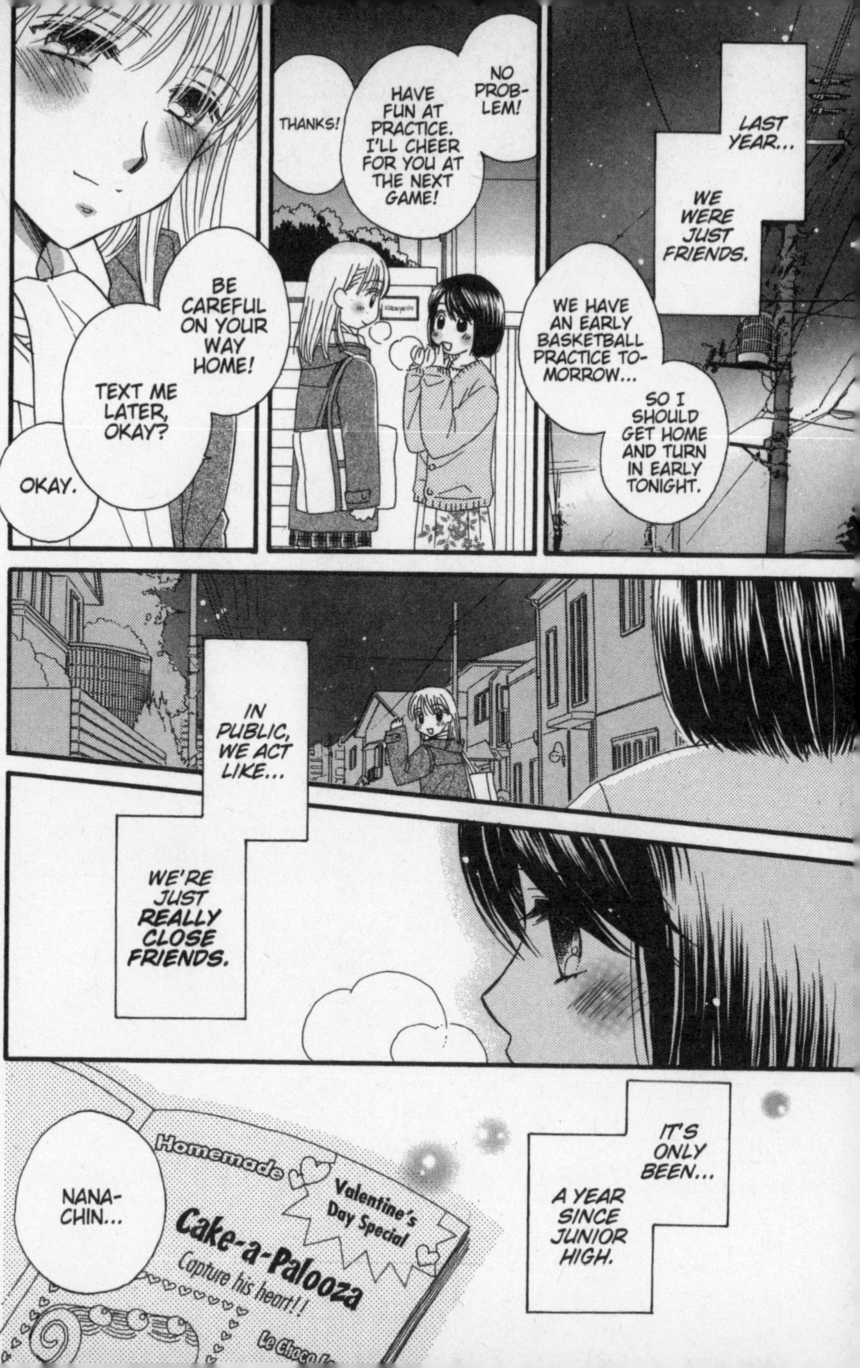
LAST YEAR...
WE WERE JUST FRIENDS.
WE HAVE AN EARLY BASKETBALL PRACTICE TO-MORROW...
SO I SHOULD GET HOME AND TURN IN EARLY TONIGHT.
NO PROB-LEM!
HAVE FUN AT PRACTICE. I'LL CHEER FOR YOU AT THE NEXT GAME!
THANKS!
BE CAREFUL ON YOUR WAY HOME!
TEXT ME LATER, OKAY?
OKAY.
IN PUBLIC, WE ACT LIKE...
WE'RE JUST REALLY CLOSE FRIENDS.
IT'S ONLY BEEN...
A YEAR SINCE JUNIOR HIGH.
NANA-CHIN...
Homemade
Valentine's Day Special
Cake-a-Palooza
Capture his heart!!

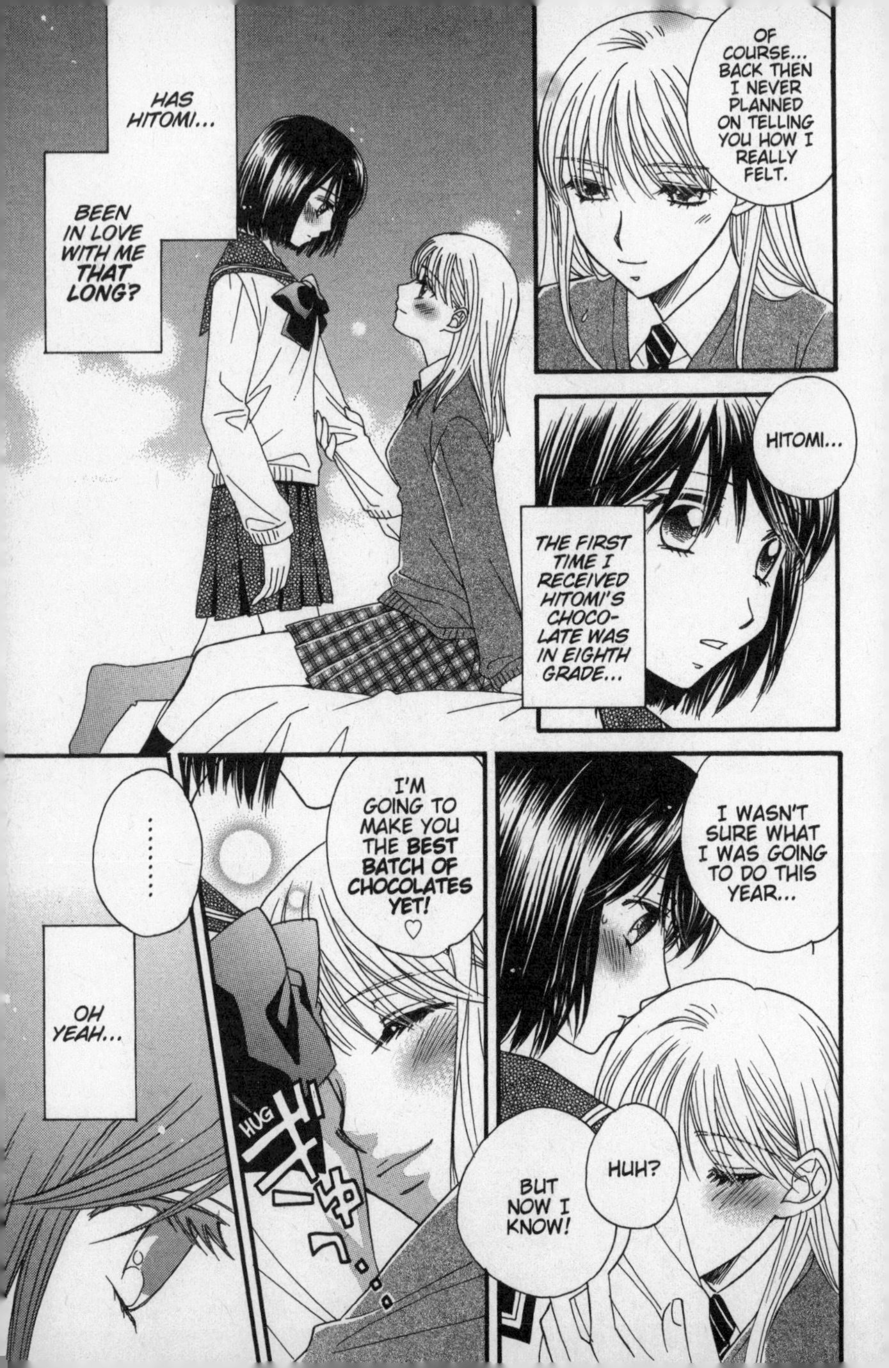
OF COURSE... BACK THEN I NEVER PLANNED ON TELLING YOU HOW I REALLY FELT.
HITOMI...
THE FIRST TIME I RECEIVED HITOMI'S CHOCOLATE WAS IN EIGHTH GRADE...
HAS HITOMI...
BEEN IN LOVE WITH ME THAT LONG?
I WASN'T SURE WHAT I WAS GOING TO DO THIS YEAR...
HUH?
BUT NOW I KNOW!
I'M GOING TO MAKE YOU THE BEST BATCH OF CHOCOLATES YET! ♡
HUG
......
OH YEAH...

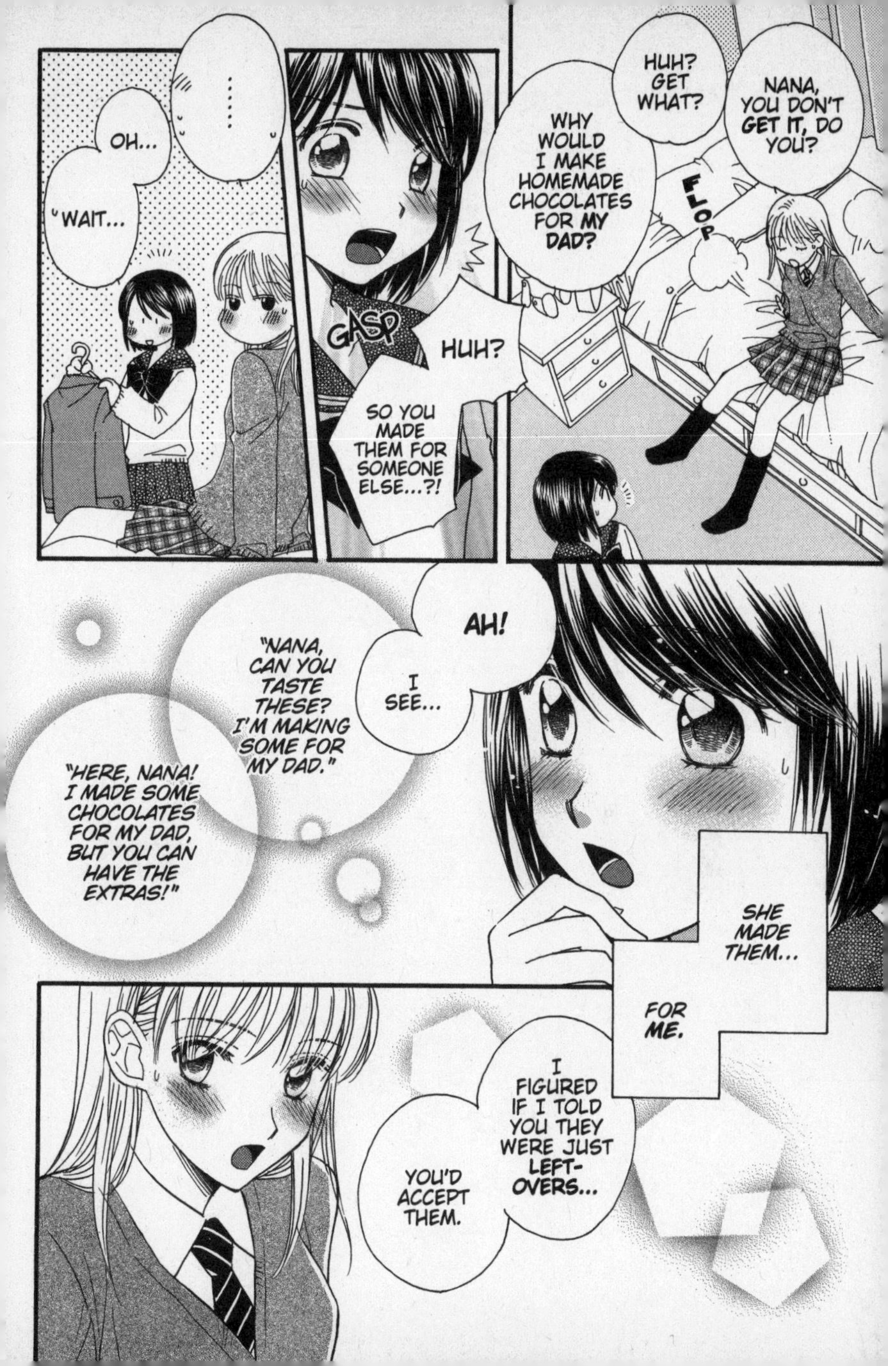
NANA, YOU DON'T GET IT, DO YOU?
HUH? GET WHAT?
WHY WOULD I MAKE HOMEMADE CHOCOLATES FOR MY DAD?
FLOP
GASP
HUH?
SO YOU MADE THEM FOR SOMEONE ELSE...?!
......
OH...
"WAIT...
AH!
I SEE...
"NANA, CAN YOU TASTE THESE? I'M MAKING SOME FOR MY DAD."
"HERE, NANA! I MADE SOME CHOCOLATES FOR MY DAD, BUT YOU CAN HAVE THE EXTRAS!"
SHE MADE THEM...
FOR ME.
I FIGURED IF I TOLD YOU THEY WERE JUST LEFT-OVERS...
YOU'D ACCEPT THEM.

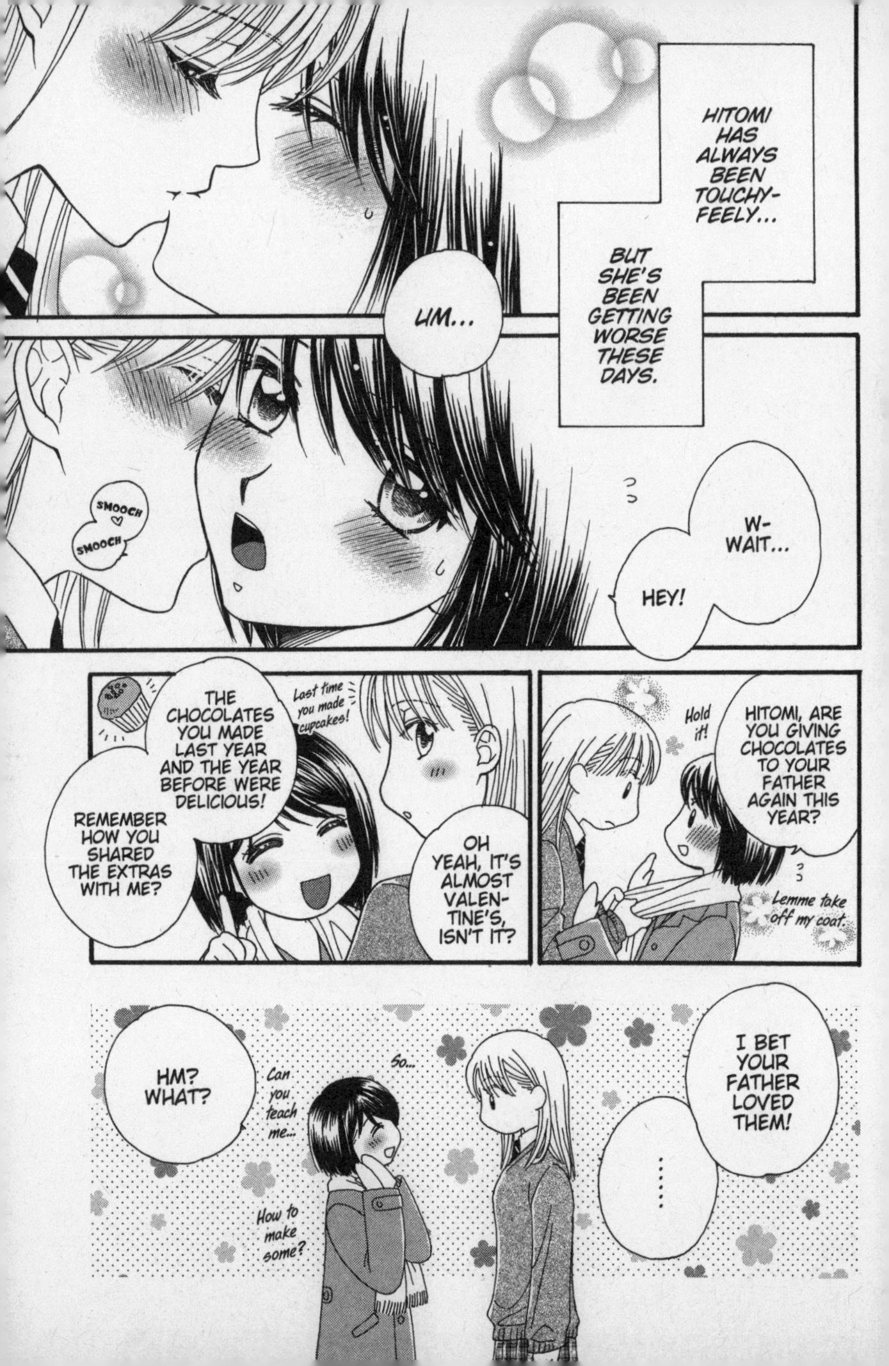

HITOMI HAS ALWAYS BEEN TOUCHY-FEELY...
BUT SHE'S BEEN GETTING WORSE THESE DAYS.
UM...
W- WAIT...
HEY!
SMOOCH ♡ SMOOCH
Hold it!
HITOMI, ARE YOU GIVING CHOCOLATES TO YOUR FATHER AGAIN THIS YEAR?
Lemme take off my coat.
OH YEAH, IT'S ALMOST VALEN-TINE'S, ISN'T IT?
Last time you made cupcakes!
THE CHOCOLATES YOU MADE LAST YEAR AND THE YEAR BEFORE WERE DELICIOUS!
REMEMBER HOW YOU SHARED THE EXTRAS WITH ME?
I BET YOUR FATHER LOVED THEM!
......
So...
Can you teach me...
HM? WHAT?
How to make some?

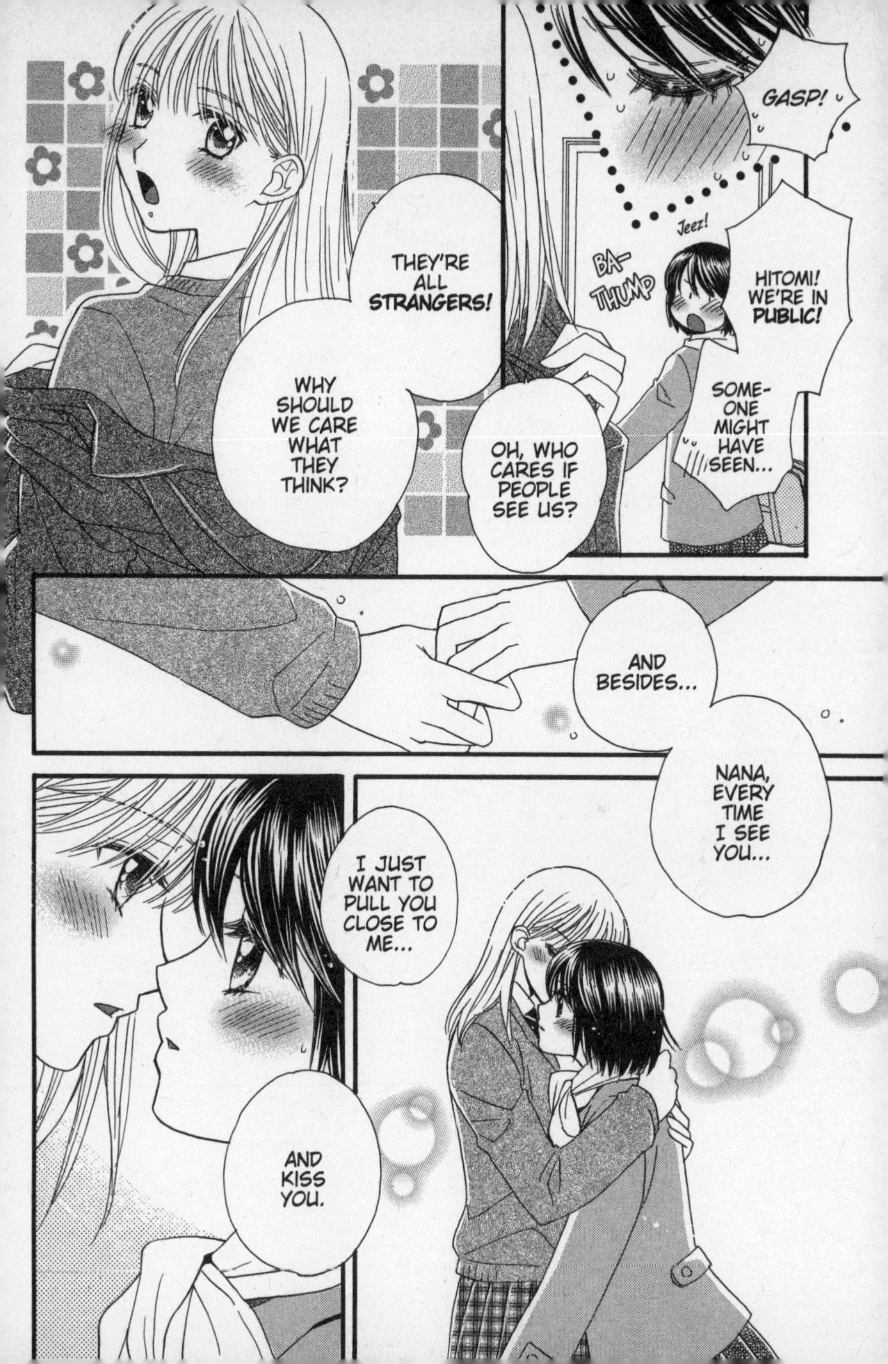
GASP!
Jeez!
BA-THUMP
HITOMI! WE'RE IN PUBLIC!
SOME-ONE MIGHT HAVE SEEN...
OH, WHO CARES IF PEOPLE SEE US?
THEY'RE ALL STRANGERS!
WHY SHOULD WE CARE WHAT THEY THINK?
AND BESIDES...
NANA, EVERY TIME I SEE YOU...
I JUST WANT TO PULL YOU CLOSE TO ME...
AND KISS YOU.

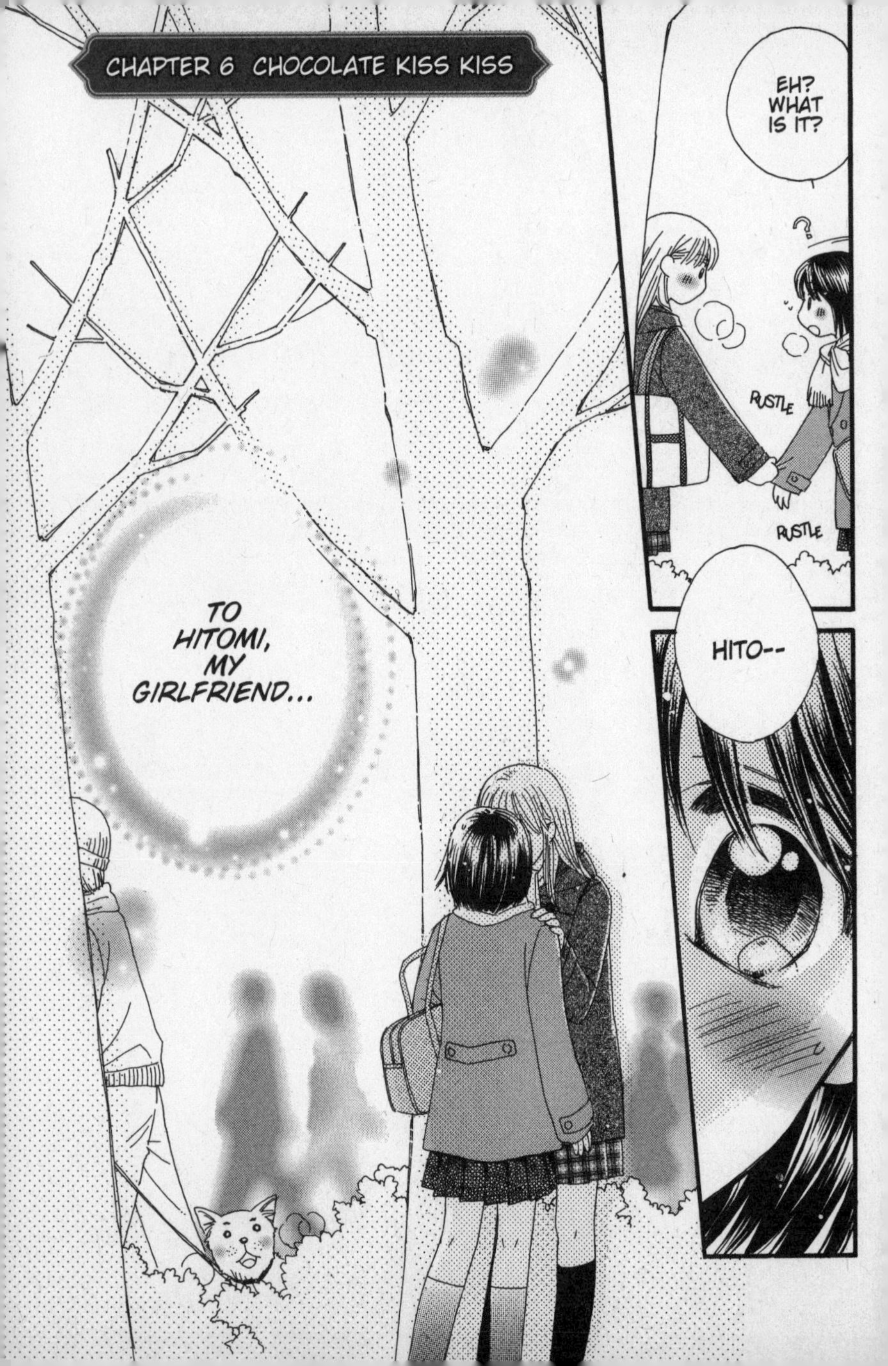
EH? WHAT IS IT?
?
RUSTLE
RUSTLE
HITO--
CHAPTER 6 CHOCOLATE KISS KISS
TO HITOMI, MY GIRLFRIEND...

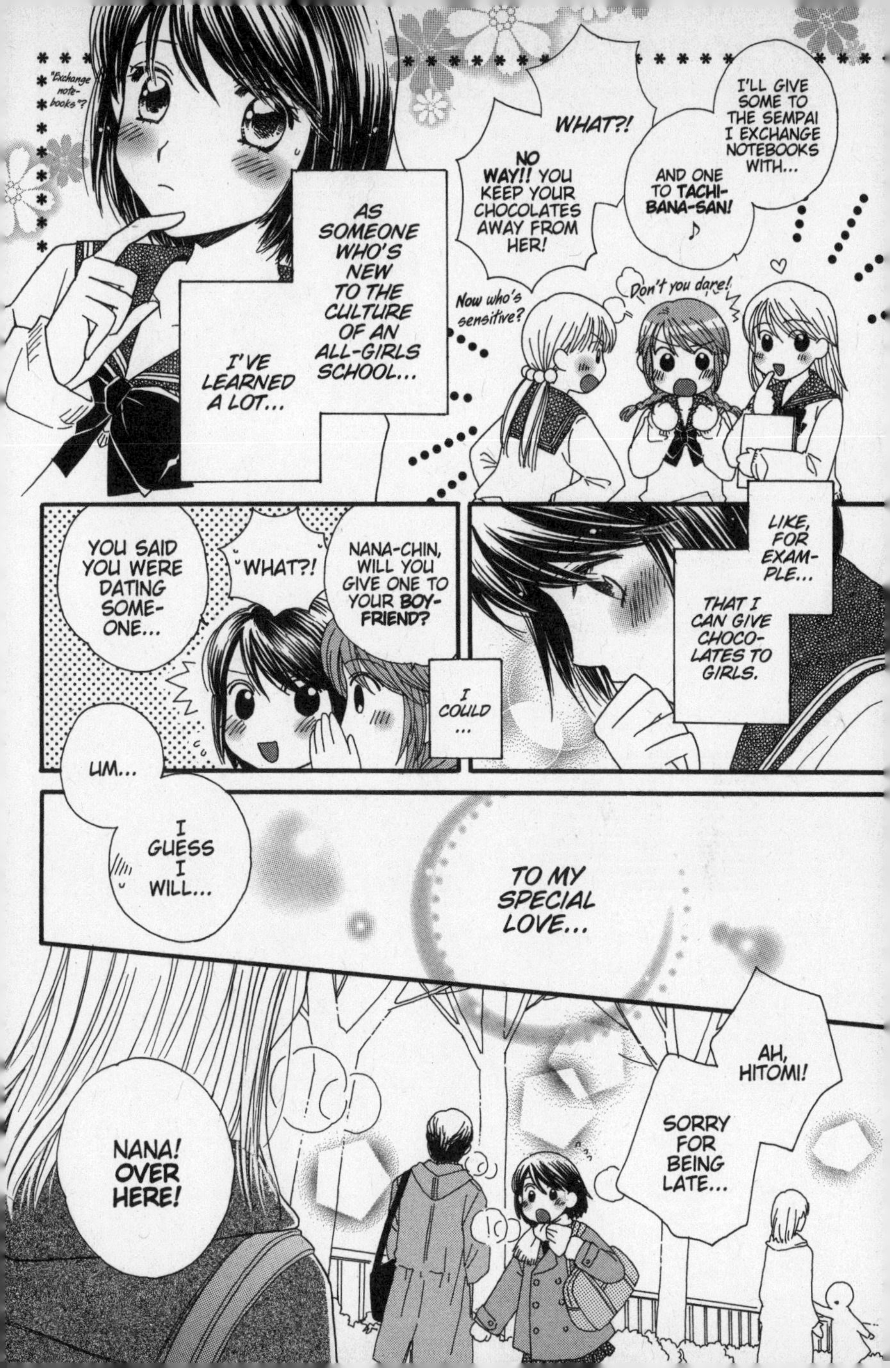
I'LL GIVE SOME TO THE SEMPAI I EXCHANGE NOTEBOOKS WITH...
AND ONE TO TACHIBANA-SAN! ♪
WHAT?!
NO WAY!! YOU KEEP YOUR CHOCOLATES AWAY FROM HER!
Don't you dare!
Now who's sensitive?
AS SOMEONE WHO'S NEW TO THE CULTURE OF AN ALL-GIRLS SCHOOL...
I'VE LEARNED A LOT...
*"Exchange notebooks"?
LIKE, FOR EXAMPLE...
THAT I CAN GIVE CHOCOLATES TO GIRLS.
I COULD...
NANA-CHIN, WILL YOU GIVE ONE TO YOUR BOYFRIEND?
WHAT?!
YOU SAID YOU WERE DATING SOMEONE...
UM...
I GUESS I WILL...
TO MY SPECIAL LOVE...
AH, HITOMI!
SORRY FOR BEING LATE...
NANA! OVER HERE!

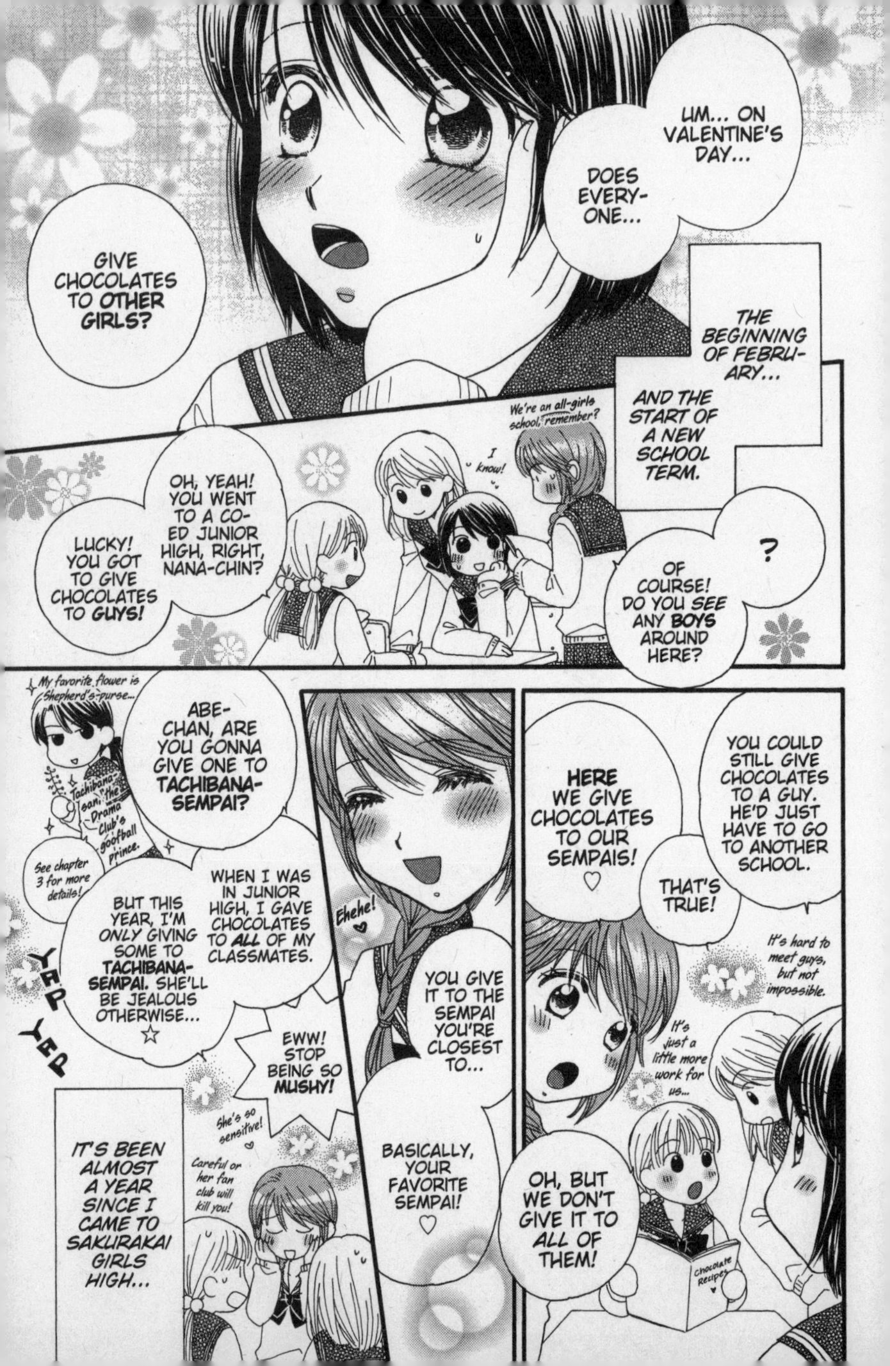
UM... ON VALENTINE'S DAY...
DOES EVERY-ONE...
GIVE CHOCOLATES TO OTHER GIRLS?
THE BEGINNING OF FEBRU-ARY...
AND THE START OF A NEW SCHOOL TERM.
?
OF COURSE! DO YOU SEE ANY BOYS AROUND HERE?
We're an all-girls school, remember?
I know!
OH, YEAH! YOU WENT TO A CO-ED JUNIOR HIGH, RIGHT, NANA-CHIN?
LUCKY! YOU GOT TO GIVE CHOCOLATES TO GUYS!
YOU COULD STILL GIVE CHOCOLATES TO A GUY. HE'D JUST HAVE TO GO TO ANOTHER SCHOOL.
HERE WE GIVE CHOCOLATES TO OUR SEMPAIS! ♡
THAT'S TRUE!
It's hard to meet guys, but not impossible.
It's just a little more work for us...
OH, BUT WE DON'T GIVE IT TO ALL OF THEM!
Chocolate Recipes
YOU GIVE IT TO THE SEMPAI YOU'RE CLOSEST TO...
Ehehe! ♥
BASICALLY, YOUR FAVORITE SEMPAI! ♡
ABE-CHAN, ARE YOU GONNA GIVE ONE TO TACHIBANA-SEMPAI?
My favorite flower is Shepherd's-purse...
Tachibana-san, the Drama Club's goofball prince.
See chapter 3 for more details!
WHEN I WAS IN JUNIOR HIGH, I GAVE CHOCOLATES TO ALL OF MY CLASSMATES.
BUT THIS YEAR, I'M ONLY GIVING SOME TO TACHIBANA-SEMPAI. SHE'LL BE JEALOUS OTHERWISE... ☆
YAP YAP
EWW! STOP BEING SO MUSHY!
She's so sensitive! ♡
Careful or her fan club will kill you!
IT'S BEEN ALMOST A YEAR SINCE I CAME TO SAKURAKAI GIRLS HIGH...

くちびるためいきさくらいろ

KuchibiruTameikiSakurairo.

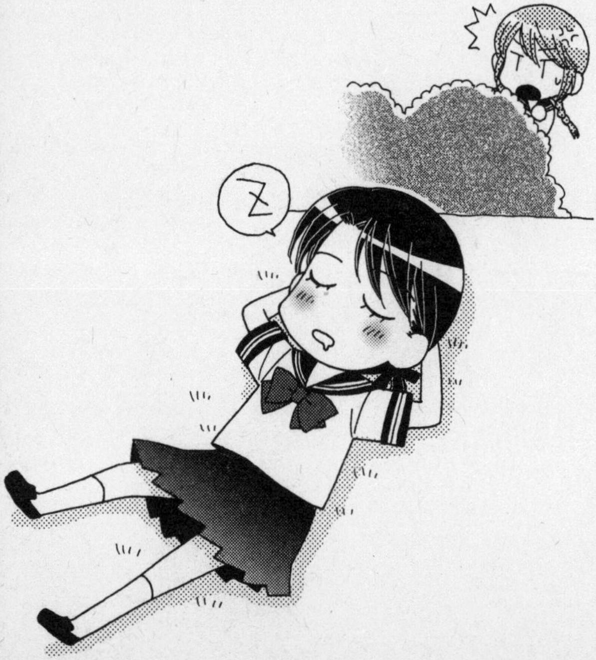
Z

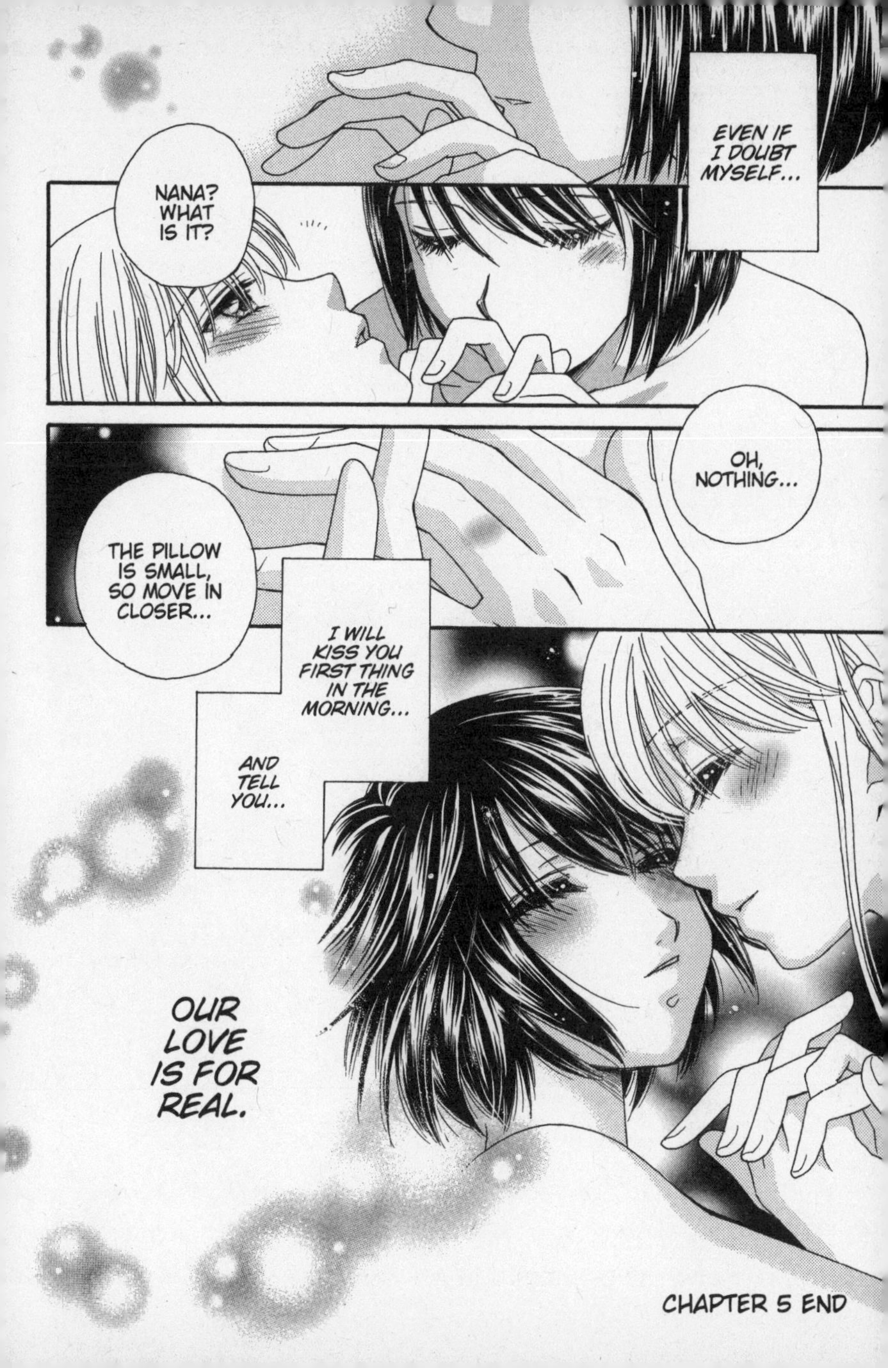
EVEN IF I DOUBT MYSELF...
NANA? WHAT IS IT?
OH, NOTHING...
THE PILLOW IS SMALL, SO MOVE IN CLOSER...
I WILL KISS YOU FIRST THING IN THE MORNING...
AND TELL YOU...
OUR LOVE IS FOR REAL.
CHAPTER 5 END

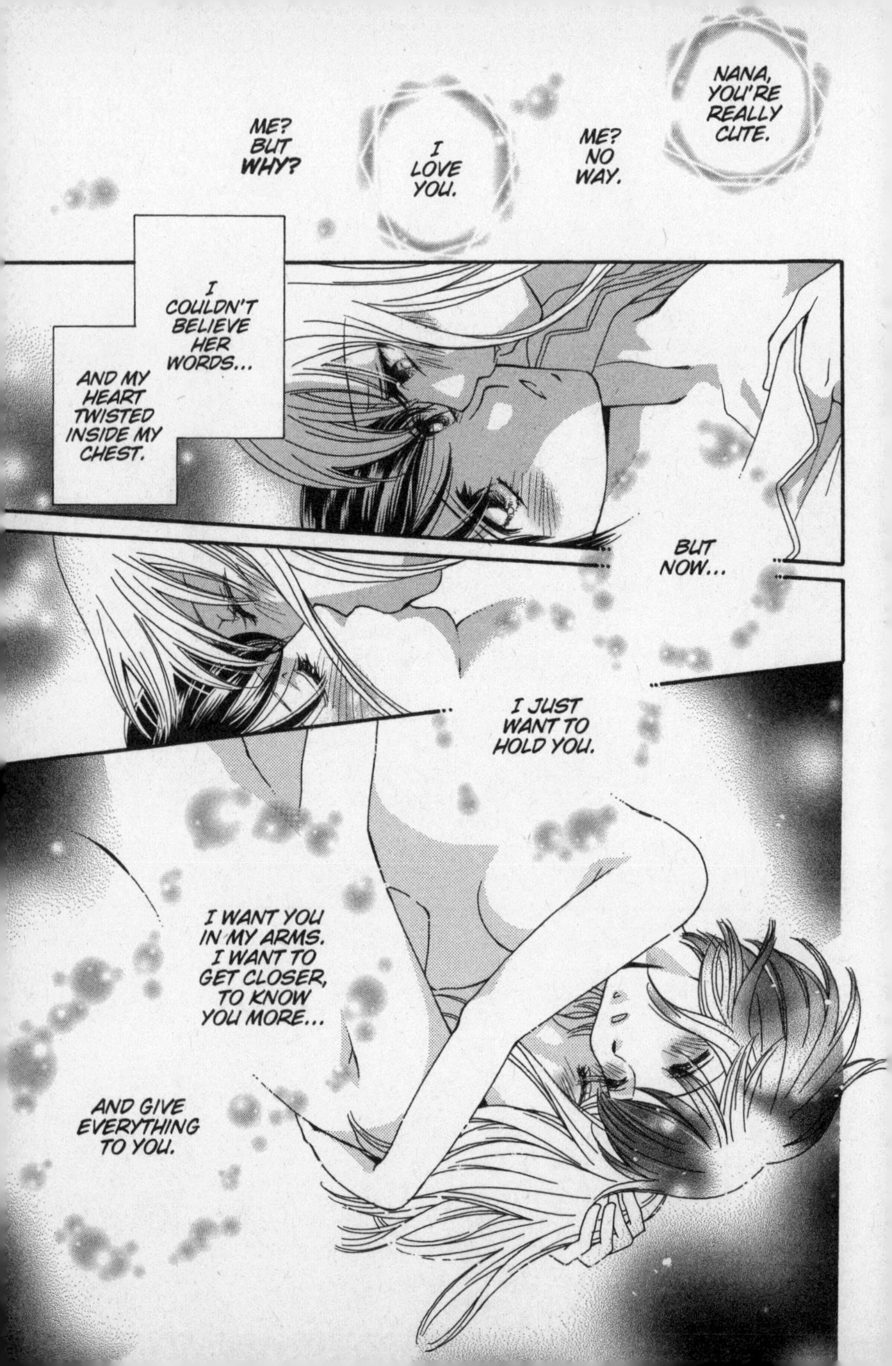
NANA, YOU'RE REALLY CUTE.
ME? NO WAY.
I LOVE YOU.
ME? BUT WHY?
I COULDN'T BELIEVE HER WORDS...
AND MY HEART TWISTED INSIDE MY CHEST.
BUT NOW...
I JUST WANT TO HOLD YOU.
I WANT YOU IN MY ARMS. I WANT TO GET CLOSER, TO KNOW YOU MORE...
AND GIVE EVERYTHING TO YOU.

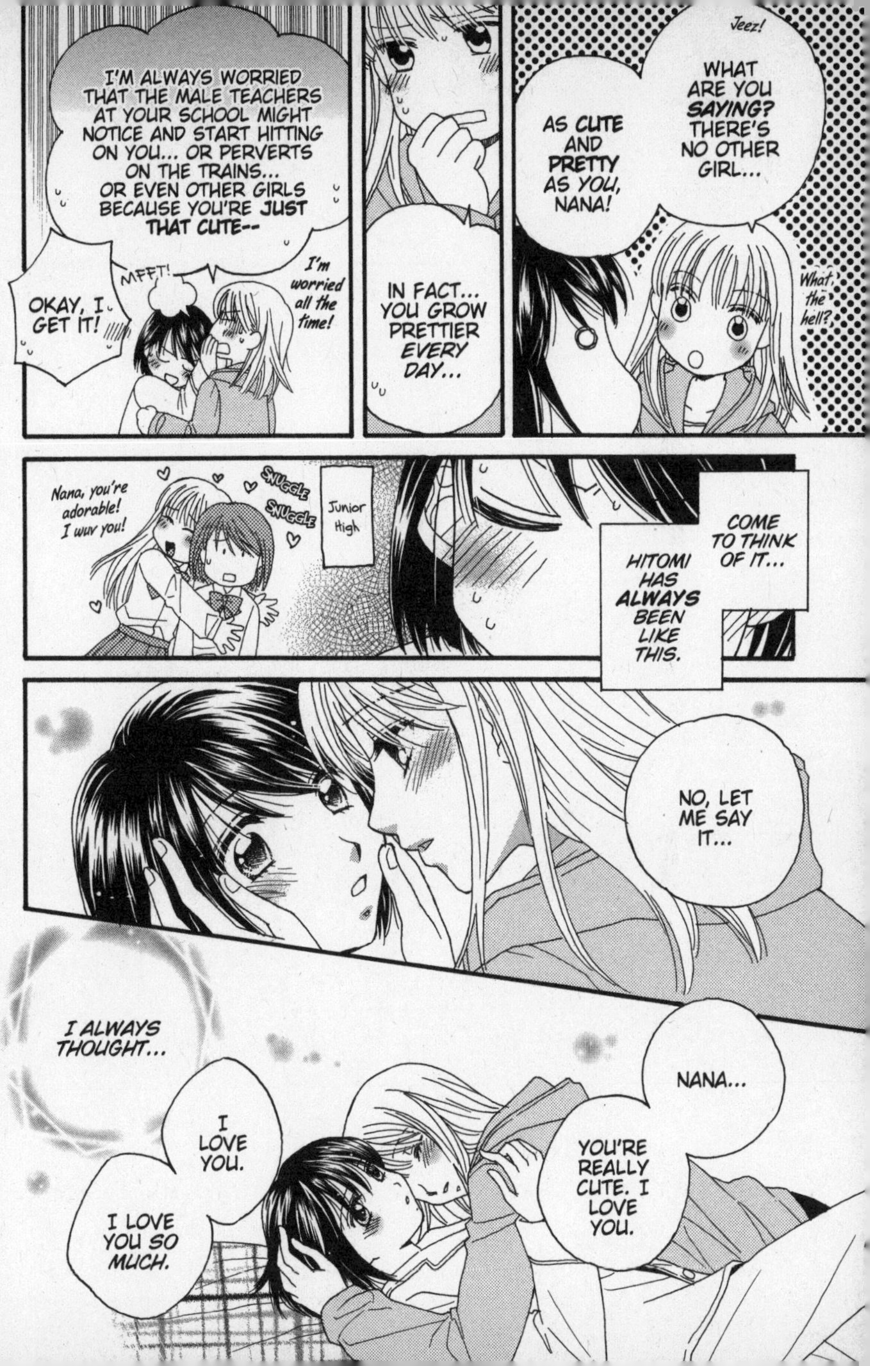
Jeez!
WHAT ARE YOU SAYING? THERE'S NO OTHER GIRL...
AS CUTE AND PRETTY AS YOU, NANA!
What, the hell?
IN FACT... YOU GROW PRETTIER EVERY DAY...
I'M ALWAYS WORRIED THAT THE MALE TEACHERS AT YOUR SCHOOL MIGHT NOTICE AND START HITTING ON YOU... OR PERVERTS ON THE TRAINS... OR EVEN OTHER GIRLS BECAUSE YOU'RE JUST THAT CUTE--
I'm worried all the time!
MFFT!
OKAY, I GET IT!
COME TO THINK OF IT...
HITOMI HAS ALWAYS BEEN LIKE THIS.
Junior High
SNUGGLE
SNUGGLE
Nana, you're adorable! I wuv you!
NO, LET ME SAY IT...
NANA...
YOU'RE REALLY CUTE. I LOVE YOU.
I ALWAYS THOUGHT...
I LOVE YOU.
I LOVE YOU SO MUCH.

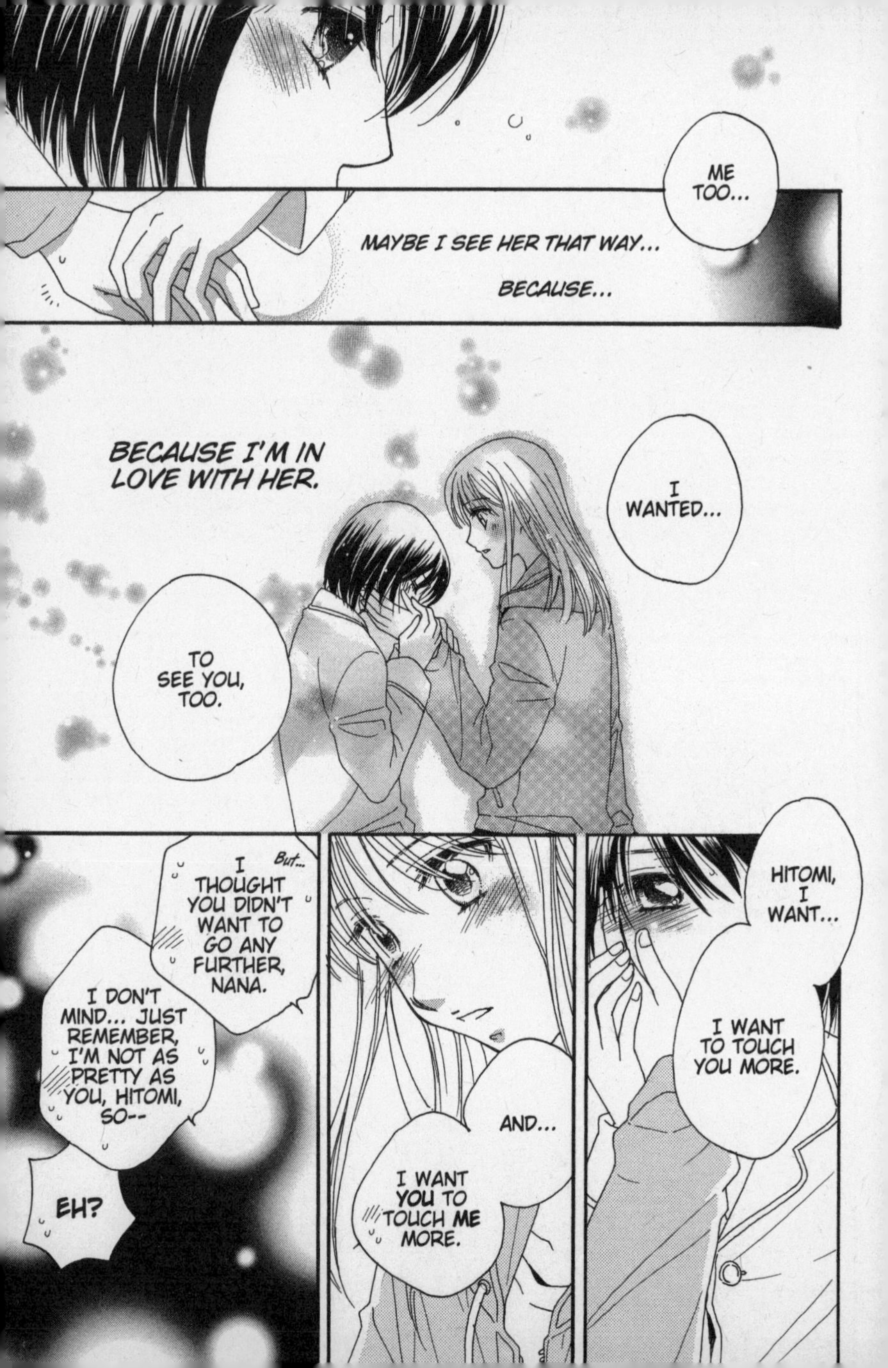
ME TOO...
MAYBE I SEE HER THAT WAY...
BECAUSE...
I WANTED...
BECAUSE I'M IN LOVE WITH HER.
TO SEE YOU, TOO.
HITOMI, I WANT...
I WANT TO TOUCH YOU MORE.
AND...
I WANT YOU TO TOUCH ME MORE.
But...
I THOUGHT YOU DIDN'T WANT TO GO ANY FURTHER, NANA.
I DON'T MIND... JUST REMEMBER, I'M NOT AS PRETTY AS YOU, HITOMI, SO--
EH?

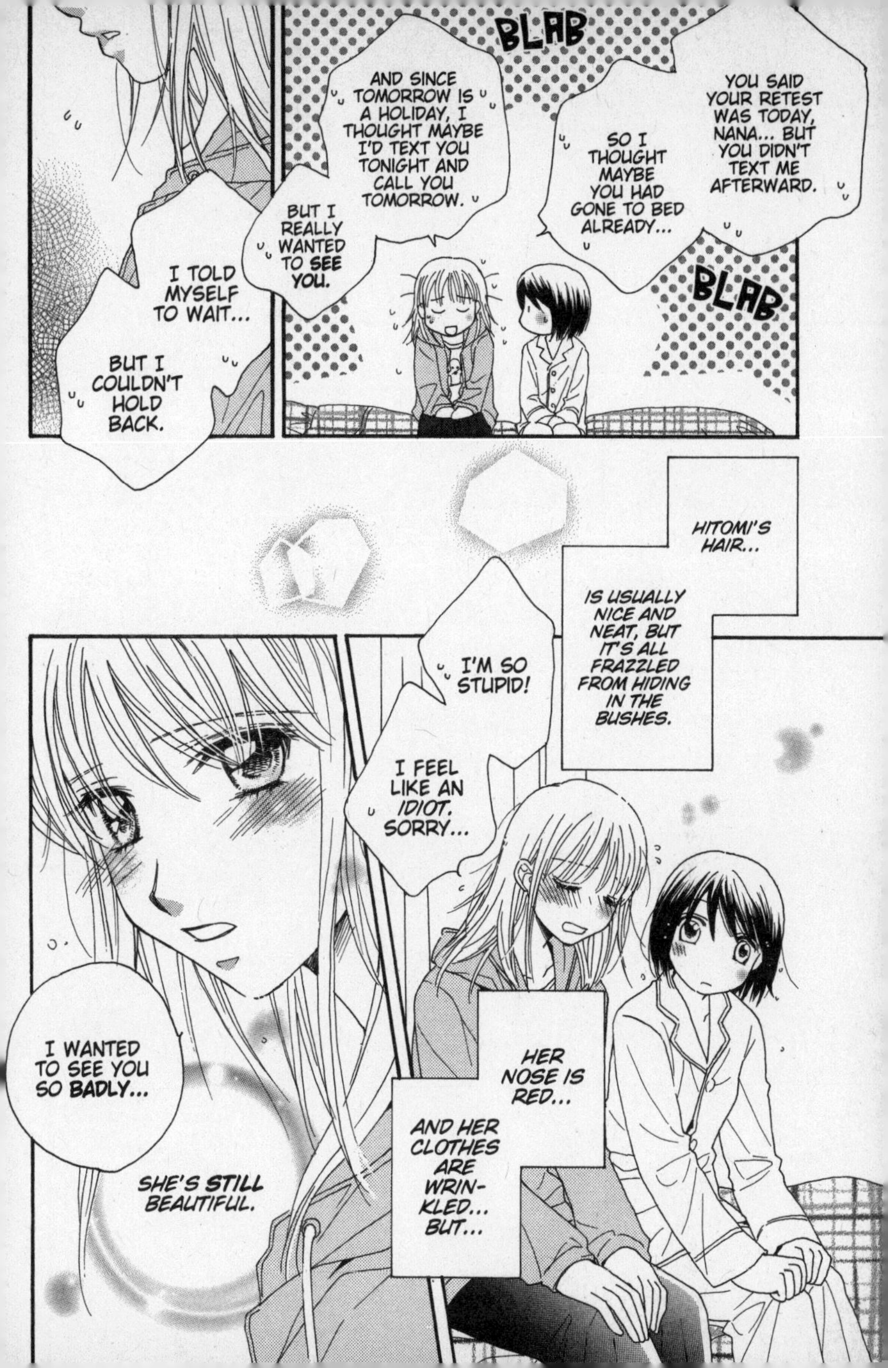
BLAB
YOU SAID YOUR RETEST WAS TODAY, NANA... BUT YOU DIDN'T TEXT ME AFTERWARD.
SO I THOUGHT MAYBE YOU HAD GONE TO BED ALREADY...
AND SINCE TOMORROW IS A HOLIDAY, I THOUGHT MAYBE I'D TEXT YOU TONIGHT AND CALL YOU TOMORROW.
BUT I REALLY WANTED TO SEE YOU.
BLAB
I TOLD MYSELF TO WAIT...
BUT I COULDN'T HOLD BACK.
HITOMI'S HAIR...
IS USUALLY NICE AND NEAT, BUT IT'S ALL FRAZZLED FROM HIDING IN THE BUSHES.
I'M SO STUPID!
I FEEL LIKE AN IDIOT. SORRY...
HER NOSE IS RED...
AND HER CLOTHES ARE WRIN-KLED... BUT...
I WANTED TO SEE YOU SO BADLY...
SHE'S STILL BEAUTIFUL.

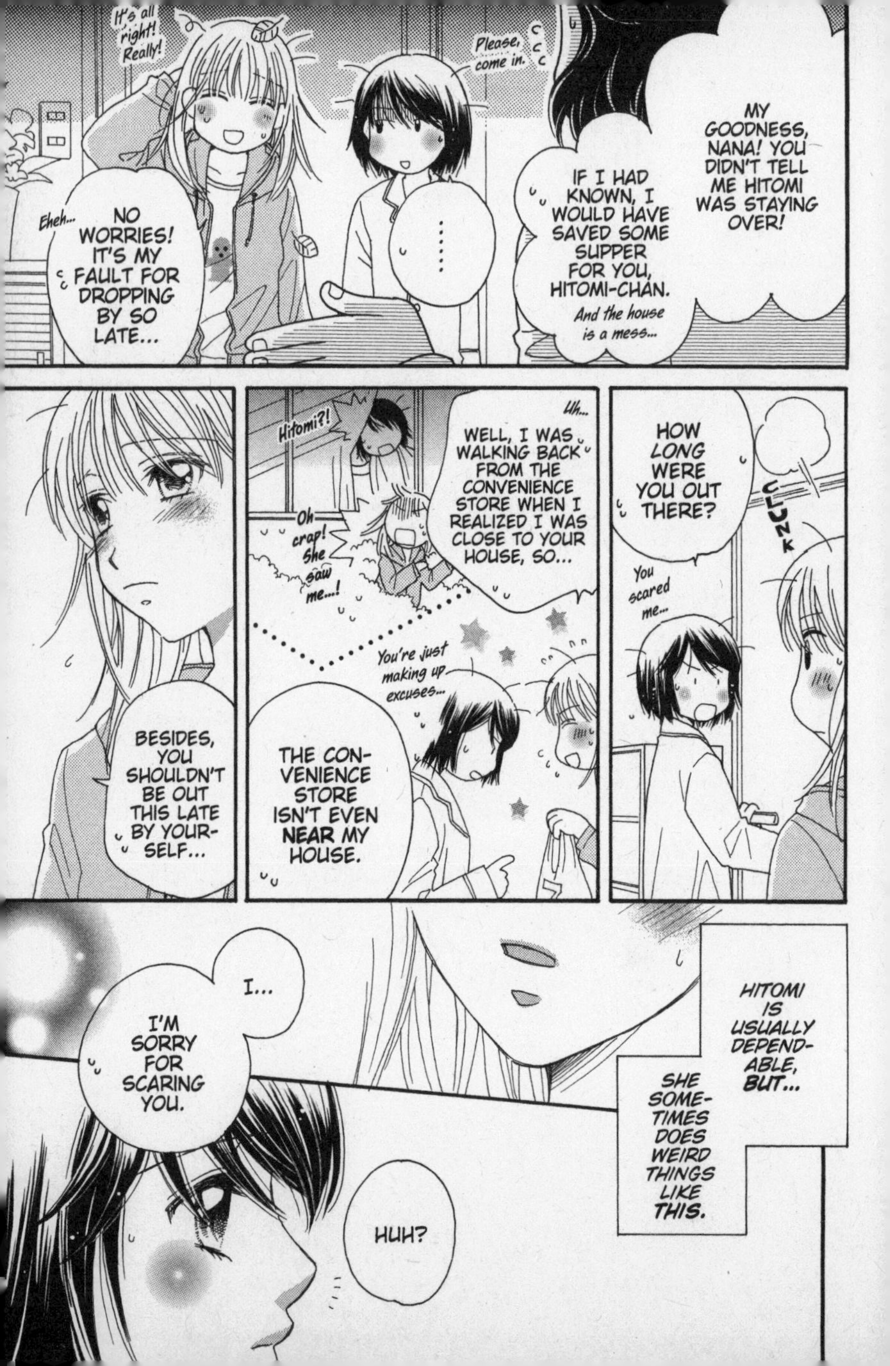

MY GOODNESS, NANA! YOU DIDN'T TELL ME HITOMI WAS STAYING OVER!
IF I HAD KNOWN, I WOULD HAVE SAVED SOME SUPPER FOR YOU, HITOMI-CHAN.
And the house is a mess...
Please, come in.
......
It's all right! Really!
NO WORRIES! IT'S MY FAULT FOR DROPPING BY SO LATE...
Eheh...
HOW LONG WERE YOU OUT THERE?
CLUNK
You scared me...
Uh...
WELL, I WAS WALKING BACK FROM THE CONVENIENCE STORE WHEN I REALIZED I WAS CLOSE TO YOUR HOUSE, SO...
Hitomi?!
Oh crap! She saw me...!
You're just making up excuses...
THE CON-VENIENCE STORE ISN'T EVEN NEAR MY HOUSE.
BESIDES, YOU SHOULDN'T BE OUT THIS LATE BY YOUR-SELF...
HITOMI IS USUALLY DEPENDABLE, BUT...
SHE SOMETIMES DOES WEIRD THINGS LIKE THIS.
I...
I'M SORRY FOR SCARING YOU.
HUH?

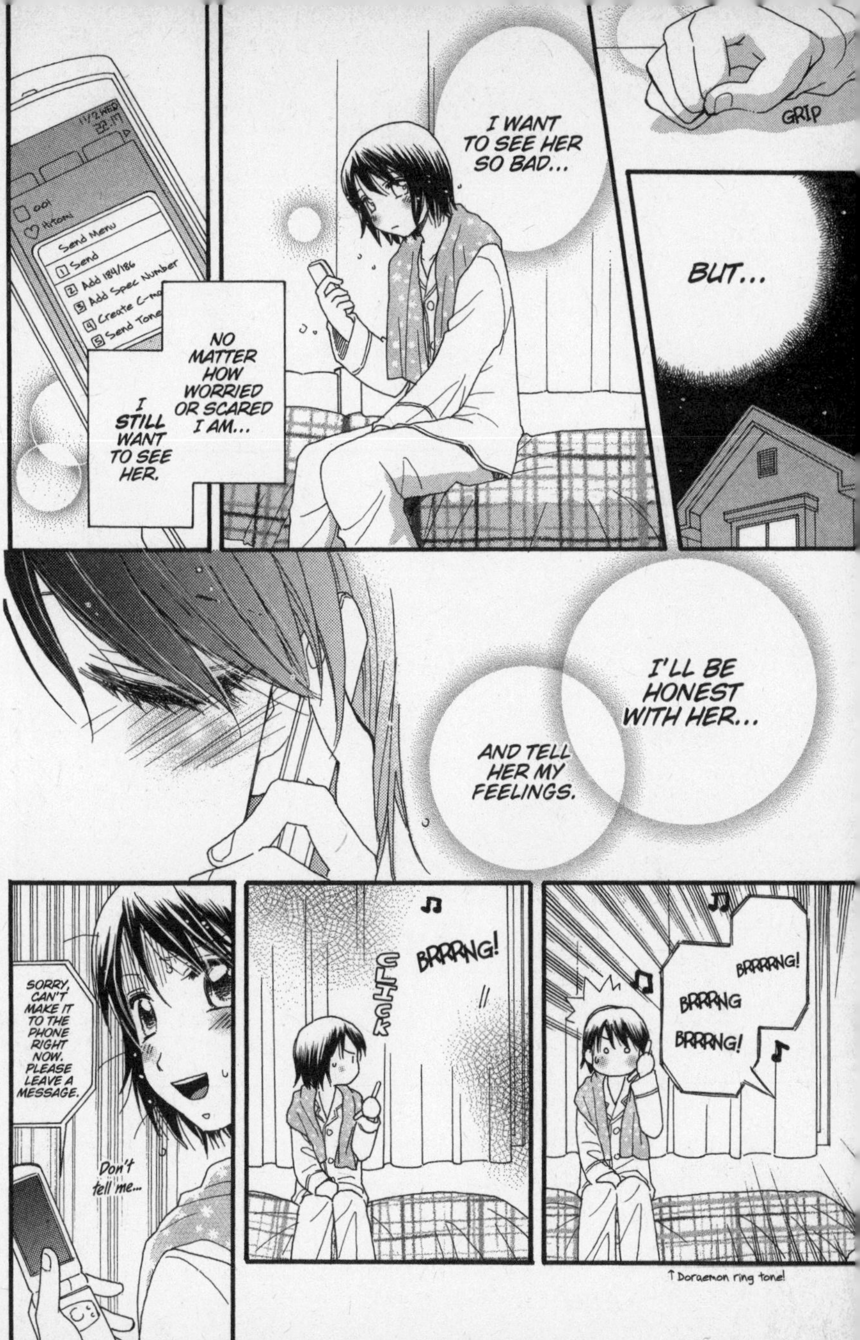
GRIP
BUT...
I WANT TO SEE HER SO BAD...
11/2 WED 22:17
ooi
Hitomi
Send Menu
1 Send
2 Add 184/186
3 Add Spec Number
NO MATTER HOW WORRIED OR SCARED I AM...
I STILL WANT TO SEE HER.
I'LL BE HONEST WITH HER...
AND TELL HER MY FEELINGS.
BRRRRNG!
BRRRNG
BRRRNG!
BRRRNG!
CLICK
SORRY, CAN'T MAKE IT TO THE PHONE RIGHT NOW. PLEASE LEAVE A MESSAGE.
Don't tell me...
↑Doraemon ring tone!

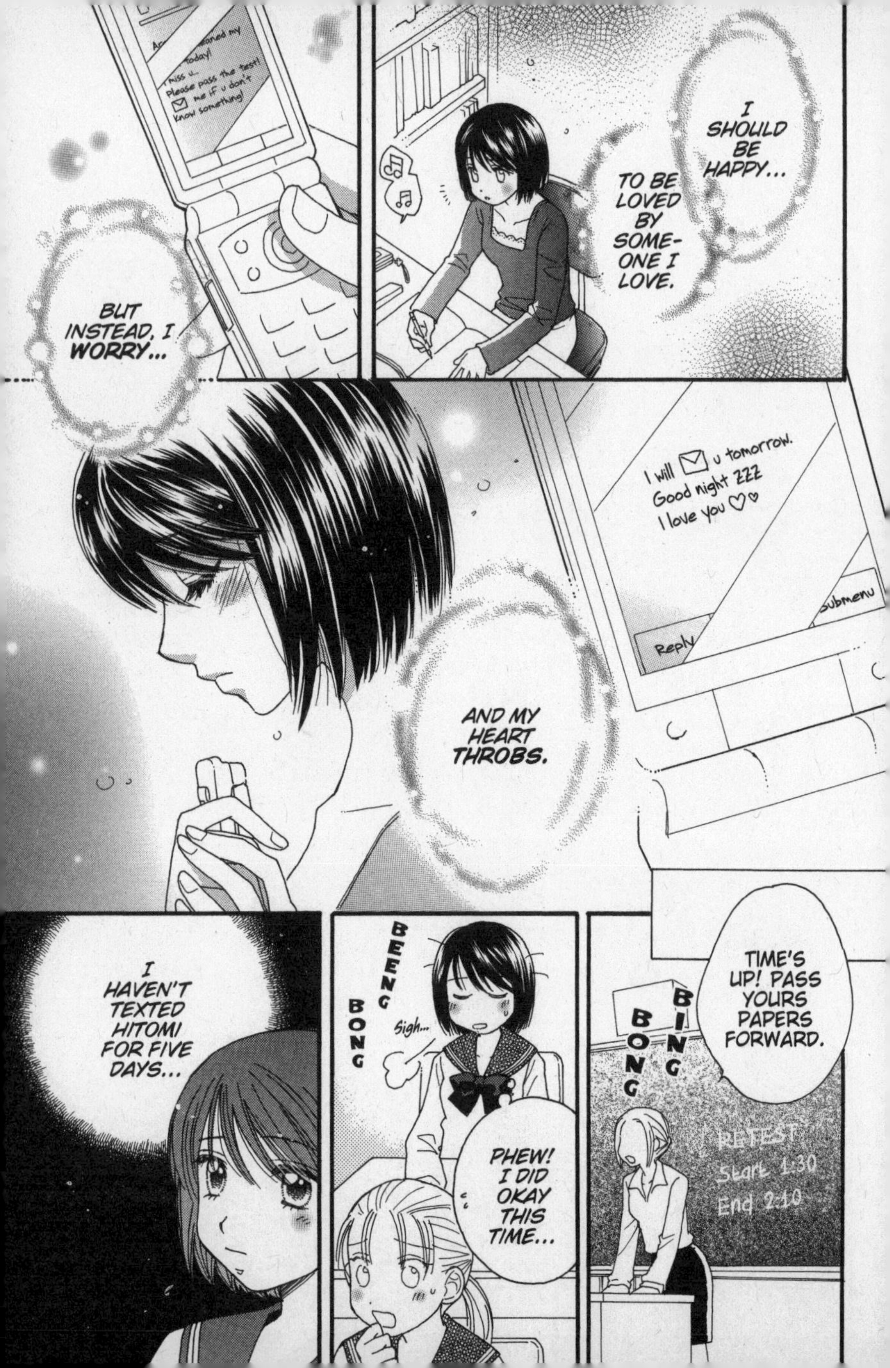
I SHOULD BE HAPPY...
TO BE LOVED BY SOMEONE I LOVE.
today!
I miss u..
Please pass the test!
me if u don't know something!
BUT INSTEAD, I WORRY...
I will u tomorrow.
Good night ZZZ
I love you
Submenu
Reply
AND MY HEART THROBS.
TIME'S UP! PASS YOURS PAPERS FORWARD.
BING
BONG
RETEST
Start 1:30
End 2:10
BEENG
BONG
Sigh...
PHEW! I DID OKAY THIS TIME...
I HAVEN'T TEXTED HITOMI FOR FIVE DAYS...

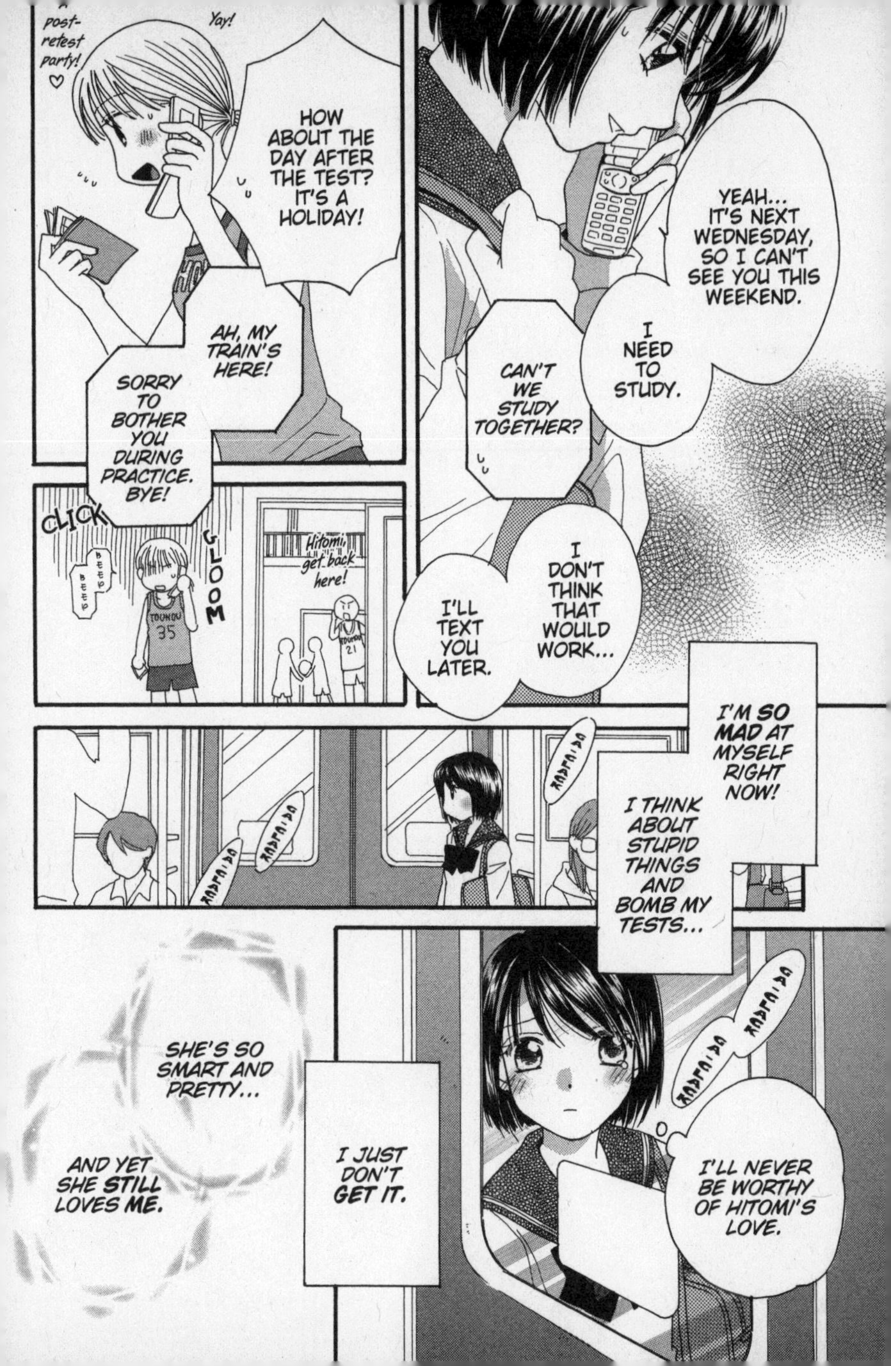

YEAH... IT'S NEXT WEDNESDAY, SO I CAN'T SEE YOU THIS WEEKEND.
I NEED TO STUDY.
CAN'T WE STUDY TOGETHER?
I DON'T THINK THAT WOULD WORK...
I'LL TEXT YOU LATER.
Yay!
post-retest party! ♡
HOW ABOUT THE DAY AFTER THE TEST? IT'S A HOLIDAY!
AH, MY TRAIN'S HERE!
SORRY TO BOTHER YOU DURING PRACTICE. BYE!
CLICK
GLOOM
BEEP BEEP BEEP
Hitomi, get back here!
I'M SO MAD AT MYSELF RIGHT NOW!
I THINK ABOUT STUPID THINGS AND BOMB MY TESTS...
I'LL NEVER BE WORTHY OF HITOMI'S LOVE.
SHE'S SO SMART AND PRETTY...
AND YET SHE STILL LOVES ME.
I JUST DON'T GET IT.

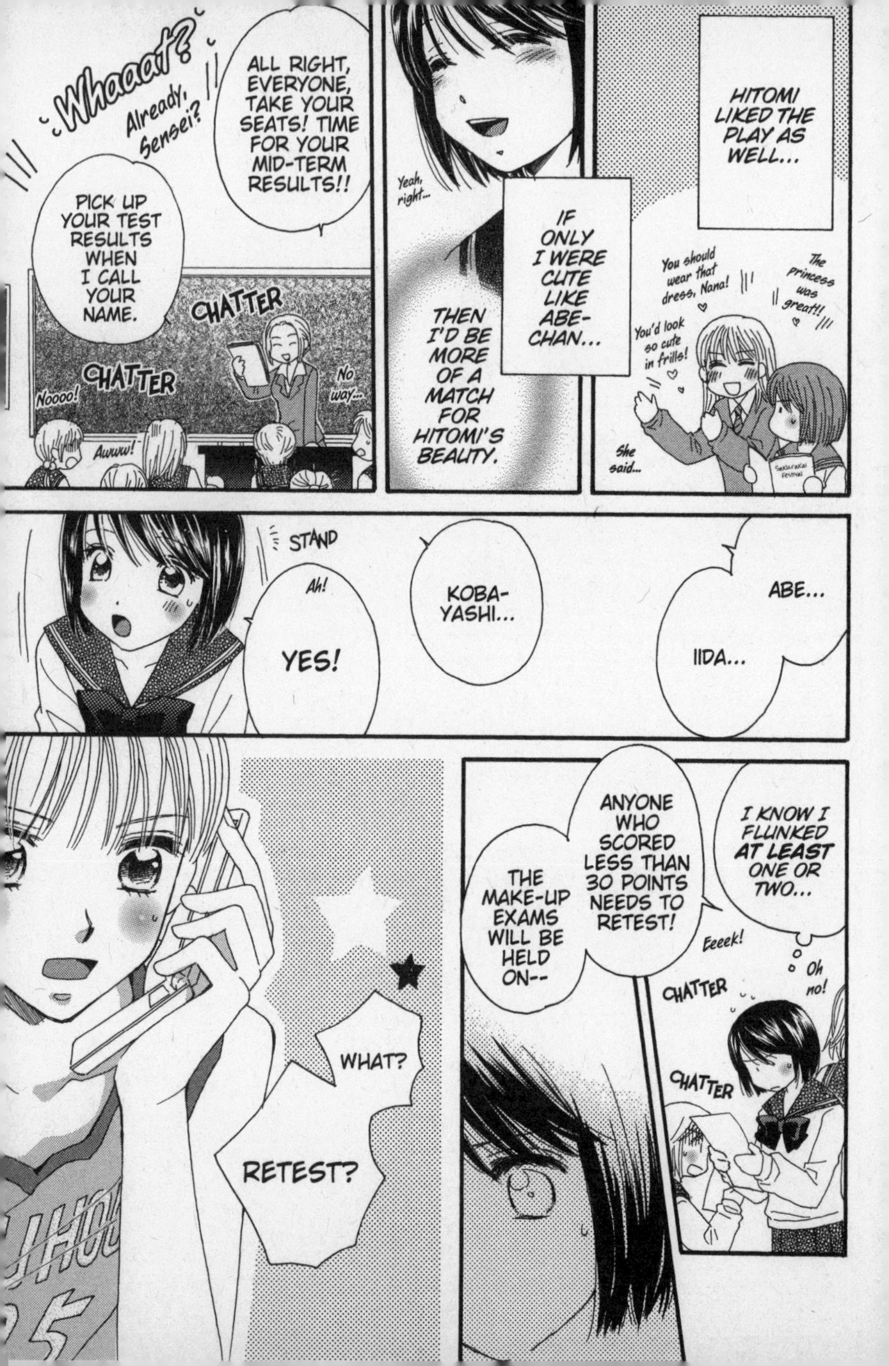

HITOMI LIKED THE PLAY AS WELL...
The princess was great!!
You should wear that dress, Nana!
You'd look so cute in frills!
She said...
IF ONLY I WERE CUTE LIKE ABE-CHAN...
THEN I'D BE MORE OF A MATCH FOR HITOMI'S BEAUTY.
Yeah, right...
ALL RIGHT, EVERYONE, TAKE YOUR SEATS! TIME FOR YOUR MID-TERM RESULTS!!
Whaaat?
Already, Sensei?
PICK UP YOUR TEST RESULTS WHEN I CALL YOUR NAME.
CHATTER
No way...
CHATTER
Noooo!
Awww!
ABE...
IIDA...
KOBA-YASHI...
Ah!
YES!
STAND
I KNOW I FLUNKED AT LEAST ONE OR TWO...
ANYONE WHO SCORED LESS THAN 30 POINTS NEEDS TO RETEST!
THE MAKE-UP EXAMS WILL BE HELD ON--
Eeeek!
Oh no!
CHATTER
CHATTER
WHAT?
RETEST?

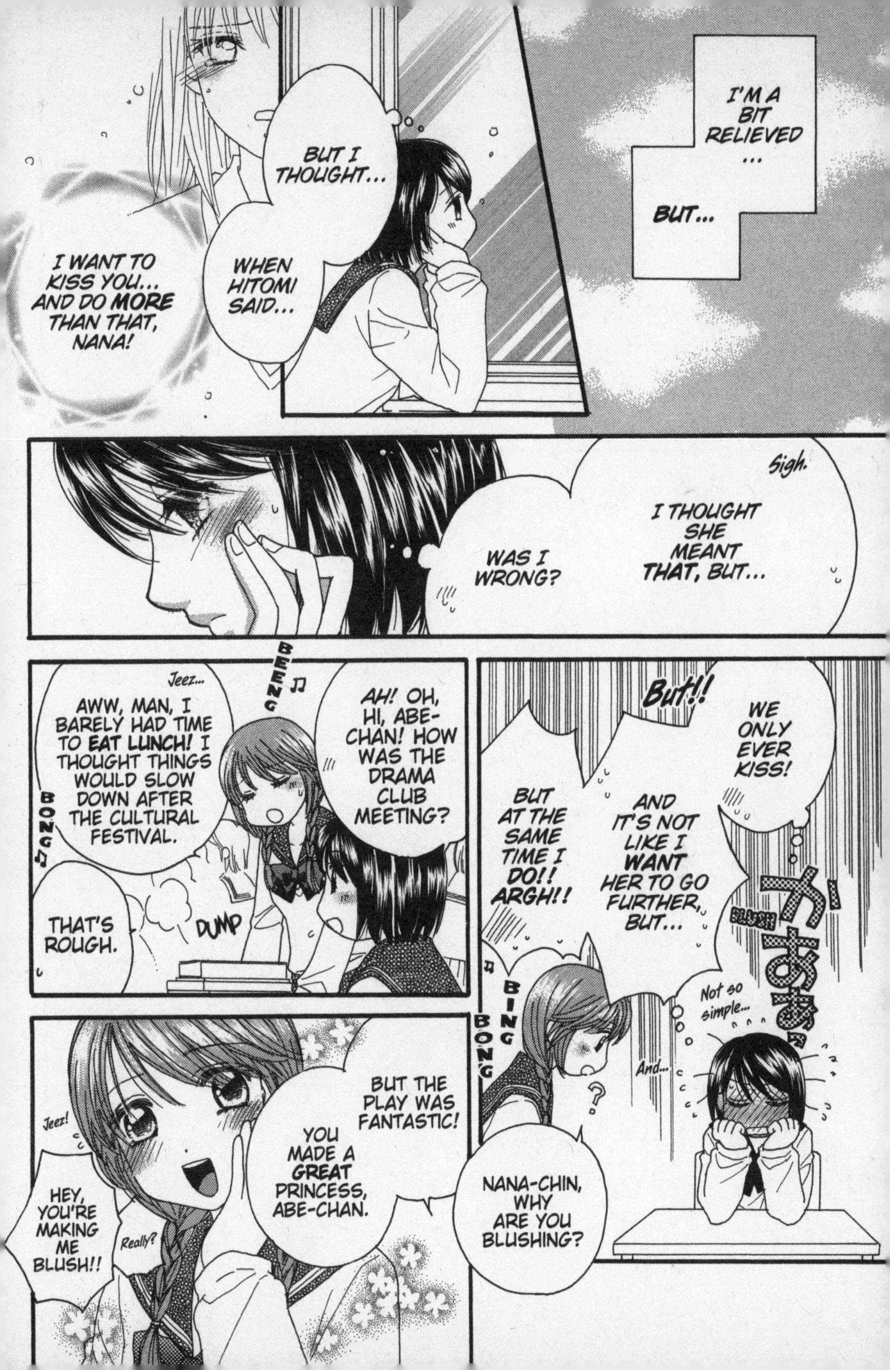

I'M A BIT RELIEVED...
BUT...
BUT I THOUGHT...
WHEN HITOMI SAID...
I WANT TO KISS YOU... AND DO MORE THAN THAT, NANA!
Sigh.
I THOUGHT SHE MEANT THAT, BUT...
WAS I WRONG?
But!!
WE ONLY EVER KISS!
AND IT'S NOT LIKE I WANT HER TO GO FURTHER, BUT...
BUT AT THE SAME TIME I DO!! ARGH!!
かぁぁ
BLUSH
Not so simple...
And...
BING
BONG
?
NANA-CHIN, WHY ARE YOU BLUSHING?
BEEENG
BONG
AH! OH, HI, ABE-CHAN! HOW WAS THE DRAMA CLUB MEETING?
Jeez...
AWW, MAN, I BARELY HAD TIME TO EAT LUNCH! I THOUGHT THINGS WOULD SLOW DOWN AFTER THE CULTURAL FESTIVAL.
DUMP
THAT'S ROUGH.
BUT THE PLAY WAS FANTASTIC!
YOU MADE A GREAT PRINCESS, ABE-CHAN.
Jeez!
HEY, YOU'RE MAKING ME BLUSH!!
Really?

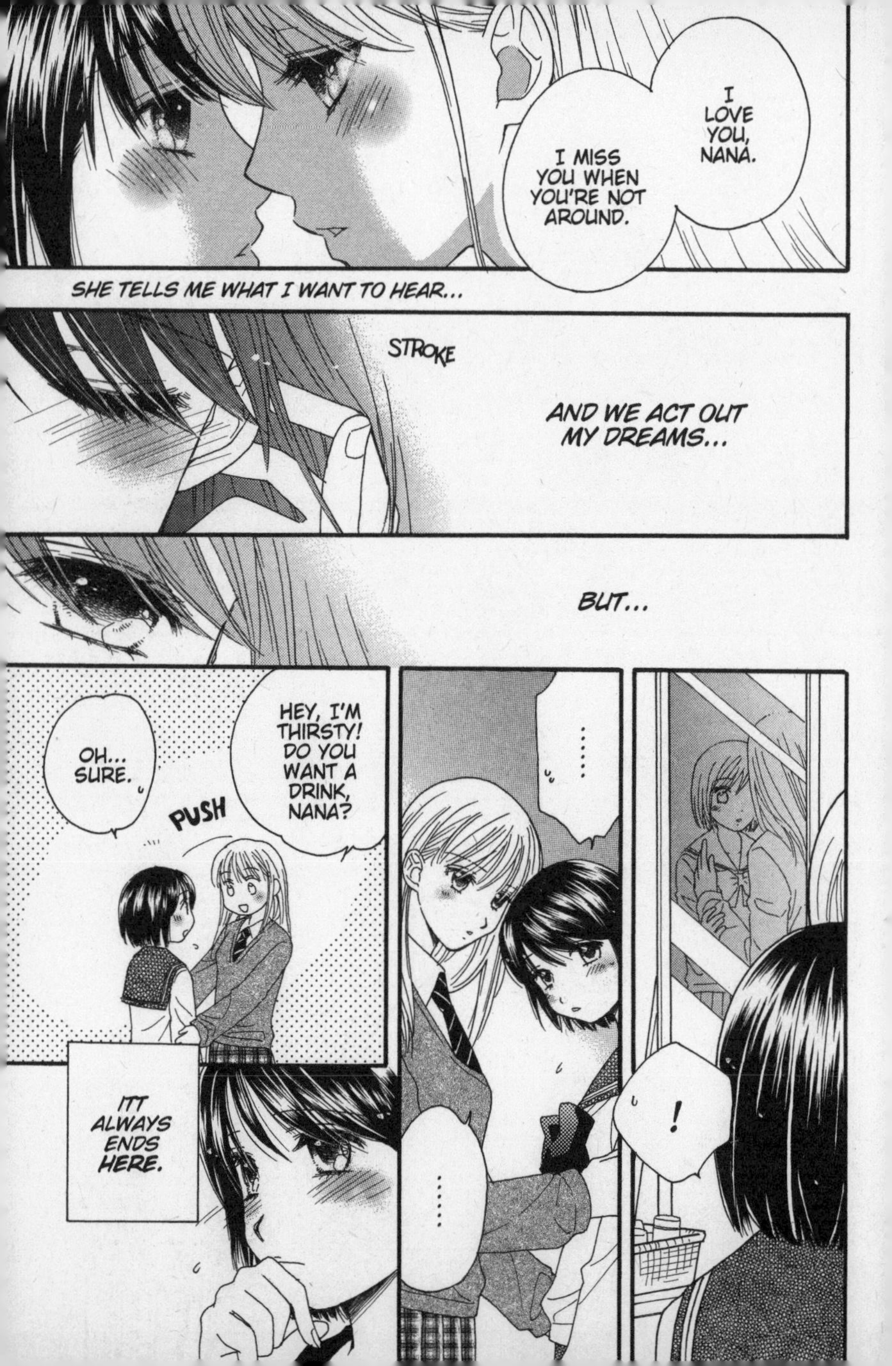
I LOVE YOU, NANA.
I MISS YOU WHEN YOU'RE NOT AROUND.
SHE TELLS ME WHAT I WANT TO HEAR...
STROKE
AND WE ACT OUT MY DREAMS...
BUT...
!
......
......
HEY, I'M THIRSTY! DO YOU WANT A DRINK, NANA?
PUSH
OH... SURE.
ITT ALWAYS ENDS HERE.

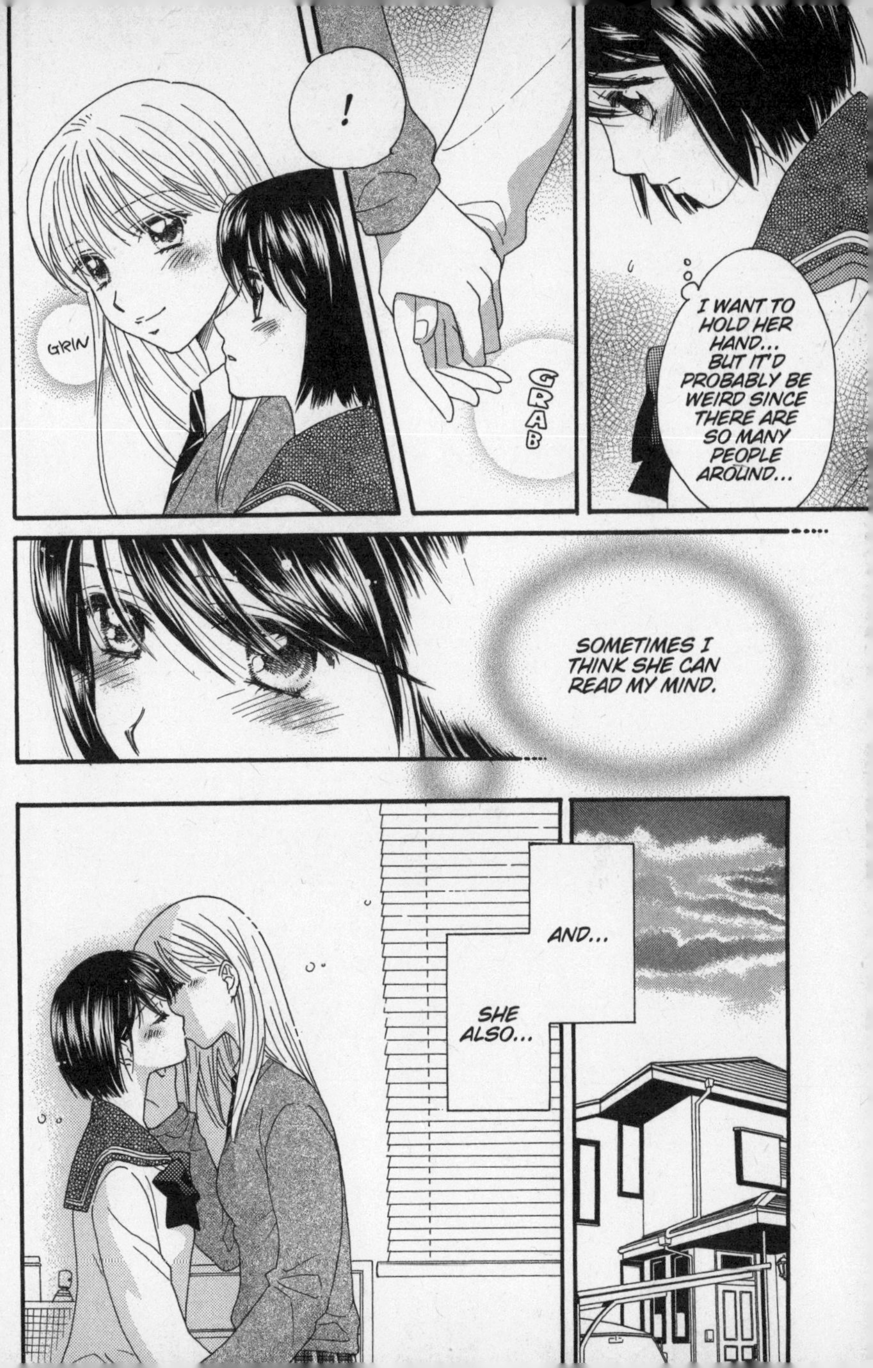
I WANT TO HOLD HER HAND... BUT IT'D PROBABLY BE WEIRD SINCE THERE ARE SO MANY PEOPLE AROUND...
!
GRAB
GRIN
SOMETIMES I THINK SHE CAN READ MY MIND.
AND...
SHE ALSO...

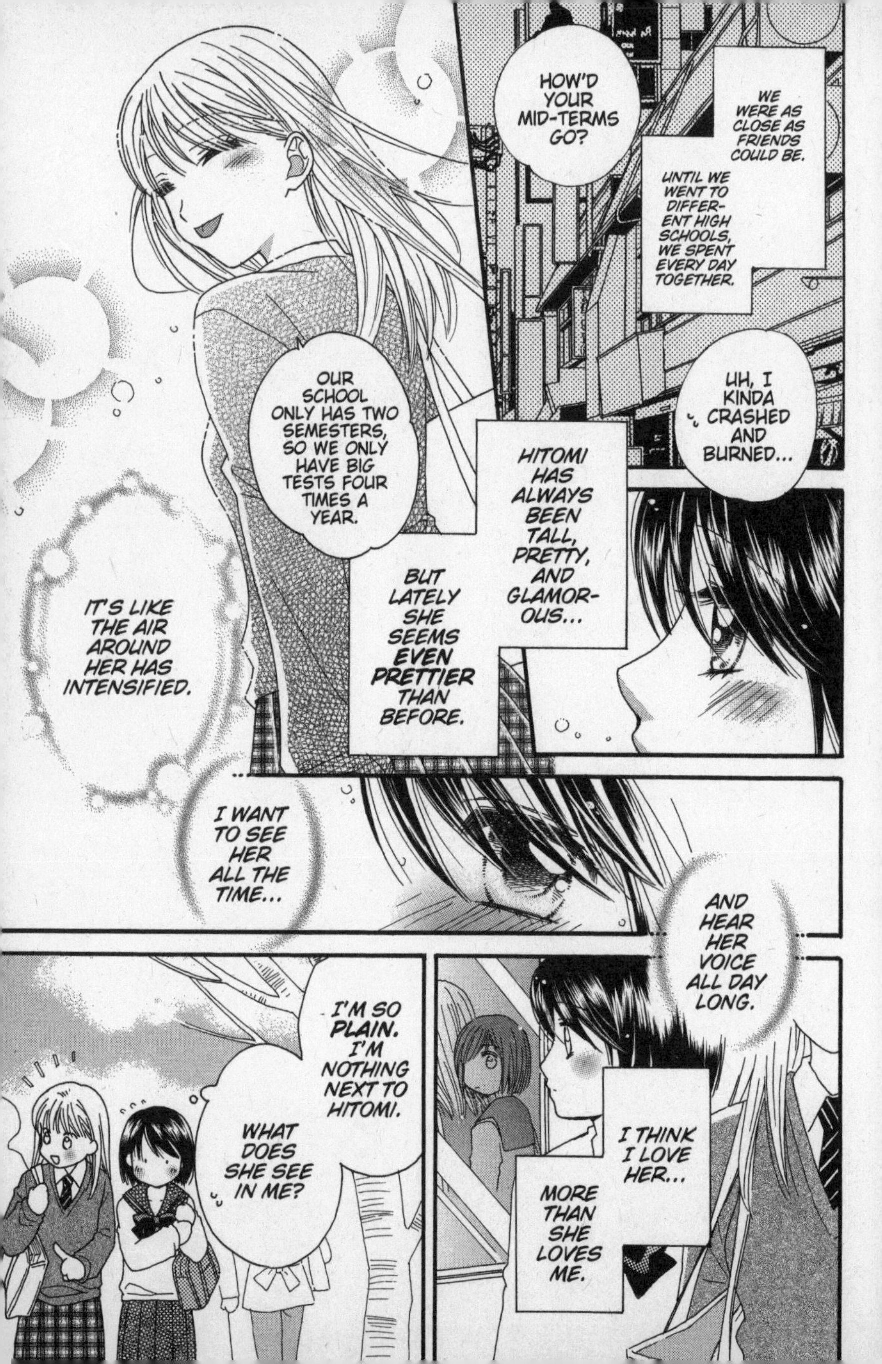
HOW'D YOUR MID-TERMS GO?
WE WERE AS CLOSE AS FRIENDS COULD BE.
UNTIL WE WENT TO DIFFERENT HIGH SCHOOLS, WE SPENT EVERY DAY TOGETHER.
UH, I KINDA CRASHED AND BURNED...
HITOMI HAS ALWAYS BEEN TALL, PRETTY, AND GLAMOROUS...
BUT LATELY SHE SEEMS EVEN PRETTIER THAN BEFORE.
OUR SCHOOL ONLY HAS TWO SEMESTERS, SO WE ONLY HAVE BIG TESTS FOUR TIMES A YEAR.
IT'S LIKE THE AIR AROUND HER HAS INTENSIFIED.
AND HEAR HER VOICE ALL DAY LONG.
I WANT TO SEE HER ALL THE TIME...
I THINK I LOVE HER...
MORE THAN SHE LOVES ME.
I'M SO PLAIN. I'M NOTHING NEXT TO HITOMI.
WHAT DOES SHE SEE IN ME?

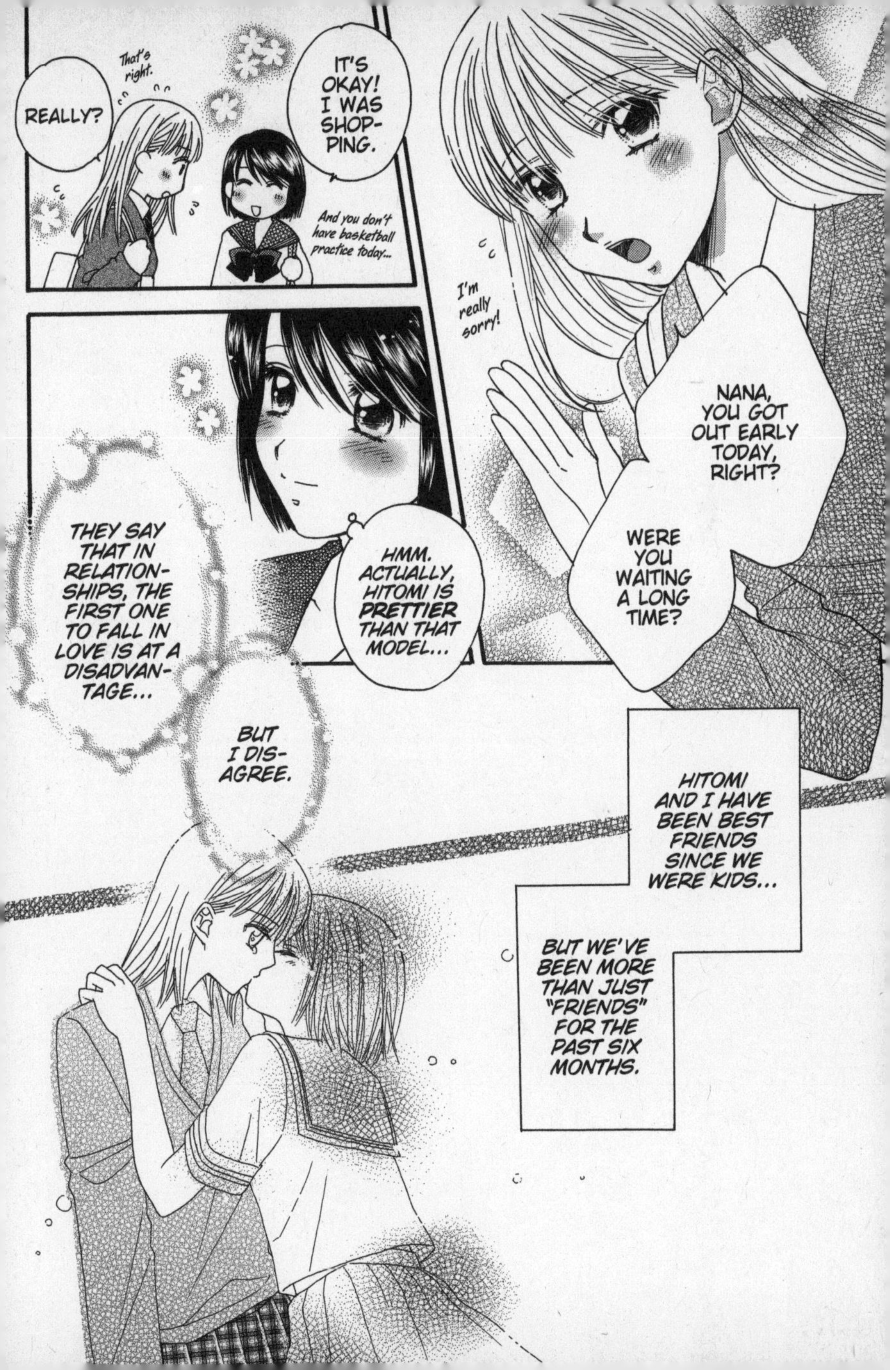

I'm really sorry!
NANA, YOU GOT OUT EARLY TODAY, RIGHT?
WERE YOU WAITING A LONG TIME?
IT'S OKAY! I WAS SHOP-PING.
And you don't have basketball practice today...
That's right.
REALLY?
HMM. ACTUALLY, HITOMI IS PRETTIER THAN THAT MODEL...
HITOMI AND I HAVE BEEN BEST FRIENDS SINCE WE WERE KIDS...
BUT WE'VE BEEN MORE THAN JUST "FRIENDS" FOR THE PAST SIX MONTHS.
THEY SAY THAT IN RELATION-SHIPS, THE FIRST ONE TO FALL IN LOVE IS AT A DISADVAN-TAGE...
BUT I DIS-AGREE.

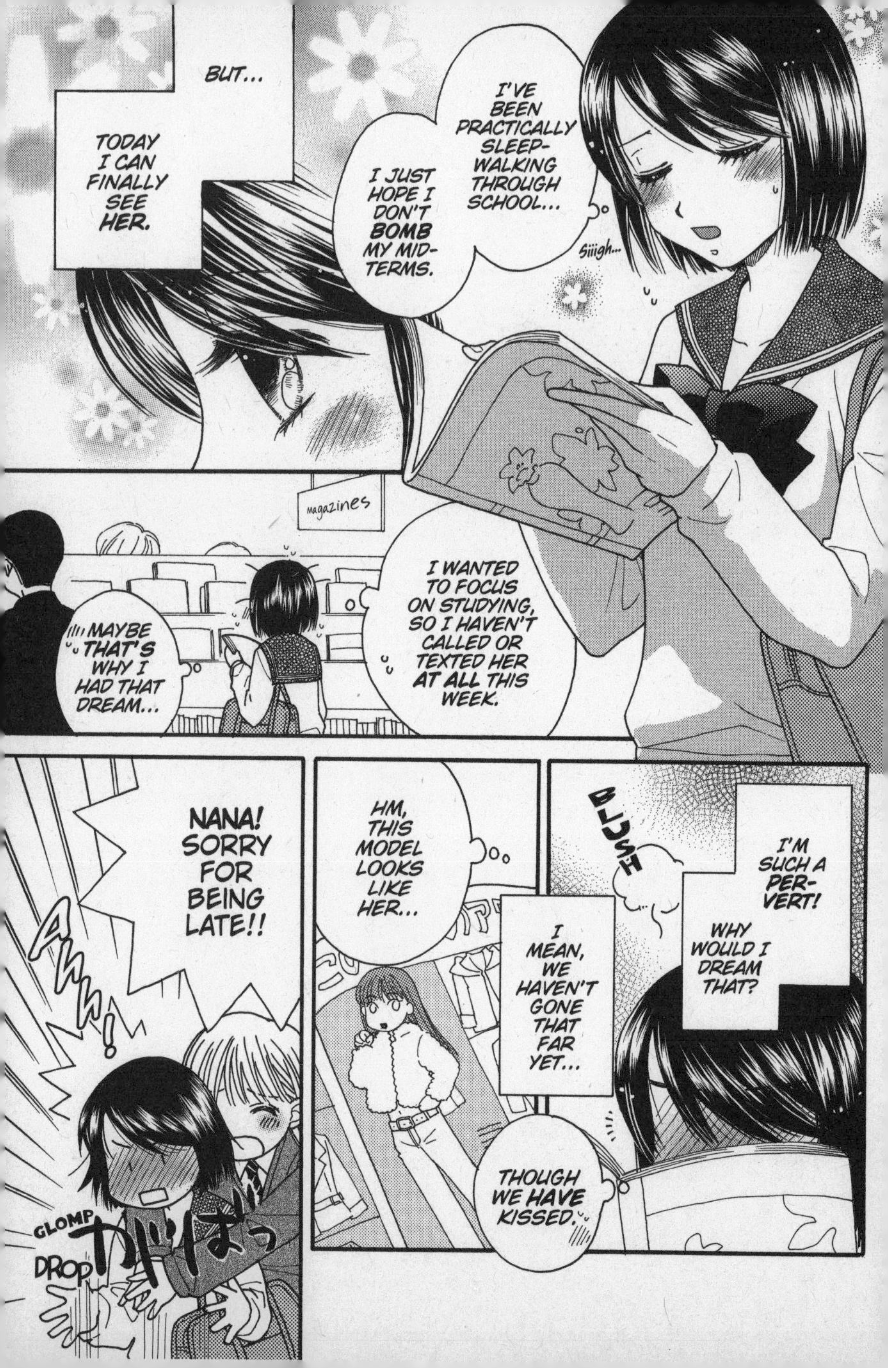

I'VE BEEN PRACTICALLY SLEEP-WALKING THROUGH SCHOOL...
Siiigh...
I JUST HOPE I DON'T BOMB MY MID-TERMS.
BUT...
TODAY I CAN FINALLY SEE HER.
magazines
I WANTED TO FOCUS ON STUDYING, SO I HAVEN'T CALLED OR TEXTED HER AT ALL THIS WEEK.
MAYBE THAT'S WHY I HAD THAT DREAM...
BLUSH
I'M SUCH A PER-VERT!
WHY WOULD I DREAM THAT?
I MEAN, WE HAVEN'T GONE THAT FAR YET...
THOUGH WE HAVE KISSED.
HM, THIS MODEL LOOKS LIKE HER...
NANA! SORRY FOR BEING LATE!!
AWW!
GLOMP
DROP

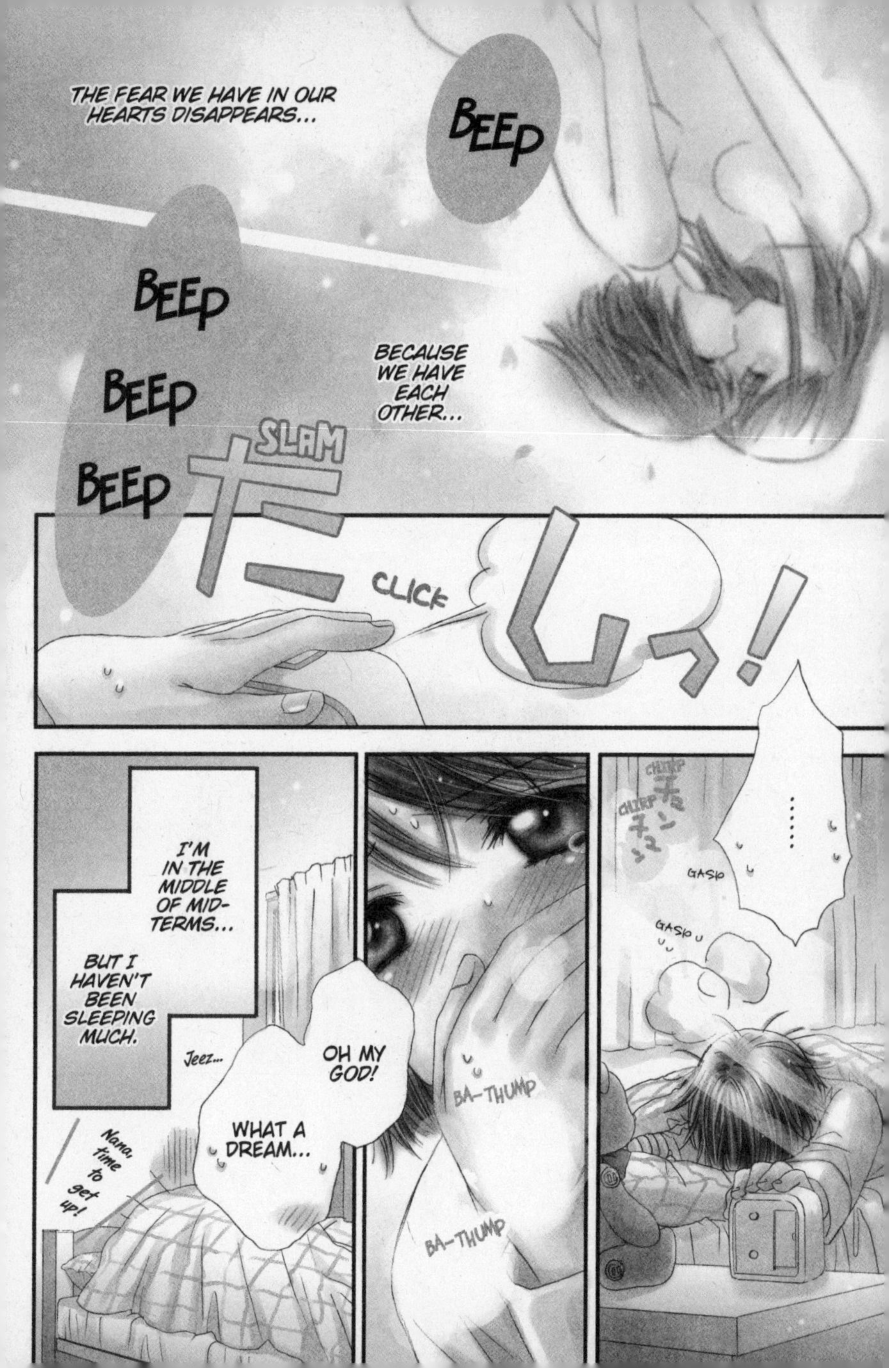
THE FEAR WE HAVE IN OUR HEARTS DISAPPEARS...
BEEP
BECAUSE WE HAVE EACH OTHER...
BEEP
BEEP
BEEP
SLAM
CLICK
CHIRP
CHIRP
......
GASP
GASP
OH MY GOD!
WHAT A DREAM...
BA-THUMP
BA-THUMP
I'M IN THE MIDDLE OF MID-TERMS...
BUT I HAVEN'T BEEN SLEEPING MUCH.
Jeez...
Nana, time to get up!

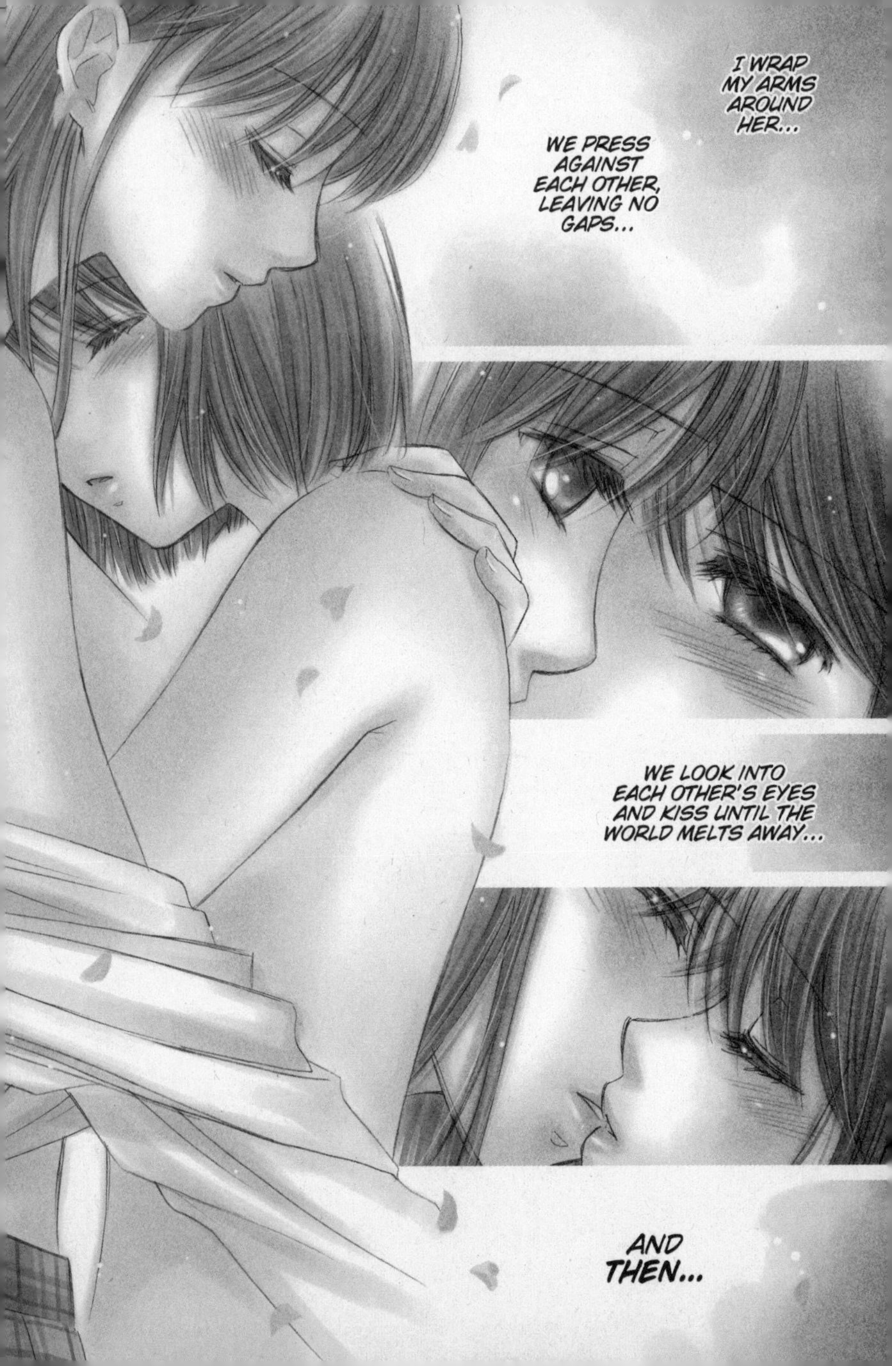
I WRAP MY ARMS AROUND HER...
WE PRESS AGAINST EACH OTHER, LEAVING NO GAPS...
WE LOOK INTO EACH OTHER'S EYES AND KISS UNTIL THE WORLD MELTS AWAY...
AND THEN...

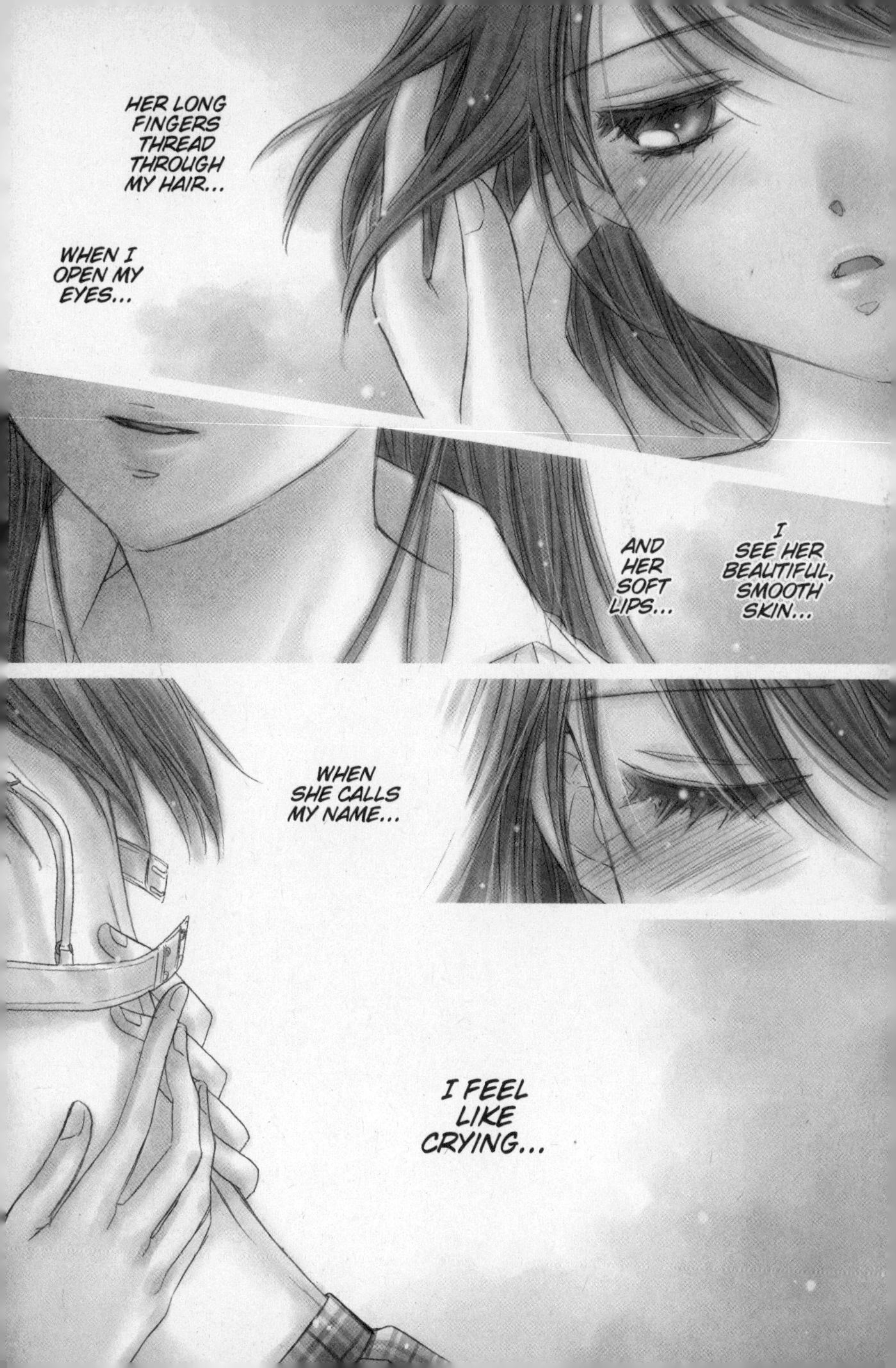
HER LONG FINGERS THREAD THROUGH MY HAIR...
WHEN I OPEN MY EYES...
I SEE HER BEAUTIFUL, SMOOTH SKIN...
AND HER SOFT LIPS...
WHEN SHE CALLS MY NAME...
I FEEL LIKE CRYING...

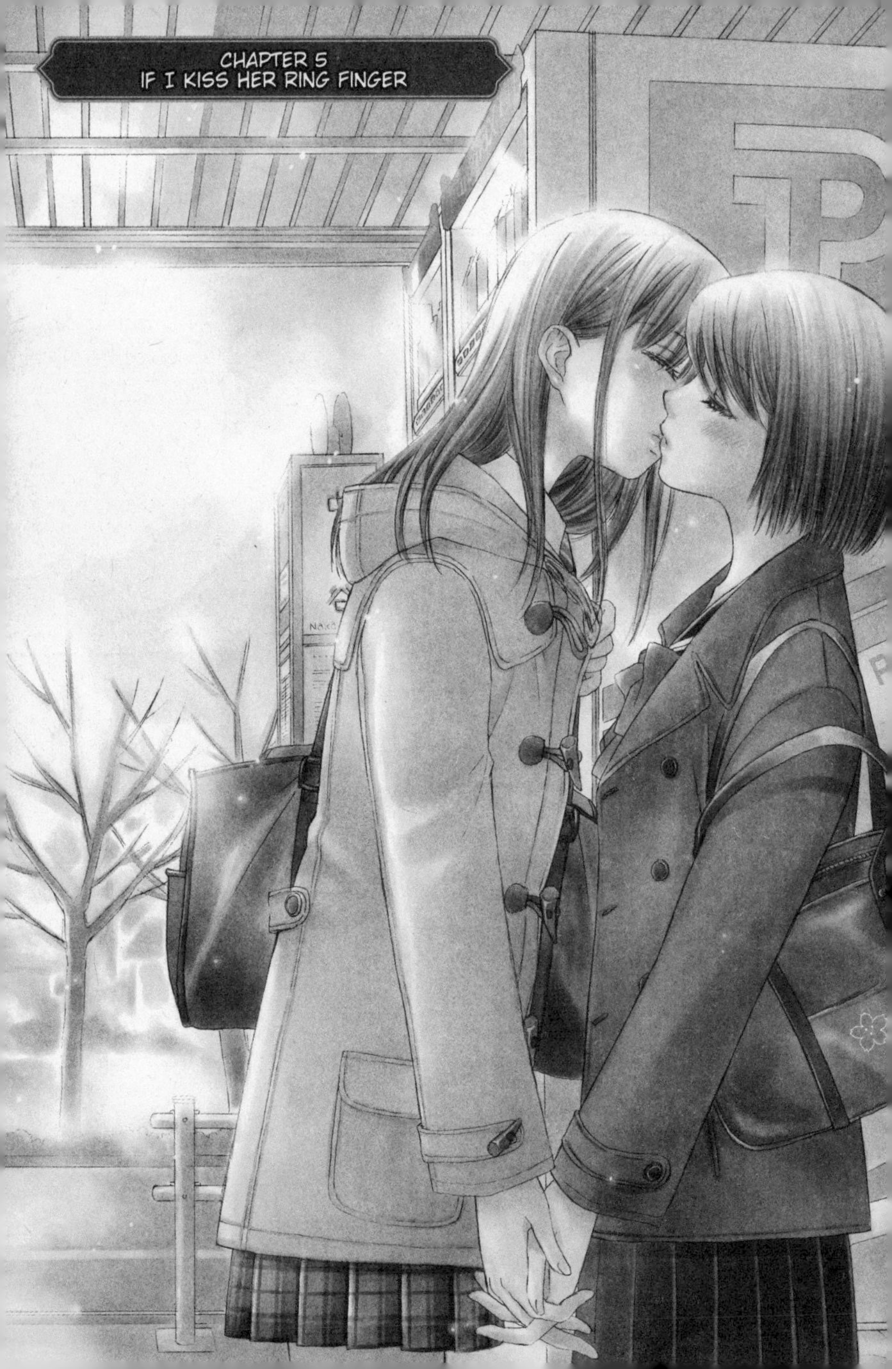
CHAPTER 5
IF I KISS HER RING FINGER

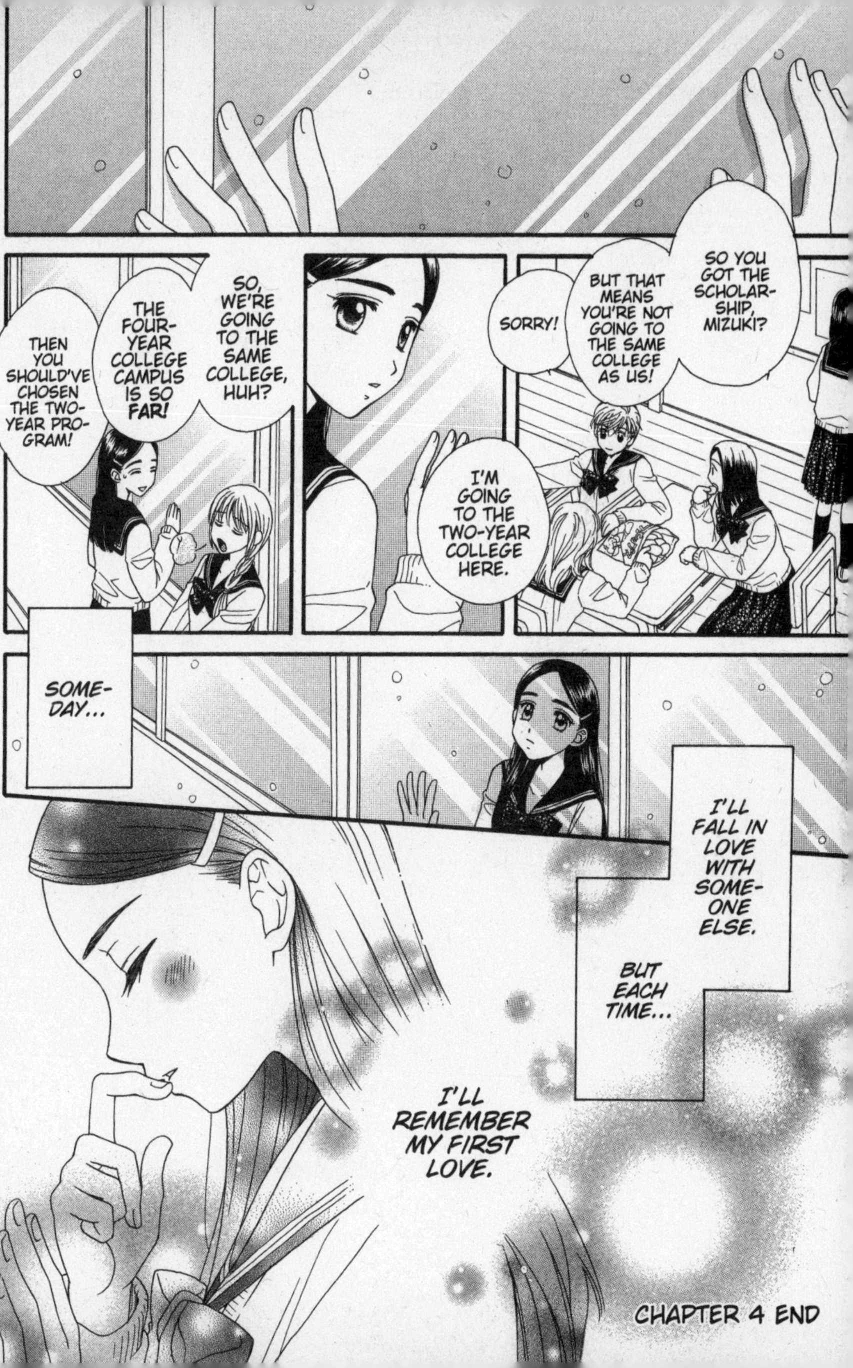
SO YOU GOT THE SCHOLAR-SHIP, MIZUKI?
BUT THAT MEANS YOU'RE NOT GOING TO THE SAME COLLEGE AS US!
SORRY!
I'M GOING TO THE TWO-YEAR COLLEGE HERE.
SO, WE'RE GOING TO THE SAME COLLEGE, HUH?
THE FOUR-YEAR COLLEGE CAMPUS IS SO FAR!
THEN YOU SHOULD'VE CHOSEN THE TWO-YEAR PRO-GRAM!
SOME-DAY...
I'LL FALL IN LOVE WITH SOME-ONE ELSE.
BUT EACH TIME...
I'LL REMEMBER MY FIRST LOVE.
CHAPTER 4 END

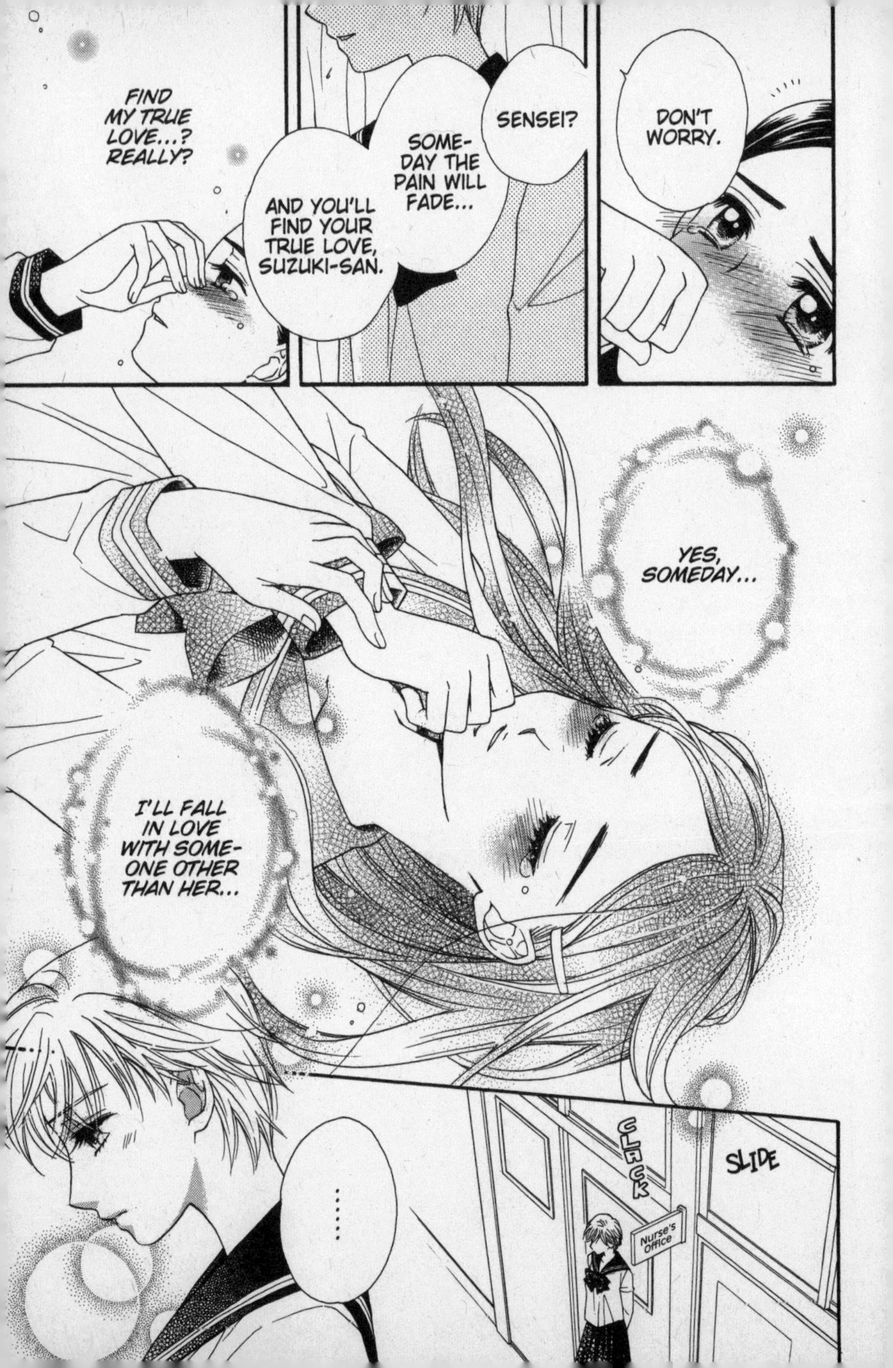
DON'T WORRY.
SENSEI?
SOME-DAY THE PAIN WILL FADE...
AND YOU'LL FIND YOUR TRUE LOVE, SUZUKI-SAN.
FIND MY TRUE LOVE...? REALLY?
YES, SOMEDAY...
I'LL FALL IN LOVE WITH SOME-ONE OTHER THAN HER...
SLIDE
CLACK
Nurse's Office
......

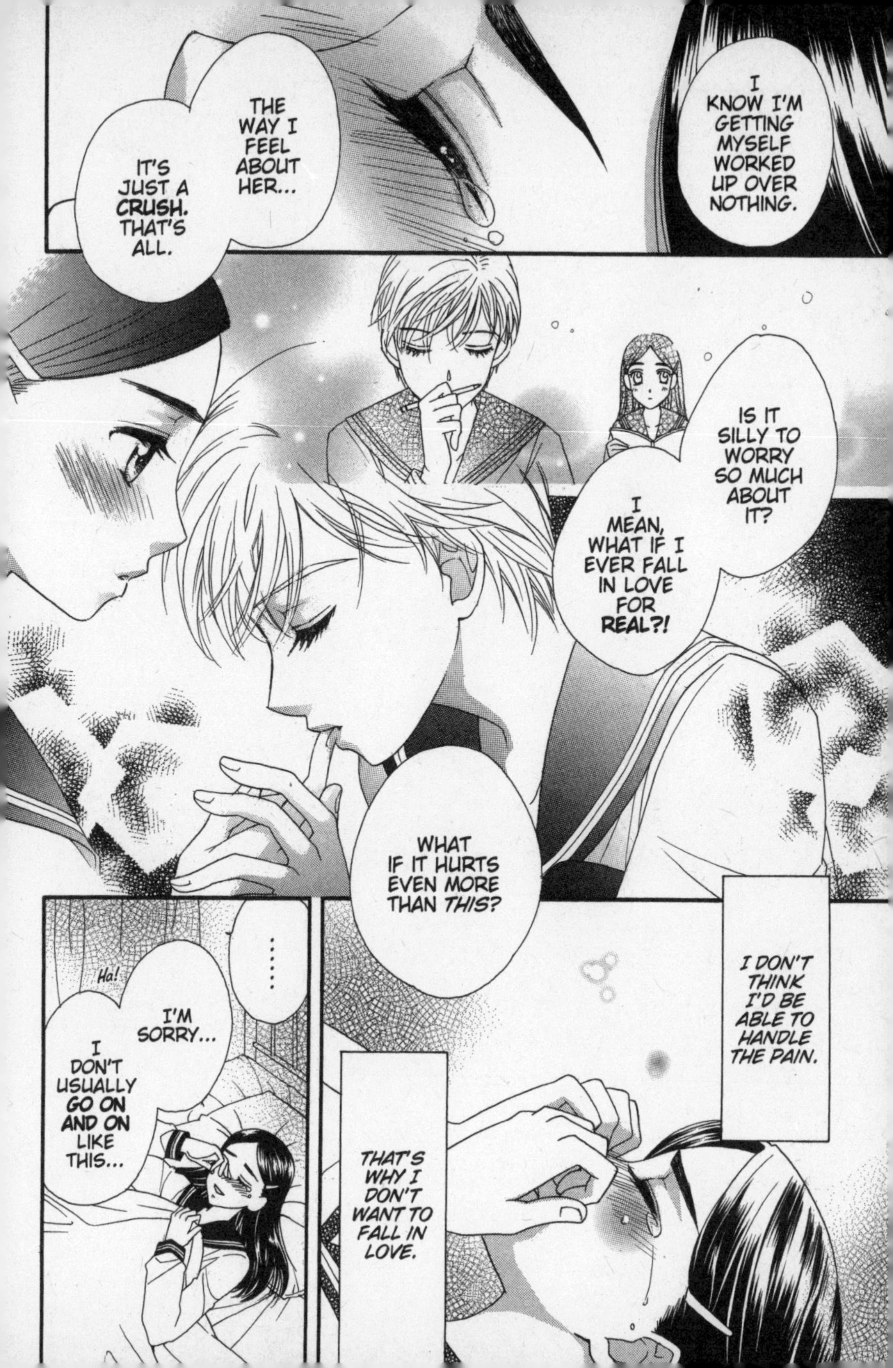
I KNOW I'M GETTING MYSELF WORKED UP OVER NOTHING.
THE WAY I FEEL ABOUT HER... IT'S JUST A **CRUSH.** THAT'S ALL.
IS IT SILLY TO WORRY SO MUCH ABOUT IT? I MEAN, WHAT IF I EVER FALL IN LOVE FOR **REAL?!**
WHAT IF IT HURTS EVEN MORE THAN *THIS?*
I DON'T THINK I'D BE ABLE TO HANDLE THE PAIN.
THAT'S WHY I DON'T WANT TO FALL IN LOVE.
......
Ha!
I'M SORRY... I DON'T USUALLY **GO ON AND ON** LIKE THIS...

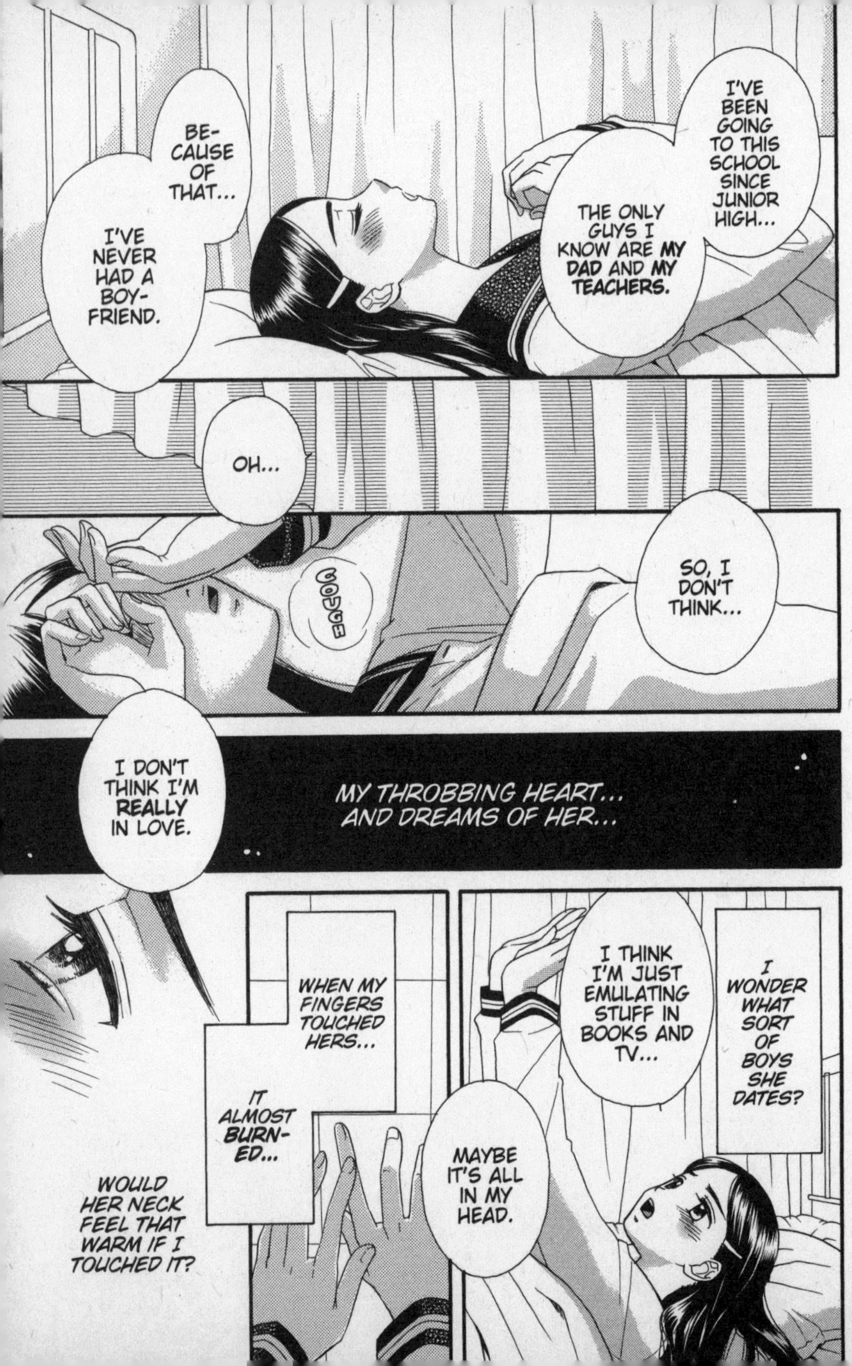
I'VE BEEN GOING TO THIS SCHOOL SINCE JUNIOR HIGH...
THE ONLY GUYS I KNOW ARE MY DAD AND MY TEACHERS.
BE-CAUSE OF THAT...
I'VE NEVER HAD A BOY-FRIEND.
OH...
SO, I DON'T THINK...
COUGH
I DON'T THINK I'M REALLY IN LOVE.
MY THROBBING HEART... AND DREAMS OF HER...
I WONDER WHAT SORT OF BOYS SHE DATES?
I THINK I'M JUST EMULATING STUFF IN BOOKS AND TV...
MAYBE IT'S ALL IN MY HEAD.
WHEN MY FINGERS TOUCHED HERS...
IT ALMOST BURNED...
WOULD HER NECK FEEL THAT WARM IF I TOUCHED IT?

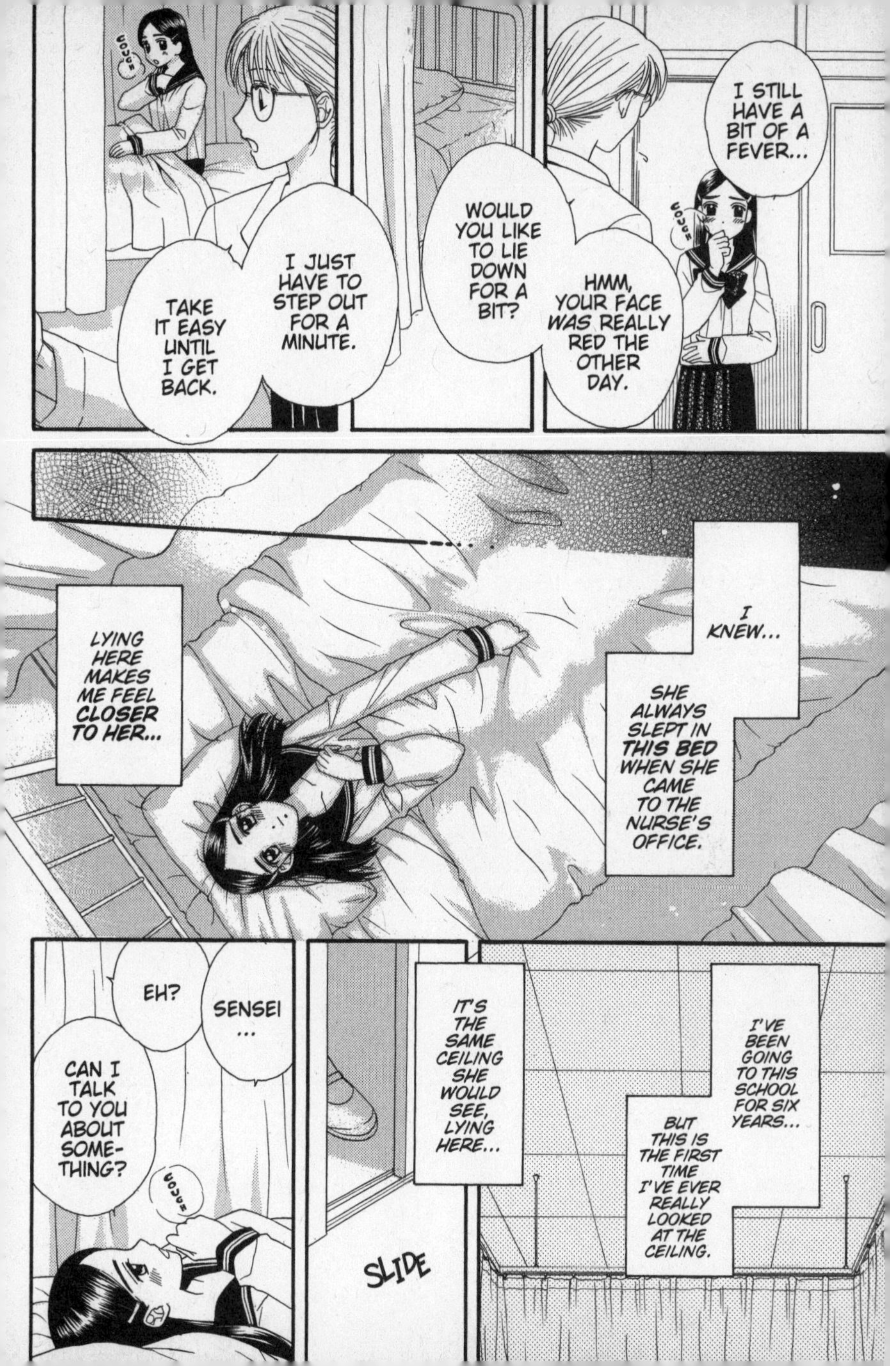
I STILL HAVE A BIT OF A FEVER...
COUGH
HMM, YOUR FACE WAS REALLY RED THE OTHER DAY.
WOULD YOU LIKE TO LIE DOWN FOR A BIT?
COUGH
I JUST HAVE TO STEP OUT FOR A MINUTE.
TAKE IT EASY UNTIL I GET BACK.
I KNEW...
SHE ALWAYS SLEPT IN THIS BED WHEN SHE CAME TO THE NURSE'S OFFICE.
LYING HERE MAKES ME FEEL CLOSER TO HER...
I'VE BEEN GOING TO THIS SCHOOL FOR SIX YEARS...
BUT THIS IS THE FIRST TIME I'VE EVER REALLY LOOKED AT THE CEILING.
IT'S THE SAME CEILING SHE WOULD SEE, LYING HERE...
SLIDE
SENSEI...
EH?
CAN I TALK TO YOU ABOUT SOMETHING?
COUGH

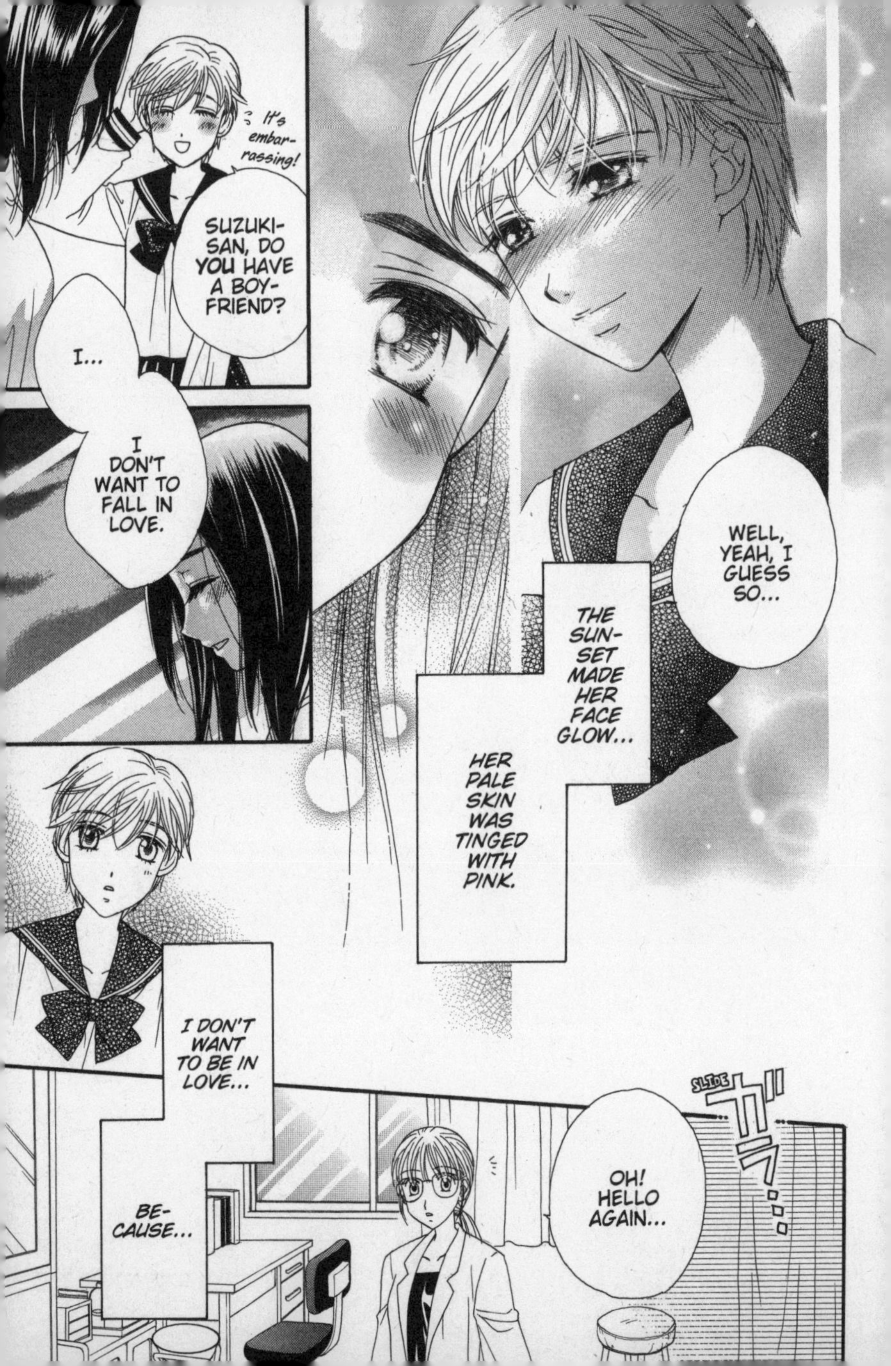

WELL, YEAH, I GUESS SO...
THE SUN-SET MADE HER FACE GLOW...
HER PALE SKIN WAS TINGED WITH PINK.
It's embar-rassing!
SUZUKI-SAN, DO YOU HAVE A BOY-FRIEND?
I...
I DON'T WANT TO FALL IN LOVE.
I DON'T WANT TO BE IN LOVE...
BE-CAUSE...
SLIDE
OH! HELLO AGAIN...

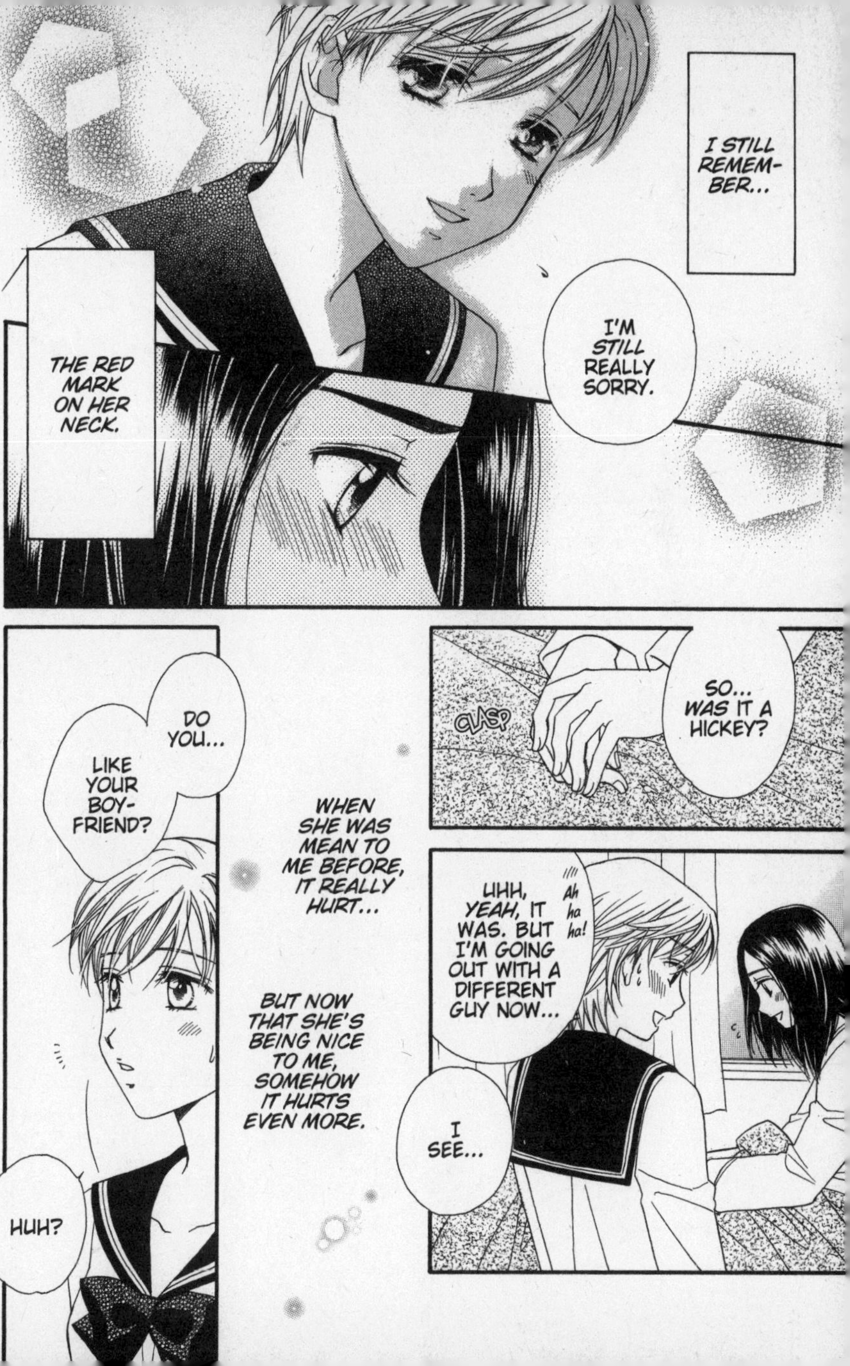

I STILL REMEMBER...
I'M STILL REALLY SORRY.
THE RED MARK ON HER NECK.
SO... WAS IT A HICKEY?
CLASP
UHH, YEAH, IT WAS. BUT I'M GOING OUT WITH A DIFFERENT GUY NOW...
Ah ha ha!
I SEE...
WHEN SHE WAS MEAN TO ME BEFORE, IT REALLY HURT...
BUT NOW THAT SHE'S BEING NICE TO ME, SOMEHOW IT HURTS EVEN MORE.
DO YOU... LIKE YOUR BOY-FRIEND?
HUH?

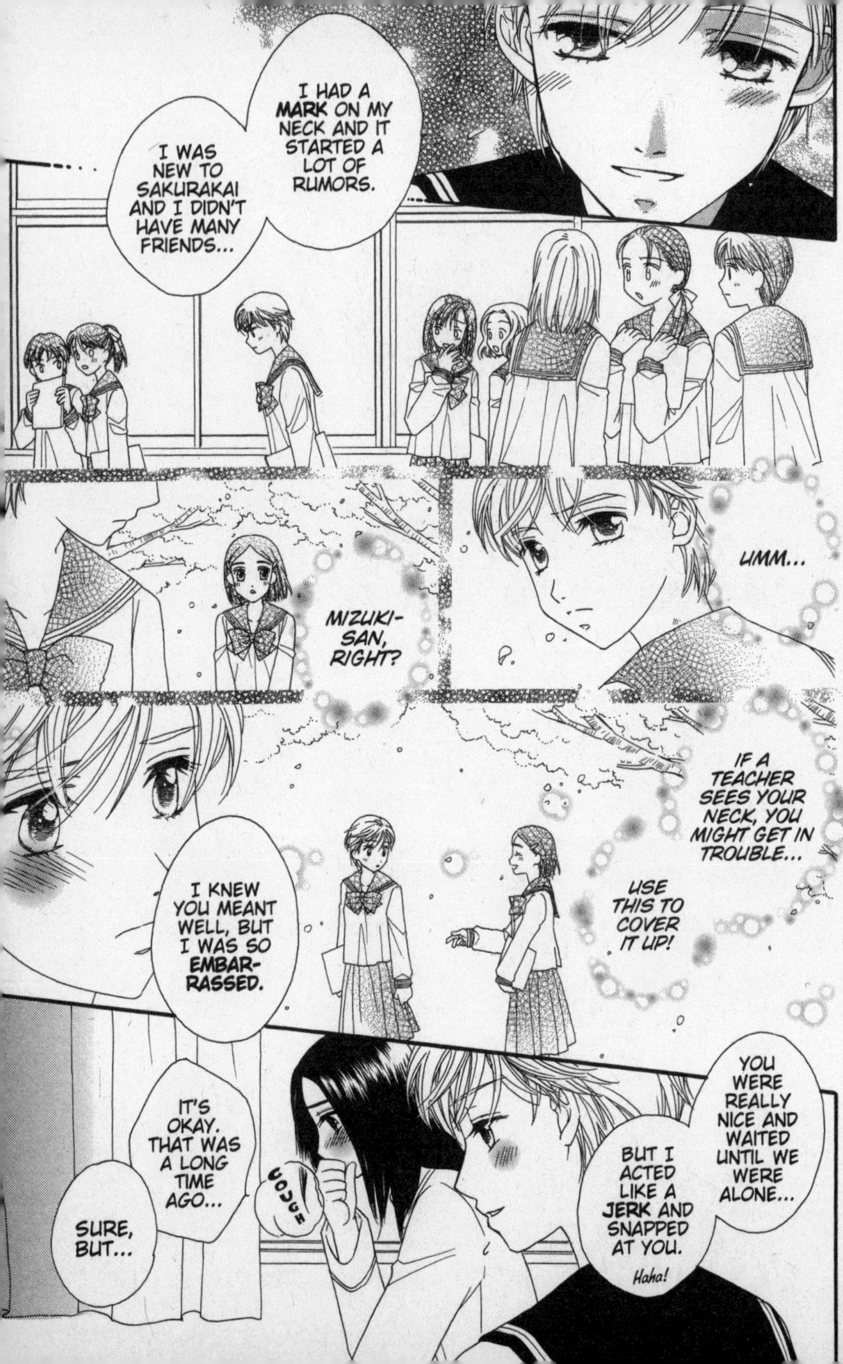
I HAD A MARK ON MY NECK AND IT STARTED A LOT OF RUMORS.
I WAS NEW TO SAKURAKAI AND I DIDN'T HAVE MANY FRIENDS...
UMM...
MIZUKI-SAN, RIGHT?
IF A TEACHER SEES YOUR NECK, YOU MIGHT GET IN TROUBLE...
USE THIS TO COVER IT UP!
I KNEW YOU MEANT WELL, BUT I WAS SO EMBARRASSED.
YOU WERE REALLY NICE AND WAITED UNTIL WE WERE ALONE...
BUT I ACTED LIKE A JERK AND SNAPPED AT YOU.
Haha!
COUGH
IT'S OKAY. THAT WAS A LONG TIME AGO...
SURE, BUT...

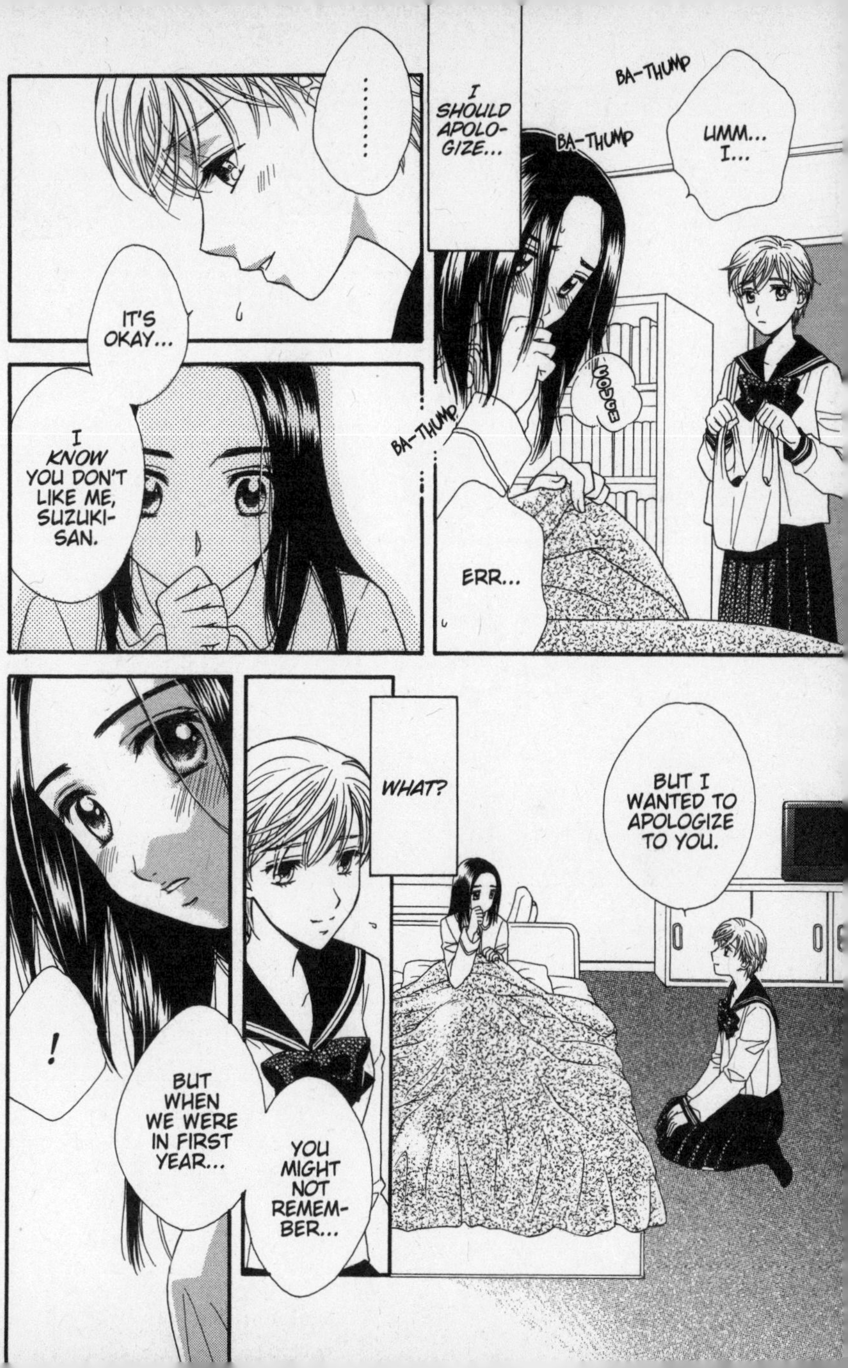
BA-THUMP
UMM... I...
BA-THUMP
I SHOULD APOLOGIZE...
COUGH
BA-THUMP
ERR...
......
IT'S OKAY...
I *KNOW* YOU DON'T LIKE ME, SUZUKI-SAN.
BUT I WANTED TO APOLOGIZE TO YOU.
WHAT?
!
BUT WHEN WE WERE IN FIRST YEAR...
YOU MIGHT NOT REMEMBER...

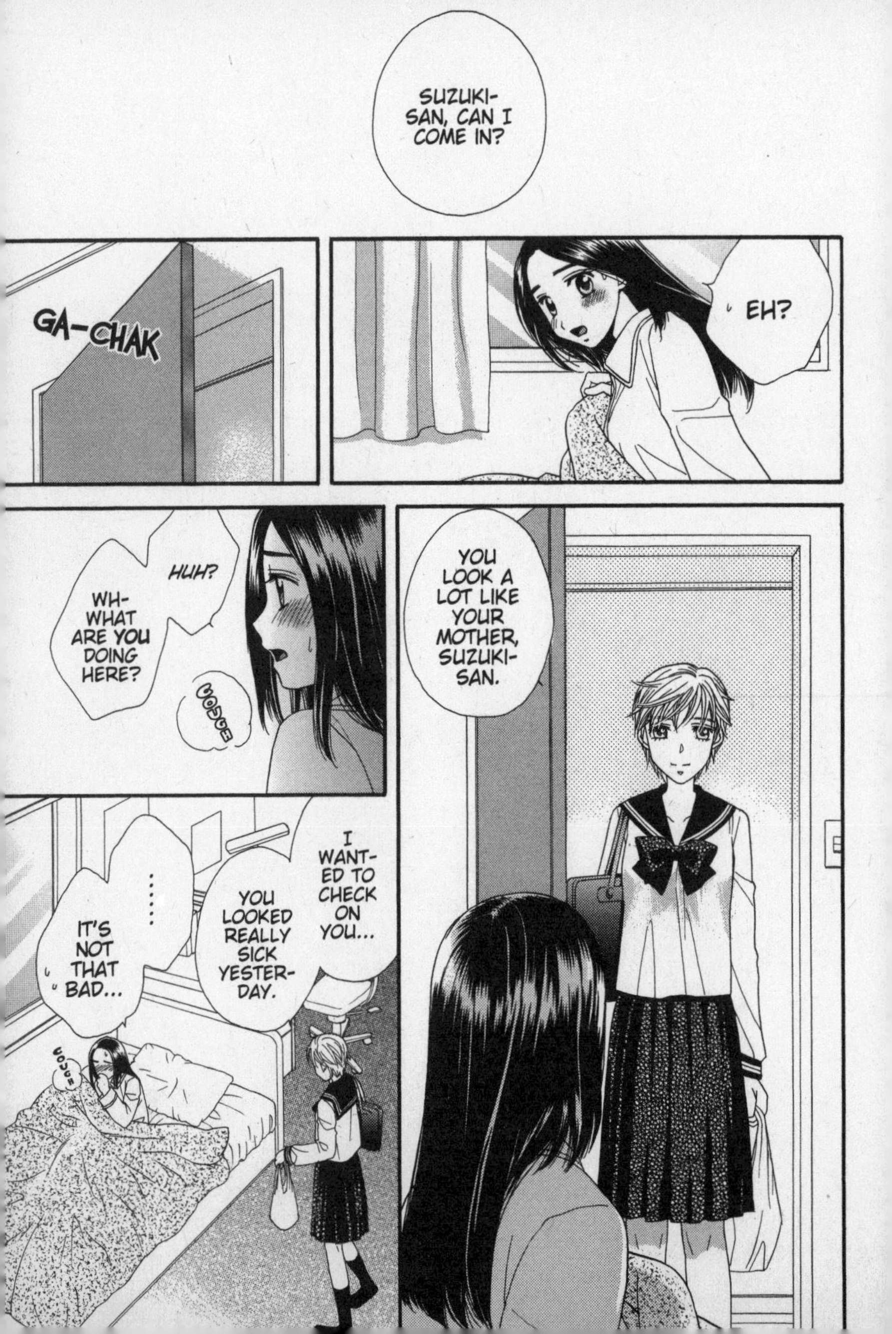
SUZUKI-SAN, CAN I COME IN?
EH?
GA-CHAK
YOU LOOK A LOT LIKE YOUR MOTHER, SUZUKI-SAN.
HUH?
WH-WHAT ARE YOU DOING HERE?
COUGH
I WANTED TO CHECK ON YOU...
YOU LOOKED REALLY SICK YESTERDAY.
......
IT'S NOT THAT BAD...
COUGH

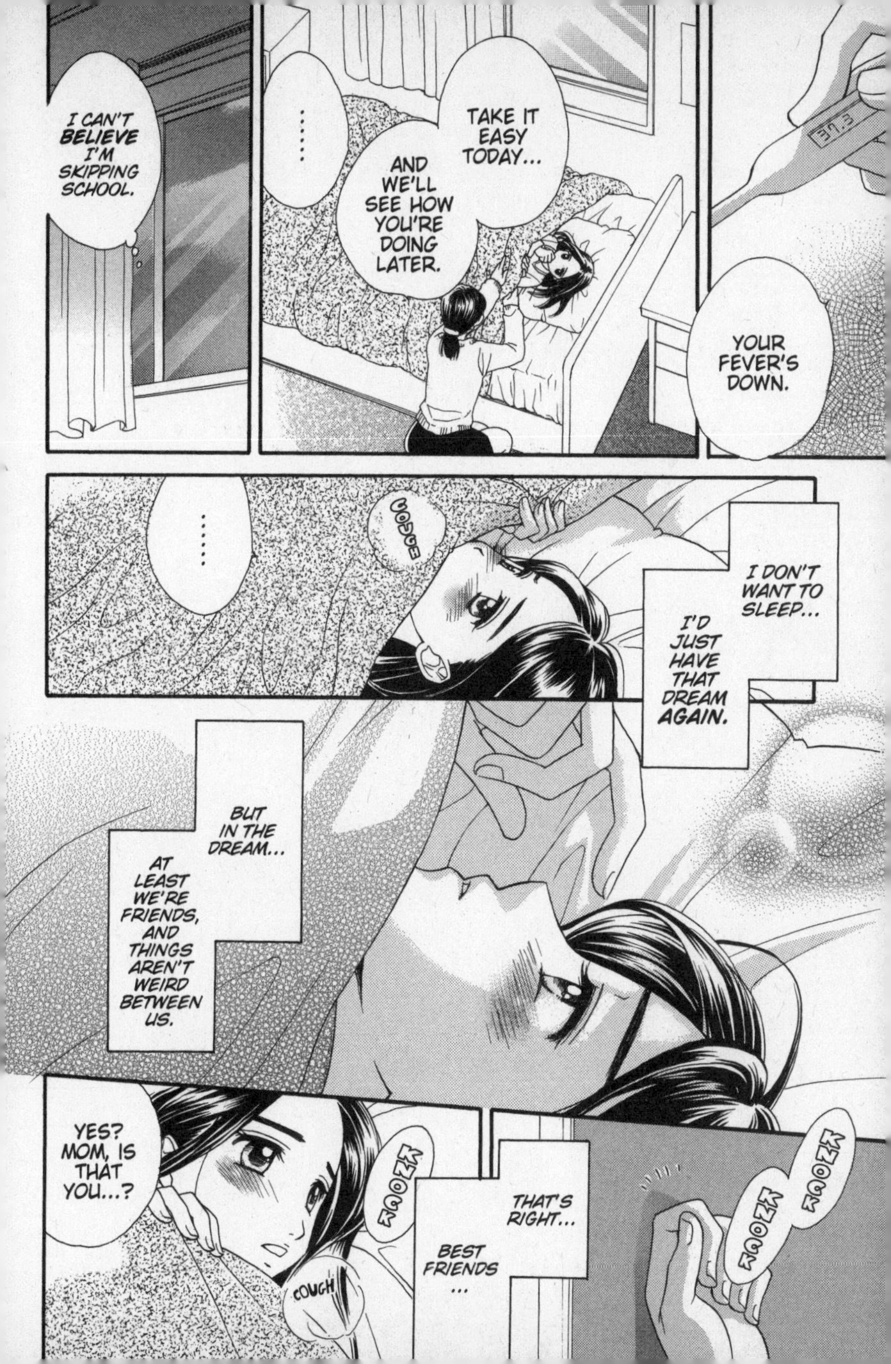
YOUR FEVER'S DOWN.
TAKE IT EASY TODAY...
AND WE'LL SEE HOW YOU'RE DOING LATER.
......
I CAN'T BELIEVE I'M SKIPPING SCHOOL.
I DON'T WANT TO SLEEP...
I'D JUST HAVE THAT DREAM AGAIN.
COUGH
......
BUT IN THE DREAM...
AT LEAST WE'RE FRIENDS, AND THINGS AREN'T WEIRD BETWEEN US.
KNOCK
KNOCK
KNOCK
THAT'S RIGHT...
BEST FRIENDS...
KNOCK
YES? MOM, IS THAT YOU...?
COUGH

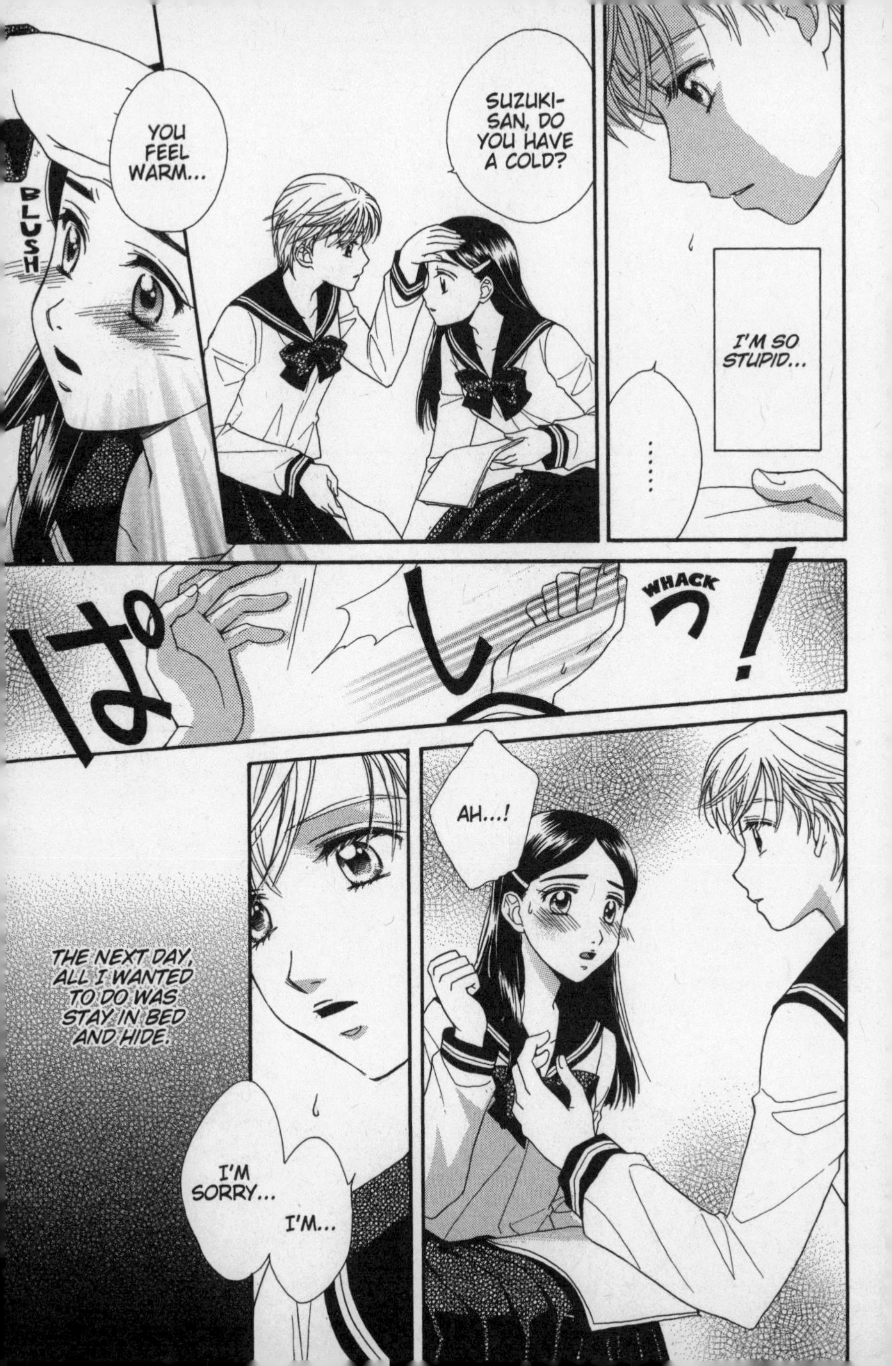
I'M SO STUPID...
......
SUZUKI-SAN, DO YOU HAVE A COLD?
YOU FEEL WARM...
BLUSH
WHACK
ぱしっ!
AH...!
THE NEXT DAY, ALL I WANTED TO DO WAS STAY IN BED AND HIDE.
I'M SORRY...
I'M...

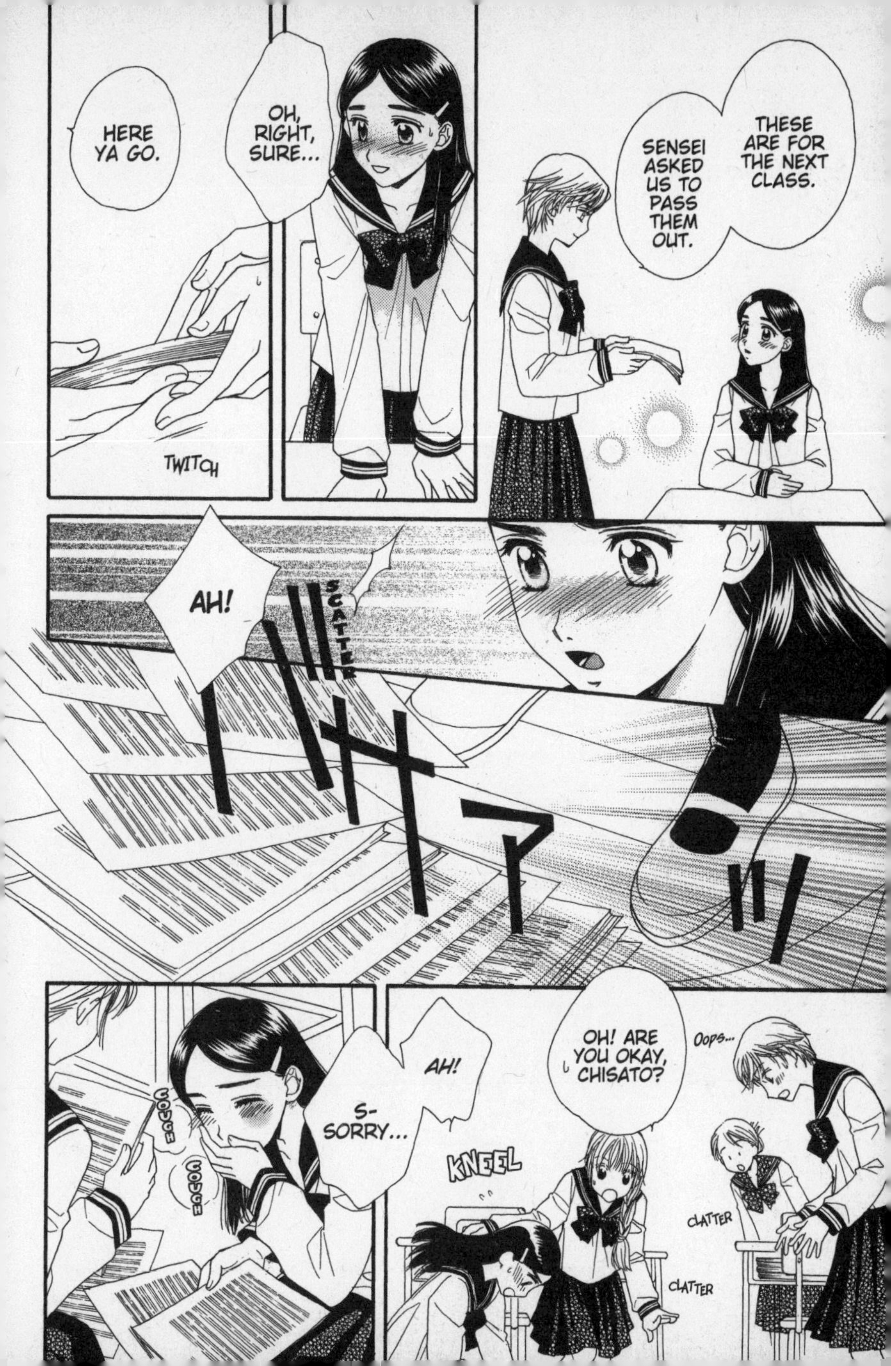
THESE ARE FOR THE NEXT CLASS.
SENSEI ASKED US TO PASS THEM OUT.
OH, RIGHT, SURE...
HERE YA GO.
TWITCH
AH!
SCATTER
OH! ARE YOU OKAY, CHISATO?
Oops...
KNEEL
CLATTER
CLATTER
AH!
S-SORRY...
COUGH
COUGH

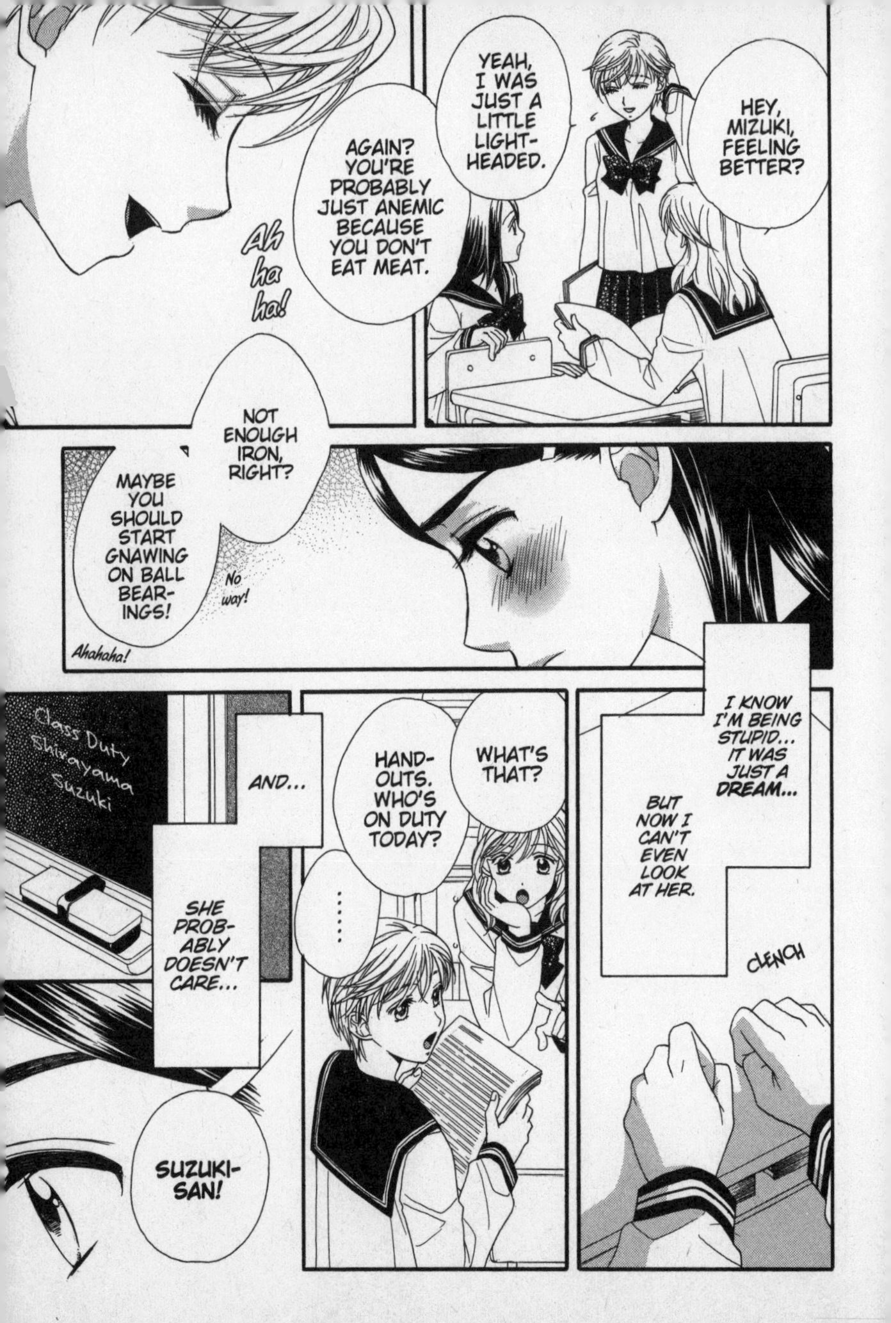

HEY, MIZUKI, FEELING BETTER?
YEAH, I WAS JUST A LITTLE LIGHT-HEADED.
AGAIN? YOU'RE PROBABLY JUST ANEMIC BECAUSE YOU DON'T EAT MEAT.
Ah ha ha!
NOT ENOUGH IRON, RIGHT?
MAYBE YOU SHOULD START GNAWING ON BALL BEARINGS!
No way!
Ahahaha!
I KNOW I'M BEING STUPID... IT WAS JUST A DREAM...
BUT NOW I CAN'T EVEN LOOK AT HER.
CLENCH
WHAT'S THAT?
HAND-OUTS. WHO'S ON DUTY TODAY?
......
Class Duty Shirayama Suzuki
AND...
SHE PROBABLY DOESN'T CARE...
SUZUKI-SAN!

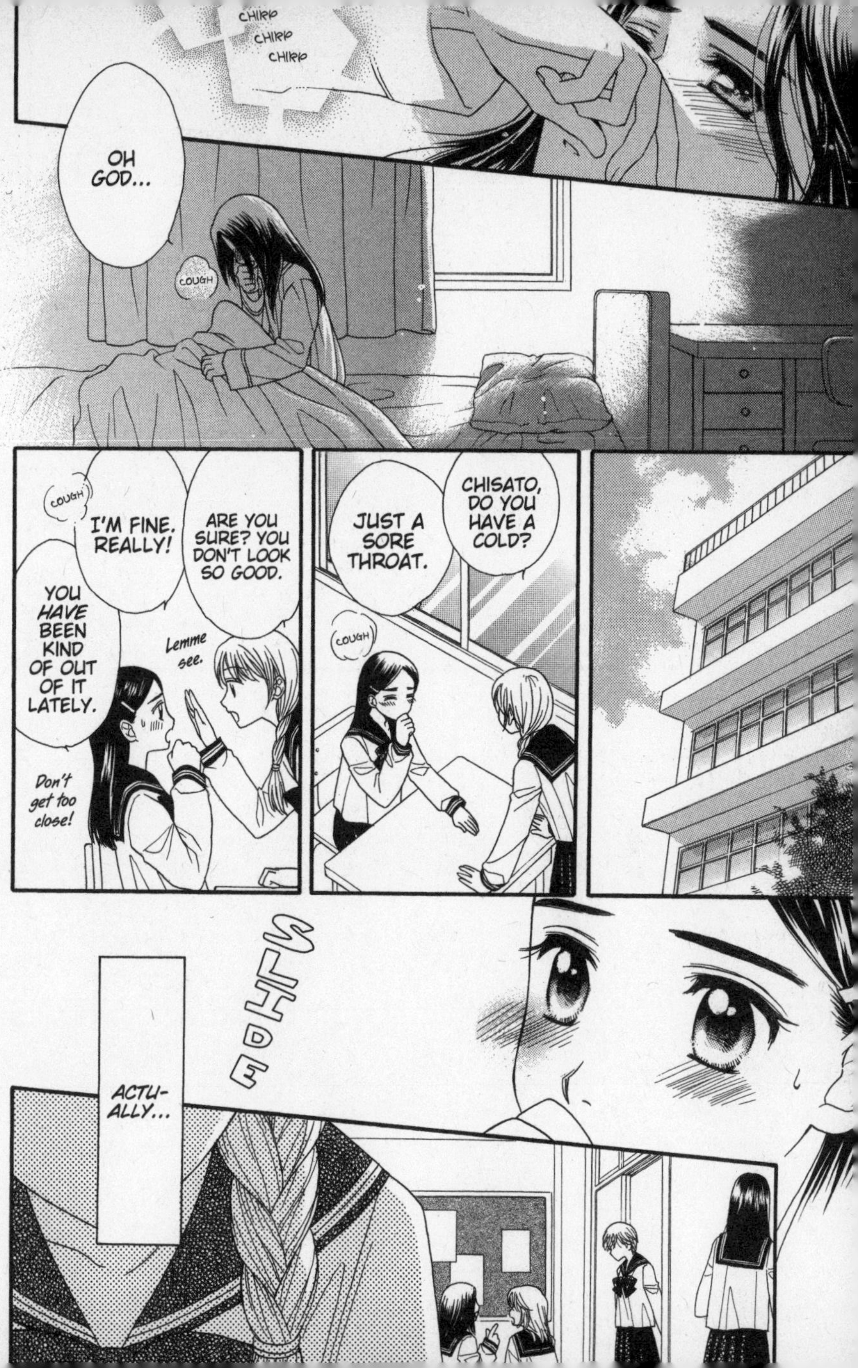
CHIRP
CHIRP
CHIRP
OH GOD...
COUGH
CHISATO, DO YOU HAVE A COLD?
JUST A SORE THROAT.
COUGH
ARE YOU SURE? YOU DON'T LOOK SO GOOD.
COUGH
I'M FINE. REALLY!
Lemme see.
YOU HAVE BEEN KIND OF OUT OF IT LATELY.
Don't get too close!
SLIDE
ACTU-ALLY...

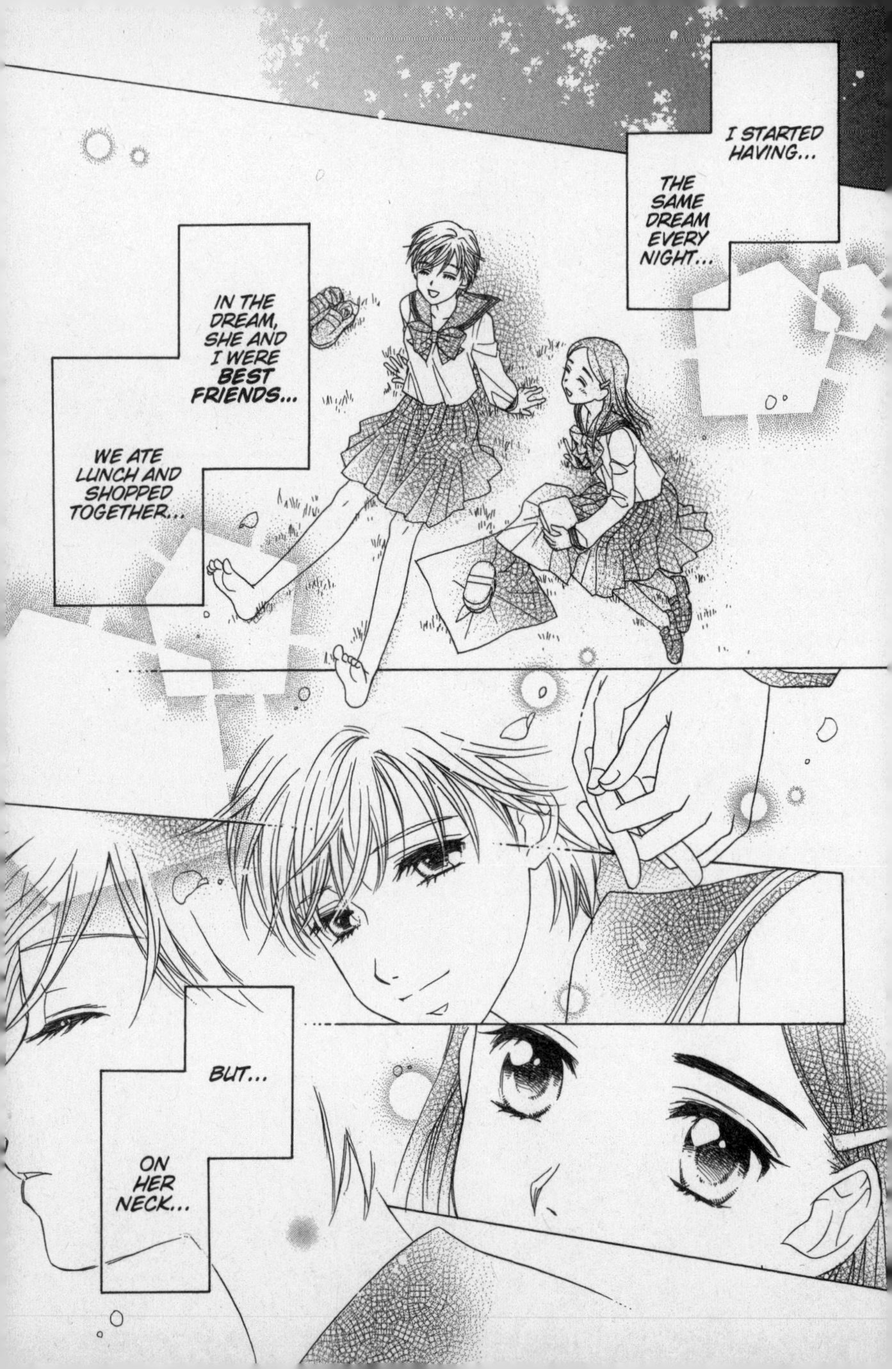
I STARTED HAVING...
THE SAME DREAM EVERY NIGHT...
IN THE DREAM, SHE AND I WERE BEST FRIENDS...
WE ATE LUNCH AND SHOPPED TOGETHER...
BUT...
ON HER NECK...

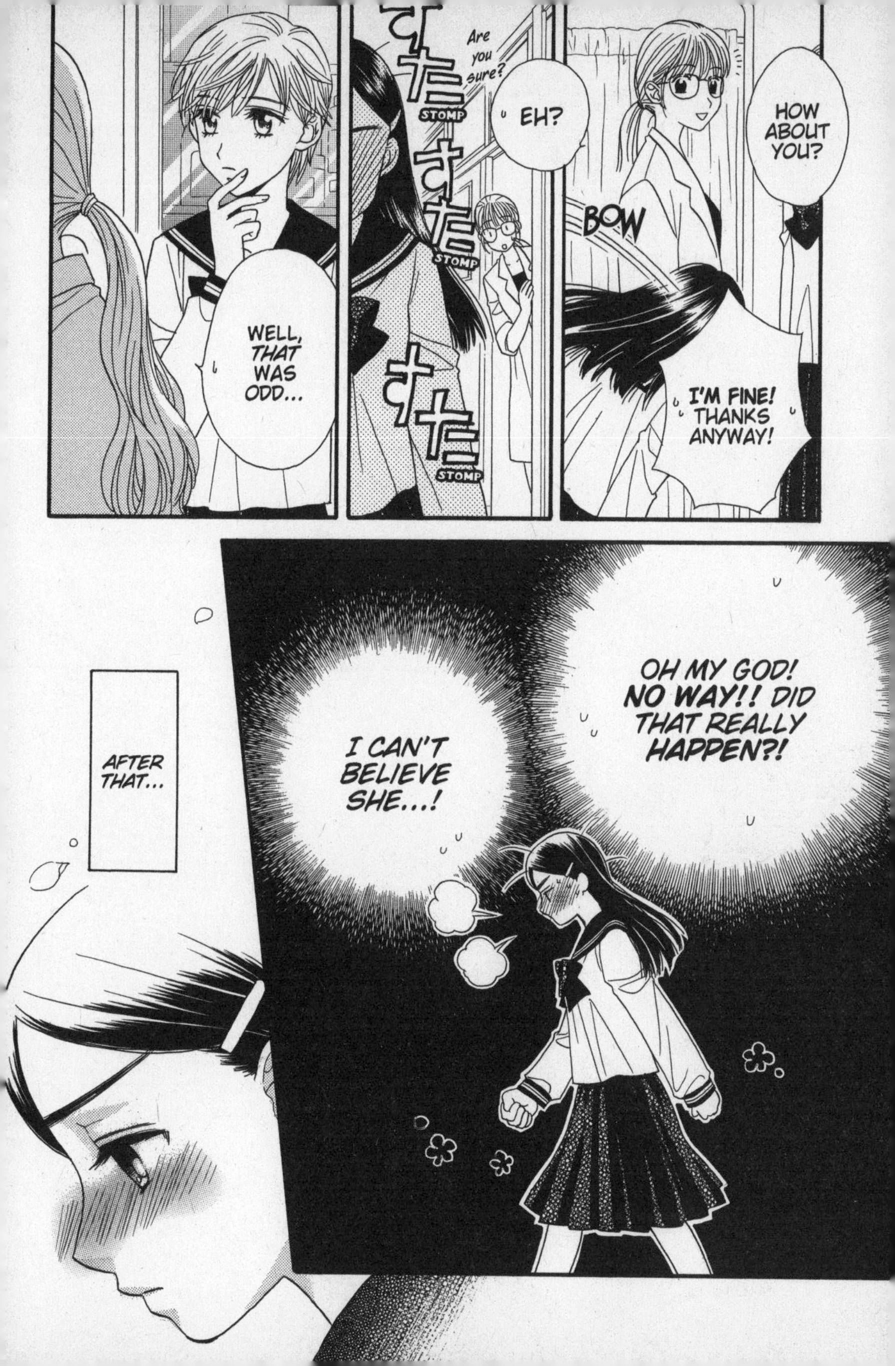
HOW ABOUT YOU?
BOW
I'M FINE! THANKS ANYWAY!
EH?
Are you sure?
STOMP
STOMP
STOMP
WELL, THAT WAS ODD...
OH MY GOD! NO WAY!! DID THAT REALLY HAPPEN?!
I CAN'T BELIEVE SHE...!
AFTER THAT...

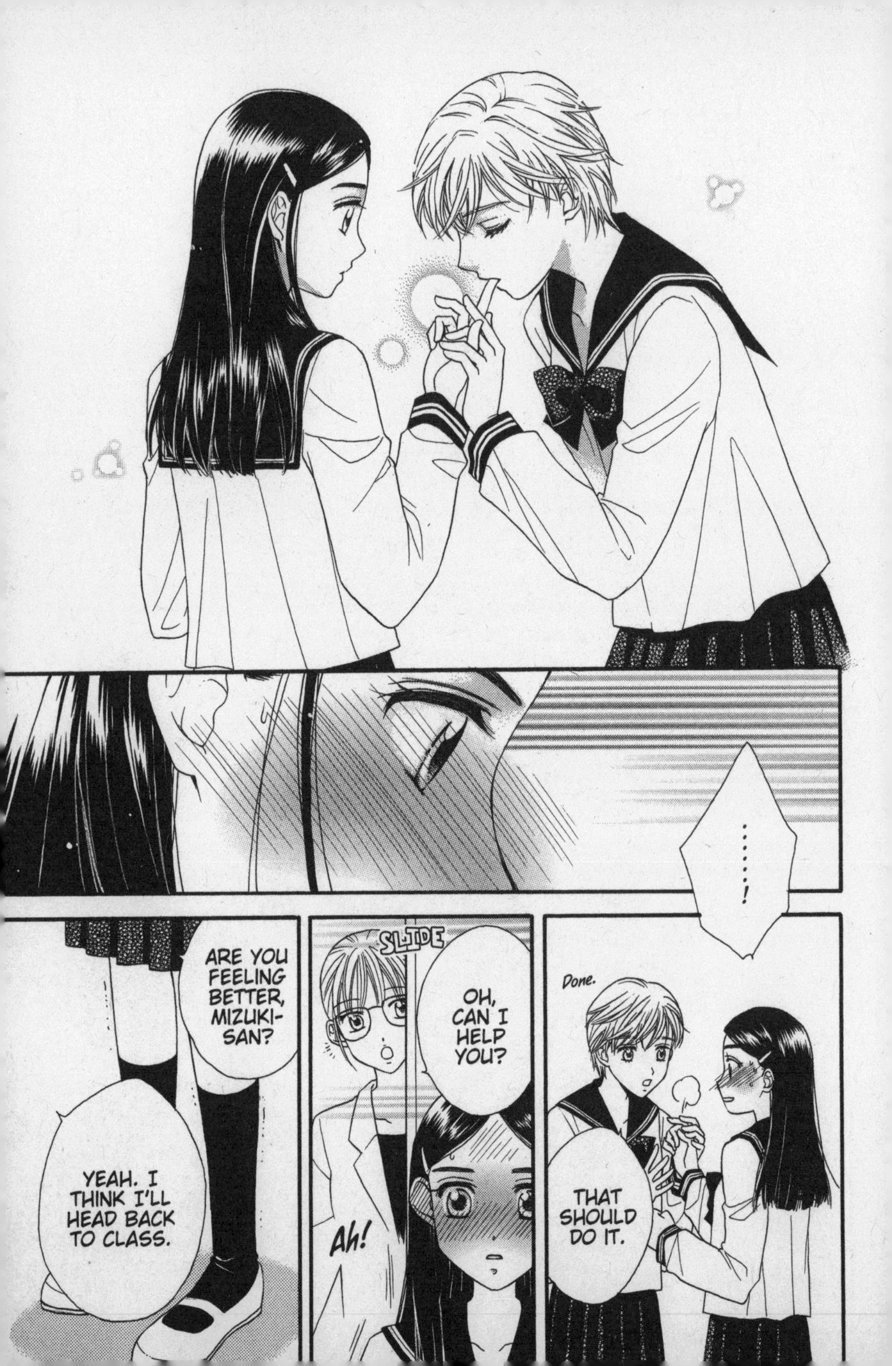
......!
Done.
THAT SHOULD DO IT.
SLIDE
OH, CAN I HELP YOU?
Ah!
ARE YOU FEELING BETTER, MIZUKI-SAN?
YEAH. I THINK I'LL HEAD BACK TO CLASS.

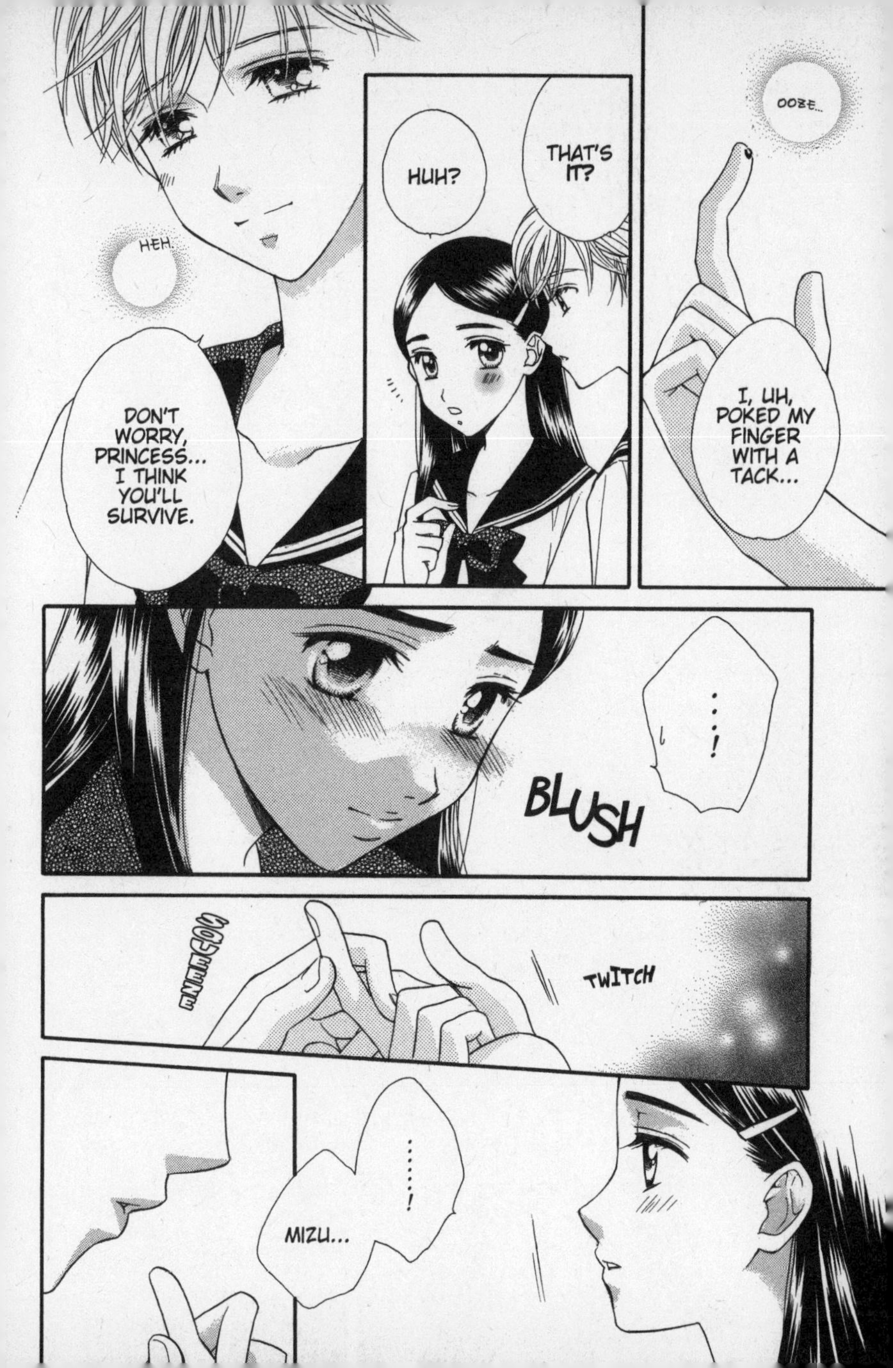
OOZE...
I, UH, POKED MY FINGER WITH A TACK...
THAT'S IT?
HUH?
HEH.
DON'T WORRY, PRINCESS... I THINK YOU'LL SURVIVE.
...!
BLUSH
TWITCH
SQUEEEZE
......!
MIZU...

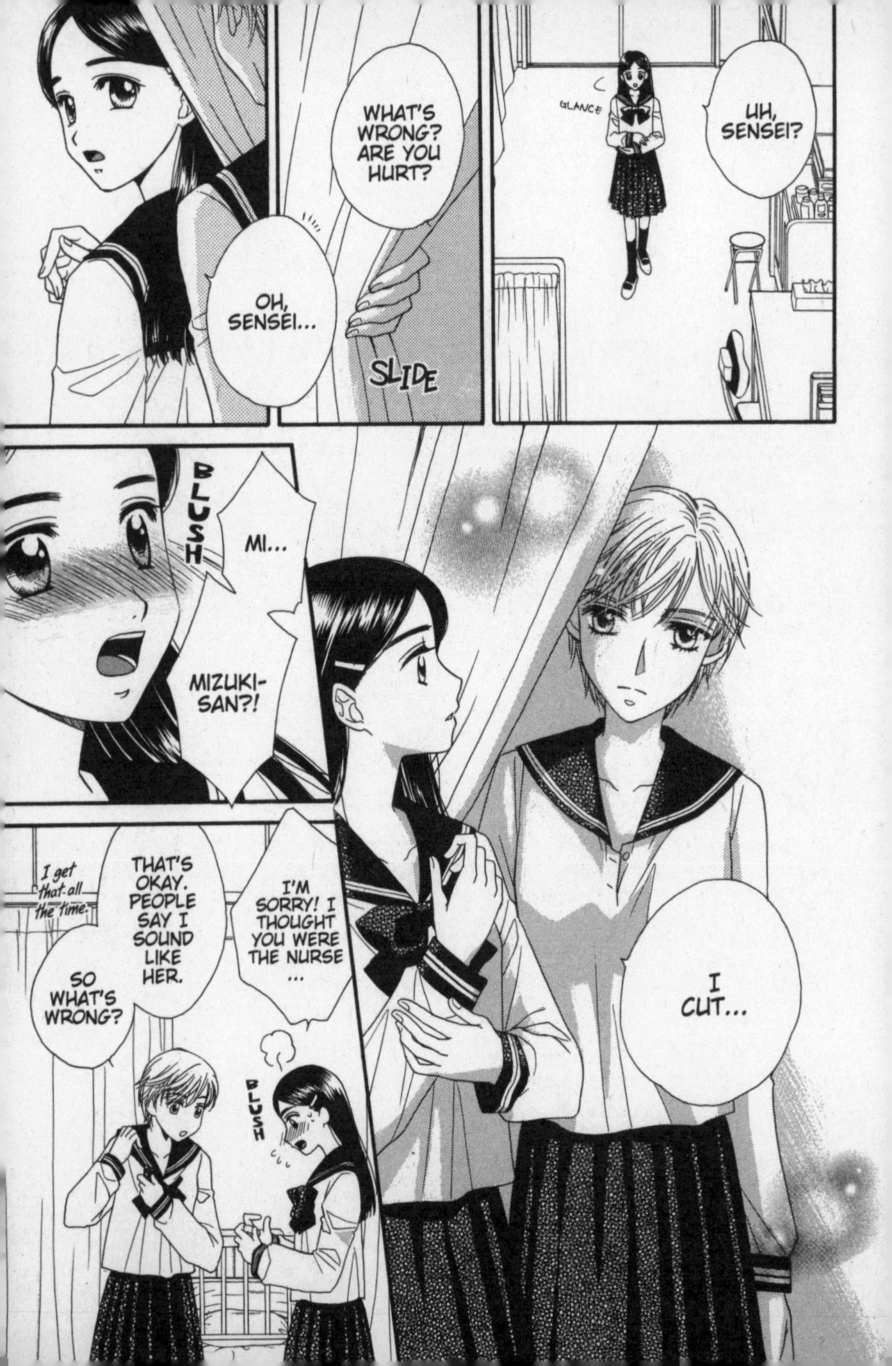
GLANCE
UH, SENSEI?
WHAT'S WRONG? ARE YOU HURT?
SLIDE
OH, SENSEI...
I CUT...
BLUSH
MI...
MIZUKI-SAN?!
I'M SORRY! I THOUGHT YOU WERE THE NURSE ...
BLUSH
THAT'S OKAY. PEOPLE SAY I SOUND LIKE HER.
I get that all the time.
SO WHAT'S WRONG?

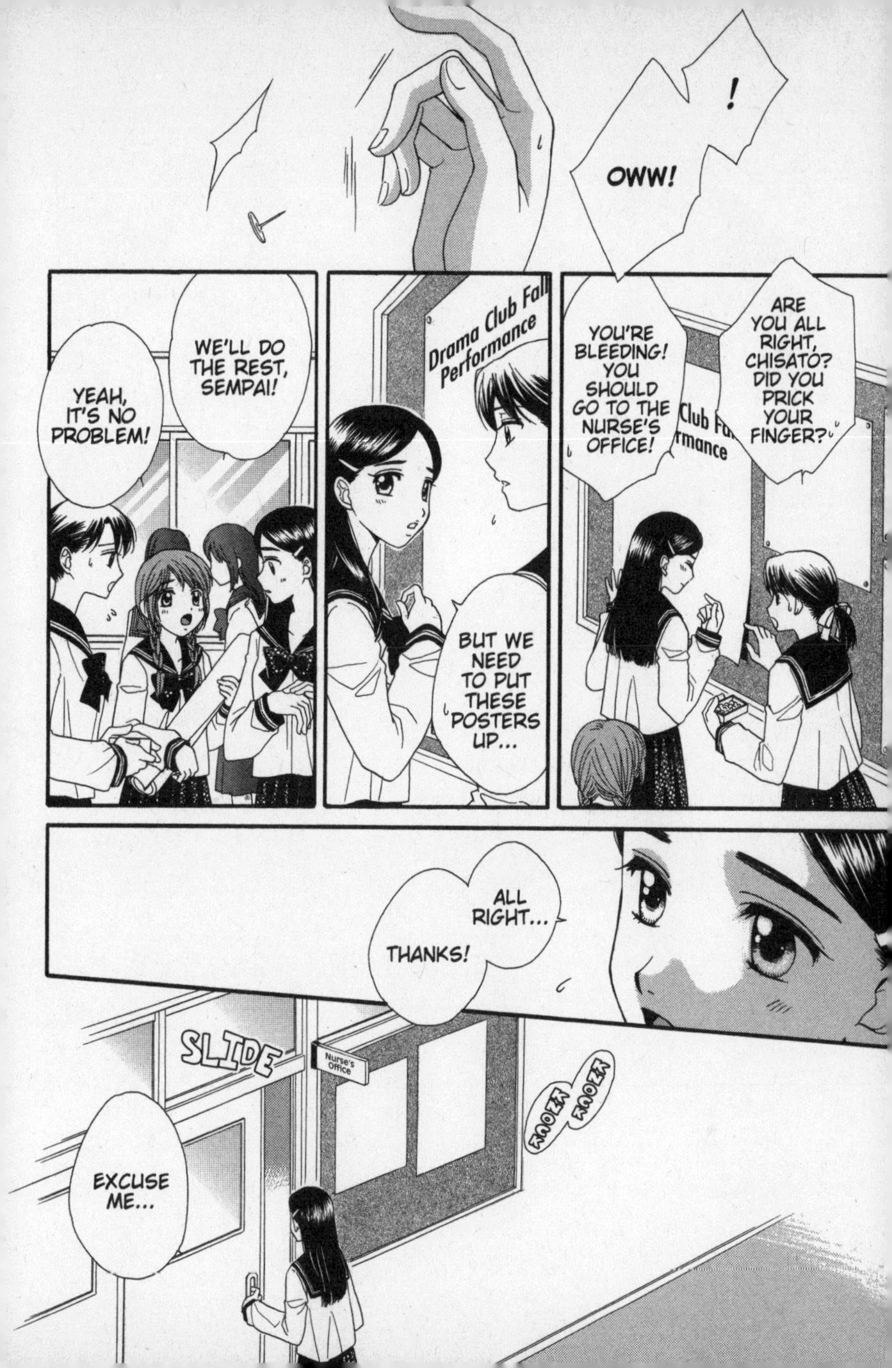
!
OWW!
ARE YOU ALL RIGHT, CHISATO? DID YOU PRICK YOUR FINGER?
YOU'RE BLEEDING! YOU SHOULD GO TO THE NURSE'S OFFICE!
Drama Club Fall Performance
BUT WE NEED TO PUT THESE POSTERS UP...
WE'LL DO THE REST, SEMPAI!
YEAH, IT'S NO PROBLEM!
ALL RIGHT...
THANKS!
SLIDE
Nurse's Office
EXCUSE ME...

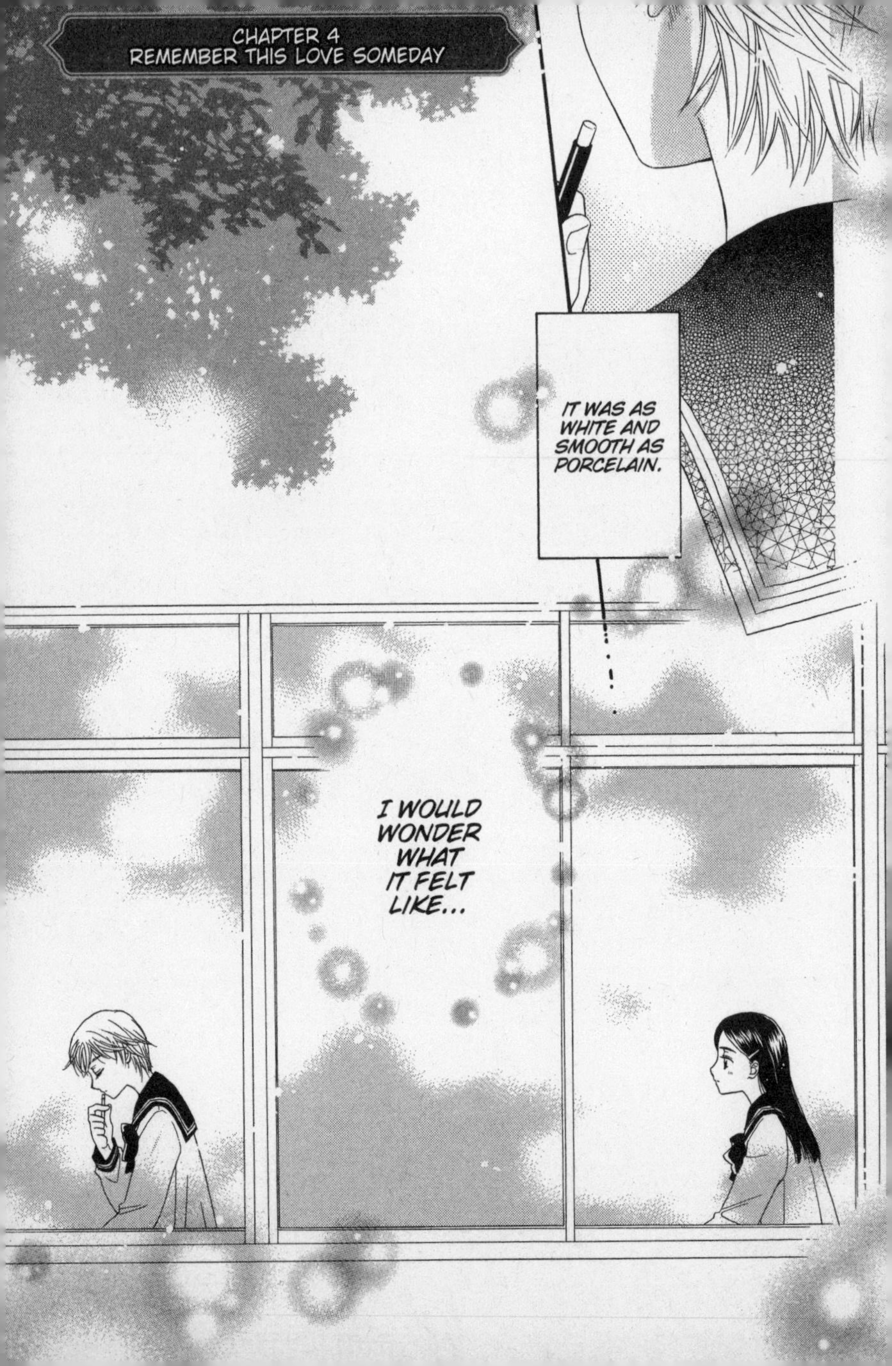
CHAPTER 4
REMEMBER THIS LOVE SOMEDAY
IT WAS AS WHITE AND SMOOTH AS PORCELAIN.
I WOULD WONDER WHAT IT FELT LIKE...

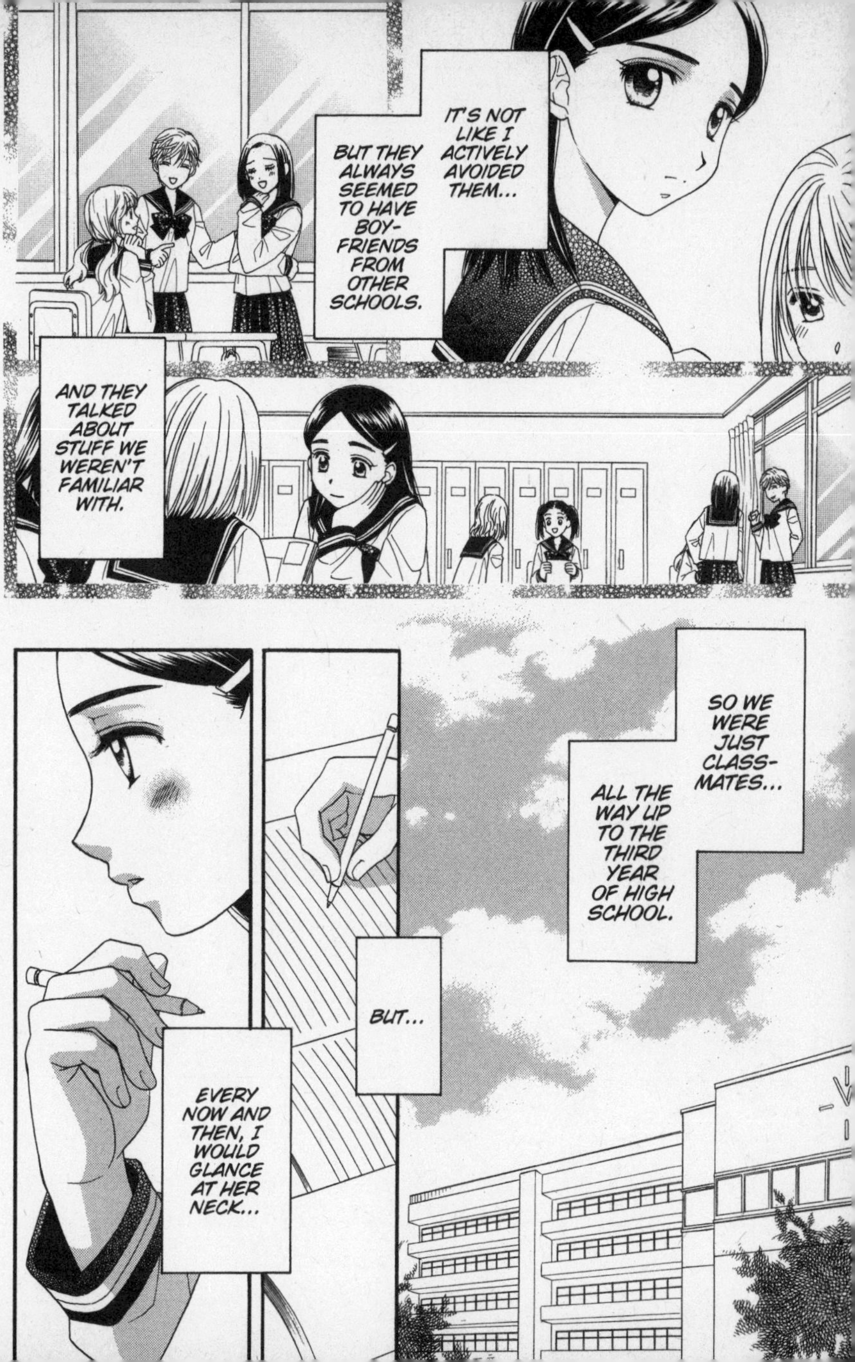
IT'S NOT LIKE I ACTIVELY AVOIDED THEM...
BUT THEY ALWAYS SEEMED TO HAVE BOY-FRIENDS FROM OTHER SCHOOLS.
AND THEY TALKED ABOUT STUFF WE WEREN'T FAMILIAR WITH.
SO WE WERE JUST CLASS-MATES...
ALL THE WAY UP TO THE THIRD YEAR OF HIGH SCHOOL.
BUT...
EVERY NOW AND THEN, I WOULD GLANCE AT HER NECK...

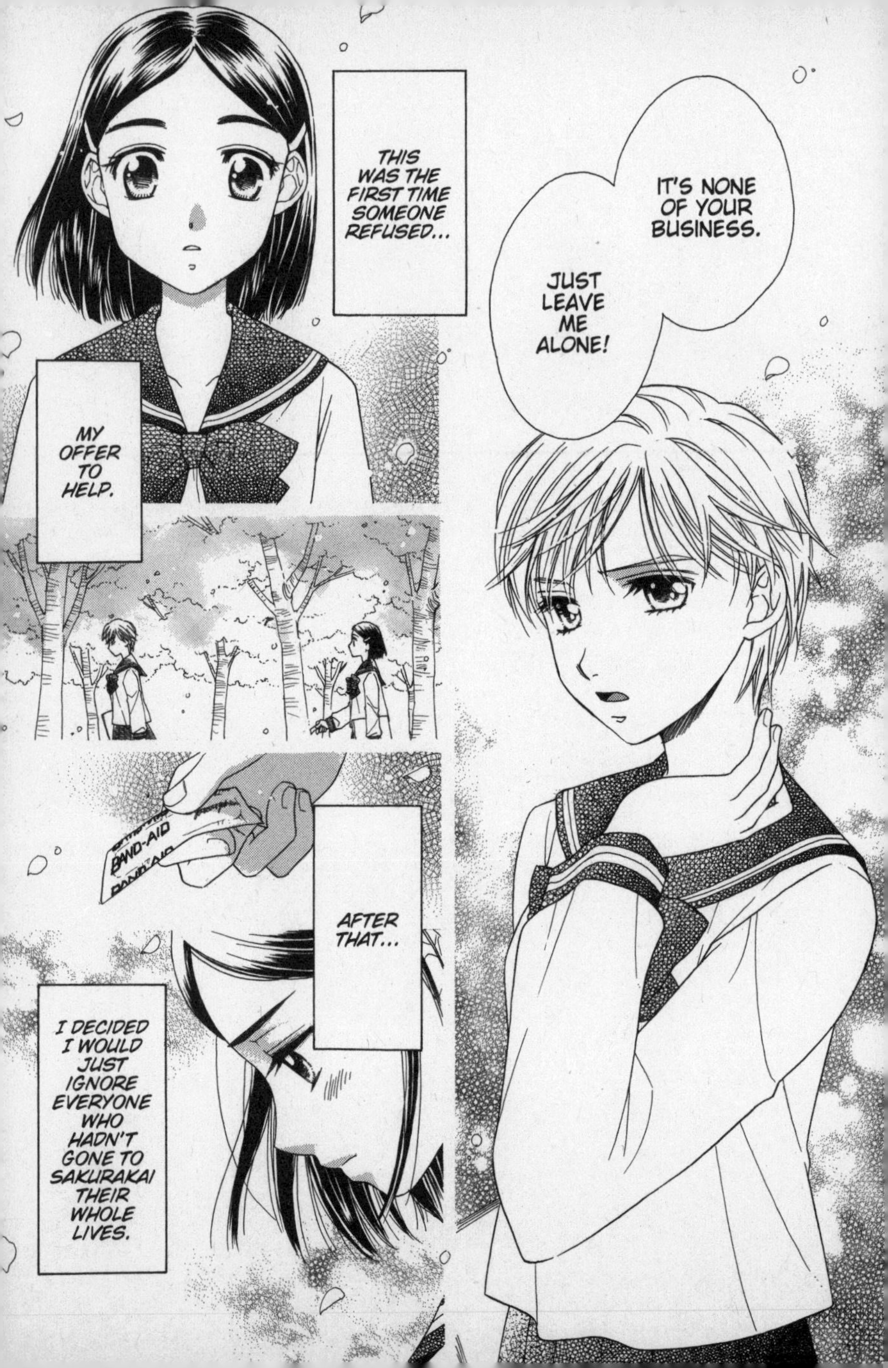
IT'S NONE OF YOUR BUSINESS.
JUST LEAVE ME ALONE!
THIS WAS THE FIRST TIME SOMEONE REFUSED...
MY OFFER TO HELP.
BAND-AID
AFTER THAT...
I DECIDED I WOULD JUST IGNORE EVERYONE WHO HADN'T GONE TO SAKURAKAI THEIR WHOLE LIVES.

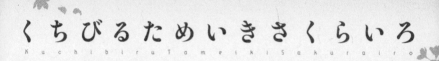

くちびるためいきさくらいろ

KuchibiruTameikiSakurairo。

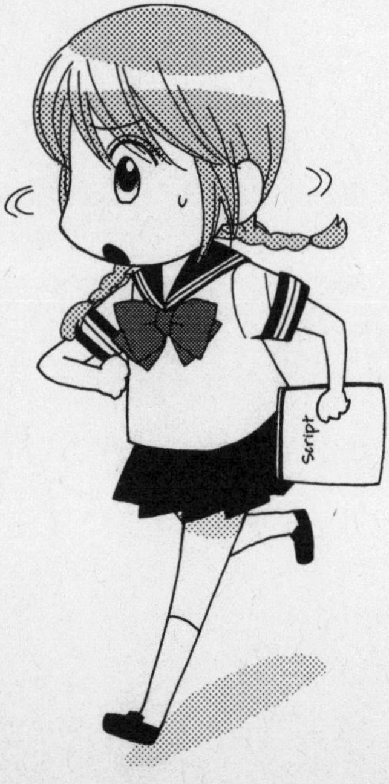
Script

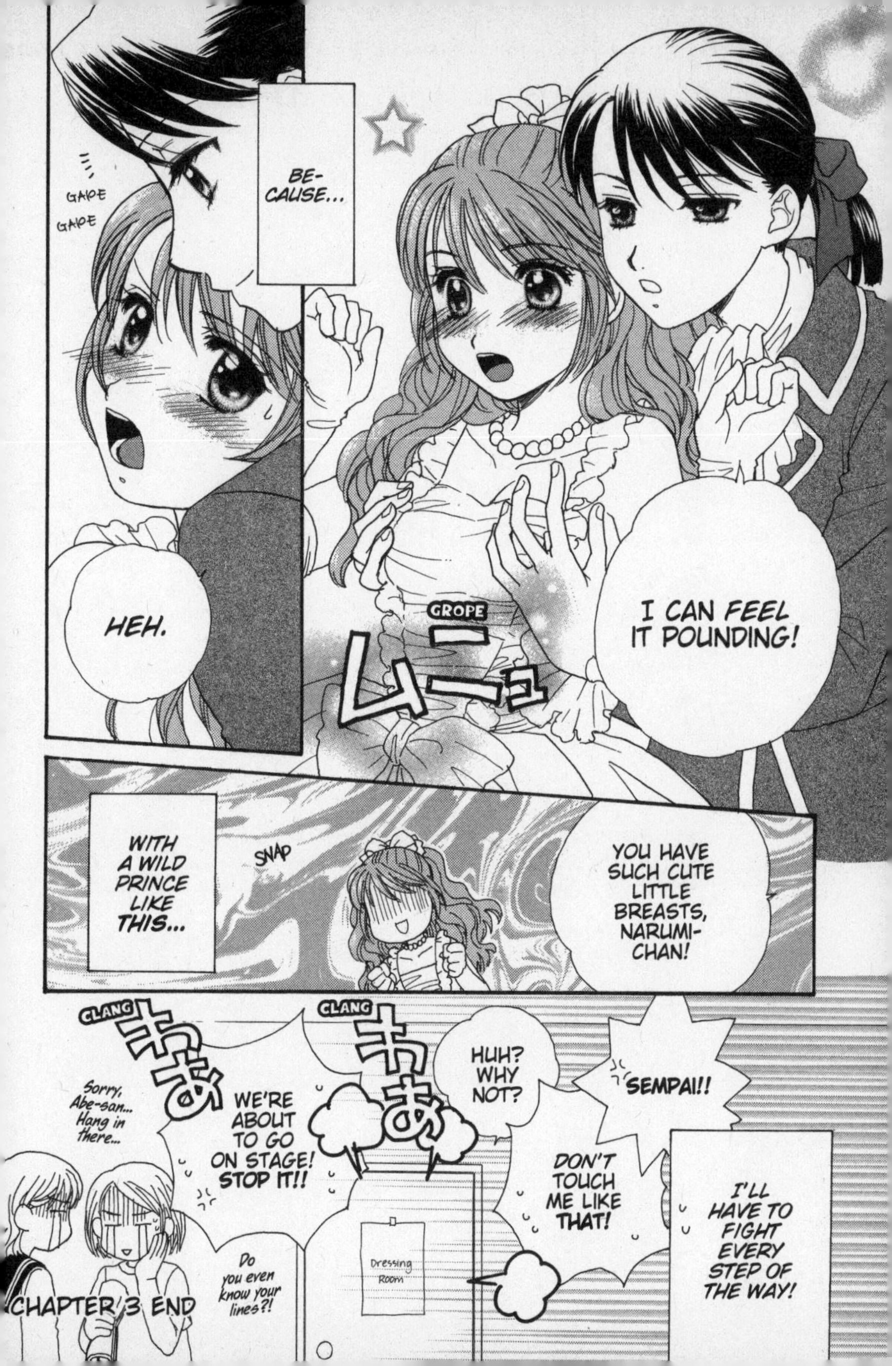
BE-CAUSE...
I CAN FEEL IT POUNDING!
GROPE
ムニュ
GAPE
GAPE
HEH.
YOU HAVE SUCH CUTE LITTLE BREASTS, NARUMI-CHAN!
SNAP
WITH A WILD PRINCE LIKE THIS...
I'LL HAVE TO FIGHT EVERY STEP OF THE WAY!
SEMPAI!!
DON'T TOUCH ME LIKE THAT!
HUH? WHY NOT?
CLANG
おあ
WE'RE ABOUT TO GO ON STAGE! STOP IT!!
CLANG
おあ
Dressing Room
Sorry, Abe-san... Hang in there...
Do you even know your lines?!
CHAPTER 3 END

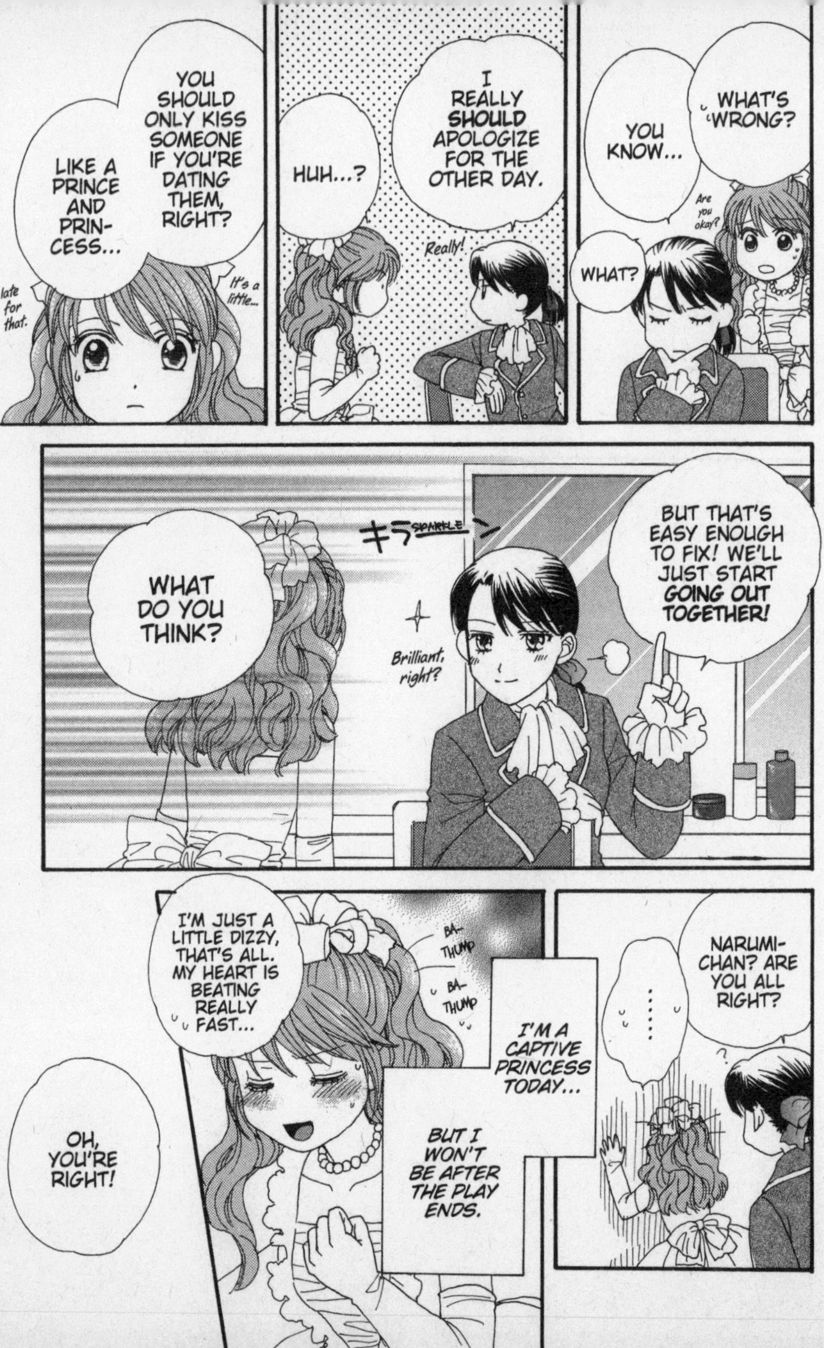
WHAT'S WRONG?
Are you okay?
YOU KNOW...
WHAT?
I REALLY SHOULD APOLOGIZE FOR THE OTHER DAY.
Really!
HUH...?
YOU SHOULD ONLY KISS SOMEONE IF YOU'RE DATING THEM, RIGHT?
It's a little...
LIKE A PRINCE AND PRIN-CESS...
late for that.
BUT THAT'S EASY ENOUGH TO FIX! WE'LL JUST START GOING OUT TOGETHER!
キラ SPARKLE
Brilliant, right?
WHAT DO YOU THINK?
NARUMI-CHAN? ARE YOU ALL RIGHT?
......
I'M A CAPTIVE PRINCESS TODAY...
BUT I WON'T BE AFTER THE PLAY ENDS.
BA-THUMP
BA-THUMP
I'M JUST A LITTLE DIZZY, THAT'S ALL. MY HEART IS BEATING REALLY FAST...
OH, YOU'RE RIGHT!

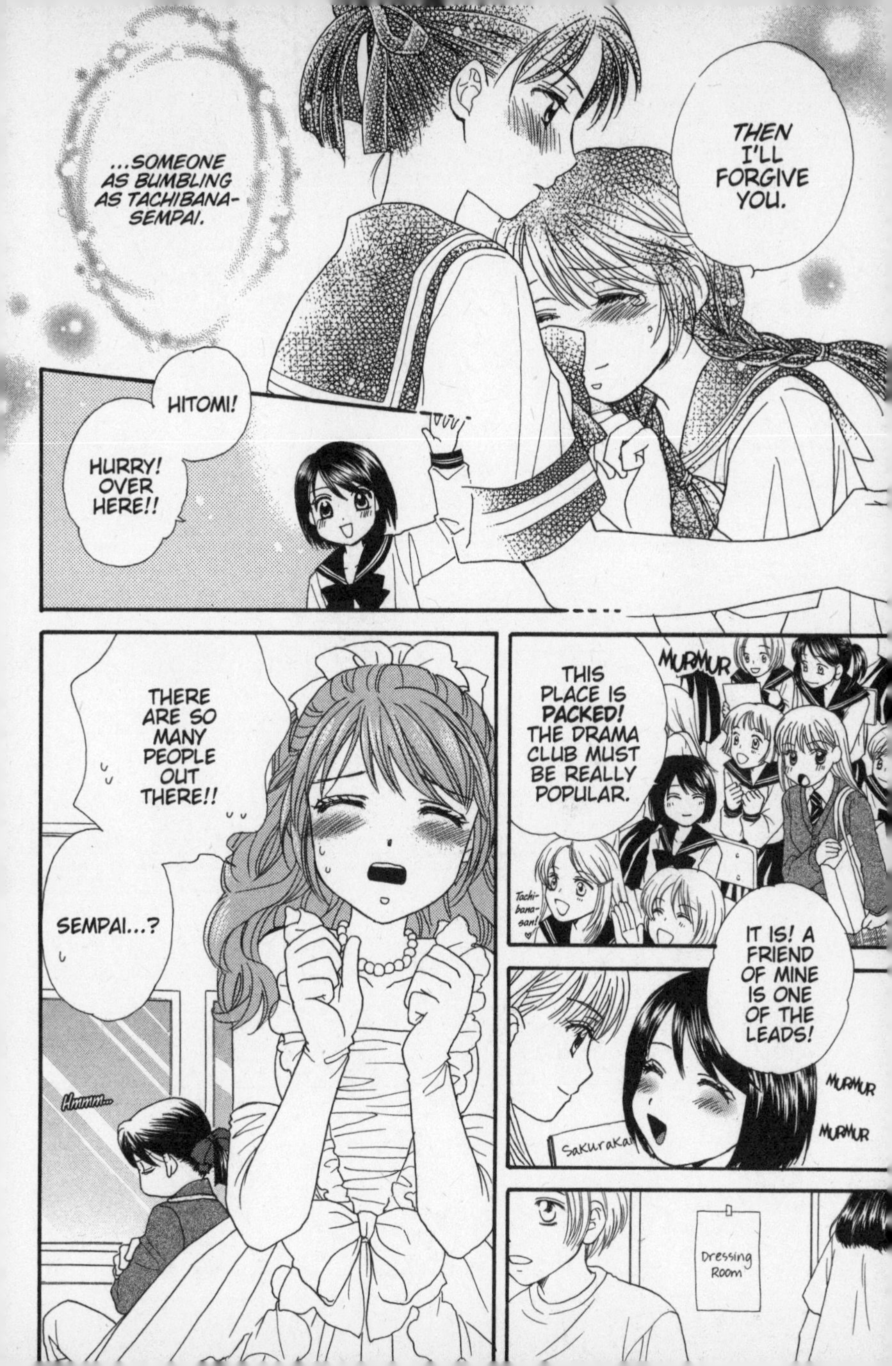
THEN I'LL FORGIVE YOU.
...SOMEONE AS BUMBLING AS TACHIBANA-SEMPAI.
HITOMI!
HURRY! OVER HERE!!
MURMUR
THIS PLACE IS PACKED! THE DRAMA CLUB MUST BE REALLY POPULAR.
Tachibana-san!
IT IS! A FRIEND OF MINE IS ONE OF THE LEADS!
MURMUR
MURMUR
SakuraKai
Dressing Room
THERE ARE SO MANY PEOPLE OUT THERE!!
SEMPAI...?
Hmmm...

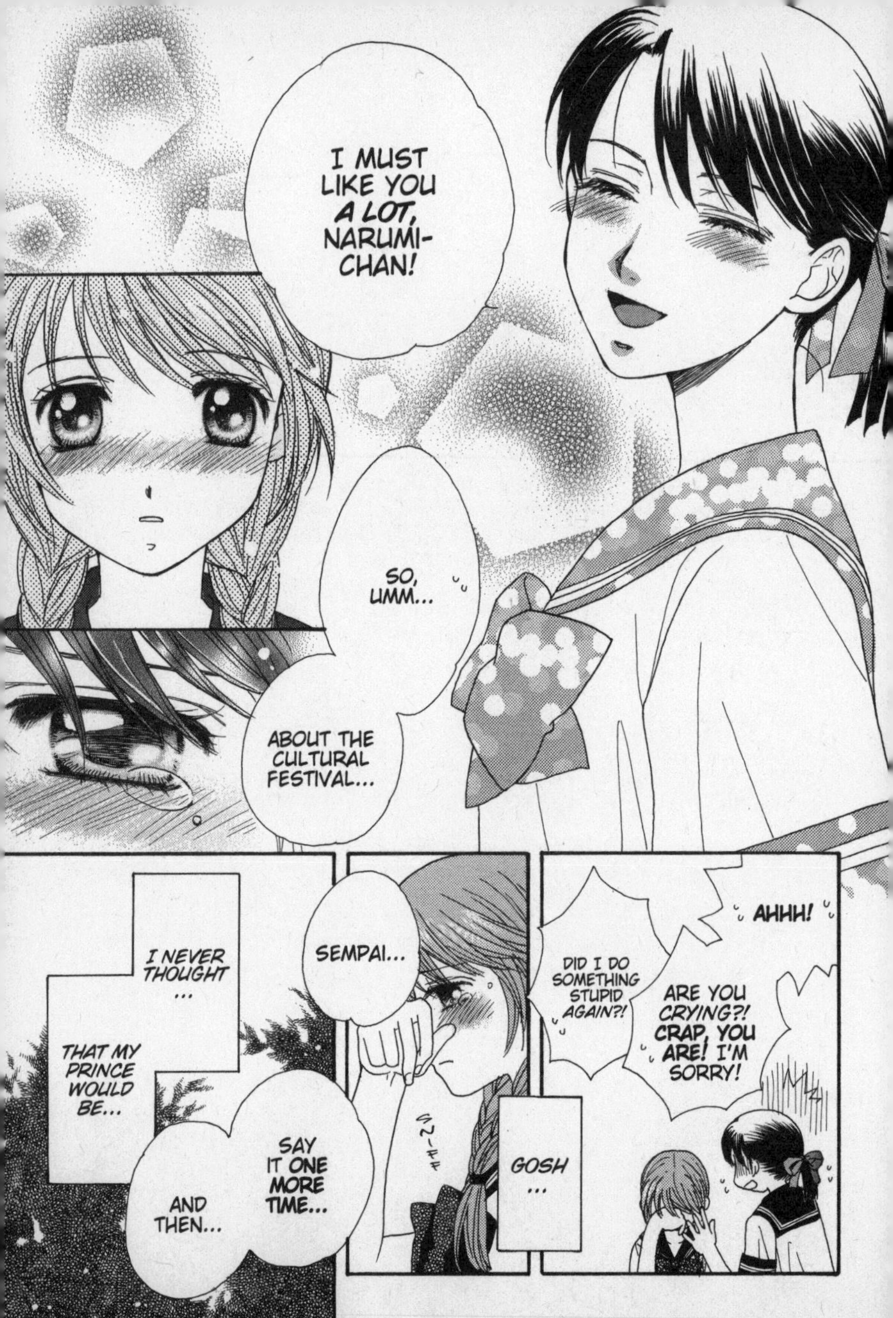
I MUST LIKE YOU A LOT, NARUMI-CHAN!
SO, UMM...
ABOUT THE CULTURAL FESTIVAL...
AHHH!
ARE YOU CRYING?! CRAP, YOU ARE! I'M SORRY!
DID I DO SOMETHING STUPID AGAIN?!
GOSH...
SEMPAI...
SNIFF
I NEVER THOUGHT...
THAT MY PRINCE WOULD BE...
SAY IT ONE MORE TIME...
AND THEN...

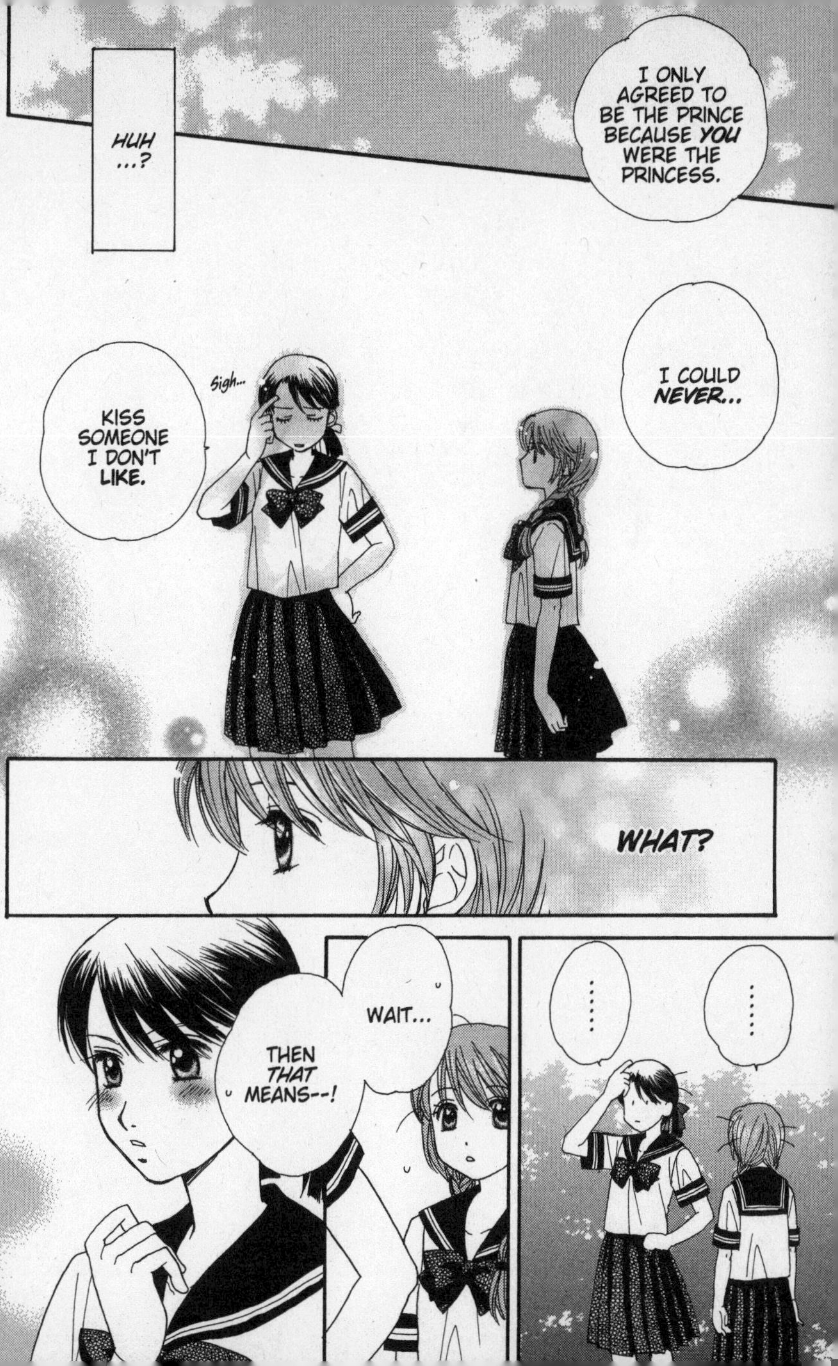
I ONLY AGREED TO BE THE PRINCE BECAUSE *YOU* WERE THE PRINCESS.
HUH ...?
I COULD *NEVER...*
Sigh...
KISS SOMEONE I DON'T LIKE.
WHAT?
......
......
WAIT...
THEN *THAT* MEANS--!

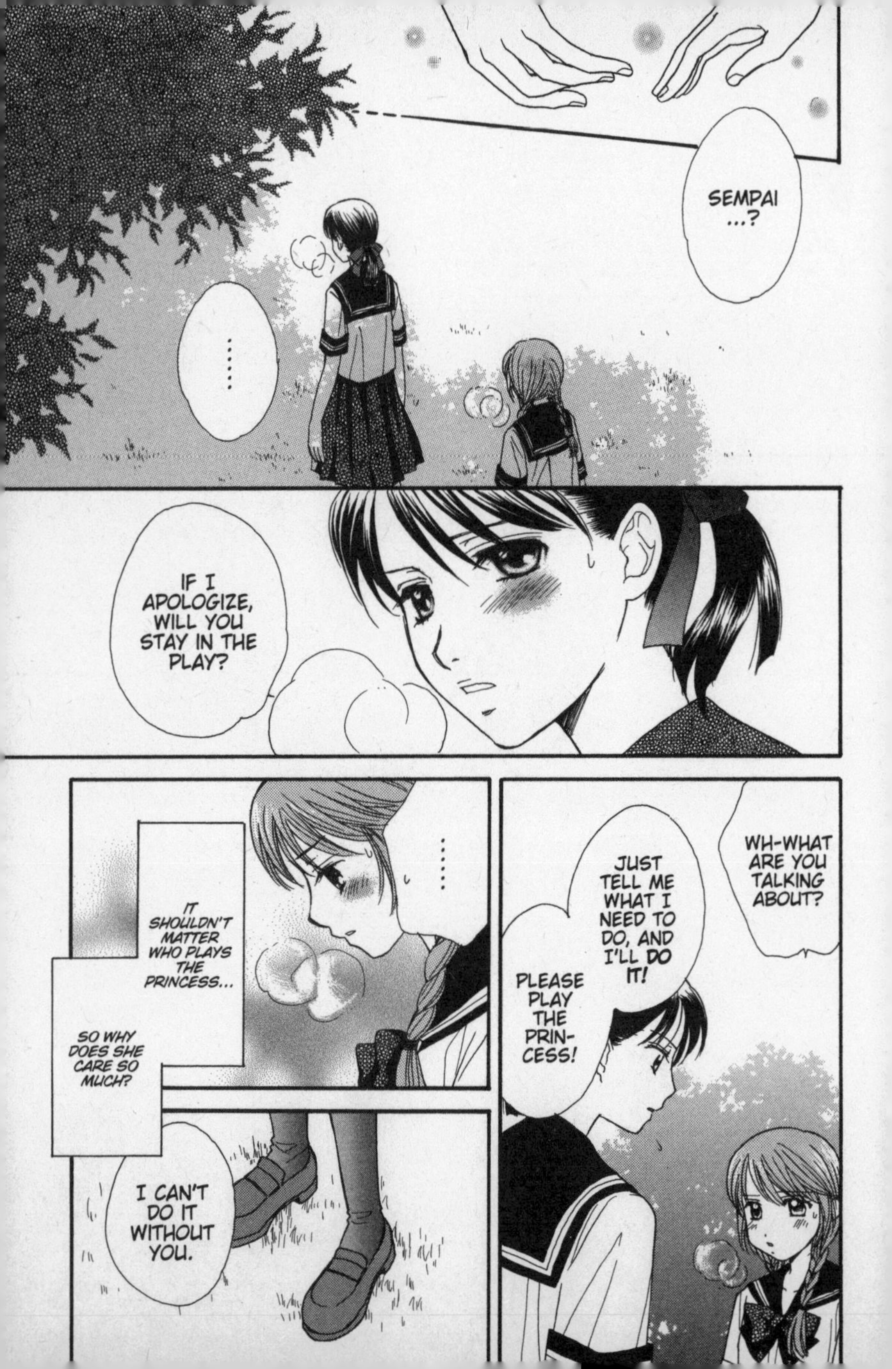
SEMPAI ...?
......
IF I APOLOGIZE, WILL YOU STAY IN THE PLAY?
WH-WHAT ARE YOU TALKING ABOUT?
JUST TELL ME WHAT I NEED TO DO, AND I'LL DO IT!
PLEASE PLAY THE PRIN-CESS!
......
IT SHOULDN'T MATTER WHO PLAYS THE PRINCESS...
SO WHY DOES SHE CARE SO MUCH?
I CAN'T DO IT WITHOUT YOU.

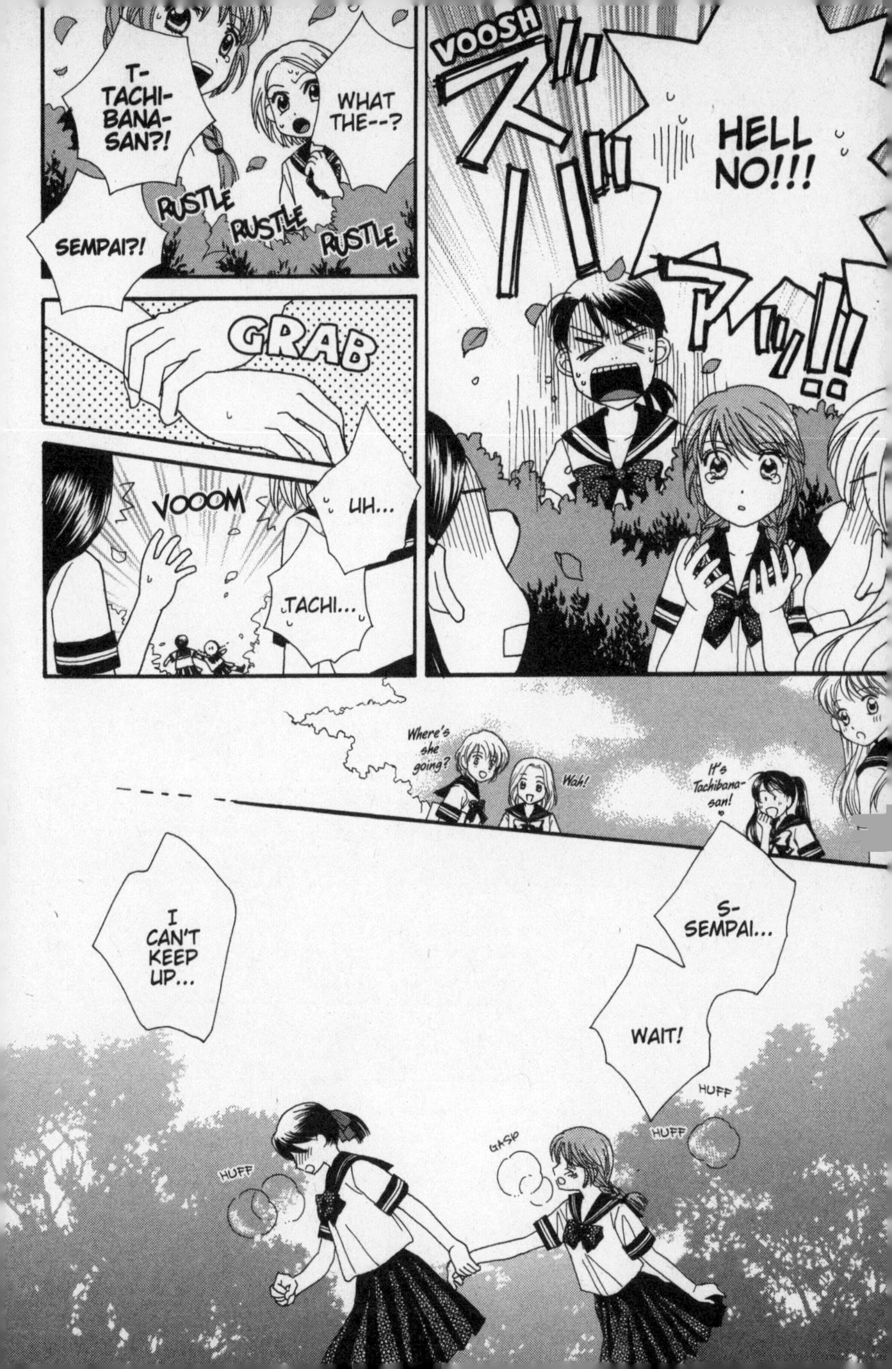

VOOSH
ズバーアッ!!
HELL NO!!!
WHAT THE--?
T-TACHIBANA-SAN?!
RUSTLE
RUSTLE
RUSTLE
SEMPAI?!
GRAB
UH...
TACHI...
VOOOM
It's Tachibana-san!
Wah!
Where's she going?
S-SEMPAI...
WAIT!
I CAN'T KEEP UP...
HUFF
HUFF
GASP
HUFF

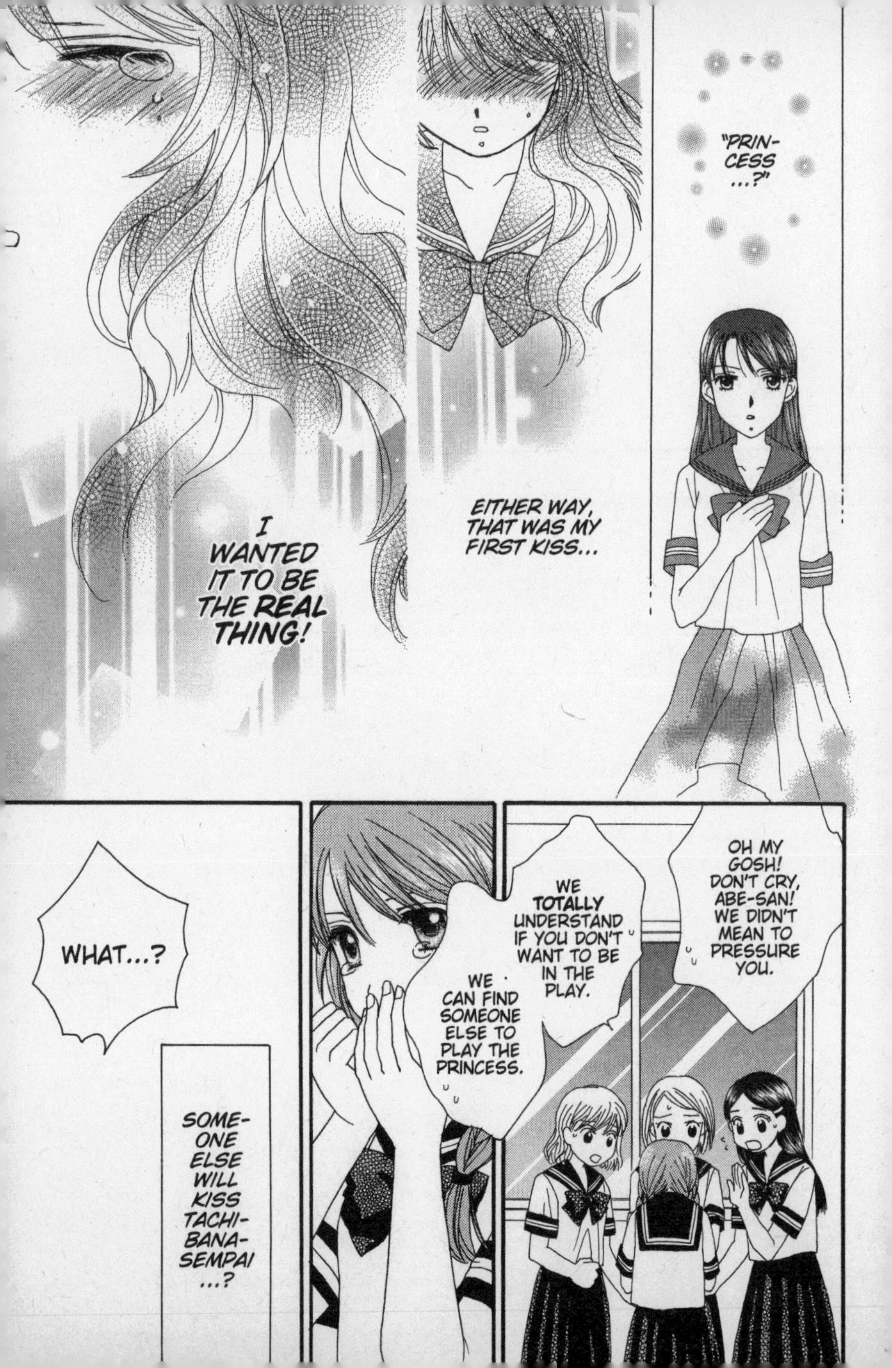
"PRIN-CESS ...?"
EITHER WAY, THAT WAS MY FIRST KISS...
I WANTED IT TO BE THE REAL THING!
OH MY GOSH! DON'T CRY, ABE-SAN! WE DIDN'T MEAN TO PRESSURE YOU.
WE TOTALLY UNDERSTAND IF YOU DON'T WANT TO BE IN THE PLAY.
WE CAN FIND SOMEONE ELSE TO PLAY THE PRINCESS.
WHAT...?
SOME-ONE ELSE WILL KISS TACHI-BANA-SEMPAI ...?

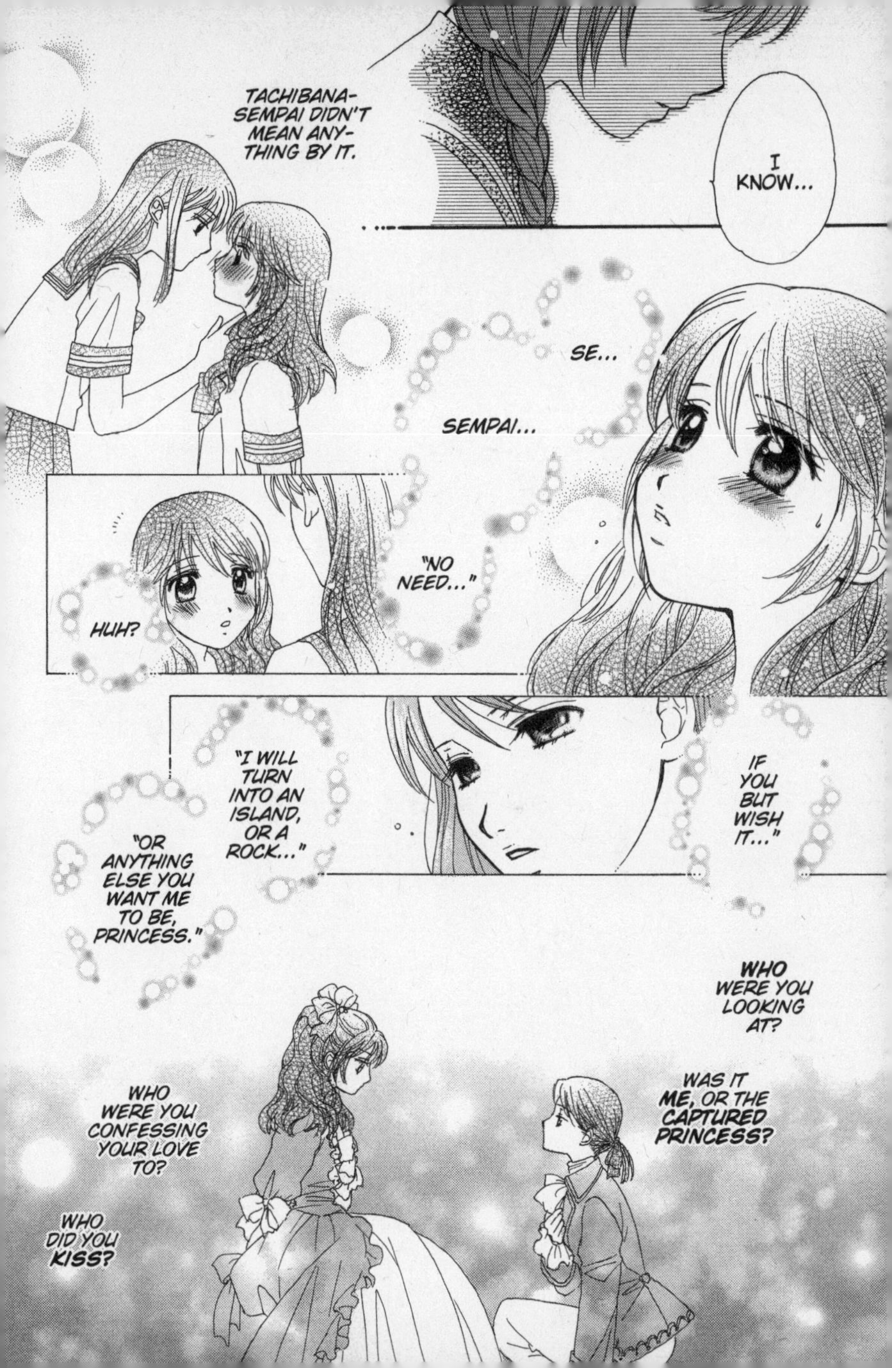
I KNOW...
TACHIBANA-SEMPAI DIDN'T MEAN ANYTHING BY IT.
SE...
SEMPAI...
"NO NEED..."
HUH?
"IF YOU BUT WISH IT..."
"I WILL TURN INTO AN ISLAND, OR A ROCK..."
"OR ANYTHING ELSE YOU WANT ME TO BE, PRINCESS."
WHO WERE YOU LOOKING AT?
WAS IT **ME**, OR THE **CAPTURED PRINCESS?**
WHO WERE YOU CONFESSING YOUR LOVE TO?
WHO DID YOU **KISS?**

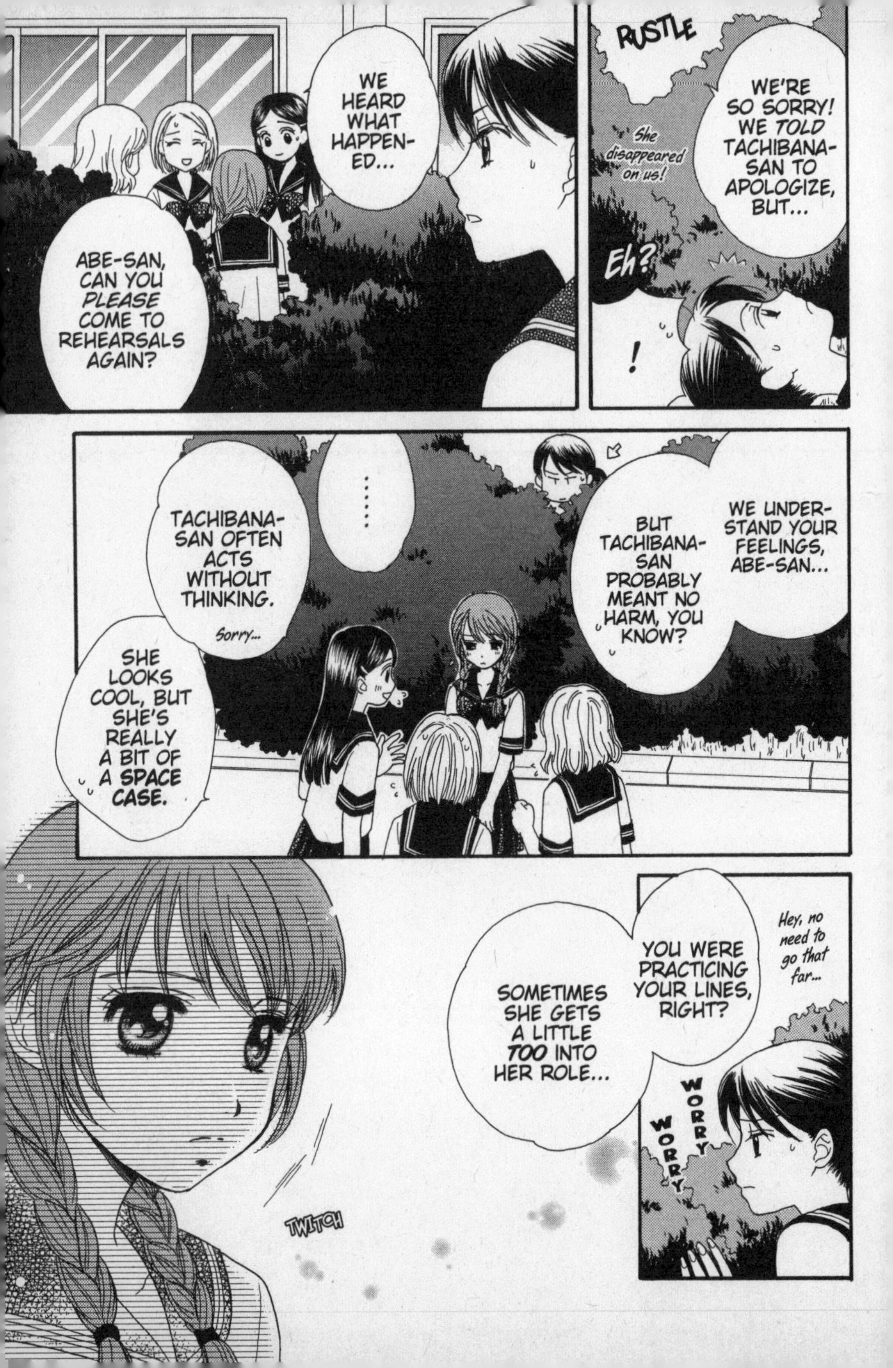
RUSTLE
WE'RE SO SORRY! WE TOLD TACHIBANA-SAN TO APOLOGIZE, BUT...
She disappeared on us!
Eh?
!
WE HEARD WHAT HAPPEN-ED...
ABE-SAN, CAN YOU PLEASE COME TO REHEARSALS AGAIN?
WE UNDER-STAND YOUR FEELINGS, ABE-SAN...
BUT TACHIBANA-SAN PROBABLY MEANT NO HARM, YOU KNOW?
......
TACHIBANA-SAN OFTEN ACTS WITHOUT THINKING.
Sorry...
SHE LOOKS COOL, BUT SHE'S REALLY A BIT OF A SPACE CASE.
Hey, no need to go that far...
YOU WERE PRACTICING YOUR LINES, RIGHT?
SOMETIMES SHE GETS A LITTLE TOO INTO HER ROLE...
WORRY WORRY WORRY
TWITCH

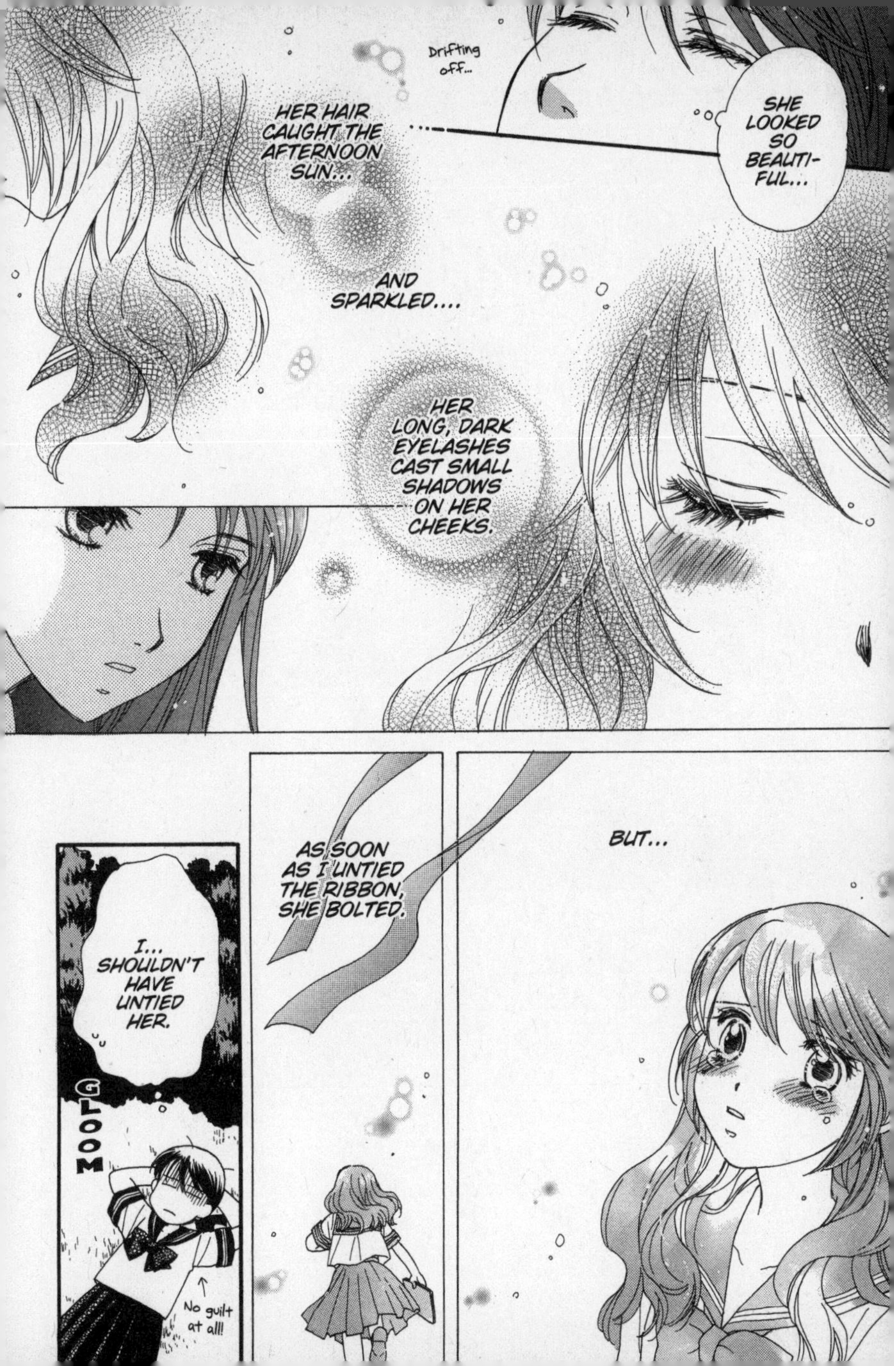
Drifting off...
SHE LOOKED SO BEAUTIFUL...
HER HAIR CAUGHT THE AFTERNOON SUN...
AND SPARKLED....
HER LONG, DARK EYELASHES CAST SMALL SHADOWS ON HER CHEEKS.
BUT...
AS SOON AS I UNTIED THE RIBBON, SHE BOLTED.
I... SHOULDN'T HAVE UNTIED HER.
GLOOM
No guilt at all!

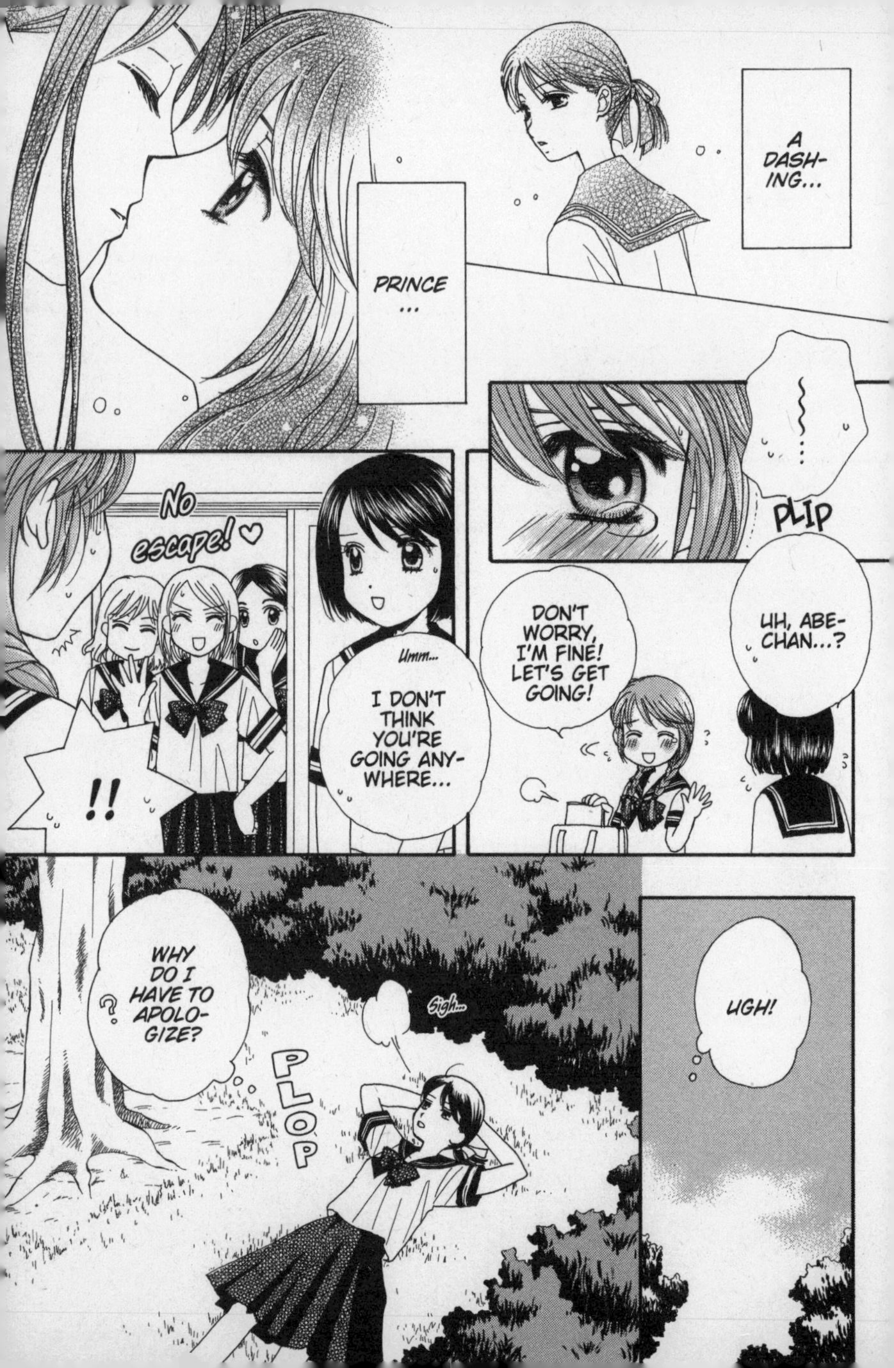
A DASHING...
PRINCE ...
PLIP
UH, ABE-CHAN...?
DON'T WORRY, I'M FINE! LET'S GET GOING!
Umm...
I DON'T THINK YOU'RE GOING ANYWHERE...
No escape! ♡
!!
UGH!
Sigh...
WHY DO I HAVE TO APOLOGIZE?
PLOP

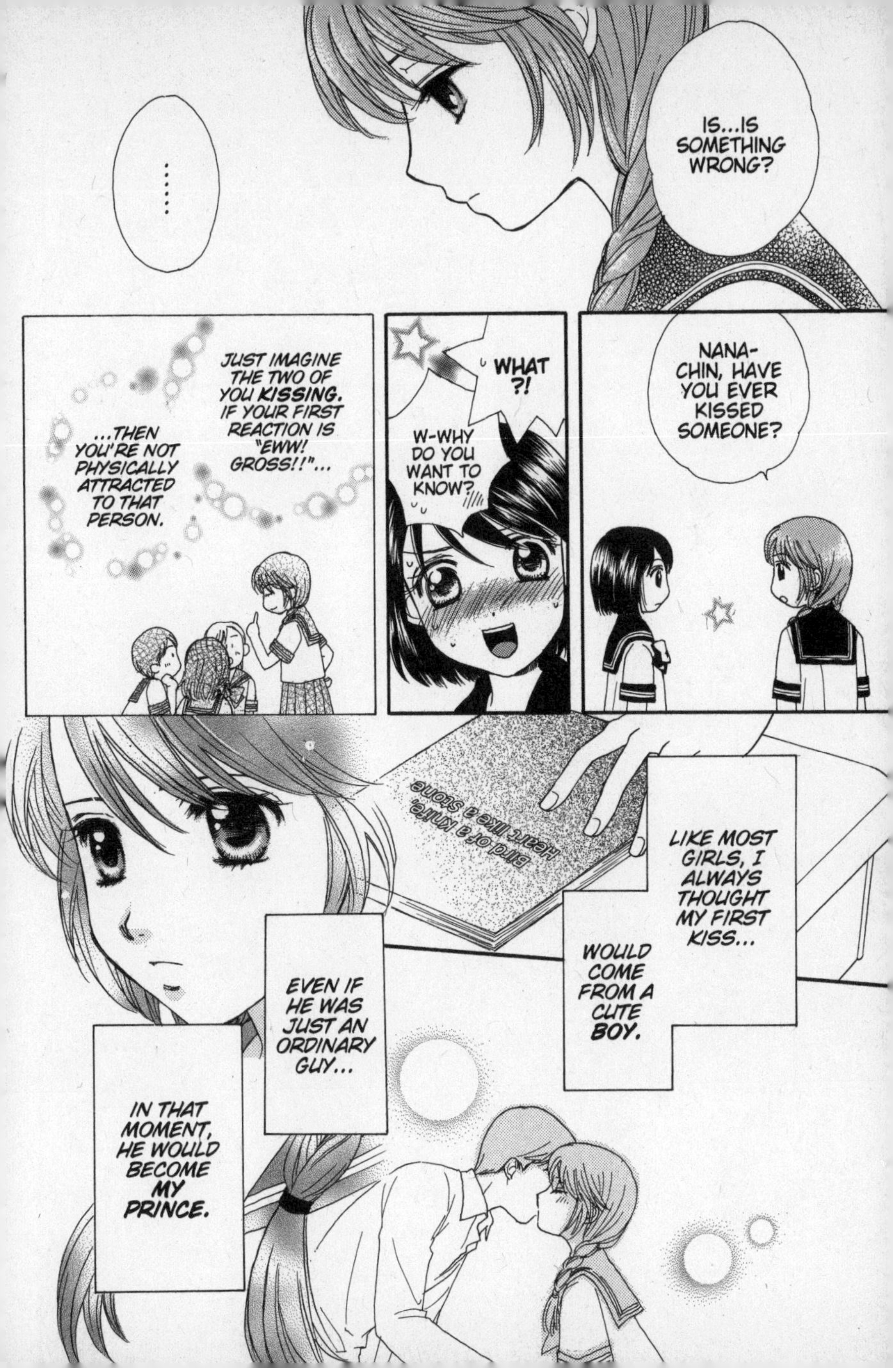
IS...IS SOMETHING WRONG?
......
NANA-CHIN, HAVE YOU EVER KISSED SOMEONE?
WHAT?!
W-WHY DO YOU WANT TO KNOW?
JUST IMAGINE THE TWO OF YOU **KISSING.** IF YOUR FIRST REACTION IS "EWW! GROSS!!"...
...THEN YOU'RE NOT PHYSICALLY ATTRACTED TO THAT PERSON.
Bird of a knife, Heart like a stone
LIKE MOST GIRLS, I ALWAYS THOUGHT MY FIRST KISS...
WOULD COME FROM A CUTE **BOY.**
EVEN IF HE WAS JUST AN ORDINARY GUY...
IN THAT MOMENT, HE WOULD BECOME **MY PRINCE.**

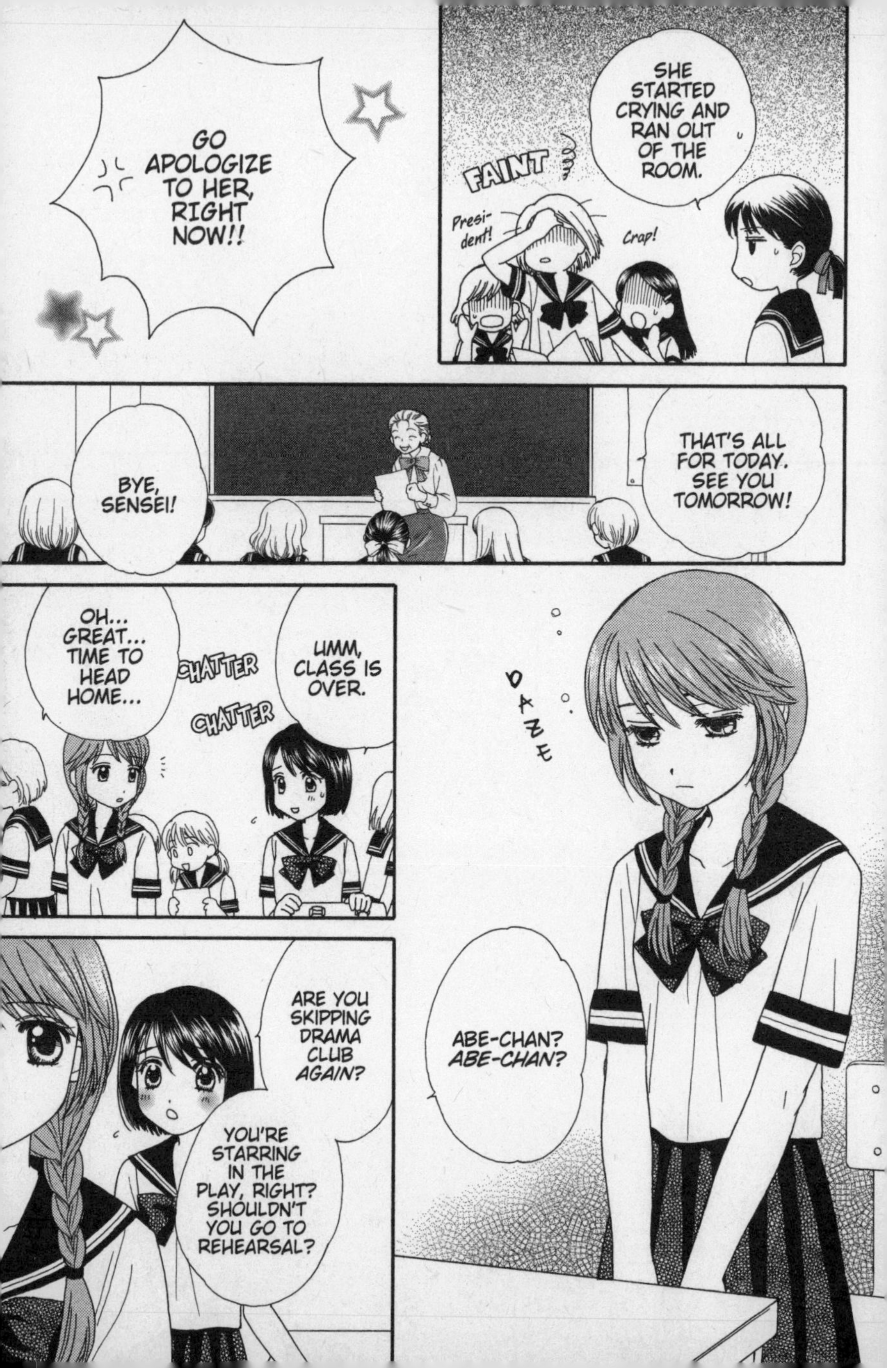
SHE STARTED CRYING AND RAN OUT OF THE ROOM.
FAINT
President!
Crap!
GO APOLOGIZE TO HER, RIGHT NOW!!
THAT'S ALL FOR TODAY. SEE YOU TOMORROW!
BYE, SENSEI!
DAZE
ABE-CHAN? ABE-CHAN?
UMM, CLASS IS OVER.
CHATTER
CHATTER
OH... GREAT... TIME TO HEAD HOME...
ARE YOU SKIPPING DRAMA CLUB AGAIN?
YOU'RE STARRING IN THE PLAY, RIGHT? SHOULDN'T YOU GO TO REHEARSAL?

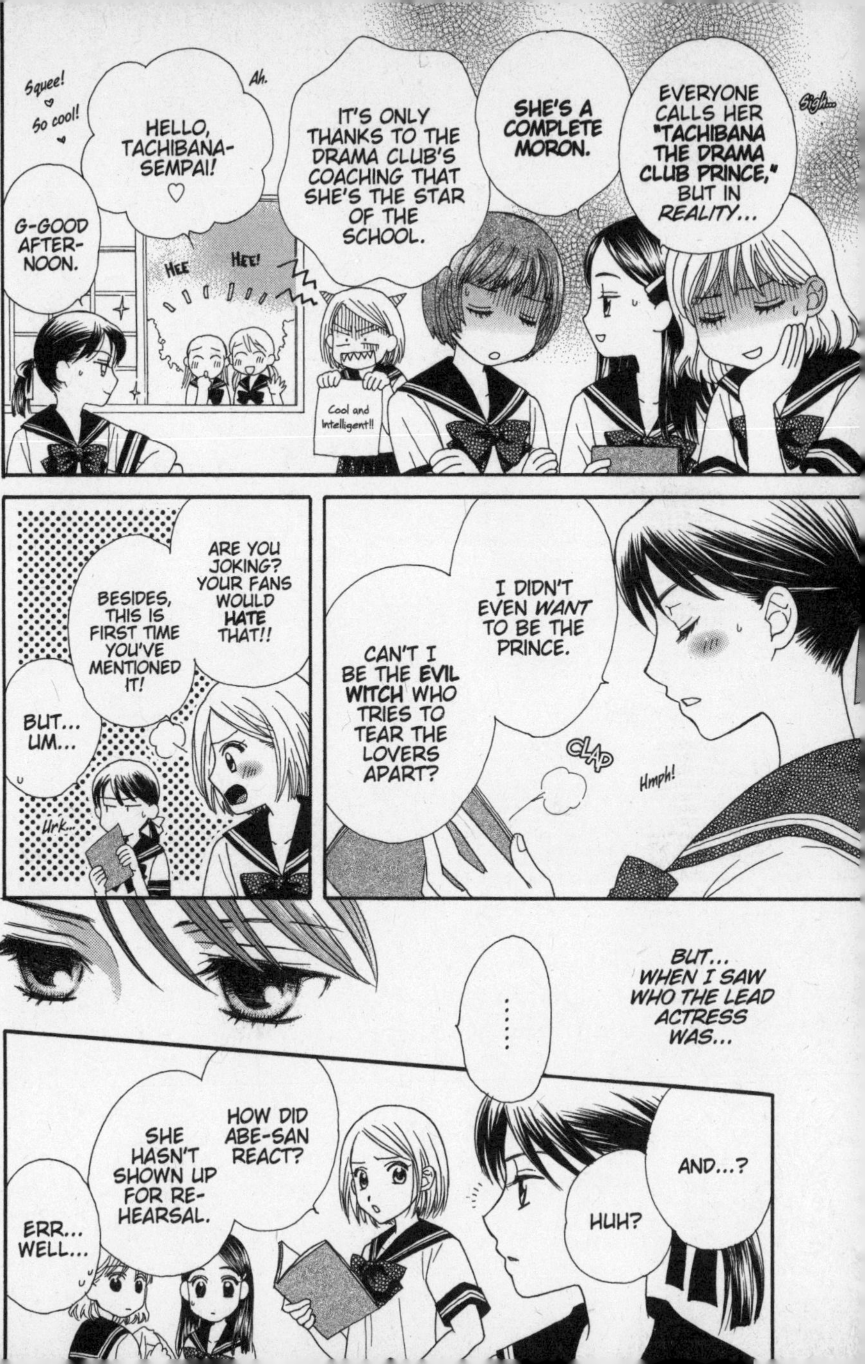
Sigh...
EVERYONE CALLS HER "TACHIBANA THE DRAMA CLUB PRINCE," BUT IN REALITY...
SHE'S A COMPLETE MORON.
IT'S ONLY THANKS TO THE DRAMA CLUB'S COACHING THAT SHE'S THE STAR OF THE SCHOOL.
Ah.
HELLO, TACHIBANA-SEMPAI! ♡
Squee! ♡ So cool! ♡
HEE HEE!
G-GOOD AFTERNOON.
Cool and Intelligent!!
I DIDN'T EVEN WANT TO BE THE PRINCE.
CAN'T I BE THE EVIL WITCH WHO TRIES TO TEAR THE LOVERS APART?
CLAP
Hmph!
ARE YOU JOKING? YOUR FANS WOULD HATE THAT!!
BESIDES, THIS IS FIRST TIME YOU'VE MENTIONED IT!
BUT... UM...
Urk...
BUT... WHEN I SAW WHO THE LEAD ACTRESS WAS...
......
AND...?
HUH?
HOW DID ABE-SAN REACT?
SHE HASN'T SHOWN UP FOR RE-HEARSAL.
ERR... WELL...

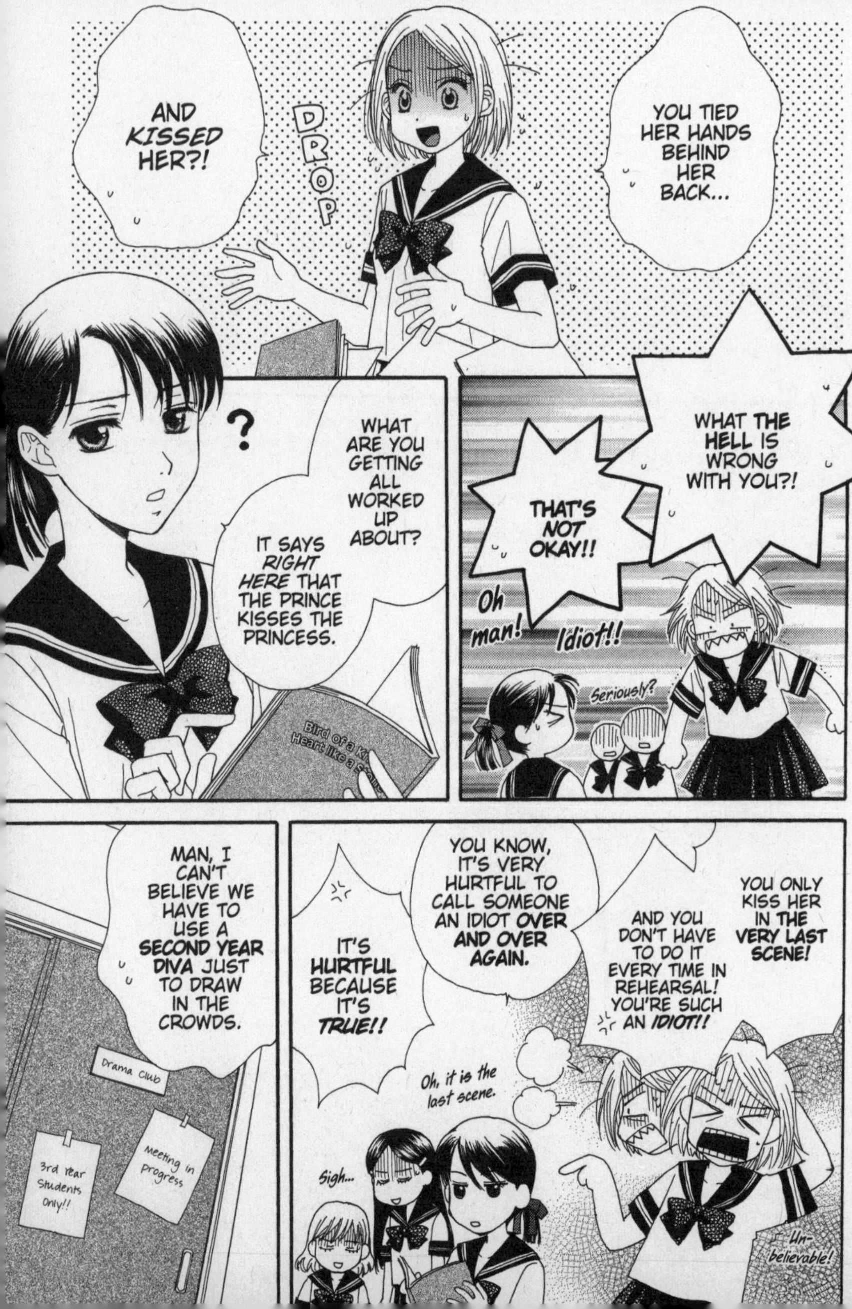
YOU TIED HER HANDS BEHIND HER BACK...
DROP
AND KISSED HER?!
WHAT THE HELL IS WRONG WITH YOU?!
THAT'S NOT OKAY!!
Oh man!
Idiot!!
Seriously?
WHAT ARE YOU GETTING ALL WORKED UP ABOUT?
IT SAYS RIGHT HERE THAT THE PRINCE KISSES THE PRINCESS.
YOU ONLY KISS HER IN THE VERY LAST SCENE!
AND YOU DON'T HAVE TO DO IT EVERY TIME IN REHEARSAL! YOU'RE SUCH AN IDIOT!!
YOU KNOW, IT'S VERY HURTFUL TO CALL SOMEONE AN IDIOT OVER AND OVER AGAIN.
IT'S HURTFUL BECAUSE IT'S TRUE!!
Un-believable!
Oh, it is the last scene.
Sigh...
MAN, I CAN'T BELIEVE WE HAVE TO USE A SECOND YEAR DIVA JUST TO DRAW IN THE CROWDS.
Drama Club
Meeting in Progress
3rd Year Students Only!!

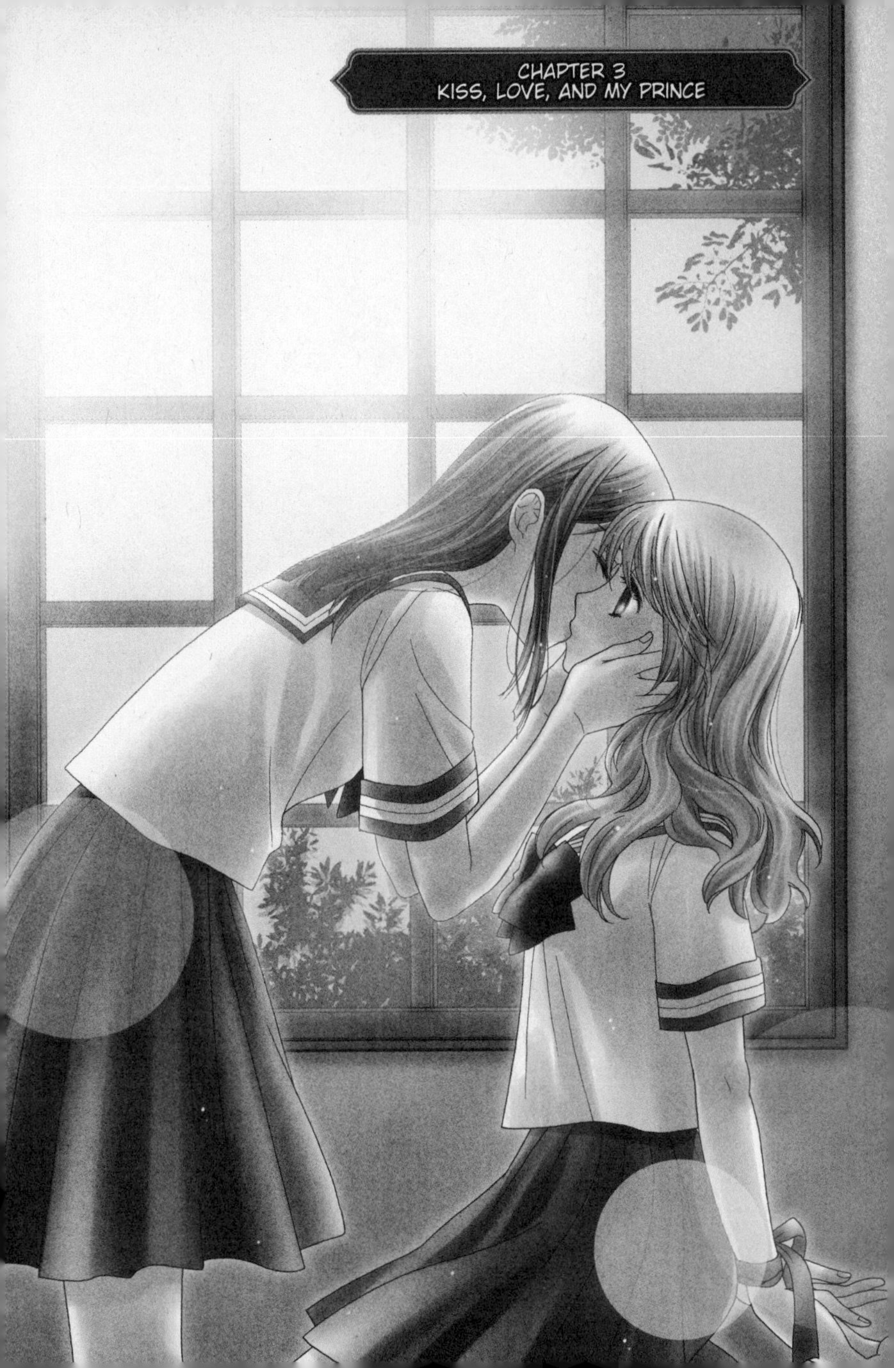
CHAPTER 3
KISS, LOVE, AND MY PRINCE

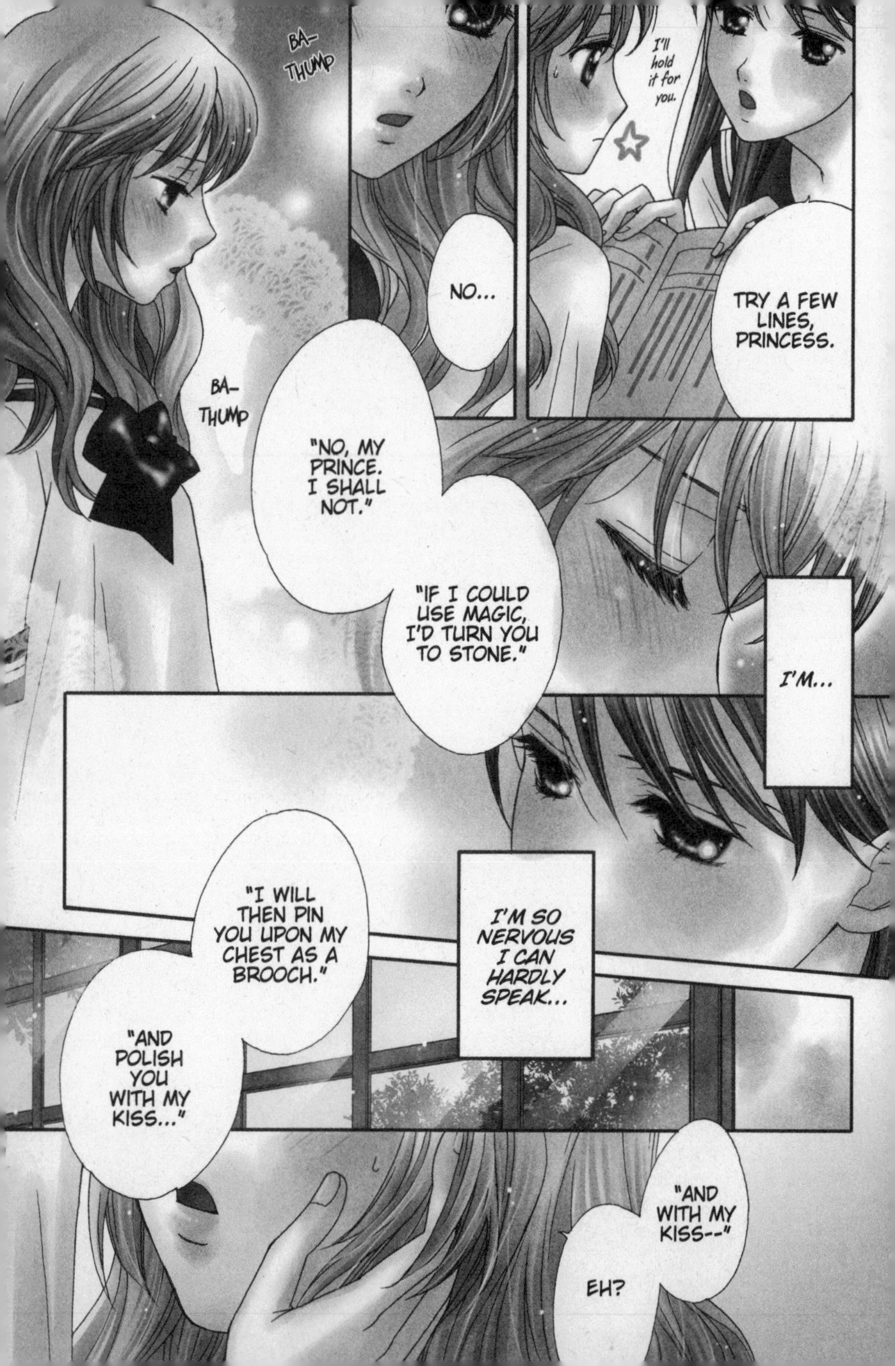
I'll hold it for you.
TRY A FEW LINES, PRINCESS.
NO...
BA-THUMP
BA-THUMP
"NO, MY PRINCE. I SHALL NOT."
"IF I COULD USE MAGIC, I'D TURN YOU TO STONE."
I'M...
I'M SO NERVOUS I CAN HARDLY SPEAK...
"I WILL THEN PIN YOU UPON MY CHEST AS A BROOCH."
"AND POLISH YOU WITH MY KISS..."
"AND WITH MY KISS--"
EH?

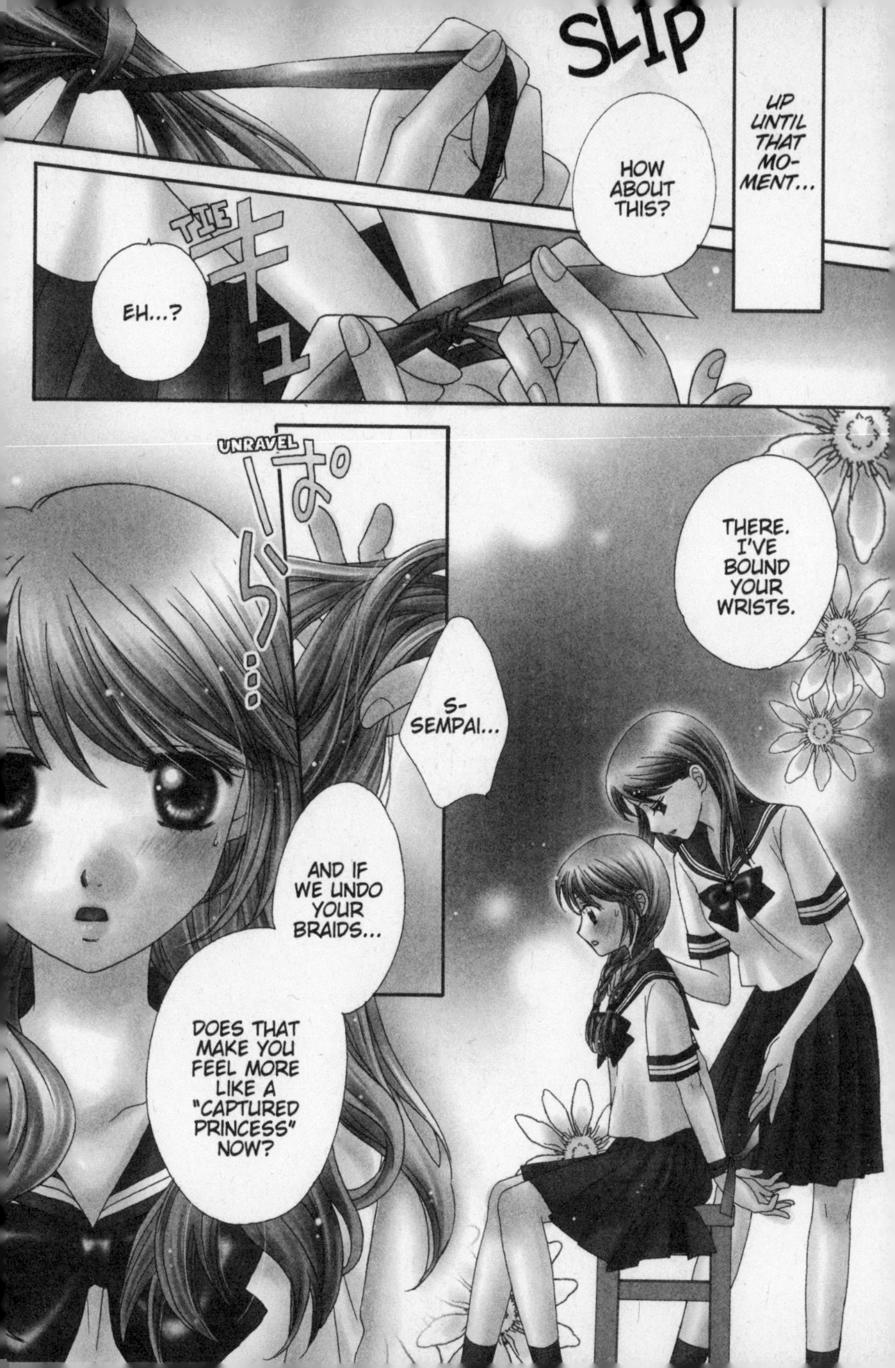
SLIP
UP UNTIL THAT MOMENT...
HOW ABOUT THIS?
TIE
EH...?
THERE. I'VE BOUND YOUR WRISTS.
UNRAVEL
S-SEMPAI...
AND IF WE UNDO YOUR BRAIDS...
DOES THAT MAKE YOU FEEL MORE LIKE A "CAPTURED PRINCESS" NOW?

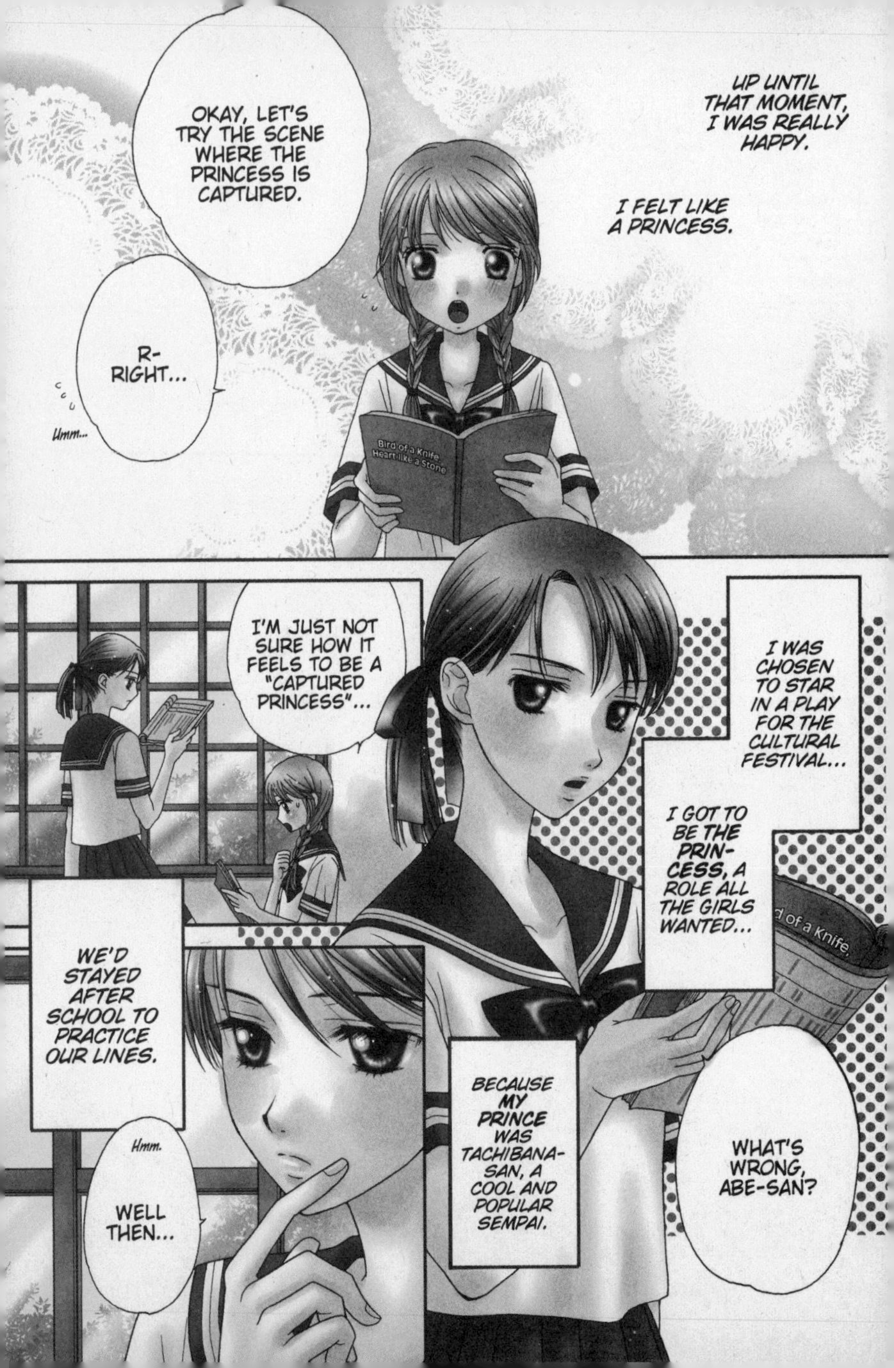
UP UNTIL THAT MOMENT, I WAS REALLY HAPPY.
I FELT LIKE A PRINCESS.
OKAY, LET'S TRY THE SCENE WHERE THE PRINCESS IS CAPTURED.
R-RIGHT...
Umm...
Bird of a Knife, Heart like a Stone
I WAS CHOSEN TO STAR IN A PLAY FOR THE CULTURAL FESTIVAL...
I GOT TO BE THE PRINCESS, A ROLE ALL THE GIRLS WANTED...
I'M JUST NOT SURE HOW IT FEELS TO BE A "CAPTURED PRINCESS"...
WHAT'S WRONG, ABE-SAN?
BECAUSE MY PRINCE WAS TACHIBANA-SAN, A COOL AND POPULAR SEMPAI.
WE'D STAYED AFTER SCHOOL TO PRACTICE OUR LINES.
Hmm.
WELL THEN...

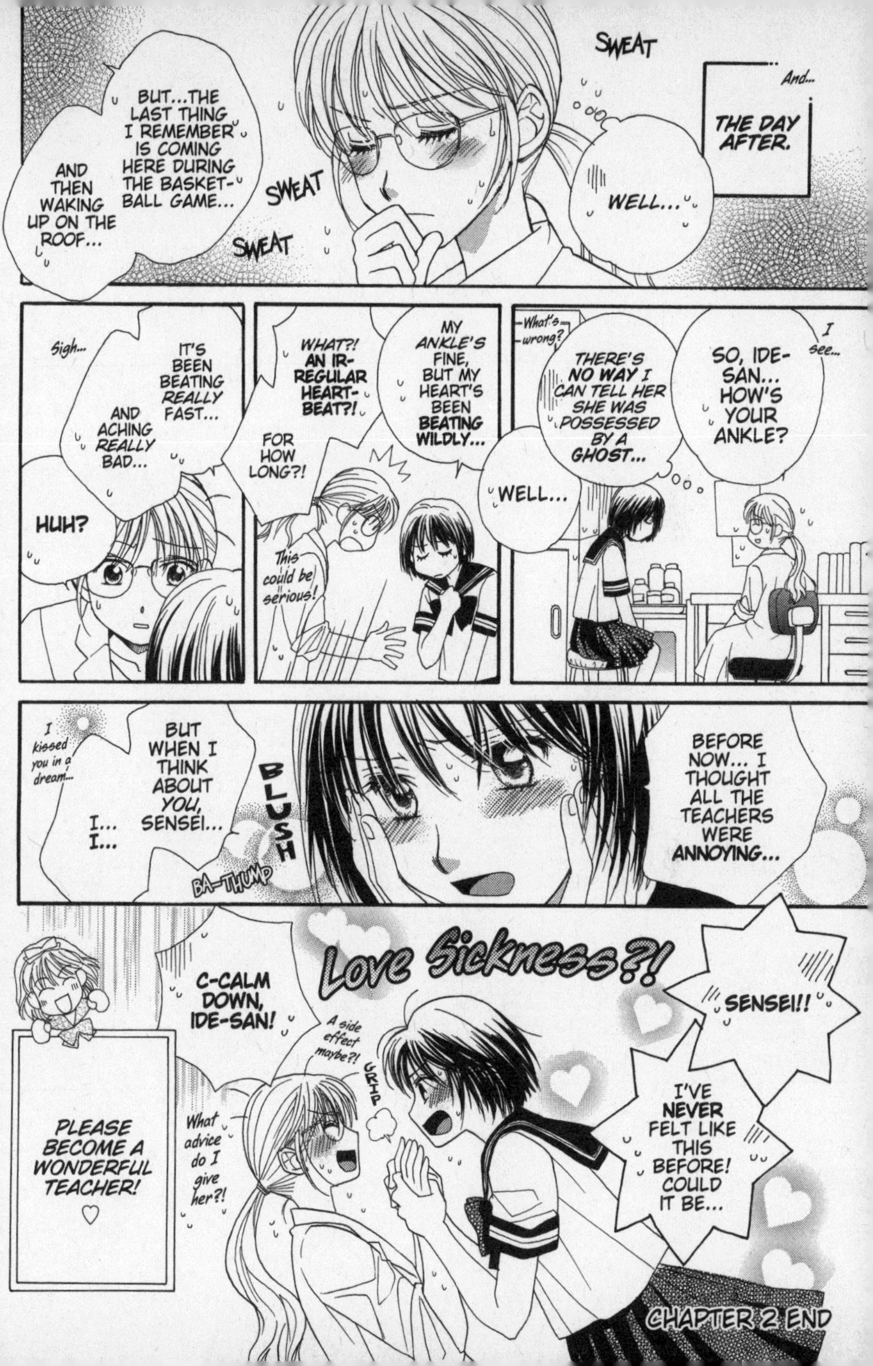

And... THE DAY AFTER.
WELL...
SWEAT
SWEAT
SWEAT
BUT...THE LAST THING I REMEMBER IS COMING HERE DURING THE BASKET-BALL GAME...
AND THEN WAKING UP ON THE ROOF...
I see...
SO, IDE-SAN... HOW'S YOUR ANKLE?
What's wrong?
THERE'S NO WAY I CAN TELL HER SHE WAS POSSESSED BY A GHOST...
WELL...
MY ANKLE'S FINE, BUT MY HEART'S BEEN BEATING WILDLY...
WHAT?! AN IR-REGULAR HEART-BEAT?!
FOR HOW LONG?!
This could be serious!
IT'S BEEN BEATING REALLY FAST...
AND ACHING REALLY BAD...
Sigh...
HUH?
BEFORE NOW... I THOUGHT ALL THE TEACHERS WERE ANNOYING...
BLUSH
BUT WHEN I THINK ABOUT YOU, SENSEI...
I... I...
I kissed you in a dream...
BA-THUMP
SENSEI!!
I'VE NEVER FELT LIKE THIS BEFORE! COULD IT BE...
Love Sickness?!
GRIP
A side effect maybe?!
C-CALM DOWN, IDE-SAN!
What advice do I give her?!
PLEASE BECOME A WONDERFUL TEACHER! ♡
CHAPTER 2 END

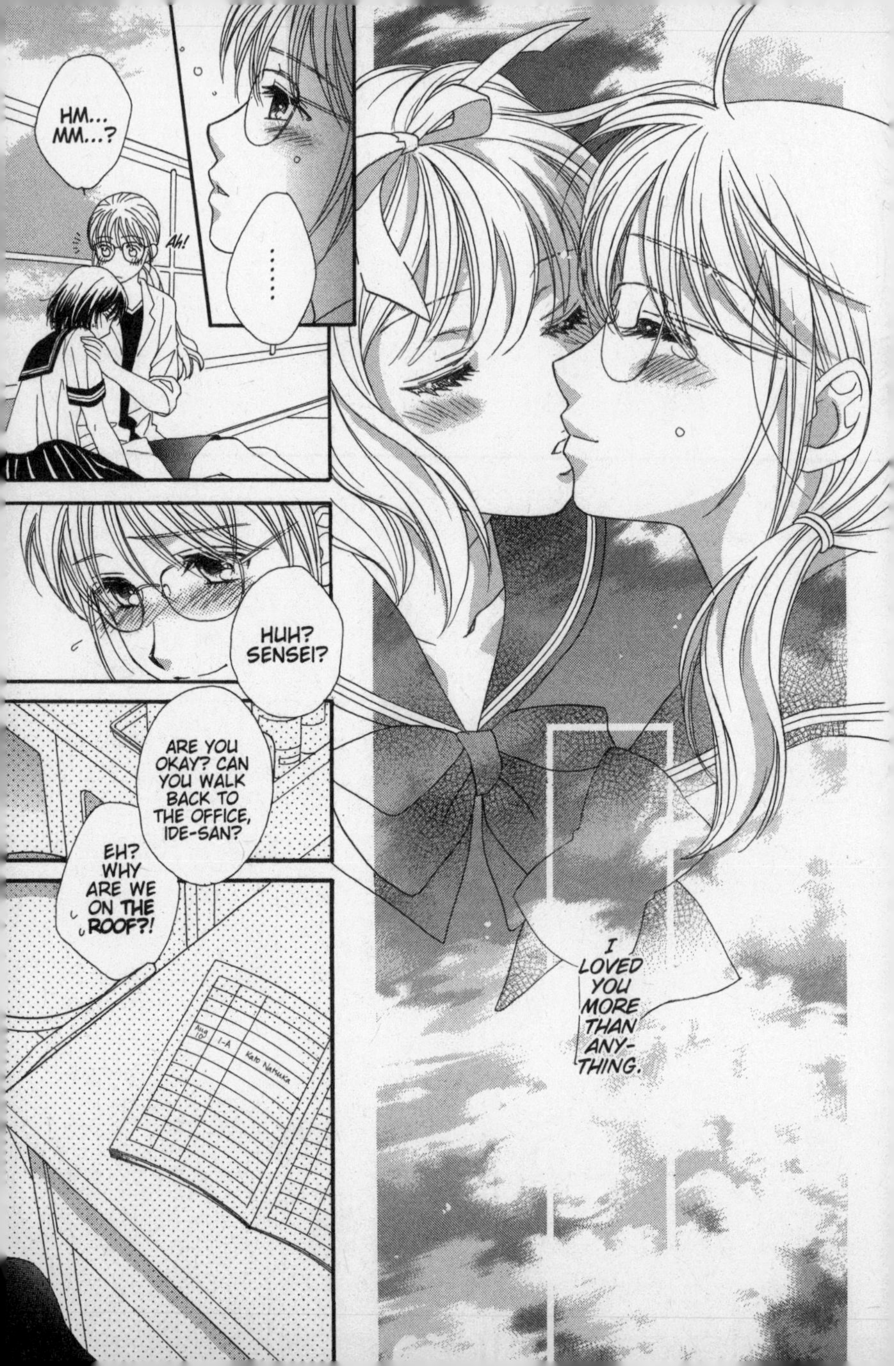
I LOVED YOU MORE THAN ANYTHING.
......
HM... MM...?
Ah!
HUH? SENSEI?
ARE YOU OKAY? CAN YOU WALK BACK TO THE OFFICE, IDE-SAN?
EH? WHY ARE WE ON THE ROOF?!
Aug 10
1-A
Kato Natsuka

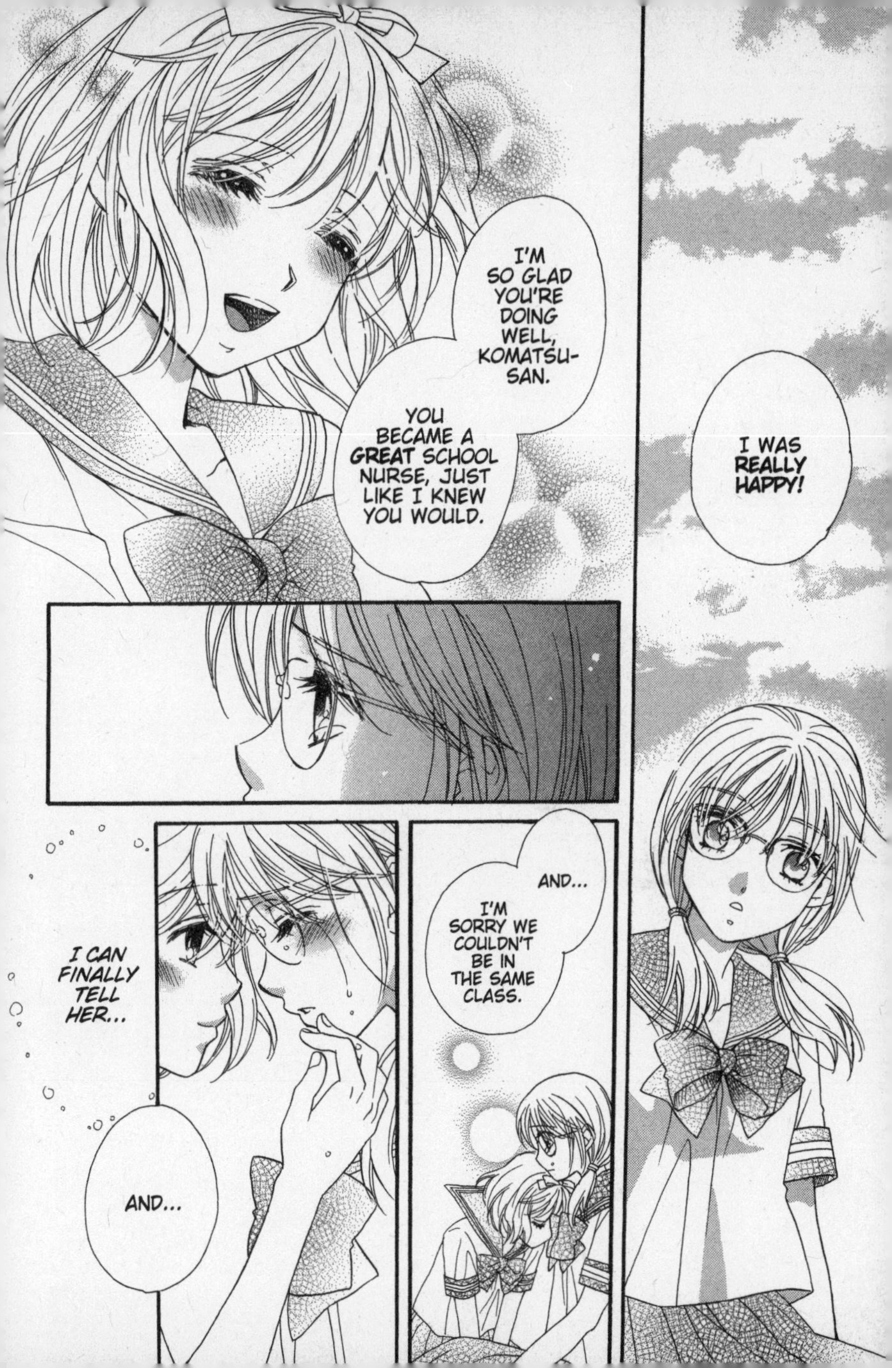
I WAS REALLY HAPPY!
I'M SO GLAD YOU'RE DOING WELL, KOMATSU-SAN.
YOU BECAME A GREAT SCHOOL NURSE, JUST LIKE I KNEW YOU WOULD.
AND...
I'M SORRY WE COULDN'T BE IN THE SAME CLASS.
I CAN FINALLY TELL HER...
AND...

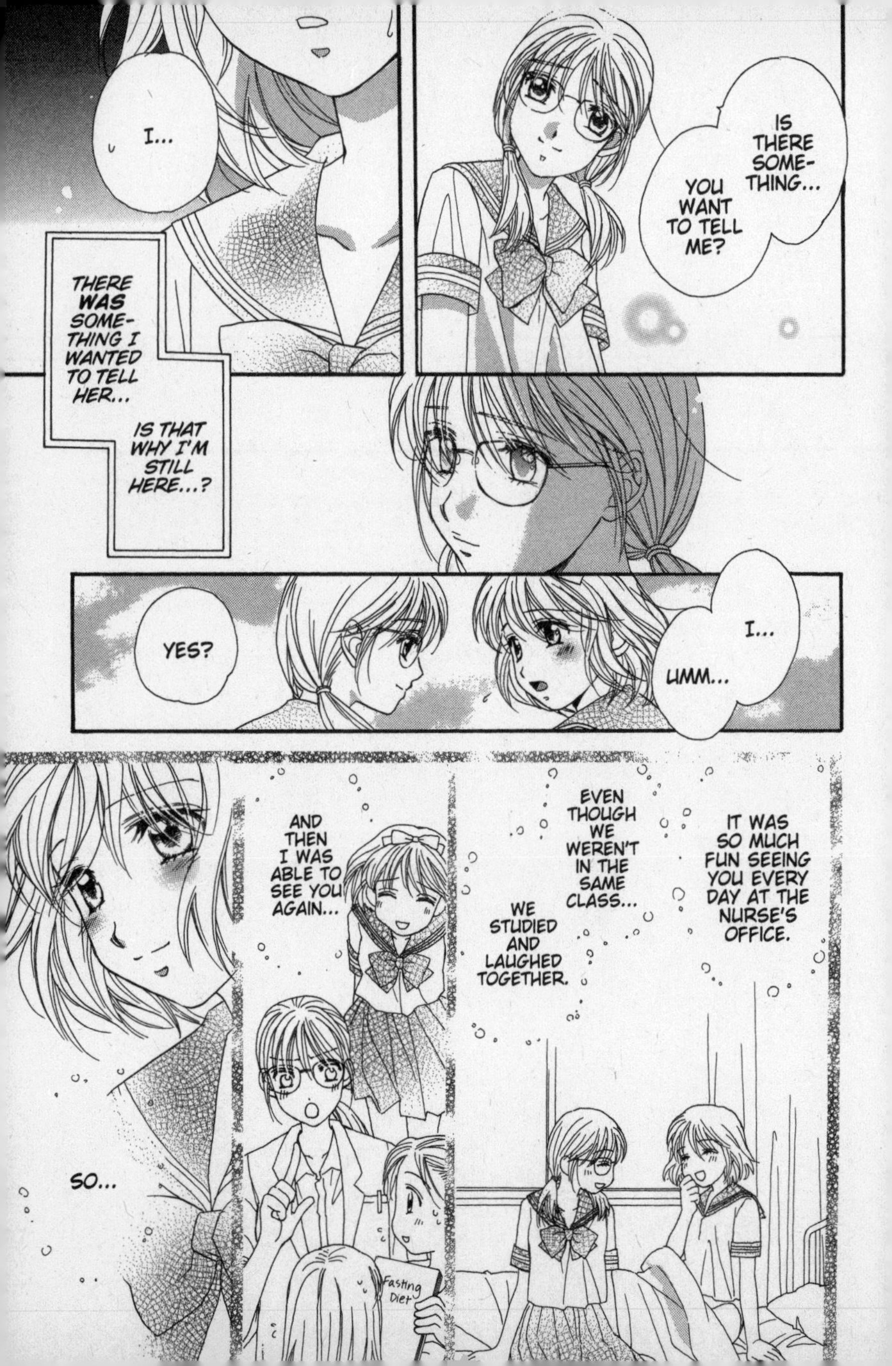
IS THERE SOME-THING... YOU WANT TO TELL ME?
I...
THERE WAS SOME-THING I WANTED TO TELL HER...
IS THAT WHY I'M STILL HERE...?
I... UMM...
YES?
IT WAS SO MUCH FUN SEEING YOU EVERY DAY AT THE NURSE'S OFFICE.
EVEN THOUGH WE WEREN'T IN THE SAME CLASS...
WE STUDIED AND LAUGHED TOGETHER.
AND THEN I WAS ABLE TO SEE YOU AGAIN...
Fasting Diet
SO...

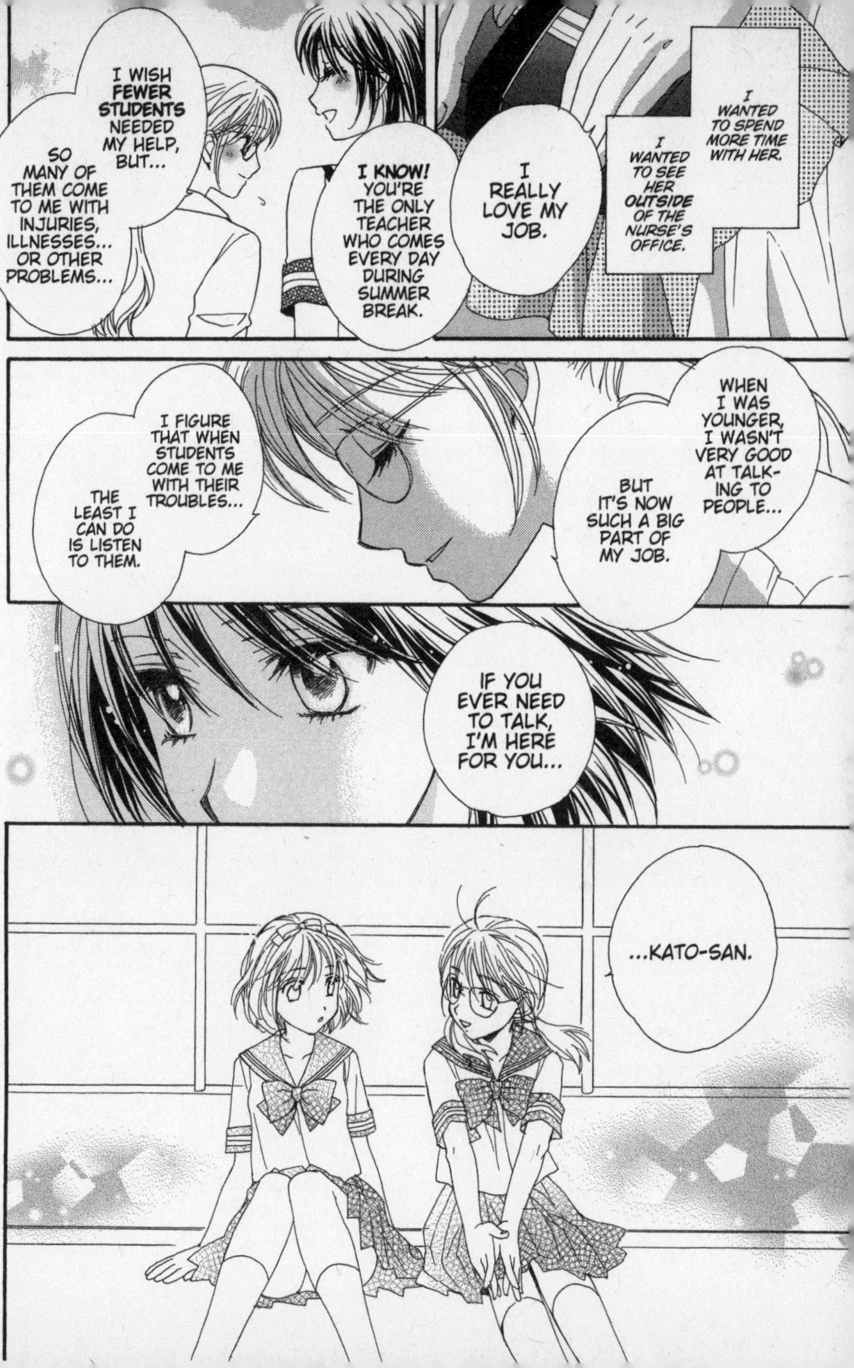
I WANTED TO SPEND MORE TIME WITH HER.
I WANTED TO SEE HER OUTSIDE OF THE NURSE'S OFFICE.
I REALLY LOVE MY JOB.
I KNOW! YOU'RE THE ONLY TEACHER WHO COMES EVERY DAY DURING SUMMER BREAK.
I WISH FEWER STUDENTS NEEDED MY HELP, BUT...
SO MANY OF THEM COME TO ME WITH INJURIES, ILLNESSES... OR OTHER PROBLEMS...
WHEN I WAS YOUNGER, I WASN'T VERY GOOD AT TALK-ING TO PEOPLE...
BUT IT'S NOW SUCH A BIG PART OF MY JOB.
I FIGURE THAT WHEN STUDENTS COME TO ME WITH THEIR TROUBLES...
THE LEAST I CAN DO IS LISTEN TO THEM.
IF YOU EVER NEED TO TALK, I'M HERE FOR YOU...
...KATO-SAN.

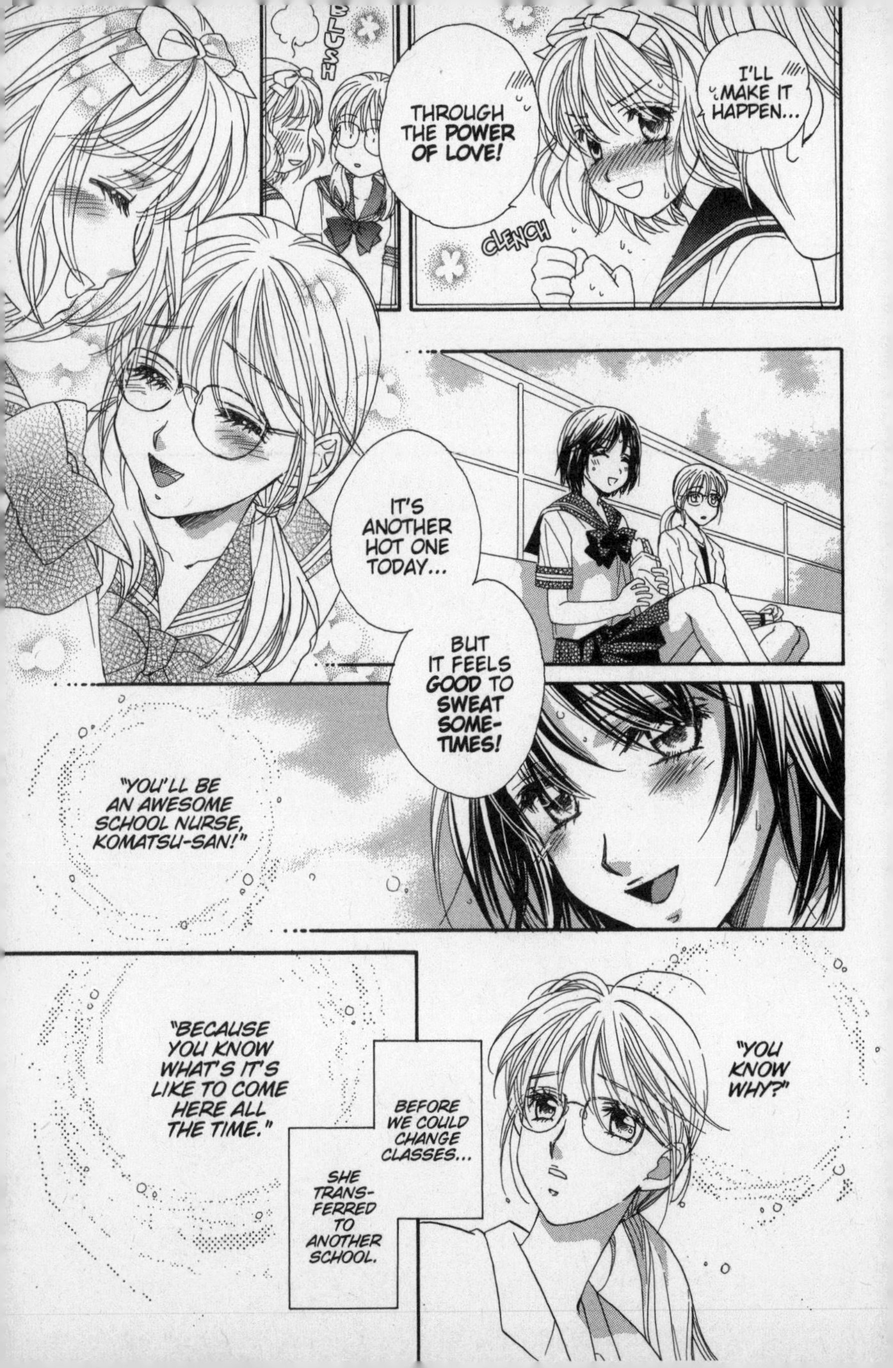
I'LL MAKE IT HAPPEN...
THROUGH THE POWER OF LOVE!
CLENCH
BLUSH
IT'S ANOTHER HOT ONE TODAY...
BUT IT FEELS GOOD TO SWEAT SOME-TIMES!
"YOU'LL BE AN AWESOME SCHOOL NURSE, KOMATSU-SAN!"
"YOU KNOW WHY?"
"BECAUSE YOU KNOW WHAT'S IT'S LIKE TO COME HERE ALL THE TIME."
BEFORE WE COULD CHANGE CLASSES...
SHE TRANS-FERRED TO ANOTHER SCHOOL.

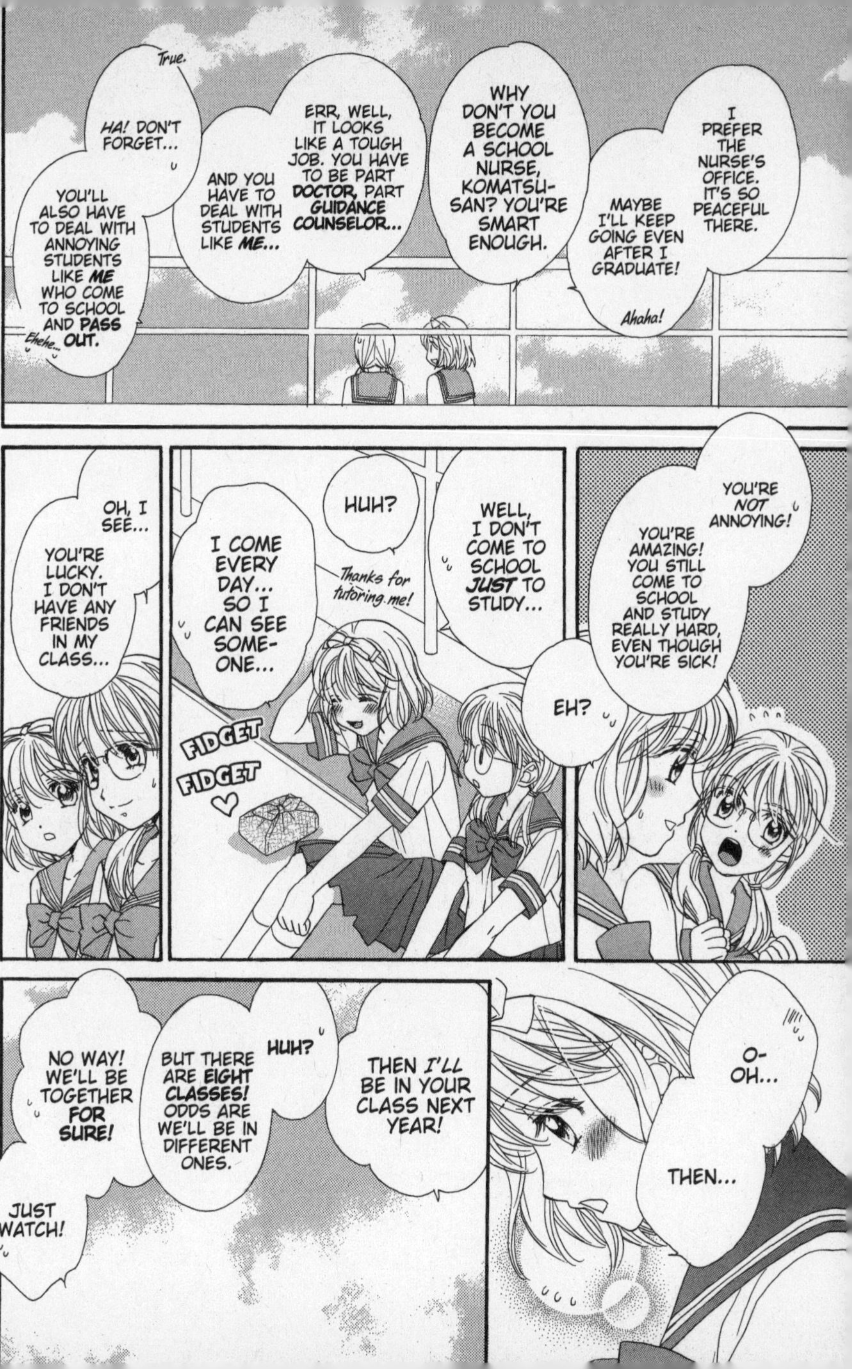
I PREFER THE NURSE'S OFFICE. IT'S SO PEACEFUL THERE.
MAYBE I'LL KEEP GOING EVEN AFTER I GRADUATE!
Ahaha!
WHY DON'T YOU BECOME A SCHOOL NURSE, KOMATSU-SAN? YOU'RE SMART ENOUGH.
ERR, WELL, IT LOOKS LIKE A TOUGH JOB. YOU HAVE TO BE PART **DOCTOR,** PART **GUIDANCE COUNSELOR...**
AND YOU HAVE TO DEAL WITH STUDENTS LIKE ***ME...***
True.
HA! DON'T FORGET...
YOU'LL ALSO HAVE TO DEAL WITH ANNOYING STUDENTS LIKE ***ME*** WHO COME TO SCHOOL AND **PASS OUT.**
Ehehe...
YOU'RE *NOT* ANNOYING!
YOU'RE AMAZING! YOU STILL COME TO SCHOOL AND STUDY REALLY HARD, EVEN THOUGH YOU'RE SICK!
EH?
WELL, I DON'T COME TO SCHOOL ***JUST*** TO STUDY...
HUH?
Thanks for tutoring me!
I COME EVERY DAY... SO I CAN SEE SOME-ONE...
FIDGET
FIDGET
OH, I SEE...
YOU'RE LUCKY. I DON'T HAVE ANY FRIENDS IN MY CLASS...
O-OH...
THEN...
THEN *I'LL* BE IN YOUR CLASS NEXT YEAR!
HUH?
BUT THERE ARE **EIGHT CLASSES!** ODDS ARE WE'LL BE IN DIFFERENT ONES.
NO WAY! WE'LL BE TOGETHER **FOR SURE!**
JUST WATCH!

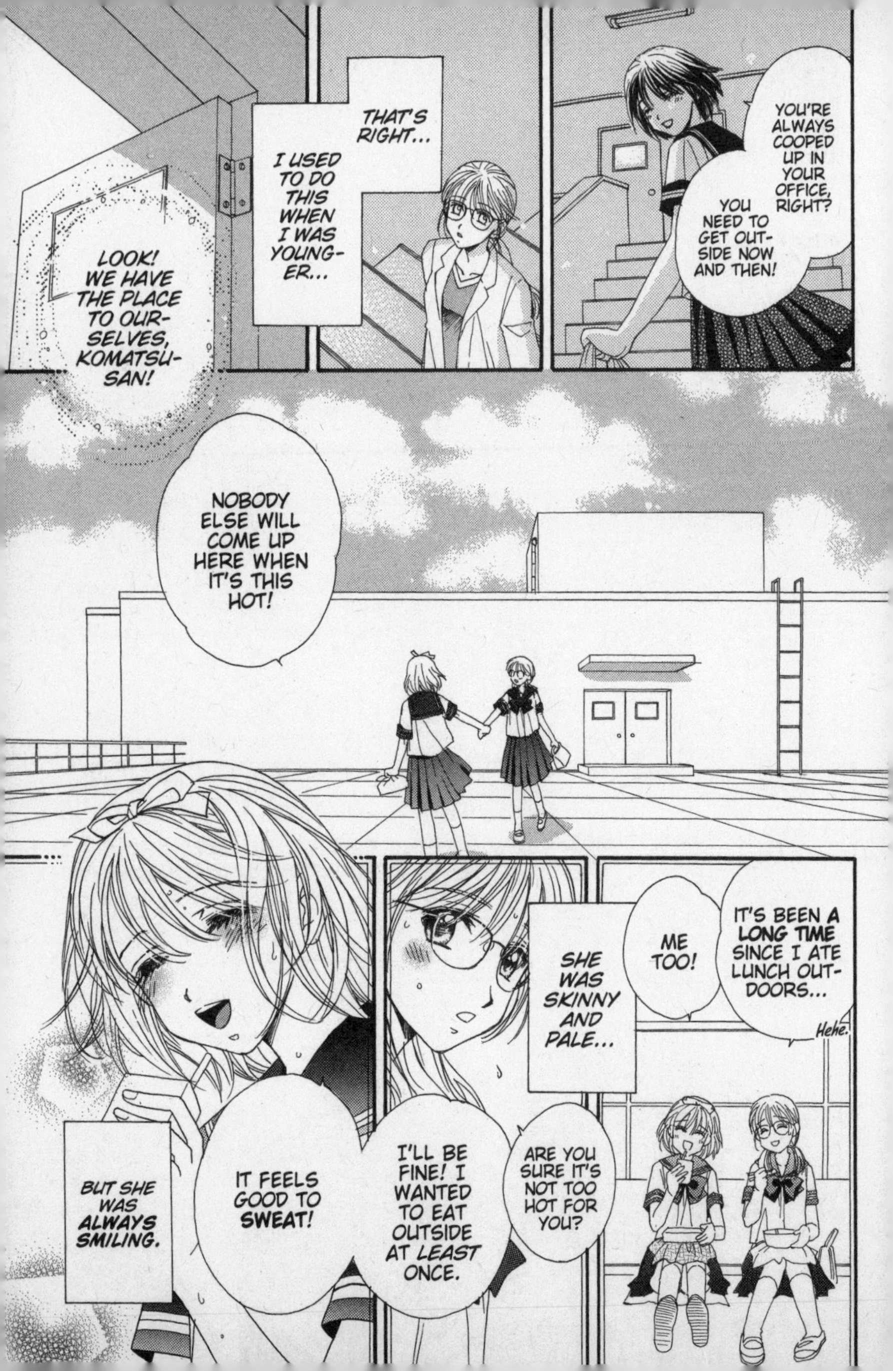
YOU'RE ALWAYS COOPED UP IN YOUR OFFICE, RIGHT?
YOU NEED TO GET OUT-SIDE NOW AND THEN!
THAT'S RIGHT...
I USED TO DO THIS WHEN I WAS YOUNG-ER...
LOOK! WE HAVE THE PLACE TO OUR-SELVES, KOMATSU-SAN!
NOBODY ELSE WILL COME UP HERE WHEN IT'S THIS HOT!
IT'S BEEN A LONG TIME SINCE I ATE LUNCH OUT-DOORS...
Hehe.
ME TOO!
SHE WAS SKINNY AND PALE...
ARE YOU SURE IT'S NOT TOO HOT FOR YOU?
I'LL BE FINE! I WANTED TO EAT OUTSIDE AT LEAST ONCE.
IT FEELS GOOD TO SWEAT!
BUT SHE WAS ALWAYS SMILING.

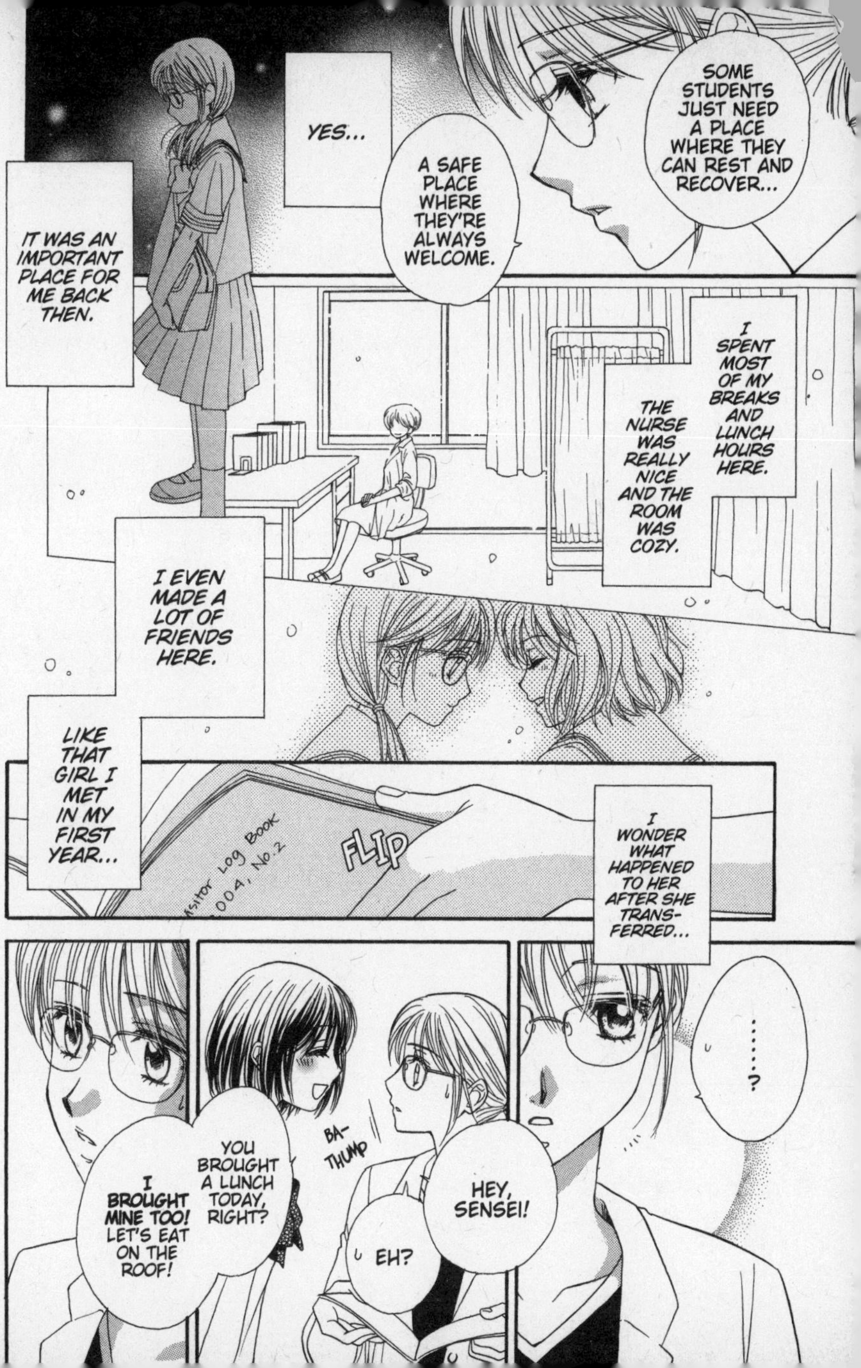

SOME STUDENTS JUST NEED A PLACE WHERE THEY CAN REST AND RECOVER...
A SAFE PLACE WHERE THEY'RE ALWAYS WELCOME.
YES...
IT WAS AN IMPORTANT PLACE FOR ME BACK THEN.
I SPENT MOST OF MY BREAKS AND LUNCH HOURS HERE.
THE NURSE WAS REALLY NICE AND THE ROOM WAS COZY.
I EVEN MADE A LOT OF FRIENDS HERE.
LIKE THAT GIRL I MET IN MY FIRST YEAR...
I WONDER WHAT HAPPENED TO HER AFTER SHE TRANSFERRED...
FLIP
isitor Log Book
004, No.2
......?
HEY, SENSEI!
EH?
BA-THUMP
YOU BROUGHT A LUNCH TODAY, RIGHT?
I BROUGHT MINE TOO! LET'S EAT ON THE ROOF!

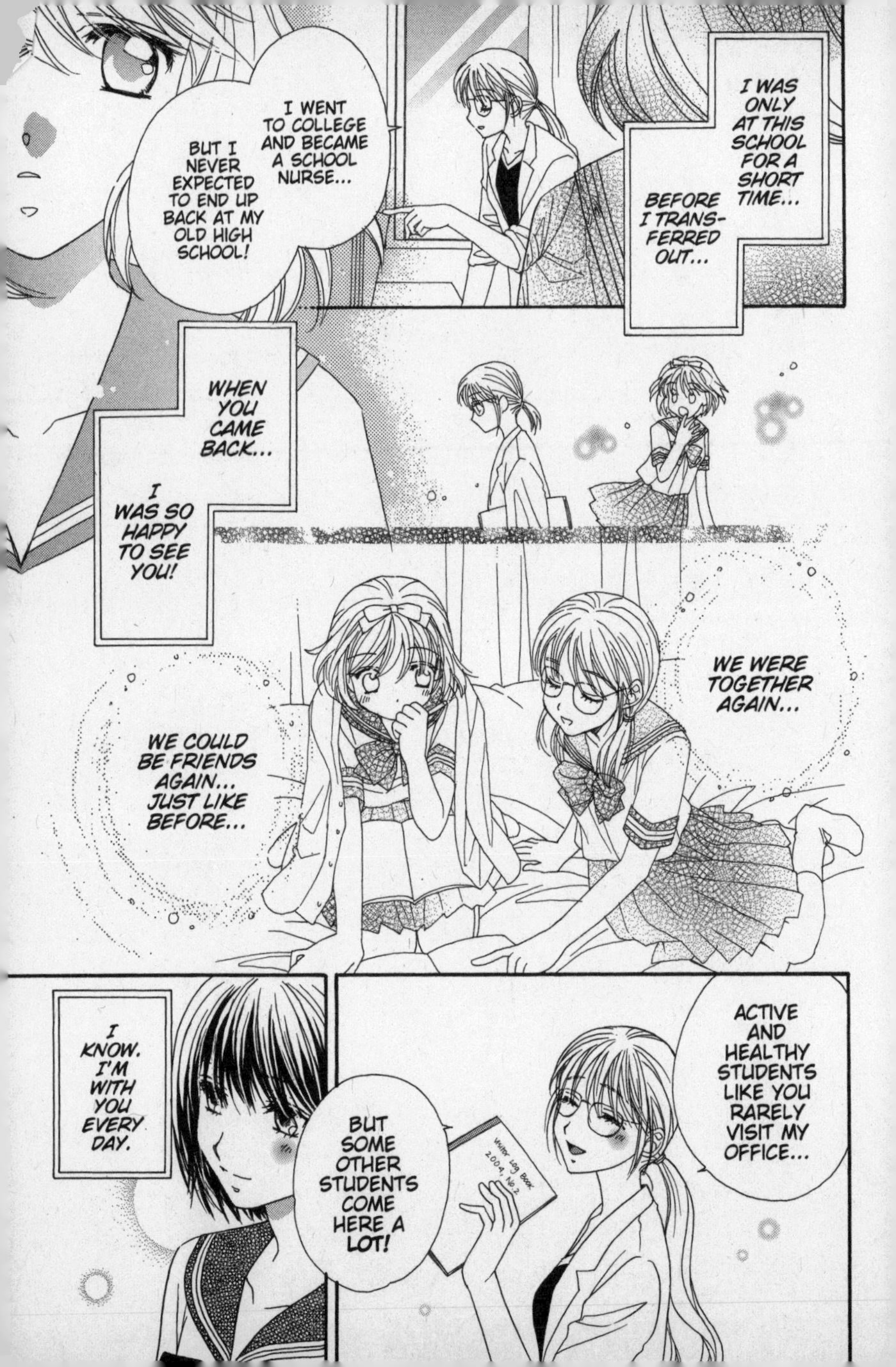
I WAS ONLY AT THIS SCHOOL FOR A SHORT TIME...
BEFORE I TRANSFERRED OUT...
I WENT TO COLLEGE AND BECAME A SCHOOL NURSE...
BUT I NEVER EXPECTED TO END UP BACK AT MY OLD HIGH SCHOOL!
WHEN YOU CAME BACK...
I WAS SO HAPPY TO SEE YOU!
WE WERE TOGETHER AGAIN...
WE COULD BE FRIENDS AGAIN... JUST LIKE BEFORE...
ACTIVE AND HEALTHY STUDENTS LIKE YOU RARELY VISIT MY OFFICE...
Visitor Log Book 2004, No.2
BUT SOME OTHER STUDENTS COME HERE A LOT!
I KNOW. I'M WITH YOU EVERY DAY.

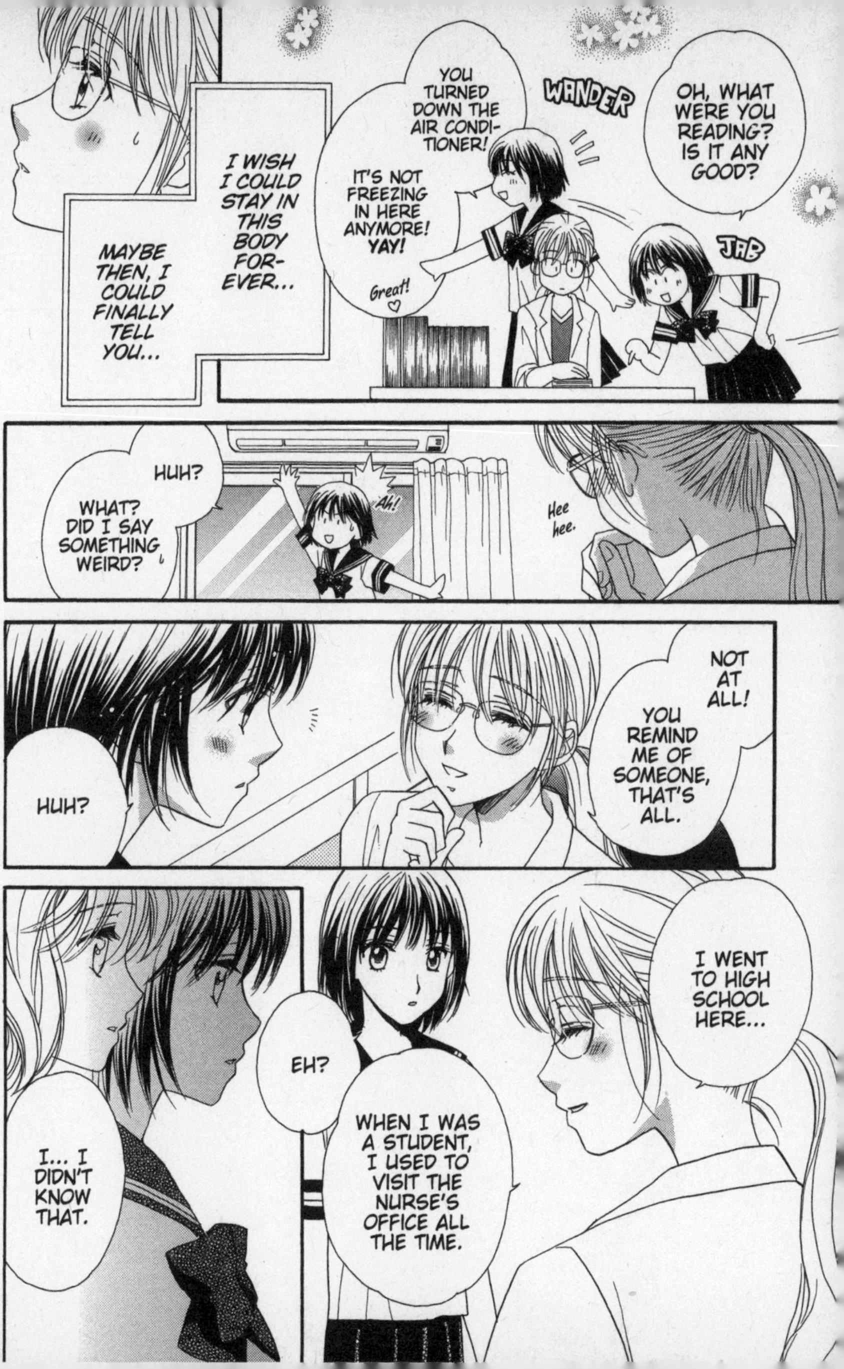
OH, WHAT WERE YOU READING? IS IT ANY GOOD?
JAB
WANDER
YOU TURNED DOWN THE AIR CONDITIONER!
IT'S NOT FREEZING IN HERE ANYMORE! YAY!
Great! ♥
I WISH I COULD STAY IN THIS BODY FOREVER...
MAYBE THEN, I COULD FINALLY TELL YOU...
Hee hee.
HUH?
WHAT? DID I SAY SOMETHING WEIRD?
Ah!
NOT AT ALL!
YOU REMIND ME OF SOMEONE, THAT'S ALL.
HUH?
I WENT TO HIGH SCHOOL HERE...
EH?
WHEN I WAS A STUDENT, I USED TO VISIT THE NURSE'S OFFICE ALL THE TIME.
I... I DIDN'T KNOW THAT.

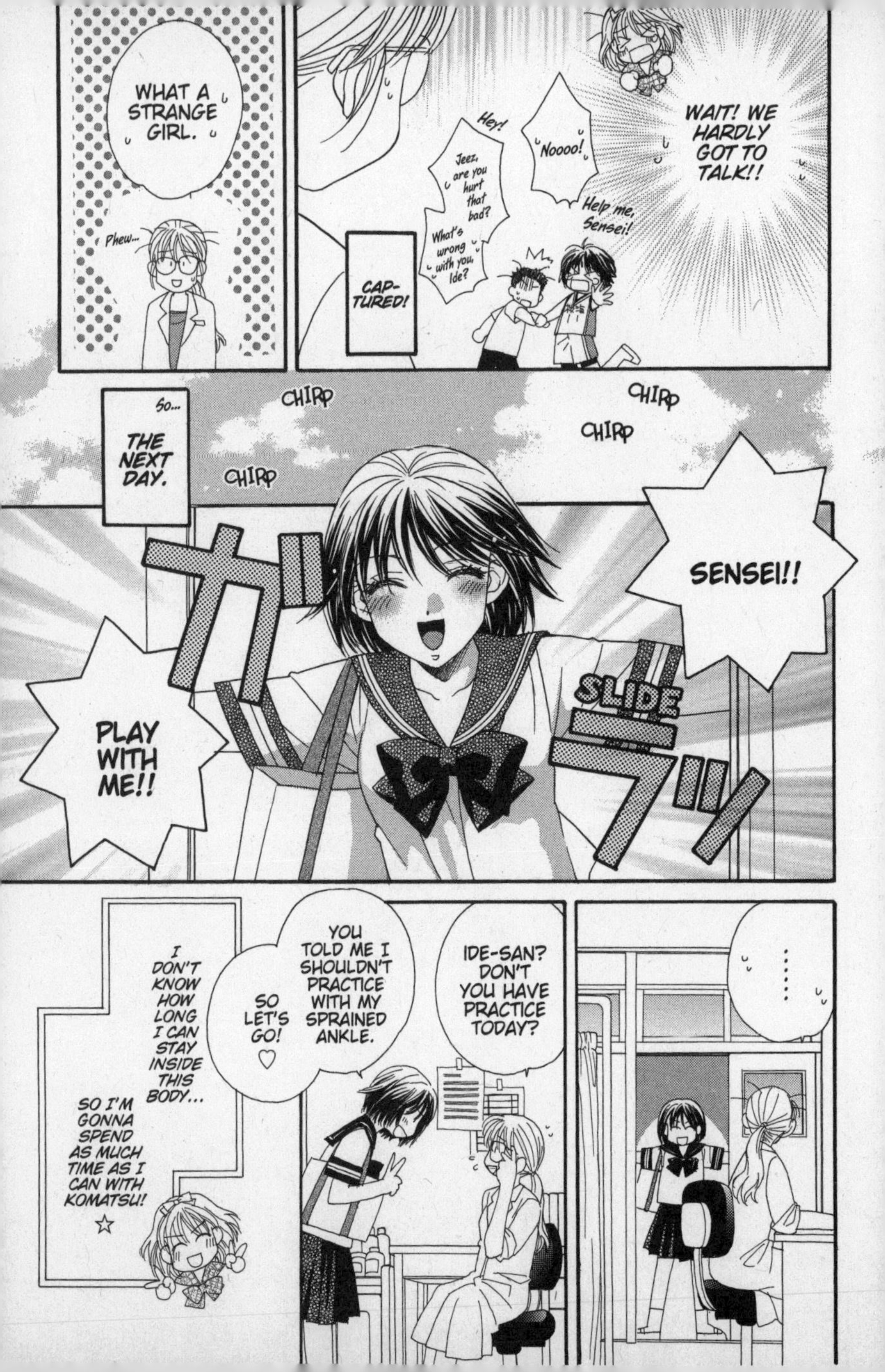
WAIT! WE HARDLY GOT TO TALK!!
Noooo!
Help me, Sensei!
Hey!
Jeez, are you hurt that bad?
What's wrong with you, Ide?
CAP-TURED!
WHAT A STRANGE GIRL.
Phew...
CHIRP
CHIRP
CHIRP
So... THE NEXT DAY.
CHIRP
SENSEI!!
SLIDE
ガラッ
PLAY WITH ME!!
......
IDE-SAN? DON'T YOU HAVE PRACTICE TODAY?
YOU TOLD ME I SHOULDN'T PRACTICE WITH MY SPRAINED ANKLE.
SO LET'S GO! ♡
I DON'T KNOW HOW LONG I CAN STAY INSIDE THIS BODY...
SO I'M GONNA SPEND AS MUCH TIME AS I CAN WITH KOMATSU! ☆

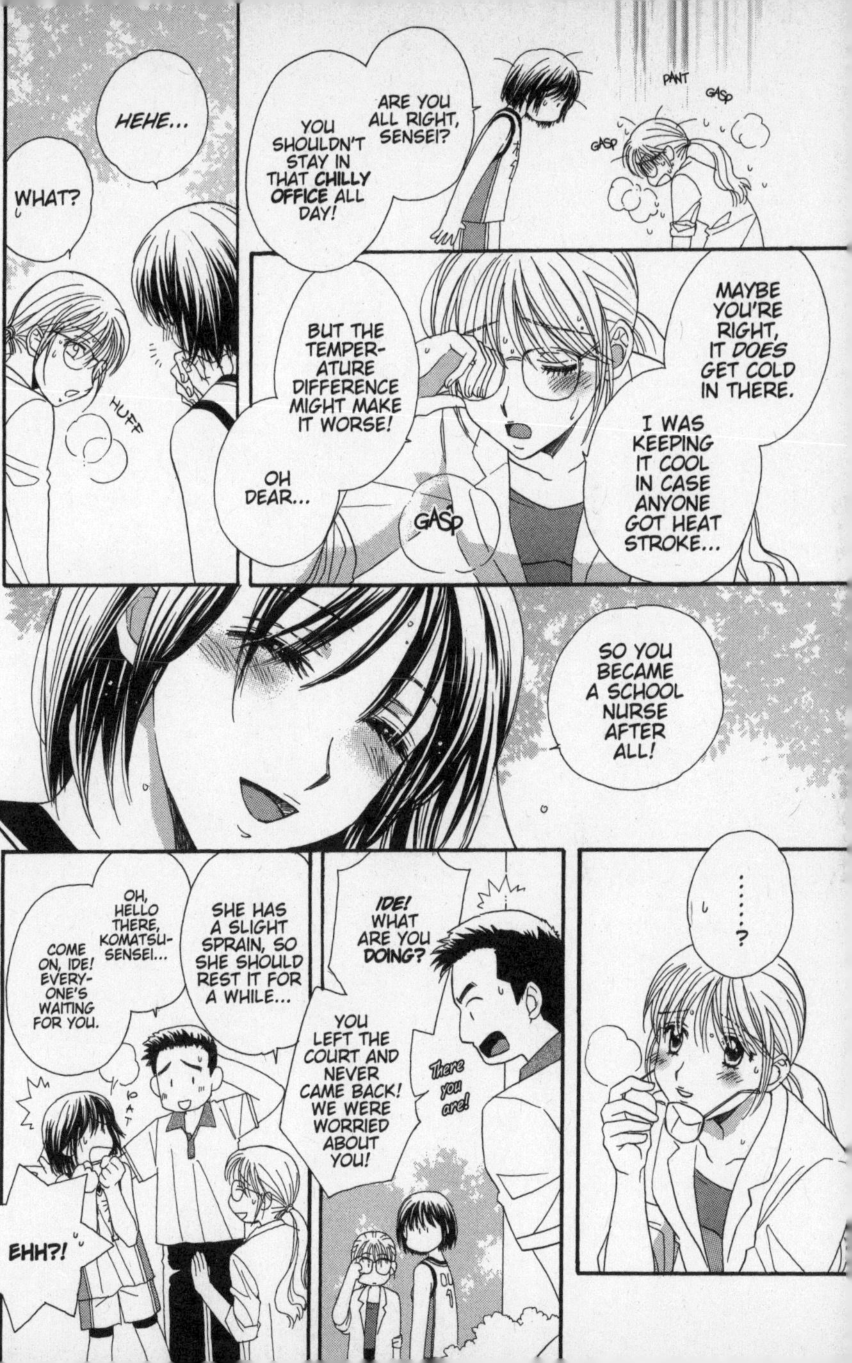
PANT
GASP
GASP
ARE YOU ALL RIGHT, SENSEI?
YOU SHOULDN'T STAY IN THAT CHILLY OFFICE ALL DAY!
MAYBE YOU'RE RIGHT, IT DOES GET COLD IN THERE.
I WAS KEEPING IT COOL IN CASE ANYONE GOT HEAT STROKE...
GASP
BUT THE TEMPERATURE DIFFERENCE MIGHT MAKE IT WORSE!
OH DEAR...
HEHE...
WHAT?
HUFF
SO YOU BECAME A SCHOOL NURSE AFTER ALL!
......?
IDE! WHAT ARE YOU DOING?
YOU LEFT THE COURT AND NEVER CAME BACK! WE WERE WORRIED ABOUT YOU!
There you are!
SHE HAS A SLIGHT SPRAIN, SO SHE SHOULD REST IT FOR A WHILE...
OH, HELLO THERE, KOMATSU-SENSEI...
COME ON, IDE! EVERYONE'S WAITING FOR YOU.
PAT
EHH?!

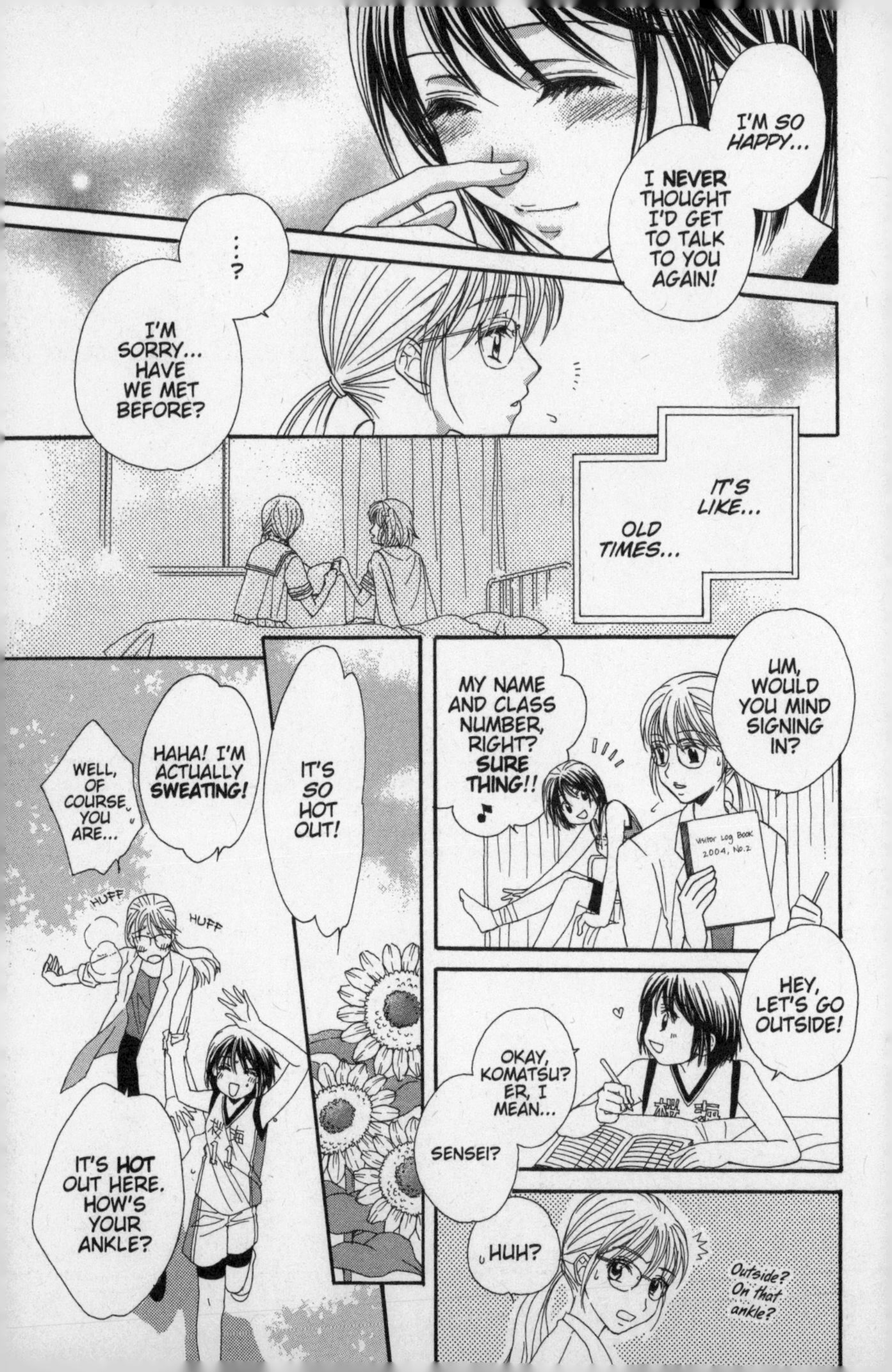
I'M SO HAPPY...
I NEVER THOUGHT I'D GET TO TALK TO YOU AGAIN!
...?
I'M SORRY... HAVE WE MET BEFORE?
IT'S LIKE...
OLD TIMES...
UM, WOULD YOU MIND SIGNING IN?
Visitor Log Book 2004, No.2
MY NAME AND CLASS NUMBER, RIGHT? SURE THING!!
HEY, LET'S GO OUTSIDE!
OKAY, KOMATSU? ER, I MEAN...
SENSEI?
HUH?
Outside? On that ankle?
IT'S SO HOT OUT!
HAHA! I'M ACTUALLY SWEATING!
WELL, OF COURSE YOU ARE...
HUFF
HUFF
IT'S HOT OUT HERE. HOW'S YOUR ANKLE?

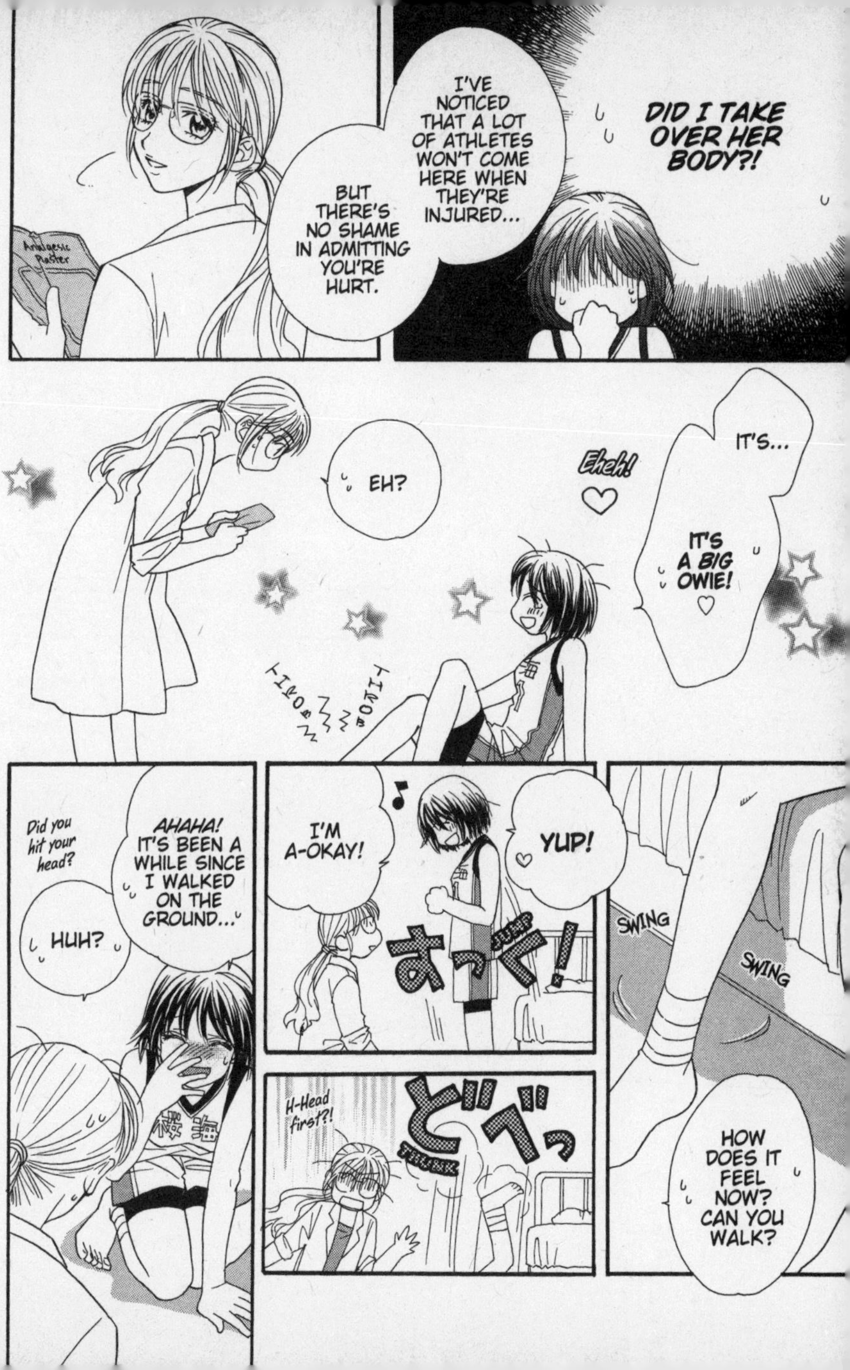
DID I TAKE OVER HER BODY?!
I'VE NOTICED THAT A LOT OF ATHLETES WON'T COME HERE WHEN THEY'RE INJURED...
BUT THERE'S NO SHAME IN ADMITTING YOU'RE HURT.
Analgesic Plaster
IT'S...
IT'S A BIG OWIE!
Eheh!
EH?
THROB
THROB
HOW DOES IT FEEL NOW? CAN YOU WALK?
SWING
SWING
YUP!
I'M A-OKAY!
すっく!
H-Head first?!
どべっ
AHAHA! IT'S BEEN A WHILE SINCE I WALKED ON THE GROUND...
HUH?
Did you hit your head?

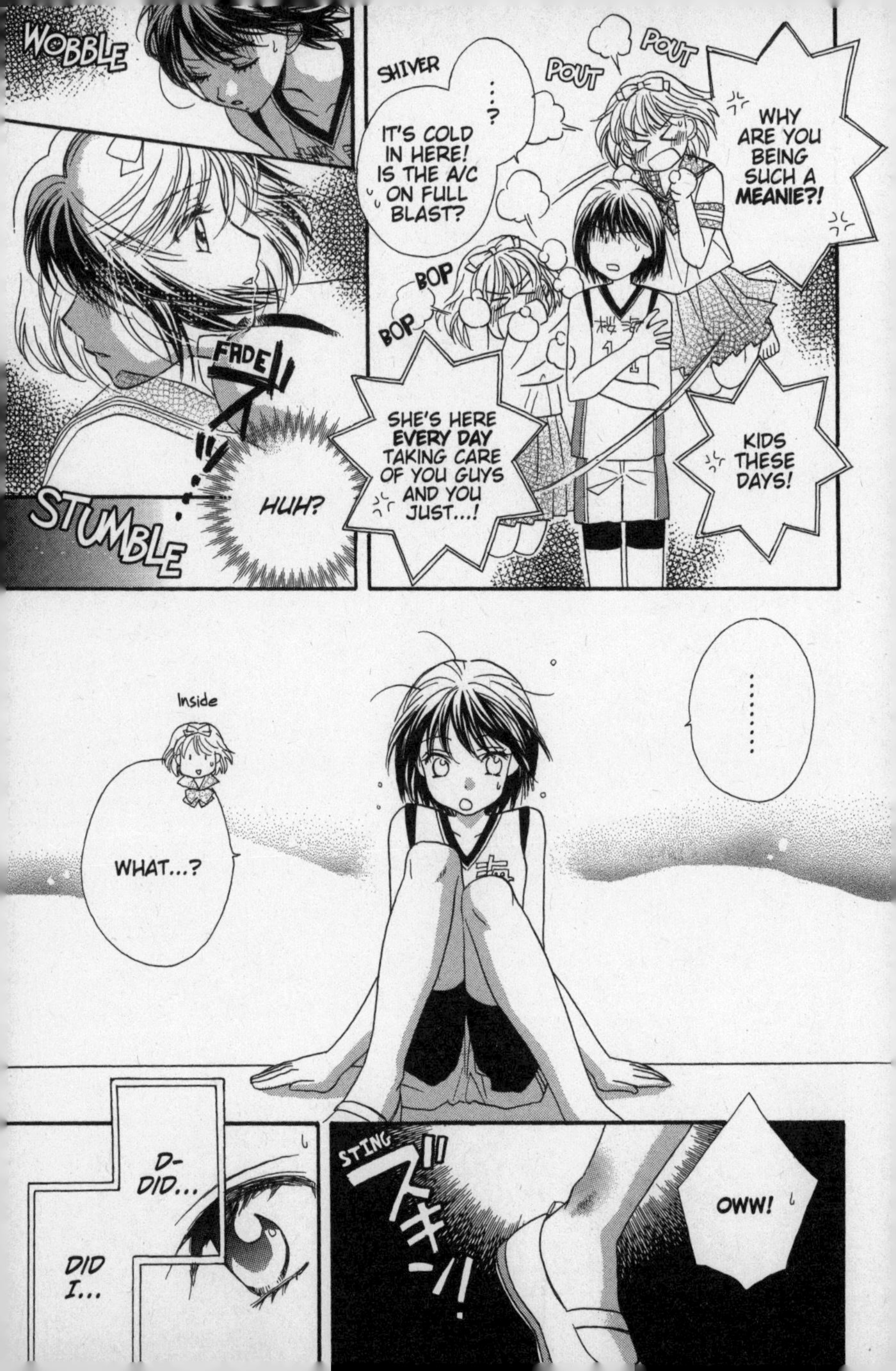
POUT
POUT
WHY ARE YOU BEING SUCH A MEANIE?!
SHIVER
...?
IT'S COLD IN HERE! IS THE A/C ON FULL BLAST?
BOP
BOP
KIDS THESE DAYS!
SHE'S HERE EVERY DAY TAKING CARE OF YOU GUYS AND YOU JUST...!
WOBBLE
FADE
HUH?
STUMBLE
......
Inside
WHAT...?
OWW!
STING
ズキー!!
D-DID...
DID I...

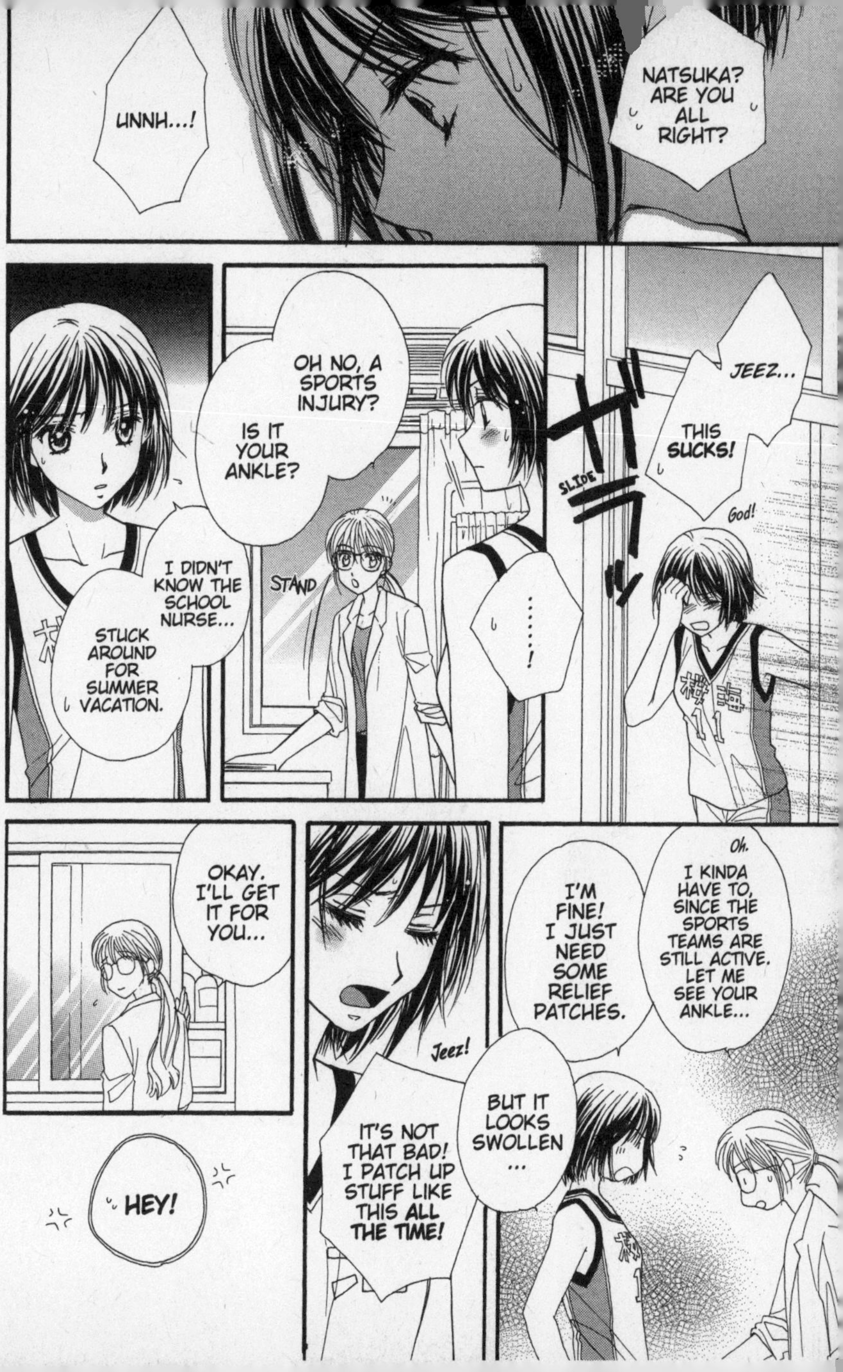
NATSUKA? ARE YOU ALL RIGHT?
UNNH...!
JEEZ...
THIS SUCKS!
God!
ガラッ
SLIDE
OH NO, A SPORTS INJURY?
IS IT YOUR ANKLE?
STAND
......!
I DIDN'T KNOW THE SCHOOL NURSE...
STUCK AROUND FOR SUMMER VACATION.
Oh.
I KINDA HAVE TO, SINCE THE SPORTS TEAMS ARE STILL ACTIVE. LET ME SEE YOUR ANKLE...
I'M FINE! I JUST NEED SOME RELIEF PATCHES.
BUT IT LOOKS SWOLLEN...
Jeez!
IT'S NOT THAT BAD! I PATCH UP STUFF LIKE THIS ALL THE TIME!
OKAY. I'LL GET IT FOR YOU...
HEY!

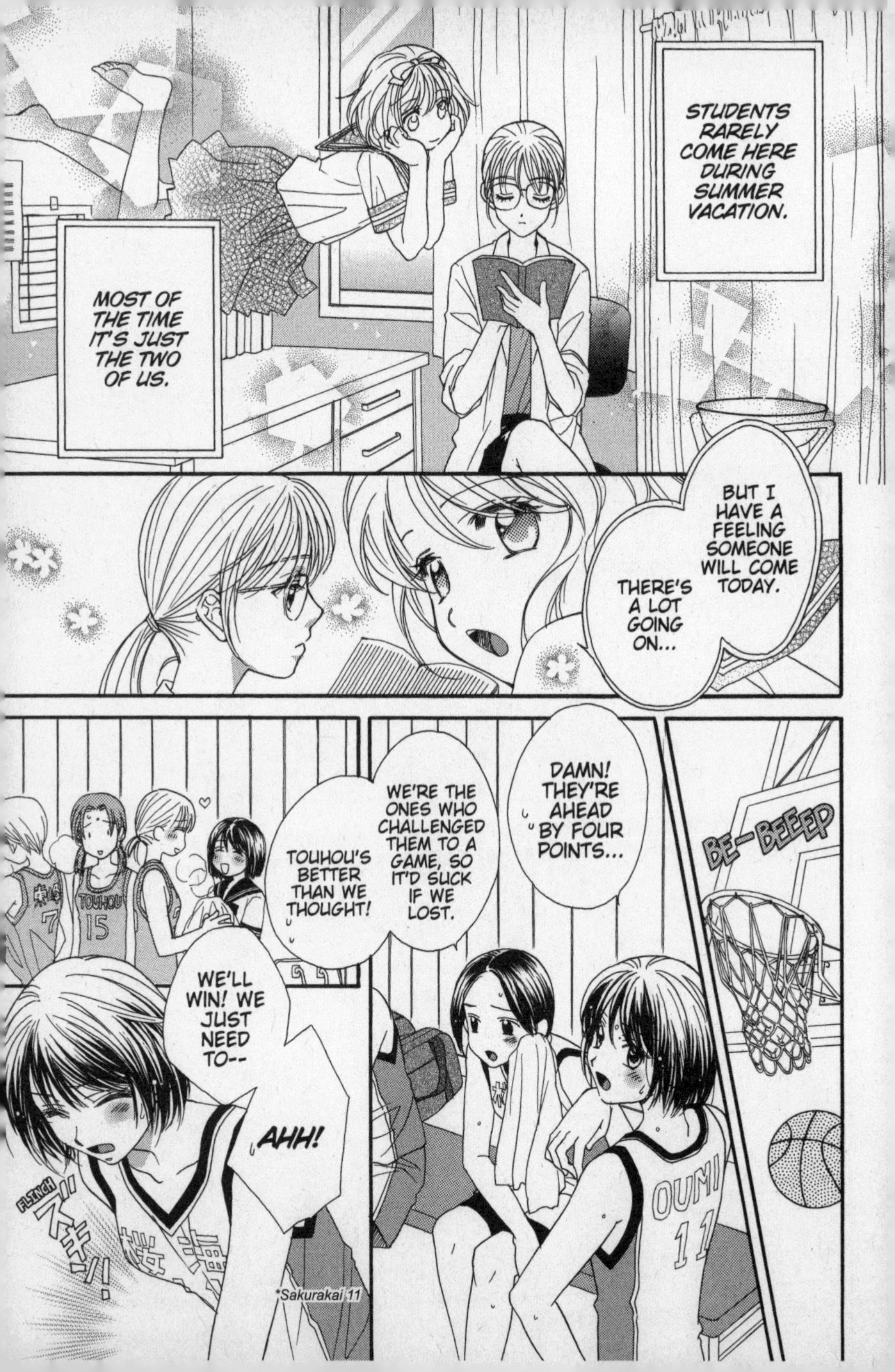
STUDENTS RARELY COME HERE DURING SUMMER VACATION.
MOST OF THE TIME IT'S JUST THE TWO OF US.
BUT I HAVE A FEELING SOMEONE WILL COME TODAY.
THERE'S A LOT GOING ON...
BE-BEEEP
DAMN! THEY'RE AHEAD BY FOUR POINTS...
WE'RE THE ONES WHO CHALLENGED THEM TO A GAME, SO IT'D SUCK IF WE LOST.
TOUHOU'S BETTER THAN WE THOUGHT!
WE'LL WIN! WE JUST NEED TO--
AHH!
FLINCH
*Sakurakai 11

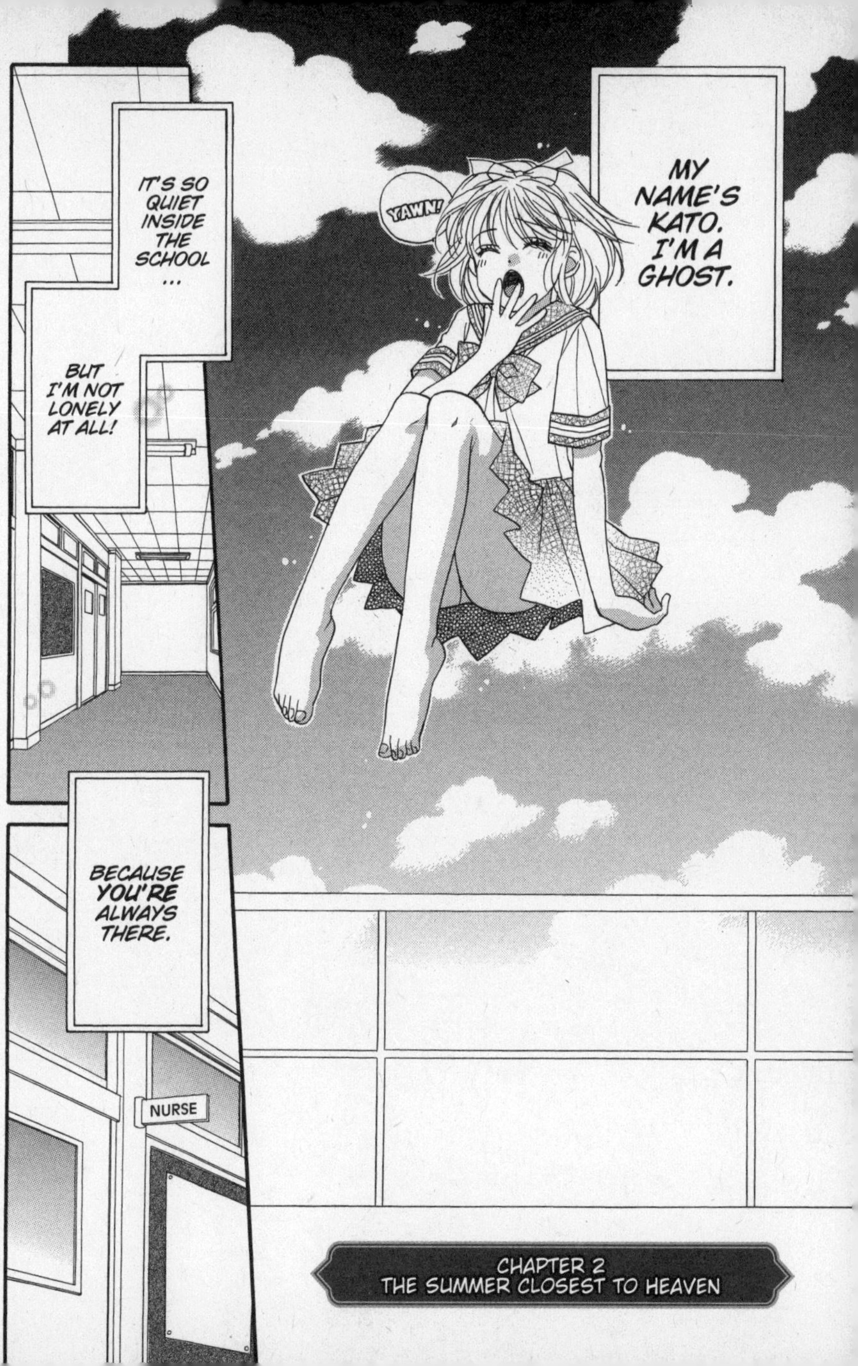
MY NAME'S KATO. I'M A GHOST.
YAWN!
IT'S SO QUIET INSIDE THE SCHOOL ...
BUT I'M NOT LONELY AT ALL!
BECAUSE YOU'RE ALWAYS THERE.
NURSE
CHAPTER 2
THE SUMMER CLOSEST TO HEAVEN

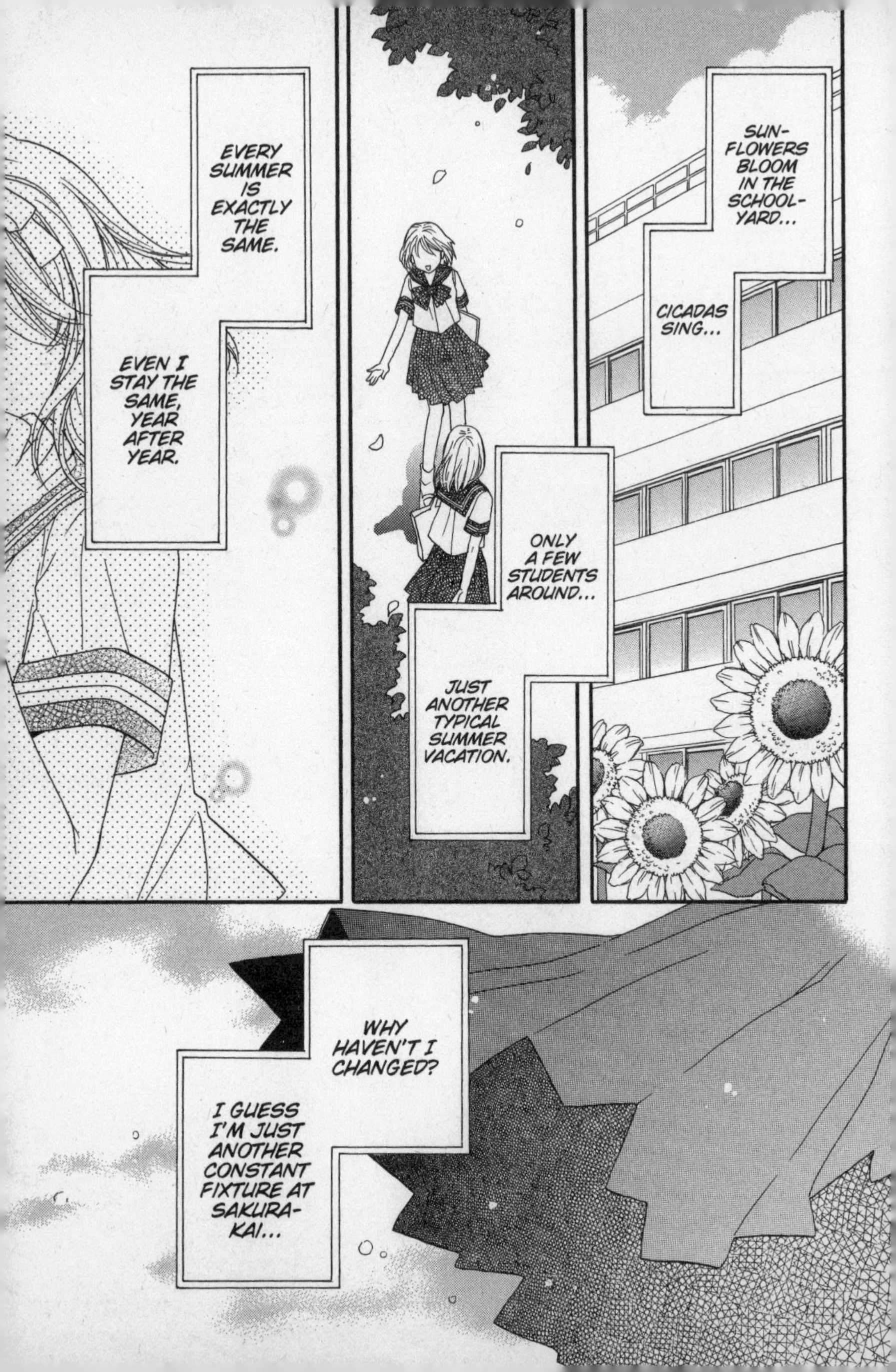
SUNFLOWERS BLOOM IN THE SCHOOLYARD...
CICADAS SING...
ONLY A FEW STUDENTS AROUND...
JUST ANOTHER TYPICAL SUMMER VACATION.
EVERY SUMMER IS EXACTLY THE SAME.
EVEN I STAY THE SAME, YEAR AFTER YEAR.
WHY HAVEN'T I CHANGED?
I GUESS I'M JUST ANOTHER CONSTANT FIXTURE AT SAKURA-KAI...

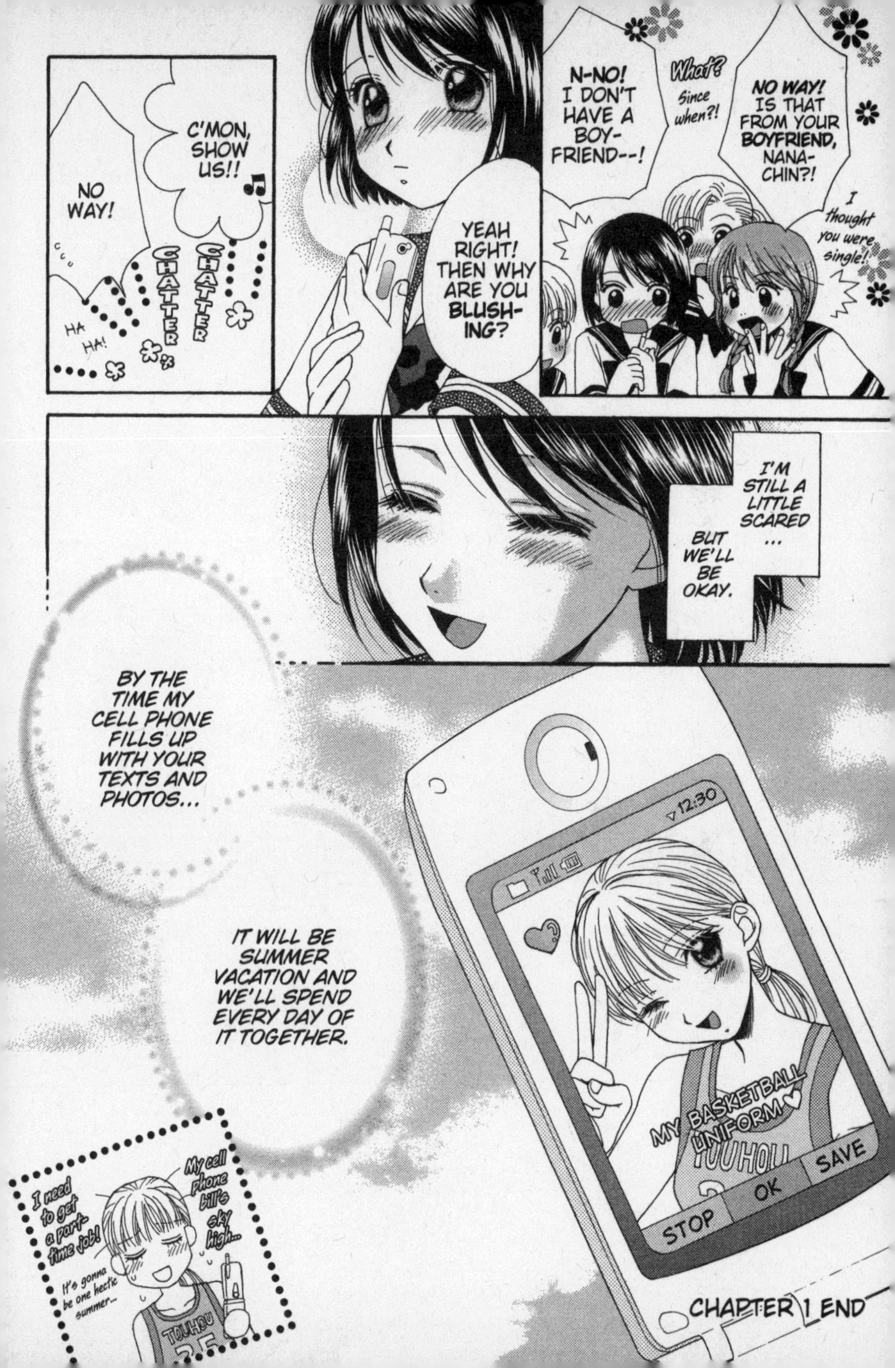
NO WAY! IS THAT FROM YOUR BOYFRIEND, NANA-CHIN?!
What? Since when?!
N-NO! I DON'T HAVE A BOY-FRIEND--!
I thought you were single!
YEAH RIGHT! THEN WHY ARE YOU BLUSH-ING?
C'MON, SHOW US!!
NO WAY!
CHATTER CHATTER
HA HA!
I'M STILL A LITTLE SCARED...
BUT WE'LL BE OKAY.
12:30
MY BASKETBALL UNIFORM♥
TOUHOU
SAVE
OK
STOP
BY THE TIME MY CELL PHONE FILLS UP WITH YOUR TEXTS AND PHOTOS...
IT WILL BE SUMMER VACATION AND WE'LL SPEND EVERY DAY OF IT TOGETHER.
My cell phone bill's sky high...
I need to get a part-time job!
It's gonna be one hectic summer...
TOUHOU
CHAPTER 1 END

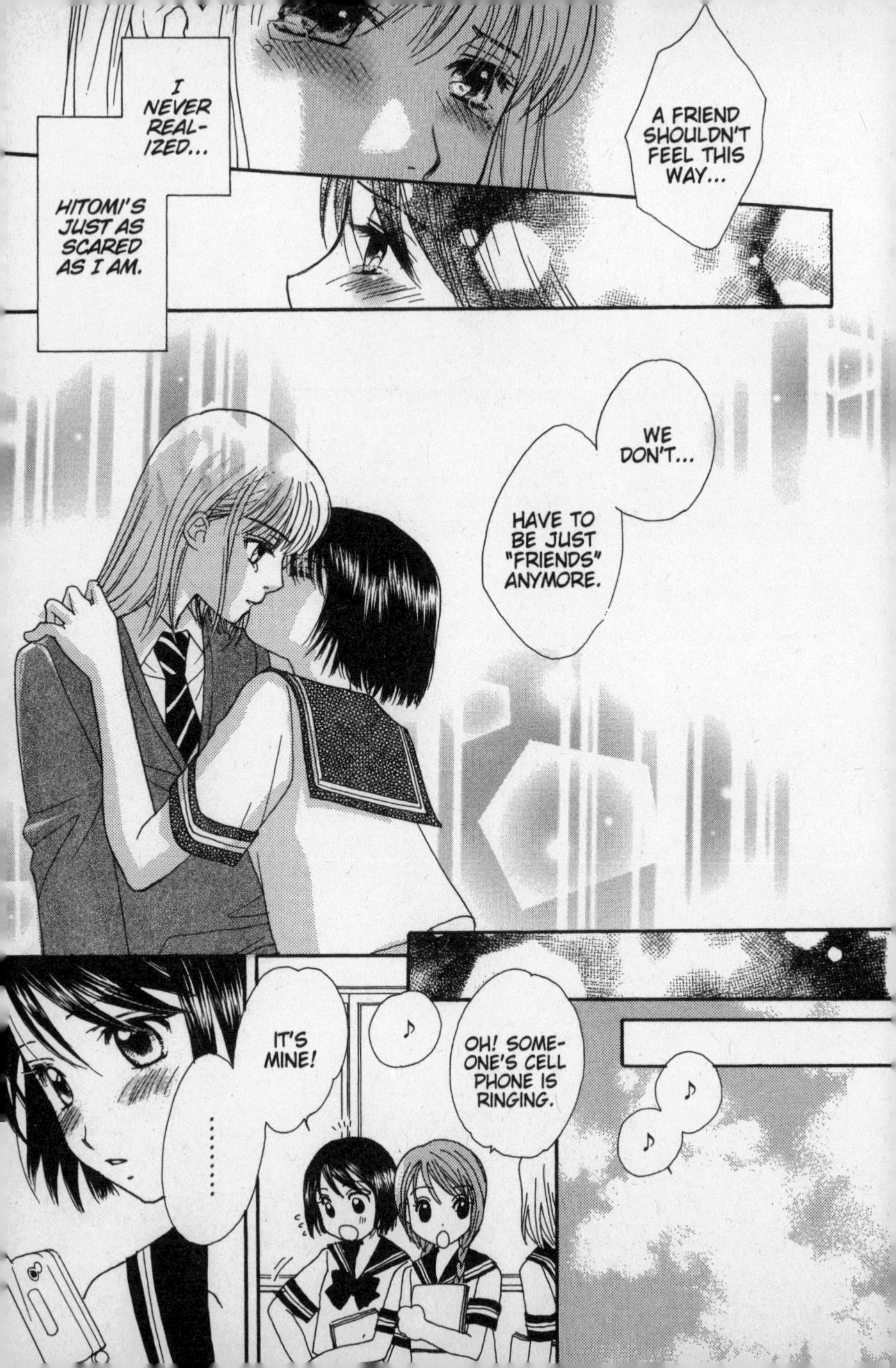
A FRIEND SHOULDN'T FEEL THIS WAY...
I NEVER REALIZED...
HITOMI'S JUST AS SCARED AS I AM.
WE DON'T...
HAVE TO BE JUST "FRIENDS" ANYMORE.
♪
♪
♪
OH! SOME-ONE'S CELL PHONE IS RINGING.
IT'S MINE!
......

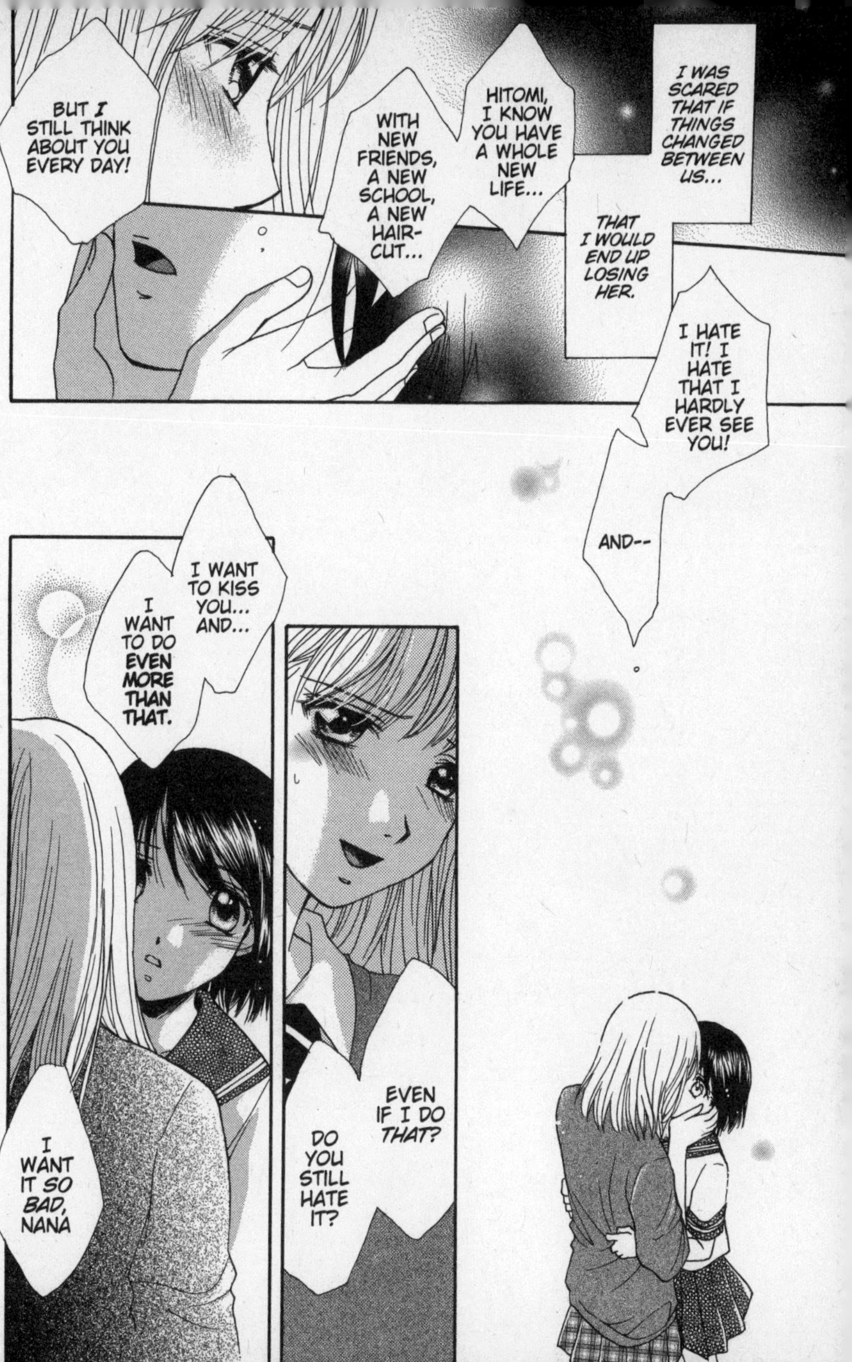
I WAS SCARED THAT IF THINGS CHANGED BETWEEN US...
THAT I WOULD END UP LOSING HER.
HITOMI, I KNOW YOU HAVE A WHOLE NEW LIFE...
WITH NEW FRIENDS, A NEW SCHOOL, A NEW HAIR-CUT...
BUT *I* STILL THINK ABOUT YOU EVERY DAY!
I HATE IT! I HATE THAT I HARDLY EVER SEE YOU!
AND--
I WANT TO KISS YOU... AND...
I WANT TO DO EVEN MORE THAN THAT.
EVEN IF I DO *THAT*?
DO YOU STILL HATE IT?
I WANT IT *SO BAD*, NANA

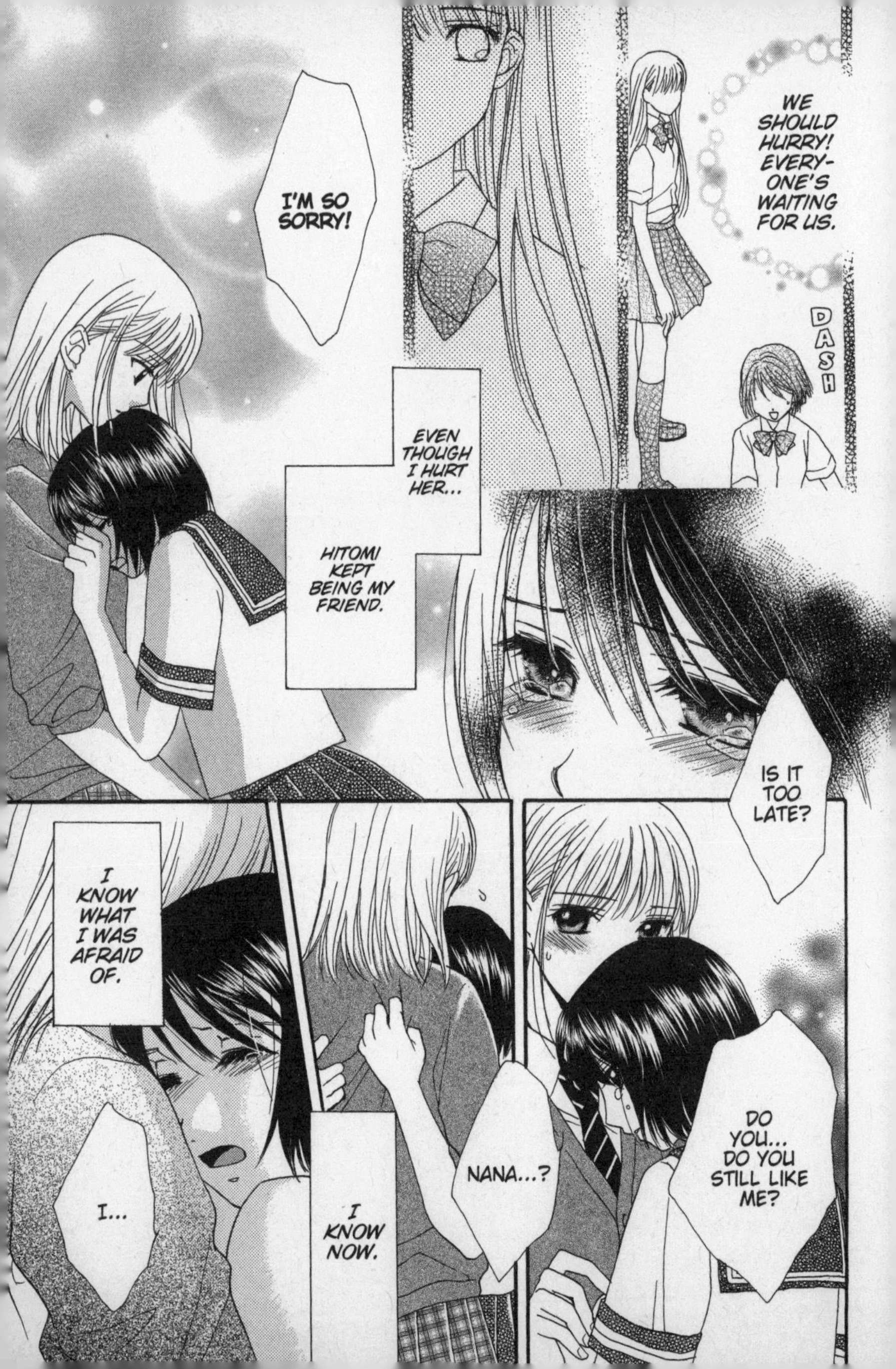
WE SHOULD HURRY! EVERY-ONE'S WAITING FOR US.
DASH
IS IT TOO LATE?
I'M SO SORRY!
EVEN THOUGH I HURT HER...
HITOMI KEPT BEING MY FRIEND.
DO YOU... DO YOU STILL LIKE ME?
NANA...?
I KNOW WHAT I WAS AFRAID OF.
I...
I KNOW NOW.

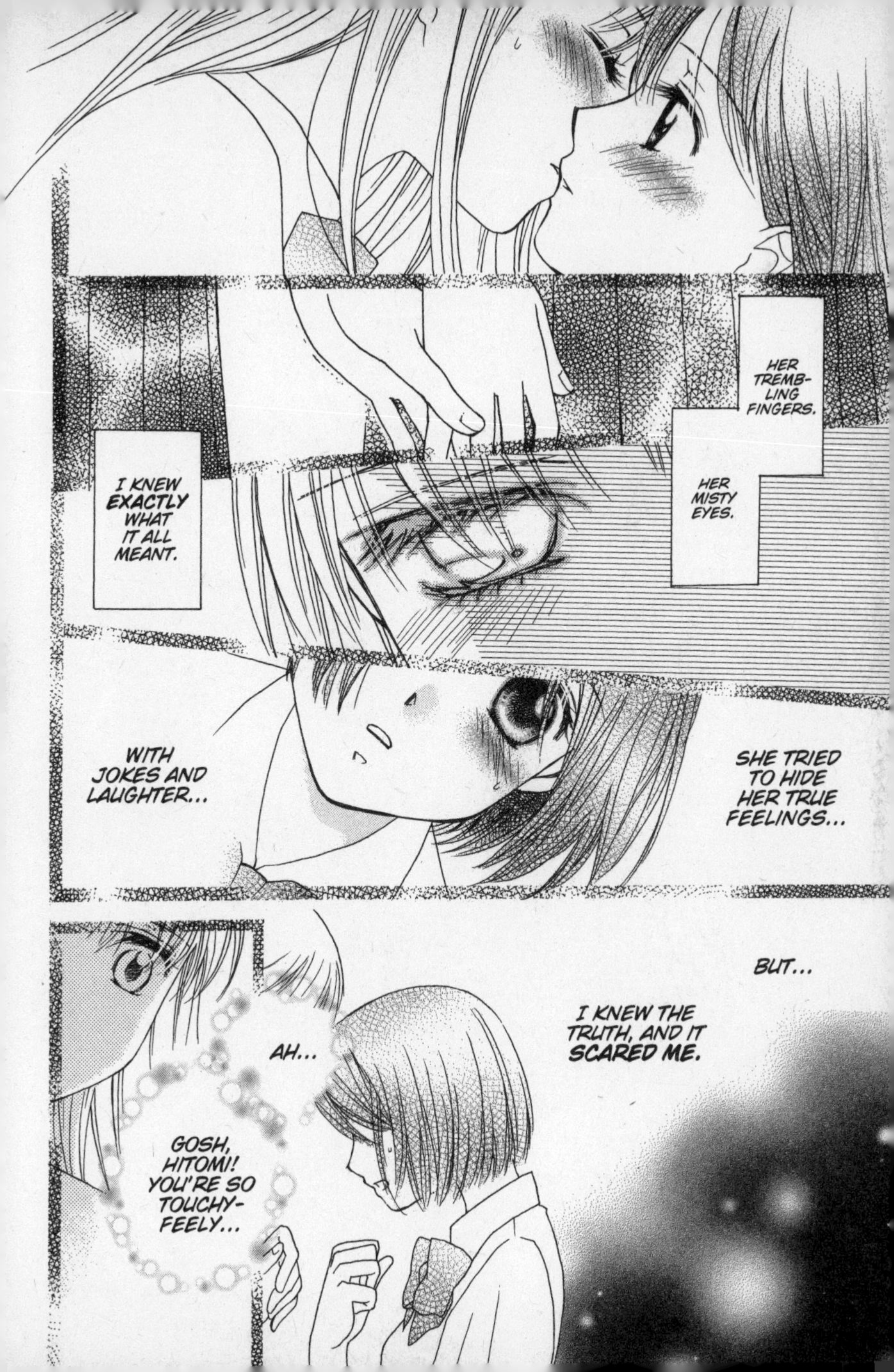
HER TREMBLING FINGERS.
HER MISTY EYES.
I KNEW EXACTLY WHAT IT ALL MEANT.
SHE TRIED TO HIDE HER TRUE FEELINGS...
WITH JOKES AND LAUGHTER...
BUT...
I KNEW THE TRUTH, AND IT SCARED ME.
AH...
GOSH, HITOMI! YOU'RE SO TOUCHY-FEELY...

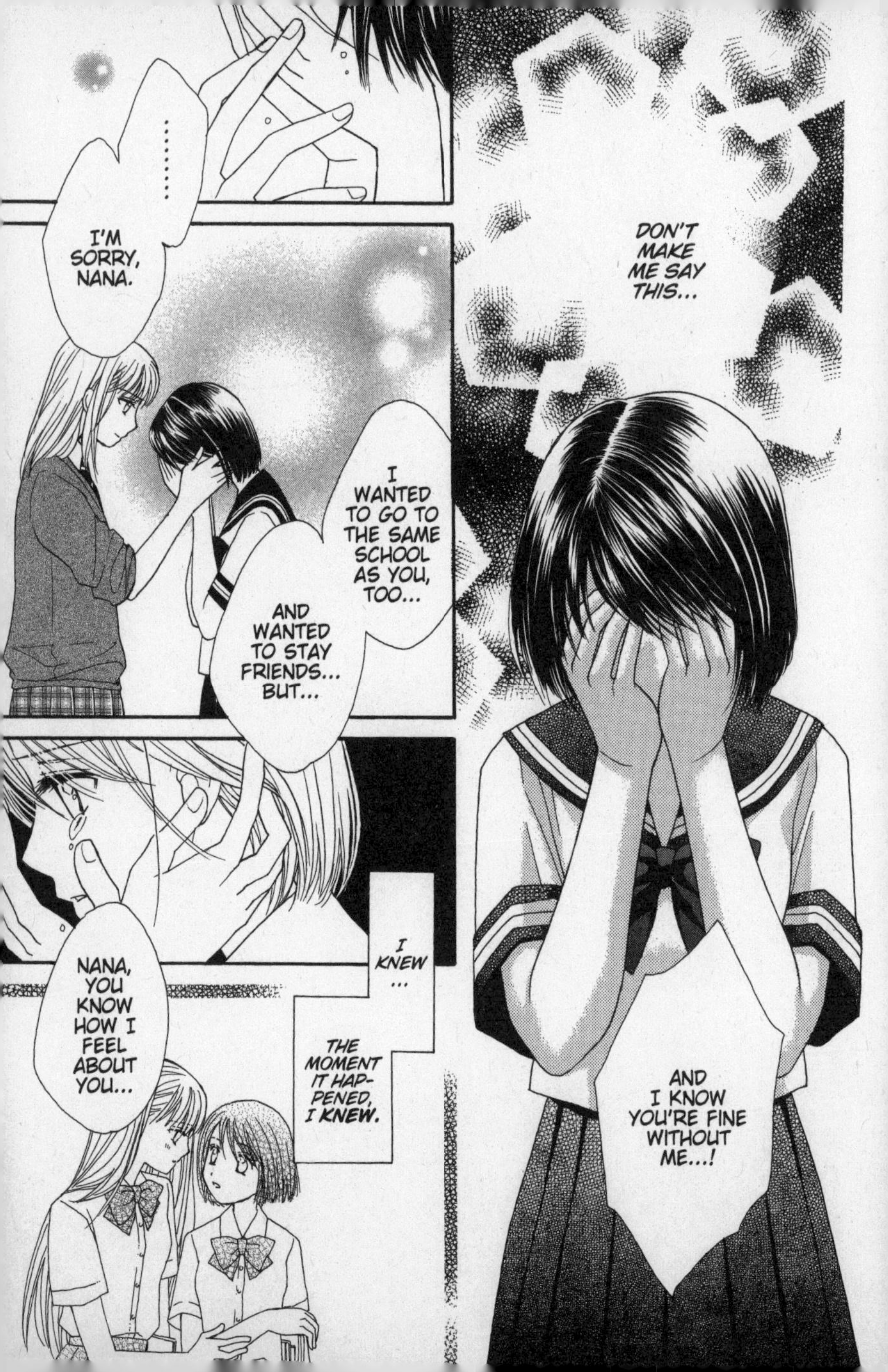
DON'T MAKE ME SAY THIS...
AND I KNOW YOU'RE FINE WITHOUT ME...!
......
I'M SORRY, NANA.
I WANTED TO GO TO THE SAME SCHOOL AS YOU, TOO...
AND WANTED TO STAY FRIENDS... BUT...
I KNEW ...
NANA, YOU KNOW HOW I FEEL ABOUT YOU...
THE MOMENT IT HAPPENED, I KNEW.

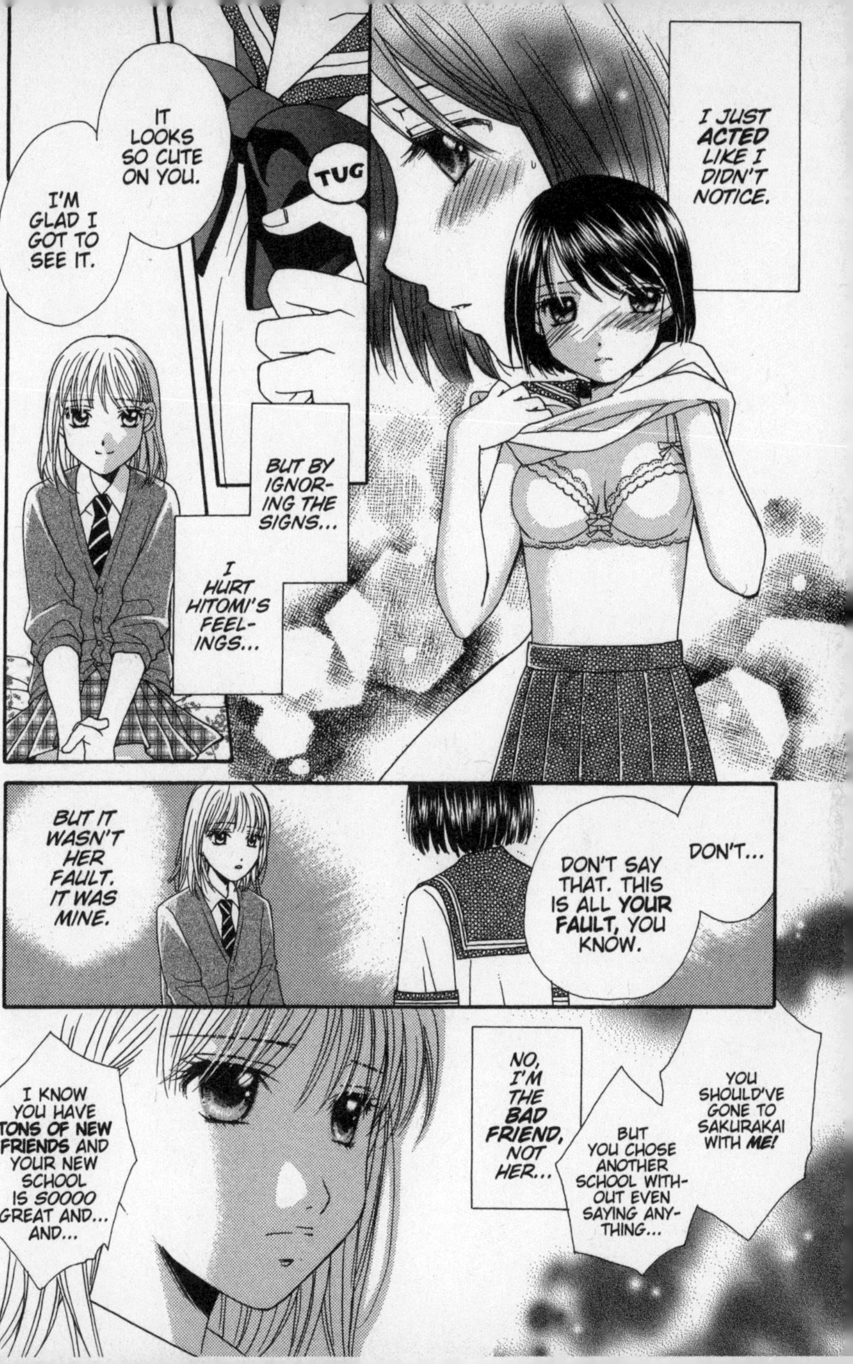
I JUST ACTED LIKE I DIDN'T NOTICE.
TUG
IT LOOKS SO CUTE ON YOU.
I'M GLAD I GOT TO SEE IT.
BUT BY IGNORING THE SIGNS...
I HURT HITOMI'S FEELINGS...
DON'T...
DON'T SAY THAT. THIS IS ALL YOUR FAULT, YOU KNOW.
BUT IT WASN'T HER FAULT. IT WAS MINE.
YOU SHOULD'VE GONE TO SAKURAKAI WITH ME!
BUT YOU CHOSE ANOTHER SCHOOL WITHOUT EVEN SAYING ANYTHING...
NO, I'M THE BAD FRIEND, NOT HER...
I KNOW YOU HAVE TONS OF NEW FRIENDS AND YOUR NEW SCHOOL IS SOOOO GREAT AND... AND...

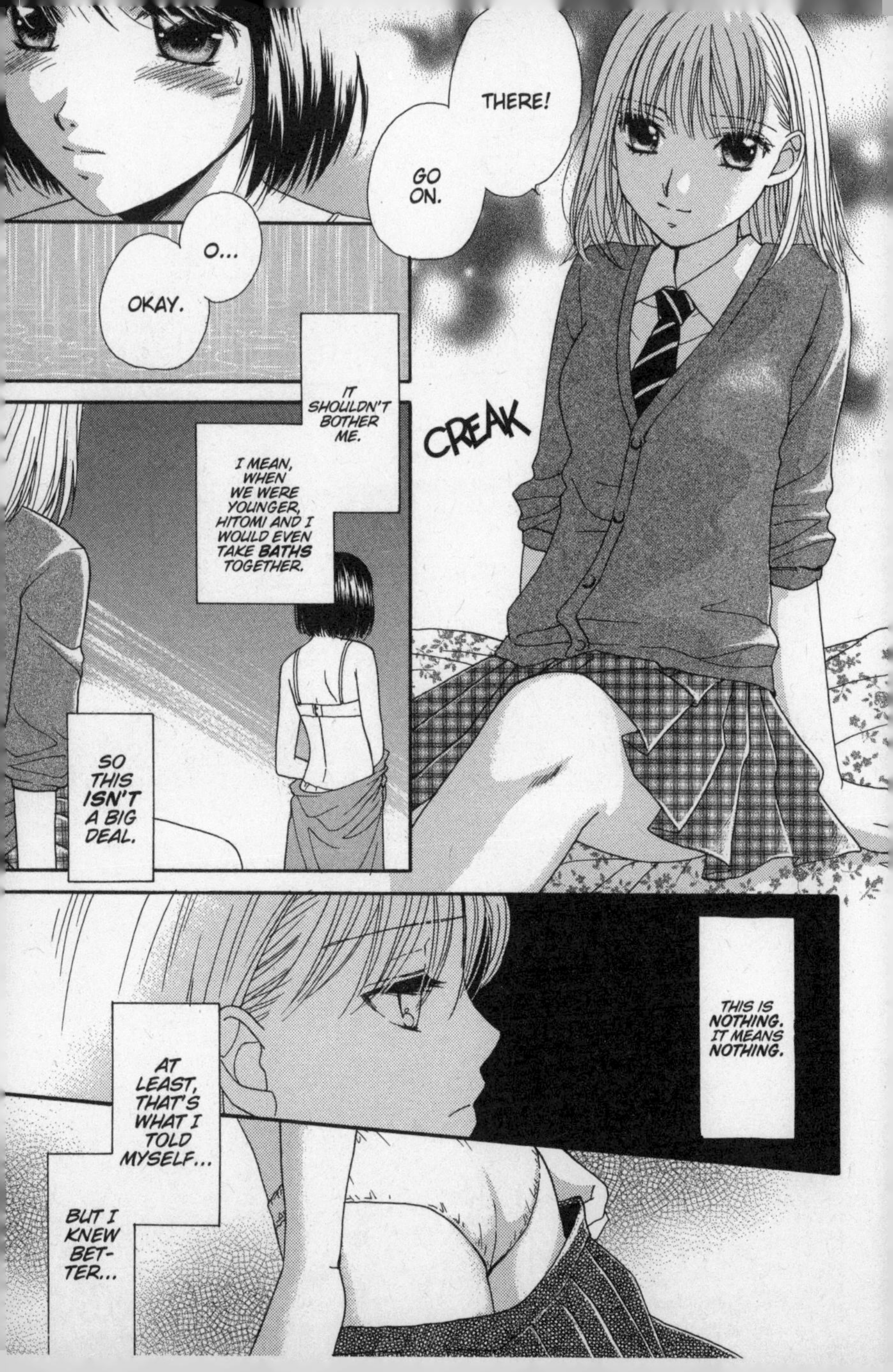
THERE!
GO ON.
CREAK
O...
OKAY.
IT SHOULDN'T BOTHER ME.
I MEAN, WHEN WE WERE YOUNGER, HITOMI AND I WOULD EVEN TAKE BATHS TOGETHER.
SO THIS ISN'T A BIG DEAL.
THIS IS NOTHING. IT MEANS NOTHING.
AT LEAST, THAT'S WHAT I TOLD MYSELF...
BUT I KNEW BETTER...

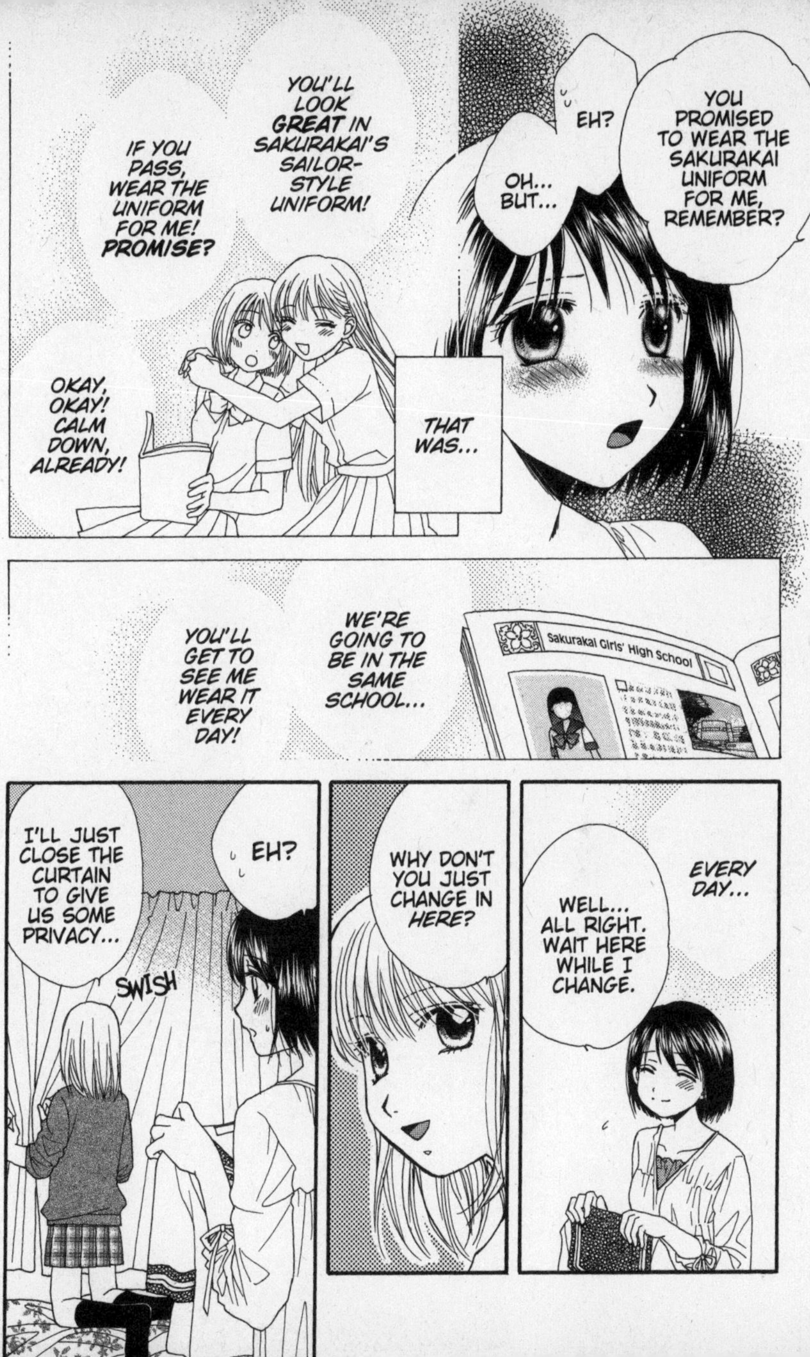
YOU PROMISED TO WEAR THE SAKURAKAI UNIFORM FOR ME, REMEMBER?
EH?
OH... BUT...
THAT WAS...
YOU'LL LOOK GREAT IN SAKURAKAI'S SAILOR-STYLE UNIFORM!
IF YOU PASS, WEAR THE UNIFORM FOR ME! PROMISE?
OKAY, OKAY! CALM DOWN, ALREADY!
Sakurakai Girls' High School
WE'RE GOING TO BE IN THE SAME SCHOOL...
YOU'LL GET TO SEE ME WEAR IT EVERY DAY!
EVERY DAY...
WELL... ALL RIGHT. WAIT HERE WHILE I CHANGE.
WHY DON'T YOU JUST CHANGE IN HERE?
EH?
I'LL JUST CLOSE THE CURTAIN TO GIVE US SOME PRIVACY...
SWISH

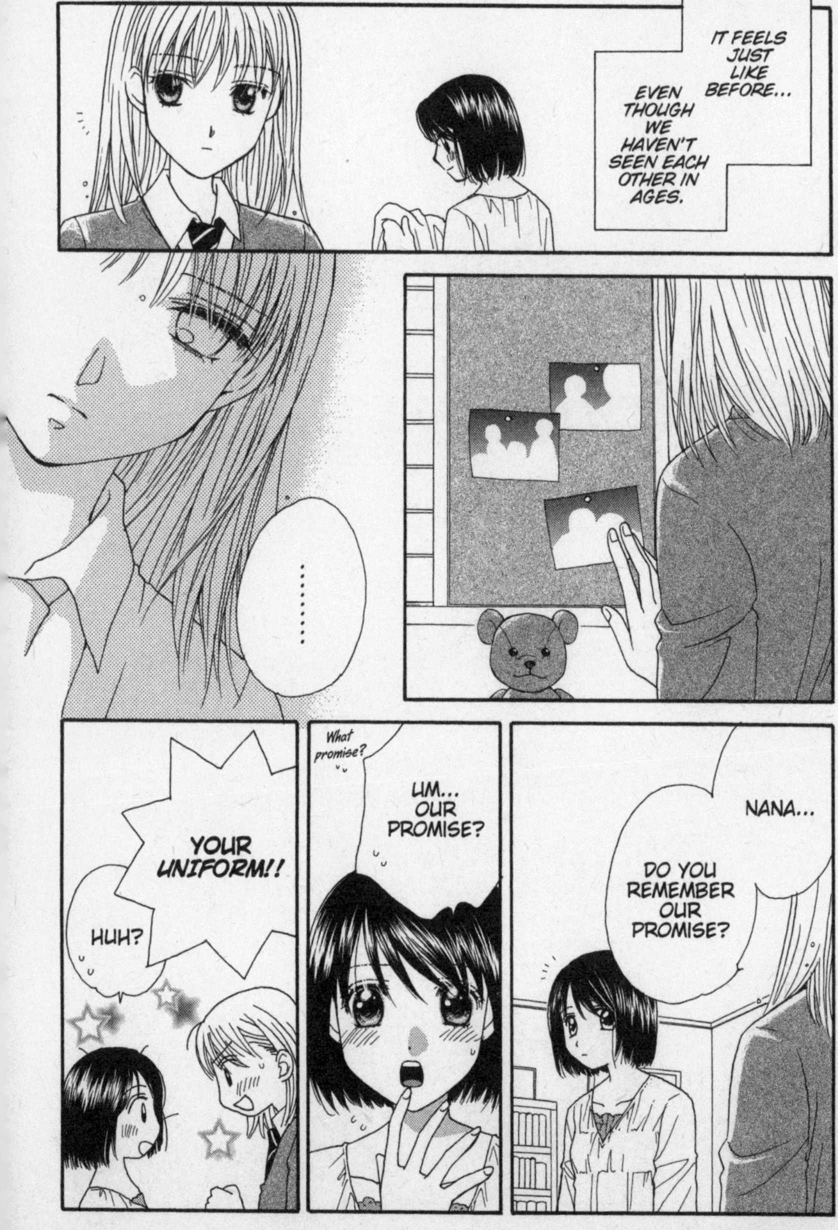
IT FEELS JUST LIKE BEFORE...
EVEN THOUGH WE HAVEN'T SEEN EACH OTHER IN AGES.
......
NANA...
DO YOU REMEMBER OUR PROMISE?
UM... OUR PROMISE?
What promise?
YOUR UNIFORM!!
HUH?

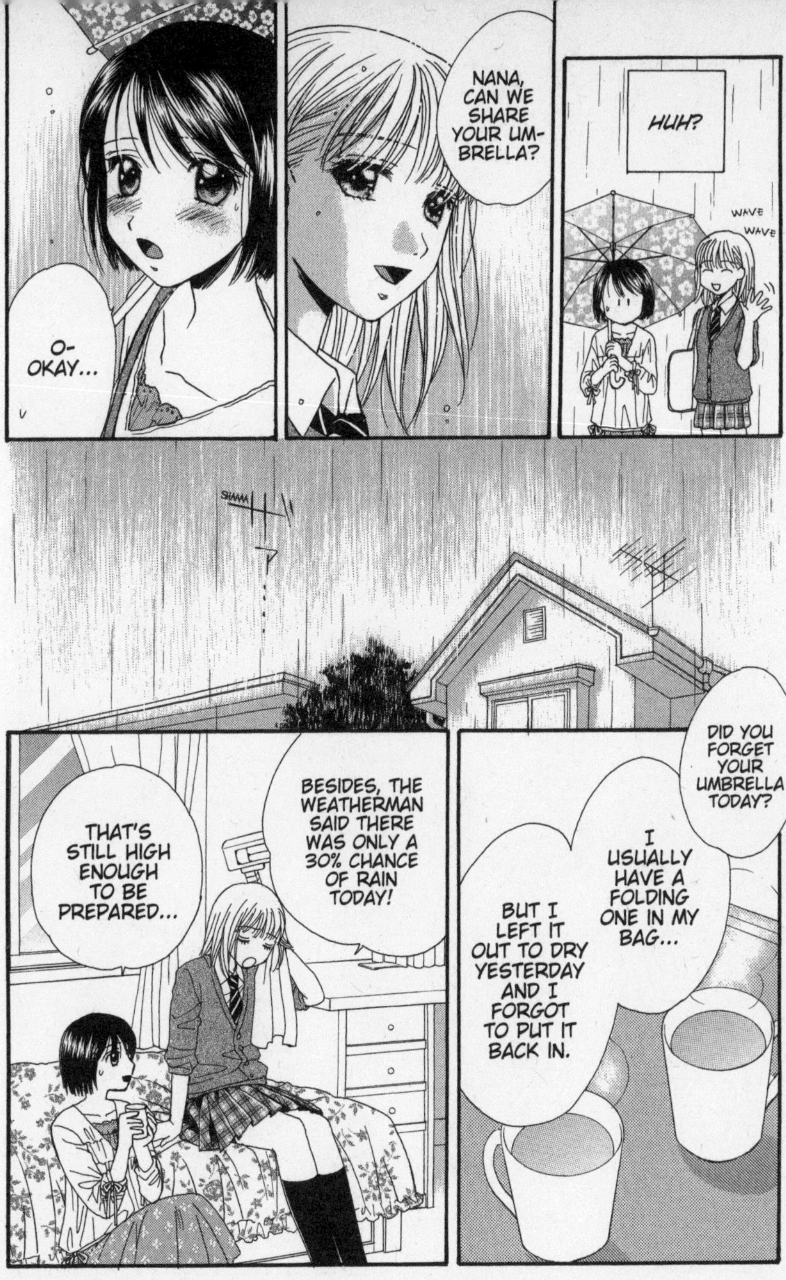
HUH?
WAVE
WAVE
NANA, CAN WE SHARE YOUR UM-BRELLA?
O-OKAY...
SHAAA
DID YOU FORGET YOUR UMBRELLA TODAY?
I USUALLY HAVE A FOLDING ONE IN MY BAG...
BUT I LEFT IT OUT TO DRY YESTERDAY AND I FORGOT TO PUT IT BACK IN.
BESIDES, THE WEATHERMAN SAID THERE WAS ONLY A 30% CHANCE OF RAIN TODAY!
THAT'S STILL HIGH ENOUGH TO BE PREPARED...

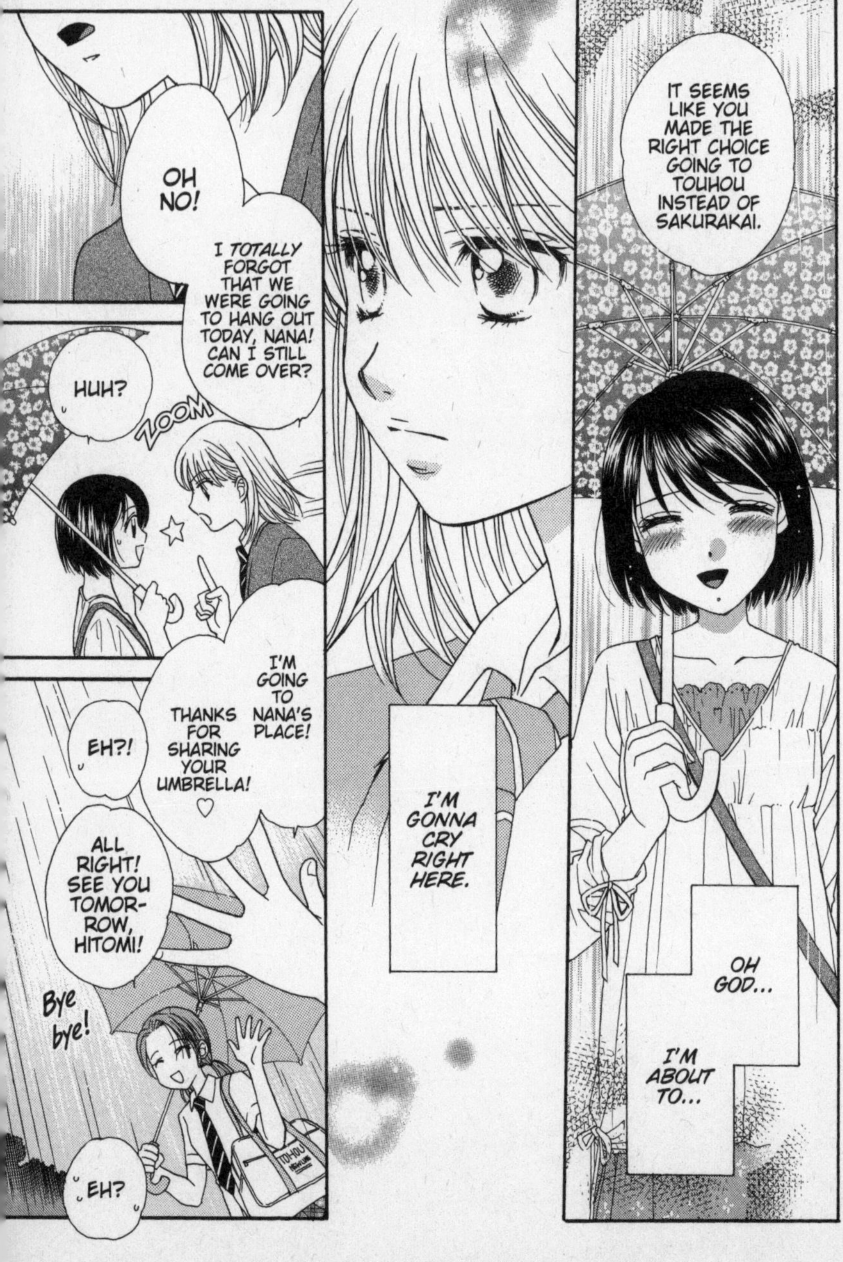
IT SEEMS LIKE YOU MADE THE RIGHT CHOICE GOING TO TOUHOU INSTEAD OF SAKURAKAI.
OH GOD...
I'M ABOUT TO...
I'M GONNA CRY RIGHT HERE.
OH NO!
I TOTALLY FORGOT THAT WE WERE GOING TO HANG OUT TODAY, NANA! CAN I STILL COME OVER?
HUH?
ZOOM
I'M GOING TO NANA'S PLACE!
THANKS FOR SHARING YOUR UMBRELLA! ♡
EH?!
ALL RIGHT! SEE YOU TOMOR-ROW, HITOMI!
Bye bye!
EH?

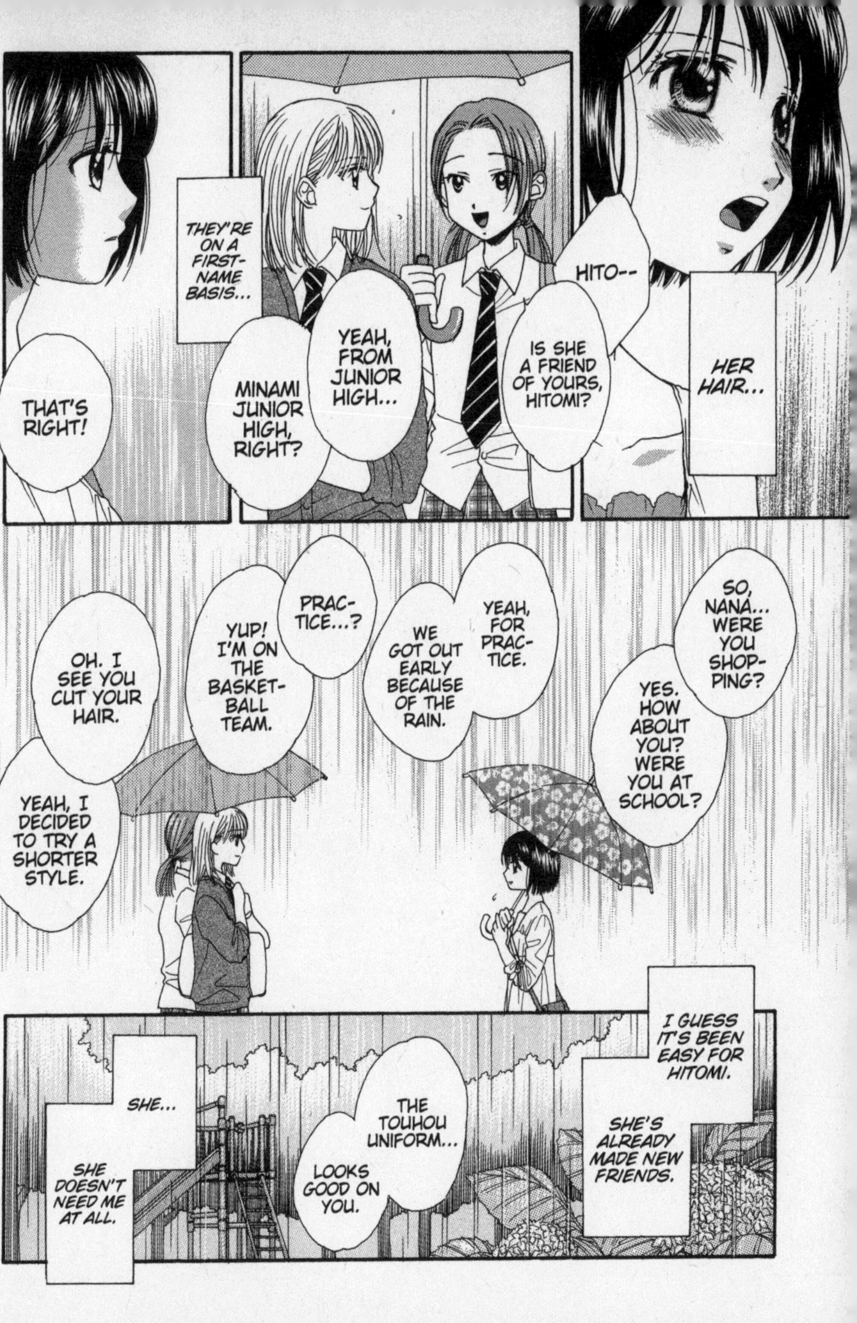
HITO--
HER HAIR...
IS SHE A FRIEND OF YOURS, HITOMI?
YEAH, FROM JUNIOR HIGH...
THEY'RE ON A FIRST-NAME BASIS...
MINAMI JUNIOR HIGH, RIGHT?
THAT'S RIGHT!
SO, NANA... WERE YOU SHOPPING?
YES. HOW ABOUT YOU? WERE YOU AT SCHOOL?
YEAH, FOR PRAC-TICE.
WE GOT OUT EARLY BECAUSE OF THE RAIN.
PRAC-TICE...?
YUP! I'M ON THE BASKET-BALL TEAM.
OH. I SEE YOU CUT YOUR HAIR.
YEAH, I DECIDED TO TRY A SHORTER STYLE.
I GUESS IT'S BEEN EASY FOR HITOMI.
SHE'S ALREADY MADE NEW FRIENDS.
THE TOUHOU UNIFORM...
LOOKS GOOD ON YOU.
SHE...
SHE DOESN'T NEED ME AT ALL.

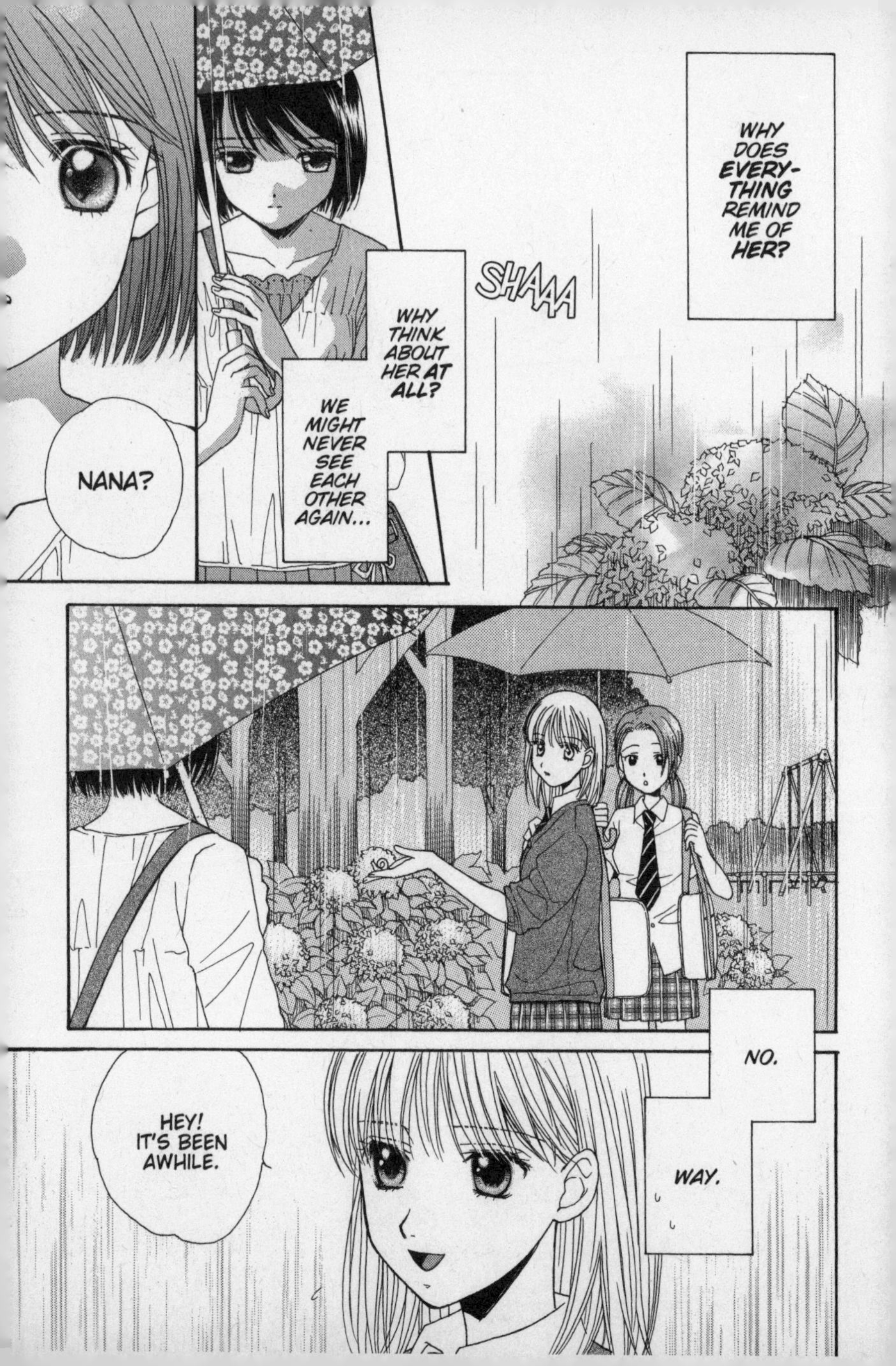
WHY DOES EVERYTHING REMIND ME OF HER?
SHAAA
WHY THINK ABOUT HER AT ALL?
WE MIGHT NEVER SEE EACH OTHER AGAIN...
NANA?
NO.
WAY.
HEY! IT'S BEEN AWHILE.

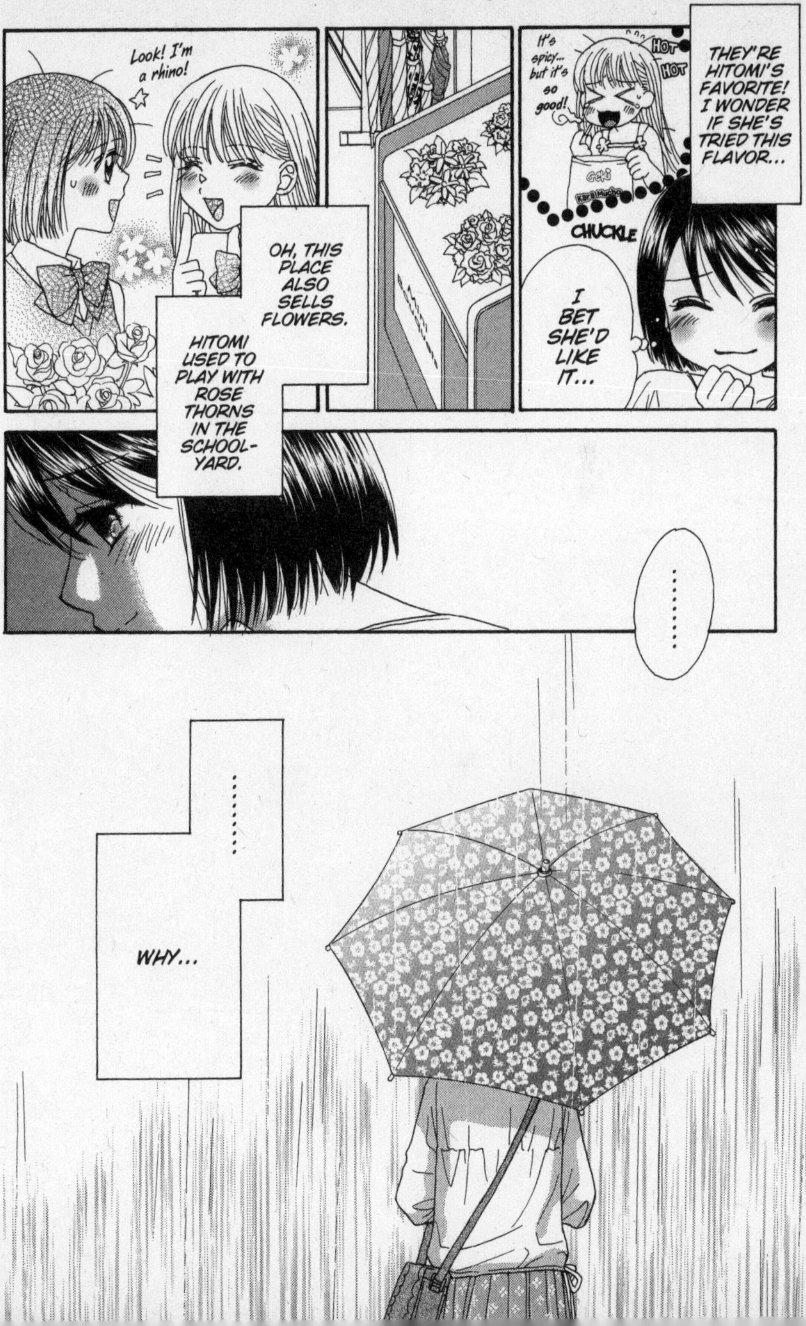
THEY'RE HITOMI'S FAVORITE! I WONDER IF SHE'S TRIED THIS FLAVOR...
HOT
HOT
It's spicy... but it's so good!
CHUCKLE
I BET SHE'D LIKE IT...
OH, THIS PLACE ALSO SELLS FLOWERS.
HITOMI USED TO PLAY WITH ROSE THORNS IN THE SCHOOL-YARD.
Look! I'm a rhino!
......
......
WHY...

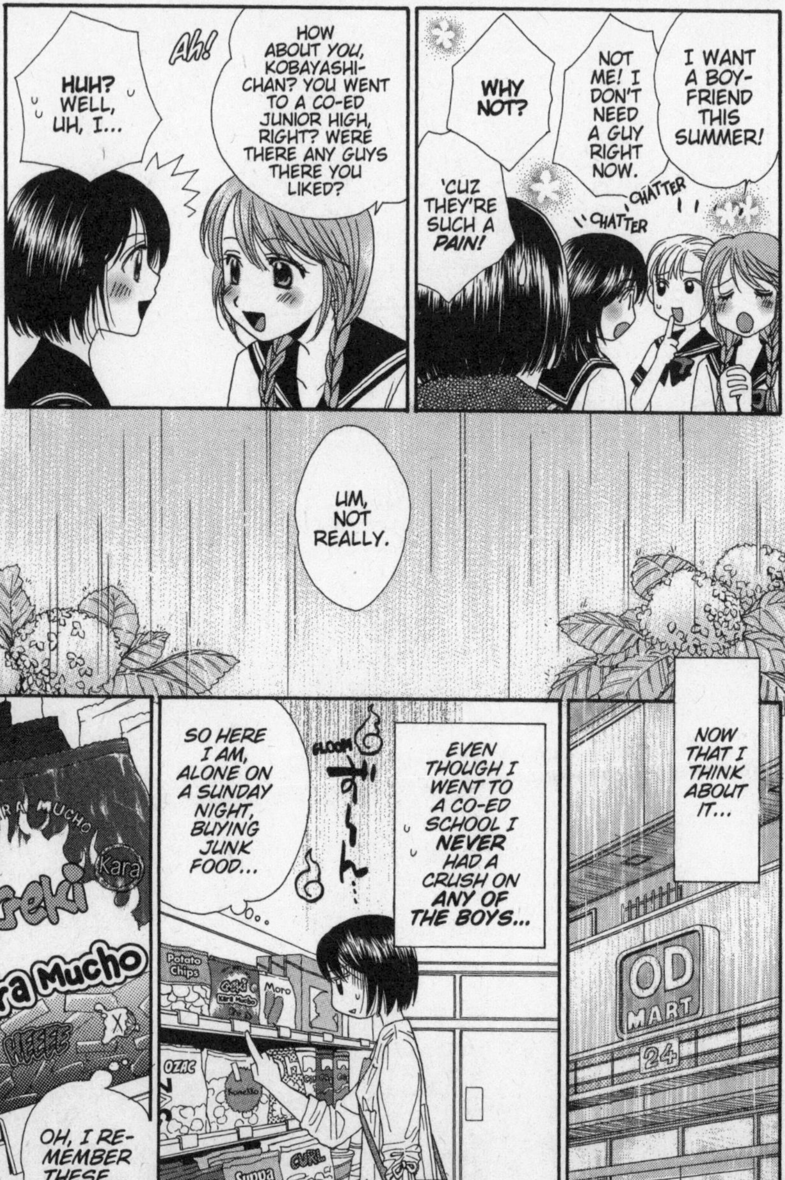

I WANT A BOY-FRIEND THIS SUMMER!
NOT ME! I DON'T NEED A GUY RIGHT NOW.
CHATTER
CHATTER
WHY NOT?
'CUZ THEY'RE SUCH A PAIN!
HOW ABOUT YOU, KOBAYASHI-CHAN? YOU WENT TO A CO-ED JUNIOR HIGH, RIGHT? WERE THERE ANY GUYS THERE YOU LIKED?
Ah!
HUH? WELL, UH, I...
UM, NOT REALLY.
NOW THAT I THINK ABOUT IT...
EVEN THOUGH I WENT TO A CO-ED SCHOOL I NEVER HAD A CRUSH ON ANY OF THE BOYS...
GLOOM
SO HERE I AM, ALONE ON A SUNDAY NIGHT, BUYING JUNK FOOD...
OD MART
24
Potato Chips
Moro
OZAC
Suppa
CURL
GEKI KARA MUCHO
Geki
Kara
Kara Mucho
OH, I RE-MEMBER THESE...

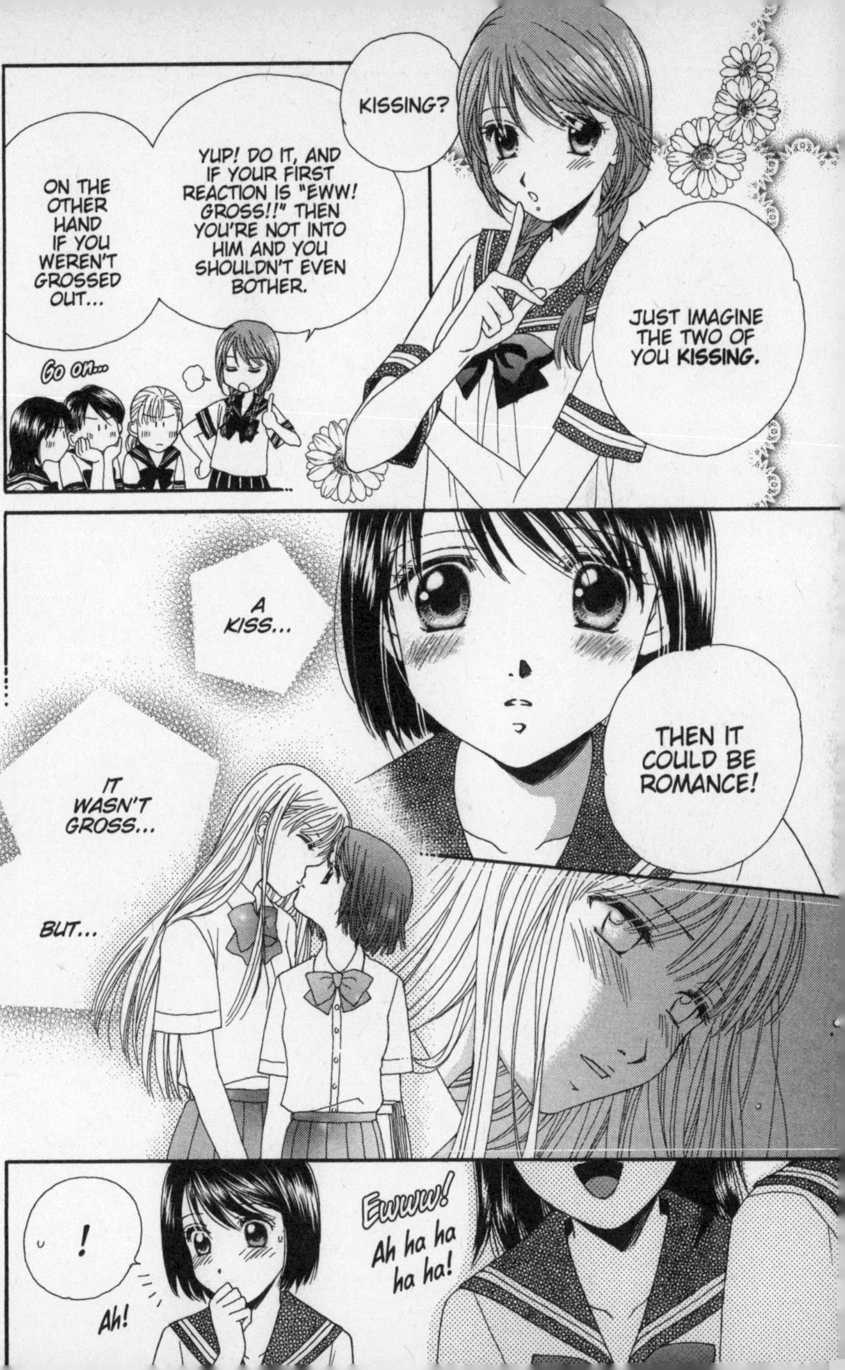
JUST IMAGINE THE TWO OF YOU KISSING.
KISSING?
YUP! DO IT, AND IF YOUR FIRST REACTION IS "EWW! GROSS!!" THEN YOU'RE NOT INTO HIM AND YOU SHOULDN'T EVEN BOTHER.
ON THE OTHER HAND IF YOU WEREN'T GROSSED OUT...
Go on...
THEN IT COULD BE ROMANCE!
A KISS...
IT WASN'T GROSS...
BUT...
Ewww!
Ah ha ha ha ha!
!
Ah!

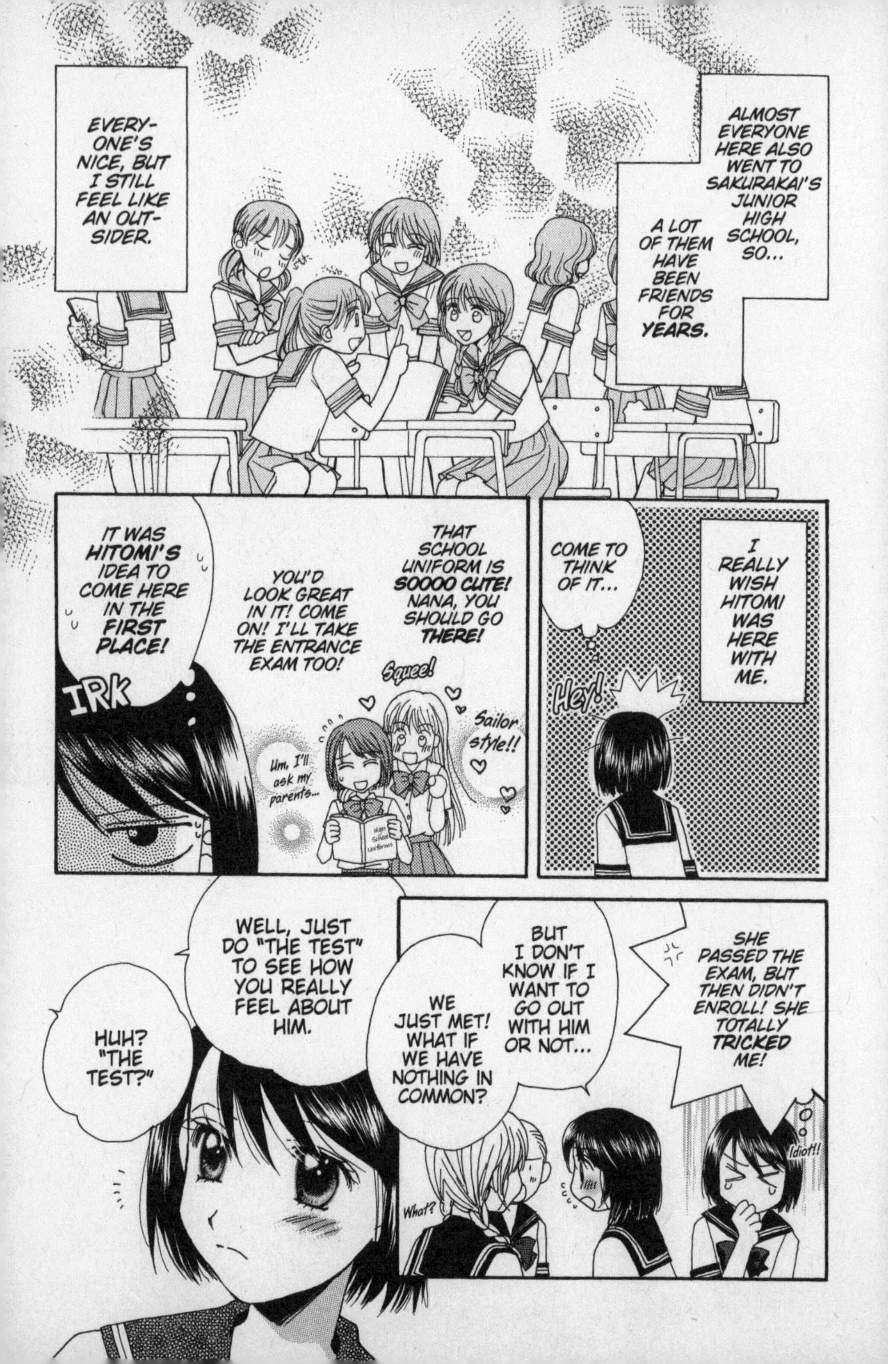
ALMOST EVERYONE HERE ALSO WENT TO SAKURAKAI'S JUNIOR HIGH SCHOOL, SO...
A LOT OF THEM HAVE BEEN FRIENDS FOR YEARS.
EVERYONE'S NICE, BUT I STILL FEEL LIKE AN OUTSIDER.
I REALLY WISH HITOMI WAS HERE WITH ME.
Hey!
COME TO THINK OF IT...
THAT SCHOOL UNIFORM IS SOOOO CUTE! NANA, YOU SHOULD GO THERE!
YOU'D LOOK GREAT IN IT! COME ON! I'LL TAKE THE ENTRANCE EXAM TOO!
Squee!
Sailor style!!
Um, I'll ask my parents...
High School Uniform
IT WAS HITOMI'S IDEA TO COME HERE IN THE FIRST PLACE!
IRK
SHE PASSED THE EXAM, BUT THEN DIDN'T ENROLL! SHE TOTALLY TRICKED ME!
Idiot!!
BUT I DON'T KNOW IF I WANT TO GO OUT WITH HIM OR NOT...
WE JUST MET! WHAT IF WE HAVE NOTHING IN COMMON?
What?
WELL, JUST DO "THE TEST" TO SEE HOW YOU REALLY FEEL ABOUT HIM.
HUH? "THE TEST?"

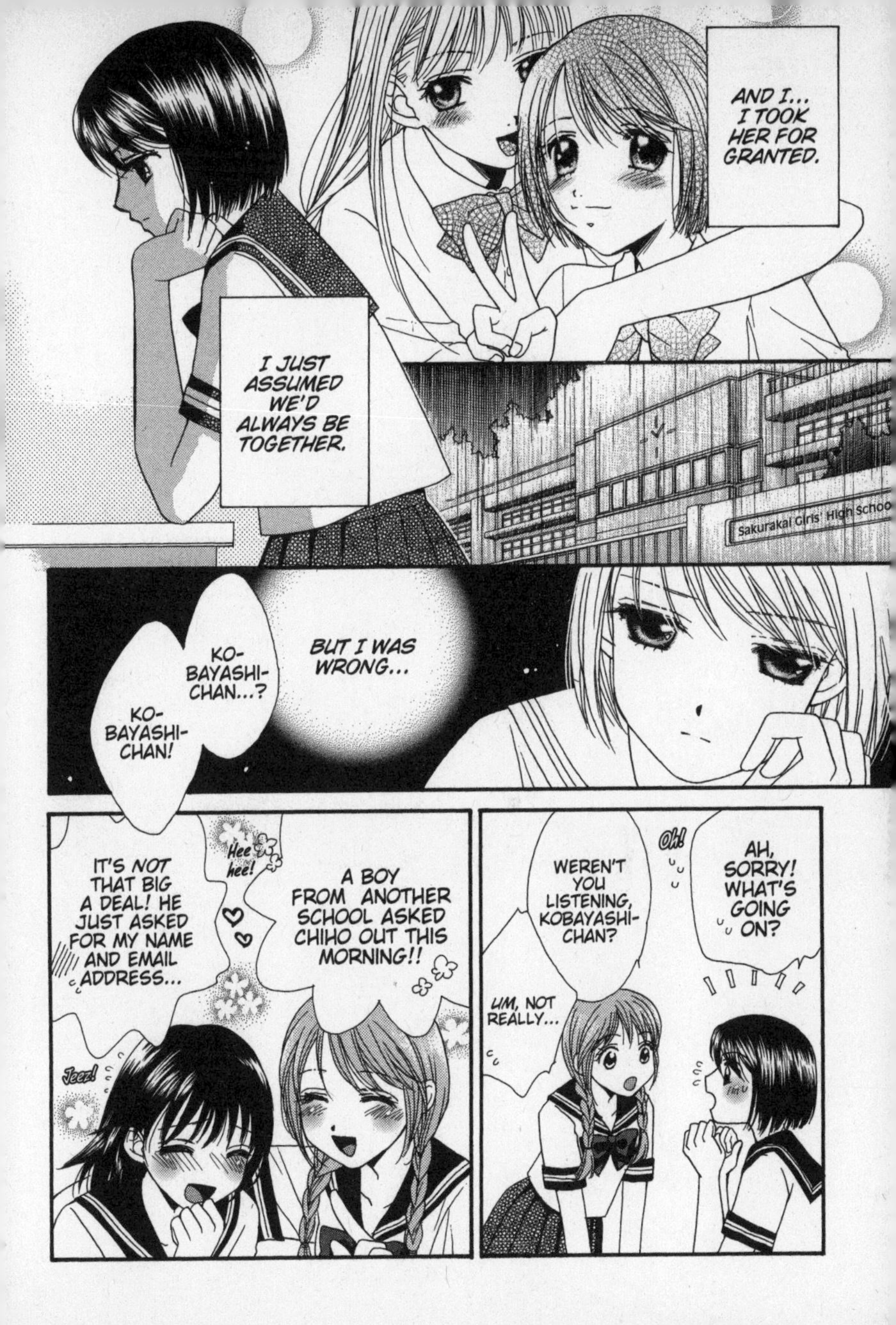
AND I... I TOOK HER FOR GRANTED.
I JUST ASSUMED WE'D ALWAYS BE TOGETHER.
Sakurakai Girls' High Schoo
BUT I WAS WRONG...
KO-BAYASHI-CHAN...?
KO-BAYASHI-CHAN!
Oh!
AH, SORRY! WHAT'S GOING ON?
WEREN'T YOU LISTENING, KOBAYASHI-CHAN?
UM, NOT REALLY...
A BOY FROM ANOTHER SCHOOL ASKED CHIHO OUT THIS MORNING!!
Hee hee!
IT'S *NOT* THAT BIG A DEAL! HE JUST ASKED FOR MY NAME AND EMAIL ADDRESS...
Jeez!

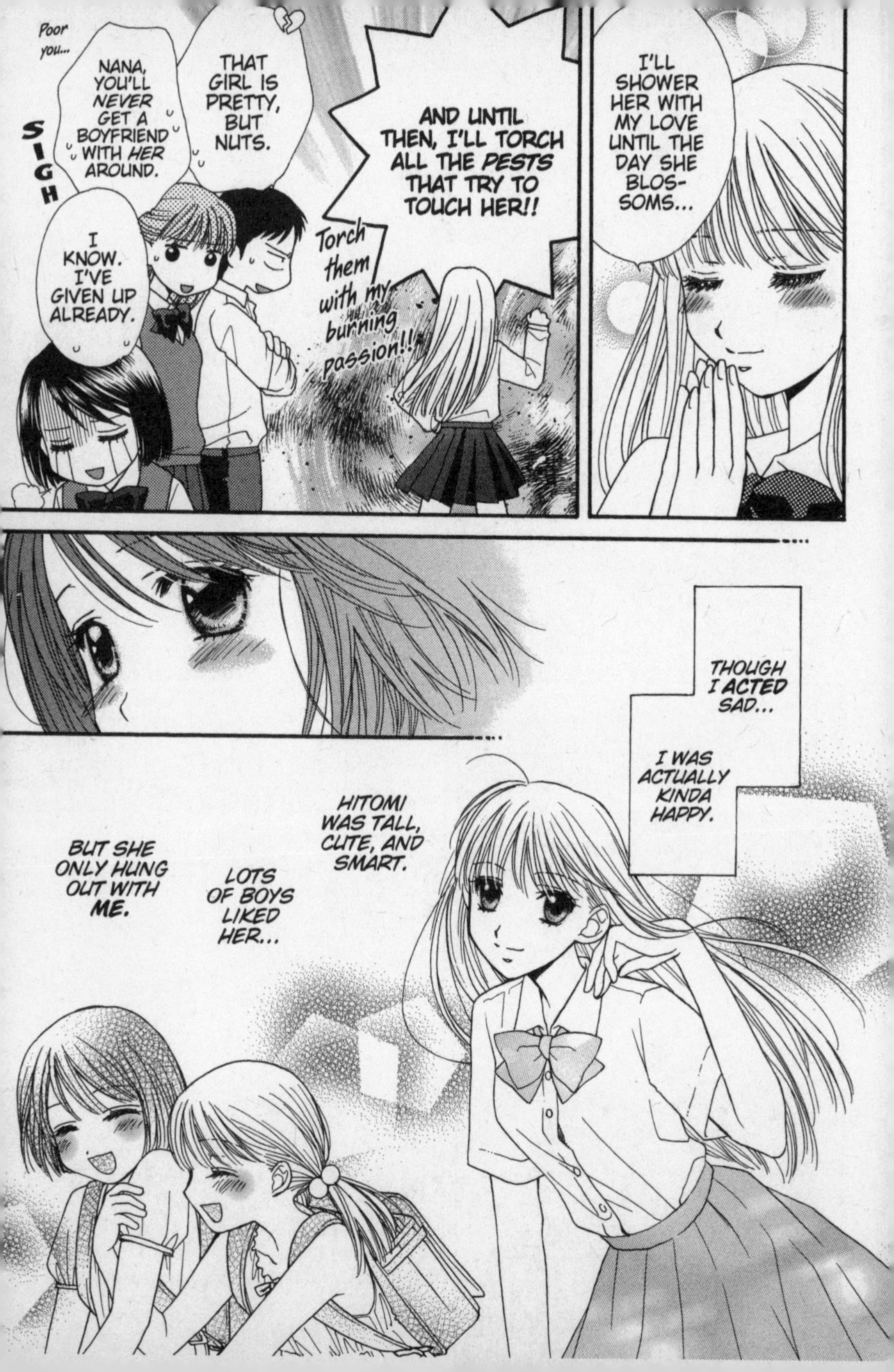
I'LL SHOWER HER WITH MY LOVE UNTIL THE DAY SHE BLOSSOMS...
AND UNTIL THEN, I'LL TORCH ALL THE PESTS THAT TRY TO TOUCH HER!!
Torch them with my burning passion!!
THAT GIRL IS PRETTY, BUT NUTS.
NANA, YOU'LL NEVER GET A BOYFRIEND WITH HER AROUND.
Poor you...
SIGH
I KNOW. I'VE GIVEN UP ALREADY.
THOUGH I ACTED SAD...
I WAS ACTUALLY KINDA HAPPY.
HITOMI WAS TALL, CUTE, AND SMART.
LOTS OF BOYS LIKED HER...
BUT SHE ONLY HUNG OUT WITH ME.

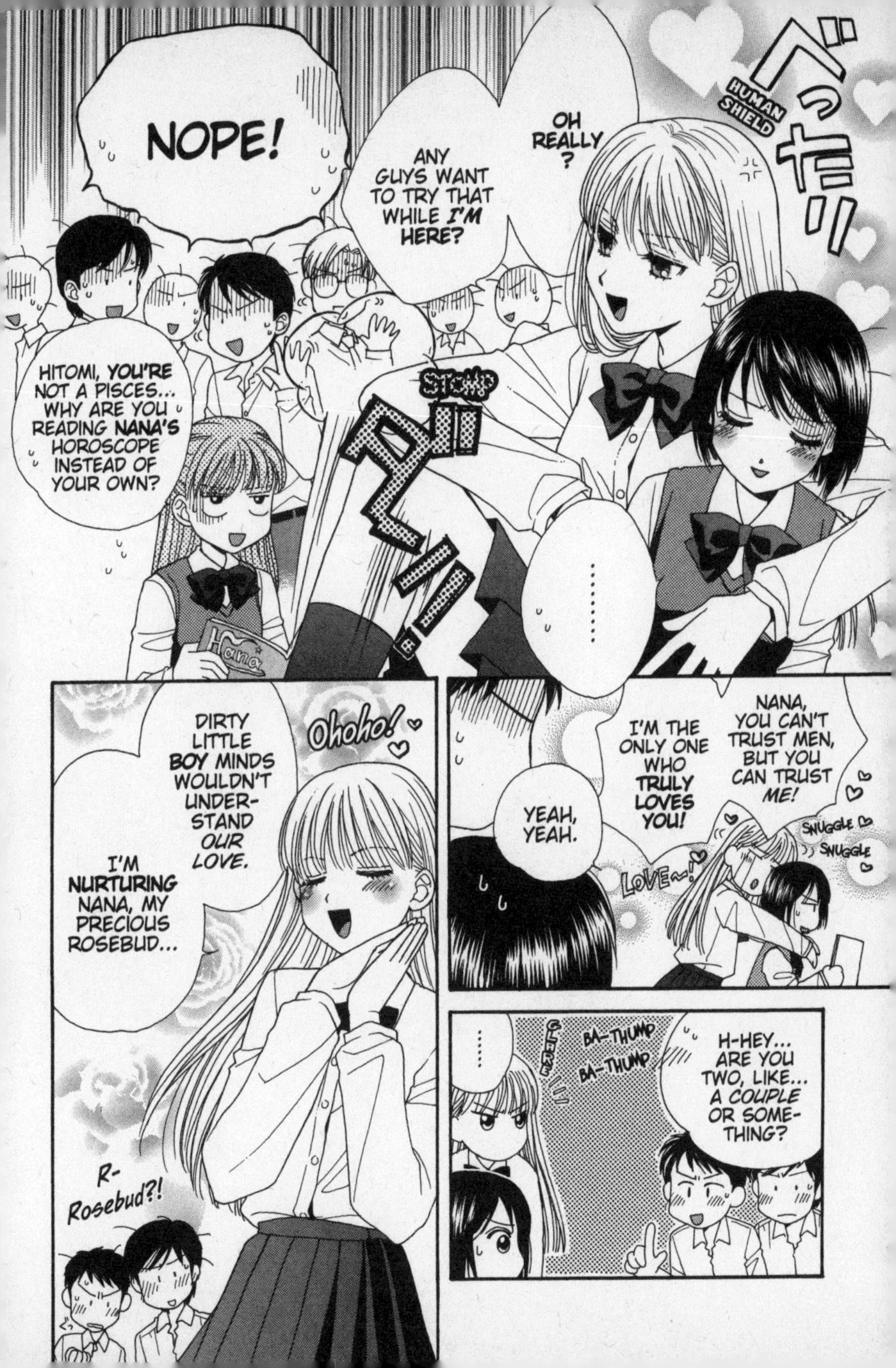
HUMAN SHIELD
OH REALLY?
ANY GUYS WANT TO TRY THAT WHILE I'M HERE?
NOPE!
STOMP
HITOMI, YOU'RE NOT A PISCES... WHY ARE YOU READING NANA'S HOROSCOPE INSTEAD OF YOUR OWN?
......
NANA, YOU CAN'T TRUST MEN, BUT YOU CAN TRUST ME!
I'M THE ONLY ONE WHO TRULY LOVES YOU!
SNUGGLE SNUGGLE
LOVE~!
YEAH, YEAH.
H-HEY... ARE YOU TWO, LIKE... A COUPLE OR SOMETHING?
BA-THUMP BA-THUMP
GLARE
......
Ohoho!
DIRTY LITTLE BOY MINDS WOULDN'T UNDER-STAND OUR LOVE.
I'M NURTURING NANA, MY PRECIOUS ROSEBUD...
R-Rosebud?!

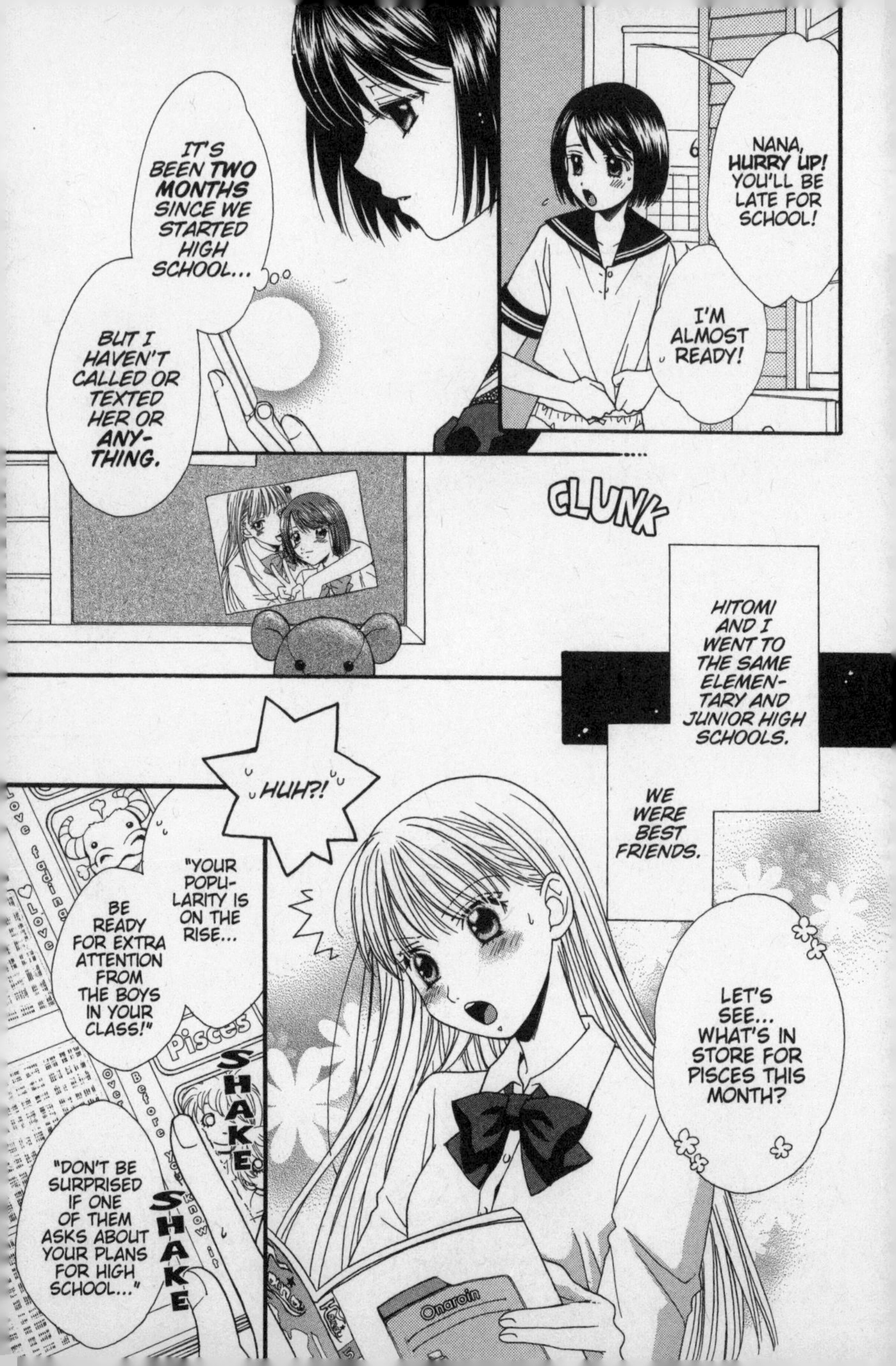
NANA, HURRY UP! YOU'LL BE LATE FOR SCHOOL!
I'M ALMOST READY!
IT'S BEEN TWO MONTHS SINCE WE STARTED HIGH SCHOOL...
BUT I HAVEN'T CALLED OR TEXTED HER OR ANY-THING.
CLUNK
HITOMI AND I WENT TO THE SAME ELEMEN-TARY AND JUNIOR HIGH SCHOOLS.
WE WERE BEST FRIENDS.
LET'S SEE... WHAT'S IN STORE FOR PISCES THIS MONTH?
HUH?!
"YOUR POPU-LARITY IS ON THE RISE...
BE READY FOR EXTRA ATTENTION FROM THE BOYS IN YOUR CLASS!"
"DON'T BE SURPRISED IF ONE OF THEM ASKS ABOUT YOUR PLANS FOR HIGH SCHOOL..."
SHAKE
SHAKE
Pisces
Onaroin

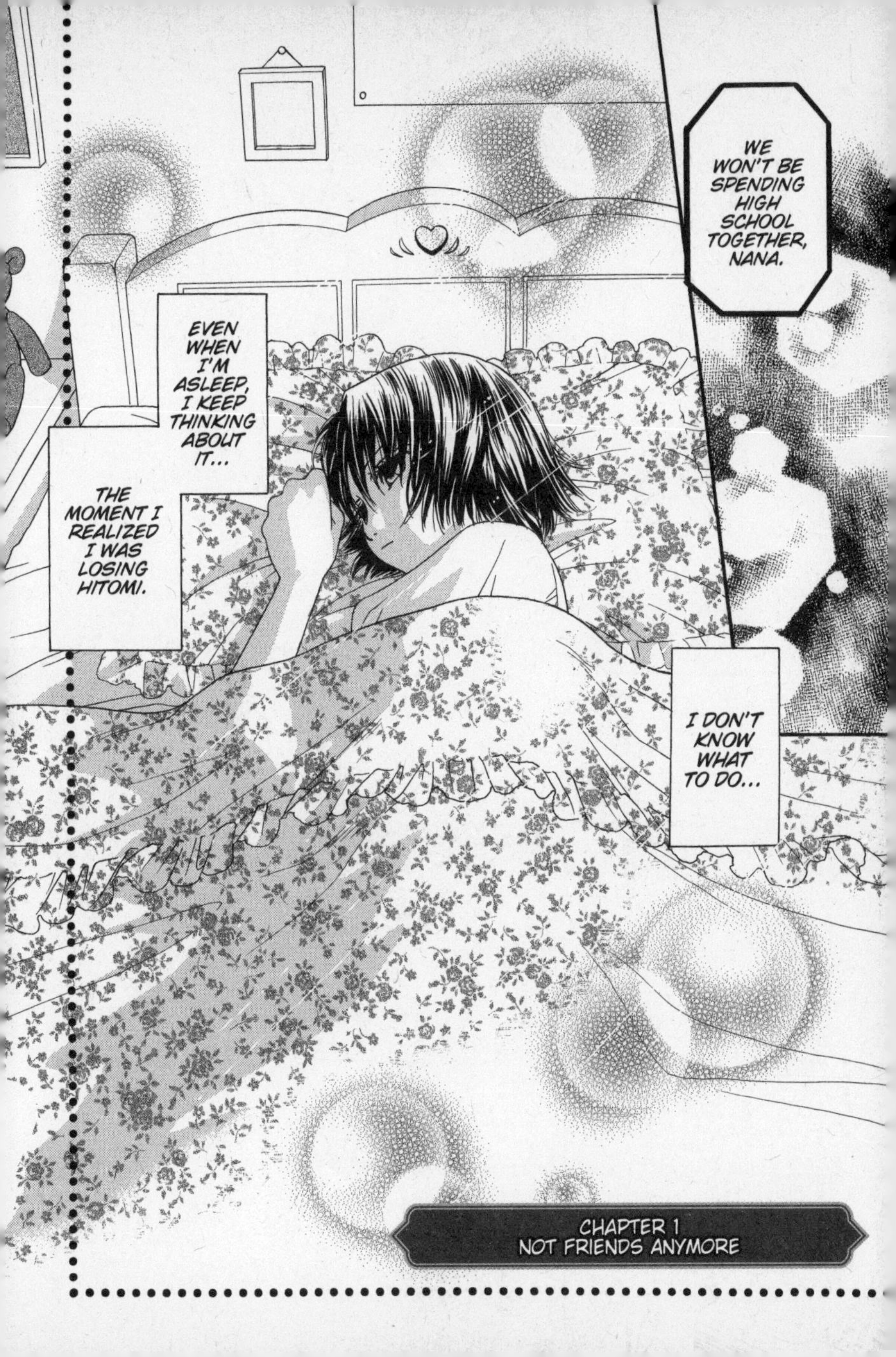
WE WON'T BE SPENDING HIGH SCHOOL TOGETHER, NANA.
EVEN WHEN I'M ASLEEP, I KEEP THINKING ABOUT IT...
THE MOMENT I REALIZED I WAS LOSING HITOMI.
I DON'T KNOW WHAT TO DO...
CHAPTER 1
NOT FRIENDS ANYMORE

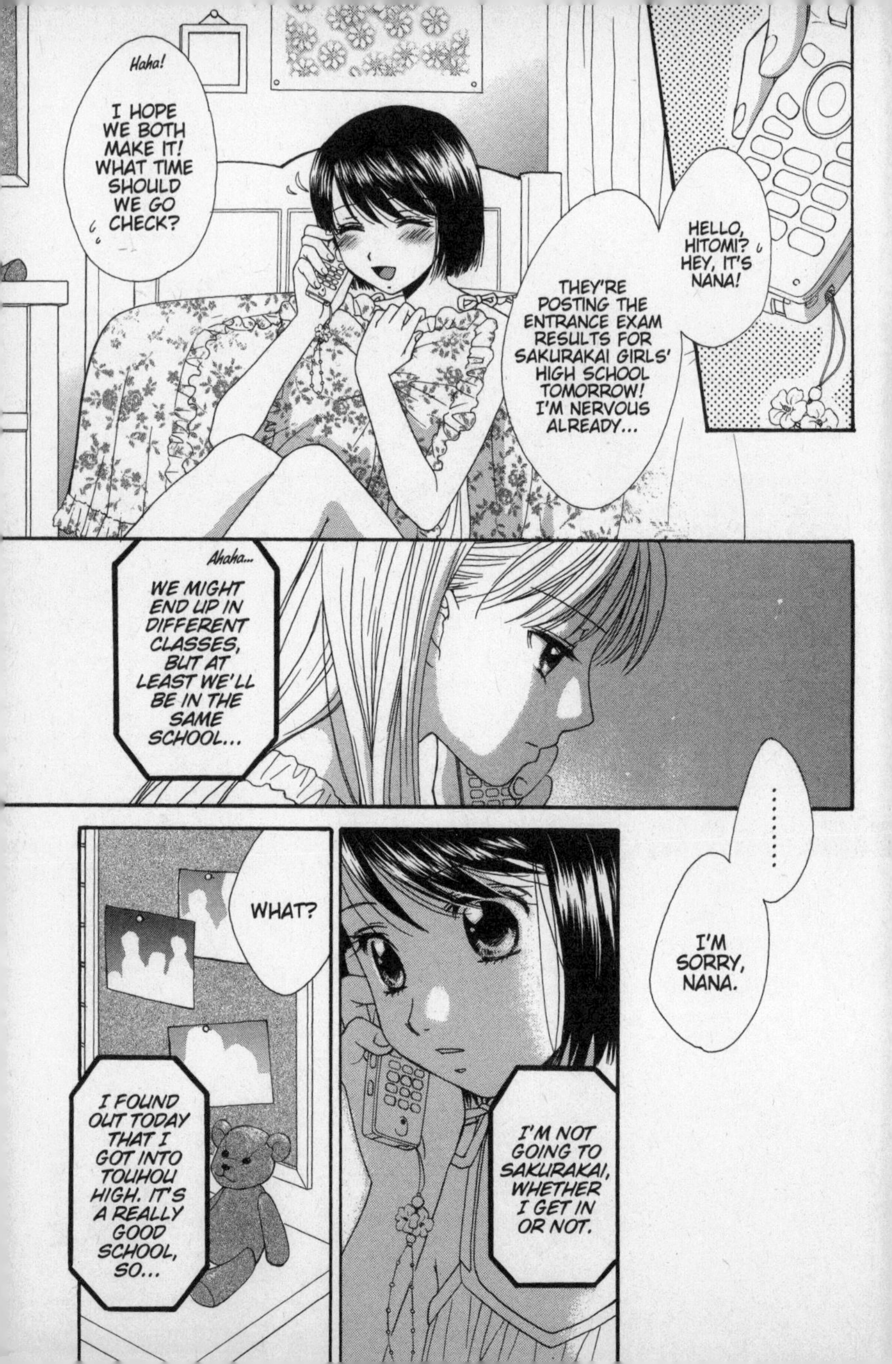
HELLO, HITOMI? HEY, IT'S NANA!
THEY'RE POSTING THE ENTRANCE EXAM RESULTS FOR SAKURAKAI GIRLS' HIGH SCHOOL TOMORROW! I'M NERVOUS ALREADY...
Haha!
I HOPE WE BOTH MAKE IT! WHAT TIME SHOULD WE GO CHECK?
Ahaha...
WE MIGHT END UP IN DIFFERENT CLASSES, BUT AT LEAST WE'LL BE IN THE SAME SCHOOL...
......
I'M SORRY, NANA.
I'M NOT GOING TO SAKURAKAI, WHETHER I GET IN OR NOT.
WHAT?
I FOUND OUT TODAY THAT I GOT INTO TOUHOU HIGH. IT'S A REALLY GOOD SCHOOL, SO...

Kisses, Sighs, and Cherry Blossom Pink

THE COMPLETE COLLECTION

STORY & ART BY
Milk Morinaga

STAFF CREDITS

translation	**Anastasia Moreno**
adaptation	**Shannon Fay**
lettering & retouch	**Jennifer Skarupa**
cover design	**Nicky Lim**
assistant editor	**Holly Kolodziejczak**
editor	**Adam Arnold**
publisher	**Jason DeAngelis** **Seven Seas Entertainment**

KISSES, SIGHS, AND CHERRY BLOSSOM PINK: THE COMPLETE COLLECTION
© MIRUKU MORINAGA 2003
All rights reserved.
First published in Japan in 2012 by Futabasha Publishers Ltd., Tokyo.
English version published by Seven Seas Entertainment, LLC.
Under license from Futabasha Publishers Ltd.

ISBN: 978-1-937867-31-7

Printed in Canada

First Printing: June 2013

10 9 8 7 6 5 4 3 2 1

FOLLOW US ONLINE: **www.gomanga.com**

READING DIRECTIONS

This book reads from *right to left*, Japanese style. If this is your first time reading manga, you start reading from the top right panel on each page and take it from there. If you get lost, just follow the numbered diagram here. It may seem backwards at first, but you'll get the hang of it! Have fun!!

Kisses, Sighs, and Cherry Blossom Pink

THE COMPLETE COLLECTION

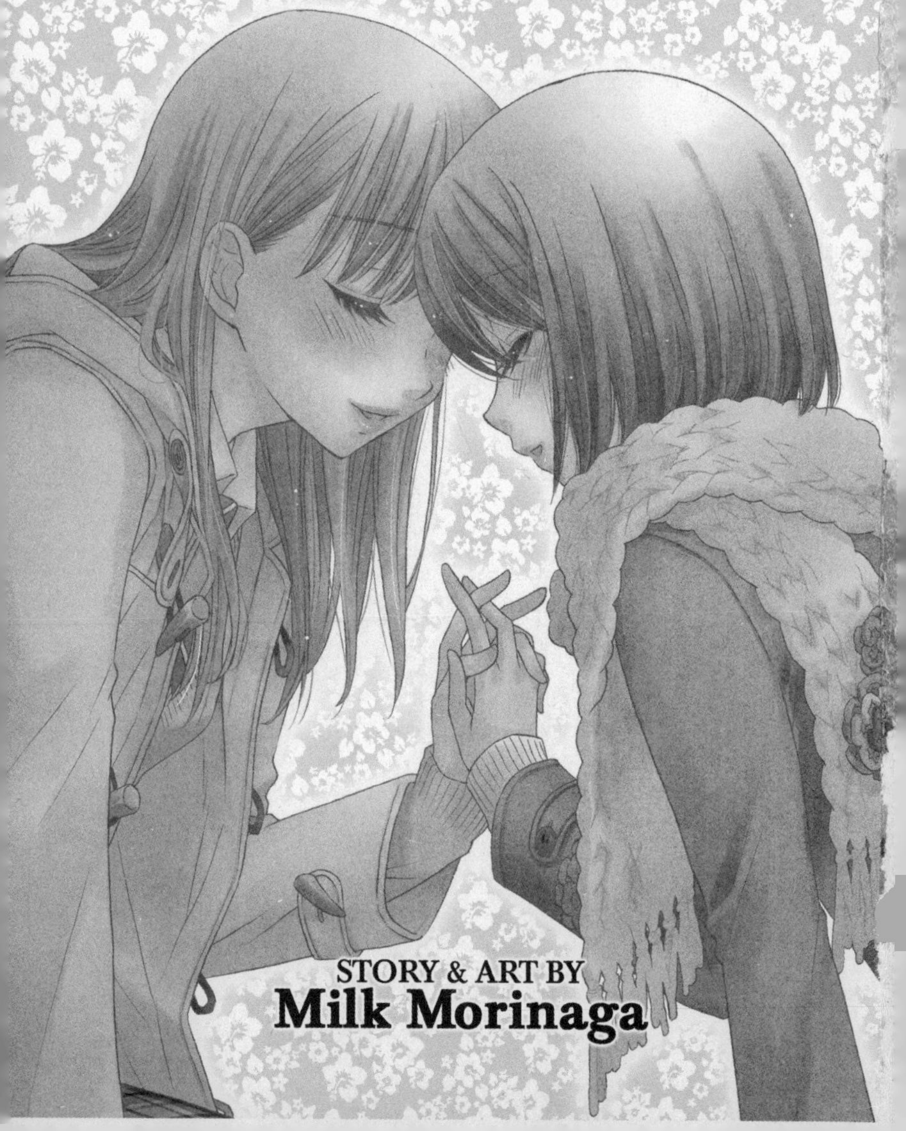

STORY & ART BY

Milk Morinaga